scope p.128
annotation p.137

Living with Books

NUMBER 2
COLUMBIA UNIVERSITY STUDIES
IN LIBRARY SERVICE

Helen E. Haines

Living with Books

THE ART OF BOOK SELECTION

SECOND EDITION

Columbia University Press NEW YORK

COPYRIGHT 1935, 1950, COLUMBIA UNIVERSITY PRESS, NEW YORK

First edition 1935
Second printing 1935
Third printing 1937
Fourth printing 1940
Fifth printing 1946
Sixth printing 1947

Second edition 1950
Second printing 1950
Third printing 1951
Fourth printing 1952

PUBLISHED IN GREAT BRITAIN, CANADA, AND INDIA
BY GEOFFREY CUMBERLEGE
OXFORD UNIVERSITY PRESS
LONDON, TORONTO, AND BOMBAY
MANUFACTURED IN THE UNITED STATES OF AMERICA

TO LIBRARIANS
IN POSSE AND IN ESSE
FRIENDS AND FELLOW WORKERS
OF A LIFETIME

Foreword

OF ALL THE THOUSANDS who are waiting to welcome the second edition of *Living with Books* the thirty-six most joyous ones are the teachers of book selection in the country's library schools. I have not established by questionnaire that it is used as a text universally, but any place that does not use it is entitled to a certificate of lost opportunity. Library text books are as a rule rather like the products of Battle Creek, dry, tasteless, and unmemorable. Miss Haines has achieved two that rank as literature and are so well-organized, animated, and reliable that their use is not limited to the profession. Any reader with discrimination who is lucky enough to discover *Living with Books* and *What's in a Novel* acquires them with enthusiastic gratitude as a Baedeker for a life's program of reading.

For people who are being trained for work which exists only because books exist it is important that the texts they use should embody fine physical traits as well as validity of contents. Columbia University Press has held to this belief in the series "Studies in Library Service," of which *Living with Books* is Number Two. The new edition has been entirely reset. The print, as in the first edition, is clear and readable. The quotations which introduce the chapters are chosen from Miss Haines' amazing cosmography of reading from Plato to Clive Bell. Most of the chapters end with an aid as practical as their beginnings are inspiring—an appropriate list of books. And what lists! I can think of no two adjectives to express Miss Haines's genius for selection so apt as Edward Lear's "concrete and fastidious." She has dropped many of the older authors in order to keep in the flow of today. Her amazingly retentive memory and the accretions of years when her health required that she do little but read have provided her with multitudes of authors for comparison. She rolls out the best as unerringly as the machine that grades olives. She does not flinch before the recondite. She makes Aristotle's

Nicomachean Ethics sound companionable. And what is rarer, she is in quick sympathy with the experimental and the unaccredited if it can claim sincerity and a touch of art.

Having used *Living with Books* for fifteen years as a buying list of essentials in public libraries and for five years as the basis for courses in book selection in library schools, I looked forward with some dread to a new edition. It was as if Robert Frost had started tampering with his poems, changing a word here or there. How dangerous to try to change something that is already perfect! I found myself wondering if by any hapless chance she would delete in the chapter, "Fiction Today," that description of the sentimentalized novel with its heroine who accepts "an undeserved stigma (usually accompanied by a baby) for the sake of an erring sister." But how ridiculous not to have trusted her! This new edition is not made up of omissions but of the richest additions to reading since 1935. It is the lovely, young, blooming daughter of the first book, tingling with the new life of the new half century.

No other person of the A.L.A. pioneering days is so equipped to lead the librarians of the 1950's and the 1960's forward to finer opportunities and higher capacities. It is easy to foretell what the second edition will accomplish. The classes in book selection in the next fifteen years will, largely on account of Miss Haines's emphatic urgings, be better grounded on how to evaluate, how to select, and how to enjoy books and will count these as their most vital duties. They will work for uncensored liberality and broad social sympathies. She will be immortalized in their realization that their first purpose is to interpret the world of print to their communities and that to accomplish this they must read unceasingly, read and understand and judge and enjoy.

No life of a librarian could be more vigorous or fearless than the fifty-eight years since Helen E. Haines entered the *Library Journal* office, then at 298 Broadway, in 1892. She was a girl of twenty, born in New York City, eldest of five sisters. Their mother had given their home the exhilarating atmosphere of constant reading, discussion, and ardent participation. One of Miss Haines's early assignments was editing the third supplementary volume of the *American Catalogue* (1890–1895). From the time that the American Library Association was organized at the Philadelphia Centennial until it began the publication of its proceedings in 1907, the *Library Journal* was the official organ of the national association. Miss Haines went to most of the annual conventions during the sixteen years of her editorship, from 1892 until her resignation from Mr. Bowker's office in February of 1908. There was a lilt and shine in the accounts of the trips year after year which make our present meetings of several thousands appear as feverish catastrophes.

"By the time the coaches had gone up and down through the pines from Paul Smith's to Bloomingdale the star-spangled banner had waved, the gem of the ocean had sparkled, Bonnie had been brought back several times, Nellie had been seen home assiduously, and the yearnings of the librarians had found vent in musical appeals for mush, mush, mush."

Her duties as recorder also included the most painstaking accounts of the official meetings and the indexing of the proceedings, for which she was paid $10.00!

Mr. Bowker soon discovered her aptitude for book reviewing. Her estimates of the first volume of the *Catalogue of Printed Books in the Bibliothèque Nationale*, of the first edition of *Baker's Guide to Fiction*, and of many other important books were frank and careful analyses.

Of course local library clubs and state associations soon realized the acceleration she would bring to any program. Her annual estimates of the fiction of the year came to be an established prize-winner at the New York (City) Library Club.

The demands increased without mercy. She was elected vice-president of the New York State Library Association. Her services to the American Library Association came to include membership on a committee to get out library tracts and on the program committee, and in 1907 she was elected second vice-president. She even scaled one of the unscalable peaks in every library author's dreams—the general magazine, getting two articles on the growth of libraries into the *World's Work* in 1903 and 1904. With William I. Fletcher she edited the *Annual Library Index* in 1905.

A breakdown in health came in the fall of 1906. She with her mother and two sisters went to Pasadena in 1908. By 1914 she was well enough to join the faculty of the training class of the Los Angeles Public Library as a teacher of book selection. She organized the Pasadena Library Club. She has given series of book talks to clubs and in the adult education programs of the Long Beach, Los Angeles, and Pasadena public libraries. For thirty years she has been staff reviewer for the Pasadena *Star-News*. The California Library Association and the School Librarians Association have constantly had the stimulus of her talks on catch-words, on recent books, on intellectual freedom. Scarcely a year has gone by without an incisive article by her in the *Library Journal*, the *Publishers' Weekly*, the *A.L.A. Booklist* or *Bulletin*. From 1924 to 1936 Miss Haines served at intervals on the faculty of the Library School of the University of California. She taught also at the summer sessions of Columbia University School of Library Service from 1937 to 1945. From 1937 she has been visiting professor at the University of Southern California School of Library Science. From that university she received the honorary degree of Master of Arts. She is proudest of having organized the Committee on Intellectual Freedom in the California Library Association in 1937, and served ten years as its chairman.

Like all personalities of the upper atmosphere it is as a friend that she is the most complete success. Her tremendous drive is in inverse ratio to her strength. Her sensitiveness reaches out intensely even to persecuted people she has not known. All of her close friends cherish for life bits of her own verses or quotations of unique appropriateness which have come on Christmas cards or at times of crisis. They are in her delicate, connoisseur's handwriting.

Above all else she stands for precision of understanding.

ALTHEA WARREN

University of Michigan
Department of Library Service

Preface to the Second Edition

THIS PREFACE is in itself a fulfillment of the purpose and hope which underlay the original preface to *Living with Books*, written fifteen years ago. Books as the basis of library service; librarianship as the only calling that has direct public responsibility for the exercise of discriminating judgment among conflicting book values and for the widest possible application of the potencies of books to the enrichment of life were foundation principles on which that volume was built. They are principles that demand wider recognition and have more immediate vital significance today. For the years since 1935 have opened an era of human history weighted by man's new powers of destructiveness, darkened by world-wide uncertainties, fears, and suspicions. Only by a higher general level of public intelligence, more knowledge of peoples and countries other than our own, and a mutual will to international understanding can human survival be assured and the possibilities be realized that this age of mass-power also offers for material, social, and spiritual well-being among all peoples. To the public library as the great community agency of informal self-education this obligation to raise the level of public intelligence comes as a challenge, an opportunity, and a great adventure. In library school training, in the routine of familiar library techniques, in the approach of youth to a rewarding vocation there should be wider radiation and deeper understanding of the Power of the Book in librarianship and in everyday life. *Living with Books* seeks to develop that radiation and instill that understanding.

The second edition is not a remaking; the first organic structure with its four main divisions, the scope and method, are unchanged. But it is expansion and revision; and an endeavor to discern in the flow of books through these years the general direction or way in which history is moving. In doing this trends and tendencies are emphasized that are shaping themselves in thought and action today, and I have sought to show that book selection for library service should be known and practiced as the expression of, the accompaniment to, the surging stream of history we are living in. Strongest trends are social, philosophic, scientific, economic, and political. Race relationships, national and international; the rise of socialism; intellectual and spiritual aspects of philosophic thought; preoccupation with psychology are influences affecting all classes of literature. These and other dominant subjects I have sought to present in broad synthesis with fair consideration of variant viewpoints, and to strengthen the illustrative lists by recent distinctive titles—though the close limitation of those lists have regretfully forced many omissions that should have been included. The lists of a bibliographical or reference character have been somewhat augmented. As full attention as possible has been given to the field of book production, with its many mechanical innovations, to the enormous increase in editions, anthologies, and collections, to the range and trends of contemporary book reviewing—all important factors in selection and appraisal of books by librarians, by teachers and other workers with books, and of interest and usefulness to many general readers. Throughout, the selective background has been reinforced by continuing years of professional book reviewing, and by a rich usufruct of rewarding personal contacts with a generation of library school students, whose clear-sighted recognition of inevitable world change must strengthen and stabilize their use of books as materials for the building of the future: "Consciousness the will informing, till it fashion all things fair."

Help and encouragement received from many friends are gratefully recorded in the preface to the first edition. The same incentive and sustenance made possible the present revision, which has had the cooperation of friends previously enlisted and of many more who have given stimulus, counsel, and practical participation in supplying desired information and tracing bibliographical detail. Through Carl White, Director of Libraries, Columbia University again sponsored this undertaking on behalf of the School of Library Service, and Columbia University Press has been, as for more than a decade, a bulwark of friendly confidence. Among those who have especially shared in bringing this second edition to completion sincerest appreciation must go to John Askling; to Dr. Hazel Pulling, associate professor of the School of Library Science of the University of Southern California (now assistant director of the School of Library Training and Service, State University, Tallahassee, Florida); to Dr. Hazel Dean, associate professor of the School of Library Science of the University of Southern California; to Dorothy Bevis, assistant professor of the School of Librarianship of the University of Washington; to Mary Murdoch, librarian of the South Pasadena (California) Public Library; to Carroll Richardson, professor in the Department of Sociology of Occidental College; to Althea Warren, now on the faculty of the Department of Library Science of the University of Michigan; to Dorothy and Roy Rosen; to Lewis Galantière; to Elizabeth Connor, librarian of Mount Wilson Observatory, Pasadena; to Norma Cuthbert, of the staff of the Henry E. Huntington library; to Leslie I. Hood, manager of the Library Department of A. C. Vroman, Inc., Pasadena; to Faith Holmes Hyers; to Mary Helen Peterson, Mary Alice Boyd, Katherine Garbutt, Rhoda Marshall, Hazel Thomas, Armine Mackenzie, and others of the staff of the Los Angeles Public Library; and to Lulu Littlejohn and Faith Green, of the staff of the Pasadena Public Library. From the Alumni Association of the School of Library Science of the University of Southern California have come continuing fellowship and appreciation that are both tonic and recompense.

Grateful acknowledgment is made to the following publishers for permission to quote from various works: Oxford University Press, for the passage from Arnold J. Toynbee, *A Study of History*, Abridgement by D. C. Somervell; Henry Holt and Company, Inc., for quotations from Lancelot Law Whyte's works, *The Next Development in Man* and *Everyman Looks Forward*; Harcourt, Brace and Company, Inc., for the excerpt from Virginia Woolf, *The Common Reader, Second Series*; The Macmillan Company, for the passage from Phyllis Bentley, *Some Observations on the Art of*

Narrative (copyright 1947 by Phyllis Bentley); and International Publishers Company, Inc., for the quotation from Christopher Caudwell, *Illusion and Reality*.

HELEN E. HAINES

Pasadena, California
March 22, 1950

Preface

THIS VOLUME is the outgrowth of courses in Book Selection and related subjects given during the years 1914 to 1931 at the Library School of the Los Angeles Public Library, and also at intervals at the School of Librarianship of the University of California and in university extension teaching. It includes the substance of the Home Study course in Book Selection conducted for the School of Library Service of Columbia University; and it is also based on material collected during many previous years of work as managing editor of the *Library Journal*, and upon regular and continuing book reviewing.

It is not designed to be a complete text upon the subject of Book Selection for libraries, but an introductory presentation centering on aspects that relate to general book use through library service; to principles and methods developed in the practice of book selection for libraries; to use of the simpler bibliographical aids; to the more obvious information essential to librarians concerning series, editions, publishers, and characteristics of standard and current publications; and to survey and synthesis of leading classes of literature. My hope especially is that it may prove a means of self-development for library students and those untrained or inexperienced in book service whose work lies with books and readers in educational or social fields or in book-trade relationship, and that it may be useful to librarians, particularly in small public libraries and school libraries, in their own routine practice of book selection. While it should be practical as a text in library-school teaching of book selection, it is primarily for students rather than for teachers, who will have to supplement and build upon it in their class work. It will not take the place of Mr. Drury's manual of book selection, which must long remain the encyclopedic compendium of the subject, nor does it offer the extended bibliographical information that makes the *Book-*

man's Manual indispensable to the worker with books. If it imparts a deepened sense of the significance of books as the basis of library service, if it strengthens discriminating judgment of conflicting book values and stimulates realization of the inexhaustible potencies of books for the enrichment of common life, it should be an acceptable complement to those standard works, and should give something of its own besides. That those who select books for library service can develop proficiency and vitalize their work only by themselves "living with books," is the essential theme I have sought to convey.

In plan and treatment, my aim has been to simplify and reduce technical and bibliographical detail and to stimulate students to exploration and discovery for themselves in certain great regional divisions of literature. For this reason, while books recommended for study in the various short reference lists receive the usual bibliographical record (place of publication, publisher, and date), author and title only are indicated in the illustrative lists designed simply as representative of distinctive work in various classes of literature and not intended to guide to specific editions or to serve a bibliographical purpose. Most of the books included in these lists are well-known standard or contemporary works, many of them appear in various editions, information concerning them is available in the familiar library aids, and with a few possible exceptions all should be readily accessible in any representative library collection.

Help and encouragement generously accorded by many friends must have grateful acknowledgment. On Charles C. Williamson, Dean of the School of Library Service of Columbia University, rests the responsibility for this book's existence; for it was undertaken at his suggestion, the writing of it was made possible by the grant he obtained for the purpose from Columbia University, and through every step of its preparation he has given sympathetic encouragement, unfailing consideration, and valued counsel. From Frederic G. Melcher, editor of the *Publishers' Weekly* I have had responsive interest and friendly cooperation and the benefit of his expert knowledge for the chapters dealing with bookmaking and publishing. For helpful counsel and suggestions, sincerest appreciation goes also to John S. Cleavinger, Mary M. Shaver, and Lucy E. Fay, of the faculty of the School of Library Service of Columbia University; to Sydney B. Mitchell, director of the School of Librarianship of the University of California, Berkeley; to Mrs. Theodora R. Brewitt, librarian of the Long Beach (California) Public Library; to Winifred E. Skinner, librarian of Pasadena (California) Junior College; to Elizabeth Connor, librarian of the Mount Wilson Observatory, Pasadena; to Leslie I. Hood, manager of the library department of A. C. Vroman, Inc., Pasadena; to C. C. Parker, of Los Angeles; to Joseph L. Wheeler, librarian of the Enoch Pratt Free Library, Baltimore, Md.; to Zaidee Brown, librarian of State Teachers' College, Upper Montclair, N.J.; to the staff of the Los Angeles Public Library, for countless kindnesses and painstaking services; and to friends in the Pasadena Public Library, the Henry E. Huntington Library, the Mount Wilson Observatory, and the California Institute of Technology.

HELEN E. HAINES

Pasadena, California
January 2, 1935

Contents

FOREWORD BY ALTHEA WARREN vii

INTRODUCTION: THE WORLD OF BOOKS 3

Part One: Foundations and Backgrounds

1. PEOPLE AND BOOKS 15
   Education through reading; purpose of library service; book selection is basis of library service; evolution in reading; community interests and needs; library supply in relation to community demand

2. BOOKS FOR PEOPLE: PRINCIPLES IN SELECTION 29
   What people read; tastes and tendencies; group reading; McColvin's study of book selection; study and comparison of library use; fundamental selection principles that apply to community demand and supply; books mentioned in this chapter

3. TESTING BOOK VALUES 45
   Kinds of book knowledge necessary in selection; range and proportion of a library collection; interlibrary relation and cooperation; apportioning the book fund; fundamental selection principles that apply to book values; books of inspiration; books of information; books of recreation; analysis of book values; rapid reading; proportional representation of classes; a dozen books for background reading

4. FAMILIAR FRIENDS AND COMPANIONS 63
   Standard aids and guides in selection; *A.L.A. Catalog* series; *Booklist*; *Book Review Digest*; characteristics and use of standard aids; annotations analyzed and compared; *Bookman's Manual*; Shaw's *List of Books for College Libraries*; aids mentioned in this chapter

5. DAILY HELP FOR DAILY NEEDS 78
   Other aids and guides; Wilson bibliographical publications; *Publishers' Weekly*; English book-trade tools; Sonnenschein's *Best Books*; general and special bibliographical aids; bulletins, lists, catalogues; pamphlets and other free printed material; keeping record of selection; chief aids mentioned in this chapter

Part Two: Values and Appraisals

6. CURRENT BOOK REVIEWING AND LITERARY COMMENTARY 99
    Development, range, and variety of book reviewing; tendencies in present-day reviewing; use of reviews in book selections; qualities of a good book review; leading review periodicals

7. BOOK EVALUATION AND REVIEWING BY LIBARIES 122
    Why libraries review books; principles and methods of book evaluation; use of book review slips; analyzing books for evaluation; how to prepare a library review; speech and delivery in oral reviewing

8. THE ART OF ANNOTATION 137
    Annotation writing as a product of evaluation; readers' notes; librarians' notes; how to write an annotation for nonfiction; how to write an annotation for fiction; examples and contrasts; aids to the art of annotation

Part Three: Substance and Product

9. BOOKS IN THEIR TEXTUAL AND PHYSICAL ASPECTS 159
    The art of the book; familiarity with book history essential; the physical book; wartime books; tendencies in modern bookmaking

10. MAKERS OF BOOKS: THE TRADE AND ITS PRODUCTS 185
    "The great trade" (publishing and bookselling); censorship in book history; copyright and its relation to the development of American publishing; present-day American publishing and publishers; English publishing backgrounds; relationship between English and American publishing; changed titles; general and special publishers; knowledge of publishing houses necessary; bibliography on bookmaking and bookmakers

11. EDITIONS, SERIES, TRANSLATIONS 218
    Knowledge of editions necessary; development of the popular reprint; "Bohn's Library" and its successors; editions and series; points to be considered in choosing editions; subject series; a brief selection of representative editions and series; some modern translators of authority and distinction

Part Four: Exploration and Discovery

12. BIOGRAPHY: SPECULUM VITAE   249

Range and appeal of biography; its relationship to history, science, art, sociology; types of autobiography; types of biography; points to be considered in selection; books on biographic art; fifty biographies indicative of variant older and modern forms and methods

13. HISTORY   275

The literature of history; relationship to other classes of literature; nature and basis of history; art of the historian; old and new methods in history; types of historical writing; Montaigne on historians; historiography; bibliography of history; reference works; source books and collections; historical textbooks; edited or cooperative histories; histories by individual historians; World War II and after; points to be considered in selection; fifty histories representative of different kinds of historical writing; twenty-five background books on World War II and after

14. TRAVEL   302

Range and variety of travel literature; history and bibliography of travel; atlases, maps, guidebooks; different kinds of travel literature; characteristics and qualities of travel books; present trends in travel literature; points to be considered in selection; ten classics of travel; fifty books, old and new, that represent aspects of travel

15. NATURE AND SCIENCE   324

The modern age created by science; transformations effected in life and thought; growth of the literature of science; increasing specialization of research; atomic bomb and public responsibility; popular interest in science; humanization of science in books for the general reader; divisions of science; "nature books" and the literature of natural science; astrophysical research and changed conceptions of the universe; modern research in biology; pseudoscience; points to be considered in selection; twenty-five books on nature and animal life; fifty books in modern science

16. SOCIOLOGY; THE SOCIAL SCIENCES   354

Sociology in library classification; growing interest in social problems; increase of literature in the social sciences; historical development of the literature; scientific method in sociology; agencies in social research; documents and pamphlets; selection for the general reader in political science and economics; conflicting values in sociological literature; points to be considered in selection; aids and guides in selection; fifty books on questions of the times, indicating trends and tendencies

LIVING WITH BOOKS

17. RELIGION; PHILOSOPHY   385

Importance and range of literature of religion; relationships to other classes; trends in general religious reading; principles that govern libraries in provision of religious literature; points to be considered in selection; philosophy, in older and modern development; literature of philosophy for the general reader; the literature of vagary and delusion; points to be considered in selection of philosophy; aids and guides in selection of religion and philosophy; fifty books, old and new, in religion, philosophy, ethics; twenty-five books indicative of emergent trends

18. LITERATURE; ESSAYS   418

World literature; limitations and specialization of library collections in literature; literary prize awards; importance of works in literature to writers and students; bibliographies and lists; dictionaries and encyclopedias of literature; works on history of literature; works of literary criticism; essays: qualities, characteristics, development; types and trends in essays; points to consider in selection of essays; books of humor; twenty-five books representative of significant modern criticism; fifty volumes of essays, chiefly contemporary, illustrating types and characteristics

19. POETRY   446

Poetry the highest and oldest form of expression; nature and art of poetry; rise of new currents in American poetry; what poetry demands of the reader; trends and tendencies in poetry today; anthologies; older and standard poetry; present-day poetry; books on poetry; a few books and essays about poetry; fifty names chosen to indicate patterns and variations in modern poetry

20. DRAMA   475

Growing importance of drama in community life; pioneer influences in development of community interest; "little" theatres and community drama; Federal Theatre Project; ANTA and Unesco; importance of drama collections in libraries; popularity of the printed play; richness and diversity of contemporary literature of drama; types and characteristics of modern plays; collections of plays; individual plays; the classics; history of drama; manuals of playwriting and stage technique; aids and guides in selection; fifty books on drama and the theatre

21. FICTION TODAY   506

Fiction as a mirror of human experience; dominance of fiction in literature today; development of English fiction since 1800; novels of a century ago; nineteenth-century influences in development of English fiction; Jane Austen; Sir Walter Scott; twentieth-century influences, trends, tendencies; range and diversity of modern fiction; distinctive types in contemporary fiction, standards of value applied to fiction; requirements of truth and art; character consistency; style; other points to be considered in selection; development of modern English fiction indicated in a chronological sequence of fifty novels; twenty-five books about fiction; fifty postwar novels

22. ASPECTS OF FICTION   538
Historical fiction; foreign fiction in translation; ethical influence of fiction and problem of censorship; the short story; aids in selection of fiction; brief panorama of history as presented in chronological order in fifty historical novels; fifty contemporary foreign novels in English translation

EPILOGUE   568

INDEX BY JOHN ASKLING   571

Living with Books

Introduction: The World of Books

> All that Mankind has done, thought, gained, or been: it is lying as in magic preservation in the pages of Books. . . .
> All that a university or final highest school can do for us, is still but what the first school began doing—teach us to read.
>   Thomas Carlyle: *The Hero as Man of Letters*

As CHILDREN learning to read, we step with indifference into the world of books. How we fare in it afterwards depends on how soon and in what measure indifference gives place to inclination and selection. And inclination and selection find their stimulus chiefly in the influence of what has been read upon the will to choose what shall be read. "Evolution in reading" proves its truth in the personal experience of everyone who knows and uses books. Standards are raised, intelligence is enlarged, perceptions are deepened, through the simple process of reading. Books that meant nothing to a reader ten years ago, today penetrate his understanding and stimulate his own deepening realization of human experience; books that ten years ago were revealing or inspiring, have long since been outgrown and forgotten. "What may have sounded like balderdash at twenty, may be the very tissue of truth when forty winters besiege the brow," says John Mistletoe.

Formal education applies its patterns to the mind; but only through books does the mind itself enrich, deepen, apply, modify, and develop those patterns in individual life fulfillment. Intelligence must be kept active, playing over the education it is receiving, drawing its own conclusions, making its own observations and its own tests; otherwise we have simply a thin surface coating of applied instruction. Books are the instruments of intelligence. They are also, of course, the instruments of aberration and fallacy; for they are the expression of all the qualities and defects of the human mind. The more we know them, love them, and use them, the more their inexhaustible riches, their ever increasing potencies, are made manifest.

Consider what books may mean in individual development: in the formation of character, in the activation of intelligence, in the enrichment of resources, and in the deepening of sensitivity.

They offer building material for the formation of character through knowledge and thought. Such character making is a continuous unconscious process of self-education in the school of daily life. We may grow in maturity of judgment, in knowledge of the world, in ideals and principles; or we may remain stationary, gleaning nothing from the ripening harvests of experience; or we may narrow and diminish in intelligence, indifferent to changing thought and expanding knowledge, or intolerant and antagonistic toward all that is outside our immediate experience. Growth is a determinate process of change—not in the essence of the individual being; the germ is unchangeable—but in mutation to broader, deeper understanding, to deeper insight and freer range. We may learn much simply from living and working; but the enduring materials of knowledge, prepared for us through centuries of thought and labor, are stored for our use in books.

Through books we gain what John Morley called "the historic sense of progress through the ages," in other words, a background of understanding, a basis of familiarity with the interlocking of events and with the great undercurrents that run, forever changing yet forever the same, through human experience, past and present. There cannot be broad intelligence or sound judgment without this. No one can form valid opinion or pass fair judgment on what is, who has not some ability to compare, to contrast it, with what has been. Man's possessions and equipment today—achievements and realizations that would have been miracles to the men and women who lived only a hundred years ago—are but later waymarks along paths of human effort and research worn slowly through four thousand years. Ambroise Paré plodded toward the shining highway of modern surgery; Copernicus helped break the pathway to Palomar. Every succeeding generation widens and makes more firm the path;

INTRODUCTION

but take away the knowledge gained by the labor expended before our own day and what should we have left? Through books we have bridged the centuries and built the world's structure of achievement; through books we receive and enlarge the heritage of the human mind.

This background of understanding in some degree, is indispensable to enjoyment of good reading; and it builds itself from that enjoyment. To care for good reading, to keep on with good reading because you care for it, means that little by little this background takes on substance in the mind, and unconsciously every new subject contemplated, studied, or enjoyed enlarges and enriches it. From every book invisible threads reach out to other books; and as the mind comes to use and control those threads the whole panorama of the world's life, past and present, becomes constantly more varied and interesting, while at the same time the mind's own powers of reflection and judgment are exercised and strengthened. Poetry, drama, novels—books that set the imagination at work—are potent agents in background-building, weaving color and personality into the fabric of history and social progress.

Background reading may be built forward or backward. The present gives stimulus to explore the past; the tides of the past ebb and flow into the present. As the new physics teaches, there is no solid matter—all is change and motion in ourselves and our universe. Through reading we are borne along on this flow and movement of life.

Books give a deeper meaning and interest to living. There is nothing in daily work, in the most humdrum occupation, that cannot be made more interesting or more useful through books. They are means to proficiency in every calling. They are inexhaustible sources of pleasure. They bring to us the life of the world as it was and as it is now. They supply increased resources. Those able to turn to books for companionship are seldom lonely; nor do they suffer from the need of finding some action, however trivial, to fill an empty hour. They have friends who will come when desired, bringing amusement, counsel, or some absorbing confidence; friends who, unlike the human variety, may be dismissed when their conversation palls, and who may be chosen to suit whatever mood or interest is uppermost.

Books impart deepened sensitiveness to ideals, to beauty, to pleasure, to the best emotions of life. Living is feeling, and the more responsive the spirit becomes, the fuller and richer life it enjoys. There can be no true culture without sensibility. Every thought and every feeling has overtones that can be apprehended only through refinement and extension of the mind's perceptions. To recognize these overtones, to catch their delicate implications and glimpse their variant elusive radiations, is one of the keenest and most enduring pleasures of life. This is the "meaning of culture," as John Cowper Powys says:

A mind that is totally uncultured gets its own special thrills, no doubt, from a raw, direct contact with unmitigated experience; but a cultured mind approaches everything through an imagination already charged with the passionate responses of the great artists: so that what it sees is a fragment of Nature, double-dyed, so to speak—a reach, a stretch of time's whirling tide, that carries upon its chance-tossed eddies the pattern of something at once transitory and eternal.

Reading transmits the current that keys and charges the mind to this responsiveness. Every class of literature—religion, philosophy, biography, history, science, poetry, fiction—conveys its voltage of inspiration, wisdom, and knowledge. The influences that good reading can shed upon life are no procrustean compulsions, but flow in manifold expression from "the free spirit of mankind." Ideals of courage and endurance and purpose are created for thousands through such biographies as those of Jeanne d'Arc, Lincoln, or Florence Nightingale. Sensitiveness to natural beauty is quickened through poetry, or essay, or vivid word-picture. Sensitiveness to humanity—the ill-used race of man—is deepened through the pages of the great story-tellers and dramatists.

Changing currents of thought and purpose, conflict and turmoil, come to us through books. The present is always tumult and transition. In our immediate present the impact of global war has shattered

INTRODUCTION 7

old stabilities and imposed new compulsions on man's relationship to man. Under the application of modern science everyday life has accelerated and expanded as never before, and the whole form of civilization is changing. The books of today reflect the thoughts, the ideals, the weaknesses, and strength of today; they indicate the paths on which its course is set; they illuminate and interpret its conflicts and its problems. With all its diversity and multiplicity this modern literature is infused with a common purpose—the pursuit of truth: truth in the individual use of the mind, truth in the understanding of man's physical organization, truth in recording the past, truth in recognition of inequalities and shortcomings in the social fabric, truth in the testing and development of human relationships. It is a long pursuit, hampered, contested, deflected by inadequacies and dogmatisms, but stronger and freer today than ever before.

What is good reading? The question is easier to ask than to answer. All reading, any reading, is better than none. Books that have lived long have in that fact proved their power. Books that have given the greatest pleasure to the greatest number of readers are lifted above others by that tidal wave of felicity. Even books born only to die, like the coral insect have left their trace of vital substance in the substructure of the world of literature. It is futile to attempt to specify what are the ten, twenty-five, or fifty "best books." That familiar phrase means only "the books that are the best to me." The choice of books must always be influenced by individual personality. Among any dozen persons who love books, I doubt if there is one who, if honest, would not confess indifference or aversion for some acknowledged masterpiece. Yet the "books that everyone should know" are all worth knowing; from them every reader can draw his own measure of inspiration and wisdom; they are the sources of, the means to, background in understanding and appreciation of literature. As John Mistletoe says: "One of the truisms about books is this: that the things you have heard since childhood were great, really *are* great."

Shakespeare's advice is still sound: "No profit grows where is no pleasure ta'en. In brief, sir, study what you most affect." If you prefer history, or poetry, or biography, or science, or novels, or philosophy, or the discussion of economic and social problems, let your taste have free rein. But though personal taste predominate, it must not wholly rule. Cultivate catholicity; savor the tang of adventure and discovery. There must be a certain rounding out of literature as a whole in reading if breadth of background is to develop. There must be an effort to keep mental elasticity and not let selection settle into a rut, as time goes on and the mind's youthful demand for novelty is blunted. Variety is here both spice and substance of life.

Under the high pressure of present-day living, how is time for reading to be found? This question is often propounded as unanswerable. Its only answer is that those who care for books will somehow, slowly, as years go by, come to know them widely and well. Those protestants who "love reading, but never have a minute for it," in that plea invalidate their claim; for we all find time for the things most vital to us. Even half an hour of daily reading will after six months have brought a rich reward. An hour a day, retrieved perhaps in fragments from the grasp of daily routine, counts for more than would seem possible until its results are seen in perspective. Arnold Bennett wrote in his diary in 1908: "Decided that I must confine reading newspapers to odd moments, and read every day some part of a serious work of instruction and also some verses. So yesterday and today I swallowed the whole of Hayes' *Secret of Herbart*. Now I understand what Herbartianism is." As for reading in bed, that practice long inhibited by traditional family disapproval has received scientific vindication in the researches of Laird and Muller on *Sleep*. Eugene Field discovered long ago that it is the improving and pleasing avocation of all true booklovers; and its justification was put in a sentence by Sir William Osler when he said: "With half an hour's reading in bed every night as a steady practice the busiest man can get a fair education before the plasma sets in the periganglionic spaces of his grey cortex."

It is most useful to keep a record of one's reading. Abbé Dimnet, in *The Art of Thinking*, emphasizes the value of note making—of writing down what has been read or observed and has made an impression on the mind that is felt to be of value. Of course, the fuller the note taking (indicating the subject of the book, the opinion held concerning it, or copying some striking extract), the greater its value in deepening background of book knowledge and developing critical judgment.

Magazines are far more widely read than books; but not by those who know the joys and values of reading. Magazines and newspapers—both dominant factors in American mass culture—are no more than accessories or deterrents to reading; they do not signify that wide ranging and rich adventure in the world of books that is real reading. Magazines have their place, their own usefulness; but no magazine can take the place of standard books. There are periodicals of literary value, of scholarly, technical, or specialized importance, essential to scholars and scientific and technical workers and to men and women in every field. But if more Americans would read good books and cease reading promiscuous popular magazines, we should have a higher level of general education and intelligence.

To bulwark and extend individual reading there must be individual possession of books. The public library, offering its ever renewing supply, is the common reservoir and dispensary of books that otherwise few could know or use. It makes the world of books part of everyday life. But all who care for books will possess some friends and intimates whose companionship cannot be restricted to a formal and limited visit. This may be the simplest and most inexpensive of indulgences, kept closely to low-priced reprint editions or to favorites salvaged from the flotsam of secondhand bookshops. It is not a question of money. Half of what most people spend without demur each month for the movies will bring beauty, wit, gossip, argument, wisdom, and glorious foolishness into any reader's intimate possession. Ownership of books has unending implications and possibilities. It may kindle the thrill of book-hunting and develop into collectorship; it may yield material assurance of investment value; it may reveal unsuspected tastes or stimulate unrealized capabilities; it will surely deepen and stabilize in any household the intangible elements of culture. Immense energies of organized and concentrated publicity are directed toward placing automobiles, radios, electric refrigerators, in every American home; but little attention is given to the value, joy, and pride derivable from the modest private library that ought to be the most indispensable of household utilities. Books are the most interesting and distinguished accessories of any home; merely as furniture, they are cheaper and better decoration than oriental rugs or overstuffed chairs. They give a house character and meaning. The discerning eye looks for them in its first appraisal; their absence is a negative finding upon the cultivation and intelligence of the household; their presence is as illuminating of social, intellectual, and personal status as a merchants' association rating is of material stability and financial integrity.

Librarianship is the only calling that devotes itself to bringing books into the common life of the world. The materials librarians work with are the materials which furnish the understanding, knowledge, and reason that can inform the mind and direct the will to meet the challenge of the time, to fit ourselves to its compulsions, to discern and guide the forces that are shaping the future. The "great trade" of publishing and bookselling, though it is the oldest and most universal agency for bringing together the reader and the printed word, has not the same range of opportunity nor the same variety and intimacy of relationship to readers of all tastes, capacities, needs, habits, and levels of education. The spirit of delight and confidence in books, the receptive and adventurous attitude toward the new and experimental, the catholicity of lifelong friendship and understanding for literature, are attributes of librarianship more than of any other calling. And those attributes must be fused in a dynamic of social consciousness, of confidence and purpose, if librarians are to rise to their potential leadership in welding public understanding and unity for the building of a safer and better world.

Of course, the taste for books is not common to all. It is a spark latent in the individual, most often implanted by heredity, kindled by training or circumstance, and fed and tended by purpose and experience. But only those who possess this spark will draw from librarianship its full measure of inspiration and reward in the interpretation and enrichment of human life through books. For the world of books is the world of man's thought and effort, joy and purpose and inextinguishable hopes, as they pass in heritage from the past to the present and as they are born of each immediate moment.

PART ONE

Foundations and Backgrounds

1. People and Books

> Every man who knows how to read has it in his power to magnify himself, to multiply the ways in which he exists, to make his life full, significant and interesting.
> Aldous Huxley: Jesting Pilate

> ... the deep
> Layers of the islanded points of mind that are peaks
> Risen from one base ... whose fatal
> Perceptions and discoveries were making the future.
> Robinson Jeffers: The Women at Point Sur

THE PROVINCE AND PURPOSE of the public library is to provide for every person the education obtainable through reading. This does not mean education in any narrow or formalized sense but, rather, the culture of mind and spirit that books can diffuse in life. Education in its ideal fulfillment is not simply fact finding nor the assiduous pursuit of information. It implies the use of books for spiritual and intellectual as well as for material and vocational profit, books for mental resource, reading for individual and personal joy—all elements in the diffusion, perhaps not of specific knowledge, but of culture in Matthew Arnold's sense—"in becoming something rather than in having something, in an inward condition of the mind and spirit, not in an outward set of circumstances."

This is the ideal that has inspired and directed the development of library service during the rounding century of the American public library movement.

When the first convention of librarians ever held met in 1853 in New York City, their purpose was concisely stated by Charles Coffin Jewett. "We meet," he said, "to provide for the diffusion of a knowledge of good books and for enlarging the means of public access to them." From 1876, when the Centennial Exposition at Philadelphia brought new values into American living, the ever broadening current of this purpose has swept steadily onward. It has deepened, widened, overflowed its original bounds, and channelled the whole surface of American life. Knowledge of good books is diffused through organized librarianship; and the means of access to books is enlarged through an ever growing multiplicity and diversity of libraries. Scholarly, scientific, educational, professional, industrial, technical, and sociological libraries, all are part of the modern library structure. Their work is specialized and intensive; but in variety and range it is represented, in some degree, in the service of the public library, which, large or small, must supply in its books all the manifestations and requirements of the community it serves.

The public library is maintained to provide books that meet human wants, needs, and tastes; that develop capacities of mind and body; that give practical aid to workers in every field; that equalize opportunities and enrich life for all. Only the rich could buy for their own use the books necessary for any extended or specialized study or research; but the library provides them freely for all. Few, however rich, could readily acquire the number and variety of books that are available in even a moderate, representative, public library collection; for bookstores (their stock, however large, always in transition) offer no such organized accumulation of older and standard literature as is built up during the life of a public library.

Library service is not only the provision of books; it is the bringing of the right book to the right reader. Without a reader a book is in suspended animation; without users a library is dead. People and books are the positive and negative poles that keep alive the current of library service.

Any kind of library service that is designed to bring together people and books, whether rendered by public libraries, or school libraries, or by libraries maintained for professional or scholarly or specialized use, must be based on intelligent book selection. Librarians must know how to choose wisely books that are the expression of human life and thought, that offer the materials of knowledge, that satisfy or stimulate individual development, that enlarge and clarify mass intelligence. To aid any worker with books to acquire this knowledge and put it to use in the service of the reading public is the purpose of the present study of the principles and practice of book selection.

Consider first the public for which the library exists. For there is no living world of books apart from the living world of readers. Only as librarianship relates and integrates the manifold influences and uses of books with the manifold interests and activities of human life does it fulfill its modern purpose.

Today the American public as a whole is potentially a reading public. Illiteracy exists, but in a limited and steadily diminishing degree. Newspaper and magazine reading bulks much larger than the reading of books. In 1949 approximately 2,000 daily newspapers, with a total daily sale of more than 52,000,000 copies, were published in the United States. (Including those published at all frequencies—daily, weekly, semiweekly, and so on—the total number of newspapers published in the United States was almost 12,000 in 1949.) Periodicals (weekly, fortnightly, semimonthly, monthly, bimonthly, quarterly, and miscellaneous) totaled more than 6,000 in 1949.[1]

Analysis of the reading of a "selected group," made in 1928, in Gray and Munroe's *The Reading Interests and Habits of Adults*, shows that about 50 percent read books, 75 percent read magazines, and 97 percent read a daily newspaper. A survey of reading interests and use of public library services, made for the American Library Association and 17 cooperating libraries by the National Opinion Research Center, University of Denver, in January, 1945, reported that 56 percent of the adults interviewed said they spent an average of an hour a day reading newspapers and magazines, 22 percent said they spent an average of an hour a day reading books. The total number of interviews held in the 17 cities was 2,114.[2] More comprehensive in scope is the survey of reading and book-buying habits of the country undertaken in 1945, by Henry C. Link and Harry A.

[1] N. W. Ayer & Sons, *Directory of Newspapers and Periodicals*, 1949 (Philadelphia, 1949), p. 11.
[2] *What, Where, Why Do People Read?* (National Opinion Research Center, University of Denver, 1946).

Hopf, and sponsored by the Book Manufacturers' Institute.³ This followed the *Middletown* method and was based on 4,000 personal interviews (1,705 men, 2,295 women) conducted between May 21 and June 8, 1945; it reported 50 percent of the population interviewed as "active readers" (one book a month or more), 21 percent as "inactive readers," and 29 percent as "non-readers"; but it dealt only with the reading of books and did not consider magazines or newspapers. Kindred statistical analyses of community book use, community book supply and demand in its relation to library service, group characteristics, preferences and interests of library users, have developed within recent years into an important division of professional library literature.⁴

The actual book-reading public (buyers of books, library book borrowers, borrowers from commercial rental libraries), estimated broadly but conservatively by Maxwell Aley at twenty-five million in 1931,⁵ was immensely increased under the stimulus of the war years, when books sold in totals never before reached, when the Army and Navy bought books by millions for men in the service, and when book club subscriptions rose to unimagined figures. Statistics in this field are as yet only approximate and generalizing. But there can be no question of the phenomenal enlargement of the book-reading public nor of the continuous expansion of the demand for education and for reading. Even prior to 1945, when the "G.I. Bill of Rights" made higher education a financial possibility for added millions, there were more persons enlisted in study of some degree or kind—college courses, extension courses, correspondence courses, reading courses—than ever before in proportion to the population. And it is significant that Liberal Arts was the first choice as preferred field of study by veterans availing themselves of the "G.I. Bill" provision for education and training.

Whatever the inflationary aspect of these "peak" years may have

---

³ Henry C. Link and Harry Arthur Hopf, *People and Books* (New York, Book Manufacturers' Institute, 1946).
⁴ See Bernard Berelson, *The Library's Public* (New York, Columbia University Press, 1949), especially pp. 5–10: "Popular Use of the Major Media of Communication" and "Book Reading Related to Other Media."
⁵ *Publishers' Weekly*, June 6, 1931.

been, they represent a fundamental development in book production and book use. Publishing activities multiply and enlarge; new publishing houses have come into existence, and the leading older firms continue to flourish. Commercial book clubs, initiated in April, 1926, within twenty years had multiplied twentyfold, ramified into many specialized fields (religious, scientific, Catholic, psychiatric, Negro, are examples), and in 1946 had a membership of three and a half million people in this country and Canada. There is steadily mounting multiplicity of book reviewing, book publicity, and book discussion. More books of high quality or specialized value are constantly rising to best-seller ranks, and individual scientific and literary work receives continuous encouragement through the enlarging system of awards made by research foundations and educational organizations.

That is one side of the shield. On the other, evidence and argument are frequently offered to show that proportionately very few Americans are readers and users of books; that books, as a matter of fact, are of relative unimportance in American life. A comprehensive study of this subject was made in 1930 by Robert L. Duffus, who was commissioned by the Carnegie Corporation to survey conditions affecting "the publication and distribution of serious, nontechnical books." Mr. Duffus [6] summarized book trade and library statistics, reviewed the development of American publishing and bookselling, traced the course of the public library movement, analyzed conditions of book distribution, through trade agencies and methods, through bookstores, book clubs, and libraries. He found "that the American public buys approximately two books per capita each year, and that it pays for books certainly not more than one-half of one percent of its annual income." From public library statistics he cited a total circulation that averaged two books a year for each man, woman, and child in the entire population; he allowed for rental use and for individual borrowing, and he arrived at: "two books a year bought outright, two books a year borrowed from the library, two books a year rented from rental libraries, one book

[6] *Books: Their Place in a Democracy* (Boston, Houghton, 1930).

a year borrowed from a friend—or a possible total of seven books a year read by the average American." His conclusion was "that a relatively small percentage of Americans read much more than seven books a year, that a relatively large percentage read much less, and that many millions, after their school days are over, read none at all. But it is plain that we are not a book-reading nation."

Mr. Duffus' study, as a whole, is thoughtful, lucid, soundly based. He was aware of the swift-moving changes that were altering conditions even as he recorded them. He recognized the immense variation in human capabilities, and he knew that the capacities of the ordinary human being are yet to be explored and developed. He believes that books must be more effectively popularized—more standardized in physical character and in methods of distribution, but not necessarily standardized in contents. He says:

I believe that the failure of the democratic majority to accept intellectual and aesthetic ideals is due rather to a lack of will to do so than to a lack of ability. And I believe that the lack of will is due to false and imperfect systems of education and to other conditions in the environment which can be altered. . . . Almost any American community will read books, including a certain percentage of good books, if it is exposed to them.

The logical supplement to the Duffus study appeared in 1938, in Louis R. Wilson's elaborate statistical survey of *The Geography of Reading*.[7] This is a landmark in present-day library development, for it defined and analyzed regional limitations and inequalities in the provision and use of books throughout the United States and furnished a base for the American Library Association's postwar planning program, initiated in 1942. Solidly packed with tables, charts, and graphs, the enormous mass of data here presented focused on the fact that 37 out of every 100 persons (35 million in all) were without access to public library service. One half of these live in the Southeast and Southwest, though these two regions contain only one

---

[7] Louis R. Wilson, *The Geography of Reading: a Study of the Distribution and Status of Libraries in the United States* (University of Chicago Studies in Library Science). Chicago, American Library Association and University of Chicago Press, 1938.

third of the population of the nation. The problem is thus primarily a rural one; and the best promise for its solution seems to lie in the now well established movement for organization and extension of library service through state and federal aid in areas without such service.[8] In analyses of amount and kind of reading done, the Wilson volume sustains the Duffus findings, with perhaps an added shade of gloom. Books are read by probably not more than 25 percent of the population; magazines are read at least twice as extensively as books; newspapers reach perhaps 90 percent of the population. Only one half of the adult public, Dr. Wilson believes, has sufficient reading skill to read and understand books published for adults; and this condition must be remedied by more widespread and more effective education and the provision of more elementary "readable" material.

Critics and pessimists have made wide use of these conclusions. The dictum that no American reads more than seven books a year has been given currency. It serves to reinforce the still lingering traditional belief that "culture" must be the privilege of the few and that the great mass of humanity is incapable of mental development. This tradition finds expression in wholesale condemnation of the "trash" circulated from public libraries and of the triviality and futility of the mass demand that the public library seeks to satisfy. Robert E. Rogers affirmed it when he said:

Literature is not and cannot possibly be the possession of the hundred million. It is idle to believe that, and it is foolish to build a vast public library system on that assumption. . . . Let the crowd that has no appreciation of what literature may mean, no interest in it, and no desire to be interested in it, go where it wants for the sort of thing it wants. And let the guardians of our public libraries be freed from the endless and tedious and futile task of serving out over the counter the canned goods of literature to people who are not even interested in the different brands of canned goods.[9]

[8] The Library Demonstration Bill, which has A.L.A. support, was reported favorably by a Senate committee late in 1949. It embodies a program for promoting interest in libraries and demonstrating their usefulness in new areas.
[9] "This Bequest of Wings," *A.L.A. Proceedings*, New Haven Conference, 1931.

To accept this doctrine is to abandon the principle of evolution on which modern life erects its structure.

But there is truth imbedded in all tradition. Mass demand considered in bulk is more weighted by ignorance and instinct than by intelligence and reason. It is supplied and stimulated by many exploiting agencies of our machine civilization. It has enforced and established crudities and superficialities in mass education. It represents the most difficult problem in library service. To deal with it constructively there must be analysis and differentiation of its various elements and a proportional representation of values for each; and above all there must be realization that its density is not solid, but a continuous flow of change and motion.

Our concern is primarily with the public library's relation to its public. In the abstract, that public is the whole body of citizens composing the community the library serves; actually, it consists of those persons who use the library. Consider it from the double aspect of mass readers and individual readers. The mass of public library readers in the ordinary American community represents an almost complete cross section of the community life: every profession, trade, calling, and occupation; every shade of opinion, prejudice, and belief; every degree of education and mentality, of understanding and narrow-mindedness; all ages, both sexes, and all conditions of living —though the very poor and the very rich are likely to be most inadequately represented.

The demand made upon the public library by this mass of readers is strongest along the line of least mental resistance—for the popular, the superficial, and the elementary in literature, whether in pursuit of pleasure or edification. This range of demand grows constantly more diversified and more flexible. Only when the mass is resolved into individuals do its finer potencies and elements become evident. Then, intelligent and purposeful and fruitful reading is revealed, to a degree that not all librarians and very few social commentators realize.[10] Such reading is done undoubtedly by a select body of book

---

[10] Interesting evidence of the extent and variety of good reading among the general public is presented by Charles H. Compton, in *Who Reads What* (H. W. Wilson

users, but these are so infiltrated in the mass, so constantly shifting from one level of book value to another, that they can hardly be separated from the whole. Thus, as the library's public has this double aspect, so is the library's task a twofold one. It must supply the mass demands of its users as effectively as possbile, and at the same time it must render intensive personal service to that minority of readers who know and love literature and have the capacity to find in books sustenance for the mind and inspiration for the spirit.

The public library is an integral part of community activity; an organ in the social body. It functions in response to or in anticipation of the whole range of community needs. Presumptively, these needs are the needs of all the people of the community, not merely of those who are library users; but, in fact, they are needs made evident by public demand; and demand upon the library comes only from those who in some measure desire to make use of it. Demand can often be elicited; it can always be stimulated and influenced; but if it does not exist, material provided to supply it will not be used.

So, in its provision of books and its plan of service the public library must always consider supply in relation to demand; it must always realize the great variation in values of demand—the strongest demand does not always represent the greatest value; and it must always relate and adjust these two factors to each other and to a third factor, the library's available resources in books and in income.

Here is the triangular base of the public library's problem and purpose. It was put in eleven words by Melvil Dewey, in a phrase that has been the motto of the American Library Association since its organization in 1876: "The best reading for the largest number at the least cost." On these three phrases hang all the law and the prophets in the scriptures of library book selection.

How to discover the needs of the community is the librarian's first

---

Co., 1934), a study of the personal backgrounds, occupations, and tastes of individual borrowers who drew from the St. Louis Public Library the Greek classics in translation, the works of William James, Shaw, Hardy, Mark Twain, and Carl Sandburg. Further studies by Mr. Compton, analyzing different aspects of the reading done by users of the St. Louis Public Library, appear in his annual reports as librarian of that library for 1940, 1942, 1943, 1945.

problem in establishing relationship with the public. How to select the books to fill those needs best is the second; and this implies a third, how to judge the value of individual books.

It should be remembered that the problems of selection are simpler in a large library than in a small one, because standard works are already purchased, the range of demand is broader, and selection need not be so closely restricted. In the large library, also, selection is usually divided among departments, each responsible for its own subject. The small public library, however, can often weld a closer, more direct, and more personal relationship with its community as a whole than can be effected by the highly organized and interrelated library system of a great city.

Various avenues open to discovery of community needs. There must be knowledge of the activities, interests, organizations, institutions, and distinctive characteristics of the community life, to give understanding of channels through which mass demand for books may be stimulated or developed. In a rural community there will be channels of interest that do not exist in a suburban town, or an industrial city, or a university center—each in its distinctive components differing from the other. New channels are constantly opening as the scope of librarianship expands. Rising interest in public relations releases fresh dynamics of personality and purpose in the library's relation to the people. Deepening social consciousness seeks to replace ignorance and prejudice by knowledge and understanding. Fuller measures of practical cooperation with civic, social, and industrial agencies strengthen unity and mutual interests in common living. Radio and moving pictures become ever more effective mediums for relating the library to its public and stimulating appreciation of books. Concurrently, there is continuous expansion in fields in which specialized library service is sought: research and semi-technical service in business, industry, applied science, public utilities, organizations, private and public institutional bodies; these are potential strands for the weaving of an over-all net of library service for the whole community.

Familiarity with all cultural and racial elements in the population is important. From foreign strains rich potencies of mind, imagination, and craftsmanship flow continuously into American culture. Through the public library these potencies can be deepened and brought to fruitful expression, and the difficulties that so often make American assimilation a tragic experience can be offset or alleviated. There should be available to foreign readers through the public library literature of their own lands in their own languages; and with this should go provision of books that will give such readers understanding of the English language and knowledge of backgrounds, conditions, and opportunities of American life. This is one of the most interesting specialized fields in present-day book selection; it offers satisfaction to any librarian who has facility in languages, sympathy for people, and enthusiasm for books.

The Negro population in any community should have full library representation, both in demand and supply. The great contributions made by Negroes to the United States are of far-reaching significance in our national development. They are building a constantly rising structure of material achievement; they have released new colors, vital rhythms, dramatic power, and sensitivity of feeling into Amercian art, music, theatre, and literature. Deep-rooted racial discrimination, economic inequality, and social injustice, creations of the ancient fetish of "white supremacy," are challenged today as never before; and the fetish itself is being swept away from the emerging postwar world by a rising mass movement that demands equality for all peoples. There is a growing strength of Negro purpose and organization directed against exploitation, suppression, and injustice; and constructive influences are at work throughout the country to prevent violence, check intolerance, and bring equality and cooperation into interracial relations. The public library, as one of the two great agencies of education and common understanding, should maintain continuous effort toward extinction of race prejudice and full integration of all minorities into a free democratic society. Whether the public library provides for Negro readers without separation or distinction is influenced by community conditions. But in any collection there should be generous provision of books by and about Negroes, the library itself should stand for freedom from all race or class distinctions, and wherever practicable it should carry on carefully organized programs for improvement of racial and cultural relations.[11] Librarians can take pride in the fact that theirs is one of the first liberal professions to welcome and develop participation of Negroes in its activities; and that what Negro librarians are doing in effective library administration and book service constantly takes on wider range and greater importance.

There must be close relationship between the library and all community agencies of education. Public elementary and high schools in many cities maintain their own library systems. When this is so, the local school library organization should be regarded by the public library as furnishing common groundwork for cooperation in book selection and for making the use of books a part of life education. So with schools of other types, with evening schools, university extension courses, institutions of higher education or of specialized research. For all, a sense of friendly alliance with the public library should be established that will be of mutual usefulness in correlating the book resources of the community and in linking the informal education through books that the public library fosters with the activities and trends of formal education.

Active cooperative relations with organized labor give the library great opportunities to fulfill its high aim as an agency of self-education through reading and to win recognition and support from the rank and file of the community. Even a small public library can maintain a deposit collection in the local labor temple, can call the attention of union members to books they should find useful and interesting, can give fair proportional representation to labor literature in its book selection, can supply the important labor periodicals, and can furnish adequate material concerning labor's educational activities in classes, institutes, and conferences.[12]

---

[11] An excellent practical, suggestive study of "Library Activities in the Field of Race Relations" was presented by Miriam Matthews as a master's thesis to the University of Chicago Library School in September, 1945, but is so far unavailable in print.

[12] Clear, practical summary of methods and values in cooperative library relation-

Local newspapers are an important link between the library and the public. From them, the librarian learns immediate community interests and needs, and gains familiarity with local celebrities and with those heterogeneous organizations that spring ready-made from the brow of Demos. In their columns there may be built up a bulwark of public support for the library that is of continuing value. To develop this sort of local press affiliation, however, demands patience and tact on the part of the librarian; also a sense of news values, as well as the ability (either personally or by proxy) to supply suitable and interesting copy—not just bald lists of "Books (Nonfiction) Recently Added."

Besides familiarity with the community in its special characteristics and needs, there must be a broad general acquaintance with the immediate problems of the day, general, national, and local. To ensure this the librarian must read regularly a daily newspaper and keep in touch with the broad range of magazine topics. This aids especially in recognizing advancing currents of popular interest and in anticipating requests by readers.

Since public library readers represent a cross section of the community, to understand community needs the librarian must have a cross-sectional knowledge of the community. It is unnecessary to recite in detail the industrial, business, political, recreational, ethical, and social manifestations of the ordinary American community: its factories and shops and institutions, its business men's associations, its labor unions, its myriad organized groups concerned with public affairs, with art, drama, music, religion, education, and every kind of individual interest and activity. The librarian's cross-sectional knowledge is not acquired through an immediate personal participation in all these activities. A surprising variety and multiplicity of contacts for the library may be developed, however, by placing upon each member of the staff the responsibility to reach some particular circle of influence. Of course, the more varied personal rela-

---

ship with organized labor is given in an article on the Work with Trade-Unions department of the Boston Public Library: "The Ins and Outs of Attracting Labor," by A. H. Kalish, *Library Journal*, January 15, 1944, pp. 54-56.

tionship that can be maintained, the better; a genuine interest in and sympathy for human beings is indispensable; but no single human being can have nonvicarious participation in the whole of human experience. The librarian's knowledge must be established by bringing together the threads that, in the use of the library, are connecting people to books. From the material of mass demand there must be traced, analyzed, and utilized the elements that produce it. Such a mastery of community life for the ends of library service is the first requirement of successful librarianship.

2. Books for People: Principles in Selection

> The purpose of art and literature is not to educate us into a state where our servants must do our living for us. It is rather, to give us increased vitality and a more passionate sense of life and living. We do not try to force our way of seeing upon people. What we try to do is to give people their own way of seeing. . . . We explain that there are a thousand aspects of even the most ordinary subject, and that we see this subject in such and such a way. This will help each person in turn to arrive at an individual view and idea of each object. All this enriches life; it adds experience: not only that, it will eventually increase the consciousness of the race.
>
> Edith Sitwell: "Poetry," in *Tradition and Experiment in Present-Day Literature: Addresses Delivered at the [London] City Literary Institute* (1929)

FROM THE BACKGROUND AND INTERESTS of the community, turn now to the reading tastes, capacities, needs, and habits of the individuals who form the public. The more thoroughly librarians know the full range and the possibilities of individual reading, the more wisdom can be exercised in book selection and the more effectively can library service be carried on. Study of reading habits is now taking shape as an organic process in professional librarianship. Best known among earlier contributions to this study are the report on *Reading Interests and Habits of Adults*, by W. S. Gray and Ruth Munroe, made at the suggestion of the American Association for Adult Education, published in 1929; and *What People Want to Read About*, an elaborate survey and analysis of group reading interests, made in 1931 by Douglas Waples and Ralph W. Tyler.

In the Gray and Munroe study, any librarian concerned with book selection will find interesting broad deductions regarding the effect upon reading habits of geographical location, age, sex, occupation, and marital condition. Statistical analyses show the highest averages in library circulation and magazine reading recorded for the Pacific Coast and three New England states. Women, apparently, read more books than do men—a conclusion shared by nearly all observers of present-day American culture; men give more time to newspaper reading than do women; the unmarried are more interested in books than the married, though married people give more time to reading newspapers and magazines; city dwellers read more than do country people. These are generalizations which will be found in most of the statistical analyses of reading; but they undoubtedly have some validity and significance.

What People Want to Read About is concerned not at all with what people do read, nor is it related to any specific use of books. It seeks to discover what people would like to read about, through submitting to small, carefully chosen groups a series of questionnaires listing 117 topics, made up from collection and classification of magazine articles published in the United States during ten years. These topics are crisply phrased, often in interrogative form. They reflect very imperfectly the subject matter most familiar in books. The study, in fact, represents an elaborate test to find out which of a selected array of subjects seem most interesting to groups of people who have certain similarities—in sex, age, amount of schooling, kind of occupation, and environment. It has, however, a definite relationship to library book selection, for by estimating the degrees of interest felt in certain subjects by different community groups and by flexible and experimental book selection directed upon those subjects, it should be possible for a skillful librarian to extend and develop reading interest in almost any community.

Different aspects of the library's book service to the public are brought out in numerous other studies, many of them linked to actual surveys of specific communities or libraries. Of basic importance as an over-all presentation is *Post-War Standards for Public Libraries,* compact, comprehensive formulation of working standards for public library service, prepared by the A.L.A. Committee on Post-War Planning and published in 1943. Every phase of library administration and development, stripped to essentials, is set forth in logical order, in clear factual and statistical statement. The chapter devoted to "Standards of the Book Collection," summarizing objectives, size in proportion to population, and broad principles of selection, may be considered an anchor and accompaniment for the present chapter and the one that follows.

A comprehensive, analytical survey and study which holds far-reaching implications for future library development is the Public Library Inquiry, initiated in May, 1947, with a Carnegie Corporation grant of $200,000. Conducted by the Social Science Research Council (at A.L.A. suggestion), under the direction of a special advisory committee with Dr. Robert Leigh as chairman, this undertaking was designed to provide a thoroughgoing evaluation of the functions, procedures, and public relationships of American public libraries, by social scientists experienced "in appraising the evolution, functioning, trends and possibilities of other social institutions." The undertaking was completed in 1949, when Columbia University Press began publication of the seven separate volumes that compose the Inquiry. Of these, the General Report by Robert D. Leigh, entitled *The Public Library in the United States*, is a critical evaluation and summing up of the total findings; the other volumes include *The Library's Public*, by Bernard Berelson; *The Public Librarian*, by Alice I. Bryan; *The Public Library in the Political Process*, by Oliver Garceau; *Government Publications for the Citizen*, by James L. McCamy; *The Book Industry*, by William Miller; and *The Information Film*, by Gloria Waldron.

In many of the studies in this field, chief trends have been toward analyses of community conditions, character and extent of all sources of community book supply and community book demand, and toward statistical investigation of reading abilities and tastes of the less literate majority of the population. *Portrait of a Library*, by Margery Quigley and W. E. Marcus, is a study of the Montclair (New Jersey) Public Library during a ten-year period of carefully planned development. While it does not deal with specific book selection, it gives much practical and provocative suggestion concerning the library's ability to discover community needs and adapt its service to community conditions. Grace Kelly's monograph, *Woodside Does Read*, describes a survey made for a section of the Queens Borough (New York) Public Library and gives examples and forms for study and analysis of what subjects are most read by library users, for record of subjects in which readers would like to read, and for record of other community agencies of book supply.

This absorption in statistical analysis of readers' capacities and readers' interests finds culmination in James H. Wellard's volume, *Book Selection: Its Principles and Practice*. Here a "social theory of book selection" is presented which disregards any approach to book selection through literary and critical consideration of the books themselves, but resolves selection into an effort to elicit and organize sociological and psychological findings as to readers; in other words, "to classify readers by homogeneous and identifiable groups, and for this purpose utilize social traits which have been found the most trustworthy bases for the description of reading as a social activity." Such traits are indicated as sex, age, occupation, education, and any others that correlate with actual reading. Then follows analysis of the groups' formal activities, social needs, and reading interests, to discover "requirements and deficiencies, some of which it will be within the province of the library to fulfill. These, when evaluated by standards inherent in the library's social and local purpose, will represent the desirable objectives of book selection. These objectives, in their turn, will be represented by corresponding subjects from which the specific books will be chosen according to standards based on the nature of the book and of reading."

Mr. Wellard is an Englishman, and the application of his theory —with its implication of a large statistical corps engaged in survey, record, and analysis—is particularly related to the English county public library system with its regional branches. His book, under its coating of what Jacques Barzun calls "educators' patois," suggests some directions in which public library service can be strengthened and intensified among groups which have not been adequately reached. But it gives little recognition to what libraries have long done and are effectively doing in these channels. There are few large public libraries that do not have in their branch relationships a fairly thorough and intensive knowledge of community factors and characteristics. There are few public libraries of any standing at all whose practice of book selection is, as Mr. Wellard says, "simply a process of choosing books from publishers' catalogs and library magazines according to the individual librarian's estimate of what his patrons would or should read." And it should be added that whatever scientific-statistical basis may be worked out for more adequate knowledge of what people read, why they read, and how they do or don't or may read, useful and proficient selection of books for library service demands knowledge of the books themselves, awareness of variant values, discriminating comparative judgment concerning them, and most of all enthusiasm for and confidence in the enrichment they bring to life.

The "readers' adviser" service, which, as part of the movement for adult education, has been developed as a specialized activity in many public libraries, is one of the most valuable means of building up materials of knowledge concerning people and books. It gives opportunity to study the tastes, needs, and capacities of individual readers, to observe the influence of specific books upon different persons, to record variations in interest, and to trace the progressive influence of reading in the experiences of individuals. In every library where this work is organized, careful and systematic records should be kept, and the findings of the readers' advisers should be reflected in book selection. Two specific studies make it possible to follow one library's observation and experience in this field through ten years of change, growth, and expansion. *A Readers' Advisory Service*, the pamphlet by Jennie M. Flexner and Sigrid A. Edge, published in 1934, is a survey of the personalized service to adult readers organized in 1929 in the New York Public Library, and of the range, character, and variations of reading demand encountered during the next five years. This was followed in 1941 by *Readers' Advisers at Work*, in which Miss Flexner and Byron C. Hopkins survey the development of the service through a decade that opened with the impact of the Depression, bringing "pressures never before encountered by this generation of librarians," as men and women turned to books to find what employment and security had hitherto supplied, and that closed on the rising tide of war, with its inflow of refugees from all over the world seeking to learn how to live in a new country.

Advisory service to readers has, of course, been a vital, continuous current in the life-stream of American public library development. When the American Association for Adult Education was organized in 1926, the American Library Association was an active participant in the new movement. In many libraries, readers' advisers' work was organized or strengthened, and cooperative relations with local forums and adult education programs were widely developed. In the immense postwar expansion of adult education activities, another kind of readers' service has also developed. This is the Guided Group Reading, conducted in libraries and schools as a carefully controlled popular book-seminar discussion under trained leadership. It stems from the course devoted to the reading of great books instituted at Columbia College in 1920, under the inspiration of John Erskine, but received its impetus in 1939, from the nationwide educational controversy ("Traditionalism" versus "Progressivism") which centered on the curriculum of St. John's College, Annapolis, with its four years of concentrated study of world classics; and from the best-selling success of Mortimer J. Adler's volume, *How to Read a Book*, which expounds an intensive technique of reading and applies it to the mastery of the "great books," as "the art of getting a liberal education." The "great books" classes, later offered at the University of Chicago by Chancellor Robert M. Hutchins and Dr. Adler, set the pattern for the university's Great Books Extension program, which by 1946 had established in Chicago, Detroit, Cleveland, and Indianapolis training classes for discussion leaders.

In 1947 the movement was established on a national basis by organization of the Great Books Foundation, a nonprofit, independent body, with headquarters at the University of Chicago and Dr. Hutchins as chairman of the board of directors. The purpose of the Foundation is to encourage the formation of discussion groups, develop training classes for discussion leaders, and cooperate in the provision of the literature required as discussion material. "Great Books of the Western World," a 54-volume set of the ancient and modern classics chosen for the discussion groups, published under Dr. Hutchins' editorship, by Encyclopaedia Britannica, Incorporated, supplies this basic material; and the Foundation sponsors publication of reprint "readings," special lists, and coordination of correlative material. Groups are conducted on a carefully worked out plan. Leaders are trained to ask questions, to stimulate discussion, and to listen sympathetically; students are required to give intensive personal reading to the books discussed; and in each city the program is administered by local organizations—universities, libraries, school systems. Such study and discussion as this Guided Group Reading represents can hold stimulus and opportunity for fulfillment of the library's great aim—"the aim," as John Powell says, "of making books more helpful, of getting more people to make more and better use of books as instruments in their attempts to make living richer, more satisfying, and more humane." [1]

From the inside of the library, and from all points of contact with the public, knowledge of readers must be constantly enlarged and clarified if book selection is to be made intelligent and adequate. The librarian who looks upon the ever-moving throng of book users only as an unending influx of unreasonable or stupid consumers of the trivial and the commonplace, should find another vocation. No one who has penetrated beneath appearances into realities of human nature and human experience can maintain this attitude. Public library readers, like Mr. Venus' collection of bones, are "assorted, human, warious." The books that meet their needs must also be "assorted, human, warious." No representative library collection is

---

[1] John Powell, "One Step Nearer Leadership," *Library Journal*, April 1, 1946, p. 443. This is a clear, compact exposition of the content, technique, and values of the first Guided Group Reading program, launched in 1945, by the Public Library of the District of Columbia.

Of closely related interest is Lowell Martin's "Guided Group Reading as a Library Service: the Chicago Project," in *Library Journal*, May 15, 1946, p. 734. "The pioneer Washington project is a demonstration, the Chicago project an application."

composed of "trash," though it must contain much printed matter of varying values—recreational, practical, educational, intellectual, ethical, and empirical. No reading public consumes only "trashy and ephemeral fiction"; nor are the books that make the bulk of any public library fiction collection correctly defined by this favorite phrase. The whole fabric of public library reading is a texture woven of different strands—weak and strong, gay and somber, shoddy and genuine; and the reading of the individual is of the texture of the whole. From Dr. Waples' intensive investigation of reading interests this truth emerges. "Most literate people," he says, "read many kinds of material for many different reasons." And he sums up the matter in a single cogent paragraph:

Other popularly accepted opinions about reading in general can be listed indefinitely: most people read trashy fiction; most people read substantial books in libraries; the movies and radio have taken the place of reading for most people; farms and sparsely settled regions supply the heavy readers; the astonishing success of the book-of-the-month clubs has made the reading of books almost universal; people read mostly about sex. Each of these is stated in terms of black and white. Hence none is correct. The fact is that most people read some of all kinds of material and for a wide variety of purposes.

In any study of readers, however, certain tendencies will be evident. To a majority of the public, reading is an agreeable occupation which bears little relation to the serious business of life and is indulged in according to well-defined personal tastes. Most readers know what they want—not specific books, perhaps, but the general kind of reading; they will test a new venture by the interest it arouses, and if disappointed are not likely to pursue it further. In their reaction to individual books there is little apprehension of critical values. Most often their judgment is either immediately personal, or it represents what I. A. Richards calls "stock responses." That is, in an immediately personal judgment, the reader considering a given book precipitates himself upon specific points which he seizes and holds up as generalizations, adjudged true or false according to whether they coincide with his own personal experience. "Stock responses," on the other hand, are views and emotions already prepared in the reader's mind, so that, in reading, a button is pressed and the old mental record starts playing quite independently of the instrument that is supposed to be receiving attention. Somewhat akin are the "doctrinal adhesions" that weight or prevent mental action when new points of view are presented. A great many readers are wholly insensitive to literary quality; to them, subject interest and moral acceptability are the only things that count. Comparatively few relate a book to its author, with any recognition of his style, his characteristics, his preceding work, and his status as a writer. Not all of these tendencies are confined to the public; some of them may be frequently observed in librarians.

Anyone whose work has lain with people and books will recognize these tendencies, and yet will recognize also the undercurrents of innate talent, of instinctive craving for beauty and wisdom in books, of purpose to enlarge opportunities and improve environment, that beneath the surface are constantly opening deeper life channels in individual experience. For in its relation to its public, library service is both impersonal and personal. People who seek counsel, incentive, or encouragement are apt nowadays to turn instinctively to books. In many personal situations the public library is the modern substitute for the religious help sought in an earlier age. The part that books can play in individual life is revealed over and over again to every librarian whose work brings any personal relationship with readers. There should be a deeper realization of this and a higher confidence in the inspiring influences that, in all library service, flow continuously through books, awakening and developing unpredictable responses in acceptant or aspiring minds.

In the annals of American librarianship there should be some record of men and women whose life paths to success, in literature, in science, in endeavor of all kinds, have opened through the public library. Sherwood Anderson, dumbly groping, through the poetry he discovered on library shelves, toward some richer life of the mind; the train boy, Edison, seizing knowledge during his noon hours in the old Detroit library; Pupin, Walcott, Hudson Maxim, drawing their early education from library books; James Stevens, common laborer, reading library books omnivorously as he worked in Oregon lumber mills and without knowing it preparing himself to become a writer. Carlos Bulosan, frail Filipino youth seeking in America education and opportunity, submerged instead in poverty, degradation, and cruelty of race prejudice, says in his autobiography: "I had only one escape—the Los Angeles Public Library." [2] Here was his home, his school; here he found sympathy and help in his purpose to prove that "an Oriental without education could become a writer in America." In *Dawn*, Theodore Dreiser gives a glimpse of the new vistas that the public library has opened to youthful minds, chained and clogged by a harsh, drab, and stultifying existence: "Books! Books! Books!" he says, as he describes his own discovery of the library—

How wonderful, fascinating and revealing! . . . Outside, overhead, might be a blue or grey sky, sunshine or rain or snow; it made little difference. For I was reading and awakening to a consciousness of many things, the mere knowledge of which appeared to coincide with power. The skies in my books were blue. One could do things with sufficient power.

So, in the fabric of library service, upon the background of mass use there emerge the infinite traceries of individual destiny.

The best definition of the purpose of book selection is still found in the familiar phrase, "To supply the right book to the right reader at the right time." This involves knowledge of the extent and character of readers' demands, knowledge of books that meet those demands, and satisfaction of those demands in terms of the highest book values.

The third factor offers the greatest difficulty: What are the highest book values, and how are they to be determined? The first original and constructive attempt at definition and analysis of this factor is that made by an English librarian, Lionel Roy McColvin, in a

---

[2] Carlos Bulosan, *America Is in the Heart: a Personal History* (New York, Harcourt, Brace & Co., 1946).

little volume, *The Theory of Book Selection for Public Libraries.* Only its most salient points can be summarized here, but it should be read and pondered by everyone concerned with library book selection.

Mr. McColvin's premise is that the public library should be the universal provider, through books, of all men's needs and desires; and that since we cannot give men all they ask, we must evaluate their needs and desires. Book selection resolves itself into two fields —demand and supply. Demand must be differentiated into volume, value, and variety. Volume of demand alone is no index; neither is value alone; because the demand of greatest volume is often of least value, and a valuable demand may have no volume (the books supplied would not be used). The two qualities must, therefore, be related. To do this a mathematical principle is applied. Each subject represented in the library's use is given an index number denoting its relative value ("value" is defined as "the force tending to the development of mind, the enrichment of experience, and the promotion of understanding and sympathy"). A similar number is given to denote the volume of demand; and the two are multiplied to arrive at a number which shall denote the proportionate representation of that particular subject in the library's supply.

From this basis there is developed a most interesting and suggestive study of kinds and variations of demand, shades and degrees of value. What is meant by "comprehensiveness" of a library collection? Not "completeness" in representation of subjects, but an inclusiveness of supply that meets and will develop demand. What is meant by "variety" of demand? Not only popular or scientific or elementary treatment of a subject, but material adapted to different classes of users and different degrees of need. How can demand be controlled and stimulated? Chiefly by increasing supply to emphasize subjects beneficial to the community at large; "but our best service will be rendered if we keep closely in touch with the definite existent needs of our readers, neither attempting to hurry forward the march of progress nor lagging behind."

Research and experiment by other librarians upon the basis that Mr. McColvin has established should make book selection in the future a more scientific process than it has been in the past.

In any public library this analytical approach to book selection may be begun through study and comparison of various records of library use. For example, statistics of circulation in adult nonfiction classes should be compared yearly with the number of books bought in the same classes; analysis will indicate what classes have been over-emphasized or neglected, and this should be rectified in later book selection. "Value" in fiction demand may be gauged by similar comparison of circulation and supply of different groups—such as classics and fine fiction, good standard fiction, light fiction, detective and western fiction. Volume of "reserves" made for individual books should be checked against supply, and supply increased according to a definite policy based on demand and value. Readers' requests should be studied for indication of "variety"; and record should be kept of books that in response to such requests have been considered for purchase but not selected, with the reason for the decision. Systematic inspection of the library shelves, noting frequency of circulation by examining the date slips in the books, is a useful means of gauging demand in small subject groups. One of the simplest and most common means of testing the range and quality of the collection as a whole is provided by the regular practice of checking the library's holdings against the titles included in trustworthy book lists and bibliographies. In building up or revising subject groups, consultation with and suggestions from outside specialists are always desirable and usually practicable.

Study, experience, observation, and experiment concentrated upon any purpose are soon resolved into principles and methods. So, in library service designed to bring together people and books and to provide for readers books that meet demands, needs, and tastes, there have emerged certain principles that are commonly accepted as fundamental in book selection. Those that apply most directly to the broader aspects of public library demand and supply with which we have been concerned are:

1. Study your community and know its general character, special characteristics, cultural and racial elements, chief activities, and leading interests.

2. Be familiar with subjects of present interest, general, national, and local.

3. Represent in book selection all subjects that apply to community conditions and that reflect community interests.

4. Make your collection of local history as extensive and useful as possible.

5. Provide for all organized groups whose activities or interests can be related to books.

6. Provide for actual and potential readers by satisfying so far as possible existent demands and anticipating demands foreshadowed by events, conditions, or increasing use of the library.

7. Avoid selection of books for which no demand is evident, and supersede books that have definitely outlived their usefulness.

8. But, while demand is primarily the basis and reason for supply, remember that the great works of literature are foundation stones in the library's own structure and therefore select some books of permanent value regardless of whether or not they will be widely used.

9. Maintain impartiality in selection; favor no special hobbies or opinions; in controversial and sectarian subjects, gifts may be accepted when purchase may be undesirable.

10. Provide as far as possible books that will meet the needs of specialists or others whose work will benefit the community. The public library is an armory of books, and those who use books as tools (writers, teachers, scholars, students) have a special claim to its services. Technical books in law and medicine and extremely doctrinal or sectarian religious books, however, are not provided by the average public library.

11. Do not attempt to build up a "complete" collection; select the best books on a subject, the best books of an author, the most useful volumes of a series, and do not make a fetish of "full sets" that possess no specific and evident usefulness.

12. A principle often affirmed, but to be applied with caution, is: Give preference to an inferior book that will be read over a superior book that will not be read. This involves opposed "values" and deserves most consideration in selection of fiction. With a wide and discriminating knowledge of books, it is almost always possible to choose a book that on its own plane possesses both value and interest.

To these principles may be added two others, perhaps less familiar:

1. Keep abreast of the changing currents of thought and opinion, and give adequate representation to the scientific, social, and intellectual forces that are reshaping the modern world.

2. Maintain, so far as possible, promptness and regularity in supplying new books. There are good arguments for delaying purchase of new books, but there is nothing that readers appreciate more than a prompt supply of recent publications, and in the case of books of assured standing and popularity there should be the least possible delay in selection and purchase.

Inconsistency of some of these principles with others is apparent. But this indicates only that balanced judgment and the constant weighing of relative values are required in successful book selection.

As we realize the place and influence of books in the personal development of the individual and therefore in the whole fabric of life education, we appreciate more fully the importance of book knowledge to all who in any kind of library service are to serve as a connecting link between people and books. Every library worker should possess an enthusiasm for books. But no one can become sincerely enthusiastic over something about which he knows little or nothing. The more we know about books, the more genuine enthusiasm they inspire. But wide reading and enjoyment of books are not sufficient qualifications for intelligent book selection. There must be a foundation of understanding of the principles upon which practice of book selection is to be based, of the tools necessary in the practice, and of the needs and demands that principles and practice must combine to satisfy.

BOOKS MENTIONED IN THIS CHAPTER

Adler, Mortimer J. How to Read a Book: the art of getting a liberal education. New York, Simon & Schuster, 1940.

Berelson, Bernard. The Library's Public. New York, Columbia University Press, 1949. (A report of the Public Library Inquiry.)

Bryan, Alice. The Public Librarian. New York, Columbia Unversity Press. (A report of the Public Library Inquiry. In preparation.)

Flexner, Jennie M., and Sigrid A. Edge. A Readers' Advisory Service. New York, American Association for Adult Education, 1934.

Flexner, Jennie M., and Byron C. Hopkins. Readers' Advisers at Work. New York, American Association for Adult Education, 1941.

Garceau, Oliver. The Public Library in the Political Process. New York, Columbia University Press, 1949. (A report of the Public Library Inquiry.)

Gray, W. S., and Ruth Munroe. The Reading Interests and Habits of Adults: a preliminary report. New York, The Macmillan Company, 1929.

Kelly, Grace O. Woodside Does Read. New York, Queens Borough Public Library, 1935.

Leigh, Robert D. The Public Library in the United States. New York, Columbia University Press. (The general report of the Public Library Inquiry, by its director. In preparation.)

McCamy, J. L. Government Publications for the Citizen. New York, Columbia University Press, 1949. (A report of the Public Library Inquiry.)

McColvin, L. R. The Theory of Book Selection for Public Libraries. London, Grafton & Co., 1935.

Miller, William. The Book Industry. New York, Columbia University Press, 1949. (A report of the Public Library Inquiry.)

Post-War Standards for Public Libraries: prepared by the Committee on Post-War Planning of the American Library Association, Carlton Bruns Joeckel, Chairman. Chicago, American Library Association, 1943.

Quigley, Margery C., and W. E. Marcus. Portrait of a Library. New York, D. Appleton-Century Co., 1936.

Richards, I. A. Practical Criticism: a study of literary judgment. New York, Harcourt, Brace & Co., 1929.

Waldron, Gloria. The Information Film. New York, Columbia University Press, 1949. (A report of the Public Library Inquiry.)

Waples, Douglas, and R. W. Tyler. What People Want to Read About: a study of group interests and a survey of problems in adult reading. Chicago, American Library Association and University of Chicago Press, 1931.

Wellard, James H. Book Selection: its principles and practice. London, Grafton & Co., 1937.

3. Testing Book Values

> Whoever has read the best books has acquired not only information but a method of thinking. Intelligence is as contagious as gracefulness and wit used to be in the eighteenth century. This is not all. Doctrines are tested and developed, methods are improved, views are completed, the work of the whole world becomes the property of each individual seeker who cares to annex its results.
> Ernest Dimnet: *The Art of Thinking*

> It is absurd to estimate the services of a librarian to his community by the number of books he issues or the per capita cost of such issues. The true measure of his service is the extent to which the great world of books has been made a living, appealing, inspiring reality through that service. The librarian who is not something of an authority on books is, whatever his technical training, as much out of place as the doctor who knows nothing of the value of his medicines.
> *New York Libraries:* July, 1911

KNOWLEDGE OF BOOKS to meet community needs involves knowledge of the kinds and qualities of books, so that they may be wisely chosen and effectively used. This means knowledge of books that are already available, as well as of the new works that flow constantly from the press. It means the ability to compare different books on a subject, to weigh the merits of opposed demands, to judge the value of individual books, and in application of principles, in working out of methods, to use the library book fund to the best possible advantage. These requirements are all essential to the successful practice of book selection.

First of all, the range and proportion of the library collection as a whole must be considered. There is now a growing tendency to regard a "well-rounded collection" as less important than a collection carefully built up to supply the most evident public demand. In a measure, this is supported by reason and common sense. "Completeness" is impossible of attainment in any library collection. Effort to maintain a fixed ratio for different classes often means that the collection becomes rigid and that fields in which there is a new or increasing public interest are inadequately represented. Nevertheless, every library collection should be built up according to a definite plan on a broad general foundation. Its development must be flexible, but constant attention must be paid to the maintaining of just proportions as a whole, so that certain classes will not be overemphasized and others neglected. The needs of the library exist and should be met, as well as the needs of its readers.

There is no fixed rule on which to base a balanced ratio of subjects. Successive volumes of the *A.L.A. Catalog* tabulate proportionate representation of different classes, and these tables give at least a basis for study of individual conditions. If a library, for example, has a fine collection in older biography and a weak, uneven representation of books in scientific subjects, or if there is an extensive, up-to-date collection of business manuals and books of technology with only a scanty showing of Greek and Latin classics in translation, these discrepancies indicate need of better balance in selection. Remember that the proportion of classes shifts with time. Problems and crises of the advancing "revolution of our time," immense development of war activities, and the effect of global war upon our civilization, have had a transforming influence on the proportional content of almost every library collection. There has been an enormous enlargement of supply and demand in technological and military publications; science has come to the forefront, as has medical research; little-known fields of history—the almost unknown Pacific and Asiatic world—have become of prime importance; there has been a flooding in of new subjects, or of different treatment of familiar subjects, in every field of literature. These changes have carried over in a steady increase in the demand for, and consequently in the representation of, sociology, vocational education, useful arts, psychology, and perhaps surprisingly, poetry and drama. A library of fifty years ago would show very different class proportions, with greater emphasis on religion, biography, history, and fiction.

In determining the needs of the library it is important to know how far there can be cooperative utilization of the resources of other libraries in the community. Libraries of research institutions, university or school libraries, medical and law libraries, and collections maintained by other specialized bodies, all contain material that the public library may thus be relieved of acquiring and that will meet occasional special demands made upon it. With all such collections the public library should be in a relation of friendly interdependence, so that duplication of expensive specialized works may be avoided and readers may know of additional channels through which information is accessible.

The needs of the library are fundamentally the needs of its readers; but there is a larger implication as well. For its own growth, its own well-being, the library should continually strengthen its equipment of bibliographical tools, should maintain its supply of "foundation" books, and should seek constant enrichment in the quality of the material that composes its substance.

Of course, the library book fund is the controlling power in the practice of book selection. Its amount varies according to individual conditions. The one certainty is that it is never adequate to meet needs and desires. It enforces constant watchfulness in buying, the exercise of expert economies, and the continual weighing of opposed demands and of the relative merits of individual books. "If you buy this, you cannot buy that" is the unspoken warning that becomes a sort of "inner check" to the intelligent, conscientious librarian.

In the average public library, under normal conditions, the book fund is about 25 percent of the total library appropriation. It is usually budgeted in three main groups, representing a ratio of approximately 40 percent for adult nonfiction, 30 percent for fiction, and 30 percent for children's books. This was the average ratio that prevailed in seventy-three public libraries in 1931.[1] According to *Post-War Standards for Public Libraries*, in 1943, normal distribution of the total library appropriation for the average public library "will approximate the following proportions: salaries of library staff, 55 percent; books, periodicals, and binding, 25 percent; other expenditures, 20 percent." Suggested allotment of the book fund is: 20 to 25 percent devoted to books for children, and at least 60 percent for

[1] Article by Karl Brown, in *Publishers' Weekly*, June 20, 1931.

adult nonfiction—which, however, implies inadequate provision of fiction, the body of literature that holds the most pervasive values for the largest public. An increasing flexibility is evident in such apportionment, and the majority of public libraries are no longer allocating a definite percentage of their book funds to the purchase of specified types of books. "Public libraries do not, as a rule, buy books because they are fiction or nonfiction but because the books meet the demands of the patrons of the library or fill a lack in the book collection." [2] Normal budgetary conditions for American libraries lapsed with the increasing economic stress of the "depression years" from 1931. In 1933 the book funds of representative public libraries throughout the country showed an average reduction of 34.5 percent, and even more drastic reductions were the rule in 1934. A slow upward trend began as the war years closed, but provision of an adequate book supply remains a crucial problem for libraries of every size and almost all types.

Administrative processes that relate to checking and recording of selected titles, the routine of recommendation and ordering and buying, belong rather with the study of book ordering and acquisition than with principles and practice of selection. They are not considered here. The simplest and most compact statement of the subject as a whole is to be found in Miss Bascom's little pamphlet [3] on book selection, which is particularly valuable to any librarian of a small library. The basic manual upon its every aspect and detail is Mr. Drury's volume [4] in the "Library Curriculum Studies," prepared for the American Library Association. Leta E. Adams' concise exposition of "Organization of Internal Processes in Book Selection for Public Libraries," included in the University of Chicago Library Institute volume, *The Practice of Book Selection*, treats the subject

[2] From Myra Simms' article, "Allocating the Book Fund to Departments and Branch Libraries," in *Library Journal*, October 1, 1946. This is an excellent analytical study of the subject, based on 34 replies received to a questionnaire sent in March, 1945, to the librarians of public libraries in the 45 largest cities in the United States.
[3] Elva L. Bascom, *Book Selection* (Rev. ed., American Library Association, 1925).
[4] F. K. W. Drury, *Book Selection* (American Library Association, 1930).

with authority and experience.[5] Our concern is with book selection as it involves the background of knowledge of kinds and qualities of books, the familiar use of bibliographical aids and guides, and the ability to compare and appraise the books themselves, in the characteristics and values of their contents.

Principles of book selection that are fundamental in relating the community to the use of the library have already been summarized. There remain two commonly accepted principles that relate to the books themselves and that underlie selection in all fields of literature.

The first of these epitomizes the whole purpose and ideal of book selection: Select books that will tend toward the development and enrichment of life.

Closely related to it is: Let the basis of selection be positive, not negative. If the best that can be said for a book is that it will do no harm, there is no valid reason for its selection; every book should be of actual service to somebody, in inspiration or information or recreation.

Consider what is meant by "books that tend toward the development and enrichment of life." Knowledge of such books requires good literary background, or knowledge of foundation books, as, for example, the value and place of Gibbon in history, of Matthew Arnold's essays in literature, of Morley's *Gladstone* in biography. But such books are found not only among older and accepted works; they come to us in the constantly flowing stream of new publications, and the library selector must be alert and keen to recognize and appreciate them. In the clashing nationalisms of the postwar world, under the shadow of atomic annihilation, many deeply imprinted patterns of mass thinking must change. On librarians rests a deepening responsibility for knowing and using books to enlighten prejudices, to enlarge understanding of vital issues, to strengthen public acceptance and practice of cooperation and race tolerance as the only solvents of many tense, resistant problems of life to-

---

[5] Louis R. Wilson, ed., *The Practice of Book Selection:* papers presented before the Library Institute at the University of Chicago, July 31 to August 13, 1939 (University of Chicago Press, 1940).

day. There must be unfailing broadmindedness and sympathy toward current literature. Don't accept the censorious objections of narrow-minded readers, or yield to personal prejudices or traditional opinions. Thought never stands still, but is an ever moving, ever changing force.

Granted that we understand the purpose of book selection and the fundamental principles that must be followed to make that selection both comprehensive and satisfactory, we come next to consider what are the particular things that must be found out about the books themselves, if they are to be judged intelligently. In learning to know books, the whole great domain of literature must be surveyed and charted. In its every division there are degrees and gradations of value and merit, standards of excellence, practical and literary requirements in substance and in style, which must be studied and applied.

Francis Bacon divided knowledge into three classes, according to the faculty of the mind employed upon them. These were: history, as based upon memory; philosophy, as based upon reason; and poetry, as based upon imagination. It can be readily seen that a great mass of literature may be regarded as falling within these divisions, and they have been used as the basis of various early systems of library classification for books.

Another broad sytematization divides literature into two classes: the literature of power, which includes all imaginative work (fiction, poetry, drama, etc.); and the literature of knowledge, which includes books of information (history, science, biography, etc.).

But through later years books have been generally regarded as falling into the following three divisions:

Books of inspiration—as religion, philosophy, poetry, fine drama, fine fiction.

Books of information—as biography, history, travel, science, useful arts, sociology.

Books of recreation—as fiction, drama, humor, essays, light reading in various fields.

In books of inspiration, wisdom and understanding find expression. Here are the utterances that have given spiritual illumination and incentive to successive generations, whether expressed in the parables of the Christian gospels, in the meditations of the Roman emperor, in the questionings of Socrates, or in the counsels of Emerson. Here poetry and drama and great fiction reflect and interpret human life. In books of inspiration, critical judgment requires creative power, vitality, sincerity, firm structure, depth and beauty in expression. These qualities, enlarged or diminished, inhere in every great work of literary art, though essentially the greatness of such art depends not upon its form but upon its substance. As Pater says:

It is on the quality of the matter it informs or controls, its compass, its variety, its alliance to great ends, or the depth of the note of revolt, or the largeness of hope in it, that the greatness of literary art depends, as *The Divine Comedy, Paradise Lost, Les Miserables*, the English Bible, are great art.

In books of information, critical judgment requires knowledge rather than creative power as the first essential. At its best such a book should be like a great tree, its unseen roots of knowledge, study, authority, equalling in extent the product that is visible. This is true of such a book as Morison's life of Columbus, *Admiral of the Ocean Sea,* or Symonds' studies of the Renaissance in Italy, or Darwin's narrative of his voyage in the "Beagle." Indeed, it is true of almost all the books of information that win a permanent place in literature. Vitality and sincerity are requisites; good structure is more important than style, though excellence of expression is an integral part of all books that live. In its finer examples the book of information becomes also a book of inspiration, for it presents ideals of character and achievement, as in biography; or imparts enthusiasm for knowledge, as in the annals of scientific discovery; or enlarges and clarifies understanding of human events, as in the record of history. But there are many books in this division that are necessary and useful on a less exalted plane and that must be examined for minor characteristics of merit.

Books of recreation may be said to fall into two broad groups that merge together but are of different quality. In great creative literature, inspiration and recreation are indistinguishably blended. Shakespeare, Cervantes, Scott, Dickens, Hawthorne, are names fragrant with pure pleasure, yet diffusing illumination and conveying interpretation of life. Even in lesser manifestation the creative imagination almost always wakens some fine emotion—a quickened understanding of human experience, or an impulse of sympathy, or just the joy that invests the sensation of simple pleasure. So, though the great mass of fiction as well as much in drama and poetry belongs to the literature of recreation, yet in varying degree it is also literature of inspiration.

These three divisions, indeed, must never be regarded as rigidly separated; their border lines are always flexible. Of course, there are many books that do belong exclusively in one division. Thomas à Kempis' *Imitation of Christ*, for example, is wholly inspiration; *The World Almanac* is wholly information; Don Marquis' *Hermione and Her Little Group of Serious Thinkers* is wholly recreation. But there are even more books that merge from one division into another. Stevenson's *Travels with a Donkey* combines information and recreation. Hugo's *Notre Dame de Paris* combines recreation and information and inspiration, in its mingling of dramatic plot and character interest, its portrayal of a historical setting, and its awakening of emotions of compassion and understanding. Wells' *Outline of History* combines information and inspiration, in conveying an impressive realization of the progression of mankind through the ages. In general, books of higher quality in the divisions of information and recreation almost always possess something of inspiration as well.

It must also be remembered that these three divisions—inspiration, information, and recreation—are simply broadly generalized characterizations that indicate the nature of a book, but not its specific class or subject. The books that fall into these divisions are also specifically defined as history, or biography, or poetry, and so on, through all the classes of literature.

To test the values of books in each of these classes, there are differing standards, or criteria, to be applied. Only the briefest indication of these can be given now, but their analysis and application will be more fully considered in succeeding chapters.

History, for example, must be based on reliable sources; biography must concern an interesting person or be made interesting in itself; travel must combine accurate observation and interesting description. Style—that is, a clear or polished or noble expression—is a necessary element in books of inspiration, but less necessary in works that deal entirely with information. Style, however, adds value to any book, and its presence or absence is the chief test of a book's quality as literature.

There are also specific tests that are common to many kinds of books. In close analysis, these will be seen to resolve themselves into tests for books of information, tests for books of inspiration, and tests for books of recreation; but in general practical application they are usually divided into two groups—tests for nonfiction, and tests for fiction. In each group, the tests are of two kinds—tests for subject matter, authority, and quality of a book, and tests for its bibliographical and physical characteristics. Consider a few examples of those most widely used:

Tests for Nonfiction

SUBJECT MATTER

What is subject or theme?
What is scope? Complete? Partial? History of the subject, or discussion of certain aspects or conditions?
Additional subjects covered?
Is the book brief? Exhaustive? Selective? Balanced?
Is the treatment concrete? Abstract?
Is it popular? Scholarly? Technical? Semitechnical?
Is it for general readers? Students? Specialists?
Date (usually important in relation to subject matter).

AUTHORITY

What are the author's qualifications? What is his education? Experience? Special preparation for writing this book?
Has he used source material? If secondary material, is it reliable?
Is his work based on personal observation or research?

Is it accurate? Inexact?
Does he understand thoroughly the period, facts, or theories with which he deals?
What is the author's point of view? Partisan? Fair-minded? Conservative? Radical?

QUALITIES

Does the work show any degree of creative power?
Is the form appropriate to the thought?
Has it originality of conception? Of expression?
Has it a clear, graphic style? Readability? Charm? Profundity? Imaginative power?
Has it vitality? Interest? Is it likely to endure as a permanent contribution to literature?

PHYSICAL CHARACTERISTICS

Is there an adequate index?
Are there illustrations? Maps? Charts or graphs? Bibliographies? Appendixes? Any other reference features?
Has the book clear type? Good paper?

VALUES FOR READER

Information?
Contribution to culture?
Stimulation of interests?
Recreation or entertainment?
What reading relationships does it offer?
To what types of readers does it appeal?

Tests for Fiction

(Some of the tests previously cited are also appropriate for fiction.)
Is it true to life? Sensational? Exaggerated? Distorted?
Has it vitality and consistency in character depiction? Valid psychology? Insight into human nature?
Is the plot original? Hackneyed? Probable? Simple? Involved?
Is dramatic interest sustained?
Does it stimulate? Provoke thought? Satisfy? Inspire? Amuse?

In even a cursory analysis of these tests it is easy to differentiate those that apply to books of information from those that apply to books of inspiration and recreation. Tests for inspirational books and for fiction emphasize the more intangible values of creative power and quality of expression; those for books of information give weight to factual values of knowledge and accuracy, and to method of treatment. Tests for author's qualifications and for physical features are of less importance in consideration of books that are inspirational and recreational—essays, plays, poetry, novels, are judged by their own qualities, not by the author's scholarly attainments or specialized experience. However, in any field of literature a writer who has an established reputation will always be judged in part on the basis of that reputation. Sound background knowledge of literature and a wide-ranging familiarity with contemporary writers are thus of the greatest possible value in the practice of book selection, for they will in time impart a swift, almost instinctive, discrimination in dealing with many current publications. Excellence of print and paper, convenience of size, and satisfactory binding, are important in books of every kind. A good index is indispensable in every book of information; notes, bibliographies, and other aids to reference are essential in many. The importance of illustrations depends in large measure upon the character or purpose of the book.

In considering tests for "authority," the distinction between "original" and "secondary" source material should be clearly understood. Original source material (primary material) means contemporaneous documents, archives, manuscripts, early narratives, "sources" of information upon the subject dealt with that spring from its immediate time or place. Napoleon's personal and official correspondence, for example, is original source material for the history of his era; the records of archaeological research conducted in Yucatan reveal original source material for study of the Mayan civilization. "Secondary source material" means material available in published form, the work of writers of authority based on original sources, but not the original material itself. A subject is said to receive "concrete" treatment when the author presents or analyzes facts and the statements made are direct, condensed, verifiable; it receives "abstract" treatment when the author presents it as part of a philosophical theory or in a speculative or hypothetical manner.

Publication date of a book is of varying importance. In the case of old, valuable, or rare works it denotes whether or not the book is an early edition, and is then, of course, of special interest to collectors or in indicating value; but the attention now given to first editions of many contemporary authors as possible "collectors' items" is not a factor in general library book selection. In standard and current inspirational and recreational literature date of publication is of minor importance, as the value of the book depends not so much on its timeliness as on its literary quality; when a critic says that a novel or play is "dated," the implication is that the theme is outworn or the expression hackneyed. In informational literature date of publication is often significant in indicating present value of a book. For example, a school history of Europe published in 1925 and not brought to date would be of little present value; a book on automobiles published in 1920 would be virtually useless to the reader of today; in all fields of science and technology, publication date is extremely important. Books of accepted value, however, keep their repute, independent of publication date, though it is usually desirable to select late, revised editions in preference to early editions. Gibbon's *Decline and Fall of the Roman Empire* is still an indispensable history, though first published in 1790; but the latest, revised edition is preferable to an edition of 1850. John Florio's sixteenth-century version of Montaigne's essays holds its own against later translations; though the edition most desirable is that presented under modern scholarly editorship.

Careful examination of a book is essential in gaining familiarity with book selection tests. Intelligent concentration on the obvious will reveal much. Concentration, indeed, is the secret lever of the mind. Thus, the title-page must be carefully examined, with attention to the author's honorary titles or any other clue to his qualifications and with regard to any subtitles or amplification of the title. Observe the date, and turn the page to see if publication date on the title-page differs from the date of copyright or first printing. Note the publisher's name, as publishing houses of established reputation are usually identified with books of merit; an unknown publisher, a printing house in some out-of-the-way place, an author publishing his own books, usually demand more critical attention. Preface or introduction should always be read, or at least carefully examined, as it usually casts light upon a book's purpose, scope, and point of view, or upon the author and his work. Take, as an example, a current biography by an unfamiliar author. To make a rapid, concentrated examination, note the points already indicated, and observe the general make-up and readability of the volume. Glance over the chapter headings and give special attention to the first and last chapters, as these often epitomize the treatment and purpose of a book. Pick out some chapter that may be controversial and read enough to determine whether the author shows definite bias or some fixed idea, and whether his attitude appears to be bulwarked by authoritative information. If the treatment is fictionized, consider whether the manner is restrained or sensational; if the form is scholarly, note whether the style has vigor and ease, or is diffuse, or pedantic. Observe the kind and extent of references made to sources of information. Test the index by referring from it to some item in the text, and vice versa; if there is no index, the factual usefulness of the biography is lessened, though it may possess high values in interpretation or appreciation.[6]

Ability to compare and contrast books of similar type or character is one of the best qualifications for effective book selection. It can be acquired only by building up a background of personal acquaintance with literature. This background, although it must be formed by reading—for reading is the fundamental basis of book knowledge—may be developed through the faculty of attentive observation, the habit of dipping into a book and of browsing here and there through many diverse volumes. Library attendants who handle books with any intelligent attention must inevitably acquire a sort of intangible book familiarity; at least they will associate names

---

[6] Mortimer Adler's *How to Read a Book* gives pithy counsel on these essential points of book-examination technique, in Chapter 8, "Catching On from the Title." The processes of analytical reading for appraisal of book values are also expounded with elaboration and pungency in Chapter 9, "Seeing the Skeleton," and Chapter 10, "Coming to Terms."

and subjects; they will know that *Penguin Island* is a novel, not a place; that Georgian poetry belongs to the present day. Anyone who works in any way with books can develop this faculty of attentive observation, through a process of attrition that rubs off into the mind something from the books worked with, and in this way constantly enlarges the background of book familiarity.

Successful book selection demands not only a living background of book familiarity, but sound critical judgment and discriminating literary taste. No one can correctly appraise a book's creative power, or originality, or style, or plot structure, who is unable to recognize and estimate those qualities. Sound critical judgment is acquired chiefly through the application of intelligence, concentration, and reflection to good reading. No one is born with discriminating literary taste, nor is it absorbed simply by accepting other people's opinions. Probably the greatest aid to its development is a childhood familiarity with good literature—I believe that books read before the age of sixteen have a stronger formative influence on the mind than all the reading of later years—but there can be no sound critical judgment that is not based upon constant familiarity with books. As the background of book knowledge deepens, the reader will change his mind about many books. No one ever acquired sound critical judgment without building it on many unsound and immature opinions, first accepted, later modified, and then discarded and forgotten. But there must also be familiarity with good critical writing, to establish fundamentals and to clarify perception of distinctions and differences. Matthew Arnold's essays on literature represent the finest essence of the English critical spirit, and even today they will give to any intelligent reader a keener perception of what constitutes the difference between worthy intention and worthy accomplishment in literary expression. Walter Pater's *Essay on Style*, Santayana's crystalline presentation of *The Sense of Beauty*, Ludwig Lewisohn's provocative and penetrating analysis of American literature, and, at the opposite pole, Van Wyck Brooks' fragrant garnering from *The Flowering of New England* in the early nineteenth century—the reading of such books as these will do more to strengthen the ability to choose books wisely than will any textbook exposition of literary structure.

Critical judgment, however, must not be static. It must be fine-fibered and strong, but also flexible. It must enable the librarian to recognize and use all the values that a book may hold for different readers, without regard to its immediate personal appeal. There are varied values in many books that may not be of the highest importance from a single, specific aspect. William Ellery Leonard's autobiography, *The Locomotive God*, for example, holds its deepest values for the psychologist and lover of literature, rather than for the general reader of biography; Will Durant's *Story of Philosophy* is negligible for the scholar, but has strong values for the untrained mind of the average man with a natural curiosity concerning life. There are books of mediocre literary quality that possess values of spiritual reinforcement, or psychological stimulation, or practical self-development, for many readers of different needs and capabilities.

The ability to perform the act of reading with rapidity, concentration, and spontaneous apprehension is an indispensable aid to proficiency in book selection. The expert book selector must be an expert reader. If such expertness has not developed through the unconscious exercise of eye and mind, it should be deliberately acquired. For the novice, the following suggestions may be useful: practice reading as rapidly as possible, first for short and then for longer periods, until the general reading pace has quickened; never read word for word, but take in at a glance single groups of words, phrases, and sentences; do not turn back to pick up again words or lines already read, except under special necessity—in time there will develop a remarkable visual aptitude for seizing what is important and passing over what is superfluous or unimportant. Thus is acquired the art of judicious skipping, the ability to extract in a few hours the essence of a substantial volume. Adapt the speed of reading to the type of material read—newspaper reading, for example, may be in ordinary practice an almost instantaneous process; the reading of a popular magazine or of a crime-and-mystery novel may be swift, almost volitionless; the ordinary, popular book of nonfiction may demand a more irregular tempo, now slowed, now speeded; while such a work as Eddington's *The Nature of the Physical World* will bring the most expert reader to a slow-paced, cautious advance.

Most of those to whom reading is a professional requirement acquire naturally and instinctively this facility to change to different kinds of reading technique: to skim, to swallow, to dip, to submerge, to swim, to float (each term conveys a different procedure and result), according to immediate obligations or opportunities. It is frequently urged, however, that effective reading must involve physical tension. Headley says: "Never suppose that you can do genuine reading when you are relaxed on a sofa or an easy chair." Adler shares the same conviction: to him all worth while reading is an intensive, closely restricted process. This dictum is not sustained by the experience of the goodly company of readers-in-bed (Mark Twain and John Shaw Billings among them) whose mental concentration and power to make productive use of books is not dependent on bodily rigidity. Proficiency in appraisal of book values is a matter of practice rather than of posture.[7]

Constant personal reading, it has been made clear, must accompany and supplement the study and the practice of book selection. But the testing of book values is not dependent upon personal judgment of individual books. No single human brain can grasp and appraise the whole content of literature. Wide range of book knowl-

---

[7] There is a large body of literature devoted to the mechanics of reading, to visual and mental maladjustments, to the need of "readability" in the materials provided for lower literacy levels, and to remedial measures, physical, psychological, and educational. Among them: J. A. Hamilton, *Toward Proficient Reading* (Claremont, California, Saunders Press, 1939), is compact but inclusive, emphasizing development of ability to comprehend and the building of vocabulary; L. A. Headley, *Making the Most of Books* (Chicago, American Library Association, 1932), offers good practical counsel on a rather elementary plane; Norman Lewis, *How to Read Better and Faster* (New York, Crowell, 1944), presents a five-weeks course for self-improvement and increased comprehension, with exercises and tests.

Daniel P. Macmillan's article, "Dyslexia (Reading Difficulty)," in *Library Journal*, June 15, 1946, describes the aims and work of the Dyslexia Memorial Institute in Chicago, devoted to the clinical study of reading disabilities among children—probably one of the most elaborate specialized undertakings in this particular field.

edge and power of instinctive sound critical judgment must be established. On this foundation proficiency in book selection is made possible through knowledge and use of the "tools of the trade," the aids, guides, bibliographies, which record and appraise current and standard literature, and through the rapid, discriminating gleaning of literary reviews and news about books. It is this aspect of book selection that now demands attention.

A DOZEN BOOKS FOR BACKGROUND READING

The following titles are suggestive of books that will enrich and enlarge understanding of good literature.

Arnold, Matthew. Essays in Criticism. 2 vols. New York, The Macmillan Company, 1924.
Brooks, Van Wyck. The Flowering of New England, 1815–1865. New York, E. P. Dutton & Co., 1936.
Canby, Henry Seidel. Seven Years' Harvest. New York, Farrar & Rinehart, 1936.
Drew, Elizabeth. The Enjoyment of Literature. New York, W. W. Norton & Co., 1935.
Erskine, John. The Delight of Great Books. Indianapolis, Bobbs-Merrill Co., 1928.
Hearn, Lafcadio. Interpretations of Literature. New York, Dodd, Mead & Co., 1915.
Lewisohn, Ludwig. Expression in America. New York, Harper & Brothers, 1932.
Mott, Frank Luther. Golden Multitudes: the story of best sellers in the United States. New York, The Macmillan Company, 1947.
Rogers, Robert E. The Fine Art of Reading. Boston, Stratford Co., 1929.
Swinnerton, Frank. The Georgian Scene: a literary panorama. New York, Farrar & Rinehart, 1934.
Wendell, Barrett. Traditions of European Literature from Homer to Dante. New York, Charles Scribner's Sons, 1920.
Woolf, Virginia. The Common Reader. New York, Harcourt, Brace & Co., 1925.

PROPORTIONATE REPRESENTATION OF CLASSES IN BOOK SELECTION

Proportions of classes of literature represented in successive volumes of *A.L.A. Catalog*, 1904 to 1941, are as follows:

CLASS	A.L.A. CAT. 1904 [a] Percent	A.L.A. CAT. 1926 [a] Percent	A.L.A. CAT. SUPP. 1926–31 [a] Percent	A.L.A. CAT. SUPP. 1932–36 Percent	A.L.A. CAT. SUPP. 1937–41 Percent
General works	2.0	2.2	4.0	2.9	1.6
Philosophy	2.	2.7	3.	3.4	2.6
Religion	4.	3.3	3.	3.8	3.
Sociology	8.	10.	10.	11.	10.
Philology	1.6	1.3	.7	.7	.4
Natural Science	6.2	3.5	3.	4.2	3.6
Useful Arts	6.	8.6	8.	6.8	10.2
Fine Arts	4.7	8.9	8.	12.1	10.9
Literature	13.4	13.6	12.	8.9	5.8
History	13.3	7.8	5.7	6.6	8.2
Travel	9.1	9.	9.6	5.5	8.5
Biography	13.5	8.4	10.	9.3	8.7
Fiction	16.3	10.9	9.	8.1	6.
Children's books [b]	...	9.2	10.	15.9	19.7

[a] From *A.L.A. Catalog, 1926–1931*, p. v.
[b] In *A.L.A. Catalog, 1904*, the children's books were counted with the other books in each class.

4. Familiar Friends and Companions

> From my point of view, a book is a literary prescription put up for the benefit of some one who needs it. It may be simple or compounded of many ingredients. The ideas may unite in true chemical union or they may be insoluble in one another and form an emulsion. . . .
>
> A book being a literary prescription, it should be carefully put up. Thus I learned, in looking up the subject, that a proper prescription contains:—(1) A basis or chief ingredient, intended to cure. (2) An adjuvant, to assist the action and make it cure more quickly. (3) A corrective, to prevent or lessen any undesirable effect. (4) A vehicle or excipient, to make it suitable for administration and pleasant to the patient.
>
> I do not propose to go into literary pharmacy any more than to say that there are sufficient tests of what is called literary style. In regard to a book, I ask, Does it have any basis or chief ingredient? Does the Author furnish any corrective for his own exaggerations? Above all, is the remedy presented in a pleasant vehicle or excipient, so that it will go down easily?
>
> S. M. Crothers: "A Literary Clinic," in
The Pleasures of an Absentee Landlord

LINES FROM A fifteenth-century morality play that the small volumes of "Everyman's Library" have made known to two generations of English readers best characterize the aids and guides that are familiar friends and companions in the practice of book selection:

> I will go with thee and be thy guide,
> In thy most need to go by thy side.

These form the working equipment, the tools always at hand, without which there can be no professional mastery of books. Their importance to any librarian or other worker with books is fundamental.

For it is obvious that as the selection and purchase of books for libraries developed into a specialized calling, it became more and more impossible to depend upon the immense and unorganized mass of general literary criticism and current book reviewing for guidance and information. No librarian could make a satisfactory selection in every field of literature, without guidebooks representing the specialized study and knowledge of those familiar with the material in each field. So, within the years that cover the history of the modern library movement there has been established a steadily increasing equipment of professional book-selection tools. These tools, it must be remembered, are apart from the general reviewing and literary periodicals and the contemporary works of literary criticism. They are prepared specifically for library or book-trade use, or for scholars, teachers, and students. Every field of literature now possesses its bibliographical aids, varying in excellence, perhaps, but at least recording the material of information for all readers. One of the signs of book ignorance is the plaint that "nothing exists" on a given topic; it is almost a certainty that material does exist, but that the complainant does not know where to find it. He who has learned where to look for the recorded literature of his subject is no longer an amateur but a proficient in the use of books.

Aids and guides available in the practice of book selection range from the bibliographical publications of the American Library Association, of other library organizations, of individual libraries, of educational institutions and associations, through the bibliographical publications of special or general publishing firms, to the catalogues and lists issued by book dealers, and the bibliographical material that appears in library, or literary, or other specialized periodicals. They merge indistinguishably into the varied literature of bibliography—general, special, and trade bibliography; and to the expert in book selection there is fascination and value in almost any kind of list, catalogue, or other record of printed material—as Christopher Morley says: "There is a pang in consigning any book catalogue at all to the rubbish heap. You never know what bird of strange plumage will twitter on an unexpected branch."

Even in the present limited study of simpler basic aids, the student should try to gain a sense of the interest and information that may be found in any record of books. Every available work of bibliography should be examined, when opportunity offers; unfamiliar titles encountered in other lists or in reviews should receive a mental note.

It is possible to make every printed record of book titles (advertisements, publishers' catalogues, booksellers' lists and announcements) add to one's familiarity with books. In observing them, consider whether or not the author's name is familiar, whether the book is new or old, whether you have seen it or heard of it, who publishes it, and what is its apparent interest or appeal. The development of such a habit of mind will gradually build up a background of book acquaintance, constantly useful although necessarily superficial. It must be remembered also that it is highly important to be intelligently informed concerning books that for one reason or another have not been included in selection. The blanket response, "No; we don't have that," when a request is made for a particular book, is an easy but unjustifiable evasion of responsibility. There should be some understanding of why the book is not available—some knowledge of the authority upon which selection has been based, some familiarity with comparative book values, some valid indication that a reasoned judgment has directed selection.

In many professional book selection aids, information concerning books listed is presented in the form of annotations; that is, in a condensed note concerning the essential characteristics and apparent value of the book. In other words, the "annotation" conveys the "evaluation" made for guidance of the book selector or for information of the reader. The term "book evaluation" was given its special library significance in the late 1890's, by George Iles, whose original mind and generous enthusiasm were devoted to practical experimentation with his idea of centralized, comprehensive "evaluation" of literature as a function of librarianship. Its meaning may be given as a definitive, authoritative statement of book values, presented in comment so brief that it is an "annotation" and not a "review." Thus, annotations are constructed upon a definite plan and for a definite purpose, although both may vary according to the medium used for presentation. Their study is an important part of training in book selection. Competent workers with books should know what an annotation ought to be, should be able to detect a poor or unsatisfactory annotation, and should themselves be able to write a satisfactory one. Throughout the present study of book selection special attention will be directed to analysis of annotations in the "evaluation" they convey and in the method of their construction.

First among standard aids in selection for smaller American libraries is the *A.L.A. Catalog*. It was in 1879 that the project of a cooperative printed catalogue prepared by librarians for librarians and intended as a primary guide in book selection was proposed to the American Library Association by Melvil Dewey. An experimental edition, imperfect in details and without annotations, was prepared for the A.L.A. exhibit at the World's Columbian Exposition in Chicago in 1893, with the title, *Catalog of A.L.A. Library*. The collection of books on which it was based is still preserved in the library of the Bureau of Education in Washington. This imperfect catalogue proved so useful that plans were undertaken in 1894 for the projected *A.L.A. Catalog*.

The work was carried through by the united effort of the Publishing Board of the American Library Association, the New York State Library (under direction of Melvil Dewey), and the Library of Congress; and the *A.L.A. Catalog: 8,000 Volumes for a Popular Library, with Notes, 1904*, was completed in time for publication and distribution at the A.L.A. conference at the St. Louis Exposition in 1904. This catalogue was the first fulfillment of a purpose held by the American Library Association almost from its origin. Selection was cooperative, made by specialists and by librarians judging and testing the needs of their public. Although experimental in method, it nevertheless established two principles that have been consistently followed in later publications—the selection of books by consensus of professional judgment and their evaluation in a compact note of characterization. Annotations were not an important feature, for this was a first attempt on a large scale and was carried out under many difficulties; but the annotations that were given were either contributed by qualified judges or drawn from authentic sources. For more than twenty years this catalogue was in constant use as a basis for selection for small library collections and as a guide to selected standard books. It had many shortcomings, and time naturally impaired its practical value; but it is still useful for indication of older standard editions and for some books which are no longer of first importance but which still possess merit and hold their places in the affections of many readers.

The *A.L.A. Catalog, 1926*, prepared in commemoration of the fiftieth anniversary of the American Library Association, appeared in 1927, replacing the 1904 volume as general selection aid for smaller public libraries. As it represents a quarter-century leap in the practice of library book selection—both in increase and variation of demand to be supplied and in technical method—it deserves close attention. It records 10,295 books, as against the 7,520 (exact figures) included in the 1904 volume. A note of evaluation is given for virtually every book recorded, and although these annotations are uneven in quality they condense an immense amount of valuable descriptive, critical, and bibliographical information. Selectively, the volume represents the cooperative work of more than 400 collaborators, and its 10,295 entries are the ultimate reduction of 50,000 collected, recommended, or suggested titles. The chief weakness of the catalogue lies in this high-pressure reduction. A limit of 15,000 volumes instead of 10,000 would have given a basic list of much greater value. For the average small public library, which in 1904 had an estimated collection of from 8,000 to 10,000 volumes, had after twenty-two years of expanding library use undoubtedly increased to a collection ranging from 15,000 to 20,000 volumes; and the steady proportionate gain in book production during the same period also required a larger margin of allowance. The rigid limitation to which the catalogue was held means that representation of many classes (history, biography, literature, and fiction especially) is distinctly inadequate.

Comparison of the two catalogues reveals the far-reaching changes that twenty-two years effected in range of knowledge and in modes of literary expression. Classes that showed the greatest increase were bibliography, philosophy, sociology, applied science (or useful arts), and fine arts. Natural (pure) science was considerably reduced; history was cut from 973 volumes in 1904 to 806 in 1926;

and fiction, which was represented by 1,226 volumes in 1904, had only 1,129 in 1926. Some of these reductions are explained by the fact that books for children which in 1904 were scattered through all the adult classes were later grouped by themselves in an independent list which represented 9.2 percent of the total collection. One of the most significant changes was the trend toward informational literature—bibliographies, conspectuses, outlines, yearbooks, all part of the modern consolidation, condensation, and popularization of knowledge. Sociology, especially, revealed the changes of a quarter-century; for example, the Negro was represented in 1904 by two books on slavery, but in 1926 we find fifteen titles, covering social, historical, and economic relations of the race. There was a great increase in the literature of labor, prison reform, population problems, child welfare, and a flood of new subjects in the literature of education. Mental tests, psychoanalysis, publicity, sexual ethics, industrial management, concrete construction, were among the many subjects unrepresented in the catalogue of 1904. There were significant changes in the literature of philosophy and religion. Philosophy was improved, strengthened, and organized, with 284 titles as against 143 in 1904. Religion was vigorously pruned and was modernized, and the implication inherent in the Dewey classification that religion is synonymous with Protestantism was almost eliminated. Drama and poetry were greatly enlarged. Fiction, though much too closely limited, had far greater catholicity and richness than in 1904; foreign fiction in English translation was intelligently gleaned, the inanely "harmless" was avoided, and distinctive work of modern writers was adequately represented. Fuller contrast and comparison of the two volumes is well worth making, for it will indicate not only the broadening and changing trends of public demand and the rich expansion of contemporary literature, but also an increasing catholicity and discrimination in library book selection.

Five supplements bridge the years between and succeeding the two basic "A.L.A. Catalogs." These are: *A.L.A. Catalog, 1904–1911.* 1912 (3,000 titles); *A.L.A. Catalog, 1912–1921.* 1923 (4,000 titles); *A.L.A. Catalog, 1926–1931.* 1932 (3,000 titles); *A.L.A. Cata-*

FAMILIAR FRIENDS AND COMPANIONS 69

log, 1932–1936. 1938 (4,000 titles); *A.L.A. Catalog, 1937–1941.* 1943 (4,000 titles). In each of these, almost all books listed are given annotations, representing careful evaluation, and basic catalogues and supplements alike are largely built upon semi-monthly issues of the *Booklist* during the periods covered, both for titles included and for annotations. Thus, the *A.L.A. Catalog* series will guide to a general, limited collection of standard and popular literature available during the preceding forty years, representing books considered by experienced librarians to be desirable for the average small public library. As a basic aid, however, of later years its primacy has yielded to the practical streamlined efficiency of the H. W. Wilson *Standard Catalog for Public Libraries,* which receives consideration in the following chapter.

The current continuation of the *A.L.A. Catalog* supplied by the *Booklist* is on a more comprehensive scale and of value to libraries of all sizes and types. This "guide to new books" has been published by the American Library Association since 1905, in ten monthly issues a year for many years, once each month from 1931 to 1938, and twice a month thereafter. It is edited with the cooperation of fifty American libraries, and the votes of these collaborators are registered by plus and minus signs against the titles submitted to them in mimeographed "tentative lists." These votes determine the final selection made from new books sent to the editorial office by the publishers and reviewed by the *Booklist* staff. Each issue of the *Booklist* contains several short lists in addition to the classified, annotated list of general literature (usually including from 150 to 200 titles) which is its main content. Selected titles suitable for high school libraries or other small collections, special lists of carefully chosen foreign books or of books on subjects of timely interest, and excellent lists of new editions, of pamphlets, and government documents, are features that help to make the *Booklist* indispensable in current selection. In all its details of method, as well as in general content, it should become thoroughly familiar to every student of book selection.

From 1919 to 1940 the *Booklist* issued each year an additional publication called *Booklist Books.* This was a selection of about 300 titles chosen chiefly from the year's issues of the *Booklist* as especially desirable for small library purchase. It had also wider usefulness, as giving in compact form a careful gleaning of "books of the year" that had particular significance or generally accepted excellence. Discontinued in 1941, it deserves revival as a stimulus to discriminating comparative library appraisal of values in current literature.

In the practice of current selection for libraries of almost every type, the *Book Review Digest* is the indispensable accompaniment to the *Booklist*. It is also a familiar source of information for the reading public concerning the range and values of current literature and literary criticism. Students, teachers, editors, reviewers, writers, and many nonprofessional readers turn to it constantly for fact and opinion about books and writers of the day. It is more important in selection for larger libraries; if a small library must choose between the two, it should choose the *Booklist*. New books are more promptly recorded in the *Booklist*, as its annotations are not based on published reviews. But in most libraries neither the *Booklist* nor the *Book Review Digest* cover new books promptly enough always to give information before it is necessary for the librarian to order them. Often books must be ordered before any reviews are available, and in such cases the book knowledge and critical judgment of the librarian are directly tested. The *Book Review Digest* was established in 1905 by the H. W. Wilson Company, and is published monthly, on the cumulative method that is a fundamental feature of the Wilson bibliographies.

Cumulation may be described as making printed catalogues in the same way that card catalogues are made, by filing new entries into a catalogue and so keeping it up to date. It is based on the use of the linotype machine in printing. In cumulation, the catalogue entry is a "linotype slug," that is, a separate title or bibliographical record on a small bar of metal. So, the first issue of a monthly cumulated list prints the record of the books of that month; the slugs are preserved in proper order; for the next issue, slugs for the record of the new books are filed among the slugs of the month already covered, and the books of the two months will appear in one uniform printed list. This will continue until the size of the list so increases as to make the printing too expensive. Then a small supplement is issued and cumulated; then all the slugs are filed together and a full cumulated catalogue is printed. In the *Book Review Digest*, the main list is fully cumulated twice a year; a six-month cumulation appears in August, and a bound annual cumulated volume in February. The index is cumulated continuously all through the year with a complete cumulation every five years. It is readily seen that the principle of cumulation—the use of the linotype slugs in any combination desired—makes possible a great variety of catalogues, by reducing or expanding or adapting the material to meet various demands. There is, of course, a limit to the expansion possible in any cumulative record, and the sequence and extent of cumulation vary in different lists, but the method itself is so far the twentieth century's most valuable contribution to mechanical efficiency in bibliographical publishing.

The *Book Review Digest* is broader in scope than the *Booklist*. It presents each month a full author record of current publications (a total of about 4,000 a year), giving for each a descriptive, noncritical annotation, followed by an ingenious digest of opinions and commentaries of reviewers. These are conveyed in brief excerpts, with use of symbols and abbreviations to indicate detailed information; plus and minus signs, for example, appended to the citations from reviews, indicate whether the reviewer's final opinion is favorable, unfavorable, or divided in judgment. Thus, it gives at a glance a consensus of reviewing opinion upon a specific book and so aids in the librarian's decision as to advisability of purchase. In many libraries this record is clipped and pasted, sometimes on the inside cover or flyleaf of the book reviewed, sometimes on the card filed in the catalogue, to give readers information about the book. The subject-and-title index which supplements the main list deserves consideration for its ingenious indication of different kinds of books in broad classes. Fiction, for example, is so analyzed that novels of particular type or special interest are brought directly to attention. There are subdivisions for Cheerful Stories, Ghost Stories, Mystery Novels, Novels of Locality (with places alphabetically listed), Historical Novels (listed by country); and for novels that center on a particular theme, as Marriage, Sex, School and College, etc. This intelligent, modernized form of indexing, which supplies so many quick clues to books that possess a varied appeal, is another of the achievements of the Wilson bibliographical method, which has come into wide use. Other useful features of the *Book Review Digest* include the list of "Publications from Which the Digest of Reviews Is Made" (in itself a good brief guide to the chief reviewing periodicals, American and English) and special lists that appear from time to time, particularly the list of public documents desirable for small libraries. The expansion that is evident in all these aids may be indicated by the fact that the first volume of the *Digest* (1905) contained 386 pages while there are 1,067 pages in the volume for 1948.

In all the aids so far considered there are accessory details that must be thoroughly familiar if these tools are to be used to best advantage. For example, students should analyze the arrangement and method of the *A.L.A. Catalog, 1926*, noting that it is a classed list according to the Dewey classification, supplemented by an elaborate author-title-and-subject index, which is its indispensable key; they should observe that in the main list a serial number is given for each entry, and this number is used for reference in consultation of the index, instead of a page reference. This method, which has distinct advantages of compression and rapidity in use, was adopted and tested in Larned's remarkable bibliographical guide, *The Literature of American History*, which at the opening of the present century gave the fullest practical exemplification of George Iles' ideals of "annotation and evaluation" in book selection. In all these aids (*A.L.A. Catalog, Standard Catalog, Booklist, Book Review Digest*) the bibliographical record of nonfiction includes indication of Dewey class numbers and class headings, intended to aid in the correct cataloguing of the book for library use. In all of them, including also (beginning in August, 1947) the "Weekly Record" of the *Publishers' Weekly*, for every title listed the Library of Congress card numbers are indicated whenever possible—these being the numbers by which printed catalogue cards for the individual books may be ordered from the Library of Congress to be used in the library card catalogue, thus saving labor for the individual cataloguer. Each aid has its own distinctive characteristics, its own personality, developed to meet the constantly increasing comprehensiveness, the curiously interfused standardization and specialization, of modern library book selection.

Careful study and comparison should be made of the annotations that are a feature of each of these aids. While the annotations in the *A.L.A. Catalog* and the *Booklist* are of the same general character and purpose, there are distinct differences between them. In the earlier *A.L.A. Catalog* volumes, annotations are more uneven in quality and less workmanlike in construction. In the 1926 volume there will be noted a marked improvement in the effective condensation of information and in the emphasis given to *comparative* evaluation, by means of references to other editions or other works of an author, or through comparison of other books on a subject. Annotations in the *Book Review Digest* must always be differentiated from the excerpts from reviews that accompany them. Often unusually detailed, the former are almost wholly descriptive; they tell what the book is about and indicate distinctive features, but rarely give evaluation of quality.

Another aid must take its place among friends and companions in general book selection. This is the *Bookman's Manual*, by Bessie Graham, first published in 1921, and since issued in revised, enlarged editions by the R. R. Bowker Company of New York. The *Bookman's Manual* is an indispensable general guide to modern and classical literature in print, not designed as a specific library aid in book selection, but of such practical usefulness in building up a broad professional acquaintance with books that it belongs in the first-aid equipment of librarians.

Its origin goes back to 1914, when Miss Graham opened the first bookselling school in the United States. The Philadelphia Booksellers' School, as it was called, was begun as part of the public school system of Philadelphia, meeting in the William Penn Evening High School for Women. Miss Graham planned it to combine bookselling education with instruction in library methods valuable in book-trade work. Her purpose was to impart a general acquaintance with "the vast subject of all literature," and her curriculum was based on the Dewey classification. The literature of each of the ten classes was studied as a whole and in rotation. Much interest was aroused throughout the book trade by Miss Graham's school. The lessons prepared for her classes were revised for publication and printed serially in the *Publishers' Weekly* during 1917–18, under the title, "The Home School for Booksellers." It was then decided to publish the material in book form as the *Bookman's Manual*. The first edition was used as a textbook in many library schools and in the school for booksellers later conducted in New York under the auspices of the New York Booksellers' League; it also proved a valuable reference tool in bookstores and in libraries. The revised editions issued from 1924 at from three- to six-year intervals have been enlarged by additional chapters, improved in detail, and kept carefully up to date. But the sixth edition, published in 1948, is a remaking rather than a revision—a remarkable bibliographical and literary achievement, carried through by Hester R. Hoffman, as Miss Graham's successor, with the dynamic thoroughness, the vitality and range of book knowledge, and the magnetic current of book sympathy that are the qualities of creative bibliography. It fulfills Miss Graham's devoted life work and holds enlightenment and allure for every worker with books.

In plan and purpose, the *Bookman's Manual* centers on giving an approach to books from the point of view of the experienced bookseller, which is very similar to that of the professional librarian. Familiarity with standard and popular books in the chief fields of literature, wide acquaintance with authors in their chronology and their works, discrimination between respective editions, and a background of long fellowship with publishers past and present—this knowledge is of prime importance to the worker with books, whether bookseller or librarian, who needs "to visualize literature as books to be bought from the right publisher and fitted to the right reader."

Primarily the *Bookman's Manual* summarizes facts. Emphasis is laid upon reference books and upon books that give information concerning books. Each chapter presents a particular class or subdivision of literature, in a sequence approximating that of the Dewey classification. As a rule, authors are listed in chronological order, thus giving an idea of the development of literature in each field presented; birth and death dates are given; biographical information is scanty and much compressed, but there is brief characterization of an author's works, which are recorded in order of publication, and a wealth of out-of-the-way information is concealed in this commentary. For standards and classics various editions are indicated, and there is record of leading series in history, philosophy, and other classes. The *Bookman's Manual* is not of importance for critical appraisal of books or writers, nor as a means to discriminating literary judgment; but it will build book background for any user, and is of constant practical usefulness to the library worker, the bookstore clerk, to all who are Companions of the Order of the Book.

In selection for college and high school libraries there are two basic aids that in their particular fields are comparable to the *A.L.A. Catalog* volumes in selection for the public library. These are Shaw's *List of Books for College Libraries*, published by the American Library Association in 1931 with a supplemental volume, 1931–38, published in 1940; and the *Standard Catalog for High School Libraries*, published in successive editions since 1926 by the H. W. Wilson Company. The Shaw list includes in careful, authoritative selection, about 14,000 titles, with publishers and prices, arranged in twenty-three divisions that correspond to the subjects of college instruction instead of to library classification, including under each group periodicals, reference books, and general works. Compiled for the Carnegie Corporation Advisory Group on College Libraries, selection was made on recommendation of 200 college teachers, librarians, and other advisers. There are no annotations, but the selection itself represents an "evaluation" that offers indispensable guidance in building up any college collection. The 1931–38 supplemental volume includes 3,600 titles, and for most of them cites evaluations from reviewing journals. In the *Standard Catalog for High School Libraries*, 5th ed. (1947), 4,555 books are fully recorded, with excellent annotations, and 842 are briefly listed, in a discriminating selection for junior and senior high schools; 773 pamphlets are also listed and there is a list of sources for pictures. This edition is much enlarged, arranged in two sections (a dictionary catalogue and a classified list according to the Dewey system), with valuable expansion of index range and detail.

AIDS MENTIONED IN THIS CHAPTER

A.L.A. Catalog: 8,000 volumes for a popular library, with notes; prepared by the New York State Library and the Library of Congress under the auspices of the A.L.A. Publishing Board; editor, Melvil Dewey. Washington, Government Printing Office, 1904.

A.L.A. Catalog, 1904–1911. Class list: 3,000 titles for a popular library; edited by E. L. Bascom. Chicago, A.L.A., 1912.

A.L.A. Catalog, 1912–1921. An annotated list of 4,000 books; edited by May Massee. Chicago, A.L.A., 1923.

A.L.A. Catalog, 1926. An annotated basic list of 10,000 books; edited by Isabella M. Cooper. Chicago, A.L.A., 1926.

A.L.A. Catalog, 1926–1931. An annotated list of approximately 3,000 titles; edited by Marion Horton. Chicago, A.L.A., 1933.

A.L.A. Catalog, 1932–1936. An annotated list of approximately 4,000 titles; edited by Marion Horton. Chicago, A.L.A., 1938.

A.L.A. Catalog, 1937–1941. An annotated list of approximately 4,000 titles; edited by Marion Horton. Chicago, A.L.A., 1943.

The Booklist: a guide to current books (semimonthly). Chicago, A.L.A., 1905–date.

Booklist Books: a selection (annual, 1919–40). Chicago, A.L.A.

Book Review Digest (monthly). New York, The H. W. Wilson Company, 1905–date.

Graham, Bessie. The Bookman's Manual: a guide to literature. 6th ed., rev. and enl., by Hester R. Hoffman. New York, R. R. Bowker Company, 1948.

Shaw, Charles B., ed. A List of Books for College Libraries. 2d preliminary ed. Chicago, A.L.A., 1931.

—— A List of Books for College Libraries, 1931–1938 [Supplement]. Chicago, A.L.A., 1940.

Standard Catalog for High School Libraries. A selected catalog of 4,555 books; Part 1, Dictionary catalog; Part 2, Classified catalog; [5th ed.] comp. by Dorothy E. Cook and others. New York, The H. W. Wilson Company, 1947.

5. Daily Help for Daily Needs

> No sooner had we made our bow to Mr. Cambridge, in his library, than Johnson ran eagerly to one side of the room, intent on poring over the backs of the books. . . . Mr. Cambridge, upon this, politely said, "Dr. Johnson, I have the same custom which I perceive you have. But it seems odd that we should have such a desire to look at the backs of books." Johnson instantly started from his reverie, wheeled about and answered, "Sir, the reason is very plain. Knowledge is of two kinds. We know a subject ourselves, or we know where we can find information upon it. When we inquire into any subject, the first thing we have to do is to know what books have treated of it. This leads us to look at catalogues and the backs of books in libraries."
>
> Boswell: *Life of Johnson*

BESIDES THE simple standard aids that have been considered, there are many others that are tools in constant use in the practice of book selection. They may be roughly grouped as aids in selection for small and medium-sized libraries, and aids that belong in the more extended bibliographical equipment of larger or specialized collections. They resolve themselves also into aids in current book selection, and aids in the selection of older books. The *Booklist* and the *Book Review Digest*, for example, are guides to the selection of new books; the *A.L.A. Catalog* and *Standard Catalog* volumes and the *Bookman's Manual* are guides to older, standard, and contemporary literature.

The extent of a library's bibliographical equipment depends upon the size of its collection and the amount of its book fund, but every competent librarian seeks to build up as strong and varied a supply of bibliographical tools as possible, for they are the means of strengthening the library's own structure and of making its service more useful. Thus a bibliographical list that contains no books included in the library collection has its value, for it indicates, at least, the existence of material that may possibly be available through other channels. And today almost every library can borrow from other libraries, for special use, books that it cannot provide from its own shelves. Every kind of booklist has potential usefulness: bulletins, catalogues, and reading lists of other libraries; publishers' and booksellers' catalogues and announcements; club or school or study programs with reading or reference notes—all should be gleaned and organized so that they can be quickly and effectively used.

For very small public or school or other general libraries (say under 10,000 volumes) the *A.L.A. Catalog* or *Standard Catalog* series and *Booklist* are often found adequate; the *Book Review Digest* is perhaps of next importance. Whenever possible, in addition to these aids, a minimum equipment should include the chief booktrade bibliographies, the *Bookman's Manual* (6th edition), the *Publishers' Weekly*, and several representative book reviewing periodicals.

From the H. W. Wilson Company comes the basic work of American book-trade bibliography that is indispensable in any extended ordering and purchase of books and is constantly used for reference in selection. This is the *United States Catalog*, which began in 1900 [1] and was continued in successive period-volumes, culminating in the fourth edition, a mammoth volume (3,164 pages and 25 pounds weight) that lists all books in print in the United States on January 1, 1928. In it are indexed, under author, title, and subject, 190,000 titles of books, requiring a total of 575,000 entries. These great period-volumes are kept up to date by the current record of the *Cumulative Book Index*, published monthly, with annual cumulations and also in period-supplements (that for 1938-42 covering 2,722 pages, appeared in 1945). Beginning with 1929, the *Index* assumed an international bibliographical range by including in its record books printed in English, regardless of the country of origin. In 1948, as an alternative to higher subscription rates, it was decided to discontinue this practice and confine the *Index* to listing books published in the United States and Canada only. But later in the year subscribers, by a majority of 72.7 percent to 27.3 percent,

---

[1] The first edition, covering books in print, 1899, was published in 1900; 2d edition, 1903; the first important period-volume covered books in print on January 1, 1912.

voted for increased rates and the continuance of the *Index* as a world list of books in English.

Prepared especially for small and medium-sized libraries is the Wilson Company's *Standard Catalog for Public Libraries*, which since the 1920s has become a basic aid, in large measure superseding the *A.L.A. Catalog* series. First published in eight separate subject sections (Fiction, Biography, Social Sciences, Fine Arts, History and Travel, Natural Sciences and Useful Arts, Literature and Language, Philosophy and Religion), it appeared as a consolidated one-volume Nonfiction Section in 1934, preceded by a revised Fiction Section in 1931, which together listed with annotations nearly 14,000 volumes. This segregation of fiction from nonfiction has continued. The *Standard Catalog for Public Libraries, 1940 Edition* (nonfiction) listed more than 12,000 titles and covered 2,192 pages; the five-year supplement, 1941-45, published in 1946, lists 3,908 titles in its 796 pages. These catalogues represent excellent selection of popular type, drawn in large part from library recommendation, good annotations, extremely full and useful analytical indexing. Of the books included, about one fourth are recommended for first purchase by libraries with very limited book funds; this recommendation, indicated by an asterisk prefaced to the title, is helpful in choosing books for very small collections, or in compilation of short reading lists. The *Fiction Section*, first published in 1908, with succeeding supplements, had expanded by 1942 into the substantial *Fiction Catalog, 1941 Edition;* this is considered in a later chapter among other aids in selection of fiction. An offshoot of the *Standard Catalog*, chiefly for distribution by libraries to readers, is *Readers' Choice of Best Books*, a recommended selection of about fifty new books, which appears as a section of the *Wilson Library Bulletin*, monthly periodical (except for July and August) devoted to library and bibliographical articles and widely used, especially in school libraries.

Of the full range of the Wilson bibliographical publications only a word can be said. They represent, I believe, the most extensive and intensive system of extracting and conveying information from printed matter that has yet come into existence.² These catalogues, lists, and indexes give daily help for the daily needs of librarians, students, and book users in all the fields of knowledge. Every library student, every worker in books, should be familiar with their variety, scope, and method—from the *Book Review Digest*, the *United States Catalog* and the great *Readers' Guide* series, the *Essay and General Literature Index*, the indispensable biographical reference volumes devoted to authors, the many special indexes to periodicals, the debaters' handbooks on subjects of public interest, the study outlines, special bibliographies and reading lists, to the record and supply of pamphlet material through the "Vertical File Service." Bland acceptance of the fact that these aids exist is not enough. It is only by some personal contact—by examination, by testing, by quick and practiced handling—that the instruments of any calling can be put to expert use. Full provision of such aids, of course, is beyond the means of many libraries; but the more thoroughly the librarian knows their scope and use, the more intelligently can choice be made among them, when possible, to meet the particular needs of any individual collection.

Beside the *United States Catalog* should stand that indispensable working tool of the book trade, the *Publishers' Trade List Annual*, established in 1873. It is also indispensable in the book selection and order work of almost any general library of moderate or larger size. Formerly a single huge volume running to 6,000 pages and over 20 pounds in weight, publication in two volumes was begun in 1947. Here are assembled the trade catalogues or price lists of all leading and many minor American publishers, arranged in alphabetical order. Until 1948, to use it one had to know who published the books desired, for there was no index of individual books, except as this might be included in a publisher's own catalogue. This need, however, was met with the appearance of *Books in Print, an Index to the*

---

² *Wilson Library Bulletin* for June, 1948, is the Fiftieth Anniversary Number, commemorating the founding and development of the Wilson bibliographical system in a notable autobiographical article by H. W. Wilson (pp. 779-83), and in other historical and descriptive commentary—all of permanent reference value. A history of the firm, by John Lawler, published by the University of Minnesota Press, also marks this semi-centennial.

Publishers' Trade List Annual for 1948, and its continuance yearly as a key to succeeding *Trade List* volumes. The massive index volume (of some 200,000 entries) consists of author and title indexes, giving full information as to author, title, price, and publisher, and making possible easy reference for fuller information to the appropriate publisher's catalogue in the *Trade List Annual*. In the book trade, where the publisher is the important factor in the ordering and supply of books, this *Trade List Annual* set is a necessity, for it gives up-to-date information as to whether or not a given book is still in print, whether its price has changed since date of its first publication, and whether it has gone into new or variant editions. Publishers' catalogues also often give fuller information concerning series, editions, and physical characteristics of books than can be found in the highly compressed bibliographical records. Familiarity with the *Trade List Annual* is one of the best means of gaining that expert "trade familiarity" with books in which many library workers are deficient.

The *Trade List Annual* is a publication of the R. R. Bowker Company (originally, Office of the *Publishers' Weekly*), a firm that, since 1872, has been especially identified with the development of American book-trade bibliography (through the *American Catalogue* series, which was predecessor of the *United States Catalog*) and with leading book-trade and library aids. The *Library Journal*, established in 1876, has from the beginning been published by it. So has the *Bookman's Manual*. The *Bookman's Glossary*, a useful small compendium of terms used in all branches of printing, binding, and publishing, and the *Literary Market Place*, a directory of publishers, reviewing media, and other information for authors, are among its widely used publications.

From the Bowker Company comes the *Publishers' Weekly*, the oldest and leading American book-trade periodical. This is of prime importance in all extended book selection. It furnishes the basic current record of American publications, the official statistics of American book production, and the fullest and most varied information of the publishing and book-trade world. It was founded in New

York in 1872, by Frederick Leypoldt, also the founder of the *American Catalogue* and the first publisher of the *Library Journal*, and one of the great original geniuses in American bibliography. Associated with Mr. Leypoldt from those early days was Richard R. Bowker, who later succeeded to the ownership of the *Publishers' Weekly* and in 1911 reorganized the firm as the R. R. Bowker Company. Mr. Bowker was president of the company and maintained supervisory editorship of *Publishers' Weekly* and *Library Journal* until his death in 1933. His organizing abilities were notable in many different fields, and for years he was active not only in the book trade and the library world, but in literary, political, and civic affairs. Under Frederic G. Melcher, who became editor of *Publishers' Weekly* in 1918, book-trade and library relationships have been expanded and strengthened, with a vision and a creative energy which have given guidance and stimulus to all concerned with book production and book distribution. The *Publishers' Weekly* "Seventy-fifth Anniversary Number," issued January 18, 1947, is devoted to a comprehensive and detailed history of its organization and development from the beginning, comprising also a valuable over-all survey of American publishing and book-trade history during that period.

The *Publishers' Weekly* is primarily concerned with book-trade activities rather than with literary material concerning books. It publishes no general book reviews. It is both a bibliographical record and a trade journal. The feature that gives it special value to all who work with books is its "Weekly Record" of new publications. This is a list published in every regular issue, of all books, pamphlets, and other separate printed works currently published in the United States; short descriptive annotations are given for many titles. It is based upon the actual receipt of all new publications of importance, for all American publishers of standing send their new books to the *Publishers' Weekly* office to be listed in this record, and upon careful collection of all titles of current publications that can be gleaned from many sources. Where the *Booklist* and the *Book Review Digest* are selective, the *Publishers' Weekly* record is inclusive, or as inclusive as such a record can be made. It thus furnishes what may be called the raw material of book selection—a comprehensive, nondiscriminating record, full and accurate in bibliographical detail. The *Booklist* provides this material selected and digested, prepared and ready for immediate use. The *Book Review Digest* provides it, also selected and garnished with a commentary of representative critical opinion as to its qualities and defects. The *Cumulative Book Index*, of course, gives an inclusive record, but it appears at longer intervals and so is less prompt as a source of information.

For these reasons (comprehensiveness and weekly appearance) the *Publishers' Weekly* record of new publications is checked regularly by nearly all of the larger and medium-sized libraries of this country, as a part of their process of book selection. Many small libraries also check it; but, of course, a library with a very limited book fund will usually depend upon the selective record of the *Booklist*. Every worker with books who can do so, however, should know and use the *Publishers' Weekly*, not only because it gives a continuous and comprehensive record of all the books published in this country, but for its wide gleaning of book news, its special indexes of books announced for publication, its many articles and lists suggestive to librarians (both the *Bookman's Manual* and the *Bookman's Glossary* appeared in its pages in serial form), and its value in imparting "book-trade familiarity." No other single periodical seems to me so valuable in establishing expert working knowledge of books, not from the standpoint of literary appreciation or criticism, but from the realistic and practical aspects of production, distribution, publicity methods, economic influences, and tendencies in public demand.

Several English book-trade tools are used in current book selection for moderate-sized American libraries. Of first importance is the *Reference Catalogue of Current Literature*, which in its history parallels both the *Publishers' Trade List Annual* and the *United States Catalog*. Originally modelled upon the *Trade List Annual*, and published usually at four-year intervals, it gave in two immense volumes the current price-lists or catalogues of almost all British publishing firms, in alphabetical sequence, and in a third and smaller volume provided a complete author-and-title index (with partial subject indication) to all books recorded in the publishers' lists. After fifty years of existence in this incarnation, it appeared in 1936 as a single-volume 1,200-page "national inclusive book-reference index of all books in print and on sale in the British Isles," in a pattern approximating the basic period-volumes of the *United States Catalog*. Two-volume form was returned to with the period-volume for 1940, covering books in print to the end of 1939.

The *Reference Catalogue*, in its present index form, is supplemented by *Whitaker's Cumulative Book List*, begun in 1924. This is an alphabetical class list, followed by an author-and-title index, which first appeared in an annual volume and quarterly cumulative bound issues—roughly paralleling the American *Cumulative Book Index*—but added a five-year period-volume with the publication in 1945 of *Whitaker's Five-Year Cumulative Book List, 1939–1943*, which records in a single alphabetical list all books published during the years covered; its succeeding volume, *Whitaker's Four-Year Cumulative Book List*, appeared in 1949. Current record of new publications is given by two English book-trade weeklies, the *Publishers' Circular* and the *Bookseller*. On the *Publishers' Circular* record are based the annual volumes of the *English Catalogue of Books*, which has registered English book production through more than a century, while the *Bookseller* record links with that of *Whitaker's Cumulative Book List*. There are some irregularities in the period-sequence of these aids, owing to the destruction wreaked by the war on the London publishing trade, to wartime limitations of production, and to continuing increases in production costs. But these disasters were met with unflagging determination and resourcefulness; and the basic bibliographical record was maintained—to receive notable impetus in 1950, when the weekly *British National Bibliography* began record of books filed in the British Museum. English literature is so much a part of American life and thought, past and present, that the information supplied by English book-trade catalogues, journals, and review periodicals is constantly useful in American book selection.

There are many bibliographies and lists designed as guides to the "best books." Most of them are more suggestive to the general reader or student than in the practice of library book selection. Some of them will be indicated in later consideration of different classes of literature. But there is one, so unusual and so valuable that it must have attention here. This is *The Best Books: a Readers' Guide*, by William Swan Sonnenschein (1855–1931)—the life work of a veteran English bookman and publisher, whose story, told by his son in the preface to his father's great work, completed after his death, is an inspiring chronicle of bibliographical devotion, excitement, and achievement.

William Swan Sonnenschein was an Austrian by birth, but an English citizen from young manhood. During the First World War he took his mother's surname, Stallybras (as was then done by many Englishmen of German descent), and this appears on the title-page of several of the *Best Books* volumes. A man of great erudition and even greater powers of application, enthusiasm, and purpose, as a youth he entered the English book and publishing world, established his own publishing firm of Swan Sonnenschein and Company, and later was for thirty years senior director of the Routledge firm. For fifty years *The Best Books* was his dominating absorption and the center of his family life. His wife was his assistant through the whole period; his daughter devoted thirteen years to helping complete the task. His son says: "The compilation of *The Best Books* would have been a remarkable achievement for one man had he been able to give all his time and energies to it. It is almost incredible that it should be the work of a man who from the beginning to the end was fully engaged during all the ordinary working hours in the business side of publishing, and who night after night was bringing home the work of authors in order to prepare their manuscripts for the press." He adds: "All my life my memory is of my family working at *The Best Books*—my father consulting bibliographies, checking dates, making entries in his beautiful clear handwriting, and my mother working away at the great index." Both husband and wife were always young in spirit, finding unflagging stimulus and satisfaction in the structure they were building. "Let it not be thought," says their son, "that my father's life of unremitting industry was unhappy or dismal. Never was there a man of gayer spirit than he" —he had written fanciful tales for children in his youth—"and the community of interest and of work—the shared joys, the shared disappointments and sorrows—made a perfect foundation of family happiness." This vivid glimpse of bibliographic genius in action evokes for me the picture of Frederick Leypoldt in the making of the great 1876 *American Catalogue*, as his wife so often described it. But there was more tragedy than well-being in the carrying out of the Leypoldt achievement.

The Best Books is a comprehensive and scholarly bibliography of contemporary literature in English, offering in its six volumes an immense and rewarding field for exploration by any hardy adventurer in book selection. The first two volumes, recording books in nine subject groups, were published in 1910–12. Then the First World War intervened, and the three volumes that followed, in 1923, 1926, and 1931, show a virtual breakdown of the bibliographic method under the immense accumulation of material. There are about 100,000 books listed in these volumes, in a selection that represents encyclopedic book knowledge and catholicity in critical judgment. Structure and arrangement throughout are elaborate and confusing. The classification is an original scheme of broad subject groups, designated by letters, with numerical sections and subdivisions. Condensation and abbreviation are carried to extremes. Annotations are included sparingly in the first two volumes; they are made cryptic by abbreviations and contractions, but beneath this forbidding stubble they offer for study some of the finest examples of expert book evaluation that I have ever discovered. The index volume, published in 1935, crowns the work and assures its continuing use and usefulness.

Probably only those in whom the "bibliographic urge" is innate will admit the lure of "Sonnenschein." But in any extended study or practice of book selection, especially in rounding out or building up a full representation of standard and older contemporary literature in religion, philosophy, sociology, history, science, and other nonfiction, this remarkable work, with all its oddities and shortcomings, is rich in suggestion and practical value.

To pursue much further this survey of bibliographical aids and guides is beyond the purpose of the present study. For the tools of library book selection belong with the apparatus of general and special bibliographical research and are to be chosen and used according to the extent and purpose of selection. Systems of national book-trade bibliography, similar to those of the United States and England, exist in France, Germany, and many other countries. In all large libraries these bibliographies and all other available works of bibliographical reference—general and special bibliographies of earlier and rare books, records of book prices for older or contemporary books of value, guides to books in every class of literature—are part of the equipment for the selection, ordering, and purchase of books. Knowledge of their distinctive characteristics must be gained through study; facility in their use is imparted only through experience. Compact and immediate information concerning them is to be found in the *Guide to Reference Books*, by Isadore Mudge (with its continuing supplements), one of the indispensable aids in any extended or specialized selection, now carried on by Constance Winchell. In all work with books that relates to or depends upon scholarship or research, there should be constant personal exploration and discovery in the immense storehouse of bibliography, with its intersecting passageways to specialized book knowledge and its great depositories of information that guide to the literature and the learning of all ages and all countries.

Bulletins, lists, and other publications of libraries are commonly used in selection, on the principle that books carefully chosen as desirable for one library of a particular type will be suitable for others of the same general character. Popular appeal in selection and annotations of the "readers' notes" type are emphasized in most of the public library bulletins (Cleveland, Detroit, Brooklyn, are good examples); and the New York Public Library *Branch Library Book News* has for many years been a valuable and suggestive aid, notable for excellent special lists and discriminating selection and characterization.

Every small library should receive the library publications of its own state—bulletins, lists, and reports of the state library commission or state library, and of the individual libraries themselves—most of which may be obtained without cost; for these reflect prevailing standards and practice in selection, give many suggestions for local application, and strengthen the spirit of cooperative service.

Of the scholarly bibilographical work found in many of the publications of the larger libraries, the *Bulletin* of the New York Public Library is an example. Its lists are of high authority, often exhaustive bibilographies of important collections, and always valuable as reference or research material. *About Books,* the bulletin of the Boston Public Library, mingles notable bibliographical articles and grouped reviews with special and general lists.

But the library publication of foremost importance as an aid in current book selection is the *United States Quarterly Book List,* initiated in March, 1945, by the Library of Congress and published (after completion of volume 3), by Rutgers University Press. Originating from a recommendation of the Inter-American Congress for the Maintenance of Peace, held in Buenos Aires in 1936, this is designed to introduce important United States books abroad, and to serve especially as a contribution to systematic exchange of bibliographical information with the Latin American republics. Dignified and substantial, it offers authoritative and scholarly appraisal by a large cooperative staff of readers and annotators, of current literary, learned, and scientific books published in the United States. Necessarily highly selective, it is comprehensive in scope and of immediate timeliness and significance. More than 200 books are included in each quarterly issue, under broad subject classification, in compact reviews that are explicit, factual, and have authority of judgment. This is a bibliographical undertaking of far-reaching importance and value—an aid to the improvement of our own library collections and a means of deepening international understanding and cooperation in the postwar world. In all larger libraries and those of important specialized character, bound sets of such publications as these are carefully built up, for use in reference work and as sources of information in selection of books in many different fields of knowledge.

Printed library catalogues were formerly (in the days before printed catalogue cards and cumulative bibliography) indispensable aids in book selection and in bibliographical method. The great catalogues of the Boston Athenaeum, of the Peabody Institute of Baltimore, of the Brooklyn Library, and the Detroit Public Library, were famous in their day, and some of them still possess high reference value. But the printed catalogue cards of the Library of Congress have replaced them by a centralized, authoritative, flexible, and continuous book record, used by libraries all over the country. There are still some printed catalogues, however, that are standard aids to selection in many subjects, chief among them the *Classified Catalogue* of the Carnegie Library of Pittsburgh, which represents a great general collection, especially strong in technology.

Indeed, every kind of special catalogue, reference or reading list has potential usefulness in expert book selection. None of them should be used blindly, for each has its own particular purpose, its possible bias in selection, and most of them give little detailed information about individual books. The use of library lists and bibliographies for older books almost always requires search of other records to find publisher and price, or to make sure that there are no later and better editions, or that some more recent book on the same subject is not preferable.

It is obvious that lists, bulletins, and fugitive publications that record or recommend books may be of possible value in book selection. But in building up any library there should be a constant gleaning of all useful printed material that can be obtained free of cost or at nominal expense. Today's immense and varied literature of commercial publicity, of high-powered modern advertising; publications distributed by public organizations, institutions, and foundations; "separates" of university addresses, programs of lecture courses, circulars of travel agencies; all this, and much more of the same general character, is grist to the mill of library reference service. In any small library where economy in buying is imperative, through knowing and using such material an intelligent librarian can, at very little cost, enlarge and enrich the collection. It is unnecessary to indicate the extent and value of public documents—national, state, and municipal—that are freely available to any library. But not all library workers realize the use to be made of publications of by such groups as the Carnegie Endowment for International Peace, the American Association for the United Nations, the Child Study Association of America, the World Calendar Reform Association, the National League of Women Voters, the American Civil Liberties Union, the Federal Council of the Churches of Christ in America, the National Association for the Advancement of Colored People, the C.I.O. Department of Research and Education, and many others. A mass of timely reference information on contemporary writers and their books is available through the little pamphlets of "appreciation" distributed by many publishing firms as publicity for authors whose books they carry. Compilations of household hints or recipes may help to meet readers' demands, even though they center on the virtues of some individual food product or labor-saving device.

Much of this matter, of course, is propaganda, designed to influence public opinion or to establish sales response. It must be sifted with discrimination, but it yields genuine and often unexpected values. Guides to these values are included among the everyday aids in book selection. Both the *Booklist* and the *Book Review Digest* offer from time to time excellent selective lists of pamphlets and documents; the *Publishers' Weekly* currently supplements its record of new publications with a small-type list of "pamphlet material and books of lesser trade interest"; and the H. W. Wilson Company, in its "Vertical File Service," has established a careful and extensive record and supply of pamphlet material, through publication of a monthly cumulative catalogue, and the provision, through a centralized clearinghouse method, of pamphlets desired by subscribing libraries.

Processes by which books are ordered and acquired after their selection has been made are not within our province. They vary in minutiae and organization according to the size and character of the individual library. But perhaps the simple mechanical routine by which selection is recorded should be briefly indicated. It is based on regular systematic checking of current lists, reviews, and other sources of information. For each title checked, a card record is made, giving author, title, publisher, price, and indication of the source of information concerning it. Sometimes this record is made by clipping and pasting titles on the cards instead of copying them; very often both methods are used. Later information discovered concerning individual books is noted on the cards; often descriptive notes or excerpts from reviews are pasted to them or atttached by clips. If systematic book reviewing is done by the library, the review slips are sometimes used for this card record, and sometimes simply filed back of the original card. Books recommended by readers are included, with notation of further information and the ultimate decision made; books on special subjects, new editions, replacements, all find place here.

This is the "possible order file" or "possible purchase file"—its name is variable. Its cards are kept under author or class number, usually divided, according to the apportionment of the book fund, into nonfiction, fiction, reference books, children's books, etc., and often further separated into groups roughly classed as, "titles approved for prompt purchase," "titles for later purchase," "titles that demand further investigation," or any other designation that applies. In even moderate-sized libraries such a file often contains several thousand titles. From these cards the actual ordering is done. They represent the whole body of material that is passing through the various stages of selection, from immediate acceptance to suspended judgment or reasonable doubt. In its extent and detail such a file is a register of the volume and quality of selection and a manifestation of the skill with which it is practiced. When books are purchased, their cards are withdrawn, to pass into the permanent record of orders and accessions; for this file represents simply the pros and cons of book selection—the evolutionary process of library creation.

So far, we have laid the first row of foundation stones in our study of book selection. Consider them in brief recapitulation. We realize that books furnish the means of individual development in character, in intelligence, and in work; that the provision of books is the basis of all library service and the reason for the library's existence as an agency of public education. Such knowledge of books as will make it possible to select them intelligently and use them to the best advantage of the individual reader and the community is necessary to every librarian, and to any worker with books who deals also with the reading public. Intelligent book selection for library use is based on definite principles and carried on with the aid of tools planned for the purpose.

Principles to be applied in selection fall into two divisions: first, knowledge of the needs of the community and of the individual reader; second, knowledge of the books to meet those needs.

To select books for a community, you must know its character. To meet the needs of individual readers, you must know their tastes, their interests, and whether or not the library is adequate to meet their needs.

Knowledge of books to meet community and individual needs, requires a background of book familiarity, built up through wide and general reading; the ability to analyze and judge book values, acquired through study and observation; and a proficiency in selection made possible through wide knowledge and intelligent use of the bibliographical equipment that is available to all professional workers with books.

From professional book selection aids, we turn now to consider appraisal and evaluation of books through the materials of current literary reviewing and criticism, and through systematic book analysis and book annotation.

CHIEF AIDS MENTIONED IN THIS CHAPTER

Books in Print: an index to the *Publishers' Trade List Annual*. New York, R. R. Bowker Company, 1948–date.

Boston Public Library. About Books (monthly bulletin).

Cumulative Book Index: a world list of books in the English language (monthly, with annual cumulation and period-supplements). New York, The H. W. Wilson Company, 1898–date.

Fiction Catalog, 1941 edition. New York, The H. W. Wilson Company, 1942.

Holden, John A. The Bookman's Glossary: a compendium of information relating to the production and distribution of books, 2d ed., revised and enlarged. New York, R. R. Bowker Company, 1931.

Library of Congress. The United States Quarterly Book List. New Brunswick, N. J., Rutgers University Press, 1945–date.

The Literary Market Place: a directory for publishers, broadcasters, and advertisers (revised annually). New York, R. R. Bowker Company, 1940–date.

Mudge, Isadore G. Guide to Reference Books. 6th ed., 1936 (with successive supplements). Chicago, A.L.A.

New York Public Library. Branch Library Book News (monthly).

New York Public Library. Bulletin (monthly).

Pittsburgh, Carnegie Library. Classified Catalogue. 11 vols. Series 1–4, 1895–1916.

Publishers' Trade List Annual. New York, R. R. Bowker Company, 1872–date.

Publishers' Weekly. New York, R. R. Bowker Company, 1873–date.

Reference Catalogue of Current Literature, 1940. 2 vols. London, Whitaker; New York, R. R. Bowker Company, 1940.

Sonnenschein, W. S. The Best Books: a readers' guide to the choice of the best available books in every department of science, art and literature, with the dates of the first and last editions, and the price, size and publishers' name (both English and American) of each book: a contribution toward systematic bibliography. 3d ed. 6 vols. New York, G. P. Putnam's Sons, 1905–35.

Standard Catalog for Public Libraries, 1940 edition, compiled by Dorothy E. Cook and Isabel S. Monroe (Standard Catalog series). New York, The H. W. Wilson Company, 1940.

Standard Catalog for Public Libraries, 1949 edition, compiled by Dorothy E. Cook and Dorothy Herbert West (Standard Catalog series). New York, The H. W. Wilson Company, 1950.

United States Catalog: Books in Print, January 1, 1928. New York, The H. W. Wilson Company, 1928.

Vertical File Service. New York, The H. W. Wilson Company, 1932–date.

Whitaker's Cumulative Book List (annual volume and quarterly issues). London, Whitaker; New York, R. R. Bowker Company, 1924–date.
Whitaker's Five-Year Cumulative Book List: 1939–1943. London, Whitaker; New York, R. R. Bowker Company, 1945.
Whitaker's Four-Year Cumulative Book List: 1944–1947. London, Whitaker; New York, R. R. Bowker Company, 1949.
Wilson Library Bulletin (monthly, except July and August). New York, The H. W. Wilson Company, 1926–date.

PART TWO

Values and Appraisals

6. Current Book Reviewing and Literary Commentary

> Criticism is neither the scales that weigh nor the icing that sweetens, but the yeast that, for readers, leavens the lump. A good reviewer must have cool brains and a warm heart. He must have enthusiasms and guard them, and his likings must be as strong as his hates.
> H. S. Canby: "A Sermon for Reviewers," in *Saturday Papers*
>
> Yes, sir, puffing is of various sorts: the principal are—the puff direct—the puff preliminary—the puff collateral—the puff collusive—and the puff oblique, or puff by implication.
> R. B. Sheridan: *The Critic*

BROAD ACQUAINTANCE with review periodicals and discriminating use of book reviews are essential in book selection. In earlier years this unorganized material of literary criticism was the only source of information concerning the merits of current or standard publications. Up to the later years of the nineteenth century, the reviewers of the quarterlies, the literary periodicals, and the newspapers were virtually the only book evaluators. The organized bibliographical apparatus to which librarians and book users turn today has been the product of the enormous increase in the provision of books for educational use, the development of libraries, the extension of agencies of public education; it has aided to develop the causes which produced it—has been, in a way, both their origin and their effect.

But current book reviewing still makes the most direct personal appeal to readers and still sets the fashions in popular literary taste. Study of book reviews and familiarity with general literary criticism are important to all whose work lies with books and readers, both as aiding in the choice of books in every class of literature and as strengthening and sharpening individual judgment; also in making it possible to give desired information about books and to discuss or recommend books intelligently.

Our concern is not with literary criticism as that philosophy of aesthetics through which, since Aristotle, men have sought to define and denote beauty in creative expression. It is with the immediate criticism, opinion, and commentary through which readers, book users, and the general public are kept in touch with current literature.

Reviews are the most familiar form of critical exposition concerning books. In the past they were apt to take the guise of long, comparative articles, analytical and descriptive, conveying ethical homily, or political polemic. In the great English quarterlies a hundred years ago famous reviewers volleyed and thundered against writers of opposed political faith, or vied with one another in the ferocity of their attack upon books they found unpleasing. Sydney Smith told Harriet Martineau how he and his fellow reviewer, Brougham, who "had got hold of a poor nervous little vegetarian who had put out a poor silly little book," sat late one night over their review, "trying to find one more chink, one more crevice, through which we might drop one more drop of verjuice to eat into his bones." The cruel ridicule, the savage and reckless condemnation, that made the "scorpions" of the *Edinburgh Review* famous in its early days were in lesser measure common to much current English criticism until the mid-nineteenth century. But at the same time, throughout the nineteenth century, the art of literary criticism was strengthened in principle and clarified in application by the work of such writers as Hazlitt, Macaulay, Leslie Stephen, F. W. H. Myers, Matthew Arnold, and John Morley, whose work nearly all appeared as critical reviews in the quarterlies and later literary periodicals.

Present-day reviewing ranges from an extended critical essay by a scholar of authority to a "notice" of three or four paragraphs turned out by a hack writer. "Notice" is the word that the editors and reviewers themselves have for it; and the term indicates the difference between current literary criticism today and that of sixty years ago. The "notice" may range in length from a dozen lines to two columns or more. It may be the production of a "literary" aunt or niece of the country editor, who runs the book department of the agricultural weekly; or the compact, lively summary of an experienced journalist turning his hand to any odd job; or the magisterial pronouncement of self-conscious youth serving a novitiate in "literary work"; or the thoughtful, balanced, responsive utterance of a competent professional reviewer.

There is as much difference in the mediums in which book reviews appear as in the reviews themselves. Probably the most uneven and unsatisfactory reviewing is found in newspaper columns, though it must be remembered that sound and intelligent reviews constantly appear in the book pages or literary sections of many newspapers, and that two of the most important reviewing periodicals of the day are weekly supplements to great New York dailies. Any local newspaper in which book reviews appear is of value in book selection for the library of that community, for its notices indicate books that are being brought to local attention and through its columns it is often possible for the library to stimulate interest in good reading.

The best reviewing is found in the few periodicals that are entirely devoted to literary criticism and in the review columns of periodicals of general or specialized interest. Reviews in professional and trade periodicals are usually limited to books that relate to subjects with which the periodical is concerned. They represent the judgment of specialists, and are indispensable aids in the selection of books in these subjects. History, education, art, science, technology, business, are but a few of the many fields in which the book reviews in specialized periodicals must be carefully and constantly used for guidance in current book selection.

Newspapers and the book-reviewing weeklies have, of course, the advantage of frequency of issue and therefore can review books more promptly than can the monthlies or quarterlies. Usually, in the case of books of popular appeal, leading current reviews are based on advance copies—sometimes on galley proofs—sent out by the publishers for review well ahead of publication, so that the review may appear simultaneously with the appearance of the volume on bookstore counters. But very often the rapidity with which books are "covered" to ensure timeliness in reviewing means vagueness or superficiality or a publicity-inspired enthusiasm in the review. This is particularly true of nonfiction; the careful, authoritative consideration of an important work by a reviewer who knows the subject and deals with it deliberately seldom appears until several weeks, perhaps months, after the publication of the book; but such a review is worth waiting for.

In the general field of book reviewing the prevailing attitude today is not critical, but rather one of enthusiastic appreciation or noncommittal acceptance. A deliberately censorious approach, a chronically caustic characterization, is found in very few reviewers. The great mass of reviews are superficial, but ardent; they indicate excellences, they convey subject or theme in as lively and entertaining a fashion as possible; they are eager to discover and celebrate "greatness." This tendency to praise and accept is registered in the preponderance of plus signs over minus signs in any issue of the *Book Review Digest*. In a compilation and tabulation of reviews appearing in some fifty metropolitan newspapers and literary periodicals in one year, Louis Bromfield found that 137 novels had, during that particular year, been acclaimed as "the best novel of the year"; the same verdict had been bestowed upon twenty-seven biographies. There was evident also a bewildering and baffling confusion in critical appraisals: "Side by side were to be found reviews condemning the author as a tyro and praising him as the best writer of the past decade. Side by side were articles praising his style and condemning it. The total value was very often nil: the things cancelled each other." [1] This comment is still valid. Although through succeeding years the enormous growth of the commercial book clubs and their far-reaching, inwoven relationship to publishers, reviewers, and writers have made exuberant acceptance and admiration the dominant note in current reviewing, the flow of contradiction and dissent in judgments rendered is perennial.

Why, then, it may be asked, is the study of reviews valuable in book selection? The answer is that in spite of contradictions and

---

[1] Louis Bromfield, "A Critique of Criticism," in *The Mirrors of the Year* (New York, Stokes, 1928).

stultifications in judgment, there emerge from the mass of current criticism a certain consensus of opinion concerning the literature of the day, and a certain indication of its trends, tendencies, and qualities, that must be known and heeded in book selection and supply. Familiarity with current reviewing strengthens discriminating judgment and deepens background acquaintance with literature. It brings out aspects that probably otherwise would not be so quickly evident; it reveals the many different kinds and degrees of impact produced by the same stimulus applied to different varieties of gray matter. In expert library use of book reviews individual prejudices and proclivities of individual reviewers are allowed for, the points of view of the various reviewing publications are understood. The pulsating praise of such an enthusiast as Christopher Morley will be noted for calmer confirmation; the review of a book on social trends in the *Nation* will be instinctively compared with a review of the same book in the *New York Times Book Review*, and the result will usually be a more reasoned judgment of its scope and value than could be based on either review alone.

Reading reviews is not a substitute for reading books. But it is the quickest and most effective aid to their discriminating selection, for reviews give a certain amount of advance information concerning a book which enlarges and clarifies the information obtained in its rapid examination. The reviewer of a biography, for example, will almost surely tell something about the subject, will indicate whether the treatment is factual or fictionized, and will convey some impression of the book's interest or importance. Thus review material, when checked against the findings derived from an expert concentrated examination of the book itself, makes possible a rapid and fairly accurate appraisal of the book's intrinsic merit or of its suitability to a given demand. This appraisal is more trustworthy for nonfiction than for fiction. In dealing with novels, the advance information imparted by reviews is chiefly valuable in at once ruling out many novels by an often unconscious exposure of crudities, trivialities, or sensationalism, and indicating for others qualities of style or theme interest that demand consideration.

Reviews may be roughly grouped as usually of three kinds. There is the long critical or descriptive review of the work of a single writer; the notice, ranging from a quarter-column or less to two columns or more; and the omnibus review of a number of books grouped together.

Work in the first group represents the best in current criticism; from such reviews have been compounded many of the volumes that define qualities of contemporary literary art, denote new currents of purpose, or analyze changing modes of expression. Excellent examples of reviewing of this caliber are to be found in the anthology [2] published by the *Saturday Review of Literature* to celebrate its tenth anniversary. The collection of reviews there given are classed according to character or type (that is, critically analytical, appreciative, severe), and offer helpful examples to the student or amateur reviewer. John Drewry's volume, *Book Reviewing* (Boston, The Writer, 1945), treats the subject with compact, readable thoroughness, from definitions and background through technique, evaluation of different types of literature, suggested reference aids, and other practical aspects. There is analysis of a typical newspaper book page, and good examples are cited of the work of expert critics.

Stimulating and useful and of more "literary" quality is *On Judging Books*, by Francis Hackett (New York, John Day, 1947), which surveys the craft of author, critic, and reviewer in relation to reading-public levels. Inclusion of selected reviews of books of the past few years gives an effective base for critical appraisal and aesthetic judgment. There is condemnation of commercialized publishing and reviewing as vitiating appreciation and acceptance of the true values of reading. The volume, chiefly made up of the author's previously published essays and articles, constitutes also an interesting evaluative review of modern writing.

The "notice" varies greatly in type and quality. It may represent intelligent and fair-minded appraisal, unbridled enthusiasm, bored indifference, or native stupidity. There is the synthetic notice, in

---

[2] *Designed for Reading:* an anthology drawn from the *Saturday Review of Literature*, 1924–1934 (New York, Macmillan, 1934).

which the reviewer has fallen victim to the insidious text printed as a slip sent out with the review copy of the book or as a "blurb" upon its jacket. This is the "puff direct," ingeniously conceived and compactly expressed. Its bits of personal information about the author, its skillful intimation of significant revelations, its fervid tribute to brilliancy or charm of style, all save the reviewer the trouble of reading the book or coining phrases; and the result is the appearance of identical sentences in reviews published in every state of the Union.

Another familiar type of notice may be called the "unfolding of the tale." It deals chiefly with fiction, and holds up remorselessly the skeleton that the novelist has sought to endue with flesh and life; it has no critical value, but in book selection it serves a useful purpose in immediately removing many novels from further consideration by the bald recital of what they are about.

A more unsatisfactory type is the notice that proves to be an amusing or discursive little article upon the subject treated in the book, but pays no attention whatever to the text. Of similar general type is the review that is entirely devoted to the reviewer's emotions on reading the book, or his own knowledge of the subject about which the author is writing; these, in fact, are reviews of a reviewer, not of a book, and they are, quite naturally, most often written by authors, or by specialists in a particular subject. For this reason the custom of assigning a novelist to review a novel, a biographer to review a biography, and a college professor to review almost anything in the way of "serious" literature, regardless of individual experience in reviewing, seems to me to militate against the best kind of current criticism—catholic, supple, finely tempered, keenly perceptive. The finest body of general reviewing, from Hazlitt to Canby, has been the work of critics who were professional reviewers as well as men of letters, steeped in books and deeply concerned with every manifestation of creative thought.

During recent years there has been a marked increase in intelligent book reviewing in this country, just as there has been a still greater increase in the mass of printed matter that deals with books in general. Book review departments in magazines, book sections or columns in newspapers, commentary sent out by the various book clubs, and the enormous mass of publicity material supplied by publishers and booksellers, all combine to invest books with more immediate and widespread interest than they have ever had before; and as this interest grows, so does the body of professional reviewing that possesses authority and insight. Personal tastes and personal opinion must always infuse individual criticism, even of the highest caliber, but the standards supported by such editors and reviewers as Dr. Canby, Howard Mumford Jones, Joseph Wood Krutch, F. O. Matthiessen, Clifton Fadiman, David Daiches, Albert Guerard, Edmund Wilson, Lewis Galantière, and many others, are establishing a current criticism that honestly seeks to denote the qualities and defects of current literature and is helping to improve literary expression in form and to clarify and strengthen it in standards.

There remain always, however, influences that weaken the critical fiber of current reviewing and turn reviewers into publicity agents for the book trade. The tidal waves of sudden popularity that sweep a book along on a surge of acclaim are too often set in motion by elaborate, powerful, commercial machinery designed to improve sales, not to appraise qualities. Mechanics of exploitation as they affect reviewing are in large measure personal. Such, for example, are the teas, cocktail parties, receptions by publishers, at which their authors may meet editors, reviewers, and others who can influence the reading public. This is a method long familiar, but within the last few years it has been more generally and vigorously applied in this country than ever before; its influence is, I think, reflected in the pervasive aimiability and evasion of forthright critical judgment that prevail in much minor reviewing. Radio contributes an important reviewing medium to the mechanics of book promotion, in many of the varied "book programs" that are continuously popular. Usually these offer commentary by a reviewer on selected new books; or the reviewer-conductor deputes an author to tell about his work; or a mock tribunal is staged, where "author meets critics" for discussion pro and con of the merits of his book. Such programs have many values. They stimulate public book-consciousness, they bring out the vital relationship of books to personal problems and to national and world questions, they are entertaining and informing; but as a rule, they transmit the infection of "bestselleritis" rather than the tonic of disinterested, discriminating, and independent appraisal.

A further word should be said on the relationship of publishers and booksellers to reviewing. Naturally, this is a fundamental relationship, for book production and distribution must be sustained by public response, which reviewing can create, or strengthen, or discourage. Thus, commercial influence exists and often has strong effect. Analyze any of the three leading review weeklies and note how many of the books reviewed in a given issue are also advertised there—of course, not all books reviewed are advertised, but virtually all books advertised are or have been or will be reviewed. Most editors, I believe, try not to yield, or yield as little as possible to pressure from the business office, but it is doubtful if the relationship can be wholly dissevered. Also there is the influence of reviewers' fellowship, family connections, cliques, common acquaintance, and mutual interests. Sisters, brothers, wives, cousins, aunts, mothers, sons, and daughters of our leading reviewers all are pursuing authorship in their own right, and their work is fairly sure to get good reviewing attention. All this constitutes a bloc of influence, a barrier hard for those outside to pass; it often limits or withholds recognition of work of finer quality by writers without personal contacts or direct sponsorship.

Fundamental qualities of good book reviewing may be summarized as follows:

Good literary form: expression should be easy and effective, though it may vary greatly in manner, from the leisurely and graceful, to the dynamic or the analytical.

Authoritative treatment: it should be written by someone who has read the book and knows something (the more the better) about the subject presented. This need not be profound, scholarly erudition; often there is more practical effectiveness in the broader, more flexible, mastery gained from a good background of information, wide book knowledge, and experienced critical judgment. The leading review periodicals aim at the expression of sound authority, but it does not generally prevail. Arnold Bennett, in *The Truth about an Author*, gives illuminating details of the various ways reviewers have of judging a book quickly.

Judicious comparison with other books in the same field, or with work of similar character.

Comprehensiveness: it should cover most of the points that have already been noted as important in testing book values—that is, authority, scope, form, treatment, literary quality, and physical characteristics.

Unbiased judgment: it should, so far as possible, be free from personal prejudices of the reviewer and uninfluenced by the editorial point of view of the publication. Many reviewers—among them some of the most brilliant and penetrating critics—are biased, either by antagonisms or sympathies. Certain reviewing periodicals of high standing have an editorial bias that must be recognized and discounted —as the *Nation* and the *New Republic*, with a radical attitude on social and political questions, the *New York Times*, with a strong tendency to conservatism.

There are other attributes of satisfactory reviewing. It should not be dull; but what seems dullness to an ignorant reader may be informing or stimulating to one who possesses greater knowledge. It should not be overenthusiastic—the adjective is the enemy of the substantive; but it should transmit to other minds the illumination that radiates from beauty and power in literature. It should possess the "wise skepticism" that Lowell said was the first attribute of a good critic; but this should mean detachment of judgment, not a carping or derogatory habit of mind. And it must be remembered that even the best reviewing is intended not for formal guidance in professional book selection, but for the enjoyment and enlightenment of the general reader, whose interest is in books as a reflection of life and satisfaction of personal tastes.

There are no rigid rules binding critical judgment to a given formula. In book reviewing, as in every human activity, there are "many men of many minds." For literary criticism is essentially an attempt to define the qualities of a certain piece of writing and to decide whether or not it has been well done. The decision will be influenced by the standards of judgment that the individual critic accepts and applies—whether traditional and erudite, as in the critical writings of Paul Elmer More, or vigorously factual and ironic, as in the reviewing of Bernard De Voto, or intellectualized and psychoanalytical, as in much of the work of Edmund Wilson. Beyond certain boundary lines, however, critical judgment does not function, and we enter a region of bad taste and fatuous opinion, where adult infantilism seeks and finds books of its own caliber. Within the canons that establish literature as an art, though all critics agree on fundamentals, not many think alike. In all his years of critical writing Howells was a champion of realism and disliked romantic literature. Stevenson loved romance and continually pleads for it in his charming critical essays. Paul Elmer More was indifferent to the most vital and significant modern literature. Stuart Sherman in his earlier critical work sharply attacked writers whose powers he later recognized. The intense anti-Puritanism of Ludwig Lewisohn leaves its tinge on his critical judgments. Individual convictions of political or social faith, personal intensities of partisanship, find violent expression in contemporary reviewing. In the literature of the war and postwar years the clash of nationalisms, the conflict of ideologies, kindled impassioned warfare; and the great reviewing combat arena of the period is that devoted to books about Russia. Balanced judgment and fair understanding were obscured and the scales of American public opinion were weighted by prejudice and hostility of a strong anti-Soviet "bloc" of well-known reviewers, so that impartial, adequate book selection in this field deteriorated in many library collections.

In any continued reading of current literary criticism there should develop a sense of personal acquaintance with individual reviewers. All who know and love books have their favorites among critics, chosen, perhaps, as we choose our friends, because their temperaments or their minds match, or supplement, or stimulate our own.

In the use of reviews in book selection, the larger this imaginary acquaintance is, the more discrimination there will be in striking a balance between conflicting opinions of a book, discounting extravagant enthusiasms, offsetting captious disapproval, and extracting essential values from apparent confusion. Especially in selection for small libraries, there should be no complete dependence on any single review, and, whenever possible, decision should be based upon examination of the books themselves.

Probably the review periodicals at present most generally used in book selection for American libraries are the *Saturday Review of Literature*, the *New York Herald Tribune Weekly Book Review*, and the *New York Times Book Review*. Each has its distinctive characteristics and special merits. Together they glean widely from the whole field of current book production; and while all handle virtually the same material, yet each finds some residue that escapes the other. For the many books that receive almost simultaneous consideration, these reviews serve as a triple mirror, bringing out different aspects, pointing variant details, and offering a basis for reasoned comparative judgment. Any public library that can afford it should make use of all three in book selection, and also encourage the interest they hold for readers as a constant influence towards making books more important in everyday life. Smaller libraries must often choose among the three according to values that best meet individual needs.

The *Saturday Review of Literature*, long the only independent American weekly periodical entirely devoted to books, later enlarged its field to include art, music, theater, and cinema. It maintains high critical standards and possesses an individual editorial personality that is lacking in the *Book Reviews* of the *Times* and the *Herald Tribune*. Its first editorial staff formerly conducted the *Literary Review*, established in 1920 by the *New York Evening Post* as successor to its earlier book page.[3] Four years later, when the *Post* was bought by the Curtis publishing organization, the *Literary Re-*

---

[3] Dr. Canby tells this early history with informality and charm in "Adventures in Starting a Literary Magazine," *Saturday Review of Literature*, October 13, 1945.

view staff resigned and established its own periodical, which, as the *Saturday Review of Literature*, appeared on August 2, 1924, with Henry Seidel Canby as editor, William Rose Benét, Christopher Morley, and Amy Loveman as associates. Dr. Canby held the editorship until 1936, then continuing as chairman of the executive board. He was followed successively by Bernard De Voto, George F. Stevens, and Norman Cousins, and with an enlarging group of associate and contributing editors. Dr. Canby's own editorials and reviews, many of them eventually collected in book form, make a body of short critical essays on contemporary trends in literature that are cogent and fair-minded, direct and pleasing in manner. Through the interest of William Rose Benét, himself a poet, poetry has always received particular consideration in the *Saturday Review*. Christopher Morley was identified with an early department, "The Bowling Green," in which most of *John Mistletoe* first appeared. Under Norman Cousins' editorship political discussion was emphasized. There has been steady expansion of scope as new departments have been added to the earlier ones for children's literature, foreign books, and other subjects; special numbers (poetry, music, regional literature, university presses, etc.) are a valuable feature. Besides special articles, correspondence, and departmental commentaries, from fifteen to thirty books are reviewed in an ordinary issue, about half of them in notices running from two columns to a page. The review is regularly indexed in the Wilson *Readers' Guide*.

As *Books*, the weekly book review supplement of the *New York Herald Tribune* made its first appearance on September 1, 1924; on January 31, 1943, its name was changed to *New York Herald Tribune Weekly Book Review*. Its early history, however, is somewhat akin to that of the *Saturday Review of Literature*, for it began as the book page of the Sunday edition of the *New York Tribune*, which, in 1922, was made a separate section, with Burton Rascoe as literary editor. When the *Tribune* bought the *Herald*, reorganization followed, and *Books*, in its present form, was launched under the editorship of Stuart Sherman. In the two years of Mr. Sherman's direction he inspired the vitality and catholicity that are still characteristic of this review; his death, in September, 1926, was an enduring loss to American literary criticism. Irita Van Doren succeeded Mr. Sherman as editor. Through ensuing years she built up a strong staff of reviewers and maintained a dynamic development, closely linked to book-trade interests, through the "bookstore plan" of individual subscriptions made in cooperative arrangement with booksellers in different cities, and through joint sponsorship of the popular "book and author luncheons," started in 1937 in New York by the American Booksellers Association. The *Review* expresses no editorial opinions; its trend is toward the commendatory rather than the critical. Its special departments deal with children's books (begun under direction of Anne Carroll Moore and later conducted by May Lamberton Becker), "The Reader's Guide" (by May Lamberton Becker), "Notes for Bibliophiles," detective and mystery fiction (by Will Cuppy until his death in 1949), and "Reprints, New Editions"—a department of much interest and usefulness in library book selection, for its judicious comment on important editions and translations of world literature. Perhaps its most distinctive department was the idiosyncratic column, "Turns with a Bookworm," in which, from the first issue until her retirement in 1949, Isabel Paterson dispensed lavish malisons and chary benisons on current literature. This publication reviews more books in an ordinary issue than does the *Saturday Review*—usually from thirty to forty—but gives no space to editorials or literary miscellany. Like the *New York Times*, the *Herald Tribune* has also a daily literary column, long conducted by Lewis Gannett, and devoted to "Books and Things."

The *New York Times Book Review* is the oldest of these weeklies, and perhaps for that reason the most conservative and equable. Ranking as the most widely circulated literary periodical in English, it is regarded by the book trade as one of the solid factors in American book distribution, covering more books more promptly than any other of the American reviewing media. With calmness, dispatch, and dignity, for more than half a century it has disposed of from thirty to sixty new books a week, in reviews that, long or short, have a certain family resemblance. In the beginning, under the editorship of F. W. Halsey, it was the *Times Saturday Book Review Supplement;* the first issue as supplement to the Sunday *Times* was that of January 29, 1911. There have been many changes of editorship (although Donald Adams held that post continuously from 1925 until 1943), but its columns give no current record of the editor's name and the *Review* maintains an impervious impersonality. The "Fiftieth Anniversary Issue," of October 8, 1946 (reproducing the first page of the original issue, for October 10, 1896), commemorates its history in a comprehensive, well organized presentation by skilled expositors of distinctive phases and aspects of American literary history through that period—trends in public taste and literary art, changing standards and interests of readers, record and comparison of books that have expanded and enriched every field of knowledge and culture. Both this issue and the twentieth anniversary issue of the *Saturday Review of Literature*, published on August 5, 1944, and devoted to "Literature between Two Wars," possess permanent usefulness as informational and evaluative reference material in library book selection. The twenty-fifth anniversary issue of the *Saturday Review of Literature*, which appeared August 6, 1949, contains similar values and covers a more widely varied field of subjects.

Times reviews are seldom critical in tone; a favorable attitude prevails, especially toward minor fiction, but the treatment is so impersonal and the "unfolding of the tale" so direct and factual that the quality of a novel may usually be fairly inferred. Children's literature, rare books, reprints and new editions, and other classes, are considered in special departments; among them, the Queries and Answers department, long famous as the happy hunting ground of myriad seekers for some half-forgotten poem or obscure quotation —a quest in which Miss Louella D. Everett, of Boston, is answerer-extraordinary. The range of books covered and the promptness with which reviews appear are special values of the *Times Book Review* in current book selection, and make it often the first choice of small libraries that can afford only one book-reviewing periodical. It is indexed in the *New York Times Index*. "Books of the Times," a department of review and discussion, appears in every weekday issue of the *Times*, and makes an excellent supplement to the *Book Review*.

Much other interesting reviewing is done by newspapers. The literary pages and supplements of the leading Chicago newspapers offer vigorous and interesting critical opinion, with *Chicago Sun Book Week* (from 1943) and *Chicago Sunday Tribune Magazine of Books* (from 1946) foremost competitors. The *Boston Evening Transcript*, for many years one of the most firmly established reviewing mediums, a cornerstone of literary judgment throughout New England, went out of existence in 1941. The *Christian Science Monitor* has excellent reviewing and is widely used by librarians. More and more newspapers in cities all over the country maintain adequate book pages or literary sections, and among southern newspapers, particularly, there has been evident a steadily increasing volume of intelligent reviewing.

Among general weekly periodicals, the *Nation* and the *New Republic* are of first importance for book reviews. Both enlist skillful and experienced reviewers and have been strong influences in the breakup of tradition and the application of modern ideas to creative expression. Both represent radical and liberal thought, in politics, art, and drama, as well as in literature; and both jettisoned much of their cargo of former consistent opinion under the fierce storm of anticommunist feeling engendered by the "cold war." *New Republic*, with the issue of December 10, 1946, came into a "second blooming" under the short-lived editorship of Henry A. Wallace, with popularized make-up and a more pictorial treatment of political and literary interests; but this "progressive" affiliation was transitory. The extreme left wing in political and social opinion was long represented by *New Masses*, old-established, vigorous communist weekly, which in March, 1948, wrecked by the anticommunist storm, was merged as a monthly with *Mainstream*, a periodical launched in January, 1947, under the editorship of Samuel Sillen, as a Marxian counterinfluence to the noncommunist, socialist-progressive movement. As *Masses & Mainstream* this little periodical leads a precarious existence, but holds the allegiance of many able American and international writers and as a stimulative book-reviewing medium deserves fuller recognition than it receives. From six to a dozen books are covered in each issue by competent reviewers, who are likely to bring out qualities and significances, not indicated elsewhere, which have value in comparative appraisal. *Time*, "the weekly news magazine," summarizes from four to six books a week in a clear-cut review pattern, and has frequent fuller articles, with interesting and illuminating detail, on books and writers of special timeliness. The book pages of the *New Yorker* are invested with a light sophisticated irony, but also with keen perceptiveness for originality and literary quality; full length, masterly reviews frequently appear here. The *Commonweal*, representing the liberal Catholic point of view in public affairs, literature, and art, contains competent book reviews in each weekly issue.

In many of the leading monthlies there are departments of book commentary, varying greatly in extent and quality. Among them, the *Atlantic* "Bookshelf" is of particular interest to librarians for its informal review comment and articles, supplemented by compact, discriminating notices of a few significant books. *The World in Books*, a monthly book review magazine in familiar newspaper supplement format, made its appearance in May, 1946, under the editorship of Edwin R. Brown, published by the United Publishers' Association, Incorporated, Boston. Each issue brings together under class headings a comprehensive gleaning of the publications of the month, summarized in brief, signed reviews, generally well advised in judgment although with appreciative emphasis.

There is much other material on which librarians draw in estimating values and probable reading appeal of current books. The Virginia Kirkus bookshop service, known as the New York Office (38 Bank Street, New York City), primarily intended to supply booksellers with advance information about new and forthcoming books, is also widely used by libraries as both a guide and forecast in buying. Mimeographed lists, sent bimonthly to subscribers, give crisp, stimulating characterization of individual books in a well-aimed quick-fire appraisal. *American News of Books*, monthly bulletin of the American News Company, is relied on by booksellers as a guide to popularity and sales possibilities. Here the books of the month are classified by dates of publication, also by a code of symbols which indicate prognosis of how each book will rent, how it will sell, and how suitable it is for a small public library. Somewhat akin is the *Retail Bookseller's* monthly "Almanac" of forthcoming publications, each compactly characterized. Purpose and point of view in these lists are commercial, but they represent shrewd judgment and practical experience and are useful in many libraries in checking over titles under consideration. The *Library Journal's* department, "New Books Appraised," gives valuable advance information each month in the annotations of forthcoming books, written by librarians with library values in mind; and the *Wilson Library Bulletin* as already noted includes in each issue a separate supplementary section, *Readers' Choice of Best Books*, a monthly selection of fifty new books of varied popular appeal.

American quarterlies give consideration to almost all aspects of contemporary literature. There are many of them, sponsored by universities or by noncommercial organizations. They range from specialized fields of scholarship, as in the *American Historical Review*, *American Literature*, and the *Journal of Religion*, to general intellectual and literary scope, as in the *Sewanee Review*, or in the "little magazine" type, chiefly concerned with ideas and experimentation in literary expression (*Accent* is a leading example); and to presentation of special trends of thought, as in *Social Research*, published by the New School for Social Research in New York. A dominating tendency is toward greater tendentious exposition and discussion of the problems of war's aftermath, postwar development, and world relationships, and of the opposed ideologies that are factors and portents in the "revolution of our time." *Science and Society*, founded in 1936, is the leading quarterly centering scholastically on Marxist interpretation of natural and social science, of philosophy, history, and literature. *The Partisan Review*, which includes also fiction, poetry, and essays, was founded in 1934, changed three years later from communism to anticommunist liberalism and became a monthly in January, 1948.[4] These are examples of the seething crosscurrents of present-day thought and opinion.

Nearly all the quarterlies contain authoritative book reviews, but these are seldom timely enough to be useful in prompt selection of current books; their value is chiefly in rounding out selection, by making possible critical comparison of books in the same field, or by giving clue to important books that have not had sufficient consideration. The *Yale Review* is the most widely known for the number, authority, and distinction of its reviews.

There is one quarterly, however, that should be known to every librarian and every student or user of contemporary literature. *Books Abroad: an International Literary Quarterly* has been published since 1927 by the University of Oklahoma, at a nominal subscription price. Dr. Roy Temple House, whose seventieth birthday and twenty-first year as editor were jointly celebrated in 1948, retired as its active editor in 1950 and was succeeded by Ernst Erich Noth. Each issue contains several short studies of foreign literature and foreign writers, followed by brief reviews, classed in subject groups, of from 250 to 300 current publications in many foreign countries, contributed by reviewers from American universities. The reviews are compact, usually descriptive, with perceptive critical qualities and responsive appreciation of values, and extremely varied in range. *Books Abroad* is valuable to any library, however small, for the information of students, and indispensable where current book selection includes provision of foreign literature.

English review publications are constantly useful in book selection for American libraries. Among them the London *Times Liter-*

[4] *The Partisan Reader: an Anthology*, representing the contents of this magazine during the first ten years of its existence, was published in 1946 (Dial Press). *Accent Anthology*, also published in 1946 (Harcourt), is a selection of stories, poems, and critical essays that have appeared in *Accent* during its first five years (1940–45). Of interest in this general field is *The Little Magazine: a History and Bibliography*, by F. J. Hoffman (Princeton University Press, 1946), which records and appraises the "advance-guard" magazines of the last forty years and their contribution to contemporary literature.

ary Supplement for comprehensiveness and promptitude stands in importance with the three leading American review weeklies. Indeed, for many books its reviews are more prompt than are the American reviews. This is because so many important current American publications (particularly in fiction and general literature) are by English writers and are published in England before they are brought out in an American edition—so that judicious gleaning of the *Times* reviews often makes it possible to order in advance books of evident merit, or provides advance information to compare later with the American reviews. In an ordinary issue the *Times* reviews from forty to forty-five books, and gives brief descriptive record to sixty or seventy-five more. As a whole, it represents a more complete cross section of the literature of the day than is to be found elsewhere.

Another English weekly, of lighter and more popular literary flavor, is *John o' London's Weekly*. Many of its reviews appear as entertaining descriptive articles; its tone is enthusiastic rather than critical; but it covers in interesting fashion many books in different fields. It mingles a little fiction and poetry with its reviews, articles on authors, and lively literary gossip; and under its editorial sponsorship "literary circles" are organized and conducted in various towns and cities, devoted to book lectures, literary study, and discussion. *Time and Tide*, akin in range and popularity, enlists many well-known contributors and maintains sound judgment and varied interest in the reviews and literary articles that have always been a special feature.

Traditional authority in English reviewing lingers in the *New Statesman and Nation*. This represents the merging, in 1921, of the older English literary organ, the *Athenaeum*—which had been established in 1828 and was for generations foremost in distinction of scholarship and critical power—with the *Nation*, later journal of liberal political opinion; and a further merging, several years later, with the *New Statesman*, brilliant representative of labor party interests. In its day, for nearly a hundred years, no paper was such a power as the *Athenaeum* in the English-speaking literary world; and the review pages of the present periodical, conducted as the "Athenaeum Section," still manifest scholarship and literary excellence and enlist many able reviewers. The *New English Weekly and the New Age*, another survivor of the war years, is liberal in point of view, "trying to work out a political philosophy for our time," and includes a few reviews in each issue. The *Spectator*, inclining toward liberalism, has many excellent reviews and maintains established standards of critical judgment.

Compared with similar American reviewing, these English reviews have a more easy and assured scholarship and a richer background of book knowledge. Their tone is more impersonal and they maintain more fully the tradition of anonymity. In the *Times Literary Supplement*, for example, all articles and reviews are unsigned, and there is no indication of the editor's identity. The reviews, as a rule, are more consistently critical and have a more literary expression; but they lack the lightness and variety of treatment and the incisiveness of phrasing that American readers expect and enjoy.

From 1919 to 1939, the *London Mercury* was the foremost English monthly of wide literary range, notable for excellent reviewing and masterly critical articles. The "General Index" to the twenty volumes covering its first ten years, published in 1932, is of permanent value to any library as a conspectus of English writers of the period. Discontinued in April, 1939, the *Mercury* was followed in that year by *Horizon*, a monthly "review of literature and art," founded and edited by Cyril Connolly, who carried it successfully through the war years and brought it to wide general recognition. *Horizon*, in format and contents, was more the type of a "coterie organ" than was the *Mercury*; it included, poetry, literary and critical articles, reviews, and emphasized European influences in literature. Among its contributors were most of the talented younger English writers of today; and its tone (strongly anti-Soviet) was that of socialist-progressive opinion, with a futile cynical awareness of world disintegration and transition. In January, 1950, it suspended publication for an indefinite period. A selection of Mr. Connolly's own literary essays from 1927 to 1944, most of them contributed to

Horizon, appeared in the volume, *The Condemned Playground* (Macmillan, 1946).

Among English quarterlies, T. S. Eliot's *Criterion* held high literary distinction under his editorship from its founding in 1923 until discontinuance in January, 1939. *Scrutiny,* established in 1932, succeeded it as a medium for the "New Criticism" of the Eliot dispensation and is given entirely to literary articles, reviews, and appraisal notes. The tone, at once hortatory and truculent, is predominantly one of drastic denigration of virtually all values in contemporary literature since the mid-twenties; contributors are drawn from professional academic critics rather than from creative writers; but the publication has been a factor in maintaining the so-called New Criticism in England. An anthology of essays from its volumes, entitled *The Importance of Scrutiny*, edited by Eric Bentley, published in 1948 (New York, George W. Stewart), is a useful addition to any collection of materials of present-day literary criticism. Although *The Nineteenth Century and After,* general conservative-liberal quarterly begun in 1877, still continues, reduced in bulk, the *Quarterly Review* remains the chief surviving example of the traditional English type its name perpetuates; entirely devoted to extended and scholarly reviews of books in all fields of literature, it represents authority and maturity of critical judgment.

Only leading general American and English periodicals have been touched upon. There are many more: French, German, Italian, and other foreign mediums for the record and appraisal of current books, journals of critical opinion and scholarly research. In expert book selection all this material fits into place, its values gleaned and utilized according to needs and opportunities.

And in all selection of books—general, special, limited, or extensive—it must be remembered that immense, pervading influences of publicity and commercialism constantly qualify and modify the validity of current literary criticism. The printed material lavishly distributed by publishers, that so often sets a model for reviewers, is essentially ingenious, skillfully disguised advertising. It is often useful in giving information—the experience or personality of an author, what a book is about, details as to illustrations, indexes, or special features. But it is frequently misleading; its cardinal sin is concealment of the fact that a book is a reissue and not a new work; and it should never be accepted as authority for a book's merit. This publicity material appears on book jackets, in advertisements, in the columns of literary gossip and paragraphs about authors; it infiltrates the commentary of the columnists; it often takes on the semblance of bona fide book reviews; and it finds expression in multifarious attractive and entertaining leaflets and booklets, published primarily for distribution by booksellers. All this is transitory newsprint of the daily life of books, entertaining as commentary and episode, but conveying no genuine critical values.

7. Book Evaluation and Reviewing by Libraries

Every discourse ought to be a living creature, having a body of its own, and a head and feet; there should be a middle, beginning and end, adapted to one another and to the whole.
        Plato: "Phaedrus," in *Dialogues;* Jowett translation

Accuracy of diction means accuracy of sensation, and precision of accent, precision of feeling.
        John Ruskin: *Praeterita*

PRINTED ANNOTATED AIDS represent the finished tools of book selection. Book reviews are the raw materials of opinion and judgment on which selection is based. With so many of these aids and accessories available, it might seem that no personal reviewing or annotating of books would be necessary; but this is not so. Books must frequently be purchased before they are recorded in the *Booklist* or *Book Review Digest*, even before they can be judged from reliable printed reviews. Very often, neither aids nor reviews tell all that an individual library needs to know, especially a library that purchases many duplicate copies. Besides these immediate practical reasons, it must be remembered that in the last analysis the selection of books is an individual exercise of individual purpose and intelligence. Sound personal judgment of qualities and values in literature, of requirements and opportunities in reading demand, is a first essential; and this judgment must be established and developed in all who work with books and readers.

So, in some of the larger libraries and in many of moderate size, so-called library reviewing has become a well-established and carefully systematized practice, primarily as an aid in selection, but also as a means of making library workers more familiar with the books they work with. Even in small libraries, regularly held "book-order meetings" are of great value to all members of the staff; while among individual workers, the school librarian, the librarian of a specialized collection, or the custodian of a small branch who can tell in a clear and pleasing way what a book is about or can write compact, interesting notes on new books for school bulletin or local paper increases the efficiency of the library's service and improves the professional status of the librarian.

Ability to review a book in a manner that interests and informs is a valuable asset to any worker with books. Even more valuable is the ability to write a sound, well-expressed, effective book annotation, compressed within less than a hundred words. At its best, this sort of work presupposes or demands a native gift of literary taste and facility in expression; but with intelligence and perseverance almost anyone can learn how to give an interesting review of a book or write a workmanlike annotation. Even if reviewing or annotating books is not a part of a librarian's required duties, some knowledge of method is helpful in sharpening critical judgment and making clearer the points that are to be weighed in forming and expressing opinions about books.

Some of the principles to be applied and the points to be observed in judging book values have already received attention. We are now to consider principles and methods that particularly apply in the book evaluation and reviewing practiced by individual libraries, either as part of the book selection process or as a means of enlarging public interest in worthwhile books.

According to familiar principles of literary criticism, the first requirement for any book is that it shall interest the reader, shall give some kind of pleasure, which implies a certain degree of value. The next step in forming judgment of its worth is to test the kind and degree of interest aroused or pleasure given. The third step is to analyze the book's qualities according to those canons that represent permanent beauty and value in literature. These are the three most important ways to judge a book: by the immediate personal impression received from reading it; by judgment of its usefulness or value to others; by dissection and appraisal of its intrinsic qualities. The last of these is the method of literary criticism in its finest manifestation, and in practical library reviewing is drawn upon only for the simplest and most obvious standards of judgment. It demands differentiation of a book's qualities. There is the idea, the subject, that the author has set out to present; there is the pattern in which that subject has taken shape; and there is the personality, the attitude toward life, that the author transmits to his work. In other words, there is the book's content, its form, and its spirit. Analysis directed upon these three aspects seeks to elicit the values that inhere in each; the validity, importance, truth to human nature and experience of the *content* (matter); the unity, excellence, vitality, of the *form* (treatment and style); the sincerity, power, beauty, dignity, of the *spirit*.

The term "evaluation" has been defined as an authoritative summarized statement of book values; but it applies both to the testing process by which values are determined and to the product of that process—"an evaluation" is the result of "evaluation." It denotes analysis of the form and content of a book, the testing and comparison of its quality and significance. In library practice, annotations and reviews alike are based upon a common technique of evaluation. The field of book evaluation is really the whole field of analysis and appraisal of books from the point of view of library selection. But there are so many different terms in use that apparent distinctions and differences create confusion. "Evaluation" and "appraisal" usually mean the same thing, that is, analysis or testing of book values for guidance in selection. "Evaluation" and "annotation" are also interchangeably used to indicate the compact statement in which the analysis of value is recorded, but "annotation" is now more generally accepted.

Distinction between library reviewing and annotation should be clearly borne in mind. "Library reviewing" usually means an oral review of a book, limited to from three to ten minutes and based upon definite points of analysis. "Annotation" means a brief written characterization of a book, also based upon definite points of analysis. In library reviewing the analysis (or evaluation) upon which the review is based may be indicated by a record of separate points briefly noted but not unified in form. In annotation, from the same points of analysis must be welded a compact statement, clear, well expressed, and interesting, suitable for use in a printed bulletin or annotated list.

Frequency of book-order meetings varies in different libraries. Their organization and procedure also differ; but their common purpose is to recommend or reject for purchase new books received on approval, to bring to attention books that will meet different types of demand, and to indicate the amount of duplication desirable for books recommended. Books are assigned for review to staff members at least a week before the meeting, and assignments are made so far as possible according to individual interest in different classes of literature. In highly departmentalized libraries, assignments are as closely specialized as possible: books in technology, science, religion, education, and so on, are given to librarians whose work lies in those departments. In smaller libraries, meetings are usually held once a month; there is less specialization in reviewing and more informal discussion of divergent opinions. Most of this library reviewing is based upon printed report forms, usually called "review slips." These furnish the evaluation of the book—the text from which the oral review is given; and the slips themselves are usually preserved in a reference file for further consultation if necessary or for possible later use in the preparation of annotated lists.

Such library reviewing always has practical administrative usefulness. In large libraries with many branches and other agencies of distribution it helps to unify the book structure of the whole library system and at the same time to discover and supply varying demands. In all libraries its greatest value should be the vitalizing and energizing of library service by stimulating book interest in individual workers. Any book-order meeting should at least waken in its participants an immediate, even though transitory, consciousness of the values and potencies that current literature draws from and instills into current living. Many fail to do this, through overmechanization, too insistent "speeding up," or the inadequacy of individual reviewers. Even the living spirit of books cannot penetrate and illuminate the densities of automatic routine and conscientious monotony.

There are many useful channels and opportunities in library reviewing, as guidance to readers, as a publicity medium, as community service. Book talks by librarians to clubs and special groups are always in demand. Skillful review commentary for library discussion groups can be made incentive and influence for broader, more enlightened, opinion on world problems. A weekly column of reviews and book news contributed by the library to a local newspaper may become of continuing value to the library, the paper, and the community. Radio is perhaps most commonly used for bringing book information and library news to the general reading public; many libraries carry regular or intermittent radio reviewing programs as stimulus to library use and find them effective, but success depends upon cooperation of the radio station and on the skill and vitality of the radio reviewer.

Consider now the process of book evaluation that forms the basis of library reviewing and that furnishes the material for annotations.

Report forms on which evaluation is made differ in size, in name, and in details in different libraries. The form most commonly used is the "review slip" of standard catalogue card size, printed on thin strong paper, which is filled out by the reviewer after reading the book. Review slips used by different libraries vary only in minor detail; in general form they derive from the slips (now long discontinued) originally used by reviewers for the *Booklist*. Different forms are used for nonfiction and fiction, as each require somewhat different treatment. Children's books also have their own special review slips, for they represent a special field of book selection for which in almost all libraries separate provision is made. Representative examples follow:

Nonfiction Review

Author
Title   vols.
Publisher   Date   Price
Illus.   maps   diagr.   indexes   bibl.
Subject or form
Scope
Sources
Literary merit
Treatment: popular, scholarly, technical, accurate, careless, partisan, unbiased, dull, interesting.
Of interest to: adults, young people, students, teachers, specialists
Recommended for: Main, Branches, Stations, Pay, Open Shelf
Author's qualifications, see reverse of slip
                                    Signature of reviewer

Fiction Review

Author
Title
Publisher   Date   Price
Illustrator   Translator
Literary merit
Moral tendency
Type: romantic, symbolic, realistic, psychological, expressionistic, humorous
Period and locality
Subjects for fiction lists
Of interest to:
Recommended for: Main, Branches, Stations, Pay
Reason for purchase or rejection
Outline of plot: on reverse of slip
                                    Signature of reviewer

Observe that author, title, and publisher are the first items of information given on all review slips, as these are the first absolutely necessary facts to know about a book. In filling out these slips the general practice is to underline words that indicate specific facts. Thus, if the book examined has illustrations, the word "Illus." is underlined, unless more specific detail can be written in, as "Illus. & 2 col." (that is, "Illustrations and two colored plates"). Underlining is used also to denote characterizations, for example, "popular," "scholarly," etc., for nonfiction; "romantic," "realistic," etc., for fiction.

It is apparent that the evaluation indicated on these review slips condenses and selects from tests that have been outlined in Chapter 3. Comparison will make clear that all analysis of book values is based on fundamental principles of criticism applied, however partially or superficially, to the informational content, the aesthetic quality, and the physical attributes of individual books; it will also indicate specific tests that are considered of first importance in making a rapid, valid characterization of a book.

Examination of the two review slips will bring out certain primary points. On the nonfiction slip, distinction and differentiation is indicated between "subject" and "form." For example, "study of crime" would be subject; "textbook" or "essays" would be form, as would any unusual framework, such as the separate chapters by specialists in *One World or None*. "Scope" is important as indicating how fully a subject is presented, whether comprehensively (ranging from past to present), partially, or in a special aspect. "Sources" have already been defined; but it must be remembered that in the case of many books of general, popular, or literary character no indication of sources is practicable or necessary. To pronounce authoritatively on "literary merit" requires discriminating critical judgment; the inexperienced reviewer can only indicate the impression as to literary quality that the book has made in reading it. In all reading, however, there should be a constant endeavor to develop sensitiveness to style, to recognize the difference between what is crude and what is dignified, what is commonplace and what is graphic, in the manner of writing. Many books will require several characterizations of "treatment." For example, a "popular" book may also be "accurate" and "interesting"; a "scholarly" book may be "partisan" or "unbiased." There are many other possible combinations of these characterizations. Remember that a book is not made "partisan" just because it presents a definite thesis or holds a specific point of view, but because it presents such a thesis or advocates such a point of view in a one-sided or violent manner. "Author's qualifications" are not included on the face of the slip, but are to be more fully given on its reverse; here information drawn from preface, from title-page, or from available reviews will cast light upon the authority or timeliness of a book.

On the fiction slip, the more common kinds of fiction may be indicated either under "subject" or by underlining one of various "type" characterizations. On some review slips, various kinds of fiction (adventure, western, mystery, historical, sea, etc.) are listed, to be underlined according to the character of the book. "Period and locality" of a novel should have clear factual statement (for example, *Death Comes for the Archbishop* deals with New Mexico and Colorado, from 1850 to 1888). "Subject" should be differentiated from "theme." It should be observed that the "outline of plot" to be noted on the reverse of the slip (as "qualifications of author" are noted for nonfiction) must come within the space of a standard catalogue card and therefore cannot be more than 150 to 200 words in length. Some libraries divide the space on the reverse of the fiction review slip into two equal sections: one assigned to "outline of plot," the other to compact "evaluation." On neither of these review slips is there any characterization of the physical make-up (print, paper, binding, etc.) of the book. Such details are sometimes included, but in general practice it is considered that these points will be observed in the routine handling of a book that has been received on approval, and the evaluation made for a library review is intended particularly to state facts that are not apparent on the surface.

Evaluation begins with the reading of the book. And in reading any book for review some degree of personal interest in the book is a first essential. No book can be judged fairly if it is read simply as a task. To plod doggedly through four hundred pages in reluctant performance of a distasteful duty or to skim scornfully over the same number of pages in aloof indifference is equally fatal to any clear and judicious appraisal. The reader should at least be receptive, should give the author the courtesy of polite attention until politeness becomes no longer a virtue. Be open-minded; allow other people to have a different point of view from your own. As you read, try to appreciate and define the style in which the book is written, whether it seems to you brilliant, graceful, monotonous, commonplace, or unusual. For style is always the hallmark of literature, the sign manual of a writer's credentials; if you doubt this, compare a page of Philip Wylie and a page of Santayana, a page of Tomlinson and a page of Aldous Huxley. Always read with pencil available, and make brief notes (even if no more than page references jotted on a bookmark) of facts or statements that will help you in grasping a book's character and quality.

In reading any book of nonfiction, note especially the tendency or purpose evident in its presentation and the point of view implied or expressed by the author. For example, the emphasis given to national economic trends greatly enlarges the scope of *Brookings: a Biography*, Hermann Hagedorn's life of the founder of the Brookings Institution; comparison and contrast between modern mechanized industry and primitive conditions is the dominant purpose of Stuart Chase's *Mexico;* the point of view of Katherine Mayo's *Mother India* is narrow and intensely prejudiced, while that of Allen's *Only Yesterday* is impersonal and comprehensive. Salient points and distinctive qualities of a book must be apprehended, such as the psychological character study in Strachey's *Elizabeth and Essex;* simple, practical admonition in Dimnet's *Art of Thinking;* the counterplay of brilliant, charming personalities in the Terry-Shaw correspondence. If apparent misstatements or distortions of fact are encountered that can be readily verified, they should be noted and some later effort made to prove or disprove them. For though sympathy is necessary to discover a book's best qualities, there must also be the critical attentiveness that observes seeming discrepancies, exaggerations, or omissions, and the discrimination that is repelled by pretentiousness and platitudes. Valid appraisal of nonfiction depends chiefly on the amount of general information and general or specialized knowledge possessed by the reviewer.

In reading a novel for evaluation, facts of setting and period should be noted with as much exactitude as possible; not, vaguely, "Kentucky in Revolutionary period" for *The Great Meadow*, or "Modern American life" for *Years of Grace;* but for the former, "Virginia and Kentucky, 1770–1778," for the latter, "Chicago, New York, New England, 1888–1930." The abbreviation "c." (circa: about) is useful to indicate an approximate date. Any distinctive form of presentation (autobiographical, told in letters, diary, allegory) should be indicated. Designation of subject may also convey the theme; but theme and plot must always be differentiated: theme is the underlying subject or principle, as avarice in *Eugénie Grandet* and *Riceyman Steps*, race prejudice in *Earth and High Heaven*, old age in *All Passion Spent;* plot is the skeleton of the story. If a title subtly conveys theme or subject, its meaning should be made clear—as, *The Left Hand Is the Dreamer, The Great Meadow, The Plumed Serpent, Point Counter Point.* Such titles are most common in fiction, poetry, and drama, but may also be found often in studies of literature (as in Edmund Wilson's *Axel's Castle*) and less frequently in other nonfiction classes (as in Bradley's *No Place to Hide*). In considering character delineation, it is unimportant whether or not you find the characters "pleasant" or highly reprehensible. What is important is whether they come to life, move, speak, and feel as individual human beings; whether they remain carefully composed types, recognizable but artificial; or whether they are simply conventional, contrasted patterns of vice and virtue. Observe the structure of the book, whether long, rambling, elaborate, well-knit, or highly compressed; determine the degree of unity it possesses, both in form and expression; consider its significance as a valid reflection or intepretation of the phase of life with which it deals; and be perceptive of the spirit or atmosphere, whether delicate, satirical, somber, passionate, or miasmic, that infuses it. All these are important elements in establishing the literary qualities of a novel.

Fiction is the most difficult class of literature to evaluate. To judge a novel in brief appraisal requires concentrated attention, intelligent analysis, a background of good reading, and sympathetic or specialized interest. As a rule, note taking is less necessary in reviewing fiction than in reviewing nonfiction. It is often better simply to read the book and enjoy it (if you can); then analyze and formulate the impression it has made. It must be remembered that a sympathetic interest in fiction does not mean indiscriminate approval. On the contrary, library reviewing is necessarily critical and must often unqualifiedly condemn; but the condemnation should represent candid, mature, discriminating judgment, not sentimental moralism nor intellectual preciosity. No novel can be fairly judged by a reviewer who is inspired only by an earnest and painstaking moral purpose. Personal prejudices should be eliminated, so far as possible: a reader who dislikes historical novels should not review them; a literal-minded person should not review De la Mare, Dunsany, Robert Nathan, or others who weave their webs of imagination and fantasy. Anyone who does not enjoy fiction or recognize its importance should not be a fiction reviewer. Independent judgment, however, is not dislike or prejudice, and a reviewer's opinion should be independent and frankly expressed, not timorously noncommittal because other people may think differently. Undue severity and undue leniency should alike be avoided. Many library reviewers are still too easily shocked; remember that all subjects are fit for fiction, if in skill and truth the fiction is fit for the subject. Don't welcome the inane because you fear the significant. And always indicate any special points of interest (local setting, timeliness, popular appeal) for these often make a book desirable for library use although some other qualities may be lacking.

In critical consideration of all creative literature there must be broad and balanced judgment. The younger and more inexperienced a critic is, the more likely he is to be ruthless and sweeping in condemnation, contemptuous rather than appreciative. Knowledge and experience mellow judgment. Literature is art. Almost every book represents grueling work; a writer's lifeblood runs in the pages of his book. Often a book that embodies a year or more of labor, thought, effort of mind and body, is dismissed with a few flippant words by someone who has merely glanced indifferently at its surface. Try to approach literature as something that holds the finest achievements of the creative power, not as a pastime undeserving serious consideration. And again I say, eliminate moral rigidity from your attitude. The tendency to judge literature, which is art, by narrow dogmas of "moral judgment" is the tendency most characteristic of American librarians and most responsible for their limitations as booklovers. The immature critic is inclined to see everything in the terms of immediate personal experience; to reason, "I never met anyone like that," "I never would have acted in that manner,"—therefore, it is either wrong or impossible. In much library reviewing of fiction, the moral judgment expressed is sound, the point of view normal, and there is little tendency to be fascinated by the picturesquely decadent or to surrender common sense to the exaggerated depiction of the dramatic or the emotional; but there is an immaturity that does not see beyond the obvious and that blunts perception of the artist's purpose and expression. There is a great deal of fiction that requires for appreciation as much definite training and concentration as is needed to study philosophy and history. Forster's *A Passage to India* has depths and implications that many readers will never know. There is an entire national social commentary running beneath Dreiser's *An American Tragedy*. If you really love books and read them as part of daily living, time brings ripeness and insight to your critical judgment.

On the basis of such evaluation as this, a library review is formulated and presented. A satisfactory oral review depends almost as much upon formulation and presentation as upon the accuracy of the preliminary evaluation. The information assembled must be organized as a clear and logical summary, accented and enlarged by fuller comment than the review slip record permits, made interesting, effective, and (above all) audible. For nonfiction, the subject of the book should be linked with the author's experience or qualifications for writing it, for some reflection of a writer's life experience or personality not only arrests the attention of an audience, but also often explains or justifies his work. Bring out the most striking characteristics of the book, factual, descriptive, or controversial; emphasize definitions, facts, conclusions. Convey point of view and manner of writing in a few salient sentences, or, if time permits, in brief quotations; and compare and contrast with other current or recent work in the same domain. Points of criticism should be definitely stated and sustained, when possible, by reference to printed comment, for any printed reviews available should be used to supplement the original evaluation.

In oral reviewing of fiction, the chief pitfall is the synopsis of plot. This may be given on the review slip in bare and disconnected outline, but it must be molded into more attractive form to interest an audience. Treat the plot as the outgrowth, the expression, of the theme; specify its chief elements and suggest its course and climax of action as clearly and vividly as possible. Try to transmit a sense of the book's own personality and thus convey its strength or weakness; but shun prolixity and evade entanglement in detail. The "telling of the story" in a long, involved narrative that relentlessly pursues hero or heroine to the ultimate gasp is the certain sign of incompetent reviewing.

For good oral reviewing, notes are advisable. Only expert, experienced speakers can maintain clarity, brevity, and good expression in the impromptu exposition of a subject. Carefully prepared notes, accurate in fact and precise in phrasing, are the soundest basis, the best assurance, of effective speaking. Radio broadcasting, whatever its sins, has established time limits in word production and eliminated the hesitations, repetitions, and footless wanderings of impromptu speechmaking. Its example might be usefully followed in book talks and review programs. Spontaneity in effect need not be lost, even though notes are used. The review slip itself will often serve as sufficient anchor or safeguard for the brief summary of a book; but for longer reviews additional notes are desirable. These should be unobtrusive in size (never larger than half a letter sheet), typewritten, clearly folioed, and used as casually as possible. They furnish not a formal text to be read aloud, but the framework within which speech is shaped and given substance. They should be tested beforehand for time required in delivery and kept rigorously within the limit set.

In radio book reviewing a script is essential, timed to the exact speaking time required, double-spaced, and clearly typed. A speaking average of about 125 words a minute is generally considered satisfactory, but careful word-counting is desirable to ensure correct timing until technique is thoroughly familiar. A script must be carefully written, with factual precision, logical organization, and sustained interest, but without stiffness or formality; then read aloud, for timing, effect, and tone; checked for pronunciation and clarity, revised, and rehearsed at least once for simplicity and ease in speaking. Careful preparation, and spontaneous, magnetic sincerity and personal warmth of interest are basic requirements for a successful radio book review.

Here a word must be added on the importance of clear speech and good delivery in all public speaking about books. Almost all librarians are called upon at some time to speak before an audience—in staff or professional meetings, as part of club and school work, or to the invisible audience of the radio realm. The majority of such library speakers are women. And any impersonal general observation must recognize that, however sound the substance of thought their words convey, the manner of conveyance is too often sadly ineffective. Inaudibility is the most common weakness—a gentle, monotonous murmuring that induces audience-coma; but there is often also a curious inarticulateness of utterance that confuses and impedes clear communication. Women's voices are thinner and lighter than men's; but a woman speaker with good training and presence can be heard and enjoyed by any audience. Public speaking, it may be said, is not important in book selection. This is true; but as one of the means of making books vital and interesting to readers it is important in library service, and instruction and practice in effective use of the voice should, I believe, be given in all library school training. Speaking should be practiced as the art it is. There should be vibrancy and inflections in tone that make the voice carry shades of meaning, facility in phrasing sentences that "speak well" and catch the ear, accent and pronunciation that denote cultivation, a simplicity and directness of manner that puts the hearers in accord with the speaker, and an unflagging awareness of the flight of time. To acquire a good speaking technique is for almost any intelligent person only a matter of will and exercise. Without it few library reviewers and speakers can successfully fulfill the three simple requirements expected of them: to be heard, to be understood, to end.

8. The Art of Annotation

> Have you begun to detect the two main vices of Jargon? The first is that it uses circumlocution rather than short straight speech. . . . The second vice is that it habitually chooses vague woolly abstract nouns rather than concrete ones. . . . "How excellent a thing is sleep," sighed Sancho Panza, "it wraps a man round like a cloak"—an excellent example, by the way, of how to say a thing concretely: A Jargoneer would have said that "among the beneficent qualities of sleep its capacity for withdrawing the human consciousness from the contemplation of immediate circumstances may perhaps be accounted not the least remarkable." How vile a thing—shall we say?—is the abstract noun! It wraps a man's thoughts round like cotton wool.
> Sir Arthur Quiller-Couch: *On the Art of Writing*

ANNOTATION, or characterization of a book in a compact descriptive or critical note, is a familiar bibliographical practice. It is a feature of most of the older "literary guides" to different fields of knowledge, of reading courses and educational manuals, and of many works in general and specialized literature. Its importance in the standard and current aids and guides that are the tools of book selection has been made clear, and so has its relationship to book evaluation as carried on by the libraries themselves.

Annotation writing as a product of evaluation is now to be considered. The points of analysis that have been applied in the formulation of library reviewing apply also in the formulation of annotations. Upon these points there must be based a specific structure of method, a definite process of composition, to convey in a brief paragraph a clear, valid, and interesting summary of a book's qualities and characteristics. In writing annotations the chief essentials are: condensation, sound construction, and effective phrasing. Every word must count, every sentence must be compressed to give specific, definite fact; yet at the same time there must be indication or reflection of the color, the texture, the spirit, of the book.

The writing of annotations is not necessarily a part of book selection. It has, however, a double relationship to selection, for it is a means by which the choice of books is often determined and a means by which information about selected books is put at the service of readers. So various are the uses to which it may be applied and the opportunities to which it may lead that some proficiency in the art (for at its best it is an art, demanding concentrated intelligence and expert expression) is one of the most valuable assets of any worker with books. An experienced and skillful annotator has necessarily acquired perception of book values and facility in expression. Such a person should readily develop fitness for writing in other fields—particularly for effective work in library or booktrade publicity and for professional book reviewing. Indeed, the difference between an annotation and a review is rather one of size than of treatment; an apprenticeship at book annotation would give needed precision and cogency to the work of many literary critics and commentators on books.

Method of annotation varies according to its purpose. Annotations fall roughly into two classes—"readers' notes" and "librarians' notes." A readers' note is intended to impart information to the reader and at the same time awaken a desire to read the book. A satisfactory readers' note should make clear the subject of the book, its authority or special value, its treatment, and its literary quality or flavor; special features, such as important appendixes or unusual illustrations, may be noted. Such a note does not, as a rule, mention weaknesses or defects, because it assumes to treat only books that are worth reading; and it seeks to put its information into attractive and interesting phrasing. Readers' notes are most common in popular reading lists, in library bulletins, and in mediums especially intended for popular use. They are often very brief, sometimes confined to ten or a dozen words, and they are frequently misleading, in their endeavor to arrest attention and arouse enthusiasm. Among good examples for study are those appearing in *Branch Library Book News* of the New York Public Library.

A librarians' note has for its specific purpose the aiding of the librarian in the choice of books. It should give, with more fullness, the same information that is given in the readers' note, but in addition it should point out deficiencies, such as inaccuracy, overtechnicality, or features that would be objectionable to certain readers, and it should indicate a book's merit in comparison with other books in the same field. Annotations for books in specialized technical fields emphasize, of course, points of technical quality and importance.

In all annotations brevity is especially to be considered. Many readers' notes are limited to fifteen or twenty-five words. For librarians' notes, sixty words is an average length; few annotations exceed one hundred words. The annotations in the *A.L.A. Catalog* and the *Booklist* represent the type of librarians' note that is now predominant. They emphasize the critical and comparative information that is important to librarians and indicate suitability to different tastes; but (especially in the *Booklist* and generally in fiction annotations) they are also designed to arouse interest and awaken a desire to read the book.

In the *United States Quarterly Book List* the annotations, by scholars and specialists, usually exceed customary word limits, running to two hundred words or more, so that they take on the nature of short reviews. Descriptive rather than critical, they follow a formal, somewhat monotonous pattern, summarizing the content of a book with impassive factual precision; their values are in library selection and in general reader-use, rather than as models of effective annotation. The annotations contributed by librarians to the "New Books Appraised" department of *Library Journal*, however, offer unusual material for critical study. Extremely varied in quality, they range from single-track expression of personal opinion to rounded, discriminating judgment, from ineffectual construction to smooth, skillful integration; but nearly always they convey a sense of the vital relationship of books to human experience.

Booklist annotations will repay careful study. As a rule, they maintain high standards of technical workmanship and discriminating judgment. There is probably no other body of current annotation work that so competently covers the points essential in evaluation of nonfiction for library selection. These points are: subject of the book, author's qualifications, scope, treatment, point of view, literary quality, comparative value, class of readers it will appeal to. To convey this information in clear and interesting phrasing within the compass of from fifty to ninety words is the art of the expert annotator. Evaluation of fiction presents greater difficulties, but here, too, *Booklist* annotations offer useful material for analysis of method and purpose.

"Readers' notes," designed primarily to attract, usually represent descriptive annotation. "Librarians' notes," designed primarily to inform, usually represent critical annotation. But the best annotation work combines the two, in a unified, clear, and interesting characterization. Almost all libraries prepare and issue annotated lists of various kinds, from the record of new books added, printed in the local newspaper, to the carefully edited, regularly issued bulletin that is an attractive and useful library publication. Short popular lists for the general reader may contain not more than a dozen titles, with a few words of comment for each, printed on a bookmark slip; extended reference lists or study outlines in special fields may represent expert bibliographical detail and scholarly cooperation. In the preparation of such lists, annotations in current and standard bibliographical guides as well as terse comments from reviews or graphic summations from publishers' announcements are drawn upon for information, for adaptation or paraphrase. From the evaluation of the book itself and from this accessory material is welded the individual annotation intended to fit a book to a reader who will enjoy it or to make clear its usefulness to the student or serious reader in a specific field of knowledge.

To write a good annotation requires careful study of models and considerable practice. Annotations of different types should be analyzed and compared. Original annotations based upon personal evaluation of a book and prepared without suggestive material should be compared with the annotations for the same book in the *Booklist* or *Library Journal*. Such study of annotations is a fascinating exercise for anyone with a responsive mind, critical perceptions, a background of good reading, and an interest in word usage. Merits and defects are soon apprehended. Plato said, "He shall be as a god to me, who can rightly divide and define,"—and the student of annotation comes to understand and share this feeling. Effective compression is contrasted with inept disunity, flexible and magnetic expression with the monotonous reiteration of a few stock phrases. The most common defects in annotations designed to attract readers are vagueness, "prettiness," and failure to convey a true impression of the book. In annotations intended to guide to serious reading, verbosity and superficiality are the chief dangers. In both types the desire to "lure" the reader often results in false emphasis.

Points to be brought out in the evaluation of a book already have been sufficiently indicated. Consider now how to weld an evaluation into a workmanlike annotation. Structure, content, and expression are the fundamentals here. They are handled differently in the annotation of nonfiction and of fiction; and there are further differences in dealing with specific classes of literature. But here only the essentials in nonfiction and fiction annotation can be considered.

Structure should be logical and unified, but may differ in plan. If the annotation opens with statement of the author's theme, this may be linked with indication of the way that theme is presented. This is illustrated by an annotation for Rourke's *American Humor:*

The comic spirit and the part it has played in forming a national character, is the subject of this serious study. The author follows the course of American humor from its early incarnation in the Yankee peddler through its various manifestations in oral tradition, drama and literature.

If the annotation opens with a characterization of the author, this may be phrased to convey also the subject of the book: as, for Thompson's study of Mayan antiquities, *The People of the Serpent:*

The veteran archaeologist, whose work in Yucatan was described in Willard's *City of the Sacred Well,* tells the story of his forty years' study of Mayan ruins.

Exposition of theme, authority or experience of author, descriptive detail, comparative estimate or appraisal of value, appreciation of literary quality—these are all components of structure. They must not be scattered in disconnected fragments through the annotation, but, each complete in itself, built into a consistent whole. The ways in which the building is done may vary. An annotation may open with statement of theme, or with characterization of the author (as in the examples given); it may, especially for books of travel, open with a vivid descriptive summary of the subject; it may open with a salient short quotation from the book that conveys its purpose or flavor. There are many allowable openings, for variety in structure evades rigidity and monotony and makes the annotation more interesting to the reader. But there must be logical progression from one component to another and each component must be compact, definite, and complete. Perhaps the best formula for structure of an annotation is that compounded by Aristotle for the structure of a tragic plot—that it shall be "complete and whole and of a certain magnitude":

A whole is that which has a beginning, middle and end. A beginning is that which does not itself follow anything by causal necessity, but after which something naturally is, or comes to be. An end, on the contrary, is that which itself naturally follows some other thing, either by necessity or in the regular course of events, but has nothing following it. A middle is that which follows something, as some other thing follows it. A well constructed plot, therefore, must neither begin nor end at haphazard but conform to the type here described.

Content of an annotation requires first of all precision of statement. It should have exactitude as well as compression of detail. At the same time, it should be complete rather than partial; effort must be made to convey the whole of a book instead of a single aspect. An annotation for Younghill Kang's Korean autobiography, *The Grass Roof*, is an example of inadequate and confused content:

In his passage from an insular Korean village to the Western world, the author, who is now a lecturer at New York University, describes a bewildering parade of interesting characters. His biography opens the intimacy of village life to the reader so that to the discriminating the psychology of the crazy, poet uncle and the father, who uncomplainingly supported so many branches of the family, is no longer alien.

A reader will gain from this no understanding of the range and quality of a book that combines historical significance with exotic backgrounds, dramatic personal experience, and unusual literary charm. An adequate annotation would indicate each of these aspects:

Life-story of a young Korean, born just before the Japanese invasion in 1898, who tells of his happy childhood in a little village ruled by family traditions handed down through centuries. Oppression and terror fell upon his home when Japan annexed Korea in 1910, and the boy's share in student revolutionary efforts led him ultimately to a new life in the United States. A narrative of delicate clarity, picturesque and moving, possessing also humor and poetic charm.

The content of an annotation is the substance of the component parts that are united to make its whole structure. Information concerning the author, the subject, theory, or theme of the book, the manner in which the subject is dealt with, and the spirit and quality of the work, must be distilled into clear, compact statement. In books of travel, political and sociological study, science, and other fields of specialized knowledge, an author's background of experience has special importance and should be carefully and explicitly indicated. To say of George Soule's study of Anglo-American economic interdependence, *America's Stake in Britain's Future*, that it offers "cogent argument," is made more significant by the specific statement that the author is "a well-known American economist and former editor of the *New Republic*." This individualization of an author's qualifications is a means of denoting the value of the book in relation to its general subject.

As much individualization as possible should also be applied to the subject, so that it may be evident to the reader in what way this book is distinguished from other books in its field. The usefulness of Rosinger's *Restless India*, for instance, will be more evident if the annotation mentions the documentary appendix which gives the Cripps proposals and Indian answers and Attlee's statement of policy. An annotation for Northrop's philosophic-cultural treatise, *The Meeting of East and West*, should penetrate beyond descriptive summary into the book's fundamental thesis that the culture of the East centers on analysis of aesthetic immediate experience, that in Western culture science and theoretical abstractions are central, and that correlation of the aesthetic and scientific factors in experience is the only key to world understanding. But an author's viewpoint is of significance only when it affects the presentation of his subject. That Max Eastman is an irreconcilable antagonist to the Soviet state is important in the appraisal of anything he writes concerning Russia, but immaterial in consideration of his work in other fields. Hilaire Belloc's Catholic viewpoint should often be made clear in characterizing his writings in history and biography, but may be disregarded in an annotation for his essays. There must be constant discrimination between essential and nonessential information, and only facts that have specific relationship to the subject or authority or quality of a book should be included in an annotation.

Presumably, annotations are always written for readers who know nothing of the book. Thus they should make as clear and definite as possible just what it deals with and should be phrased to convey a topic of immediate interest not to present-day readers only, but to future readers as well. In biography, indication of the dates during which the subject lived or some clear indication of the period covered is desirable, unless this information is given in the book's title. In history, specific characterization of period, phase, or aspect is necessary; in travel, the region dealt with and the period covered must be noted. In all fields of literature the annotation should bring out the most salient facts that bear upon the presentation of the subject.

Whenever possible the quality of a book should be indicated simply and without too great emphasis. For superficial compilations that masquerade as authentic works some such statement as "Popular, but not to be accepted as authoritative," or "Interesting, but of slight historical value," is desirable, as a hint to readers who might otherwise think they were getting a book of serious importance. In the same way, a work of eminent authority and equally eminent dullness should receive some enlightening sentence, as "Of great value in its analysis of original authorities, but difficult reading for the inexperienced student." Annotations for editions of classics or standard works should state character and scope of the editorial treatment—whether new material is included or a new point of view offered—for this is the chief means of distinguishing between various editions of the same work.

When a title is given in full in the entry of a book, the annotation should not repeat the words, or give the same information in different phrasing, or offer information that an intelligent person could readily infer from the title itself. It is through the bibliographical entry that the book is introduced to the reader's attention; the fundamental purpose of the annotation is to explain or supplement information insufficiently conveyed through this introductory record. If, however, the title of a book is obscure but has direct relation to the book's subject or purpose, the annotation should make its meaning clear. Many titles are more or less cryptic, either to stimulate the reader's curiosity or to convey a symbolic theme; others are built upon a word or an allusion used in the book that, in itself, is likely to be misunderstood. An obscure title, left unilluminated by any annotation that I have seen, is *I. Americans,* in which Señor de Madariaga, with the epistles of the New Testament in mind, undoubtedly sought to convey a "First Epistle to the Americans" on the gospel of world unity.

Expression must have vigor and clarity. First of all, an annotation must be kept rigorously within the allotted length, whether it be thirty-five words or a hundred. Usually this length varies somewhat, according to the importance of the book or the purpose of the annotation. But brevity is the essence of annotation writing, just as skillful and graphic expression is its most necessary element. There must be logical construction and smooth dovetailing of sentences. But it is the substance of those sentences, the annotator's mastery of words, that gives effectiveness of appeal, precision of statement, and conveys the quality and spirit of the book. In all annotation writing a good thesaurus (Roget or March) is an indispensable companion. To shun the hackneyed phrase, the threadbare adjective, to find the word that conveys the nature of a book's style or distills the essence of its theme, to integrate its substance, quality, and value clearly, logically, with graphic brevity, is to practice the fine art of annotation. Always, vague phrases, long or involved sentences, must be avoided; jerkiness and disconnection that destroy continuity of effect are equally undesirable. An annotation should not read like a fragment from an oratorical disquisition, nor like a night-letter telegram. Sir Arthur Quiller-Couch's memorable chapter on "Jargon," in his *On the Art of Writing*, is golden counsel for the annotator. Eschew the abstract noun, the passive voice; be concrete, be active —if you can't be active, be as active as you can.

Certain abbreviations or contractions in wording are sanctioned by practice. A verb may be used with omitted subject when the subject is the book's name or the words "this book," thus giving a concise declarative statement, such as "Treats of family disorganization and health problems"; "Tells the story of American relations with Cuba"; "Describes a journey to Lapland." Whenever possible, avoid beginning a sentence with "A" or "The"; do not refer unnecessarily to "the author," or use such waste words as "The author's aim in this book." Articles and prepositions may be omitted in the middle of a sentence, commas may be used to indicate words eliminated, and other devices adapted to speed the process of condensation; but this must be done without sacrifice of good form or spontaneity. As an example of compression, effectiveness, and insight, consider the following annotation, from Sonnenschein, of Chesterton's *Orthodoxy:*

Exposition of author's religious philosophy, urging that an innate sense of mystery, security, romance, loyalty to ideals and to progress, is left wholly unsatisfied by Logic. Full of paradox and antithetical reasoning.

Here we have the essence of a book distilled into thirty-two words.

An annotation should not take sides on questions nor express any strong personal opinions, nor even accept and repeat an author's strong opinions without some qualification that makes it clear they are the author's views. That is, unless an annotator is an authority on the subject treated, with thorough knowledge of its various aspects, it is better to qualify dogmatic utterances. The common newspaper practice of disclaiming responsibility by the use of such phrases as "it is stated," "it is asserted," is useful in annotation writing. It is better to say "apparently a fair and judicious presentation," than to say "entirely unbiased and absolutely fair"; better to point out that "the author says" such and such a thing, than that "the author convinces his readers" of the same thing, although such a comment as "a convincing presentation" is legitimate. Annotations should not be dogmatic; they should be devoid of any condescending hortatory tone, and they should equally eschew an ecstatic "come-and-read-me" appeal that is irritating to most intelligent minds. The language used should be as simple as possible; but words should be carefully chosen for their vividness and fitness, and there must be constant endeavor to avoid monotony of effect in the annotation as a whole.

Defects and qualities of nonfiction annotation may, perhaps, be best summarized by a few examples and comparisons.

The shorter the annotation, the more difficult it is to convey adequate information. Many short annotations, therefore, attempt to give simply a tang of the book's flavor, or a glimpse of its most salient aspect. Such an annotation as the following, however, is essentially meaningless:

Lamb, Harold. *The Crusades: Iron Men and Saints.*
To read this book is to join the greatest adventure in history.

The following annotation of exactly the same word-length transmits a sense of the subject and quality of the book it deals with:

Guedalla, Philip. *Second Empire.*
Brilliant, dramatic, ironic picture of period, centering on portrait of Napoleon III.

Two annotations from the *A.L.A. Catalog, 1904,* offer interesting contrast. For Gibbon's *Decline and Fall of the Roman Empire*—a subject sufficiently indicated by the title to need no restatement—the annotation reads:

At once scrupulously faithful in its facts, consummate in literary art and comprehensive in analysis of forces affecting society over a very long and crowded epoch.

This is terse, effective appreciation of a masterpiece.

For Macaulay's *History of England*, we have this note:

No other historian has shown such familiarity with facts of English history. Absolutely unrivalled in art of arranging and combining facts and of presenting in clear and vigorous narrative the spirit of an epoch.

This also is an "appreciation," but defective because it gives no clue to the exact period covered (very few readers are likely to remember that Macaulay's history covers only the seventeen years from 1685 to 1702) and no intimation of the historian's Whig bias. These defects are remedied in the admirable annotation given in *A.L.A. Catalog, 1926*.

Here is a longer annotation, of Calverton's volume, *The Liberation of American Literature:*

"In a sense, this book is as much a study of American culture as it is of American literature, for its aim is to interpret American literature in terms of American culture."—*Preface*. Applying sociological rather than literary standards, the author shows how literature reflects and is shaped by current cultural ideals. Not a complete history of American literature but an interesting evaluation of its relation to social forces.

This is repetitive and inadequate, with more than a hint of Jargon. Its first sentence rephrases the information conveyed in the opening quotation, and as a whole it gives no idea that Mr. Calverton's thesis is founded on Marxian philosophy and that he finds the "liberation" of American literature in the development of the proletarian spirit, represented by Dos Passos and other writers of the present day. Contrast it, for precision and clarity, with the following (which conveys also the meaning of an obscure title):

Cram, R. A. *The Nemesis of Mediocrity*.
Eloquent summary of the failure of civilization today, as due to the absence of leadership. This is the "nemesis of mediocrity"—the result and penalty of the modern democratic method of government, which prevents the rise of the master-man and produces petty demagogues or well-meaning incompetents. By a disciple of Henry Adams, it shows strongly the impress of Adams' influence.

THE ART OF ANNOTATION 149

As final example of how brilliantly an annotator can render the content, spirit, and quality of a book, take from Sonnenschein this 120-word summary of an unusual older book, still often sought for:

Oliphant, Laurence. *Scientific Religion: Higher Possibilities through Operation of Natural Forces.*
A new system of "spiritual materialism," asserting that physical, mental, and emotional forces are all material, that their manifestations are conditioned by the varieties of the atoms of which they consist, and of endless combinations and "fermentations" which may be produced by these atoms. There are thus "joy atoms" and "pain atoms"; will is an aggregation, love a perturbation, and worship a current of atoms. Immortality depends on strength rather than on virtue or vice, and, as the latter "weigh more," the wicked sink into nonentity, whilst the good rise continuously. A curious book, not without much suggestion, and written by a most capable *littérateur*—the first two parts said to have been written under inspiration of the late Mrs. Oliphant, an inhabitant of the spirit world.

Most of the suggestions that have been made concerning the structure, content, and expression of nonfiction annotations apply also to the annotation of fiction. Fiction, however, is more difficult than nonfiction to annotate with discrimination and effectiveness. It is creative literature, and it demands a certain creative quality of expression to convey its spirit and its character. In structure, fiction annotations have fewer component parts to be welded into unity. An author's qualifications seldom demand specific comment, for a novel is a work of imagination, not a product of learning or factual knowledge. The kind of novel, its theme, setting, plot interest, literary quality, and reading appeal are the usual components, to be brought together logically and in as unstereotyped a fashion as possible. Vivid or provocative indication of theme or setting makes an arresting opening, to be followed by some suggestion of the book's strongest values, emotional, analytical, descriptive, or in character portrayal, while the summing up of qualities of style or the characterization of reading appeal is most logically placed in a final sentence. The climax of a novel's course of action may be hinted, but should not be fully disclosed. Indeed, the value of an annotation for any work of imagination lies in the success with which literary quality and individual personality of the book are transmitted to the reader. Novels of the finest quality are the most difficult to annotate. They are so invested with significance, so rich and many-sided in thought, purpose, and expression that it is almost impossible to adequately distill their theme and scope and implications into fifty or seventy-five words. Probably the most effective rendering of their content is by ellipsis—by conveying theme or dominant aspect in a vivid characterization that, while omitting much, still suggests the range and texture of the whole work. I doubt if an entirely satisfactory annotation can be written for such a novel as Thomas Mann's *The Magic Mountain*, or Willa Cather's *The Professor's House*, or Virginia Woolf's *Orlando*.

Historical fiction is the easiest to annotate, for it permits the most specific factual statement. Here annotation should denote period and setting as exactly as possible, and make clear the attitude of the author toward his subject and whether treatment is crude, sensational, in obvious distortion of history, or dignified and soundly based. In annotation of foreign fiction the nationality or national spirit of the author must be conveyed; setting and quality of style are important, but theme demands first consideration; and it must always be remembered that foreign literature has its own standards of taste and style and must be judged from a universal, not a provincial, viewpoint.

Fiction annotations differ greatly in length. For the ordinary novel of familiar type, brief indication of type, plot or subject, and literary quality is sufficient, and this may sometimes be conveyed in a single sentence. For books of finer texture and more varied significance, adequate annotations are often necessarily longer than are the annotations for nonfiction of similar quality.

Contrast and comparison of a few fiction annotations may help to bring out some of the foregoing points.

Here are two annotations for *Lolly Willowes, or the Loving Huntsman*, by Sylvia Townsend Warner—a book that in its subtle mingling of pastoral demureness, feminine irony, and macabre fantasy offers a complex task to the annotator:

A charmingly ironical character study that only a woman author could portray, of a sheltered English maiden aunt, whose ultimate desire it was "to have a life of her own, not an existence doled out to her by others." Reminiscent of Jane Austen, but distinguished by a wistfulness and depth of feeling lacking in her work.

This gives no indication of the central theme and conveys nothing of the fantastic element hinted at in the title. The literal-mindedness of this annotation makes it thoroughly inadequate.

The first half of this story deals with the antecedents of Laura Willowes and recounts her none too lively adventures as a spinster up to the age of 47. From realism, even in tone and shrewdly humorous, the book then changes to fantasy. Laura flings off her winter garment and with the aid of Satan embraces witchcraft. Charmingly written.

Here the triple nature of the tale is indicated, and its transition from the pastoral to the fantastic is conveyed; but the phrasing of the opening sentence is formal and awkward, and there is no indication of the theme's symbolic suggestion that the only escape for an English spinster from her barren lot is to embrace the devil and all his works.

An annotation that is excellent in conveying setting, spirit, and quality, but needs deeper perceptiveness of the underlying theme of selfless love, is:

Heyward, DuBose. *Porgy*.
The first novel of a southern poet, written with great power and beauty. The characters are the Negroes of the Charleston waterfront, particularly Porgy, the crippled beggar, and his woman, Bess. There is both comedy and tragedy with interludes of the wise, quaint philosophy of the older Negroes who have learned something from life. The story has a haunting rhythm; it rocks with Negro laughter and sways to the beat of Negro spirituals.

Broad generalization that is effective in conveying the range and texture of a masterpiece is illustrated in the following annotation for Reymont's *The Peasants:*

A vast panorama of Polish peasant life, unrolled through the four seasons with a wealth of picturesque and accurate detail. Desire for the land and the rival love of a father and son for one woman provide the thread of the plot, but even more essential to the story are the primitive elemental scenes of village ceremonies and feasts as well as the day-to-day preoccupations with the soil. A four-volume epic which was awarded the Nobel prize for literature.

What I have called annotation by ellipsis—an incomplete or partial characterization that seeks to convey a sense of the whole—may be illustrated in the two annotations that follow:

Conrad, Joseph. *Victory*.
Absorbing, tragic idyll of one of Conrad's islands of the South Seas. Hate, revenge, and careless crime are set against love, and the victory is to snatch the beloved object out of danger at the sacrifice of life. The inscrutable character of Axel Heyst is most striking; it conveys the implication that the dominating element for misfortune is inability to express emotion.

Dostoyevsky, Fyodor. *The Idiot*.
Wonderful phantasmagoria of ardent, abnormal, semi-diseased personalities. If condensed or pruned to one-third its length would have been one of the great world-books, but is too diffused, too pathless in its tangled undergrowth of detail. Character of Prince Myshkin, the idiot, is touching and deeply interesting, his epileptic affliction being an analysis and study of the author's own disease. The underlying spirit, as in all Dostoyevsky's books, is that of unalterable gentleness, Christlike sympathy and allowance for all who are afflicted in mind, body, or estate. The climax, of the murder, is an enthralling but blurred and dreamlike presentation of morbid sex-psychology.

Good annotation writing, it will be evident, demands certain qualifications. A natural gift for literary expression is desirable, but even more important are interest in books, alert intelligence, associative memory, accuracy in detail, and critical perceptiveness. A background of good reading, constantly deepening and enlarging, is indispensable; and there should be familiarity with current book reviewing and critical writing, and a spontaneous interest in sentence construction and word usage.

AIDS TO THE ART OF ANNOTATION

For students of annotation who wish to supplement the suggestions made in this chapter by further analysis of literary structure, by expert counsel on precision of expression and correct word usage, and by comparison and contrast of annotative method, the following books are recommended:

Flesch, Rudolf. *The Art of Plain Talk.* Foreword by Lyman Bryson. New York, Harper & Brothers, 1946.

Although somewhat overenveloped in elaborate analytical exposition of word use, this is essentially sound common-sense formulation of rules for producing readable, clear writing, by use of short sentences, concrete words, short words, and direct expression. Interesting and useful is the characterization of words: "live words," "crowded words," "empty words," with appropriate examples. Punctuation; easy, casual expression; idiomatic writing, are effectively analyzed. Official jargon and what Barzun calls "educators' patois" receive exemplary citations, as amusing as they are appalling. Exercises are given for rewriting involved sentences. Arithmetical formulas are used to determine sentence length and word use, and to indicate proportional relation of kinds of writing to different grades of reader ability. Fowler's *Modern English Usage,* Quiller-Couch's *On the Art of Writing* are Flesch's foundation stones.

Fowler, H. W. *A Dictionary of Modern English Usage.* New York, Oxford University Press, 1927.

A forbidding title masks this delightful repository of crusted English humor, common sense, and erudition. It is not only a guide to correct speech and writing (grammatical structure, pronunciation, etc.), but it imparts the elements of literary appreciation, an understanding of crudities, vulgarities, and cheap mannerisms in literary expression. Those who follow its exploration of "battered ornaments," "didacticism," "hackneyed phrases," "genteelisms," "pedantic humor," "stock pathos," "misquotations," and other verbal crimes and misdemeanors will find their knowledge of English clarified and invigorated. American users, however, must temper its scorn of "Americanisms" by realization that a national idiom has its own validity and justification; granting this, Fowler will do more to improve crude and slovenly writing than any other remedial agent.

Jones, Llewellyn. *How to Criticize Books.* New York, W. W. Norton & Co., Inc., 1928.

Stimulating, practical exposition of the technique of book reviewing: distinctions between creative and critical writing, the formulation and structure of reviews, fundamental critical principles, the approach to different classes of literature, and the means by which a reviewer's authority and flexibility of expression may be developed. By the literary editor of the Chicago *Daily News*, who based it on fourteen years of writing criticism and editing the book reviews of several hundred contributors. Although it deals specifically with reviewing books for newspapers, it contains much that is applicable to library reviewing and annotation writing.

Leypoldt, A. H., and George Iles. A List of Books for Girls and Women and Their Clubs. Boston, Library Bureau (for American Library Association), 1895. o.p.

One of the earliest and most interesting examples of critical evaluation for librarians, applied to a varied selection of books. It represents George Iles' original conviction that evaluation (especially of fiction) should be distinctly critical and should be applied to inferior books as well as to those of merit, so that readers might be warned of their defects. In practice, however, it was soon evident that if evaluation was not made selective it would break down of its own weight. This list is still of value for two reasons:

1. It shows both the strength and weakness of strongly critical evaluations that denote both good and bad books and distribute both praise and blame. It makes evident that expression of an annotator's personal opinions results in biased judgment (for example, in the annotations for George Meredith and Emily Brontë), and demonstrates that annotation of this kind in library lists and bulletins would be impracticable and undesirable. At the same time it also indicates the provocative quality, the sparkle and flash of personality, that make such annotations vital and interesting.

2. It is probably the only annotated list that offers pungent condemnation of certain types of fiction (E. P. Roe, Mary Jane Holmes, Mrs. Southworth) that, in different manifestation, have their successors today. Its annotations for these and many other older novels are still entertaining and suggestive. The annotations for nonfiction also are often extremely interesting and will repay study. Though long out of print this "List" may still be found in many libraries.

Masterson, James R., and Wendell Brooks Phillips. Federal Prose: how to write in and/or for Washington. Chapel Hill, University of North Carolina Press, 1948.

"Federal prose" is the language of our federal bureaucracy, closely akin to, though more legalistic than, the "educators' patois" of doctoral dissertations and the professional writing of many "educationists" and sociologists and some librarians. This cogent, amusing booklet is a priceless accompaniment to Flesch, making evident in a compact but rich repository of examples that English and Jargon are two distinct languages. The authors point out that in English one says, "Too many cooks spoil the broth." But in Federal Prose, one says: "Undue multiplicity of personnel assigned either concurrently or consecutively to a single function involves deterioration of quality in the resultant product as compared with the product of the labor of an exact sufficiency of personnel."

Quiller-Couch, Sir Arthur. On the Art of Writing. New York, G. P. Putnam's Sons, 1916.

Everyone who essays to practice writing English should know these Cambridge lectures, so rich in authority and insight and so skilled in mastery of the art they expound. The chapter on Jargon should be inscribed in letters of gold in every college and library school classroom.

Savage, E. A. Manual of Descriptive Annotation for Library Catalogues. London, Library Supply Co., 1906.

Although published many years ago this still remains the only comprehensive and detailed manual devoted to annotation writing. By an English librarian, it treats annotation as a practice in cataloguing, designed for use in library catalogues rather than in separate printed form. Its clear denotation, thorough analysis, and the great variety of examples illustrative of merits and defects of annotations for different kinds of books, make it indispensable in any study of the subject.

Shuman, E. L. How to Judge a Book: a handy method of criticism for the general reader. Boston, Houghton Mifflin Co., 1910.

Since its publication this has been a standard aid in the critical study of literature. It was designed to furnish easy standards, objective and subjective, by which the ordinary reader might form sound judgment of books and distinguish between "the best and the worst, the good and the less good." Based on long editorial and book-reviewing experience, it presents fundamental principles of criticism and effective practical methods of analysis of a book's content, character, and spirit. Although some of its principles and tests now have a rather traditional flavor, it is still unsuperseded in its particular field.

PART THREE

Substance and Product

9. Books in Their Textual and Physical Aspects

> Let me vision for you a book of the future, yet in no way beyond the bounds of practicality. It is convenient to handle, easy to read, the execution is workmanlike, the materials are good but not extravagant, the design a thing of beauty, revealing the hand of an artist. Into its make-up will go the gold refined from ore mined by many generations of printers of genius, wrought into a work of art by the taste and skill of the designer.
>
> D. C. McMurtrie: *The Golden Book*

USE AND STUDY of book reviews, practice of evaluation and annotation, center upon the content of the individual book, in denotation of its values and appraisal of its character and quality. There is, however, another field of book knowledge in which experience must be gained if book selection is to be judicious and effective. This is knowledge of books in their textual and physical aspects, as material substance of paper, ink, and fabric, and as a product of historic craftsmanship and highly specialized modern industry. It is a large field, from which many fascinating byways open, to the study of early printing, rare editions, fine bindings, and the elaborate minutiae of collectorship, or to mastery of the details of expert modern bookmaking. We cannot pursue these byways. Our concern is with those characteristics of bookmaking, those factors in the relation of publishers to their product, that must be known if books are to be chosen that in form, as well as in content, are appropriate to the needs of libraries and the use of readers.

But a word must first be said on the importance of some appreciation of the art of the book, some knowledge of book history, not only to every librarian and worker with books, but to every person of cultivated intelligence. The vast majority of those who are "fond of books" believe that this assertion makes them true booklovers.

Comparatively few understand what a good book is, in its physical and artistic aspects. Probably in no other field does ignorance masquerade so complacently and with such genuine self-delusion as in this field of book knowledge, which so many assume and so few possess. William Dana Orcutt says:

One does have to stop and think about a well made book in order to comprehend the difference between printing that is merely printing and that which is based upon art in its broadest sense and upon centuries of precedent. It does require more than a gleam of intelligence to grasp the idea that the basis of every volume ought to be the thought expressed by the writer; that the type, the illustrations, the paper, the binding, simply combine to form the vehicle to convey that expression to the reader.

Everyone who possesses some degree of book knowledge can recall terrible moments when proud friends, awaiting enthusiastic commendation, have displayed as cherished possessions pretentious and hybrid volumes—pages with gaudy rubrications, imitation parchment titles, covers of oozy, roycrofty, limp (very limp) leather, inner upholstery of satin or moiré; or "complete sets" in "de luxe" bindings (immediately identifiable, because the words "de luxe" are stamped in gold on the backbone of every volume!) with imitation watercolor frontispieces on imitation vellum. By such sad experiences are revealed the strange and God-forsaken volumes that are admired and acquired by people otherwise of good taste and culture.

As for book history, with its rich relationship to world history and world literature, it is an indispensable element in any sound background of book knowledge. To the great mass of intelligent readers it has neither existence nor meaning; but to librarians it should be the familiar heritage of their calling. Not all librarians, however, have entered into their heritage. Not so many years ago the representative of one of the greatest English rare book firms attended a reception in a large American city given by a famous American collector whose chief glory was his remarkable collection of Shakespeare quartos. In the beautiful private library, among the élite of wealth and culture assembled, was an imposing lady, richly bejewelled, who made her way a little forcibly to the cases where the quartos were displayed, uttering ecstatic cries of appreciation: "How delightful! How wonderful! What a privilege to see such treasures! Tell me," she added, turning to the librarian, "are they *all* Caxtons?" This story the observer told later to a distinguished American librarian, who listened to it attentively, and then said: "Well, were they?"

No one can be proficient in book selection who has not some basic knowledge of good bookmaking and discrimination in choice of editions. Points of chief importance in judging textual and physical characteristics of books were indicated in Chapter 3, as relating to material accessory to the text, such as index, illustrations, maps, charts, bibilographies, notes, and appendixes; to quality of paper, kind of type and quality of printing, convenience of size, and suitability of binding. These points and others must now be considered in closer detail.

In the first place, there should be clear understanding of certain terms and characterizations.

The "format" of a book, more closely defined as shape and size, is the term commonly applied to the general make-up of a book, in size, type page, margins, and binding. If these component parts, each of excellence and suitability in itself, are harmoniously combined, the finished product is a book that in intelligent design and skillful workmanship expresses its individual character and is suitable to its particular purpose. Format differs for books of different kinds. A novel, a book of poems, an essay, a textbook, a dictionary, each imply and demand differences in the component parts and in their unification.

"Edition" is a term that generally conveys three meanings: (1) the whole number of copies of a book or other publication printed and published at one time; (2) each separate printing of a book; (3) the form of a book or set of books as regards its editing or style of make-up.

The second definition, when not further qualified, is commonly regarded as illegitimate, and the term "impression" or "printing" or "issue" should be applied to separate reprintings of a work made from one setting of type. In 1897 a committee to consider these and related points was appointed by the Publishers' Association in England; and the committee report, adopted as an official decision in 1925, made clear, specific recommendations. After the first printing of a book every subsequent printing "without change" should be termed a "new impression"; a "new edition" is an impression "in which the matter has undergone some change, or for which the type has been reset"; "reissue" implies that part of the same impression is marketed in a different form—as when the unsold sheets of a published book are reissued with a reprinted title-page ("cancel title"), new preface, or in a remainder binding. There is a growing tendency among publishers to clarify these distinctions. "First printing" or "first edition" often appears immediately after the copyright notice; or edition and printing may be indicated by a symbol (letter and numeral). Librarians, bibliographers, and many publishers have accepted these official definitions; but in commercial practice many books that are, in fact, simply later printings from unchanged plates are announced and sold as new editions. The use of the word "edition," however, in connection with the term "first edition" is too widely established to be changed. Most current books appear only in one edition. Those of wide popularity go through successive printings or impressions from the same plates, such as Sinclair Lewis' *Main Street*, of which 300,000 copies were issued in successive printings from the original plates within two years. It is obviously correct to use the term "printing" or "impression" when the original plates of a book are used without change, and to designate a new "edition" only when the text has been changed or edited or new plates have been made.

In the third meaning of the word, "edition" is identified with the editor (for example, the works of Dickens as edited by Andrew Lang in the "Gadshill Edition"); or with format (such as "large paper edition" or "illustrated edition"); or with other special characteristics. Series are often counted among editions in this third meaning of the word, and the term "series" or "edition" is interchangeably applied to such sequences of books uniform in textual and physical make-up as "Everyman's Library," the "Bohn Library," the "Oxford Standard Authors," and many others. Both series and editions will be more fully considered later.

For each of the components represented in the format of a book there are requirements that determine suitability for library use. Librarians should know these requirements and when possible choose the volumes in which they are fulfilled. But choice can be made only when there is something to choose from. The first factor in book selection is the value, the timeliness, the importance, of a book's content. And since in the great majority of current books there is no alternative format to that in which they are first published, excellence of content must often offset physical deficiencies. It is only when there are two or more current books of equal importance or merit, or when different editions of older or standard works offer variety of format, that selection can give full weight to textual and physical superiority.

Textual features of a book accessory to the main body of the text include title-page, copyright page, dedication, preface, table of contents, list of illustrations, introduction, and, following the text, appendixes, bibliographies, and index, usually arranged in the order indicated. Illustrations, though accessory to the text, may perhaps be best grouped under physical characteristics. In many books, of course, not all these features appear; in others, there may be additional ones, according to the book's subject or character. In the composition, typography, and arrangement of this material expert or incompetent bookmaking is revealed.

By its wording a title-page should suggest to the reader the character of the book; by its design and typography it should be in harmony with the nature and substance of the volume. Perfection in this relationship may be observed in the title-page to Richard Aldington's *A Wreath for San Gemignano* (Duell, Sloan and Pearce), which with dramatic simplicity combines medieval richness of detail and poetic delicacy; in the vigor, realism, and pictorial individuality of Miné Okubo's title-page to her objective personal narrative, *Citizen 13660* (Columbia University Press); in the dignity of the beautifully spaced title-page to Roger Burlingame's *Of Making Many Books* (Scribner), which centers on the Scribner colophon, symbolizing the century of publishing that the volume records; and in *The Little Magazine* (Princeton University Press), where the nature of the book is reflected with wit and aptness, not only in the title-page, on which lies a thumbnail title-page of a little magazine, but in the use at each chapter opening of the same thumbnail page bearing a device that foretells the chapter's subject—and in many other volumes, neither expensive nor exotic, that represent excellence in modern bookmaking.

The publisher's name appears on the title-page, usually with year of publication. The year of copyright appears on the back (verso) of the title-page (sometimes the month of first printing), and a comparison of the two dates will often make clear whether a book is the first printing or a later impression. If, as is frequently the case, there are two copyright dates, the earlier may be for magazine or other serial publication. Among publishers of high standing it is a growing practice to add to the copyright notice indication of successive reprintings. Such full bibliographical information is valuable to librarians and important to collectors and others interested in first editions. On the verso of the title-page is usually also found the printer's (not the publisher's) imprint with the statement "Printed in the United States of America," or "Printed in Great Britain"—a compulsory indication of the country of production, which is useful in showing whether or not an English book has received American copyright. In English books, however, this is sometimes printed on the final page of text.

When a book contains both a preface and an introduction, the former is usually a brief statement of the author's purpose and the authorities on which the book is based; while the latter frequently takes on the character of a preliminary chapter, summarizing the book's theme and scope. If there is only an introduction, it should give the information otherwise looked for in the preface, but it may also include much more and run beyond ordinary preface length. Introductions written by someone other than the author are usually designed to convey appreciation and enlist public attention; Galsworthy's introduction to Hudson's *Green Mansions*, for example, was an important factor in bringing that beautiful book to belated recognition.

For reference works and other books of information the table of contents should outline the organization of the book and demonstrate the material it deals with. A table of contents that simply registers successively numbered chapters is of little use to the reader. Wells' *Outline of History* offers a good example of a workmanlike table of contents, closely condensed, yet giving a comprehensive survey of the whole subject and adequate guidance to its separate divisions. In the J. B. Bury edition of Gibbon the table of contents provides a detailed chronological conspectus of the ordered sequence of the history that is invaluable either for reference or for study; while, on the other hand, the table of contents for Ludwig Lewisohn's *Expression in America* is simply a brief list of chapter titles that in themselves convey no specific information, so that the reader can obtain no preliminary orientation to the subject nor discover its structural development.

Appendixes, notes, and bibliographies represent the apparatus that reinforces a book's informational content. Their excellence lies primarily in the added value they impart to the text. But their value may be enhanced or impaired by the way in which this supplementary or explanatory material is presented. Slipshod, indiscriminate bibliographies, neither alphabetical nor chronological, giving no clue to date or publisher of the works cited, are valueless except as a well-intentioned gesture by a too complacent author. Fine-print footnotes piled in solid blockade halfway up the page, holding up the traffic of the text, impede and irritate the reader. But when logically organized and skillfully presented, these become interesting and useful accessories, such as, for example, are the "Bibliographical Suggestions," explicit, concise, carefully arranged, that supplement Barrett Wendell's fine study, *The Traditions of European Litera-*

ture; and the practical, diversified "Selected Bibliography," crisply and judiciously annotated, that is appended to Stuart Chase's *Mexico*.

An index is the indispensable key to every book of information; its presence or absence will always turn the scale in deciding between two volumes of otherwise fairly matched excellence. Indeed, the lack of an index makes many books that are desirable in subject and interesting in treatment unacceptable for library use, while books of lesser merit, amply indexed, render useful service. As Sir Edward Cook says: "There is no book (in the category of general literature) so good that it is not made better by an index, and no book so bad that it may not by this adjunct escape the worst condemnation." [1] Fortunately, good indexes are becoming constantly more common, as publishers in growing numbers have realized their necessity and standardized their form. But far too many books are still sent out into the world indexless, their spring of practical usefulness sealed at the source. Mrs. Humphry Ward's two volumes of reminiscence, *A Writer's Recollections,* filled as they are with salient or intimate references to the whole Victorian literary world, have been made a sarcophagus of inaccessible information because their contents are not opened to use through an index. Inexcusable also is the omission of an index from Harold Laski's *Reflections on the Revolution of Our Time;* and an even worse example is that delightful composite volume, *The Legacy of Greece*—first and best of the "Legacy" series—in which scholars and enthusiasts set forth the many aspects of Greek culture; their work is deprived of its fullest usefulness through the negligence that failed to supply an index.

Indexes themselves are good, bad, and indifferent, but a poor index, although highly irritating, is better than none. At its best an index is a fine achievement of intelligence, precision, and effective organization—one of the most valuable by-products of professional bibliography. Sir Edward Cook cites as one of the best examples the index to Morley's *Recollections,* which in the English edition covers seventy-six pages; in the first American edition, however, this was

---

[1] "The Art of Indexing," In his *Literary Recreations,* p. 55.

ruthlessly cut down to ten pages and is of minor value, and though extended in later American printings, it remains a reduction of the original. Excellent also, though on a more condensed scale, is the index to Wells' *Outline of History*. John Askling's index to Carola Oman's *Nelson* biography, running to thirty-five three-column pages, is an effective example of unusual historical detail and condensed descriptive characterization. Here the indexer is given credit by name, just as the illustrator, and, sometimes, the book designer, receive recognition by name in the volumes they have helped to create. This is a notable step toward better indexing, for it should lead to general recognition by publishers that the indexer's work is not just a minor detail of publication, but an art essential to worthy bookmaking.

Because of their stupidities, absurdities, and lapses, inferior indexes have created an unintended humorous literature of their own; but in many indexes prepared by authors for their own books there are twinklings of deliberate sly humor, such as may be discovered by examining the index to Raymond Pearl's shrewd treatise on students' reading, *To Begin With*. Here you will find such entries as "Allah, piously mentioned," "Homo sapiens, ridiculous animal," "Music, the modesty of the author regarding his skill as a performer of," "Uplift, subtle propaganda against" (with a page reference inclusive of the entire book), and other demure byplay of a prankish indexer. Bertrand Russell's satiric twinkle is evident in the index to *The Amberley Papers*, where the entry under his name records "his ugliness," "his bad temper," "why not called Galahad," "fed on ass's milk," "a bookworm."

Physical aspects of a book, representing also component parts of its format, are: size, type, paper, page, illustrations, and binding. Let us consider them in the order indicated.

Size may be said to be two-dimensional, for its most important elements are thickness and height. Thickness depends on the number of pages contained in a single book and the "bulk" of the paper, and this is determined by the number of printed sheets, or "signatures," bound into the volume. A book, large or small, is well proportioned when its thickness is in appropriate relationship to its height. An elephant folio, twenty-three inches tall, carries with symmetrical dignity a six-inch bulk, while an ordinary twelvemo, which is less than eight inches high, should not exceed a thickness of an inch and a half if symmetry is to be observed. Any book that is to be read with comfort should be small enough to hold conveniently and large enough to permit a size of type that is easily read. Reference books, of course, are naturally and legitimately bulky, but for ordinary reading use a bulk of more than two inches gives clumsiness to books that are less than nine inches high. This means that for convenience of handling, from 450 to 650 pages (depending upon the kind of paper used) should be the maximum thickness of the usual twelvemo or small octavo volume.

Symmetry of effect, in books as in the human race, is less affected by thinness than by thickness; but there is more harmony of proportion in such a book as Edna Millay's *The Buck in the Snow*, with its height of seven-and-a-half inches and its eighty-three pages making a bulk of three-eighths of an inch, than there is in the taller, thinner form of Archibald MacLeish's *New Found Land*, standing nine-and-a-half inches high, with seventy-eight pages that give a bulk of two-eighths of an inch. Every degree of thickness has prevailed in present-day bookmaking, for with the use of very thin paper from 900 to 1,200 readable pages may be compressed into a volume of ordinary small octavo height.

From the 1920's through the 1930's there was an increasing production of overbulked books, so clumsy and heavy as to be a real burden upon the reader. This was, in part, literary fashion (with *Anthony Adverse* a leader in the van); in part, the tendency to compress into a single volume works originally published in sequence (such as Sigrid Undset's *Kristin Lavransdatter* and Couperus' *Book of the Small Souls*); in part, the result of the growing popularity of "omnibus" volumes and anthologies. Then wartime restrictions on book production brought sudden and drastic change. For five years the accustomed format was metamorphosed. Bulk shrank to attenuation. Type faded from black to gray and diminished to myopic smallness. Text was cut to the bone; chapters lost their headings; margins disappeared; flimsy-thin pages clung anemically together. These were extreme manifestations; but they are evident in any comparison of, say, twenty-five books published in 1938 with an equal number published in 1944. Advent of the postwar period brought return to more normal standards, but the war impact left a definite practical and aesthetic impress on format and has been a decisive factor in advancing the claims of thin books over fat ones. From the librarian's point of view, slim books mean additional shelf space (a three-foot shelf will hold thirty-eight wartime-format novels as against twenty-five of prewar proportions), they are light and comfortable to hold and cheaper to mail. Their attractiveness and popularity with the reading (and buying) public is attested by book-trade experience of the immense market built up for them during the war. Consensus of publishers' opinion indicates that as the defects of extreme wartime format are eliminated the small, compact format, symmetrical and artistic, will flourish and multiply, and the old-style, large, unnecessarily bulked-up volumes will remain in abeyance.[2]

It is height, not thickness, that defines the size of a book. The common book-trade terms used to describe the various book sizes—folio, quarto, octavo, twelvemo, sixteenmo—indicate, for each, a height in inches that establishes the standard dimensions appropriate to that size. These terms were originally derived from their relation to the folding of the printed sheets in binding the volume. The large sheets of paper used in printing have always been manufactured in certain standard sizes, and the book-trade designations for book sizes are based upon the use of a sheet measuring nineteen by twenty-five inches—which was a standard size during many years of printing. When such a sheet was folded once, two leaves (four pages) each sixteen inches wide and twenty-five inches high, were formed, and leaves of this size were termed folios. When the sheet was folded

[2] These and related points were considered at a panel discussion of "Fat Books or Thin," held by the Trade Book Clinic of the American Institute of Graphic Arts at the opening of the 1945-46 season, and reported in *Publishers' Weekly* for Nov. 3, 1945, pp. 2034-37.

twice, four leaves (eight pages) were formed, making a quarto; three foldings gave eight leaves (sixteen pages) and made an octavo; another method of triple folding made twelve leaves (twenty-four pages) and gave a twelvemo; folded to make sixteen leaves (thirty-two pages), it was a sixteenmo; and so on, through eighteenmo, twenty-fourmo, thirty-twomo, forty-eightmo, and sixty-fourmo. The folded printed sheets were called signatures, and this term also denoted the letter or number by which each signature itself was indicated, to guide the binder in bringing them together. Even in the earlier years of printing the standard sheet varied in size (a normal size in Elizabethan times was fifteen by nineteen inches) and during modern times an infinite variety of paper sizes have prevailed, so that now all book sizes designated by these traditional terms are, in fact, approximate and no longer convey either the number of leaves in a signature or the exact dimensions of the book. More exact designation is made possible by the use of the metric system, commonly followed in library cataloguing, by which the actual height of the book is recorded in centimeters.

For library use, books that fall within a medium range of height are desirable. Dictionaries, many works of reference, many books in art, music, architecture, and other special fields, must of necessity be large and require special suitable shelving. But among books intended for continuous and general reading, those over ten inches high are "oversize" for ordinary library shelving, in which the space between shelves is usually about ten-and-one-eighth inches. Such books are separated from the main body of literature on the subject and placed on special "oversize" shelves, where they are often likely to be overlooked and consequently less used. Unduly small books, on the other hand, are prone to conceal or mislay themselves on the shelves, or to be too easily slipped into a reader's pocket or handbag. Therefore, in general book selection, volumes that range in size from sixteenmo to medium octavo, or from six-and-a-half to nine inches in height, are most satisfactory, both for library handling and for reading use.

Type must first of all be legible. It must not be so small as to strain the eyes, nor so different from the norm that the reader is constantly conscious of the process of reading. It is this sense of the bizarre, of the unaccustomed, that makes the beautiful page of William Morris' "Golden" type, and of various types modelled upon it, difficult for continuous reading. The type measure, or length of the printed line, should not be more than four-and-a-half inches for an octavo page. Laboratory experiments have shown that a longer line in the type sizes ordinarily used in books slows down the process of reading and increases the fatigue of the eye; and many authorities recommend that the maximum width of line should not exceed four inches. The American Library Association publishes a list called *Books for Tired Eyes*, which is of value in suggesting editions for readers whose sight is quickly affected by close or even ordinary small type, and also in indicating for examination and comparison books that offer examples of legible typography.

Legibility is always affected by the spacing and the leading of the page. The spacing between words should be even, unobtrusive, and sufficient to give a sense of freedom to the eye. The leading between lines should not be so great that the white spaces seem to dominate the stream of print, nor so reduced that the page seems a solid mass of print with the words so closely crowded together in every line and the lines following one another in such close proximity that the eye soon experiences a sense of confusion and discomfort. Accepted standards of legibility, however, were victims of wartime restrictions on book manufacture and of paper rationing. In most of the books published during the war years, pages were monotonously crowded, for proper leading (like suitable margins) used too much paper; and the familiar 11-, 12-, and 14-point book-size types were superseded by smaller-size types in designs chosen for maximum legibility and word-count. Many skillful and effective results were achieved, but comfortable readability was not among them: in any prolonged book use a reading glass became an almost indispensable accessory. When the postwar period came, return to former standards was slow and partial. World-wide paper shortage (though without rationing) still prevailed, small types seemed to have been firmly established in book design, and there was a steadily increasing inflow of printed material reproduced by photomechanical processes on a type-scale far below the range of unaided vision. Microfilming, planographic, or offset, reproduction of typewritten manuscript and statistical and scientific records, of out-of-print volumes, and of such great bibliographical enterprises as the Library of Congress and British Museum catalogues—all have advanced research and wonderfully enriched reference collections, but they also have made eye-strain a more common liability for book users.

Offset printing, more widely known as offset lithography, is one of the useful and many-sided developments in modern bookmaking. Here the printing is done from a flat surface (hence, the term "planography") instead of from a raised surface of type or line cuts. The original type pages, or drawings, charts, or designs, are photographed and the negatives transferred to sensitive metal plates, from which, after preparatory treatment, the printing is done. Its flexibility and wide scope make this process successfully applicable to books of all types; in color work it has great advantages, especially in that it does not require the use of glossy coated paper, necessary for color reproduction of "raised type" printing. It makes available, furthermore, more color at less cost. Gay, profusely illustrated books for children have come in ever-increasing flow from offset presses, and to adult books it contributes a discriminative use of color that gives charm and distinction. *Spin a Silver Dollar*, Alberta Hannum's narrative of life on a Navaho Indian reservation, of native weaving and the work of a Navaho boy artist, is a beautiful example of sensitive pictorial reproduction of an original, delicate, primitive art. Advance and possibilities of photomechanical printing are manifested in the annual exhibit of Books by Offset Lithography, first held in the spring of 1942, and modelled upon the famous Fifty Books of the Year exhibits, sponsored since 1923 by the American Institute of Graphic Arts.

For paper, the chief requirement in library use is durability, with satisfaction to the eye and touch. It should be so opaque that the type does not show through, strong enough to stand rebinding, yet thin and light enough for ease in handling and economy in shelving. The paper used in ordinary bookmaking is made chiefly of two materials—wood pulp prepared by chemical and mechanical processes (from which is made most of the paper used in books of American manufacture), and esparto, a coarse grass, native to southern Spain and North Africa.

All paper, however, is made from cellulose (the substance which forms the mass of the cell-membrane of all plants), whether it be obtained from papyrus, flax, wood, esparto grass, or other growth. This is one of the most indestructible substances that nature produces. Its durability in paper depends largely on the methods of production. Flax cellulose is especially durable, partly because the fiber is thoroughly cleansed of extraneous vegetable matter in being made into linen; it can, however, lose its durability by lax cleansing from chemicals in making into paper.

When wood is used for paper by the chemical processes, a "chemical pulp" is made by distintegrating wood chips, usually by caustic soda or lime and sulfurous acid treatment; the quality and durability of the product depend largely upon the proper and complete cleansing of the pulp from the chemicals. The cellulose of wood is as durable as that of flax, and in compounding "chemical pulp" certain woods, like northern spruce, that produce a firm, hard surface are mixed with fibers of softer wood, such as poplar, to give a pleasant surface texture. From the wood pulp chemical processes are made the papers of varying grades and finishes that are generally used in American bookmaking; while from esparto is made the light but bulky "antique" paper (without smooth finish) familiar in many English books; but in all papermaking some rag content (flax cellulose) is necessary for paper of better quality.

Book paper was one of the great casualties of the war. In England (where six million volumes were burned in the German bombing of Paternoster Row, London's publishing center), esparto grass, chiefly imported from Spain, was completely unobtainable; the makeshift emergency substitutes used to meet immediate necessities were pitifully inferior. In the United States, native production of pulpwood could not be adequately maintained and importation of pulp was closed at the most important sources. Drastic restrictions were imposed, in allocation of pulp to paper mills and in establishing rigid quotas of paper for civilian usage by publishers and printers. Paper shortages continued long after the war ended, especially in the supply of newsprint, which diminished almost to the vanishing point, cutting down newspapers both in number and size throughout the country.

"Newsprint" is paper of so-called "mechanical stock," made of ground wood pulp with all the vegetable material left in; it is used chiefly for newspapers, for the so-called "pulp magazines," and for the cheapest kind of books. It soon turns yellow, then browns, dries, and crumbles away, so that bound volumes of newspapers in many library collections are useless after fifteen or twenty years. The library associations and other scholarly organizations of England and the United States worked for many years on the problem of this use of bad and worthless paper for publications that have permanent reference value, and one result of their efforts was the printing of special editions on rag paper for library use. The *New York Times*, for example, publishes at an increased subscription price such a rag paper edition for binding and preservation in libraries. Solution of this problem, however, has come through the advance of microphotography, by which the pages of a newspaper or book are recorded on a small roll of film, which later may be read through a projector, enlarged to more than the original size. The *New York Times* and other leading newspapers now provide microfilm editions for subscribers so desiring, and in some libraries the microfilm edition is the only one supplied, for general reading as well as for reference use. More and more microfilming is being done by libraries themselves, for preservation and compact storage of newspaper collections. A month's issues of an ordinary newspaper make two small rolls of film, contained in boxes four inches square and less than two inches deep. As these rolls take the place of ponderous bound volumes the

PHYSICAL ASPECTS OF BOOKS 175

size of a newspaper page and two or three inches thick, the shelf space saved as microphotography supplants the binding of newspapers can be readily seen.[3]

Some knowledge of the different kinds and qualities of paper is necessary in effective book selection. With even a little familiarity, the briefest examination of a book will reveal much. An older English novel, clumsy in thickness but a featherweight in the hand, declares itself made of a cheaper grade of esparto; a volume of the same size that lifts as though weighted by lead, must be made of the glossy, clay-laden "coated" or "art" paper used for half-tone illustrations. In most books containing half-tones the illustrations are printed separately on art paper, and to make an entire book of such paper—unless it is composed almost wholly of illustrations—is one of the worst of publishers' misdeeds. It is, however, of frequent occurrence; for example, *The Story of English Literature*, by E. K. Broadus, contains but twenty-four illustrations in its six hundred pages and weighs five pounds. The thin strong paper called India or Bible paper—Oxford India paper is the most famous—is widely used for "omnibus" volumes and for many other books where extreme compression is desired. It has disadvantages when used for library reference works—difficulty in rapid turning of pages and inability to stand long and hard use. Its great advantages are ease in handling and the convenience of finding the whole body of information in a single volume. When of sufficient opacity and combined with good type and adequate leading, modern thin paper gives delightful one-volume compactness to many famous books that in their former guise appear formidable to the ordinary reader. In replacing several volumes by one and reducing the bulk of individual books, it adds much to the storage capacity of library shelving.

[3] The reports of the New York Public Library for 1943 (pp. 33-34) and 1945 (pp. 71-72) offer interesting summary of the immense growth and wide usefulness of photoduplication carried on within the library. "By means of photostat and microfilm the library is able to project itself in substance as well as in spirit beyond the four walls of the institution." In December, 1945, the Department of Photographic Service was given division status. During that year it had filled 40,454 outside orders, including 433,662 photostats, 186,723 microfilm negative frames, 46,636 feet of positive microfilm.

There is great variety in all modern book papers, in surface, tint, weight, and durability, and a steady improvement in standards of quality. As a general rule, however, the most satisfactory book paper for ordinary library use is of dull or "antique" finish, and of a white that tends toward creamy rather than bluish tones; not too thin; strong, light in weight, but without the bulky "fluffiness" that expands many three-hundred-page older English novels to a width of two inches.

Paper and type produce the printed page; but the page has its own requirements in arrangement, design, and symmetry. Much of its beauty depends upon the proportions of the margins. These make the white frame for the black mass of letterpress, and between content and frame there must be balance and harmony. William Morris considered that the true page was the double page—as displayed in the open book; that the two opposite pages are and must be seen together, as presenting two columns of black, separated by the white column of the inner margin and framed in white at top, bottom, and sides by the remaining margins. These margins are of varying proportions. Traditionally, the inner margin is the narrowest; it should be about half the width of the outer (so that in the double page its width appears equal). The top margin is next in narrowness, being visually about half as wide as the bottom; the outer side margin is less in width than the bottom and more in width than the top. This greater width for the outer and bottom margins probably represents the intention of affording sufficient space for thumbs and fingers of the reader at the side and bottom of the page without covering any of the type. Preservation of these general proportions, in relation to type design and arrangement, assures the symmetry of the printed page. But from the librarian's point of view the most important of these proportions is that of the inner margin. In rebinding a book this margin is still further reduced—as a rule at least a quarter-inch is taken from it—and if it was originally unduly narrow the rebinding will pinch into the text and make satisfactory reading of the book impossible. A book with only a half-inch inner margin cannot be properly rebound. For this reason the more generous the inner margin of a book, the more practical and acceptable it is for continued library use.

The ruthless cutting down of inner margins in wartime formats proved one of the most serious library problems, and postwar continuance of the practice brought formal protest from the American Library Association at its annual conference in 1946. It was pointed out that "narrow margins make books difficult to use. They encourage the reader to 'force' opening, resulting in breaking the backs and loosening and tearing the pages; and this hazard is increased by thin or poor quality paper. If the margins are too narrow, the books are very hard to rebind; expensive hand sewing is often needed. Where re-sewing is at all possible, it naturally reduces the binding margin still more, encouraging 'forcing' and abusing the rebound book. Frequently, re-sewing is absolutely impossible. The usable life of the book is thus reduced before discarding." For these reasons, publishers and book designers were urged to "discourage the production of any more narrow margin books of the types bought by libraries"—a recommendation that does not refer to the twenty-five-cent paper-bound pocket-type books, in which narrow margins are an accepted requirement. The resolution adds: "Unless this is done, libraries will have difficulties for years to come, particularly with titles which are allowed to go out of print."

In the page design there are many details of importance. A book may have a running head (or headline) at the top of each page, or it may have none; if there is a running head, it may be the same on each page; or it may give the title of the book on the left-hand page and the title of the chapter on the right-hand page; or instead of the chapter-title it may give on the right-hand page some phrase descriptive of the immediate content of the text. The page numbers may be placed at the top of the page or at the bottom, in the center or at the side; there may be side notes, marginal or indented; dates may be indicated as part of the running head. In all these particulars and many others there are infinite variations; also, from the point of view of the experienced librarian and the intelligent reader, there are a few simple, common-sense requirements.

One of the trends in modern bookmaking is toward the elimination of headlines of any kind. It is a practice approved by disciples of William Morris, who regard the headline as a nuisance and a stupidity, destroying the unity of the page. Halliday Sparling says: "Either a reader knows and is interested in what he is reading about or he is not; in the one case he does not need, and in the second pays no attention to, a constantly repeated reminder of the title or theme of the book he is reading." This is plausible, but hard to substantiate. As a matter of fact, to both the serious and the casual reader suitable headlines are a constant, though almost unconscious, aid and satisfaction. They are of less importance in novels, in single plays and in single, long poems, but in almost all other kinds of literature their absence causes frequent annoyance or inconvenience. Very few books are read uninterruptedly from beginning to end; they are put down and taken up again; they are glanced through to judge of subject or treatment, or to find some desired information; and the running heads guide the eye in its survey or quest. Any book intended for serious reading can be made more useful by clear and effective typographical guidance. From the librarian's point of view the headlines should give both the book's title and the chapter-title (usually preferable to the descriptive phrase). In indexes, when an entry runs over from a right- to a left-hand page, the key word should be repeated at the top of the new column. In histories and biographies, when chronological treatment permits, continuous indication of dates, as part of the headline, is extremely useful. These points must be borne in mind when choosing different editions of standard works, or in deciding between important current books that deal with the same subject.

Illustrations are of ever growing interest and importance in present-day bookmaking. Advances in photography have revolutionized pictorial reproduction; and the popular picture magazines—*Life* and *Look* are leading examples—have become patterns for a continuing outflow of books in which text is superseded in significance by illustrations. Many aspects of the war have been thus recorded; social problems and regional conditions are reflected by the camera in volumes as arresting and informative as a documentary film. *You*

Have Seen Their Faces, memorable visualization of submarginal humanity, by Erskine Caldwell and Margaret Bourke-White; Wallace Stegner's *One Nation*, portraying the American meltingpot in photographs with text commentary; the series of *Look at America* regional guides, and many others of kindred type, indicate for a single field the immense influence the camera has today on book substance and appeal. Indeed, with the modern mechanical and artistic development of the book arts now in progress, illustration and decoration combine to invest the ordinary book with higher artistic excellence than it has ever before possessed. New, improved, and varied reproductive processes have reduced the cost of illustration; changed technique has brought conventional decoration and literal illustration into closer and more harmonious relationship; the mediums by which an artist may see his work reproduced in a book are now so many and so varied that the creative spirit is stimulated and given ever freer expression. In general library book selection, illustrations are of importance as they enhance the significance of the book itself; they should be a manifestation of its spirit and in harmony with its physical aspect. Thackeray and Dickens with the original illustrations, Jane Austen with Hugh Thomson's drawings, *Alice in Wonderland* as delineated by Tenniel, Benchley's humor as accented by the pencil of Gluyas Williams—in these and many other books the illustrations become a part of the book's identity. In books of travel, illustrations are often of first importance, and fine or unusual illustrations may justify acceptance of an inferior text. In history and biography, they may add indispensable enrichment; and in art works, of course, they represent a central factor in selection. But in dealing with the great mass of current publications, illustrations are to be regarded as accessories of the text and judged by the added value they impart to it, in interpretation, or information, or artistic significance.

The binding is the outer garment of the book. It should possess fitness, durability, and attractiveness; but its characteristics are unimportant beside the qualities of the text. In current book selection there is little opportunity for discrimination in bindings, for most new books are published in a single form of binding that must be accepted for what it is. In general, it is rebinding, not binding for first publication, that is of importance in library practice. Most library books will sooner or later change their binding, sometimes more than once. Popular fiction is rebound, usually after from twenty to thirty issues; and in many libraries new books (chiefly fiction and juveniles) are bought in reinforced prebinding supplied by various dealers.[4]

"Publishers' binding" or "casing" are the terms applied to the binding in which the ordinary trade edition of a book appears. And, like typography, paper, and illustration, these bindings have shared in the mechanical and artistic development of modern bookmaking. Variety and individuality in color and design have replaced the dignified but monotonous Victorian cloth bindings in somber browns, greens, blacks, and reds. Solid colors still prevail, but in wide and varied range, with emphasis on reds and warm neutral tints. Binding decoration is usually minimized to geometrical simplicity or symbolic formalism, and to end papers in which artistic originality and fascinating ornamental detail are given free play; for it is on the book jacket that the decorative receives lavish expression. Cloth (which now includes synthetic fabrics of many names), available in wide range of colors, is still the material chiefly used and most satisfactory in durability; it is often combined with boards covered with decorative paper in bindings that are artistically beautiful and rich in varied design. Some bindings are entirely of paper over boards, but these are less durable than those with board sides and cloth or linen backs, on which the title may be effectively stamped. Paper labels, though sometimes attractive, are likely to be loosened or rubbed off under steady handling, and bindings in white or delicate tints are unsuited to the wear and tear of library use. Many

---

[4] Processes and requirements in binding for library use are compactly set forth in the standard pamphlet, *Care and Binding of Books and Magazines*, by the A.L.A. Committee on Bookbinding, published by the American Library Association in 1928. *General Bookbinding*, by Chris H. Groneman (rev. ed., 1946, Bloomington, Ill., McKnight & McKnight), a pamphlet manual for students and craftsmen, is suitable and useful in the work of a library bindery. And there are good practical suggestions and much related information in *The Care and Repair of Books*, comprehensive standard textbook in that subject, by Harry Miller Lydenberg and John Archer (3d edition, 1945, New York, R. R. Bowker Co.).

librarians object to the spiral bindings, metal or plastic, which may catch or tear into the pages of other books and often necessitate that the volume be remade as a pamphlet or rebound as a book. Elaborate "gift-book" bindings, those of limp suede, of imitation parchment, or those self-styled "de luxe," are anathema in intelligent book selection. Such productions have nothing in common with the fine examples of the binder's art represented by beautiful limited editions and other admirable products of the many presses that are establishing the high standards and ideals of modern bookmaking.

All-paper bindings have become so successful and important in present-day book manufacture that they demand a special word. Long experimented with by publishers, the chief physical factor in their success has been the development of the so-called "perfect binding," which depends on the use of adhesives to hold pages and covers together and eliminates stapling and stitching from bindery operations. From 1939, when the series of twenty-five-cent "Pocket Books" was founded, cheap, attractive paper-bound books of good literary quality have established a world-wide mass market and reached into ever widening channels of distribution. During the war years they stood the test of mass use, in the enormous output of "Pocket Books" and kindred pocket-size reprints; while in less substantial octavo pamphlet form such contributions to international understanding as Wendell Willkie's *One World* and the symposium on atomic energy, *One World or None*, were brought to universal attention. From the point of view of library selection, such editions probably do not justify acquisition as permanent stock; but "Pocket Books" and their congeners are used by many libraries for inexpensive and practical duplication of popular titles, with satisfactory results. The bindings are not reinforced, but have sufficient sturdiness to give from forty to fifty issues per volume. Selection, however, must be carefully made, as some volumes are stronger and better made than others.

Indispensable companion to the modern trade binding is the book jacket, a glorification of the plain paper "dust wrapper" that once humbly served a useful purpose. Originally devised to stimulate sales by attracting buyers, it has established a phase of modern art and has become one of the most essential "extras" of publishing. Its rise to importance was indicated when, in May, 1934, the American Institute of Graphic Arts opened the first display of fifty book jackets, chosen as the best examples of the previous year, thus initiating an annual exhibit akin to that of the "Fifty Books of the Year." From jackets submitted in competition selection is made by a jury, which bases its judgment on three points: artistic and typographic excellence, display value, and selling appeal. For the jacket represents art and commercialism, its primary purpose to arrest the observer's attention and direct it to the "blurb" that proclaims the book.

While jacket designs still range from crude pictorial advertising to original compositions of high merit, their standards of excellence constantly improve. They display initiative and originality; they draw on color harmonies and contrasts, on photography and on typographic inventiveness; and they offer rewarding opportunities for many distinguished artists. Artzybasheff's imaginative power and magnificent color use, for example, have found expression in dozens of book jackets that should be cherished by collectors. Compare a row of new books duly jacketed, with the same volumes in unjacketed tranquillity, and you will realize the brilliance, individuality, and allure that the jacket imparts to the literary marketplace. Varied uses are made of the art, informational, and publicity values that the jacket possesses. Some libraries retain the jackets while the books are on the shelves and file them during circulation; others affix the jacket to the book and add a protective cover for circulation use. Many library art departments maintain extensive collections. In others, better examples are collected, studied by students of design, and often shown in public exhibitions. Almost all libraries use jackets as effective poster announcements of new books, or as decorative material in list-making and bulletin work for readers; and many other attractive utilizations are worked out by ingenious librarians. Extra jackets, made available at a nominal price, have been a much appreciated aid in this sort of jacket extension service.

In any survey of the physical aspect of the book it is evident that harmony and consistency in design and execution represent the ideal of good bookmaking. It is an ideal that may be realized in inexpensive books as well as in costly ones. As W. D. Orcutt says:

It adds little to the expense to select a type that properly expresses the thought which the author wishes to convey; or to have the presses touch the letters into the paper in such a way as to become a part of it, without that heavy impression which makes the reverse side appear like an example of Braille; or to find a paper (even made by machine!) soft to the feel and grateful to the eye, on which the page is placed with well-considered margins; or to use illustrations or decorations, if warranted at all, in such a way as to assist the imagination of the reader rather than to divert him from the text; to plan a title-page which, like the door to a house, invites the reader to open it and proceed, its type lines carefully balanced with the blank; or to bind (even in cloth!) with trig squares and with design or lettering in keeping with the printing inside.

Toward this ideal modern bookmaking advances. The twentieth century has seen a widespread revival of the book arts, mechanical and artistic progress in every phase of bookmaking, and an increasing public appreciation of beautiful and well-made books. In 1923 the American Institute of Graphic Arts held its first exhibition of "Fifty Books of the Year," chosen as the best examples of intelligent craftsmanship, as models for inspiration and study. These exhibits have been continued annually since then. They are shown in many of the leading cities and should be familiar, not only to publishers, printers, bookmakers, and librarians, but to all students and users of books, for they represent expert judgment of the qualities and characteristics of good bookmaking.[5]

Librarians have a vital interest in all that concerns the excellence of books, physically, aesthetically, and intellectually. They have

---

[5] One of the most comprehensive and useful sources of current information on aspects of modern bookmaking is the *Publishers' Weekly* section devoted to "Modern Book Design and Manufacture," which appears in one issue each month. Begun in 1923, when the first display of the "Fifty Books of the Year" was held, it has given through the years full record and commentary for this and for the various succeeding exhibits—book jackets, books by offset lithography, textbooks, and other groups—which have sprung from the Book Clinics organized in 1932 by the American Institute of Graphic Arts, for discussion of problems of book design.

aided and influenced modern bookmaking by the practical testing of its merits and defects, by urging needed improvements, and by giving preference in selection to books that best meet fundamental requirements of use and beauty. But it must be repeated that whatever the textual or physical characteristics of a book may be, selection can be exercised only when there is an alternative choice. When there are two or more editions, the best can be given preference. So in library book selection discriminating judgment is most necessary in choosing among books that are available in different editions. Different editions are in large measure the product of different publishers. Their intelligent selection demands not only a good background of book knowledge but wide acquaintance with publishers and familiarity with the characteristics of their publications. Books, in a word, are both substance and product. We cannot know them thoroughly unless we know something about their producers.

10. Makers of Books: The Trade and Its Products

> The history of typography is a chapter in literature. So is the book trade.... The effect of Goschen, the publisher, on the destinies of Schiller is well known to English readers. Aptly has it been said by one of the most brilliant writers of our day, that the great publisher is a sort of Minister of Letters, and is not to be without the qualities of a statesman.
>
> John Morley: *Recollections*
>
> The reason why the majority of books see the light is that the publisher of each book believes or has been led to hope that this particular book is a good book. He may or may not expect to make money upon it, but if he hopes to make money the hope is not discreditable to him, since the publisher is in business for business purposes. And the publisher frequently publishes a book upon which he knows he will lose money. He publishes that book because he wants to publish it. He thinks it is a good book, and he believes that what he thinks is good will appeal to other readers. In this, he is generally right. But while he is right, he often regrets his optimism, for the reason that no publisher can fail at times to be eccentric in his opinions.
>
> Frank Swinnerton: *Authors and the Book Trade*

THE PUBLISHER is the medium through which books are produced, the bookseller the medium through which they are distributed. Publishing and bookselling are thus united in a fundamental relationship: two aspects of a single function, perhaps best expressed in the primary definition of the word "publish"—"to make generally known." Together they constitute the book trade, long known as "the great trade" and today familiarly called "the trade." Each is a distinct and separate calling, but they are so closely interrelated that even today some of the greatest publishing houses are also bookstores and conduct important and extended systems of bookselling. In the earlier days of book history, they were inextricably entwined with one another. Any history of publishing must also be a history of bookselling until modern times are reached.

The booksellers of Rome and Alexandria who employed scribes

to prepare fine manuscripts and who sold them in their shops or in distant cities were the forerunners of the publishers of today. Gutenberg, Schoeffer, Caxton, Aldus, the Elzevirs—all early producers of the printed word—were printers, publishers, and booksellers combined. They selected the subject matter, often they compiled or edited it, they printed it, sold it, and distributed it for sale by others. In the most exact sense of the word, they *published* it to the world. The great printer-publishers, as they are called, flourished from the sixteenth to the eighteenth centuries. Then, as printers increased and books multiplied, distinctions between publishers and booksellers became more clearly drawn, more widely recognized, and the "great trade" organized and developed in many different directions and separate channels. No attempt can be made here to give even the briefest outline of its development; but in the rich and diversified records of book history there are no more fascinating annals than those devoted to this rise of publishing and bookselling into a vast and varied industry of the modern world.

The invention of printing, indeed, heralded the dawn of the modern world. During the first two centuries of the printing press Europe was absorbed in theological warfare: Protestantism against Catholicism, ecclesiasticism against dissent. The new art furnished an inexhaustible supply of weapons and projectiles to the combatants; it gave expression and wide popular dissemination to thought and opinion that were shattering traditional authority and inciting revolt; it naturally and inevitably incurred the condemnation of those against whom it was used, and was subject to arbitrary restrictions imposed by whatever authority was in command. Of course, from the earliest times, utterances opposing the actions or commands of temporal or spiritual rulers have been punished. Bookburning runs through history. In China in 213 B.C. the "burning of the books" (except books on medicine, astrology, and horticulture) was carried through by imperial edict. Through the manuscript age offending books were burned by church and civil authorities. In our own day the rise of fascism brought suppression of books that could express, inspire, and defend the free spirit of mankind. The mass book-burning in Berlin, on May 10, 1933, was sign and symbol of the pattern set for world conquest for Hitler's "new order."

Thus developed the practice of official censorship (the restriction or suppression of literature deemed subversive or harmful) that has continued in varying manifestations to our own day. Its course may be traced through successive phases of restrictive purpose, each according to the tenor of its age. In the age of faith, heresy brought the severest censorship. As Protestantism came into power and gave authority to what had been heresy, censorship was directed upon so-called atheism and blasphemy, or, in fact, upon antireligious opinion. As ecclesiastical authority waned and the power of political government increased, censorship turned its rigors upon treason and sedition, or, in other words, upon insubordinate political opinion. As freedom of political opinion became more firmly established, censorship—necessarily relaxed in religion and politics—centered its energies upon literature concerned with sex, or, in other words, upon utterances regarded as objectionable by accepted moral and ethical standards.

Censorship concerned with sex extends far beyond legal control of pornography into the fields of creative and informational literature. Standard works by responsible authors on sex instruction and preparation for marriage and motherhood are too often eliminated from school use by organized attack, and similar outside pressures (with religion as chief motivating force) are directed at books on evolution and birth control. It should be remembered that Tennessee still maintains its law prohibiting the teaching of evolution and that campaigns for similar legislation in other states are frequently initiated.

Political censorship, at times quiescent but never extinct, has drawn renewed strength (as was true after the First World War) from postwar reaction. Essentially nationalistic, focusing on so-called "communistic doctrine," "anti-Americanism," and "subversive literature," strengthened by deepening hostility to Soviet Russia, and intensified by development of the U.S.–Soviet "cold war," it rose in the late 1940's to a nation-wide hysteria. "Treason" was read into acts, associations, and thoughts arbitrarily defined as "disloyal"; books were suppressed or removed from libraries. Scholars accused of "liberal thoughts" were dismissed from colleges and universities; "loyalty tests" and "loyalty boards" were set in operation for workers of every grade in the framework of federal, state, county, and municipal service. In spite of protest and resistant action by writers, publishers, teachers, scientists, librarians, many leaders in social and political thought, and a minority of newspapers, sanity and fair dealing seemed in eclipse.

In both political and moralistic aspects, censorship can become a dangerous and destructive influence, not only in publishing and bookselling but in library service, in education, and in intellectual and cultural life. In library book selection, problems are constantly encountered that arise directly from traditional acceptances of its principles and methods.[1]

Closely related to censorship in publishing history is the development of property rights in literature, which began as simple trade monopoly and culminated in the elaborate, intricate modern struc-

---

[1] The Library Bill of Rights, first adopted by the American Library Association in 1939, reaffirmed and strengthened at the conference of June, 1947, thus states "the following basic policies which should govern the services of all libraries:

"1. As a responsibility of library service, books and other reading matter selected should be chosen for values of interest, information, and enlightenment of all the people of the community. In no case should any book be excluded because of the race or nationality or the political or religious views of the writer.

"2. There should be the fullest practicable provision of material presenting all points of view concerning the problems and issues of our times, international, national, and local, and books or other reading matter of sound factual authority should not be proscribed from library shelves because of partisan or doctrinal disapproval.

"3. Censorship of books, urged or practiced by volunteer arbiters of morals or political opinion or by organizations that would establish a coercive concept of Americanism, must be challenged by libraries in maintenance of their responsibility to provide information and enlightenment through the printed word.

"4. Libraries should enlist the cooperation of allied groups in the fields of science, of education, and of book publishing in resisting all abridgment of the free access to ideas and full freedom of expression that are the tradition and heritage of Americans.

"5. As an institution of education for democratic living, the library should welcome the use of its meeting rooms for socially useful and cultural activities and discussion of current public questions. Such meeting places should be available on equal terms to all groups in the community regardless of the beliefs and affiliations of their members."

ture of copyright protection. Among the earliest rights that the printer-publishers sought to have protected was the right to sole publication of a given book. Piracy, as it has long been called, naturally prevailed in the early days of printing because, before that invention, possession of a manuscript was considered to carry with it the right to make copies, if desired, and so possession of a printed copy of a book was for some time believed to carry the right to make and dispose of further printed copies. Martin Luther was among the first to call attention to the need of legislation that should secure to literary producers some rights in their property. It should be added, however, that Luther's motive was not a desire to assure a money return to authors for their work, but rather to prevent the publication of imperfect and unrevised editions of his own writings.

The early "copy rights" expressed the literal meaning of the words. They were known as special privileges, were issued by city councils, rulers, or other authorities, and were denoted by the inscription *cum privilegio* on the title-page. This inscription still exists on the title-pages of books issued with specific official authorization, such as copies of the English Prayer-Book published by the King's Printer, and in Catholic publications which have received the *imprimatur*, or approval, of church authorities. The early "privileges," besides indicating that the work had received the approval of the censors, also conveyed monopolies, permitting a single printer or publisher to have exclusive control of a specific text for a specified time. Gradually, from these privileges and authorizations, from this mingling of censorship and trade monopoly, the right of an author to control his own work and the right of a publisher to produce or reproduce it were legally established.

Thus censorship and copyright lie at the roots of publishing history. They are still important factors in the production, distribution, and selection of books—the former, as it represents mass emotional reactions to changing thought and changing *mores;* the latter, as it controls and defines property rights of authors in their work and of publishers in their product. The influence of censorship from the library point of view will be indicated in later consideration of selection in different classes of literature. The most salient facts concerning copyright as it affects the production of standard and current English and American literature must be summarized in any survey of present-day publishing.

British copyright, American copyright, and international copyright protect property rights in the mass of our current and contemporary literature. The British copyright act of 1911 is the comprehensive copyright code of the British Commonwealth, except the self-governing dominions (Canada, New Zealand, Australia) which have framed their own codes on generally similar lines. It establishes copyright protection of an author's work during his lifetime and for fifty years after his death, although under certain compensatory provisions it permits noncopyright publication twenty-five or thirty years after an author's death. The single requirement imposed is that a work must receive its original publication within the British Commonwealth or must have so-called "simultaneous" publication there not more than fourteen days after its publication in any country that is not a member of the International Copyright Union. One copy of the best edition of every work thus published must be deposited in the British Museum, and failure to do this entails a fine, but no forfeiture of copyright; provision is also made for deposit of copies, under specific conditions, in designated libraries of Scotland, Wales, and Ireland. In actual publishing practice comparatively little attention is paid to the provision for so-called "simultaneous" publication (within fourteen days) of books by English-speaking authors, and many current American books are issued in English editions that do not meet this requirement. Probably, in strict legal interpretation, they do not possess copyright; but, as Stanley Unwin says: "So long as British publishers continue to act (as they almost invariably do) on the assumption that all books in English by living writers are *ipso facto* copyright and the legality is never questioned by anyone else, the works are for all practical purposes 'copyright.'" [2]

International copyright, sometimes simply designated as "the

[2] *The Truth about Publishing*, p. 243.

Berne convention," has existed since 1887 in all countries that are members of the International Copyright Union, and is based on the agreement, or "convention," adopted in 1886 at the organization meeting of the Union at Berne and revised at successive meetings at Berlin in 1908, and at Rome in 1928, and at Brussels in 1949. It automatically ensures throughout the signatory countries the same copyright protection for all works first published in any country that is accorded them in the country of their origin. The United States, Russia, and China are the only countries that are not members of the International Copyright Union, though certain of the South American republics have their own convention and maintain only a partial relationship to the Union.

American copyright is more restrictive and discriminatory in its international aspect than is copyright in other civilized nations. According to the revised code of 1909, to receive book copyright all works except foreign works in foreign languages must be completely manufactured in the United States; notice of copyright date must be printed on the title-page or verso of the publication; and registration must be made at the Copyright Office in Washington by depositing two copies with an affidavit attesting their domestic manufacture. Copyright is valid for twenty-eight years from date of first publication, with privilege of renewal for twenty-eight years longer. The so-called "manufacturing clause," which prevents the free and general protection to works by foreign authors that is accorded in other countries, is one of the requirements that has so far debarred the United States from membership in the International Copyright Union; it has been a constant source of controversy, and has maintained confusion and difficulties in the provision of English books for American readers. A slight modification, enacted by Congress in 1949, permits an "interim copyright" in a book published abroad in the English language; this copyright lasts for five years, and may be extended to the regular term if an edition is produced in the United States before the expiration of the interim copyright. This clearly is not a perfect solution to the problem.

Obviously, only a modest proportion of current English books are assured of a sufficiently wide American market to justify American manufacture. For this reason many English publications are handled by American publishers under various arrangements—by importation, or by binding up the English sheets in America with the American publisher's imprint, or by having the printing done in America from the English plates. Such books, of course, have no legal American copyright and run the risk, if they should prove extremely popular, of being "pirated" by some unscrupulous American publisher. This risk is nowadays comparatively negligible. "None of the many excellent firms of American publishers, whose names are so well known and respected," says Stanley Unwin, "is ever guilty of taking literary property by living authors without making proper arrangements with whoever would be the copyright owner were America a signatory to the Berne convention." There are always a few publishers who will take advantage of the situation, often by promoting spurious reprints of English editions of classics or standard works, in which the original illustrations, unprotected by copyright, have been "lifted" from the genuine editions, or for which the plates of the original edition have been photographed, page for page, to produce a cheap and dishonest reproduction.

The American attitude toward international copyright has had a controlling effect upon the development of American publishing. That development falls into two broad divisions—the preinternational copyright period, or "the years of piracy," from the beginnings of modern American book production to 1891; and the post-international copyright period, from 1891 to the present.

During the first quarter of the nineteenth century, although the foundations of later growth were laid with the establishment of such firms as Harper, Wiley, Appleton, Putnam, and Dodd, in New York, and Little, Brown and Company in Boston, American publishing was confined almost entirely to reprints of English works. In 1820, when Irving and Cooper began their careers, American book production was 70 percent British. Then gradually there came increasing interest in and representation of native authors, and by the mid-century the names that still stand as first fruits of American literature—Emerson, Holmes, Hawthorne, Melville, Mrs. Stowe, Dana, and Channing—were rising upon the horizon. These years and the forty years succeeding were "the years of piracy"—a period of development, but retarded and narrowed by the immense circulation of cheap reprints of English books and by the cutthroat competition of the publishers issuing them. English authors had no rights in the United States and received little, if any, compensation from their American reprints. And native literature had slight encouragement to grow under the handicap of the flood of English reprints issued at lower prices than the copyrighted work of American writers could compete with.

Then in 1891, after thirty years of effort, the first international copyright law was enacted by Congress, and American publishing entered its second period of development. The protection extended to English authors was, however, limited and qualified by the "manufacturing clause," which was continued and reinforced when the copyright law was revised and amended in 1909. This amended measure, known as the Copyright Code, replaced all previous legislation and included in its scope not only literary works but also works of art and music. Requirements for foreign copyright were modified by providing that original works by authors in other than the English language were exempted from the manufacturing clause and could be copyrighted by registration and the deposit of a single copy of the edition of the country of origin. But the discrimination against English authors and various other restrictions made the United States still ineligible for membership in the Berne convention.

Through succeeding years the law, confusing and unsatisfactory, remained unchanged, in spite of continuing efforts for its complete revision or at least for an amendment embodying the "automatic" provisions of the Berne agreement. In 1933 a so-called "short bill" was introduced which authorized adherence of the United States to the Berne agreement, but did not include complete revision of the Copyright Code. In 1935 a bill was introduced covering complete revision. But both measures failed of enactment, and with the advent of the war the subject was shelved. In the postwar world, international protection of the literary property of all countries takes on ever growing importance. The United Nations Educational, Scientific and Cultural Organization (Unesco) in 1947 urged the development of a satisfactory universal system of international copyright and approved preparation of a world copyright charter; so there is every reason to expect that before long the United States—with China and Russia—will take its place among the nations that give full acceptance to international copyright.

Copyright revision affects the interests of many important groups, such as the music publishing trades, the manufacturers of phonograph records, the moving picture industry, the radio broadcasting studios, and the opening field of television, as well as authors, publishers, and the bookmaking industry in general. It also involves provisions that are important to libraries, especially as regards importation of books for library use, and expert knowledge concerning this aspect is essential for all librarians specializing in order and acquisition work. While the whole subject of copyright is complex and highly technical, every competent librarian should have some general acquaintance with the subject and should be able to answer the questions most commonly asked by readers and refer promptly to fuller material. There is a formidable body of copyright literature, most of it submerged in legal phraseology and citations stupefying even to the intelligent layman. Some exceptions, however, should be indicated. Most useful for general, practical, and informational use is Margaret Nicholson's *Manual of Copyright Practice for Writers, Publishers and Agents* (Oxford University Press, 1945): clear, simple, authoritative, and highly readable, it clarifies complex detail, reduces technical material to easily comprehensible language, and answers most of the questions likely to come to the reference desk. *The Copyright Law*, by Richard DeWolf (Bureau of National Affairs, Incorporated, 1942) is expert analytical exposition, comprehensive, thorough, and concise, by a former Assistant Register of Copyrights, for many years on the legal staff of the Copyright Office. International copyright receives masterly inclusive and authoritative presentation by Stephen P. Ladas, in his volume *The International Protection of Literary and Artistic Property* (Macmillan, 1938). These three books should provide the general nonspecialist knowledge of the subject requisite in professional librarianship.

International copyright, even as granted by the act of 1891, had a stimulating effect upon American book production. It encouraged native literature, for it opened a fairer field and greater prospects of reward for American writers. It developed mechanical progress in bookmaking, for it gave more effective control of the book market. It increased the price of books, and it checked and finally exterminated the multitude of cheap paper reprints of current English literature.

From 1891 to 1914 there was a continuing process of adjustment and growth, marked by the increasing supply of American books, the fostering of American writers, and the rise of the best seller. The first monthly list of best sellers was published by the *Bookman* in its first issue, for February, 1895; and a comparison of that list and of the annual list of best sellers recorded for 1945, fifty years later, gives interesting evidence of the change in purpose and spirit in literary art and of the immense increase of public interest in serious reading.[3] All through this period there were improvements in printing and better taste in typography. There was growing specialization and diversity in publishing, an inflowing of European influences enriching the older English and American currents in our literature, and a steady movement toward better book-trade organization, toward trade solidarity and effective, systematized book

[3] Leading best sellers of 1895 included: Du Maurier, *Trilby*; Crawford, *The Ralstons*; Hope, *Prisoner of Zenda*; Maclaren, *Beside the Bonnie Briar Bush*; Caine, *The Manxman*; with very scanty representation of nonfiction. Fiction best sellers in 1945 included: Winsor, *Forever Amber*; Douglas, *The Robe*; Costain, *The Black Rose*; Ullman, *The White Tower*; Lewis, *Cass Timberlane*; Langley, *A Lion Is in the Streets*; Hilton, *So Well Remembered*; Shellabarger, *Captain from Castile*; Graham, *Earth and High Heaven*; and Stone, *Immortal Wife*. Nonfiction included: Pyle, *Brave Men*; Lowell, *Dear Sir*; Mauldin, *Up Front*; Wright, *Black Boy*; Cerf, *Try and Stop Me*; Papashvily, *Anything Can Happen*; *General Marshall's Report*; MacDonald, *The Egg and I*; Thurber, *The Thurber Carnival*; and Bromfield, *Pleasant Valley*.

publicity. In 1914, American book production reached its zenith, with a total publication of more than 12,000 new books—a figure that has not been surpassed for any one of the succeeding years.

During the war years, 1915 to 1918, publishing decreased in volume and changed in character. History increased, personal narratives multiplied, books in naval and military science, on aviation, technology, food values and food resources, all came to the fore. Through the 1920's postwar disillusion, pacifist idealism, caustic social criticism were prevailing influences, in curious contrast to the extravagant optimism of the great prosperity boom which crashed to ruin in 1929. The depression years of the 1930's struck with heaviest impact on America's social consciousness: proletarian fiction reached its peak, problems of labor, of industry, unemployment and relief, crucial issues of social and political reconstruction were constant, as world tensions tightened and the decade moved through clashing opinions and antagonistic principles to the converging conflict between fascist aggression and democratic resistance, and closed as its portents were fulfilled in global war. American publishing reflected these phases, but its activities were unchecked. There was much variation in production and a marked decrease in the yearly output of new books. The low mark was set in 1933, with a total of 8,092 publications; the high mark, for 1940, was 11,328. English book production, until the Second World War, was always larger than that in the United States (16,091 new English books were published in 1938), and so was continental book production, which is increased by a greater proportion of pamphlet publications than is common in England or America.

The Second World War transformed the publishing scene. The unprecedented changes in trade conditions—limitations of production, labor shortage, restrictions of materials, paper rationing, quotas and priorities—brought combinations and mergers among leading firms and built a mass pattern of industrial centralization and control. Public demand for books on a scale never known before opened enormous markets; publishers' and booksellers' stocks were drained; and at the same time, with this enormous expansion of book distribution, the yearly output of new books steadily diminished. In 1941, 11,112 new publications were recorded. There were 9,525 in 1942, with continuing decline to a low of 6,548 in 1945. The first postwar year, 1946, saw the turn of the tide, with a total of 7,735. By 1949, a total of 10,892 was reached, surpassing the 1942 output. In England, the great trade suffered far-spread catastrophe. Six million volumes were destroyed in the great German bombing raid of December 2, 1940; the greater part of Britain's publishing center was laid in ruins; and destruction continued through the next four years. English book production for 1941 was recorded as 7,381, as against 14,904 in 1939; it fell to 6,747 in 1945, and had revived to 11,411 in 1946 and to 13,046 in 1947.

The war years had their own inspiring chapter of book-trade history, in the activities of the Council on Books in Wartime. "Books are weapons in the war of ideas" was its slogan, first suggested by W. W. Norton, rephrased and made famous by President Roosevelt; and this gave the keynote of its purpose. Initiated by a small group of New York publishers in March, 1942, this organization included publishers, booksellers, librarians, writers, and others interested in the effective use of books for public enlightenment and national morale, and was sponsored by the national associations representing those interests. Leading American publishers composed its directorate; contributions from the publishing industry provided operating expenses, and the diverse interests and personalities of the book-trade world were welded into dynamic unity for the common cause. During the four years of its operation the Council produced the "Armed Services Editions" of pocket-size reprints, of which more than 120,000,000 copies (representing some 1,100 titles) were distributed to the armed forces of the United States; supervised the publication for distribution to civilians in liberated countries of more than 3,000,000 books (35 titles in from one to three languages); produced movie shorts and conducted radio broadcasts; issued 58 carefully prepared booklists of "imperative" books on vital war aspects and backgrounds; and in many other activities gave far-reaching manifestation of the power of books to inform, to warn, and to inspire. *A History of the Council on Books in Wartime: 1942-1946* (New York, 1946; distribution through R. R. Bowker Company) is the short, official biography of this enterprise: a compact record, modest and impersonal, of permanent significance and value. Difficulties as well as achievements are here indicated with frankness and many interesting, little-known details; and appended are lists of the books dramatized in radio programs, of the books published (in English, French, German, and Italian) in the "Overseas Editions," and of the books published in the "Armed Services Editions." John Jamieson, in *Books for the Army: the Army Library Service in the Second World War* (New York, Columbia University Press, 1950) surveys the total picture of book distribution to servicemen during the war and deals with the censorship problem in book selection. He tells of the vast number of books, hard-bound as well as paper-bound, those acquired through purchase and donation as well as those specially manufactured for the armed services, which were made available under the general supervision of the Army Library Service.

The list of leading American publishers still includes those firms whose names are part of American book history—Harper; Houghton; Wiley; Little, Brown; Scribner; Putnam; Macmillan; Appleton; Dodd, Mead; Holt, and many others. With them stand notable firms of later growth—Doubleday; Knopf; Harcourt; Simon and Schuster; Viking Press; Random House; John Day Company, and their fellows; and a continuing line of more recent firms, among them Duell, Sloan and Pearce; Creative Age Press; New Directions; William Sloane Associates; and Edwards Brothers, specialists in litho-printing of scientific, technical, and bibliographical works and the great "Bach Gesellschaft." Vital currents of European culture, doomed to extinction under Nazi oppression, found outlets in the United States, with an inflow of refugee writers and publishers, and the establishment of such firms as J. J. Augustin, Roy Publishers, Pantheon Books, and many others.

In spite of the stress of the depression years there has been no serious failure in the publishing world since the turn of the century, although certain well-known firms have consolidated with others and have passed out of independent existence. More and more, publishing activities are centralized in New York City—as they are in London for England, and in Paris for France; but the historic New England houses and the old established middle western firms still flourish, and a continuing activity in modest but stable and useful publishing goes on elsewhere throughout the country.

Specialized publishing has greatly increased, notably in the fields of technology and business. Both scholarly research and creative literature are stimulated by an ever growing number of fellowships, subsidies, and awards, designed to encourage authors of ability and to provide for specific pieces of research. Indeed, publishing receives its own individual badge of merit in the Carey-Thomas Award, founded by Frederic G. Melcher in 1943, which commemorates the names of two great early American publishers, Mathew Carey and Isaiah Thomas, and is presented to a firm chosen by a competent jury as having produced the year's best example of "creative publishing."

The rise of the university presses is one of the most significant developments in American publishing history. The University of Chicago Press was among the first of these, founded in 1891, in which year it issued two books and a few pamphlets. When its fiftieth anniversary was celebrated its output had increased to about fifty publications a year and it was issuing eighteen scholarly journals. Many other university presses parallel this development, Columbia leading in the number of volumes published annually. In 1949, 673 books were published by thirty American university presses. The Association of American University Presses, organized in 1937, had in 1949 a membership of thirty-five presses. In 1949 it published a comprehensive and valuable *Report on American University Presses*, by Chester Kerr (summarized in *Saturday Review of Literature* annual university press number, for May 14, 1949), describing the organization and personnel of a body which is constantly increasing the store of materials of knowledge and—with a background of little more than half a century—emulating the work done through four centuries by the great university presses of England.

Just as English literature gave pattern and stimulus to the development of American literature, so American publishing from its beginnings has been in constant and close relationship with English book production. Even in the immense extension and diversification of book use today, the work of American and English writers makes the widest appeal to the American reading public and constitutes the greater part of the average American library collection; and the leading American publishers, in principles and practice, are intimately allied with the traditions and methods of English publishers.

Familiarity with English publishing backgrounds is, therefore, almost as important in book selection for American libraries as is knowledge of American publishers. Every worker with books should have a sense of personal acquaintance with the great dynasties in English publishing—such as Longmans, with its illustrious record of more than two centuries of honorable association with the makers of English literature; Murray, so intimately linked with memories of Byron, Scott, and Moore; Blackwood, foster-father of nineteenth-century Scottish writers; Chambers, the first great publisher of cheap books, whose life purpose was "the production of literature for the people"; Chapman and Hall, original publishers of Dickens and permanently associated with the best and most varied editions of his work; Macmillan, whose imprint marks a great body of Victorian literature, from Tennyson, Matthew Arnold, and Lewis Carroll to Hewlett, Marion Crawford, and Kipling—and should know the fascinating history and immense and varied range of activities of the Oxford and Cambridge university presses.

Such a familiarity in itself imparts a liberal education in English literature and English history. For the history of the publishing houses of any country is inextricably interwoven with the history of that country's literature, which in its turn mirrors the change and progression of human thought and national experience. Publishing also maintains a hereditary character of its own. In the American annals we may trace leading firms back through more than a century; and in England we find still active and flourishing the houses whose family history links to the first publication of *Robinson Crusoe* in 1719, and to the first appearance of the anonymous "Waverley Novels." "The story of one firm leads to another in all bookselling and publishing annals," says Mumby; "some of their histories are like the palimpsests of ancient scribes or the super-imposed paintings of the old masters." The historic publishing houses witness not only to the continuing importance and stability of "the great trade," but they also stand "for family tradition, for ideals of public usefulness and assistance to the cause of literature and science, handed on from generation to generation."

In any study of American publishers, the *Publishers' Trade List Annual* is an indispensable aid. For here the host of present publishers, large and small, old and new, general, special, and infinitely various, may be surveyed in ordered sequence and their own inventories of their product may be analyzed and compared. Besides the great general firms—Scribner, Harper, Doubleday, Dutton, Houghton, and many more—whose close-packed lists record the sweep of literature from past to present, there are the many special publishers who represent every branch of knowledge, craftsmanship, or speculative philosophy, and every variety of curious out-of-the-way information. There are publishers identified with books on sport; those who devote themselves to the literature of gardening, or poultry-keeping, or metal craft, or tea and coffee; those who are mediums for dissemination of every religious belief or esoteric way of thought. For English publishers, the *Reference Catalogue of Current Literature* supplied a similar invaluable repository until 1936. Then, as previously noted,[4] this monumental aid was remade, with "trade lists" omitted, in comprehensive one-alphabet index form akin to that of the *United States Catalog* period-volumes. It may be hoped that in the future a return to the earlier pattern may be practicable in a companion volume, thus providing double sources of essential book information, as does American trade bibliography.

Continental publishing requires minor consideration in ordinary selection for American libraries. Most continental books (French,

[4] See above, pp. 84-85.

Italian, Spanish, and many others) are published unbound, in sewed paper covers, and for library use must be bound (either abroad, by special instructions, or after importation) before they are placed on library shelves. Selection for extended foreign-language collections requires many special aids and expert proficiency. In selection of simpler current foreign literature for racial groups in a community the various foreign book lists prepared for this purpose and published by the American Library Association are widely useful; and in a wider general selection, suggestion and guidance are offered by the bibliographical quarterly, *Books Abroad*.

The close relationship between English and American publishing has established mutual connections between many of the leading houses. Certain American firms are agents and distributors for certain English firms, and vice versa. Other firms maintain both American and English houses. Others have American or English branches, subsidiary to the main establishment. Others, again, distribute their product through a number of different agents. The English and American Macmillans, for example, are independent firms in a close union that was originally a branch relationship. There is an American branch of Oxford University Press, while the publications of the Cambridge University Press, long handled by the Macmillan New York office, have been distributed by its own New York office since June, 1949. Scribner carries the Chapman and Hall editions of Dickens and many Murray publications. Lippincott has long handled some of Chambers' leading reference works, although in 1945 the *Lippincott Gazetteer* (long out of print and originally a Chambers publication) was taken over by Columbia University Press, to be made the basis of a completely new edition to be called the *Columbia-Lippincott Gazetteer of the World*. Dutton is American agent for Dent and distributor of "Everyman's Library" and the "Temple Editions," as Harcourt has been for the historic "Bohn Libraries." Many American houses—among them Putnam, Scribner, Sheed and Ward, Doubleday, Ginn, and Lippincott—have their own London offices or separate English companies. This network of relationship must be learned, chiefly through experience, by every book-man proficient in selection of current literature, whether for commercial or library use.

Most of the important current English books appear in the American book market, either in copyrighted American editions or under some of the noncopyright arrangements that have already been mentioned. Often the original English editions are cheaper or otherwise more satisfactory than are American editions (the English edition of Morley's *Recollections*, for example, contains the unabridged index), and many American libraries in their current book selection give particular attention to comparison and checking of English publishers' lists and purchase freely in the English market, under the clause in the American copyright law that permits libraries to import English books in the original edition for institutional use.

There is, however, a pitfall for the unwary in such selection; for it is a common publishing practice to bring out books in America under titles different from those in which the books appear in England. This changing of titles sometimes occurs in either country when an older book is reissued. It often prevails when American books are published in England—Nathaniel Hawthorne's *Marble Faun*, for example, has long appeared as *Transformation* in its English editions; Ernest Hemingway's *The Sun Also Rises* was published in England as *Fiesta*, and Robert Nathan's *Jonah* as *The Son of Amittai*. In American editions of current books by English writers these changes are legion. Richard Hughes' brilliant fantasy-satire of childhood, *High Wind in Jamaica*, changed its title to *The Innocent Voyage* when published in the United States and then changed back to the English title in a later edition. Nearly all the novels of G. B. Stern lost their original titles in the American editions: *Tents of Israel* became *The Matriarch*, *Children of No Man's Land* was turned into *Debatable Ground*, *Larry Munro* into *The China Shop*, and *Little Red Horses* into *The Rueful Mating*. Dorothy Sayers' *Suspicious Characters* was *Five Red Herrings* (a much better title) in the English edition; Thomas Burke's *More Limehouse Nights* has *Whispering Windows* as its original title. *Van*

Loon's Geography was published in England as *The Home of Mankind;* the first part of Thomas Mann's biblical epic appeared in England as *The Tales of Jacob* and in the United States as *Joseph and His Brothers*. Helen McInnes' novel, entitled in the United States *While We Still Live*, was *The Unconquerable* in England; the English novel by L. P. Hartley, *The Shrimp and the Anemone*, experienced strange transformation to *The West Window* in the American edition, while for America Francis Williams' *Socialist Britain* replaced the blind English title, *Triple Challenge*. In the United States there have been many recommendations that attention be called in a conspicuous manner to the former title of a book—preferably on the copyright page, on the jacket, and in the publishers' catalogues. Many publishers have adopted these recommendations into their practice, but the changes still prevail and the examples mentioned might be indefinitely extended. They indicate one of the many opportunities that book selection offers for expert detective work.

Wide knowledge of individual publishers—their standing, standards, and characteristics, their "lines," and special interests—is indispensable. Purchase of a given book is often finally decided by the publisher's imprint. Tributes and testimonials in advertising circulars lose their effect when the work they celebrate is seen as the product of some obscure or inferior firm, or of a concern known to publish only at the author's expense.

Publishers may be divided roughly into two broad classes, general and special publishers. Within these classes they fall into different ranks of importance, according to the character and quality of their publications. General firms are those that publish books in many different fields of literature, and here are found most of the largest and best-known houses; Harper, Macmillan, Dutton, Scribner, Houghton Mifflin, are examples. Special firms center on a single branch of knowledge or on several related subjects or are devoted to a particular channel of interest. Medicine, law, religion, technology, education, children's literature, for example, are important special fields of publishing, with each of which many firms have long been identified (such as Wiley for technology, Ginn for education,

Saunders for medicine). Every cult, every faith, every social and political creed, has its own particular publishing medium. Every craft, vocation, diversion, business activity, and other human interest seem to be represented by a special publisher. But nearly all the leading general publishers have their specialties also—Lippincott with its medical and scientific departments, Bobbs-Merrill and Little, Brown with their law departments, and many others—and these rank in importance with the foremost special firms; while in religion, education, children's literature, and many other subjects much of the finest literature in existence comes from the great general publishing houses.

Among general publishers there are a few known as "vanity publishers" or "authors' publishers," because they issue only books for which the author pays cost of publication. Sometimes work of real significance, particularly poetry, first makes its appearance through some such "private" publication, but as a general rule the product of these firms, no matter how disguised by enthusiastic publicity, bears the stamp of nonentity, and finds its way to library shelves only "with the compliments of the author." The publisher's imprint usually tells what the experienced librarian, bookseller, or reviewer first needs to know about the book. Publishers of assured standing also frequently "sell their imprint," or publish at an author's expense books they would not accept for publication otherwise. Some famous and successful books have appeared in this way. The practice is justified when it makes possible publication of important work that does not promise a sale sufficient to cover production costs. But its indiscriminate exercise is open to criticism, for it implies sponsorship of a book based on confidence in its merit that does not, in fact, exist.

Subscription book publishers are a class by themselves; their works are not handled through the book trade nor recorded in the trade lists. There are many of them and they carry on immense and varied activities, either as independent companies or as subscription departments of established publishing firms, by selling methods based primarily on extensive advertising and direct personal solicitation by canvassing agents or by mail. Leading encyclopedias, many important reference works, publications of artistic or scholarly quality, and genuine limited editions of works by well-known authors are sold by subscription (the monumental *Dictionary of American Biography* is an example); these represent a type of publication that probably could not have been financed by any other method. But the system is also used for much unscrupulous promotion of works of questionable value. Often such publications represent a cheap and pretentious rehashing of old reference material, sold at exorbitant prices, or they may be ready-made "aids to culture" for the self-delusion of adult infants, or synthetic "de luxe" productions designed to awe and entrance the ignorant but aspiring bookbuyer. As a general rule, subscription publications are of minor importance in current book selection, and in dealing with them librarians should be guided by the *Subscription Books Bulletin*, published quarterly by the American Library Association, which analyzes, compares, and appraises publications in this field.

Facts that it is desirable to know about individual publishers may be summarized as follows:

Location.—For established and well-known firms this should be thoroughly familiar. Obscure firms that may be identified with useful local history material, and small firms that are printers rather than publishers, are often so denoted by their location.

History.—There should be acquaintance with the historic background of the older houses; familiarity with important business changes (such as the merging of the Doran firm with Doubleday, of Appleton with Century and, subsequently, of Appleton-Century with Crofts, of Stokes with Lippincott, or the taking over of Atlantic Press books by Little, Brown); and recognition of newcomers.

Publishers' devices.—While not important in book selection, there is enjoyment and edification in enlarging acquaintance with the devices that are now so commonly used to convey publishing identity. They derive from the "colophon," or inscription with which the scribe put the "finishing touch" to his illuminated manuscript, and from the famous "printers' marks" of the early printers.

From the famous devices of Aldus and Caxton to those designed by Rockwell Kent for Viking Press and Random House, they unfold one of the most delightful chapters of book history. Every worker with books should know these emblems, and appreciate the significance of the Longmans black swan (now two hundred years old), of the Harper "ice cream cone," of the Holt owl, of the Knopf borzoi—of the varied symbolism and the artistic, historic, and literary interest of these printers' marks of ancient and modern lineage.

Standards—literary, artistic, and mechanical.—Many publishers' imprints convey reasonable assurance of high standards—of books chosen because they are believed to possess literary excellence or sound scholarship, of bookmaking that is artistic in effect and superior in workmanship. Others are associated with the commercial exploitation of the trivial or the sensational. Others, again, imply good artistic and mechanical workmanship and exotic literary expression. Others convey mediocrity with strong popular appeal.

Special interests.—Not only the product of special publishers, but the important departments and special lines developed by the larger general firms must be familiar—Appleton's Spanish educational department, with its old-established Latin-American relationships, Scribner's rich line of importations, the religious and educational interests of Macmillan and Longmans, and an infinite range of similar diversities existing in unity.

Series and editions.—It should become automatic to associate Putnam with the "Heroes of the Nations" series, Appleton with the "Great Commanders," to turn to Houghton for the "Cambridge editions," to Longmans for the "Living Thoughts Library," or to Scribner for the Gadshill edition of Dickens; to relate well-known series, standard editions, important reference works, to the publishers who produce or distribute them.

Author association.—In spite of the constant shifting and eddying of authors in the stream of publishing, there are many whose books are consistently associated with individual firms. Putnam, as Washington Irving's lifetime publisher, still has the authorized editions of Irving's works. The relationship of Houghton to Hawthorne and

Holmes, of Little, Brown to Parkman, of Harper to Mark Twain, is part of publishing history; and many later writers have had similar relationships—such as that of Cabell to McBride, Bernard Shaw to Brentano's (later transferred to Dodd, Mead), Conrad and Kipling to Doubleday, Elizabeth Madox Roberts to Viking Press, Robert Frost to Holt, and Pearl Buck to John Day Company. Quick mental association of authors with their publishers reveals the virtuoso in book selection.

Like mankind, even the best publishers are not perfect. And always in the practice of book selection there must be an awareness of their shortcomings. The changing of titles, already mentioned, is one of their most common sins—most indefensible when adopted, as it often is, to make an old book appear as new; when such a book is advertised as a new work a direct fraud is perpetrated upon the public. There is a similar imposition in bringing out older books (or early works by well-known writers) without indication of their former publication. The omission of indexes has been mentioned: a crime often committed by publishers of the first rank. Advertising that misleads and exaggerates is a common but, after all, a minor misdemeanor, for intelligence should be deaf to the blare of publicity. "Fake" authorship, in which the original and defunct creator of a popular sequence is succeeded by a "ghost" of unrevealed identity who continues the production of sequels, is practiced in a few well-known examples, but is not common.

All this general and particular knowledge of publishers and their product is a part of what may be called "book-trade familiarity." Librarians need to have much of the trade knowledge of the good bookseller if they are to practice book selection successfully. They must know, as he does, the standing and standards of all major and many minor publishing houses, the series and editions identified with particular publishers, the difference between authorized and unauthorized editions, the comparative merits of various reprints of famous works, and the physical and mechanical characteristics of satisfactory bookmaking. In all selection of standards and classics of literature such knowledge as this is indispensable. Indeed, there can be no really satisfactory choice or purchase of current books, even for a small collection, without some background of this "book-trade familiarity." The most effective means to its development is twofold: frequent and friendly visiting of bookstores, to browse, to examine, and to compare; and regular, thorough reading of the *Publishers' Weekly*.

BOOKMAKING AND BOOKMAKERS

This selected list will help students to pursue further the study of the book in its physical aspect and to enlarge their acquaintance with "the great trade."

Bookmaking, Historic and Modern

Aldis, H. G. The Printed Book. Revised and brought up to date by John Carter and E. A. Crutchley. New York, The Macmillan Co., 1941.

First published in 1916 as one of the little "Cambridge Manuals"; of standard value and continuing usefulness as a compact, informative, and interesting account of printing, of typographic art, of illustrating and binding; with a final chapter on the care and treatment of books.

Esdaile, Arundel. A Students' Manual of Bibliography. London, Allen & Unwin, for the Library Association, 1931.

A well-known English work, clear, simple, succinct, not too popularized. The description of collation and the chapter on bibliography are particularly good.

Lehmann-Haupt, Hellmut. One Hundred Books about Bookmaking: a guide to the study and appreciation of printing. New York, Columbia University Press, 1949.

Third edition of the little volume, *Fifty Books about Bookmaking*, an annotated list of books chosen for an exhibition representative of the various branches of book art, published by Columbia University Press in 1933. A second edition, *Seventy Books about Bookmaking*, appeared in 1941. Includes works on book origins, writing and lettering, printing history, printing practice, printing types and decorations, illustration, bookbinding and papermaking, bookmaking periodicals. The annotations are clear, authoritative, and informing to any student. A brief introduction indicates the critical and aesthetic values that are established by a background knowledge of the graphic arts: "I am not suggesting that every printer should be a librarian (incidentally, however, I do believe that every librarian should be a bit of a printer)." The appended "A Bibliographical Note about the First Edition of This Checklist" is a beautiful example of bibliographical analysis.

McKerrow, R. B. An Introduction to Bibliography for Literary Students. New York, Oxford University Press, 1927.
Authoritative, detailed, extremely valuable analysis of the mechanical side of book production, applied to the methods that prevailed in England up to about the year 1800. Attention is centered on the Shakespearean period; but the volume gives a clear and fundamental understanding of the making of the printed book. It treats of composition, imposition, the technique of printing, signature, title-page, colophon, paper, decoration, and many other details. A brief general sketch of the rise and spread of printing is given in the appendix. Designed especially for students of literature as an aid in tracing the "bibliographical evidence" that is often so important in scholarly textual criticism of early works; but of value and interest to every student of book history.

McMurtrie, Douglas C. The Book: the story of printing and bookmaking. 3d revised ed. New York, Oxford University Press, 1943.
A rewriting of McMurtrie's earlier volume, *The Golden Book: the story of fine books and bookmaking—past and present*, published in 1927 (Chicago, Pascal Covici),[5] of which four editions appeared in eight years. The first edition of the work under its present title appeared in 1937; and the present volume is recorded in the copyright entry as "7th edition as successor to four editions of *The Golden Book*." Revision has been comprehensive and thorough; in the main the original outline has been followed, but previous omissions and inadequacies have been rectified; much important material is added; the fine illustrations and reproductions are augmented, and the result is a volume indispensable to library students, interesting and delightful to the general reader in its simplicity, conciseness and readability. An immense field is covered, beginning with primitive human records and origins of the alphabet, including origins, production, and use of paper; the manuscript age; invention and development of printing; great names in early printing, with an admirable chapter on printers' marks; type design, book illustration, and binding; the beginning and spread of printing in America; the rise of modern typography, modern book illustration, present processes of bookmaking; and the art and ideals of bookmaking today. *The*

---

[5] See *Living with Books*, 1st ed., p. 192.

Golden Book has 406 pages; *The Book* contains 674, with an authoritative 42-page classed list of bibliographies. More solid, more ample in detail and richer in illustrations, it supersedes *The Golden Book* in completeness and authority, but has lost some of the spontaneous vividness and idealism of expression that distinguished the earlier volume.

Orcutt, W. D. In Quest of the Perfect Book: reminiscences and reflections of a bookman. Boston, Little, Brown & Company, 1926.

Seven chapters in which Mr. Orcutt (for many years head of the University Press at Cambridge, Massachusetts) describes his experiences and work "in quest of the perfect book." These include study in famous libraries, study of manuscripts and the work of the early printers, acquaintance with scholars and with printers like Cobden-Sanderson, and his own experiments and designs in type fonts and bookmaking. There are many beautiful illustrations and reproductions of pages from famous books, and of printers' devices.

Orcutt, W. D. The Kingdom of Books. Boston, Little, Brown & Company, 1927.

Succeeds and supplements *In Quest of the Perfect Book*, centering more exclusively on printing and design in the making and clothing of the book. The seven chapters deal with famous early printers (Aldus, the Etiennes, the Plantins, the Elzevirs, and John Baskerville), the renaissance of printing through William Morris and Cobden-Sanderson, famous examples of bookmaking and binding, and the Plantin Museum in Antwerp, as a shrine of early printing history.

Orcutt, W. D. Master Makers of the Book. New York, Doubleday, 1928.

A consecutive story of the making of the book from a century before the invention of printing through the era of the Doves Press, featuring the lives and achievements of the great printers.

Updike, D. B. Printing Types, Their History, Forms and Use. 2d ed. 2 volumes. Cambridge, Harvard University Press, 1937.

A monumental work, the accepted authority in its field, by the master-printer, founder and head of the Merrymount Press, who was a pioneer in the renaissance of the printing art in America. It is both a work of book history for the booklover and a foundation source and manual for the technical student of printing. With more than 300 beautiful illustrations, Mr. Updike sets forth the history of printing types in different countries, analyzing the characteristics that have kept different varieties alive through the centuries, and deducing principles for the perfecting of modern typography. The most beautiful modern type of today is based upon the famous examples of the early great masters: Jenson, the world's first great type designer, whose work in fifteenth-century Italy still lives in the Jenson type of today; Geoffry Tory and Claude Garamond, of sixteenth-century France, whose names carry on in modern typography; John Baskerville and William Caslon, whose type still is used both for model and without variation; and many more great artists and designers of the printer's font whose work has influenced the most beautiful printing of today.

Van Hoesen, H. B., and F. K. Walter. Bibliography, Practical, Enumerative, Historical: an introductory manual. New York, Charles Scribner's Sons, 1928.

Primarily a comprehensive survey and record of general bibliography and of subject bibliography in varied fields; but devotes three chapters to book history, covering History of Writing, History of Printing, and Book-Decoration, Bookselling and Publishing, in compact, comprehensive, and authoritative summary. The detailed bibliographical lists guide to an immense amount of material, from general and special bibliographical aids, reference books, and serial publications, to aids important in selection of history, biography, science, and many other classes of literature. Of great value to all librarians and library students. Preparation of a revised edition was requested by the Reference Librarians' Section of the American Library Association in 1946.

The Great Trade: Publishing and Bookselling

Boynton, H. W. Annals of American Bookselling, 1638–1850. New York, John Wiley & Sons, Inc., 1932.

Published in commemoration of the 125th anniversary of the founding of the Wiley publishing house, this is not a history of the Wiley firm, but an excellent survey of the first two centuries of the American book trade. Famous figures of American book history—John Dunton, the English bookseller who toured the colonies in 1705; William Bradford and Benjamin Franklin, the printers; Isaiah Thomas and Mathew Carey, the first important names in American publishing; and many others—move through its pages. The Wiley firm was established, by Charles Wiley, as a bookstore in 1807; later it became the publisher of Fenimore Cooper, and as Wiley & Putnam it was a precursor of the Putnam publishing house. Its history is linked with that of the historic houses of Harper, Putnam, Appleton, and Little, Brown, and with the development of modern American book production.

Burlingame, Roger. Of Making Many Books: a hundred years of reading, writing and publishing. New York, Charles Scribner's Sons, 1946.

By the son of E. L. Burlingame (who became editor of *Scribner's Magazine* in 1887) and himself on the Scribner editorial staff from 1914 to 1926, this is less formal history of the Scribner firm than a delightful, richly informative study of the relationship between publishers and authors through a hundred years. Founded as Baker & Scribner in 1846, the firm changed its name to Charles Scribner in 1851, and after two minor changes became Charles Scribner's Sons in 1891. Five Scribners (three Charles Scribners) have been president, with Charles Scribner IV now in the direct succession. Throughout its history virtually every letter, contract, and communication which has come to the firm has been meticulously preserved, to be organized and listed in 1943, thus producing probably the most complete documentary record of a long publishing history that is to be found in this country. The work and personalities of Scribner authors notable in every field of literature are here vividly and intimately depicted, and illuminating sidelights bring out varied human contacts between writers and editors, and reveal the joys and tribulations of publishing.

Cheney, O. H. Economic Survey of the Book Industry, 1930–1931. New York, National Association of Book Publishers, 1931; reprinted with statistical report of the American Book Publishers' Council, 1947–1948. New York, R. R. Bowker Co., 1948.

The findings of an exhaustive survey of the book trade. Not a history, but a searching inquiry into the economic structure of the industry; a book which stands unsuperseded in its completeness.

Dent, J. M. Memoirs of J. M. Dent, 1849–1926; with some additions by Hugh R. Dent. New York, E. P. Dutton & Company, 1928.

Simple, informal reminiscences not originally intended for publication but after Mr. Dent's death published as a memorial, with additional notes by his son. Joseph Dent as a publisher revolutionized the reprinting of standard literature by making new editions not only cheap but beautiful. He conceived and produced the "Everyman Library," the "Temple Classics," the "Temple Shakespeare," and many other publications, in a particular fashion of printing, illustrating, and designing that gave new impetus to artistic bookmaking and immensely increased the store of literature available to the great mass of readers. These memoirs are a simple, friendly, substantial record of indomitable purpose and fine achievement—entirely Victorian in their personal reticence and unawareness of modern thought, but permeated with a lifetime love of English literature and the craft of books.

Ernst, M. L., and William Seagle. To the Pure: a study of obscenity and the censor. New York, The Viking Press, 1928.
This is a summary and survey of the official censorship of literature and its development, and a commentary on the legal definitions of obscenity; the first comprehensive presentation and analysis of the subject for the general reader. It is interesting and valuable and should be read by all librarians, booksellers, and others who work with books. The authors, who are both New York lawyers, are opposed to censorship of any kind; their attitude is logical and deserves consideration, but their presentation of the subject displays undue personal bias, and would have been more effective if written with greater restraint. The book is evidently based on extensive study, and has a full and varied bibliography. It centers particularly on censorship as practiced and legally established in England and the United States, though it notes development and present practice on the continent.

Ernst, M. L., and Alexander Lindey. The Censor Marches On: recent milestones in the administration of the obscenity law in the United States. New York, Doubleday, 1940.
Supplements and continues consideration of the subject by more recent history of efforts toward censorship of literature, movies, radio, and birth control information. Important court decisions are cited, and the record shows definite progress in liberalism, freedom, and common sense. Unflagging effort is urged to defeat censorial fanaticism; and in conclusion a twelve-point legislative program is outlined which, it is believed, "is moderate enough to warrant hope of success, and yet sufficiently forward-looking to yield real gains."

Harper, J. H. The House of Harper: a century of publishing in Franklin Square. New York, Harper & Brothers, 1912.
Written in preparation for the centenary of the firm, in 1917; based on family records and personal recollections and experiences, and full of vivid glimpses of famous writers and interesting incidents in nineteenth-century publishing history. The part played by the Harper firm through many years in opposition to the enactment of an international copyright law is very lightly touched upon.

Lehmann-Haupt, Hellmut. The Book in America: a history of the making, the selling, and the collecting of books in the United States. In collaboration with Ruth Shepard Granniss, The Grolier Club; and

Lawrence C. Wroth, John Carter Brown Library. New York, R. R. Bowker Co., 1939.

The most comprehensive and important work dealing with the whole field of bookmaking, publishing, book trade, and book collecting in the United States. Organized chiefly in chronological divisions, running from the colonial period to the present. Part II, devoted to book production and distribution from 1860 to the present day, is especially valuable for information nowhere else compactly available on older and present publishing firms, on the development of printing, and on trade conditions. Part III covers the growth of libraries in the United States, with description of famous collections. Indispensable to library students and to librarians.

Miller, William. The Book Industry. New York, Columbia University Press, 1949. A report of the Public Library Inquiry.

Covers all facets of the trade: editorial policy, manufacturing, and marketing; and contains a chapter on trade publishing and public libraries. It is considered to be the first over-all view of the industry since the Cheney survey.

Morgan, Charles. The House of Macmillan (1843–1943). New York, The Macmillan Co., 1944.

Unusual in literary charm is this collective portrait of "Macmillan's," by a well-known English novelist, essayist, and critic. His concern is almost wholly with the London house and the two brothers who founded it, for the story of the American house, in commemoration of its half-century in 1946, is to be told separately, by an American author. From the small London bookshop, opened in November, 1843, by Daniel and Alexander Macmillan, rose the broadminded, far-sighted publishing house identified with the great names of the nineteenth century and after, that set in motion new currents of thought and opened fresh vistas of beauty. Essentially, this small volume is a vivid panoramic portrayal of men and books that left their stamp on the Victorian and post-Victorian age, from Charles Kingsley, Matthew Arnold, and Lewis Carroll, to James Bryce, Thomas Hardy, Maurice Hewlett, and Hugh Walpole.

Mumby, F. A. Publishing and Bookselling: a history from the earliest times to the present day. New and revised ed. New York, R. R. Bowker Co., 1949.

This is the postwar revision of Mumby's *Romance of Bookselling*, first published in 1910 and revised in 1930. It is the most comprehensive and complete work on its subject for the general reader, and has absorbing interest and continuing value for everyone connected with the book trade or with libraries. The first chapter deals with the beginnings of the book trade, in Greece and Rome; the remainder of the volume is devoted entirely to printing, publishing, and bookselling in England, from medieval times to the present. New chapters linked with the main text record the Battle of the Books in the German bombing attacks on London and the destruction and reconstruction that marked epochal years. A storehouse of information concerning older and present-day English publishers, remarkable for its detail and for the deft interweaving of innumerable facts and names into a smooth and interesting narrative. The appended forty-two-page bibliography, by W. H. Peet, is a valuable reference aid.

Swinnerton, Frank. Authors and the Book Trade; with notes by Frederic Melcher. New York, Alfred A Knopf, Inc., 1932.

Mr. Swinnerton says that this is "a little book of comment upon the publishing trade and its allied interests," and that its justification is "that I have been in the publishing trade since I was fourteen, that I was a publishers' reader from 1910 until the end of 1925, that I have written twenty books, and that from 1910 until the present day I have been a reviewer. The opinions expressed here may all of them be wrong; but they are based upon experience." Brief, vivacious, and original in flavor, the little book casts light upon the relations of authors to publishing, the vicissitudes of bookselling, the defects and qualities of reviewers, and the vagaries of the reading public. Footnotes by Frederic Melcher, editor of the *Publishers' Weekly*, point out differences between English and American practice.

Unwin, Stanley. The Truth about Publishing. London, Allen & Unwin, 1946. (Distributed by R. R. Bowker Co.)

A new edition of the most comprehensive, compact, and thoroughly competent book on modern publishing, by the head of George Allen & Unwin, Ltd. In spite of technical and business detail, it is written smoothly with a pleasant flavor of good literary taste. It is an exposition of modern book production—the processes and methods of the publishing business in its relations with authors, with booksellers, and with the public. Begins with the arrival of manuscripts in the publishers' office, and follows through agreements with authors, copyright conditions, processes of printing, format, illustration, binding, and making of jackets, to the actual selling, with the ever growing requirements of advertising, blurbs, posters, and publicity campaigns. All the problems and activities of a complex organization that is at once commercial, industrial, and professional are clearly and concisely presented. Published in an American edition in 1927, it has been generally revised, but without reference to abnormal war conditions.

Unesco Copyright Bulletin, Vol. II (1949), No. 2–3: Special number devoted to the study of comparative copyright law and the meeting of the Committee of Experts. (The *Bulletin* is bilingual and published quarterly.)

Waugh, Arthur. A Century of Publishing: being a history of the house of Chapman & Hall, from 1830 to 1930. London, Chapman & Hall, 1930.

A centenary memorial of a famous London publishing house—the original publishers of Dickens, Carlyle, Trollope, and George Meredith, and founder, in 1865, under Anthony Trollope's editorship, of the *Fortnightly Review*, which still ranks among leading English periodicals. George Meredith was for thirty years the firm's "reader" and literary advisor. Not merely a history of the firm, but an interesting and valuable contribution to publishing history as a record of evolution in English book-trade practice and conditions.

11. Editions, Series, Translations

> I had long felt that in England we had no library of classical literature, like the French Bibliotheque nationale or the great Reclam collection produced in Leipzig, of which you could buy a volume for a few pence. It is true we had the monumental collection of Bohn, but the six hundred odd volumes included many heavy and dull translations from the classics and were not representative of the world's literature of these times. Again, none of these volumes appealed to every kind of reader; the worker, the student, the cultured man, the child, the woman. I thought I could plan such a series, dividing it into sections, like History, Fiction, Biography, etc. . . . My idea was to publish a volume of five hundred pages for one shilling. The idea enthralled me.
>
> J. M. Dent: *Memoirs*

> There are no more reliable judges of the values of books than the best translations, since they only become so by reason of degree of skill, experience, insight, and knowledge which are akin to the highest attainable. . . . If, therefore, a reader discovers that a translator whom he sees to be first-rate has been at work on some book unfamiliar to the reader, he can safely guess that he is not only coming across more translation which is worth attention, but also that the original is a book far beyond average value. Here, librarians can be of the greatest assistance.
>
> E. Stuart Bates: *Modern Translation*

WE COME NOW to chart a course through flood waters. The great books of the past that are classics today; the books that live and multiply themselves in contemporary literature by their appeal to successive generations of readers; the current books that enlarge their market by changing their clothes; the books that may be fitted and refitted and re-refitted to different patterns of purpose or form—these make the infinite range and diversity of editions, reprints, series, "libraries," and "sets" that challenge even the expert in book selection.

Nothing is more bewildering to the inexperienced worker with books than to be confronted with the responsibility of choice among the many editions of a famous classic. Consider the number and variety of editions of Shakespeare that fill sixteen solid columns in the 1928 volume of the *United States Catalog,* and six columns in the five-year volume of the *Cumulative Book Index, 1938-42*. How many should be found in a moderate-sized public library, or in a high school library, or in a small branch of a large library system? What individual editions will best meet the particular requirements of the mature student; the cultivated general reader; the undeveloped or adolescent mind? And, further, what editions mean economy in purchase, so that the supply available for different kinds of readers may be as representative as possible? What editions of Dickens are best suited for the wear and tear of general circulation? Which are the most pleasing for the booklover's own library? In the continuous process of replacement of books that hold their readers through the years—*Les Miserables, The Three Musketeers, Lavengro,* Dana's *Two Years before the Mast*—which editions offer satisfactory values to the reader at the least cost to the library?

Such questions as these must be continually answered. To answer them requires familiarity with books in the textual and physical aspects that have already been broadly surveyed. It requires recognition of implications latent in different publishing imprints. It requires observation, comparison, and contrast of the books themselves, and constant study of publishers' catalogues. Even with the aid and suggestion to be found in the standard guides—the selected editions listed in the *A.L.A. Catalog* and the *Standard Catalog,* and recorded in alternate current issues of the *Booklist,* in the Orton *Catalog of Reprints in Series,* with its successive editions and supplements (H. W. Wilson Company), and the great amount of information given in the *Bookman's Manual*—this specific personal knowledge is indispensable in the building up of a worthy and representative library collection.

The Choice of Editions, by Pearl G. Carlson (A.L.A., 1942), is a valuable aid in laying a foundation of proficiency in this field. Practical and compact, it summarizes types of editions and the kind of demand for which they are required; notes important features in a book's textual content and format; and gives brief indication of sources of information about editions and of characteristics of specific types of editions. But for the triple range of information with which the present chapter is concerned—editions, series, translations—the *Bookman's Manual*, in the revised and enlarged edition of 1948, must stand as a reservoir of factual information, a treasure store of illuminating and varied detail. The chapters on "Classics in English Translation" and on "Classical Drama" include notable translators, editions, and selective bibliographic lists; similar information is given for French literature, Russian literature, and other foreign literatures; and the whole volume offers invaluable guidance in dealing with these important and often complex details of selection, so essential to the values of a representative collection.

Materials for such a collection were never so excellent and abundant as they are at present. Well made, inexpensive, and attractive reprints of standard literature are becoming more and more a staple product of many publishing firms. Older books, unusual or half forgotten, are rediscovered for introduction to modern readers. Scholars and popularizers are constantly reworking masterpieces of literature and bringing them to a new and different public. The reprint now includes what is virtually current literature—history, biography, travel, science, fiction, first published only two or three years before being launched in popular low-priced form. Inexpensive editions range from the "special" reprints of notable and much more expensive books (the *Oxford Book of English Verse* and Audubon's *Birds* are examples), through the substantial, well-printed "dollar books," into the immense, far-reaching field of the twenty-five cent paper-bound reprints, and the lower-lying regions over which the Haldeman-Julius "Little Blue Books," at five cents apiece, long fluttered their paper wings.[1]

It must be remembered that many of these publications are unsuited to library use. Most paper-bound books, unduly small books (the "Little Blue Books," for example), books printed on wood pulp and flimsily bound, books with margins cut almost to the text,

---

[1] The rise in inexpensive reprints has brought the need for legal measures to prevent misrepresentation. Conspicuous display of the original title of a book retitled in reprinting, and of the word "abridged" in the case of an abridgment, has been ordered by the Federal Trade Commission to guard against deception of the book-buyer.

"giants" or "omnibuses" so heavy that they will pull apart after three or four readings, are impracticable or wasteful for library buying, no matter how inexpensive they may be. The fact that publication of paper-bound reprints continues to increase and publication of hard-bound reprints continues to decrease makes a serious problem for librarians. The justification and service of paper-bound editions is in bringing good reading to the multitude, enlarging "the democracy of literature," and in making it possible for almost anyone to have personal companionship with the great books of the past.

One of the most inspiring chapters of book-trade history is that which unfolds the rise and development of the popular reprint. Benjamin Franklin in his autobiography says of the library he planned and organized in Philadelphia: "It is become a great thing in itself, and continually increasing"; and these words epitomize the growth and influence of low-priced literature through more than a century in England and America. The education of the common man through cheap and enlightening publications was the aim of Robert Chambers, John Cassell, and Charles Knight, the pioneers, who with their popular libraries and reprints sold at a few pence or a shilling a volume first broke the path that is now a main-traveled road. "Bohn's Libraries" made their advent in 1846, establishing half-a-dozen well-made series devoted to reprints of standard English works and of classic and European literature in English translation. There were more than 600 volumes in the original "Bohn's," and though in their old-fashioned bindings of solid, blistery black, maroon, or blue they now seem dingy and forbidding, they were indispensable companions in the households of two generations, doing, as Emerson said, "as much for literature as railroads have done for internal intercourse."

As the reading public steadily enlarged through the advancing nineteenth century the flow of reprints increased immensely in volume and improved in quality. But it was not until 1904 that "Bohn's Libraries" found their successor in "Everyman's Library," whose compact, attractive volumes represent the next far-reaching achievement in modern reprint publishing. Since then the supply has been continually augmented. The "Modern Library," which in 1919 published as its first volume Oscar Wilde's *Portrait of Dorian Gray*, vies with "Everyman," bringing within its range books of all times and all lands that are modern in spirit, from Voltaire and *Don Quixote* to Steinbeck and Hersey, and proliferating into the two sub-series of massive "Giants" and charming, distinctive "Illustrated Modern Library." The "World's Classics" (so closely akin to "Everyman"), the "Black and Gold Library," the "Blue Ribbon Books," the "Bonibooks," "Modern Age Series," and many other reprint series of related purpose have drawn all currents of world literature into a flood tide of reading for the multitude.

The important part played by the leading twenty-five cent reprint series in this expansion of book use should be noted. First stimulus came from the success of the "Penguin Books," started as a sixpenny fiction reprint series in London, in 1935; these were later joined by "Pelican Books" (devoted to art and science) and "Pelican Specials" (politics, current events, and war). In their first three years 23,000,000 "Pelican Books" were sold, and their scope was enlarged by the inclusion of original books as well as reprints; by 1945, of the 1,000 titles 85 percent were original works. In 1939, a sales office was opened in New York, and in 1942, Penguin Books Incorporated was established as an independent American firm, in close relation with the "Penguin Books" of London, "Pelican Books" at thirty-five cents continuing as a companion series devoted to nonfiction. This direct British affiliation ended in 1948, when Penguin Books, Incorporated, changed its name to the "New American Library of World Literature, Incorporated," with its twenty-five cent "Penguin" fiction transformed into "Signet Books," and its former thirty-five cent "Pelican" nonfiction and classics rechristened "Mentor Books."

"Pocket Books," American pioneer in this field, made their appearance in 1939, coming later under the ownership of Marshall Field. Six million sold in the first full year, nine million in 1941; a total of two hundred million was reported in January, 1948, and the flow has not lessened. "Pocket Books" are excellently designed, with clear type and attractive covers, on which the mother kangaroo ("Gertrude") stamps the sign manual of the series. They include well-known older and contemporary books, many in specially prepared editions, much standard reference material (the *Merriam-Webster Pocket Dictionary* is an example), and a strong representation of original works—most notable among them, *Franklin Delano Roosevelt: a Memorial*, an impressive record and tribute, beautifully carried out, which was originated, prepared, and published within one week (April 13-18, 1945) and of which the first edition has long been a collectors' item. "Bantam Books"—jointly controlled by Grosset and Dunlap (now owned by five large publishing firms) and the Curtis Publishing Company—by 1946 had successfully set up a similar pattern. It has been estimated that in 1949 distribution by sixteen publishers of twenty-five cent books, representing 659 titles, amounted to 184,000,000 copies. The secret of the immense mass market reached by these series lies in their distribution not through regular book-trade channels, but through the highly organized system of magazine distribution, which provides some 60,000 outlets —newsstands, small neighborhood stores, and all kinds of crossroad centers, radiating throughout the country.

Consider now some of the points and principles to be observed in choosing from this immense body of literature worth-while, readable, and attractive editions.

First of all, a few definitions and specifications are necessary, for there is much looseness and confusion in the use of the various terms applied to publications in this general field.

Edition in its several meanings and in its interchangeable relationship with *series* and *library* has already been defined. But it may be repeated that *an edition* is the whole number of copies of a book or other publication printed and published at one time.

A later printing, from unchanged plates, is a *printing*, an *impression*, or an *issue*.

Reprint is commonly applied to a new printing from unchanged plates, in cheaper form than the original and often issued by a specialized "reprint publisher." But the term is often collectively applied to reissues and later editions in general—as "reprint literature," "reprint series," "reprint publishing."

Copyright reprint denotes a reprint from the original plates of a current copyright book made after it has had its first sale in the original form at a higher price. Such reprints have increased enormously in number, for four reasons: they are satisfactory to the author, because they give him a new source of income; to the publisher, because they bring in revenue from titles whose sales are lessening; to the bookseller, because they enlarge the market and reach a different group of buyers; and to the public, because they make the most successful books of recent years available at low prices. They are, of course, of great value for replacement purposes, if not for first purchases, in all library selection.[2]

Reissue is an alternative term for a reprint.

New edition is an edition from new plates, or in which there are changes in the text, or additions to or revision of the original content. A "new, revised, enlarged edition" is a self-explanatory term. A "school edition" is most commonly a reprint for classroom use, made on cheaper paper, reduced in size and more cheaply bound; sometimes, however, the term denotes a new edition equipped with notes, or questions, or other teaching material.

Trade edition (like "trade binding") is the regular edition of a book printed for and supplied to the book trade, as distinguished from a *limited* edition, issued in large paper or other special form, or signed by the author, or otherwise designed to command the particular interest of collectors.

Special edition is usually a new edition of standard work with special features or accessories, such as new introductions, illustrations, specially designed type, distinctive binding; sometimes sold only by subscription. The "Outward Bound" edition of Kipling, the "Thistle" Stevenson, the "Centenary Edition" of Parkman, are familiar examples.

---

[2] Many publishing contracts include a provision that no cheap edition may be published less than a year after publication of the trade edition.

Edition de luxe should denote an edition of fine workmanship and high artistic quality, usually limited in number, printed on special paper, often with drawings by distinguished illustrators or other decorations, and handsomely bound. The term has been so cheapened by unscrupulous selling usage that it is now rarely applied to the publications that justify it. Many editions so designated do not conform to any requirements of fine bookmaking and are the product of publishers without approved standing, or of pretentiously named "societies" or "presses," often obviously intended to suggest a non-existent relationship with famous originals (as, for example, the "Kelmscott Society," publisher of "editions de luxe" at two dollars a volume). These products should not be confused with the publications of the many responsible "private presses," American and English, whose beautiful "limited editions"—a term now preferred to "editions de luxe"—represent the best modern achievements in fine printing and bookmaking.

Facsimile is an exact copy or reproduction, printed from plates made by photographic processes. Formerly, facsimiles were usually made only for rare originals—as, for example, the fine facsimile of the first folio Shakespeare, published by Oxford University Press in 1902; in a *facsimile reprint* the original text was reset in type of identical character. But with the great development of planographic processes, facsimile editions of important older reference and scholarly works are made more and more available—as in the specialized lithoprinting of Edwards Brothers, the Peter Smith reproductions of pioneer works of American trade bibliography, and other similar undertakings.

Sets may be complete works of authors, often in special editions or editions de luxe; or uniform editions of classics; or many-volumed compilations of extracts and selections; or a uniformly bound sequence of volumes dealing with historical or scientific or other informational subjects. "Great Books of the Western World" (Chicago, Encyclopaedia Britannica, Incorporated), which began publication in 1948, is a recent example combining several of these factors. This 54-volume set of ancient and modern classics in standard reprint is integrated by able editorial organization, and sponsored by the Great Books Foundation (organized in 1947), which is the outgrowth of the Great Books Discussion Groups developed by the University of Chicago in 1944-46, and noted in an earlier chapter.[3] The 432 individual works included in these volumes provide basic material for the organized discussion groups now operating in many communities; and the set is supplemented by low-priced reprints of the "readings" (18 titles) required for each year's course in a four-year discussion program.

In this general field, many sets are sold only by subscription. They must be cautiously dealt with in selection, for as a general rule the purchase of complete sets for library use is undesirable, except for representative or definitive editions of leading standard authors. Single titles that are in assured demand are preferable—several copies of *Henry Esmond*, for example, should be available in any moderate-sized library, but *Yellowplush Papers* would be adequately represented as found in a single complete authoritative edition of Thackeray's works.

Series may be said to fall roughly into two general types, *publishers' series* and *subject series*. But it is difficult to make rigid definition or denotation of what constitutes a series in book publication. For just as there are various meanings to the word "edition," so the term "series" is applied to books published in uniform style, in related sequence, or as a correlated presentation of a specific subject. In broadest usage, it is applied to books that are usually reprints of older or standard literature, ranging widely in their subject matter, but possessing the same textual and physical characteristics and published in a definite sequence by a single publisher. These are *publishers' series*, also called *trade series* or *reprint series*, and interchangeably known as "editions" or "libraries." In more specific and familiar usage, the term is applied to two or more books, not reprints, dealing with different phases of a single subject or with a special field of literature, frequently prepared under the supervision of a single editor, though usually by different individual authors, uni-

---

[3] See above, pp. 34-35.

form in textual and physical characteristics and published by a single publisher. These are *subject series,* exemplified in "Rivers of America" series, or in "Our Debt to Greece and Rome" series. There are constant variations and exceptions in series characteristics. Often a reprint series is also a subject series—as with Houghton Mifflin's "Cambridge Poets," or Dent's "Open-Air Library," devoted to attractive reprints of memorable books dealing with nature and country life. There is also a third type of series, as the term is applied to sequences of closely related novels (such as Trollope's "Chronicles of Barsetshire") and to the continuous fiction sequels beloved of youthful readers, such as the "Little Colonel Series" and the "Sue Barton" books; but these do not come within present consideration.

In any well-selected library many books must be available in several editions. There must be generous duplication to meet the demand for old and well-loved books as well as for the popular literature of the day. There must be familiar texts in recent scholarly revision as well as in the best earlier presentation, the various distinctive renderings of the classics into English, the definitive editions of the work of standard writers, the latest important revisions of necessary works of information and reference; and there must be a watchful continuous replacement, in the best possible form, of all books that have proved their worth. Intelligent, discriminating replacement, indeed, is of first importance; too many books of continuing value are allowed to die after a short library existence, and too many older editions of enduring merit are superseded by less satisfactory modern renderings. Different kinds of editions have different kinds of values, and in judicious selection these must be recognized and represented.

Points to be observed in selection of editions are:

Text.—Whether unabridged, abridged, or expurgated; whether accurate or imperfect.

Editor or translator.—Authority, skill and special qualities.

Size.—As regards convenience and practicability.

Date.—As it may affect the value or timeliness of the book.

Price.—In comparison with that of other acceptable editions.

Type, paper illustrations, and binding.—Important as they fulfill the physical requirements of a well-made book; have already had consideration.

Text and editor demand particular attention in choosing among different editions of older and standard works. In many famous books the text appears in various forms. It may be unabridged and unaltered; it may have undergone expurgation—the elimination of words or sentences or scenes regarded as coarse or otherwise offensive; or it may be given piecemeal, in arbitrary selection. Montaigne's essays, for example, in the series, "French Classics for English Readers," are given in a limited selection, with careful elimination of a word here and a sentence there. The "Modern Readers' Series" expurgates and drastically abridges Dumas' *Three Musketeers*. Expurgation or bowdlerization (so called in memory of the Reverend Thomas Bowdler, whose expurgated "family edition" of Shakespeare was published in 1818) exists in some degree in all standard school editions of Shakespeare. Indeed, in almost all editions of famous works prepared for school or college use, there is likely to be abridgment or expurgation, or both, justified by the requirements for which they are designed. Such editions, also, in their apparatus of explanatory notes, references, and appendixes, and in their format, are apt to take on a desiccated officialism that checks or forbids spontaneous adventure of the mind. Bernard Shaw, refusing consent to a school edition of his plays, wrote his publisher:

By a school edition they mean an edition with notes and references, full of material for such questions as "Give the age of Bernard Shaw's great-aunt when he wrote 'You Never Can Tell' " and "Give the reasons for believing that the inscription on her tombstone at Ballyhooley is incorrect." The inexperienced student reads these notes and prefaces and not the plays and forever after loathes my name.

School editions, however indispensable in their own field, are undesirable in selection intended for the general reader.

For intelligent adults, editions should be chosen that present an unabridged text. This principle applies to such writers as Rabelais, the early English dramatists, the eighteenth-century novelists and many others whose work is of an earlier age, as well as to contemporaries. There are, however, various famous works that reach the general reading public only in expurgated or selective form. The *Arabian Nights* is an example, in all editions most satisfactory for general reading. Rabelais, in "The Modern Library," is given with many excisions, but with comparatively slight dilution of flavor. But as a rule, whenever possible, unabridged editions should be preferred to those that have been cut down to some prescribed measure.

Judicious abridgment, however, gives wide availability to works that in their full extent are unduly formidable to readers. Probably the most remarkable example is Frazer's one-volume edition of his many-volumed study of primitive religion, *The Golden Bough*, in which the distinction of expression, fascinating pictorial quality, and personality of the original are kept unimpaired. A similar achievement is Professor D. C. Somervell's masterly abridgment of the first six volumes of Arnold Toynbee's monumental *Study of History*, in which an original of more than 3,000 pages is transmitted in its own creative unity within the compass of 565 pages. Edna Kenton's excellent one-volume selection from the seventy-two volumes of the great Thwaites edition of the *Jesuit Relations* conveys the original quality of this memorable historic chronicle to many who could otherwise never know it. The single-volume *Selection of the Principal Voyages, Traffiques and Discoveries of the English Nation* has value in attracting new readers to Hakluyt's narratives; but in basic selection first choice should go to the complete text in the eight volumes of "Everyman" or in the more expensive ten-volume edition.

Compilation, compression, and collectivity have been strong recent influences in the production of editions. In 1935 the *Woollcott Reader* set a pattern of popular allure, and through succeeding years anthologies, omnibuses, cavalcades, treasuries, companions, digests, and condensations have flourished and multiplied. Ranging through every subject field and every degree of merit, they represent an ever present problem in library book selection. Many are superfluous, pretentious, and repetitive; an immense amount of duplication in content is always to be allowed for. Others, impressive as gifts, are unwieldy or unsatisfactory in format for library use. In selection, particular consideration should be given to collections based on a genuine and unifying idea (such as Abramowitz's *Great Prisoners*, linking prison writing through 2,000 years, from Socrates to Dostoyevsky); to those which garner scattered, obscure, or neglected material of merit (as *The Practical Cogitator*); to those that present in well organized sequence authoritative contribution in some field of knowledge (as in *A Treasury of Science*); and to those that give illuminating presentation to the individual work of important writers. The "Viking Portable Library" is an admirable example here, with compact, well-made volumes, easy to handle and pleasing to read, in which editors of authority present with discerning introductory commentary a comprehensive selection of the writing of modern and classic authors (the *Portable Walt Whitman*, the *Portable James Joyce*, and many others).

Incomplete or abridged editions that give no indication of the fact on the title-page are always open to suspicion. As a rule they contain such portions of a writer's work as the publisher could easily secure or that are no longer protected by copyright. Volumes of standard poets entitled "Poems of," "Poems by," and "Poems," are frequently of this type and should never be accepted as "complete poetical works." As copyrights expire on the work of famous writers a flood of reprint editions come into existence, but the earlier publisher still holds the author's later work and through long identification and the possession of original material is likely for many years to produce the best and most authoritative editions. Houghton Mifflin, for example (in succession to Ticknor and Fields, and Osgood), were the copyright publishers of Nathaniel Hawthorne, and though Hawthorne's work has long outlived its copyright and dozens of reprint editions exist, they are still the "authorized publishers," with editions in greater variety and of more even excellence than are to be found elsewhere. Chapman and Hall as the early publishers of Dickens, John Murray as the lifetime publisher of Byron, are, in the same way, identified with the most complete and varied later editions of those writers.

Accuracy of text is important, and varies greatly in different editions. As a general rule, "authorized" editions are superior in accuracy to standardized popular reprints. Also, English editions of English works and American editions of American works are usually to be preferred for accuracy. Poe's famous cryptogram tale appears in popular English editions as "The Gold-Beetle" (the explanation is that in ordinary English speech "bug" indicates a single most unsavory species of insect). American editions of Lowell, Irving, Hawthorne, and their fellows are more satisfactory than English reprints. In the same way, English editions of Keats, Coleridge, Byron, and other English writers are often preferable to American editions. This point hardly applies to the standard editions produced by leading publishers; for example, the "Cambridge Poets," Houghton Mifflin's famous one-volume editions, begun in 1893, are accepted and relied upon in all American libraries. Yet, even there, where the English poets are concerned I admit a preference for the editions published by Oxford or Macmillan. The best standard editions are sometimes at fault in textual details. For example, in both the American "Cambridge" and the English "Oxford" editions of Keats, there is perpetuated the first clumsy revision of "La Belle Dame Sans Merci" —which in its pristine perfection may be found in the "Everyman," Macmillan, and numerous other editions.

An editor's authority, skill, and purpose are often determining factors in selection. Many editions of famous books have their values enhanced by the work of their editors; others are sources of constant annoyance to the reader because of the superfluous or pedantic editorial information dispensed. Fitzgerald's version of the *Rubáiyát* and Browning's works are among those that have suffered most acutely from editorial commentary and the elaboration of explanatory footnotes and appendixes.

There must always be differentiation between editions that represent scholarship and research, primarily for students and specialists, and those that make their appeal to the intelligent, cultivated general reader. Every library that can afford it should have the great Furness "Variorum" edition of Shakespeare as a part of its equipment for Shakespeare students; but first choice in selection must go to editions for the general reader in which Shakespeare's text marches easily along a companionable page, unchecked by scholastic steppingstones or explanatory stiles. The seven volumes of Skeat's authoritative edition of Chaucer are indispensable for serious study; but in the ordinary public library a good one-volume edition such as "Globe" or "Cambridge" and the *Canterbury Tales*, both in original form and in some skillful retelling in modern English verse, will satisfy a larger and equally legitimate demand. All editors leave their impress on the works they sponsor, many of them most helpfully. They are at their best when in sympathy with their author, neither fulsome nor diffuse. Sometimes they tend to the opposite direction and are carping, contentious, or determined to establish some conviction of their own. This was true of Dean Milman's famous edition of Gibbon, peppered with footnotes rebuking the historian's anti-Christian utterances; long superseded by the more judicial edition of J. B. Bury.

Translators and translations are as important in their comparative values as are editors and editions. The masterpieces of world literature come to the majority of English readers only in translation. Homer, the Greek dramatists, the *Arabian Nights*, Dante, *Don Quixote*, Goethe, and others of the glorious company in which they are numbered, must be found in any adequate library collection in the English renderings that best transmit their original quality. The creative literature of contemporary racial cultures must be supplied to English readers of intelligence and imagination, as offering constant enrichment of human experience and enlargement of mental horizons. And as modern communication, abolishing distance, forces mankind (for good or ill) into constantly closer relationship, the work of the translator becomes more immediate and more necessary, as a key to the common human understanding on which human survival must depend.

While there is a steadily increasing supply of classic, standard, and contemporary work available in good English translation, the work of the best earlier translators remains unsuperseded. No modern rendering of Rabelais—such, for example, as the American version by Samuel Putnam—can take the place of the seventeenth-century translation of Urquhart and Motteux, itself an English classic, recreating in its own tongue the rushing fullness, the torrential ribaldry and grotesquery of the great jester, humanist, and philosopher of the Renaissance world. John Florio's contemporary translation of Montaigne (which Shakespeare must have known and used) is another English masterpiece, perhaps with more Elizabethan floridity than quite fits the intellectual temper of Montaigne, but alive, racy, and felicitous. It still demands first place in any collection, second choice going to the excellent modern translation by E. J. Trechmann, as preferable to either the familiar Cotton translation or the elaborate version by G. B. Ives, which is so thoroughly expurgated that Stuart Sherman proposed it should be called the "Fig-Leaf Edition." For the student, the translation by Jacob Zeitlin, publication of which was begun in 1934, is one of the notable works of modern scholarship.

In English translation of the Greek and Latin classics, the work of earlier and later translators must have discriminating recognition. For Homer, the prose versions of the *Iliad* by Lang, Leaf, and Myers and of the *Odyssey* by Lang and Butcher have merits that, in my judgment, give them precedence. But there must also be acceptance of the values that exist in Chapman, Pope, Bryant, Palmer, Shaw (T. E. Lawrence), and others whose work has proved its excellence. No one should exercise judgment upon classic translations—indeed, upon translations of any kind—unless that judgment has been fortified and sharpened by Matthew Arnold's essay, "On Translating Homer," that quintessence of the critical spirit, penetrating and illuminating the fundamental qualities of the translator's art. C. F. MacIntyre, in the "Translator's Note" appended to his brilliant translation of Goethe's *Faust*, denotes in utmost compression the essentials of a good translation and the chief pitfalls and temptations to be avoided. In all selection of the classics in translation, an indispensable aid and guide will be found in the extended, well-planned bibliographical manual of F. S. Smith,[4] now out of print but available in many libraries, which gives Greek and Latin authors in alphabetical order, indicating and evaluating the most notable English translations of their work.

The crowning achievement in English translation of the classics is the "Loeb Classical Library." For it represents one of the greatest modern undertakings in literature, impossible on an ordinary publishing basis, and established—like so many of our educational and humanitarian "foundations"—by private purpose and philanthropy. It was founded by James Loeb, to bring to English and American readers, in the original text and parallel English translation, "all that is of value and of interest in Greek and Latin literature from the time of Homer to the fall of Constantinople," a period of approximately two thousand years. It thus includes not only the literature of ancient Greece and Rome but that of early Christianity—the great body of recorded thought that has been a continuous and dominating force in our civilization. The first volumes appeared in 1912; in 1919 the "first hundred" set up the first milestone; to date more than three hundred fifty titles have been published; and the number to which the series will extend if the plan is fully carried out (Mr. Loeb's will provided for its completion under the trusteeship of Harvard University) is usually estimated at between four and five hundred. Individual translations vary in quality; some of them have proved less acceptable than are earlier well-known renderings; but many are of unusual excellence, and the series offers a bulk and variety of literature never before freely available in English. Although moderate in price it cannot be considered an inexpensive series; but every library that can afford it should have a judicious representation of the Loeb volumes. It was published by G. P. Putnam's Sons until July, 1934, when publication was taken over by Harvard University Press.

While much important foreign literature is available in several

---

[4] F. S. Smith, *The Classics in Translation:* an annotated guide to the best translations of the Greek and Latin classics into English; with a preface by H. B. Van Hoesen (New York, Scribner, 1930).

translations, the work of most of the leading present-day writers—such as Sigrid Undset, Marcel Proust, Thomas Mann—usually appears in a single English rendering. And always a foreign writer's work is made or marred by the translator. Wherever choice of editions is possible, it should be careful and discriminating, and when good translations appear they should replace less satisfactory ones. Balzac, Flaubert, and Maupassant are among the writers most commonly sacrificed in clumsy or vulgarized or emasculated translation. For Balzac, the skillful, devoted, though somewhat overfeminized translation of Katharine Wormeley and the more full-bodied translation of Saintsbury are still unsuperseded, while Ernest Boyd's translation of Maupassant represents the more vigorous and franker work of competent modern translators. Curiously enough, the work of modern literature for which a thoroughly good English translation is most needed is Hugo's *Les Miserables*. Translation at its best must be not only accurate, but must transmit the spirit and flavor of the original work. Lafcadio Hearn's exquisite translation of *The Crime of Sylvestre Bonnard* is an example of perfection in miniature; the many translations of Alexander Teixeira de Mattos reveal the sensitive emotional response and rich scholarship that must exist in the finest art of the translator; and Scott Moncrieff's translation of Marcel Proust is enduring evidence of a translator's power to transmit the most evasive subtlety of atmosphere and recreate the most complex inner texture of expression.

An effort to clarify and standardize the publishing of translations was begun in 1932 by the International Institute of Intellectual Cooperation under the League of Nations.[5] It was urged that publishers in all countries shall henceforth print on the cover and title-page of all books they publish in translation both the name of the translator and the name of the work in its original language; that if it is a first translation the fact shall be stated; that complete translations shall be indicated by the phrase "translated from," and abridgments by "adapted from"; that indication shall be given on

[5] The recommendations made are given in *Publishers' Weekly*, August 13, 1932, p. 512.

cover, flyleaf, or title-page, of the city where the work was first published, the date of publication, and the edition from which the translation has been made; and that distinction be made between first editions of a translation and reprinted editions. The International Institute also, in 1932, began the publication, from its Paris office, of *Index translationum*—a quarterly index to current translations, recording all translations published during the previous quarter and listing under different countries the languages from which they were translated. With the advent of the war further development became impracticable. The *Index translationum* was "temporarily suspended" with the issue of January, 1940; and the League of Nations "Report on the Work of the League during the War," published in Geneva in October, 1945, says (p. 126): "Although the International Institute of Intellectual Cooperation suspended its official activities after the occupation of Paris and did not resume them until after the liberation, certain work was nevertheless carried on in Paris during the occupation." Establishment of Unesco—United Nations Educational, Scientific and Cultural Organization—in November, 1945, provided opportunity to carry further the work initiated under the League, by systematizing the publication of translations, aiding in selection of material which ought to be translated, improving the quality of translations, and sponsoring bibliographical information concerning them. In May, 1948, at a conference of thirteen representatives of eleven countries at Unesco headquarters in Paris, organization of this task was begun.

A step toward improved standards in translation of foreign works into English was taken in 1933, when the Translators' Guild was organized in London, to serve as a link between publishers and translators, its particular function being "to find for the publisher the right translator and for the translator the kind of work to which he can do full justice, for even the best translator is handicapped when working on a book which violates his personal feelings and opinions." [6]

---

[6] A brief statement of the organization and purpose of the Translators' Guild, by its secretary, Cyrus Brooks, appeared in the *London Mercury*, April, 1933, p. 550.

Practical, illuminating guidance and appraisal in the whole field of translation—classical, Oriental, and European—may be found in *Modern Translation*, by E. Stuart Bates (Oxford University Press, 1936), a compact little volume, much less widely known to American librarians than it should be. It is, so far as I know, the only comprehensive treatment of a virtually untouched subject: authoritative in background knowledge and experience, discriminating in literary appreciation and comparison, and with the simple, direct, informal quality of a readable essay. There is excellent presentation of the range of translations, now expanded far beyond the former classic field with the inflow of the literature of the Orient and from all European countries. A second section is devoted to "theory and practice"—to aids, to critical standards and analyses, with examples and appraisals of work of individual translators. A separate index to translators mentioned (128 are listed) has definite reference value.[7]

In the United States during recent years English translations of contemporary literature have increased in volume and improved in quality. Three factors are chiefly responsible—the exodus of European writers, made exiles or refugees by the years of Nazi conquest, many of whom found their way to America, where their books have been written, translated, and published; the strengthening of reciprocal relations in education and much more extensive exchange of literature between the Latin American countries and the United States; and at least a beginning realization that international understanding is the only key to world peace. Since 1940 especially, the inflow of Latin American literature in English translation has been stabilized and fostered in North American book production. Brazil, Mexico, and Argentina have had strongest representation, but rich and varied work by writers of Ecuador, Chile,

---

[7] Mr. Bates, in 1943, supplemented his earlier volume with *Inter-Traffic: Studies in Translation* (London, Jonathan Cape), original and thought-provoking analyses of the art and influence of translation, exemplified by comparison of English translations of literature from China, Japan, the Near East, the classics, and of the Bible. Of much interest and value, as clarifying and strengthening standards in any study or selection of translation.

Peru, and other Latin American countries is being constantly made more available to the reading public of the United States by an experienced, competent, and enlarging group of translators.[8]

Size.—Perhaps the favorite size among popular, inexpensive editions and series is the companionable sixteenmo, the pocket-size volume, light to hold, easy to read, convenient and practical for personal use. Such are the "Everyman" volumes, the "Temple Classics," and most of the Dent editions, the "Modern Library," the Viking "Portables"—to name only a few. "Everyman" represents about the smallest size practicable for library use; as a rule, an ordinary twelvemo size is preferable. In the "Modern Library," plates intended for larger books result in many volumes with margins cut to the quick. Here chief danger-points in selection are cut-down margins and an undue weight that cannot endure continued use. The "Giants" of the "Modern Library," for example, though they offer wonderful values for the home bookshelf, are unsatisfactory for libraries, because their weight is likely to soon pull them apart and they cannot be properly rebound. But wherever practicable, one-volume editions are preferable for general library circulation.

Date is always significant in determining the value of informational works. For many of these and especially for reference books, later editions usually include new or supplementary material, or revision of text to bring it up to date; they should always be given preference over older editions that may be obsolete. But there must be careful comparison with earlier editions, to make sure that the changes are of real importance.

Prices of different editions should be compared, and choice based on textual and physical values rather than on a few cents' difference in cost: for all good literature is worthy of dignified and attractive investiture; clumsy, flimsy, uninviting editions, though they may be cheap in price, are poor economy. Often English reprint editions are cheaper than American ones and of equal or superior excellence.

---

[8] For survey and appraisal of English translations in this field, see: *What's in a Novel*, by Helen E. Haines, Chapter VIII, "Fiction from Latin America," pp. 168–96 (Columbia University Press, 1942).

As an aid in selection and purchase of editions many libraries maintain an "editions file"—a card record of standard and popular books available in different American and English editions. Such a record, besides giving publisher and price, should indicate the number of volumes to a title, size, type, paper, and binding, and any other desirable information. It may be built up from the *Publishers' Trade List Annual*, the Library of Congress cards, and from current publishers' catalogues, supplemented by notes made from personal examination of the editions, as this can be done from bookstore visiting or from copies otherwise available.

Subject series must have briefer consideration than their importance deserves, for much permanently valuable and currently popular literature is published in this form. Compact, readable presentation is most commonly given in such series, although there are many series, especially in sociology, religion, and science, that contain scholarly or technical monographs for advanced students or specialists. But, in general, most series are designed for readers who want information in condensed, accurate, and interesting exposition. The "Living Thoughts Library" is an example of such a series, with its neat little volumes each offering in sympathetic distillation the essence of the teaching of a famous explorer in philosophic, or political, social or scientific or religious thought—from Schopenhauer to Darwin, from Thoreau to Pascal. In the "Teach Yourself History Library" compact, readable biographies are planned to develop self-education in history, each conveying a significant historical theme; Lenin's biography, for example, following the course and dramatizing the issues of the Russian Revolution. There is broad national significance in "The Peoples of America Series," under the editorship of Louis Adamic, in which each volume, by a well-qualified authority, focuses on one of the national groups that have helped to shape our country; the first volume, *Americans from Holland*, by Arnold Mulder, appeared in October, 1947. Many subject series hold high rank for their authority and interest. "English Men of Letters," originally edited by John Morley, is one of these, each volume being written by a master hand with ease, charm, and unusual skill in avoiding detail.

One of the great merits of subject series is that they often include books on subjects not compactly treated elsewhere. This compact, graphic treatment is found in many historical series, in which the separate volumes deal with specific epochs or phases, campaigns, battles, or popular movements. Here one of the most interesting examples is the "Chronicles of America," published by Yale University Press, where in fifty small volumes, any one of which may be read in about four hours' time, a panorama of American history and development is presented by nearly fifty different writers of popularity and skill, each volume separate and distinctive, but fitting into its own place in the carefully worked out plan. An important series in another special field is that devoted to "Our Debt to Greece and Rome," planned to include fifty volumes, in which modern scholars set forth how much of modern thought and achievement has been shaped by classic influences; while the historic backgrounds and transformations of the world today are presented in the successive volumes of the "United Nations Series," each assigned to one of the nations in the world frame. This scholarly, objective series, published by the University of California Press, enlists an able editor for each volume, to organize and integrate material from contributory sources; the ninth volume, *Yugoslavia*, appeared in 1949.

But the richest field opened by present-day series is undoubtedly that of the American scene, of American historical, regional, and social backgrounds, as exemplified in the great "American Guide Series." This series, and the many related volumes that link to it, is the product of the memorable Federal Writers Project, initiated by the government in the early 1930's to make use of the abilities of unemployed writers and research workers. Its volumes, published by different publishers, fall into different categories. The forty-nine state Guides (including the District of Columbia), each an informational and descriptive exposition of the area dealt with, make the basic substance of the series, which was completed in 1941. Each volume follows a uniform plan in organization and in scope, but each also has distinctive individuality and conveys the "spirit of place" and the flavor of folk-life. They are supplemented by volumes devoted to individual regions and cities, which are less specifically identified with the Guides, but are also fruit of the Writers Project. Many other independent regional and historical descriptive series —"Rivers of America," "American Lake Series," "American Mountain Series," "American Folkways Series," "Look at America," are examples—help to fill out the impressive, many-sided picture of the nation's life.

Almost all subject series, it should be added, are uneven in merit. Of course, it is impossible that every volume in a series that may contain from fifteen to forty or more should have equal excellence. So the better volumes often screen the poor ones and gain a reputation for the series as a whole that it does not deserve. For this reason it is not usually desirable for a small library to buy a complete series nor to subscribe in advance to a long and expensive one. It is better to select from older and standard series individual volumes of established merit or that cover some subject of special interest, and to buy as they appear the volumes of a current series that have special appeal or will meet a known demand. It should be remembered also that a book that deals compactly with some subject on which little material is to be had in similar convenient form is usually desirable, even if it does not possess high authority or marked literary merit.

In examining or comparing subject series for library selection, the points that demand special attention are:

Importance or timeliness or intrinsic interest of the subject.

Scope and purpose of the series as a whole.

Whether or not there is a general editor, and, if so, the extent and character of his qualifications.

Authority and skill of the authors of individual volumes.

Textual and physical characteristics of the series.

Its special merits, and the class of readers to which it will appeal or be useful.

All these points are now so familiar that no further analysis or exposition concerning them should be necessary.

The third stage in our study of book selection has now been passed. We have surveyed the foundations on which it is based and examined the principles by which it is directed and the professional equipment necessary to its practice. We have sought to denote and analyze book values and to become familiar with the various methods by which those values are appraised. We have in broad survey and closer specification scrutinized the book in its material substance—in its textual and physical aspect—and as the product of the "great trade," bearing varied and potent hereditary attributes. It now remains to enter, in exploration and discovery, certain of the great regional divisions of the world of books.

A BRIEF SELECTION OF
REPRESENTATIVE EDITIONS AND SERIES

Hard-bound Series and Editions

Black and Gold Library (8vo). New York, Liveright Publishing Corp. Older and modern fiction and nonfiction.

Blue Ribbon Books (12mo or 8vo). New York, Blue Ribbon Books, Inc. Recent and standard fiction and nonfiction; extensive and very useful.

Books of Distinction (12mo or 8vo). New York, Grosset & Dunlap, Inc. Chiefly contemporary American and British fiction.

Cambridge Classics (8vo). Boston, Houghton Mifflin Company. Standard American fiction.

Cambridge Poets. Boston, Houghton Mifflin Company.

De Luxe Editions (8vo). New York, Garden City Publishing Co., Inc. Recent and older nonfiction and fiction; varied and useful.

Doubleday Illustrated Library (8vo). New York, Doubleday & Co., Inc. Standard fiction and nonfiction in handsome editions.

Everyman's Library (16mo). New York, E. P. Dutton & Co. Rather small, but contains many classics not available elsewhere. An "American Edition" of selected titles, with new format and larger type, was launched in 1947.

G. & D. Specials (12mo or 8vo). New York, Grosset & Dunlap, Inc. Fiction and nonfiction.

EDITIONS, SERIES, TRANSLATIONS 243

Globe Editions (12mo). New York, The Macmillan Company. Chiefly standard British literature.

Golden Treasury Series (16mo). New York, The Macmillan Company. Chiefly standard English poetry and translations of classics.

Great Illustrated Classics (8vo). New York, Dodd, Mead & Co. One-volume editions of standard British fiction; excellent, but sometimes abridged.

Harper Dollar Library (8vo). New York, Harper & Brothers. Nonfiction, American authors.

Harbrace Modern Classics (8vo). New York, Harcourt, Brace & Co., Inc. Fiction and nonfiction in broad range of Harcourt publications.

Heritage Editions (8vo or 4to). New York, Heritage Press. Standard and modern fiction and nonfiction; special illustrations (some in color); excellently designed.

Illustrated Modern Library (12mo). New York, Modern Library, Inc.

Imperial Editions (8vo or 4to). New York, The Macmillan Company. Nonfiction by American and British authors; handsome, unabridged reprints of more expensive Macmillan originals.

Living Library (12mo). Cleveland, O., World Publishing Company. Standard and modern fiction and nonfiction.

Modern Library (12mo). New York, Modern Library, Inc.

Modern Library Giants (8vo). New York, Modern Library, Inc.

Murray Hill Books (8vo or 4to). New York, Murray Hill Books, Inc.

Nelson Classics (small 16mo). New York, Thomas Nelson & Sons. Small for library use, but a good collection.

New Classics Series (12mo). Norfolk, Conn., New Directions. Fiction and nonfiction; distinctive modern authors.

Oxford Standard Authors (12mo). New York, Oxford University Press. Excellent editions of standard literature; many in two volumes that are more desirable than most two-volume editions.

Permanent Library (8vo). New York, Dial Press. Fiction; omnibus volumes.

Pilot Omnibus Series (8vo). New York, Duell, Sloan & Pearce. Anthologies of novels by a chosen author or of collective fiction of a specific subject, originally published by Pilot Press of London.

Popular Copyrights (12mo). New York, Grosset & Dunlap. Fiction preponderates.

Rittenhouse Classics (12mo). Philadephia, Macrae-Smith Co. Standard fiction; handsome volumes.

Riverside Library (8vo). Boston, Houghton Mifflin Company. Fiction and nonfiction by contemporary and older authors; excellent selection.

Star Books (8vo). New York, Garden City Publishing Co., Inc. Chiefly recent and older nonfiction; extensive and useful.

Sun Dial Books (12mo or 8vo). New York, Sun Dial Press. Fiction and nonfiction.

Tudor Books. Sizes vary. New York, Tudor Publishing Co. Recent and older works; chiefly nonfiction.

Viking Portable Library (16mo). New York, The Viking Press, Inc. Excellent, well-edited anthologies and comprehensive or selective collections of individual authors or famous works.

World Books of Distinction (8vo). Cleveland, O., World Publishing Co. Fiction and nonfiction, chiefly modern American authors; some standard English literature.

World's Classics (small 16mo). New York, Oxford University Press. Extensive, excellent series of world literature, but too small for satisfactory library use.

World's Classics, American Edition (12mo). New York, Oxford University Press. Launched in 1947. Fiction and nonfiction, including some reissues from the original series. Larger format, well suited to library use.

Paper-bound Series and Editions

Bantam Books (16mo). Stiff paper covers. New York, Bantam Books, Inc. Fiction and nonfiction, modern authors.

Mentor Books (12mo). Stiff paper covers. New York, New American Library of World Literature. Nonfiction and classics; formerly Pelican Books; American successor to Pelican Books, of London.

Pocket Books (16mo). Stiff paper covers. New York, Pocket Books, Inc.

Signet Books (12mo). Stiff paper covers. New York, New American Library of World Literature. Fiction; formerly Penguin Books; American successor to Penguin Books, of London.

SOME MODERN TRANSLATORS OF AUTHORITY AND DISTINCTION

Aldington, Richard. Translator of French writers.

Archer, William. Translator of Ibsen and other Scandinavian writers.

Björkman, Edwin A. Translator of Scandinavian writers.

Bone, Edith. Translator of Russian and Polish writers (Aleksei Tolstoi and Wanda Wasilewska).

Boyd, Ernest. Translator of Maupassant, of French, Italian, and German writers.
Brenner, Anita. Translator of Latin-American writers (especially Mexican).
Bussy, Dorothy. Translator of Gide and other French writers.
Cannan, Gilbert. Translator of Rolland's *Jean Christophe*.
Chambers, Whittaker. Translator of Salten and other German writers.
Chater, Arthur. Translator of Undset and other Scandinavian writers.
Chevalier, Haakon M. Translator of French writers.
Cournos, John. Translator of Russian writers.
Cowley, Malcolm. Translator of French writers.
Curtin, Jeremiah. Translator of Sienkiewicz.
De Onis, Harriet. Translator of Latin-American writers.
Flores, Angel. Translator of Latin-American writers.
Galantière, Lewis. Translator of the Goncourt Journals, of Cocteau, Mauriac, St. Exupéry, and other French writers; also of German writers.
Garnett, Constance. Translator of Chekhov, Gogol, Dostoyevsky, Tolstoy, Turgenev, and other Russian writers.
Gilbert, Stuart. Translator of Martin du Gard's *The World of the Thibaults* and other French writers.
Goldberg, Isaac. Translator of Spanish, Italian, Latin-American, and Yiddish writers.
Grummon, Stewart Edgar. Translator of Latin-American writers.
Guerney, Bernard Guilbert. Translator of Gorky, Merejkowski, and other Russian writers.
Hearn, Lafcadio. Translator of Anatole France's *Crime of Sylvestre Bonnard*, Flaubert's *Temptation of St. Anthony*.
Hopkins, Gerard. Translator of Jules Romains, Mauriac, and other French writers.
Lee, Muna. Translator of Latin-American writers.
Lewisohn, Ludwig. Translator of Wassermann, Werfel, and other German writers.
Livingston, Arthur. Translator of Latin-American, Italian, Spanish, and French writers.
Lowe-Porter, H. T. Translator of Thomas Mann and other German writers.
MacIntyre, C. F. Translator of Goethe's *Faust*, Rilke, Baudelaire.
Matson, Alexander. Translator of Finnish writers.
Maude, Aylmer and Louise. Translators of Tolstoy.
May, J. Lewis. Translator of Anatole France.

Miall, Bernard. Translator of Fabre, of French and Danish writers.
Miles, Hamish. Translator of Maurois and other French writers.
Muir, Willa and Edwin. Translators of Feuchtwanger, Kafka, and other German writers.
Mussey, Barrows. Translator of French, German, and Scandinavian writers.
O'Brien, Justin. Translator of Gide's Journals.
Paul, Eden and Cedar. Translators of Stefan Zweig and other German writers.
Putnam, Samuel. Translator of Brazilian, Italian, Spanish, and French writers.
Samuel, Maurice. Translator of Sholem Asch and other Yiddish writers; also German and French.
Scott Moncrieff, C. K. Translator of Proust and Stendhal.
Selver, Paul. Translator of French, German, and Czech writers.
Seltzer, Thomas. Translator of Russian and German writers.
Starkie, Walter. Translator of Ramón Pérez de Ayala and other Spanish writers.
Stuart, Henry Longan. Translator of French writers.
Sutton, Eric. Translator of French writers.
Teixeira de Mattos, Alexander. Translator of Couperus, Maeterlinck, Ewald, and Fabre.
Trench, Herbert. Translator of Merejkowski.
Waley, Arthur. Translator of Lady Murasaki's *Tale of Genji* and of other Japanese and Chinese literature.
Worster, W. W. Translator of Scandinavian writers.

PART FOUR

Exploration and Discovery

12. Biography: Speculum Vitae

> Each life converges to some center
> Expressed or still;
> Exists in every human nature
> A goal . . .
>
> Emily Dickinson: "The Goal"

> However difficult biography may be, it merits the devotion of our toil and of our emotions. The cult of the hero is as old as mankind. It sets before man examples which are lofty but not inaccessible, astonishing but not incredible, and it is this double quality which makes it the most convincing of art forms—the most human of religions.
>
> André Maurois: *Aspects of Biography*

> There is that marvellous, perpetually renewed, and as yet largely untapped aid to the understanding of human motives which is provided in our age by biography and autobiography.
>
> Virginia Woolf: *Three Guineas*

THERE is symbolic meaning in the name given to a group of books common in the early days of printing. They were the "Specula": the mirrors that reflected warnings of man's dangers, or visions of the mysteries of his future. The fifteenth-century Specula concerned themselves chiefly with spiritual counsel, with the penalties of vice, the rewards of virtue. Most popular among them was the famous *Mirror of Human Salvation*, scattered in tattered copies over Europe, in block book sheets and in type-printed pages. But there were many others: mirrors of wisdom, mirrors of human folly, and of human happiness, so that one feels how deep has always been the recognition of the book as the medium that reflects human life as man sees it and interprets it.

All literature, in a sense, becomes a mirror of life. In history, the life of the past as it has been recorded in many forms is reflected, clear or obscure, fragmentary or in mass. In poetry and fiction, the mirror reflects the vision of living, each image according to the power of the seer; distorted or serene, far-sighted or myopic. Biography, more than any other form of literature, transmits a mirror image of the individual human being in his immediate life experience. Fine biography may thus be truly called by the old name, *Speculum vitae*. It gives to the reader a sense of sharing in actual human experience, yet of estimating and judging it at the same time; a sense of coming in touch with living persons, not with famous names, and at the same time a realization that each character, each destiny, is molded by influences of heredity, environment, and circumstance outside individual control.

All biography, indeed, offers material for study in heredity and psychology. This is the chief reason for the development of modern methods in its presentation and treatment and for its rapid rise in popularity. In it can be traced the roots that underlie character and temperament and the conditions that produce effects in human life. The range of its appeal is expressed in its literal meaning: *biographia*, the writing of life; for it presents life in the experience of living, it turns the abstract into the concrete, gives us not the thought alone but the personality of the thinker, not the record of the deed alone, but the nature of the doer. Gamaliel Bradford described it as the study that links with and relates to all other studies and that synthesizes knowledge. He urged it as the clue to coordinating and deepening education, the means by which instruction in any subject could be vitalized and made immediate and personal to the student. He said:

If you want to interest your pupils in the varied aspects of study and research, take them right to the human element. Show them that common passions and struggles and hopes and despairs go to the making of philosophy and the making of science and the making of history and the making of life. When you have interested them in the common eternal human element, which works today as it has always worked, you will find that philosophy and science and history have acquired a new meaning.

The universality of its relationship to literature and to life, its power of inspiration, its appeal to innate, unquenchable human curiosity concerning human character and experience, have given biog-

BIOGRAPHY

raphy a place second only to fiction in the affections of readers. On account of this wide popularity and the important place it holds in any library collection, it is chosen first among the several classes of literature that we now enter for exploration and discovery. Our purpose is to survey its broader aspects, to trace its divisions and ramifications and note their chief characteristics, to indicate points of strength and points of weakness, and to direct attention upon books that are representative of each, applying fundamental principles of book selection, and summarizing defects and qualities.

In the formation of a general library collection, as already pointed out, there is no fixed rule on which to base a balanced ratio of subjects. The earlier *A.L.A. Catalog* tabulations gave to fiction, literature, biography, and history the largest proportionate representation among the different classes of literature. In the 1926 *Catalog*, however, the representation of books in the social sciences rose to third place, after literature and fiction, and biography was reduced to a slightly less proportion than was accorded fine arts and travel, while history fell lower still. These and later changes reveal the constant movement and expansion of the cycle of human knowledge and the incidence of public demand, but they do not establish any absolute ratio. It is still probably true that in the formation of a library for general community use a greater proportion of "foundation books" —work of enduring quality as literature—will be drawn from fiction, literature, biography, and history than from other classes. After the foundations of a collection are laid, however, fewer biographies proportionately will be added, partly because there are usually more current publications of immediate importance in other classes and partly on account of the many varied demands that must be met in a carefully adjusted selection.

A great increase in the production of biography began in the mid-twenties. This reached its peak in 1930 (when 792 biographies appeared), diminished during the Depression years to a low of 485 in 1934; then rose again, to drop during the war years to a low of 392; and entered upon a slow postwar rise in 1946—in accordance with the general course of book production during this period. In relation to other classes of literature, there is evident no marked diminution of the inflow of biographies, nor of the sustained public interest they command. We are still in a great era of biographic reading.[1] There are, however, fluctuations in production, in multiplication and differentiation of types, or what may be called fashions, in biographic writing; and in competent selection wide familiarity with types of current literature is of prime importance. The profusion of biographies entails constantly more thorough sifting, more careful discrimination and comparison in current selection; for though work of high quality and of varied and unusual aspect may be found in rich abundance, there is also a mounting deposit of books that are trivial, shoddy, or superfluous. Good biographies are not common. Great biographies are rare. But a good biography is a worthy companion, guide, and friend; and a great biography represents the most difficult and finest achievement of literary art.

The human appeal of biography relates it to every other class of literature. It presents every human interest and activity through the record of individual experience. So it is closely allied to imaginative literature, to history, to all fields of work or of thought, and so it wakens and stimulates interest in history, art, science, and industry. There is no calling, no branch of knowledge, in which the lives of leaders or workers in that calling do not enlarge or deepen acquaintance with the subject itself. The lives of great actors or great singers are part of the history of the theater; the lives of scientists illuminate the history of science; the lives of statesmen and rulers are a part of the texture of history.

Biography is the easiest and the most natural bridge from fiction to fact, especially for young people. Boys who delight in "westerns" and adventure tales will find a similar lure in *American*, Linderman's biography of the Crow chief, Plenty-coups; or in Stanley Vestal's graphic biography, *Jim Bridger, Mountain Man;* or for our own day

[1] From 1926 to 1949 the number of biographies published annually in the United States are recorded as follows: 1926, 551; 1927, 625; 1928, 723; 1929, 738; 1930, 792; 1931, 775; 1932, 685; 1933, 545; 1934, 485; 1935, 548; 1936, 699; 1937, 660; 1938, 662; 1939, 628; 1940, 647; 1941, 599; 1942, 542; 1943, 473; 1944, 422; 1945, 392; 1946, 456; 1947, 518; 1948, 513; 1949, 595.

in *The Big Yankee*, Michael Blankfort's stirring life story of Carlson of the Raiders. Margaret Landon's exotic, vivid biographic narrative, *Anna and the King of Siam;* Dorothy Caruso's intimate, loving memorial to her husband and their short life together, *Enrico Caruso: His Life and Death;* and *No Time for Tears,* Leora Hughes' candid life story of pioneer nursing experience, should be to many girls as fascinating as a novel. Indeed, the novel and the biography have nowadays taken on so close a likeness that they can hardly be told apart; one merges into the other. Good biographical or historical fiction, however, is to my mind preferable to overfictionized biography, which even at its best is a makeshift and a pretense—neither novel nor biography—and at its worst is crude sensationalized or sentimentalized misrepresentation.

Biography represents, of course, fundamental material of history. History deals with events, their reasons, their course, their relation to the past, their influence on the future. Biography deals with the human beings who shared or shaped those events, their natures, purposes, defeats, and triumphs. This closeness of relationship is evident in the inextricable mingling, in any library classification, of history and historical biography. The *A.L.A. Catalog, 1926,* for example, classifies Voltaire's *History of Charles XII, King of Sweden* as history, and puts Bain's *Charles XII and the Collapse of the Swedish Empire* in biography. The differentiation is apparently based on the fact that the latter is a volume in the biographical series, "Heroes of the Nations"; but both books are equally biography and history and any separation is arbitrary. There is close relationship to history in many autobiographies and diaries. Pepys' diary is a gloss on English social and political conditions during the ten years 1660–70. The several volumes of Queen Victoria's letters are material for the historian of an era. Morley's *Life of Gladstone* is one of the finest existing studies of influences and events in the history of the nineteenth century, just as General Grant's memoirs are part of the history of our Civil War. And Douglas S. Freeman's great biography, *R. E. Lee,* with its companion work, *Lee's Lieutenants: a Study in Command,* constitutes as a whole a monumental military history of the

Confederacy. Historical value exists in all biographies, memoirs, and reminiscences that present with vitality or detail authentic aspects of social life at a given period. Benvenuto Cellini's autobiography does this for Italy and France of the late Renaissance, just as the letters of John and Abigail Adams serve a like purpose for the American colonial period. And what biography is so essentially to history, it is in some degree to almost every other class of literature. Jane Addams' *Twenty Years at Hull-House* and Margaret Sanger's *My Fight for Birth Control*, for example, are more important as contributions to sociology than they are as individual life experiences; Jennie Lee's simple, eloquent autobiography, *This Great Journey*, is an intimate, colorful, and precise story of the rise of the British Independent Labour party and the movement of the working people toward socialism.

Of the inspirational value of biography it is hardly necessary to speak. Is there anyone who has not responded to the ideal conveyed in some record of accomplishment, or to the revelation of what others have endured and suffered and overcome? Perhaps it is true that "the evil that men do lives after them; the good is oft interred with their bones" (though throughout that speech Mark Antony meant just the reverse of what he said); but there is more evident truth in the almost miraculous achievements possible in the lifework of a single human being. The reader of biography comes to realize that every difficulty or handicap may be overcome by the unconquerable mind of man—physical weaknesses or disabilities, lack of advantages, lack of the commonest necessities; that the spirit can dominate the material conditions of life. Mr. Larned has said:

What we ought to seek everywhere in books is escape from the commonplace—the commonplace in thought and the commonplace in character with which our daily life surrounds us. Our chief dependence is on books to bring us into intercourse with the picked choice examples of human kind; to show us what they are or what they have been, as well as what they have thought—what they have done, as well as what they have said—with what motives, from what impulses, with what powers, to what ends, in what spirit, the work of their lives has been

BIOGRAPHY

done. When biography does that for us, it is one of the most precious forms of literature.[2]

This is true, but it is also true that the older belief that biography owes its inspiration to the nobility of its subject no longer prevails. Knowledge of common human nature, in its defects as well as in its qualities, is stimulating, valuable, and developing. The inspiration of biography is that it is the mirror of man as he is. And in that mirror more and more readers seek to study themselves, to learn their own nature and observe the inner traits that make for self-conquest or self-defeat. As Mark Longaker says:

The inner conflicts of others are now regarded as a mirror in which one's own struggles can be viewed clearly and with profit. Identification is sought, and in the comparisons which are drawn between the struggles of others and one's own conflicts, there is much satisfaction. To compare one's own feelings and inward experiences with those of others is bound to afford pleasure, for in so doing man finds comfort, resignation, and at times aspiration.[3]

The literature of biography takes on various forms, which may be grouped in the two broad divisions of *Autobiography* and *Biography*. Autobiography in its simplest definition is the story of one's life written by oneself; Biography is the written life of a person by another. Closely related as they are, they are yet organically different. Autobiography is primarily subjective, built from within outward. Biography is objective, modeled from the outside inward. The former is firsthand information; the latter is information assembled from all available sources and molded to the representation of its subject.

Autobiography in its primary form is a continuous, organized story of a life experience, complete or partial. When complete it carries the life of its writer into late maturity. Benjamin Franklin, for instance, taking us to his fifty-first year, may be said to have given a complete autobiography, though he left unrecorded the last thirty-

---

[2] J. N. Larned, "A Familiar Talk about Books." In his *Books, Culture, and Character*, pp. 32–33.
[3] Mark Longaker, *Contemporary Biography*, p. 12.

three years of his life. Gibbon in half a dozen separate strands wove a fairly complete texture. Henry Adams' autobiography is complete, although a period of twenty years is deliberately omitted; so are the autobiographies of Benvenuto Cellini, Isadora Duncan, Anthony Trollope, William Allen White, and many others.

But probably the majority of autobiographies are partial, dealing especially with childhood or youth, or presenting certain phases of a career, certain periods of experience. W. H. Hudson's beautiful self-chronicle, *Far Away and Long Ago* carries only to his eighteenth year; Ruskin's *Praeterita* does not extend beyond early manhood; Gosse's *Father and Son*, forerunner of psychological analysis of personality in biographic art, is essentially a record of the struggle for freedom of an individual soul under crushing restrictions of family relationship during childhood and youth. There is something especially appealing and interesting in almost anyone's story of his childhood, and this is usually the most charming part of autobiography—naturally enough, for there is no one of us who in later years does not look back with mingled affection, pity, and curiosity at a small figure, remote, half-forgotten but keenly cherished, that in some unbelievable way was once oneself.

Good autobiography should be honest, simple, and above all, interesting. Interesting it always is, in the almost unconscious portrayal of temperament and personality that can hardly be avoided when one writes upon that always absorbing and delightful subject, Myself. Even the partial autobiographies, that give only the early years of the writer, give the person himself—the ego that with all of us remains unchanged through life. As Ruskin says, in *Praeterita*:

Now, looking back to that brook-shore, whence I could see the whole of my youth, I find in myself nothing whatsoever changed. Some of me is dead, more of me is stronger. I have learned a few things; forgotten many; in the total of things, I am but the same youth, disappointed and rheumatic.

Probably very few autobiographies are thoroughly honest, honestly simple. It could hardly be otherwise, for we see ourselves through a medium different from that in which we are seen by others. Oliver Wendell Holmes described the six persons who participate in the dialogue between John and Henry: John's John, Henry's John, and God's John; Henry's Henry, John's Henry, and God's Henry; and in all autobiographies three persons are hidden—the writer as he sees himself, the writer as he appeared to others, and the writer as the reader sees him. Benvenuto Cellini recounts both his knavish and his worthy deeds with the same self-satisfaction and cheerful swagger; Benjamin Haydon is often unconscious of the implications of his behavior. Yet these and all other autobiographies convey more and different truth than their writers could ever realize. The complete self-revelation that was the purpose of Rousseau is now sought by many autobiographers, and represents a definite trend in modern biographic writing. It was undertaken on a monumental scale, but never completed, by Theodore Dreiser, in his *History of Myself*, with two volumes of elaborate, unabashed self-portrayal (*Dawn; Newspaper Days*), that will long remain unsurpassed as a firsthand life study of what the French call *l'homme moyen sensuel*. Robert Graves' autobiography, *Goodbye to All That*, in its vigorous compression and fine literary art is one of the best examples of this modern effort to look within with a vision cleared of self-consciousness and set down one's findings with ruthless candor and entire unconcern for what others will think or feel. H. G. Wells' *Experiment in Autobiography* is primarily self-scrutiny, self-appraisal—a candid and earnest effort, in reviewing his life, to analyze changes and phases in his own character and temperament, so far as he can study and interpret them. There are in contemporary autobiography infinite variations upon this theme of unsparing psychological self-study—some complacently egocentric, some erotic, some psychotic, many carrying self-revelation into nudism. But whatever their defects, all autobiographies that live are alive themselves, vital, interesting. Dullness is the one fatal defect that autobiography cannot survive.

Autobiographical writing takes various forms. Most familiar are memoirs, reminiscences, diaries, journals, confessions, letters, and correspondence.

Memoirs represent a form that belongs both in autobiography and biography. In the plural, "memoirs," the term usually denotes autobiographical narrative or reminiscences, informal and often more or less fragmentary. Such are the memoirs of the Duke de Saint Simon, the *Memoirs of a Highland Lady*, and many others. Sometimes also it is used for a life that is partly autobiographical and partly biography by some relative or friend of the subject, as in the memoirs of Augustus Saint Gaudens. In the singular, "memoir" usually means an account of a person's life from another hand—such as Fielding H. Garrison's *John Shaw Billings: a Memoir*. There is no single rule of practice in the use of either term. Thus, the word "memoirs" or "memoir" does not always indicate the exact biographical form, and examination of the book itself is necessary before the form can be definitely stated.

Reminiscences at their best are both valuable and delightful. In them observation and experience stored up in a rich and varied life are drawn from memory and told simply and spontaneously to a reader-listener, illuminating byways of life and thought and casting revealing side-lights on famous or interesting people. Morley's *Recollections*, the *Memories* of Lord Redesdale, Julian Hawthorne's *Shapes That Pass*, are examples of such rich and rewarding volumes. But quality is apt to be submerged in quantity, and no form of biography needs more discriminating selection than reminiscences. Of the enormous number published, many are gossip, trivial, or pretentious, or scandalous. Those dealing with political and literary affairs, or with experiences in some active field of life, are generally the best. Social reminiscences are the most variable in quality—often simply the self-glorification of some egotistical lady, intended primarily to reveal to the world how many distinguished friends and acquaintances she possessed. There is always an unconscious glamour about reminiscence; it cannot be wholly trusted. It is a natural human tendency to exaggerate in memory the splendor of our past, or the degree of intimacy we have enjoyed with well-known persons. Many celebrities, I am sure, are quite unable to recall some of the persons who boast a childhood friendship with them.

BIOGRAPHY

Memoirs and reminiscences which are personal material of history-in-the-making pour out after every great war. This was true of World War I. And now from World War II there rises a far more overwhelming flood of memoirs, recollections, and autobiographical records from military leaders, statesmen, public men, and civilian participants. All this is basic substance for the historian, but also it is current literature of information from which the great body of readers must shape a common background of opinion and understanding concerning the issues and the conditions that confront the postwar world. In ordinary library selection there can be little more than a gleaning from the mass, but the gleaning should be directed by a reasoned sense of comparative values and intrinsic merit, not by automatic acceptance of highly publicized popular appeal. Thus, Winston Churchill's *Memoirs of the Second World War* holds enduring primacy as magnificent literature in the finest English tradition, as well as in all-inclusive range, historical, political, military, and personal, of firsthand knowledge.

Diaries and *journals* are virtually the same, yet some differentiation exists in the use of the terms. Diaries generally connote a factual consecutive record of objective experience. Pepys' diary and Evelyn's diary are famous examples of the completeness and accuracy with which such a simple, scrupulous personal record can disclose the everyday life of a period. The diaries of Wilfred Blunt, suppressed on their first publication in England, are materials for the political and social history of the decline of British imperialism. Ambassador Dodd's diary records first intimations of Nazi Germany's war menace to the world; and William Shirer's *Berlin Diary* stands as a foundation document for the opening years of World War II history. Journals usually offer a fuller, more subjective, or more specialized record. Very often they are serious contributions to the writer's philosophy of life, and they have furnished some of the finest and most familiar studies in personal religion. John Woolman's journal, Fox's journal, Amiel's journal, each in its own vein, are enduring documents of the inner life. The ten volumes of Emerson's journals are, in fact, an introspective, philosophic record of the development of Emerson's structure of thought and teaching. The famous journals of Edmond and Jules de Goncourt mirror French literature and social life through the second half of the nineteenth century. Many journals, however, deal with active enterprises, as do the journals of the great explorers. Indeed firsthand records of travel and exploration very frequently take journal form. Of course, neither diaries nor journals give the rounded story of a life as it is given in autobiography and biography.

Confessions are subjective and introspective, outpourings of inner conflict, closely allied to the journals that reveal the inner life. The confessions of Saint Augustine set the earlier religious type of self-examination and self-accusation in endeavor to purge the conscience of remembered sins. Such are Tolstoi's confessions, and many others; materials for the study of every phase of religious experience. Rousseau's confessions set the later type of psychological self-revelation, designed, in laying bare motives and actions, to unveil the whole nature of man—a type that under the stimulus of psychoanalysis now multiplies and diversifies itself through the entire field of modern biography.

Letters and correspondence are closely allied to journals. Letters, especially, often deal with subjects or experiences of specialized interest. Lady Duff-Gordon's *Letters from Egypt*, Lord Dufferin's *Letters from High Latitudes*, rank among famous books of travel. Such letters as those of Walter H. Page and Emily Dickinson are of enduring biographical importance; and Gertrude Bell's letters not only paint her own full-length portrait but give historical record of the British statecraft that held Mesopotamia for the allies during World War I. *The Amberley Papers*, in which Bertrand Russell sets forth in masterly organization and illuminating comment the letters and diaries of his parents, is one of the most delightful and permanently valuable records in this field—a repository of personalities and activities in the social, cultural, and political life of England in the finest flower of Victorianism. Correspondence, which implies more than one letter-writer, is less common. Often it preserves the juiceless dregs of diplomacy or statesmanship; but now and then it is a medium that transmits warmth of personality and friendship. The correspondence of Adams and Jefferson does this; so, rooted in a lifetime's mutual absorption in law and literature, do the *Holmes-Pollock Letters;* and so, in sparkling radiance of wit and charm, does the Terry-Shaw correspondence.

Biography falls into two main classes, *individual biography* and *collective biography,* with various minor subsidiary forms. Individual biography is commonly implied by the word, "biography," and includes within itself all variations of substance and treatment. It is the oldest type of biographical writing, the art fathered by Plutarch, whose objective life-studies of the men who made the world he knew are still the admiration of biographers. Its modern range has widened far beyond the limits of the earlier biography that confined itself chiefly to lives of those eminent in leadership or in attainment. Lives of rulers, soldiers, generals, statesmen, religious teachers, pathbreakers in art, learning, or science, represent an old and familiar type of biography. Of later development is the biographical study of personality—often invested with its appeal by the art or power of the biographer, as in Barrie's *Margaret Ogilvy.* With the growth of modern psychology and the deepening popular interest in all aspects of human life and human nature, biography now turns to lives of any and every degree of significance—obscure, or abnormal, or commonplace (though no life is really commonplace)—as material for character interpretation, or analysis of personality, or merely for pictorial rendering of human traits and emotions. Most pervasive among the innumerable variations that have evolved in biography centering on character study are the family chronicles for which Clarence Day's *Life with Father* set a pattern. Basically personal reminiscence rather than impersonal biography, these range from objective critical portrayal—as in Daphne Du Maurier's two family pieces, *Gerald* and *The Du Mauriers,* Victoria Sackville-West's unveiling of patrimonial skeletons in *Pepita,* and the brilliant, many-angled Sitwell volumes based on family annals— to highly popularized chronicles of distinctive family backgrounds, erratic relatives, and uncommon experiences, of which *Mother*

Wore Tights, Chicken Every Sunday, The Egg and I, and *Cheaper by the Dozen* are typical examples.

In considering biographical literature it must be remembered that autobiography remains the same in import whether published during the lifetime of the writer or after his death; for it is the expression of personal, individual temperament and experience, in the person's own words, and will be interesting or dull, valuable or worthless, no matter when it was written. Biography is seldom of permanent value when written during the lifetime of the subject. It is too difficult a task for any biographer to write comprehensively, impartially, and frankly under the eye of the person he is writing about. Biographies of present-day celebrities are often useful as sources of information or as conveying aesthetic or critical appreciation, though even here perspective gives better values, but they are not likely to have lasting importance as definitive biography.

By *collective biography* is meant lives of a number of persons selected, or grouped, or assembled in encyclopedic form. Sometimes they are by a single author (Plutarch's *Lives* is the most famous example), sometimes of composite authorship. One of the greatest works of collective biography in English is *Dictionary of National Biography,* published by Oxford University Press, model and inspiration for the *Dictionary of American Biography,* publication of which, under the auspices of the American Council of Learned Societies and largely financed by the New York *Times,* was begun in 1928 and completed in 1936. The volumes of *Who's Who,* with their *Monthly Supplement* for current record, the Wilson monthly *Current Biography,* with its *Yearbook,* and the many biographical dictionaries exemplify collective biography in its condensed reference form. Here an ambitious undertaking of a "Who's Who" in global form is *World Biography,* published in 1948, which records some 40,000 people of importance from sixty nations, about half of them duplicating names that may be found in British and American *Who's Who* volumes. There are many inconsistencies and inadequacies, but some 20,000 of the sketches (including 1,200 Russians) furnish information that in many libraries it is difficult to supply. More general and popular presentation of collective biography is in grouped lives that convey achievements in different fields of knowledge, as in De Kruif's *Microbe Hunters*, or that illuminate historical backgrounds, as in Holbrook's *Lost Men of American History*.

Collective biography is usually more material of information than is individual biography; it is more condensed, more a record of dates and facts, less capable, on account of its brevity, of reproducing personality and character, therefore less inspiring and less interesting than individual biography. Its great usefulness is as a quick guide to information concerning a number of persons. Modern collective biography, however, has established a distinctive art form of its own, in brilliant, penetrating short character studies, concerned not with condensation of fact but with reflection or interpretation of personality; in this development the work of Gamaliel Bradford in America and of Lytton Strachey in England has been a dominant stimulating and molding influence. Here are found the "psychographs," the "thumbnail sketches," the "literary portraits," the "profiles," that are present-day successors to the "biographical essays" that enlisted the powers of Carlyle, Macaulay, and De Quincey, and that represent the application of the dramatic method which has so transformed modern biography. The biographer upon a carefully constructed framework of fact arranges, balances, studies, and interprets the material he deals with, to produce a portrait, not to make a photograph nor to cast an image. The "psychographs" of Gamaliel Bradford, in which character and temperament were studied and chronology disregarded to focus upon psychological and aesthetic aspects, set the model that found variation in the work of Lytton Strachey, with its sustained sequence of events and its stronger emphasis upon character creation, vivid scenic effect, and satiric implication.[4]

Strachey's portraits etched in caustic gave chief inspiration to the

---

[4] Bradford himself considered the resemblance between his work and Strachey's as a superficial similarity in "cleverness and direct vivacity of writing and in the use of quotations." In his published *Journal* (Houghton Mifflin, 1933), he makes an interesting comparison and analysis of the two methods of composition.

"debunking" biographies which reached their peak in the decade of the 1920's and set a pattern that still leaves its impress. Here ironical iconoclasm found full play: the altars of hero worship were overthrown; "human interest," "sex appeal," and penetration of the "inner life" of great personalities of the past were prime objectives. By most of Strachey's imitators his faults were reproduced and exaggerated; his great virtue of literary craftsmanship proved untransferable. "Debunking," startling and entertaining, held immediate popular appeal; it enlarged and brought controversial animation to the whole field of biography, long cluttered with dusty memorial wreaths and massive but dull historical monuments. But as a familiar mechanized process its shock approach lost impact, its substance was seen as too often cheap and adulterated; interest lessened, and it remains no longer a dominating type. Its defects were distortion, prejudice, crude literary expression, and what may be called a propaganda motive. Its values lay in wide gleaning from available, often unpublished, sources, in willingness to submit any reputation, however respectable, to critical examination; and in alignment with the advancing trend to social consciousness. In the long run, the influence of "debunking" was to broaden, sharpen, and clarify the biographic writing of today.

Realism, psychology, and fiction have been the most important influences in the development of modern biography. They have changed the substance and the manner of much biographical writing and are chiefly responsible for its increase in volume and its high popularity. They have established both excellences and defects. Today biography is less formalized, more flexible and vigorous, more infused with human interest, than it ever has been. The modern biographer is conceded freedom to tell his subject's thoughts (necessarily an exercise of the imagination) provided the rendering is based on psychological probability (as in Strachey's *Queen Victoria*) or on the coincident evidence of letters or diaries (as in Maurois' *Byron*). On the other hand, the desire for realism has produced biography that is sensational scavenger work, not serious and fair-minded presentation of all available facts. Preoccupation with psychology and psychoanalysis is often manifested in character delineations distorted to fit a prescribed theory; and the adoption of the novelist's technique has yielded a mass of superficial, highly spiced, or sugar-coated so-called biographies that are neither sound biography nor good fiction.

Use of the fictional element, however, when handled with restraint and judgment, is characteristic of some of the best work in modern biography. Bradford, Strachey, Maurois, Guedalla, each in a different way employs the art of the novelist in the effective organization of material, in the development of a central thread or theme of life-purpose or personality, in skillful subordination of detail to dramatic crises or climax. Their work is valid as biography and as alluring as a novel. Each in his own manner extracts an elixir of human nature from massive memoirs and many-volumed historical authorities. Such work as theirs, while it adapts the art of the novelist to the use of the biographer, is not the crude fictionized biography produced by their inexpert imitators.

It is almost impossible to make close differentiation between legitimate modern biography which employs the elements of fictional art, unduly fictionized biography, and legitimate biographical (or historical) fiction. More and more the border lines merge as the novel becomes a constantly expanding medium for serious biographical study of actual persons. Perhaps a workable general rule is to consider that constant use of the present tense in narrative, introduction of dialogue, and highly pictorial rendering of dramatic or emotional scenes, constitute undue fictionization; that a sustained dramatic framework of plot, combined with dialogue, soliloquy, and use of imaginary characters and episodes, denote a novel. E. Barrington's books are novels; so is Elswyth Thane's carefully documented chronicle of Queen Elizabeth's girlhood, *The Tudor Wench;* so is Maurice Baring's beautiful reweaving of the strands of Mary Stuart's life story, *In My End Is My Beginning*. Helen Ashton's serene narrative, *The Swan of Usk*, is putatively a novel, but it is also a valid biography of Henry Vaughan, the "poet of eternity." Irving Stone's biographical novels of Vincent van Gogh (*Lust for Life*), Jessie

Benton Frémont (*Immortal Wife*), and Eugene V. Debs (*Adversary in the House*), are factually authentic, illuminative of character and personality, touched with strong imaginative highlights, but fairly within the canons of legitimate fictionized biography. More unusual as transmutation of factual biography into an evocation of personality and life experience is James Barke's *The Wind that Shakes the Barley*, initiating a tetralogy designed as a permanent memorial to Robert Burns, which when completed will bear the title *Immortal Memory*. Of the eighty-four characters in the opening volume only twelve are wholly imagined persons, many are shaped from a line or sentence of Burns' own characterizations; and the simply told narrative, at once detailed and episodic, has authority and vitality. The same qualities are maintained in the second volume of the sequence, *The Song in the Green Thorn Tree;* and the whole enterprise holds promise of a remarkable achievement in creative rather than fictional biography: lacking perhaps in literary finish, but rich in honesty, warmth, historical accuracy, perceptive insight, and the power to evoke personality. Comparison of this with one of the standard contemporary Burns biographies (Catharine Carswell's *Life of Robert Burns* is among the best) will make clear the respective distinctions and values in these two kinds of biographic literature. This rich and varied field of biographic fiction demands careful consideration in library selection.

Modern biography, thus, has its own intellectual concept and art form. Today in psychology and ethics there are no regions of human behavior sacred from observation and analysis. To the modern biographer his subject is a human being "to be truthfully portrayed, with scientific exactitude, in the light of all available evidence." But in the performance of his task he must still display the qualifications that Plutarch brought to it nearly two thousand years ago—understanding of human nature, reason, fair-mindedness, temperate and sound ethical standards, and knowledge of the available facts and circumstances that concern his subject. Perhaps the best hint of the dangers and pitfalls that confront him is that given in Philip Guedalla's definition of biography as "a region that is bounded on the north by history, on the south by fiction, on the east by obituary, and on the west by tedium."

Chief points to be considered in selection of biography may be summarized as:

Form or type of biography.—As previously defined.

Importance or interest of subject.—The subject must be interesting in himself or made interesting by the art of the biographer. Many a dreary biography of someone of no importance whatever is published to gratify family pride or affection and to distribute to the deceased's fellow members of the Excelsior Literary Society or the descendants of the Jones Family, but a simple, uneventful life can be invested with charm and significance. Much of the permanent quality of certain famous biographies is in the way they have been told. Autobiography, in particular, must either record experiences of intrinsic interest or express distinctive personality.

Authority, accuracy, and sympathy of biographer.—A biographer should know the country, times, environment, and antecedents of his subject. In general, a better biography is written by someone who is not a relative or too close a friend, as there is then less evasion of intimate details and less adulation. Forster's life of Dickens and Tennyson's life by his son are historic examples of a reticence that repels intimate acquaintance. But a biographer must be sympathetic, otherwise the biography loses its appeal and its truth is obscured. Maurois' life of Byron represents a beautifully balanced attitude, dispassionate, yet sincerely sympathetic. The brilliancy and vigor of Woodward's *George Washington* are stultified by the personal hostility that animates it throughout. Sympathy and impartiality are the two great attributes of fine biography, for there should always be critical perception of the weaknesses or temperamental defects of the subject. For this reason husbands and wives seldom make satisfactory biographers, though Professor Palmer's biography of his wife, Alice Freeman Palmer, is one of the exceptions—beautifully proportioned and delicately sensitized. So, on a very different plane, is the rare human document, full of beauty, simplicity, and tragic emotion, in which Romola Nijinsky tells the story of her husband, the great Russian dancer. Autobiography would naturally be expected to have at least firsthand authority, but this is not always so. Life stories and reminiscences are often prepared by so-called "ghost writers," who spin a facile narrative from material furnished them by the reputed autobiographer. Such work at its best, honestly offered for what it is and transmitting the original personality, is valid and acceptable, especially when it organizes and gives effective expression to experiences of men and women who can tell vividly and explicitly of their adventures or achievements but lack facility in writing. Some of the most important narratives of world war experience are of this nature; but there are many volumes of self-styled autobiography or reminiscence that represent ghost writing in its crudest and most spurious form.

Manner of treatment.—Is it gossipy, scrappy, disconnected, diffuse; or well balanced, direct, firmly constructed? Over-diffuseness is a common fault. Albert Bigelow Paine's life of Mark Twain would have gained immensely in vitality and effectiveness by rigorous pruning. Lives of statesmen and political leaders are too often swamped by an enormous overloading of source material. Autobiography also frequently suffers from undue verbosity. One of the most remarkable examples of this may be found in the autobiography of David Starr Jordan, *The Days of a Man*—two volumes that weigh six pounds apiece and that enshrine in more than 1,600 pages an enormous, unorganized mass of material brought together with a complete unconsciousness of relative values.

Literary quality.—This is of great importance. Fine biographies require imagination, feeling, grace of style, vigor of expression—in addition to the solid materials of information assembled by scholarly labor and organized by executive skill. Beveridge's great life of John Marshall has these qualities. So has Morley's *Life of Gladstone;* and at the other end of the scale so has Arthur Benson's short biographic study of his brother, *Hugh*. They are qualities found also in all autobiographies that have permanent appeal.

Purpose or point of view.—Partisan or controversial purpose, personal bias or theory of a biographer, should be recognized. Many biographers set out to prove something, and consciously or unconsciously shape the record of their subject to produce the desired conclusions. There are many examples: in biographies centering on psychoanalysis (such as Katharine Anthony's life of Margaret Fuller, and Joseph Krutch's brilliant study of Poe); in those designed to support historical or pathological theories (as in Belloc's *Richelieu*, and Nordau's biographic studies in genius); in those written to controvert the traditional character of some famous figure in history (as in Weigall's study of Nero, and "Baron Corvo's" *Chronicles of the House of Borgia*); and in numerous present-day biographies motivated by intense political or ideological partisanship and overshadowed by personal antagonisms (as in *The Red Prussian: the Life and Legend of Karl Marx*, by Leopold Schwarzschild, and in the deadly personal enmity that imparts unintended ironic flavor to the biography of Stalin by Trotsky). Work of this sort often represents genuine research and has definite values of interpretation or information; but often—especially in the application of Freudian principles—it is based on assumptions that can never be proved and is essentially "literature of a fixed idea." It must be remembered, however, that definitely critical biography should not be dismissed as simply an expression of personal bias, but fairly appraised for authority, impersonality, factual accuracy, and significance in its special field; Keith Sward's biography, *The Legend of Henry Ford*, for example, is an important contribution to contemporary literature on labor and capital.

In the practice of selection, controversial or partisan biography frequently presents unexpected problems. It may rouse protest from persons or organizations disposed toward censorship; it may simply involve difficult decision between opposed values. The autobiography of Emma Goldman, for example, has more than once invited censorship by one hundred percent patriots as radical literature that encourages the overthrow of government; Margaret Sanger's life story has drawn protest by those averse to the cause it champions. The controversial biography of Lincoln, by Edgar Lee Masters, brought protests from military and patriotic organizations that in some cities succeeded in barring it from public library circulation. Such problems should be met with reason, knowledge, and firm purpose to maintain impartiality, and to "select books that will tend toward the development and enrichment of life." Emma Goldman's autobiography is of significance and value, both as study of personality and as a vivid, firsthand record of unrealized forces in our social history; Margaret Sanger's charts the course of an entering movement in modern life. Both are appropriate examples of books that tend toward development of life; and in all application of this principle of selection it should be remembered that "development and enrichment of life" are aided by the fullest possible knowledge of every vital issue that confronts the world in which we are living.

Comparison of the foregoing tests with those outlined in Chapter 3 will show that they are simply specialized development of fundamental principles of appraisal of book values. Their application to the literature of biography has been brief and partial, but should indicate some of the chief characteristics, defects, and qualities that must be observed and weighed in this particular field of selection. Comparison of biographies of different types and differing degrees of merit is one of the best aids to discriminating judgment. A number of such comparisons have already been suggested. Many others that will be found significant may be made—for example, comparison of Hervey Allen's rounded, sympathetic biography of Poe with the psychoanalytic study by Krutch; of Ernest Dimnet's clear, even-toned rendering of *The Brontë Sisters* with Romer Wilson's fictionized psychoanalytic conception of *The Life and Private History of Emily Jane Brontë*.

Much that is helpful and illuminating has been written on the art and work of the biographer. The *Bookman's Manual*, in chapters that offer a selective survey of the finer literature of biography, also lists well-known bibliographies, works of reference, and critical commentary.[5] These chapters should be a first aid in building up

---

[5] The *Index to Contemporary Biography and Criticism*, by Helen Hefling and Eva Richards, published in Faxon's "Useful Reference Series" (new ed., rev. and enl. by Helen Hefling and J. W. Dyde, Faxon, 1934) guides to material contained in some four hundred volumes of collective biography and criticism.

background acquaintance with the subject. In any further consideration of the qualities of biographical writing the following books will be found of particular interest and value:

Bates, E. Stuart. Inside Out: an introduction to autobiography. New York, Sheridan House, 1937.

An unusual study, by the author of *Modern Translation*, designed to show autobiography "as a great storehouse of first-hand, vivid, authentic information about human personality, in all its variety, beauty, depth, intricacy, squalor, and grandeur." In two parts: the first devoted to common experiences (being a child, growing up, looking for adventure), with chapters on "poor folk" and business industrialists; the second dealing with lives centering on religion, the arts, the professions, lives that represent failure, and lives that reveal spiritual and emotional maladjustment. Does not include the most widely known autobiographies, but chooses from work which has not had general attention. Comprises more than 400 autobiographies, drawn from 23 languages.

Bradford, Gamaliel. Biography and the Human Heart. Boston, Houghton Mifflin Company, 1932.

This posthumous volume includes several essays that analyze and illustrate Mr. Bradford's own biographic method and that are suggestive in any evaluation of biographical literature.

Cook, Sir Edward. Literary Recreations. London, Macmillan & Co., 1929.

Includes the essay, "The Art of Biography," which expresses the ripe judgment and expert knowledge of a great biographer, whose life of Florence Nightingale and life of John Ruskin are among the fine achievements of English biography.

English Institute Annual: 1942. New York, Columbia University Press, 1943.

Contains eight of the papers read at the fourth session of the Institute, held Sept. 5–7, 1942. Three are authoritative, illuminating studies on "Interpretation in Biography": "The Ethics of Biography," by André Maurois, supplements with charm and precision points set forth in his *Aspects of Biography;* "The Development, Use, and Abuse of Interpretation in Biography," by Newman D. White, maintains that "interpretation without sound factual basis is worthless"; and "The Humanistic Bases of Biographical Interpretation," by Arthur M. Wilson, sees the supreme aim of biography as being "to give us added material for experiencing vicariously the variety and complexity of human nature."

Johnson, Edgar. One Mighty Torrent: the drama of biography. New York, Stackpole Sons, 1937.

A valuable accessory to study of biographies, or to their use in list-making, characterization, annotation, and similar service to readers. It offers, not extracts or citations, but paraphrase, characterization, and summary for some fifty-odd distinctive biographies, many of them among the classics of literature, and brief mention of many others. Characterizations seem at times farfetched or ill-founded, and the writing is diffuse and, in itself, pedestrian, although it is given color and power and style from the injection of its material. The author is also editor af *A Treasury of Biography* (New York, Howell, Soskin, 1941), in which 24 well-known biographies are linked by summaries which give a condensed life history of each subject.

Longaker, Mark. Contemporary Biography. Philadelphia, University of Pennsylvania, 1934.

An excellent study of "contemporary life-writing," analyzing the emphasis upon psychology and the attention directed to personality as representative of "the inclinations which shape the modern mind." Strachey, Bradford, Maurois, Ludwig, Guedalla, and Belloc are considered in separate chapters, with balanced judgment, both critical and appreciative; and a final chapter is given to "Some American biographers." Interesting, useful, and suggestive in enlarging background and sharpening discrimination.

Maurois, André. Aspects of Biography. New York, D. Appleton & Co., 1929.

A deft, delicate, and discriminating study of qualities and characteristics of biographical writing, based on lectures delivered in 1928 at Trinity College, Cambridge. It centers entirely on English biography and asks and answers the questions, Is there such a thing as "modern" biography? Is there a literary form different from that of traditional biography? Are its methods legitimate, or ought they to be abandoned? Ought biography to be an art or a science? Can it, like the novel, be a means of expression, a means of escape, for the author as well as for the reader?

Nicolson, Harold. The Development of English Biography. New York, Harcourt, Brace & Co., 1928.

One of the "Hogarth Lectures on Literature," this is an analysis of "pure" biography (defined as "the truthful and deliberate record of an individual's life written as a work of intelligence"). It traces the course of biographical writing from the Anglo-Saxon age to the present, noting the emergence of scientific exactitude, structural art, intellectual penetration, and satirical spirit.

FIFTY BIOGRAPHIES INDICATIVE OF VARIANT OLDER AND MODERN FORMS AND METHODS

Older Biographies

Barrie, Sir J. M. Margaret Ogilvy, by Her Son. 1896.
Boswell, James. Life of Samuel Johnson. 1791.
Cellini, Benvenuto. Life, by Himself; trans. by J. A. Symonds. 1888.
Darwin, Charles. Life and Letters. 1887.
Franklin, Benjamin. Autobiography. 1868.
Gaskell, Mrs. E. C. Life of Charlotte Brontë. 1857.
Gibbon, Edward. Autobiography. 1796.
Hawthorne, Julian. Nathaniel Hawthorne and His Wife. 1884.
Lockhart, J. G. Memoirs of the Life of Sir Walter Scott. 1838.
Mill, John Stuart. Autobiography. 1873.
Morley, John. Life of William Ewart Gladstone. 1903.
Newman, Cardinal J. H. Apologia pro vita sua. 1864.
Plutarch. Parallel Lives of Greeks and Romans; trans. by North. 1579.
Rousseau, J. J. Confessions; pref. by Edmund Wilson. 1923. 2 vols.
Ruskin, John. Praeterita. 1885–89.
Tolstoy, Count L. N. Childhood, Boyhood, and Youth. 1886.
Trevelyan, Sir G. O. Life and Letters of Lord Macaulay. 1876.
Trollope, Anthony. Autobiography. 1883.

Modern Biographies

Adams, Henry. The Education of Henry Adams. 1918.
Amberley Papers: the letters and diaries of Bertrand Russell's parents. 1937.
Beveridge, Albert J. Life of John Marshall. 1916–19.
Bowen, Catherine Drinker. Yankee from Olympus. 1944.
Cecil, Lord David. The Stricken Deer, or the Life of Cowper. 1930.
Colvin, Sidney. John Keats. 1917.
Cushing, Harvey. Life of Sir William Osler. 1925.
Day, Clarence. Life with Father. 1935.
Duncan, Isadora. My Life. 1927.
Ferber, Edna. A Peculiar Treasure: autobiography. 1939.
Forbes, Esther. Paul Revere and the World He Lived In. 1942.
Gosse, Edmund. Father and Son. 1907.

Holt, Rackham. George Washington Carver. 1943.
Hudson, W. H. Far Away and Long Ago. 1918.
Keller, Helen. Story of My Life. 1902.
Leonard, William Ellery. The Locomotive God. 1927.
Maurois, André. Byron. 1930.
Morison, Samuel Eliot. Admiral of the Ocean Sea: a life of Christopher Columbus. 1942.
Nehru, Jawaharlal. Toward Freedom: autobiography. 1941.
Perkins, Frances. The Roosevelt I Knew. 1946.
Roeder, Ralph. Juarez and His Mexico. 1947.
Sandburg, Carl. Abraham Lincoln. 1926, 1939.
Santayana, George. Persons and Places. 1945.
Sitwell, Osbert. The Scarlet Tree. 1946.
Steffens, Lincoln. Autobiography. 1931.
Strachey, Lytton. Queen Victoria. 1921.
Torrence, Ridgeley. The Story of John Hope. 1948.
Webb, Beatrice. Our Partnership; ed. by Barbara Drake and Margaret I. Cole. 1948.
Wells, H. G. Experiment in Autobiography. 1934.
White, Walter. A Man Called White. 1948.
White, William Allen. Autobiography. 1946.
Wright, Richard. Black Boy: a record of childhood and youth. 1945.

13. History

> The work of the Spirit of Earth, as he weaves and draws his threads on the Loom of Time, is the temporal history of man as this manifests itself in the geneses and growths and breakdowns and disintegrations of human societies and in all this welter of life and tempest of action we can hear the beat of an elemental rhythm ... The elemental rhythm is the alternating beat of Yin and Yang; and in listening to it we have recognized that, though strophe may be answered by antistrophe, victory by defeat, creation by destruction, birth by death, the movement that this rhythm beats out is neither the fluctuation of an indecisive battle nor the cycle of a treadmill. The perpetual turning of a wheel is not a vain repetition if, at each revolution, it is carrying the vehicle that much nearer its goal ... On this showing the music that the rhythm of Yin and Yang beats out is the song of creation; and we shall not be misled into fancying ourselves mistaken because, as we give ear, we can catch the note of creation alternating with the note of destruction. If we listen well we shall perceive that, when the two notes collide, they produce not a discord but a harmony. Creation would not be creative if it did not swallow up all things in itself, including its own opposite.
> Arnold J. Toynbee: *A Study of History* (Abridgement)

HISTORY is one of the great domains of literature, one of the broadest and most varied, the richest and most rewarding; and one in which thorough specialized knowledge is necessary to any extended selection and use of books. Only a brief general survey of the broad field of historical literature can here be attempted, with some indication of its chief forms and characteristics, of trends that mark its modern development, and of elementary book selection tests by which the character and quality of individual works may be approximately gauged.

Perhaps the greatest importance of history lies in the message it bears to the present in its record of the past. James Russell Lowell said: "Time Was unlocks the riddle of Time Is." And it is only as we know the causes that lie in the past that we can understand the effects of those causes as they operate in the present, or realize the influences that are taking shape to affect the future. For history is a clearinghouse of human life; a compendium of all the facts, ideas, forces, that impel the progession of man on the earth. Thus to the general reader the great purpose and value of history is to cultivate and inform the mind, to enlighten the judgment, to establish a background of understanding and comparison for history in the making. This it does in its panorama of the past, its revelation of the continuing elemental currents of human experience and aspirations, passions and action, and its slowly massed evidence that little by little man's condition improves, man's aspirations fructify.

Primarily, history is the story of human events and actions in the past. Its assumption and purpose are to record "what really happened," accurately, impartially, from all available evidence. But it is not solely a judicial statement, based on careful sifting of fact. It is also in many of its manifestations an expression of national consciousness, a means of creating and stimulating national aspirations. In the modern scientific conception it is an endeavor to determine causes and explain results, to tell what motives impelled human actions, and why man has become what he is. Its aims, its range, and its methods have steadily broadened. It demands the patient research of the scholar, the rigid analysis of the scientist, the skillful synthesis of the literary artist, and more than a gleam of the vision of the poet. However fair, however minutely accurate a historian may be, he must have powers of expression and of personality and must give his readers something besides masses of fact. Most of the great historians have the gifts of the creative writer, in a power of setting life in action, in brilliancy or grace of style, in deft or penetrating characterization. In method, in providing and dealing with the material upon which he works, the modern historian seeks to follow the procedure of the scientist, assembling, weighing, sifting, and testing his data with rigorous precision.

In its content the literature of history is steadily expanding. Works devoted to its functions, to the principles and methods of historiography, increase in number and importance; and there is constant elaboration and enlargement of bibliographical and reference equipment. This literature of history extends into many highly specialized scholarly arts, such as paleography, epigraphy and sigillography, and into the immense region of archaeology, where the ancient world is recovered and reconstructed and knowledge gained that requires rewriting of history formerly accepted. In its own varied forms it records and interprets man's relations with his fellow man in all ages and among all peoples. It merges into biography, into travel and exploration, into literature and into fiction. It links with anthropology, psychology, the social sciences, economics, and political science. Perhaps its most significant increment has come through the development in the nineteenth century of institutional and economic history, which has its roots in the work of Malthus and Karl Marx and has attained its highest importance during the twentieth century.

The name "history" has a dual meaning: it is both the record and the event recorded. In either meaning, it is never static: there is no break between past and present, time itself is timeless; and so history is both a continuing record and a continuing process that at the same moment has been, is, and is becoming—for each successive day deposits the materials of history in the making. Because it deals, thus, with the flux of happenings seen and noted from every angle of human vision and never repeated with identical similarity, the processes and findings of history cannot be reduced to any exact formula. Such a formula was promulgated by Marx, in his communist doctrine of "historical materialism," which links the successive phases of human society to changing conditions of environment, alterations and improvement of material methods of production, and consequent, inevitable transformation of social relationships. Thus, man, through knowledge and control of these economic, political, and cultural forces of change, has power to shape his own destiny to unity and well-being by controlling human institutions as successfully as, through science, he can control the forces of nature. About a third of the population of the globe is today engaged upon the test of this formula; and only time can prove or disprove its validity. In the distant sweeping expanses and surging day-to-day currents of history, trends and tendencies may be observed, studied, and analyzed; broad or narrow, generalized or specific conclusions may be arrived at. But though the spirit and the method of the modern historian may be those of the scientific investigator there is as yet no "science of history" in the same sense that there is a science of chemistry, of physics, of biology, of astronomy.

History in its most commonly accepted form is defined as a narrative statement of happenings in the past. There is a distinction between annals and history. Annals offer a record of events in the order of their occurrence, regardless of their relationship to one another; history must have unity, coherence, and logical development. "History," says F. J. Teggart, "displays an 'action' (in the dramatic sense) with a beginning, middle, and end. In historiography, as in tragedy, the first consideration is the 'action' and the problem confronting every historian is how to bring the heterogeneous materials at his disposal within the compass of a unity." [1]

Necessarily, history is selective. Not all occurrences can be known to any historian, and of occurrences reported in data available those that seem most important must be chosen from the mass. The histories of our own times, for example, built as they are from personal knowledge, from newspapers and current material of every sort—as in Allen's *Only Yesterday* and, on a more comprehensive scale, Barck and Blake's *Since 1900*—are focused on occurrences that seem to reveal national trends and turning points. The historian of the past must sift and choose from great deposits of material concerning which he can have no personal knowledge. All the material with which the historian works has passed through human personalities in what it tells and in manner of telling, for every occurrence is described differently by each observer. Santayana says:

History, which passes for the account of facts, is in reality a collection of apperceptions of an indeterminate material, for even the material of history is not facts, but consists of memories or words subject to ever-varying interpretation. Memory, in the first place, is selective; official and other records are selective and often intentionally partial. A history is not an indiscriminate register of every known event: a file of newspapers is not an inspiration of Clio. A history is a view of the fortunes of some institution or person. It traces the development of some interest.

[1] F. J. Teggart, *Theory of History*, p. 17.

And the value of history is similar to that of poetry, and varies with the beauty, power and adequacy of the form in which the indeterminate material of human life is presented.[2]

Historical writing falls roughly into two broad divisions, as being of the "old school" or of the "new school." Lines of demarkation cannot be closely drawn, and both "schools" have characteristics in common; but differences in conception and method can be readily traced. Of the old school are the early chroniclers, with their liking for episode and anecdote, their storytelling flavor, and the older (and many present) historians whose work is predominantly "literary" narrative or centered upon the political or philosophical aspects of their subject. Of the new school are the modern historians who emphasize the scientific attitude in their work, set accuracy and impartiality above literary or emotional appeal, and seek to subordinate the political aspect and emphasize social, cultural, industrial, and scientific factors in human development.

Differentiation between old and new methods in history goes back to the early nineteenth century, when Niebuhr, whose ambition was to write a history of Rome up to the date at which Gibbon's history begins, established the principles of "scientific research"—the critical examination of actual documents that previous historians had accepted in versions handed down from one to another, the minute investigation of all existing historical evidence. From these principles developed the immense modern apparatus of historical research, which is now used both by historians whose work is of the older literary or political type and by those who are exponents of the "new history." Prescott, Motley, Macaulay, are examples of older historians who used source material diligently but whose work was never impersonal and always a dramatic composition which in its brilliancy and literary charm has kept enduring vitality. Earlier, but much more modern in method and spirit, is Edward Gibbon, the only eighteenth-century historian who remains an acknowledged master today. His great work is still unsuperseded, its fundamental historical accuracy unimpaired by the corrections and additions of modern

[2] George Santayana, *The Sense of Beauty*, pp. 141–42.

scholarship, its magnificence of sweep unsurpassed, and the stately dignity of its style shot with a rich-tinctured irony, a mordant wit, a solemn mockery, beside which even Lytton Strachey seems insipid. Bryce's *Holy Roman Empire*, masterly in authority and compression, represents the advance toward the "new" impersonal method; so does Henry Adams' *History of the United States*, remarkable for its detail and exactitude of research and its brilliancy of treatment. The "new history" that seeks to synthesize all the influences that make a national or racial culture may be exemplified in Charles and Mary Beard's *Rise of American Civilization*, with its impersonal setting-forth of causes and motives—economic, industrial, and social even more than political—that work out a people's collective destiny.

This "new history" represents the strongest modern trend of thought and purpose that now finds expression in every field of literature—the breaking away from tradition and acceptance to discover, analyze, test, and unify all the elements that make human experience. There are few illusions to cherish, few heroes to worship, in this type of history; there is realistic appraisal of all discernible values, transmutation of ideals into the material desires or necessities that generated them, much that antagonizes those who foster older traditions and loyalties. But it stimulates the mind to independent operation, it enables the vision to look objectively upon popular movements, to recognize and define the catchwords that rouse mass emotion, and it is establishing both perspective and unity in the common view of human affairs. It reached its largest public in Wells' *Outline of History*, which set universal history in brilliant synthesis, intelligible and fascinating to the untrained mind, and gave pattern and impetus to the present-day popularization of knowledge.

Within these divisions of old and new methods there are various kinds of historical writing—such as narrative and descriptive history, philosophical history, critical history, nonpolitical or social history. Among narrative and descriptive histories are included the earlier chronicles and annals, such as those of Herodotus, or Tacitus, or Froissart, and the writings of many later historians who emphasize romantic or dramatic descriptive detail, as Robertson and Macaulay in England, Prescott and Washington Irving in America. Many philosophical and critical histories are also representative of principles of scientific research. With Guizot the philosophical attitude prevailed rather than the critical, especially in his famous lectures on the history of civilization, in which he studied the development of Europe from the downfall of the Roman empire. Sismondi in his memorable history of the Italian republics is a philosophical historian, though his work is strongly narrative and descriptive. Spengler's *Decline of the West* is an arresting and provocative philosophy of world history conceived as an unending cycle of race-groups, each an organism, each passing through the same successive phases—emergence, which is preculture; fulfillment, which is culture; and death, which is civilization, bringing extinction and leaving no vital, enduring influence on any other race-group. Arnold J. Toynbee's monumental work, *A Study of History*, of which six volumes had appeared by 1939 (with three more to follow), is a philosophy of human history centered on analysis and comparison of the birth, growth, and disintegration of civilizations, and tracing a pattern of ever recurring cause and effect from which may be drawn understanding of our contemporary world. The masterly single-volume "Abridgement" by D. C. Somervell (published in 1947) has made the first six volumes of this great work available to the general reader in a unified, readable condensation that maintains unimpaired the quality and personality of the original. S. R. Gardiner represents the extreme type of critical historian in his eighteen-volume history of the English civil war period, built from sources with minute exactitude of detail and strict comparative scrutiny. Of social history, Green's *Short History of the English People* is one of the first familiar examples—history deliberately nonpolitical in emphasis, centering upon all the influences (religion, art, industry, social life, as well as government) that shape the development of a people.

It must be remembered that in much historical writing the different types overlap and merge. The work of the best historians is bulwarked by authority and research, but it is also infused with literary power, with dramatic values, with sustained human interest. Thucydides, "the great realist in history," has all the qualities of the great historians: descriptive narrative, dramatic personation, "scientific research" in use of all available materials of information, interest in the sciences, in economics, in social and cultural conditions, and philosophical consideration of the causes and results of the great war he records—his aim, to present "a true picture of the events which have happened and of the like events which may be expected to happen hereafter in the order of human things." [3] In American history Parkman holds a place unshared by any other, in his combination of thorough research with human appeal, literary charm, and balanced judgment; his histories, interesting as any romance, are authoritative in accuracy and knowledge. Many famous historians whose work combines these qualities have their own individual defects or weaknesses. Motley practiced thorough research, but was swayed by violent prejudices. Carlyle, in his *French Revolution*, is a powerful dramatist and pungent commentator rather than a judicious historian, but he penetrates and transmits the human reality of the events he narrates.

The present-day writing of history brings ever increasing development and modification of older types. All the resources of scholarship and scientific research are represented in detailed histories, elaborate, impersonal, closely specialized—such as H. L. Osgood's work on the American colonies—and in a multitude of historical monographs that from laborious critical analyses are drawing new evidence and more thorough knowledge of past events. Such work holds its greatest value for other historians, for historical students, and for readers who desire to master thoroughly some special period or subject. More popular interest is appealed to in histories that set forth comprehensively and graphically either mass movement or special phases in social development. Such lay their emphasis not on

---

[3] Louis E. Lord's *Thucydides and the World War*, Vol. XII of the "Martin Classical Lectures" (Harvard University Press, 1946), is an illuminating summation of the background, content, and qualities of the *History*, although many of the parallels drawn to World War II have been invalidated.

statesmen, rulers, or other individual figures, but on broad currents of social growth or change, political movements, progress in letters, art, and science. Thus, *Epic of America*, James Truslow Adams' brilliant, sweeping presentment of the whole structure of America, seeks particularly to trace the beginnings and growth of the American attitude toward business, toward material aggrandizement, and toward the vision of social perfectibility. In *The Age of Jackson* Arthur M. Schlesinger, Jr., centers on political and social aspects and on parallelism between Jacksonian trends and those developed under Franklin D. Roosevelt; Dixon Wecter's *The Age of the Great Depression*, with scholarship and dramatic visualization, presents the nation's experience, social, political, and economic, from the stock market crash of October, 1929, to the impact of Pearl Harbor, on December 7, 1941; while Leo Huberman's *We, the People* is specialized popularization of historical perspectives, weaving a vivid, foreshortened narrative of changing social and economic environment, development of the machine age, immense expansion of corporate business enterprise and the rise of labor, and the influences of the New Deal, as undercurrents in "the drive of common men toward equality and social improvement."

Another popular type is found in short, picturesque narratives, often with a graphic "storytelling" flavor, of particular phases or periods in national development, such as the individual volumes in the "Chronicles of America," published by Yale University Press. Many historical biographies merge indistinguishably into this kind of history. Synthetic or composite history also differs in type— sometimes a single panorama in broad perspective, on the general model of Wells' *Outline*, and sometimes a sequence of separate contributions devoted to different aspects, as in *Our Emergent Civilization*, in which, under Ruth Anshen's editorship, fourteen notable contributors outline a framework for a new unity of civilization and culture.

Nearly four hundred years ago, when scientific research was hidden in the remote future, Montaigne, in his essay "Of Books," told of the different kinds of historians he knew.

I love those historians [he says] that are either very simple or most excellent. The simple who have nothing of their own to add unto the story, and have but the care and diligence to collect whatsoever come unto their knowledge, and sincerely and faithfully to register all things, without choice or culling, by the naked truth leave our judgment more entire, and better satisfied. Such among others (for example's sake) plain and well-meaning Froissard, who in his enterprise hath marched with so free and genuine a purity, that having committed some oversight, he is neither ashamed to acknowledge nor afraid to correct the same, wheresoever he hath either notice or warning of it; and who representeth unto us the diversity of the news then current, and the different reports that were made unto him. The subject of an history should be naked, bare and formless; each man according to his capacity or understanding may reap commodity out of it. The curious and most excellent have the sufficiency to cull and choose that which is worthy to be known, and may select of two relations that which is most likely. . . . But truly that belongs not to many. Such as are between both (which is the most common fashion) it is they that spoil all; they will needs chew our meat for us, and take upon them a law to judge, and by consequence to square and encline the story according to their fantasy; for where the judgment bendeth one way, a man cannot choose but wrest and turn his narration that way. . . .

Here are noted faults and weaknesses that characterize much historical writing to the present day. Who does not know the historians who "chew our meat for us," and those who for their personal bias "wrest and turn" their narrative to fit that bias? Montaigne's judgment still holds, that the best historians are they who have the ability to "cull and choose that which is worthy to be known."

The literature of history, quite apart from the type or kind of historical writing it may represent, assumes various forms. Among them are historiography, bibliography, reference works, source books and collections, personal narratives, textbooks, edited or cooperative histories, and histories by individual historians. Let us consider them in brief summary.

Historiography, in strict definition, is the writing of history; but under this designation are commonly grouped works devoted to study and interpretation of history, to consideration of historians and their art, and to the fundamentals of historical criticism. Here, for example, are expositions of the concept and philosophy of history, as in Croce's *History, Its Theory and Practice*, and R. G. Collingwood's *The Idea of History;* analysis of the problems historians must deal with in handling, testing, and shaping their material, as in Allen Johnson's clear, stimulating discussion of *The Historian and Historical Evidence;* survey and appraisal of the development of historical research and the work of representative historians, as in Gooch's *History and Historians in the Nineteenth Century;* consideration from many angles of the "new history," as in J. H. Robinson's volume of that title and in Harry Elmer Barnes' comprehensive presentation of *The New History and the Social Studies.* James Westfall Thompson and Bernard Holm's massive, scholarly two-volume *History of Historical Writing* carries the record from the earliest times to the present, but excludes living writers and American historians. Sir Charles Oman, in *The Writing of History*, distills the qualities and defects, the individualities and universalities of historians into a delightful, invigorating compound of authority, experience, and humorous common sense. Samuel Eliot Morison, in his cogent and provocative pamphlet, *History as a Literary Art* ("Old South Leaflets," Series ii, No. 1), sets forth the mediocrities and aridities of contemporary academic history writing; and Emery Neff, in *The Poetry of History*, from his examination of historical writing since Voltaire makes it clear that to create great history literary art must be added to scholarship.

Foremost in interest and value to librarians, library students, and the general reader is Allan Nevins' *The Gateway to History*, in which the enthusiasm of a lover of history is combined with the knowledge and experience of a distinguished historian. Here, almost every aspect of the reading, writing, and study of history, of the work of the great historians and the range of historical literature is revealed in fourteen vital, informal chapters, opening with an eloquent argument "In Defence of History," then considering the variety of history, differences of treatment, suitability to diverse reader interests, problems, ideas, and influences of historians; and closing with invitation and suggestion for readers to carry on for themselves the exploration of this great domain. Of special practical interest are the three chapters that expound and analyze spurious and defective material, the practice of "ghost-writing," and values to be tested for validity of newspaper reports, press dispatches, and documentary records. In comprehensiveness, organization, and treatment and in magnetic appeal this is one of the notable present-day contributions to book selection and book use in a specific field. Its nearest successor in range and varied values is *The Use of History*, by A. L. Rowse, key volume in the "Teach Yourself History" series, of which he is editor.[4]

Bibliography of history is extensive, and indispensable to discriminating selection. Of course, it is included in all general bibliographical aids, such as Mudge's *Guide to Reference Books*, Sonnenschein, the *A.L.A. Catalog* and *Standard Catalog* volumes; but it is most detailed and valuable in its specialized form. Three works of first importance in which the immense domain of history is surveyed, charted, and appraised with expert knowledge are Larned's *Literature of American History*, C. K. Adams' *Manual of Historical Literature*, and the *Guide to Historical Literature*, prepared by a committee of the American Historical Association and published by Macmillan in 1931.

Both Larned and Adams are older works, now long out of print but still available in many libraries and still of enduring vitality and value, for both possess that infusion of creative genius that now and then illuminates the mechanical structure of bibliographical science. Larned's *Literature of American History* has previously been noted as a pioneer effort toward annotation and evaluation in book selection.[5] A monument of historical knowledge, of bibliographical enterprise and intelligence, it will repay careful study and is constantly useful in furnishing astute appraisal of an immense mass of publications dealing with American history. It applies this appraisal to books that are of minor importance and inferior value as well as to those of recognized excellence, and for this reason study of its annotations

---

[4] See above, p. 239.
[5] See above, p. 72.

offers practical training in critical judgment that, so far as I know, is not to be had elsewhere. In Adams' *Manual*, also, the annotations are of perennial value. They characterize the work of the older European, English, and American historians with a master's knowledge, and a magnetic vividness, delightful to any responsive mind.

In neither Larned nor Adams is there guidance to the historical literature that has appeared during the present century. In any present-day selection of history the comprehensive, invaluable aid is the *Guide to Historical Literature*. This was originally planned, at the suggestion of the American Library Association, as a revision and extension of Adams' *Manual*. But it soon assumed independent form and after eleven years of cooperative labor by more than three hundred American historians and scholars appeared as a new, independent work, to which Adams' *Manual* remains as a valuable supplement for the older literature of the subject. It records, with brief critical notes and references to longer critical reviews, more than four thousand historical works (most of them published before 1927), grouped in twenty-six major divisions which build a chronological framework of history of all ages and all countries. Besides the specific literature of history, there are included many works on social, religious, and cultural history, history of science, art, music, literature, and many carefully chosen biographies. Through it the whole domain of history may be explored, its features, characteristics, and relationships recognized, and the work of individual historians compared according to appraisals made by expert authority. Its range, method, and details should be thoroughly mastered.

In more limited and popular selection the "History" chapter of the *Bookman's Manual*, revised edition (1948), is of indispensable usefulness. Its sixty pages are expertly organized to cover the various kinds of historical writing, the accepted period divisions, and an extensive representation of individual historians, classic, standard, and contemporary, chosen with discrimination and characterized in clear, pithy annotations that convey an immense amount of varied descriptive and bibliographical information.

Other bibliographies and special lists that must be familiar in any extended selection of history are well summarized in Van Hoesen and Walter's manual, *Bibliography* (Chapter IV, "Subject Bibliography: Historical and Social Sciences"). Harry Elmer Barnes' book, *The New History and the Social Studies*, is full of interesting and stimulating suggestions for book selection in history, for its bibliographical references and abundant critical comments cover an immense range of histories, historical biographies, and works that are allied to history in almost every field of literature. In current selection there must be constant use of reviews appearing in the various periodicals devoted to history. Most important here are the *American Historical Review* (quarterly, Washington, D.C.), the *English Historical Review* (quarterly, London), the *Canadian Historical Review* (quarterly, Toronto), and the *Journal of Modern History* (quarterly, University of Chicago Press). *The Social Studies*, formerly *Historical Outlook* (monthly, Philadelphia), published especially for high school history teachers under editorial direction of the American Historical Association, is useful in its selection and evaluation of current books suitable for students.

Reference works include encyclopedias of history, dictionaries of dates, yearbooks devoted to historical, political, and statistical information, historical atlases, and many kindred publications. *The New Larned History for Ready Reference* is one of the most valuable standard reference works for moderate-sized and smaller libraries. There are many-angled reference values for such libraries in the "triple alliance" of historical aids edited under the direction of James Truslow Adams and published by Scribner, comprising the six-volume *Dictionary of American History*, of which publication was completed in 1940; the *Atlas of American History;* and the *Album of American History*, which in 1949 added an index volume to the four successive volumes carrying the picture history of America from the colonial period to 1947. The great series of "Cambridge Histories" are of high reference and bibliographical usefulness, and there is special reference value in many of the "universal" histories and "outlines."

Source books and *source collections* usually belong with reference works. In them are printed official documents, national archives, original records and narratives—the "source material" of historical knowledge. They range from compact source books, such as Cheyney's one-volume selection of *Readings in English History Drawn from Original Sources*, or H. S. Commager's compilation of *Documents of American History*, to the many volumes of *Diplomatic Documents Relating to the Outbreak of the European War* or the later *Documents on American Foreign Relations*, edited by R. M. Goodrich and Marie J. Carroll, covering the World War II period, and to immense source collections, such as the English medieval chronicles published in 243 volumes and known as "The Rolls Series." Source books may be shaped into unified consecutive history, made graphic and appealing to the general reader; or organized and amplified into a comprehensive, integrated historical structure. Of the first type is Mark Van Doren's *Autobiography of America*, with its seventy-four original narratives knit together into a vivid sequence of scenes and events in American life from the early settlements, through the colonial and revolutionary eras, the rise of the nation, expansion of the west, and civil war, to the social trends of the 1920's. The second type finds ambitious example in Louis M. Hacker's *The Shaping of the American Tradition*, source book and integrated history combined in a single monumental volume of 1,250 pages, so organized that its compact yet analytical original text is presented as a series of introductions to a varied selection of illustrative contemporary documents. This material is fitted into a pattern which traces for each phase of national development four specific but related aspects: the American mind, the American scene, American problems, and the United States and the world. Of high reference usefulness, this is primarily a college text, but it is also for any mature reader an arresting and stimulating general history, to which the contemporary documents impart a sense of the present still living in the past.

Personal narratives of pioneers, explorers, early adventurers, are also source material of history, and may be considered either as source books or collections, according to the form in which they are presented. Thwaites' "Early Western Travels" is a collection of such narratives, edited, annotated, and reprinted under expert historical authority. Of similar type but more closely regional is the "Southwest Historical Series," edited by Ralph Bieber; and all over the country there is a continuous increase in the assiduous gleaning, preserving, and recording of these raw materials of regional, state, and local history. Military, naval, and legal records, writings of statesmen, transcriptions of correspondence, are also brought together in collections that are part of the working material of historians.

Historical textbooks should, as a rule, be differentiated from histories for the general reader. There are exceptions to this, in such works as Breasted's *Ancient Times* or Schapiro's *Modern and Contemporary European History*, admirable as texts and so lightened and enriched in treatment that they also hold the spontaneous interest of the general reader. But the standard type of textbook in any field of knowledge, with its instructional framework and close-packed factual summarizing, is an instrument of mental discipline, not a free medium of literature.

Edited or cooperative histories are now the most common and effective form for history covering a large field. They bring work of specialized authority—each writer dealing with his own special phase or aspect of history—into a close-linked sequence, organized and developed under editorial supervision of historical scholars. Famous examples are the great series of "Cambridge Histories" (*Ancient, Medieval,* and *Modern*) initiated by Lord Acton, of which the first volume appeared in 1902 (the year of his death) and the last in 1939, with their 32 volumes of text and eight supplementary volumes of plates, maps, bibliographies, and indexes, regarded as "the most ambitious project of cooperative writing of history yet attempted in English"; and the "History of the American Nation," to which, under the editorship of Albert Bushnell Hart, twenty-four leading American historians contributed individual volumes. These two examples illustrate different methods. The Cambridge histories are massive composite volumes, each containing many separate contributions, and the "American Nation" is composed of a sequence of smaller volumes, each by an individual historian, devoted to a single phase or period. "Chronicles of America," edited by Allen Johnson and published by Yale University Press, is a more popularized example of the second method; each of its fifty volumes is complete in itself but fits into an ordered sequence as part of a continuous history from prediscovery times to the year 1920. An impressive undertaking in cooperative sectional history begun in 1947, is *A History of the South*, produced jointly by Louisiana State University Press and the University of Texas (Littlefield Fund for Southern History). Editorship is shared by W. H. Stephenson, of Tulane University, and E. M. Coulter, of the University of Georgia; and the ten volumes, running chronologically from the colonial period to 1946, are individually assigned to nine historical scholars representing leading universities. Many edited histories are interchangeably classed as historical series; for there is little, if any, distinction possible between a carefully organized subject series produced under a single expert editorship, and a sequence of individual histories planned and produced in almost identical fashion.

Histories by individual historians, of course, constitute the great mass of historical literature. Individual volumes by individual historians that form part of the cooperative histories are included here. They may be universal or general history, comprehensive in scope; or specific history, limited in scope, dealing with periods, epochs, dynasties, countries, nations, or single historic figures. Here belong most of the famous histories, such as Gibbon, Green's *Short History of the English People*, Parkman's histories of France in North America. And again within these groups history may be of its own distinctive type or kind, and scholarly, popular, or elementary in treatment.

World War II and after.—The advent of two world wars within a quarter-century brought enormous expansion to the whole body of historical literature. World War II changed global perspectives, enlarged subject fields, and set compulsions and challenges which dominate the postwar world and are reflected in every field of recorded thought, purpose, and action. Into History, the vehicle from which we appraise the past, survey the present, and forejudge the future, poured an overwhelming load of material, from which continuing problems of selection and disposition confront librarians. A few of these must be noted here:

Size of book collections must depend upon the nature and function of the library. Only the greatest libraries can attempt to build even relatively complete collections. Stanford's Hoover Library of War, Revolution and Peace, the Library of Congress, such special collections as those of Harvard, Yale, the New York Public Library, are examples of the reservoirs for research and scholarship to which students and historians must turn for the fullest, most varied materials. University libraries, specialized libraries (such as the Library of International Relations in Chicago), and many large public libraries maintain such reservoirs. With the development of regional libraries for reference, study, and interlibrary service in the principal geographic regions of the country, small and medium-size libraries should find their available resources greatly augmented and many problems of selection simplified.[6]

Background literature that preserves common understanding of the war, in its course and its crucial issues, must have place in any representative selection, however small. Much winnowing of older material is necessary, and this must be done with judicious selectivity. In current selection, new or reinforced subjects must be recognized; rising trends of thought and opinion must be discerned and emphasized. Controversial violence and suppressive pressures must be countered by objectivity and reasoned judgment. Librarians must fully accept their responsibility for maintaining balanced values in spreading public information and enlightenment amid strong currents of conflict and intensities of partisanship.

New or transformed subject fields must be given emphasis. Atomic warfare, the United Nations, the deepening struggle be-

---

[6] C. B. Joeckel and Amy Winslow, eds., *A National Plan for Public Library Service*, A.L.A. Committee on Postwar Planning (Chicago, A.L.A., 1948), pp. 39-40.

tween an old world order defending itself and a new world order rising to power have brought new critical problems of our time that must be known, understood, and acted upon by those whose present and future depend upon the solution reached. To direct attention upon and enlarge knowledge of the issues and trends that are today shaping the pattern of human history, to make them manifest and urgent to the indifferent and uninformed, and to enlist reason and understanding in their consideration are first essentials in public library book selection and community service.

Paramount among such critical issues and trends is the relationship between the United States and the Soviet Union—world powers that between them hold the postwar key to world peace and the companion key to a world war in which civilization will crumble into radioactive dust and rubble. This is a trend directed with increasing momentum toward war, incited and strengthened by a long-continuing flow of books intensifying American fear, suspicion, and antagonism toward the Soviet state, and by anti-Soviet propaganda carried on in many newspapers and periodicals, by most radio commentators and numerous public leaders. In the Soviet background are more than twenty-five years of Western hostility, beginning with armed intervention at the close of World War I and followed by continuing criticism and mistrust. World War II brought an interval of mutual confidence between the Allies as Russian resistance became chief factor in turning the Nazi tide. But with victory came swift, unnecessary deterioration of United States–Soviet relations and a rising flood of mutual ignorance, bitterness, and hostility, in which the opposed forces of capitalism and communism displaced the foundations for "one world," laid so hopefully at the war's end. To meet this issue libraries must use every resource to supply full impartial information, to clarify understanding and strengthen reasoned judgment; to make the influence of books effective, not for war, hatred, and intolerance, but for peace, for tolerance, for world cooperation and unity in diversity.

Postwar trends are toward a changing, expanding world in process of remaking for good or ill. Remote countries and peoples have become of world-wide importance in their past history, their presage for the future. A resurgent Asia—India burgeoning in rebirth, China in irresistible mass movement of its people laying foundations of a new social structure; Manchuria, Korea, Indonesia; changing vistas in Australasia and the South Pacific; conflicting forces in the Middle East; new perspectives in Africa—for these and many other regions little known to most Americans information and understanding must be drawn from an ever growing store of authoritative, illuminating literature. Race relations, as they affect the United States and are involved in the world's struggle to find peace, find expression in an enlarging body of significant work by Negro, Jewish, and other qualified writers. Scientific research has thrust us into this atomic age, with its twin portents of human annihilation and human betterment, their fulfillment depending on man's purpose and course of action. Socialism and communism, as dominating influences in an emerging world structure, demand clearer, more impartial analysis and appraisal than is supplied by the immense literature of unqualified denunciation or untempered acclaim which shapes public opinion. The aims, achievements, and vicissitudes of the United Nations, and the movement toward the ultimate goal of world government as the only means to international peace and security must have full representation in every library.

Points to be considered in selection:

The two great requirements of historical writing are truth and art: truth based on patience and accuracy in research, art expressed in sound literary structure and in vigor and ease of style. In selection of individual books these requirements must always be remembered.

Simple tests that are useful in denoting characteristics and approximate values are:

Type or *kind* of historical writing and *form* in which it is presented, as previously indicated.

Scope.—Whatever subject it deals with, whatever its form or the kind of writing it represents, the scope of the work (that is, the sweep or sphere of its outlook and action) should be determined as closely as possible. A history may be complete or partial in scope, exhaustive or condensed, uneven or well proportioned. Both Wells' *Outline* and Parsons' *Stream of History*, for example, are popular universal history, but the scope of Wells is more elaborate and intensive, that of Parsons more condensed and more evenly balanced.

Authority.—Consider the historical basis of the work, whether original or secondary sources have been used, whether all available material has been utilized. Original sources have already been mentioned; these include not only material available in printed form, but original documents, archives, manuscripts, letters, diaries, and every sort of contemporaneous record, as they exist in libraries and other institutions or in private possession. Today all historians of authority base their work on research into original records or personal examination of historic localities. Secondary sources are works by writers of established authority which are based on original research. Theodore Roosevelt's *Winning of the West*, for example, and F. J. Turner's *The Frontier in American History*, are excellent secondary sources. Indeed, nearly all histories of the first rank are acceptable secondary sources. Much popularized and superficial work, however, is based entirely upon secondary sources and so does not possess any individual authority of its own. Wells in his *Outline* used good secondary sources and had cooperation and revision from capable specialists, but shaped his narrative to his own interpretation, so that while it has value and continuing vitality for the general reader it is not accepted as authoritative history. Geoffrey Parsons' *Stream of History* has greater accuracy. Hendrik Van Loon's *Story of America* is an example of highly popularized narrative from secondary sources, superficial and opinionated, but attractive to inexperienced readers for its rapidity, vividness, and lively dogmatism. Set in comparison with the Beards' *Rise of American Civilization*, it will make evident the difference between thin and garish "popular" history and that which has sound scholarship and authority. Historians of the first rank use all available material with impartial thoroughness and cite their authorities fully and carefully. Such citation is called "documentation," and in examining any historical work the degree and manner in which it is "documented" should always be observed.

In the endeavor to determine authority, consider not only the historian's qualifications in scholarship, but his experience as a writer and his familiarity with his subject through travel or personal investigation. Does his work possess any originality of theme, does it offer any important new material, that give it greater interest or value than other works on the same subject? His personal attitude toward his work is also important—whether or not he displays prejudice, bias, strong opinions, religious or political partisanship, whether he seeks to demonstrate a thesis or prove a theory. Especially in dealing with contemporary history any strong personal attitude should be considered. This is strikingly illustrated in the later work of Charles Beard, whose deep isolationist bias is ingrained in his *Basic History of the United States*, and whose bitter personal rancor toward President Roosevelt vitiates his assumption of philosophic impartiality in his volume, *President Roosevelt and the Coming of the War, 1941*. Through many histories and narratives of the two world wars, of present-day India, of Soviet Russia—to mention only a few phases of history in the making—there run intense personal convictions, prejudices, deep-rooted loyalties, which must be recognized and balanced against one another in selection.[7] There must also be realization that in much important literature of contemporary history there exists absolute categorical contradiction by honest and responsible writers dealing with the same subject from personal observation and experience. The firsthand reports on Yugoslavia in Markham's *Tito's Imperial Communism* and in Robert St. John's *The Silent People Speak* offer one illuminating example, among many. In vital, well-balanced selection such opposed presentments should have fair comparative consideration and, within reasonable limits, be given equal representation.

[7] Oman's chapter, "On History as a Hindrance, and Poisonous History," gives admirable characterization of histories that "sometimes consciously, sometimes unconsciously, are intended to twist the record of history in some period to the profit of some cause—national, religious, political, personal, or what you please, by the methods common to all tendentious historians"; with insistence on the point that the distortion of history for propagandic purposes is and always has been poisonous.

Manner of treatment.—This may be abstruse, scholarly, elementary, designed for the specialist or the student, for the intelligent general reader or for a more undiscriminating and immature public. Quick recognition of the kind of readers to whom an individual book will appeal is essential to sound judgment in selection.

Qualities.—Structure and expression are chiefly to be considered. The able historian has the power of conceiving and presenting his subject clearly and with unity. His material must be carefully organized and built up on a sound framework with proportion and balance, according to a logical plan. Good expression demands literary skill, creative power, and forceful, graceful, or magnetic style. Almost all historians of reputation possess these qualities. There are, however, many works valuable for the material they contain, but so confused or disconnected in expression that the digging out of information is an oppressive task. There are others that so exaggerate dramatic or descriptive emphasis that their work takes on the qualities of sensational journalism.

Textual and physical characteristics.—These are of special importance in histories. Maps, genealogical or chronological tables, full chapter contents, full and accurate indexes, are essential aids to the reader. Side notes and good running heads (with indication of dates) are always helpful. Illustrations and portraits are desirable and useful. Appendixes, citations from authorities, bibliographies, notes, and references are all desirable. In choosing among different histories of a given subject or period, there should be constant observation and comparison of the extent and apparent quality of this equipment.

Subject series are of much importance in selection of histories, for many of the chief standard English and American works have appeared in this form. The *Guide to Historical Literature* offers probably the most complete information available for the widest range of historical series and serials, but this is scattered through the twenty-six sections of the work and is impracticable for quick reference.

The close relationship of history to other classes of literature must always be remembered. With biography, of course, it is inextricably entwined. A life of Jeanne d'Arc is both history and biography. Nicolay and Hay's *Abraham Lincoln* is as important as a history of the Civil War period as it is as biography; and for an earlier period this is true of Beveridge's *Life of John Marshall*. Ralph Roeder's *Juarez and His Mexico* is rightly called "a biographical history," so thoroughly does it incorporate the vast historical background with the arresting, detailed, and sympathetic full-length portrayal of the great Indian leader and statesman who was the founder of modern Mexico. It has already been pointed out that decision as to whether a work is history or biography must often be quite arbitrary, and it may be placed with equal correctness in either class. So in any selection of current books in history, the points to be considered in judging biography should be familiar and may often be usefully applied. Equally close relationship exists between history and travel, especially as concerns narratives of early explorers and adventurers and records of archaeological investigation, while in *Mont-Saint-Michel and Chartres*, Henry Adams' beautiful evocation of The Middle Ages, history takes on aspects of both travel and of art.

One of the most important accessories and by-products of history, for the general public and for younger readers, is historical fiction. Good historical novels offer the most common and the most effective approach to the reading of history. They should be constantly and systematically used to awaken and develop the impulse to read history and to give color and meaning to history that has been made task work for apathetic minds. Such a novel as Naomi Mitchison's *The Conquered* translates Caesar's Gallic wars from textbook exercise to moving human experience; *The Cloister and the Hearth* discloses the glowing pageant of fifteenth-century Europe; James Boyd's *Drums* is valid interpretation and vivid rendering of cogent aspects of the American Revolution—and these effects are produced not only upon young readers but often just as strongly upon adult minds. There are many books in which history and fiction merge almost indistinguishably: for example, in W. S. Davis' portrayal of a cross section of medieval society, *Life on a Mediaeval Barony*, which is authentic history though its scenes are linked with fictional art;

and in semi-fictional biographies of historic figures, such as Zsolt de Harsanyi's *The Star-Gazer* (Galileo).

Only with time, study, and experience can discriminating knowledge of historical literature be gained; but every intelligent worker with books should establish some personal acquaintance with this great and inspiring domain of literature, by reading some of the work of master historians, and by examining individual books whenever possible, observing their characteristics, comparing them with others of similar form and type, and considering them in relation to established standards and methods of historical writing.

FIFTY HISTORIES REPRESENTATIVE OF DIFFERENT KINDS OF HISTORICAL WRITING

Adams, Henry. History of the United States of America. 1889–1890.
Beard, Charles A. and Mary. The Rise of American Civilization. 1927–1942.
Breasted, J. H. History of Egypt from the Earliest Times to the Persian Conquest. 1909.
Burckhardt, Jakob. The Civilization of the Renaissance in Italy. 1878.
Bryce, James. The Holy Roman Empire. 1864.
Buckle, H. T. Introduction to the History of Civilization in England. 1847–1861.
Carlyle, Thomas. The French Revolution. 1837.
Channing, Edward. History of the United States. 1905–1925.
Coulton, G. G. Medieval Panorama. 1938.
Franklin, J. H. From Slavery to Freedom: a history of American Negroes. 1947.
Froissart, Jean. Chronicles of England, France, and Spain. 1523–1525.
Gibbon, Edward. History of the Decline and Fall of the Roman Empire. 1776–1788.
Gooch, G. P. History of Modern Europe, 1878–1919. 1923.
Green, J. R. Short History of the English People. 1874.
Grote, George. History of Greece. 1846–1856.
Guizot, F. P. G. A Short History of Civilization, from the Fall of the Roman Empire to the French Revolution. 1829–1832.
Helps, Sir Arthur. The Spanish Conquest in America. 1855–1861.
Herodotus. History.
Irving, Washington. Chronicle of the Conquest of Granada. 1829.
Lea, H. C. History of the Inquisition of Spain. 1906–1907.

Lecky, W. E. H. History of England in the Eighteenth Century. 1878–1890.
Leech, Margaret. Reveille in Washington. 1941.
Lowenthal, Marvin. The Jews in Germany: story of sixteen centuries. 1936.
Macaulay, T. B. History of England. 1849–1861.
Mahan, A. T. Influence of Sea Power upon History, 1660–1783. 1890.
Maurois, André. The Miracle of France. 1949.
Michelet, Jules. History of France. 1833–1867.
Morley, S. G. The Ancient Maya. 1947.
Motley, J. L. The Rise of the Dutch Republic. 1856.
Nehru, Jawaharlal. The Discovery of India. 1946.
Pares, Sir Bernard. A History of Russia. 1926.
Parkman, Francis. Montcalm and Wolfe. 1884.
Pirenne, Henri. History of Europe from the Invasions to the XVI Century. 1939.
Randall, J. H. The Making of the Modern Mind. 1926.
Roosevelt, Theodore. Winning of the West. 1889–1890.
Rostovtzeff, Michael. Social and Economic History of the Roman Empire. 1941.
Sen, Gertrude Emerson. The Pageant of India's History, Vol. I. 1948.
Smith, Preserved. Age of the Reformation. 1920.
Spengler, Oswald. The Decline of the West. 1926–1928.
Symonds, J. A. The Renaissance in Italy. 1875–1886.
Tacitus, Cornelius. Works.
Taine, H. A. Origins of Contemporary France. 1890–1894.
Taylor, H. O. The Medieval Mind. 1911, 1949.
Thucydides. History of the Peloponnesian War.
Toynbee, A. J. A Study of History. 1934, 1939.
—— Abridgement of Volumes I–VI, by D. C. Somervell. 1947.
Trevelyan, G. M. English Social History: a survey of six centuries, Chaucer to Queen Victoria. 1942.
Trevelyan, Sir. G. O. The American Revolution. 1909.
Turner, F. J. The Frontier in American History. 1920.
Van Doren, Carl C. The Great Rehearsal: story of the making and ratifying of the Constitution of the United States. 1948.
Wells, H. G. The Outline of History. 1920.

TWENTY-FIVE BACKGROUND BOOKS ON WORLD WAR II AND AFTER

Carr, E. H. The Soviet Impact on the Western World. 1947.
Churchill, Winston S. The Gathering Storm. 1948.
Crum, Bartley C. Behind the Silken Curtain. 1947.
Curtiss, John S. An Appraisal of the Protocols of Zion. 1942.
Deutscher, Isaac. Stalin: a political biography. 1949.
Dodd, W. E., and Martha, eds. Ambassador Dodd's Diary. 1941.
Glueck, Sheldon. The Nuremberg Trial and Aggressive War. 1946.
Gruber, Ruth. Destination Palestine: the story of the Haganah ship Exodus 1947. 1948.
Hersey, John. Hiroshima. 1946.
Hughes, Emmet John. Report from Spain. 1947.
Hitler, Adolf. Mein Kampf. 1939.
—— My New Order. 1941.
Jewish Black Book Committee. The Black Book: the Nazi crime against the Jewish people. 1946.
Lauterbach, Richard E. Danger from the East. 1947.
Lemkin, Raphael. Axis Rule in Occupied Europe. 1945.
Maynard, Sir John. Russia in Flux. 1941.
Millis, Walter. This is Pearl! 1947.
Roosevelt, Franklin Delano. Nothing to Fear: selected papers and addresses. 1939–1945. 1946.
Schuman, F. L. The Rise of the Nazi Dictatorship. 1935.
Sherwood, R. S. Roosevelt and Hopkins: an intimate history. 1948.
Shirer, William L. A Berlin Diary. 1941.
Smedley, Agnes. Battle Hymn of China. 1943.
Stillwell, Joseph W. The Stillwell Papers; arr. and ed. by T. H. White. 1948.
Trevor-Roper, H. R. The Last Days of Hitler. 1947.
Willkie, Wendell L. One World. 1943.

14: Travel

Along all history, down the slopes,
As a rivulet running, sinking now, and now again to the surface rising,
A ceaseless thought, a varied train—Lo, soul! to thee, thy sight, they rise,
The plans, the voyages again, the expeditions:
Again Vasco da Gama sails forth;
Again the knowledge gain'd, the mariner's compass,
Lands found, and nations born—thou born, America (a hemisphere unborn),
For purpose vast, man's long probation fill'd,
Thou, rondure of the world, at last accomplish'd.
Walt Whitman: "Passage to India"

IN THE LITERATURE of travel there is included much more than the simple definite narratives—the "travelers' tales"—that come first to mind as books of travel. It is one of the most diverse and far-reaching divisions of literature. It holds the raw materials of history in records of exploration and archaeological discovery, in annals of voyagers and adventurers. It extends into science—into zoölogy, anthropology, botany, the study of man, of nature, and of the earth. It charts and surveys the surface of the globe, and registers observation and experience against new and widening horizons. The Dewey classification imbeds Description and Travel, as a class, between History in general and Biography, places within it topography, maps, plans of cities, archaeology, historical and political divisions, and assigns it country divisions, to be subdivided just as the classification of Modern History is subdivided. Logically and realistically, as this classification indicates, both Travel and Biography are components of History regarded as the whole record of man's experience on earth.

Close as is the relationship between travel and other classes of literature, its strongest alliance is with history. Archaeological research has been the key to our knowledge of the ancient world. Through excavation of long-buried cities, invasion of the tombs of extinct civilizations, penetration of tropical jungles, we are literally digging up history, filling in gaps in the record of past events, establishing facts, confirming or demolishing theories, and building up, stone by stone, the structure of human life through past ages. Schliemann's archaeological researches on the site of ancient Troy gave information that reshaped the work of historians; Grote's history of Greece, for example, would have given a very different account of primitive Greece had the author lived at the time of Schliemann's discoveries. Excavations on the historic site of Carthage have made possible the recovery of a city that had become almost fabulous.

In America, the great pre-Columbian civilizations of Peru, Yucatan, and Mexico—the Egypts of the western hemisphere—have been recreated by archaeological skill and devotion into rich, fascinating substance of unique human history, developing its own structure of living without assistance or influence from the rest of the world. Here Sylvanus Morley's comprehensive study, *The Ancient Maya*, is the most authoritative and complete revelation of the great civilization of Guatemala and Yucatan, as through some twelve hundred years it rose, flourished, and died, astonishing and wonderful in its achievements in architecture, sculpture, and art, in scientific invention and in patterns of government and community living. Its most famous precursor in Central American archaeology is John L. Stephens' *Incidents of Travel in Central America, Chiapas and Yucatan*, published in 1841, the first modern contribution to the study of Mayan civilization; long out of print in the 12th edition, this has been restored for modern readers in the fine new edition, edited by Richard L. Predmore and published by Rutgers University Press in 1949.

Even more obvious is the fact that the narratives of explorers and discoverers are foundation material of history. The voyages of Magellan, of Cabot, the letter of Columbus in which he tells of his quest of the Indies, the narrative of Sir John Franklin's finding of the Northwest Passage; the journals of Father Marquette, of Lieutenant Pike, of George Rogers Clark—these are fountain heads of history, from which the first rills of knowledge broaden into the ocean floods of today. There is no more inspiring or fascinating literature than these records of exploration and discovery—an epic of hopes, fears, ambitions, terrors, and undaunted purpose, all centered on learning more of this mysterious world.

Geography, the science that charts and delineates the earth's surface, is both the cause and the product of travel. The blank spaces on the ancient maps were an incitement and a challenge to adventurous spirits; the maps and atlases and guidebooks that direct the modern traveler are the product of successive generations of travelers, adding their grains of observation, verification, and particularization to the body of geographic knowledge. But geography is also fundamental to history; for earth is the stage on which the drama of history is played, and knowledge of man's environment is indispensable to understanding of race movements and of the shifting currents of civilization. A nation's need of an outlet to the sea makes history; so does the migration of a nomad tribe seeking a more abundant food supply. Climate, soil, mountains, waterways, all the attributes of nature that affect man's well-being, are factors in human history and must be known as such by the historian.

Science, art, and literature are also interwoven with travel. Darwin's journal of his voyage in the *Beagle* is a record of travel; but it is also one of the great works in natural science and the book in which the principle of evolution was first indicated to the world. Reginald Farrer's delightful volumes, *On the Eaves of the World* and *Rainbow Bridge*, are not only fine works of contemporary travel but important contributions to horticulture and botany, devoted, as they are, to exploration through the Chinese-Tibetan borderland in quest of hardy shrubs and flowers that would survive in England. In the books of William Beebe and Roy Chapman Andrews travel becomes glorified into scientific adventure, in which specialized knowledge and all the devices of modern technical equipment are concentrated upon problems and secrets of nature, whether hidden in ocean depths or desert wastes. They represent, as Mr. Andrews has said, "a new era in scientific exploration, which is just as romantic, just as alluring and just as adventurous as that of Peary and Amundsen, of Stanley and Hedin. In almost every country of the earth lie vast regions which potentially are unknown, some poorly charted, and many holding undreamed-of treasures in the world of science. To study these regions, reveal their history and interpret it to the world today, is the exploration of the future."

Anthropology, the science of man, has established a varied, enlarging literature of travel which is part of the modern study of social problems. Margaret Mead's brilliant studies of primitive peoples of the South Seas are full of suggestion and significance in relation to human psychology and to root influences in the development of any social system. Ruth Benedict's impartial factual analyses of race differences (as in her interpretation of Japanese culture, *The Chrysanthemum and the Sword*) help to dispel what Ashley Montagu calls "man's most dangerous myth, the fallacy of race." Anthropological method, with its emphasis on social psychology and psychoanalytical implications, has become a strong factor not only in specialized study of isolated or primitive communities, but in more generalized descriptive travel which seeks to compare and interpret the characteristics and qualities of different peoples. Immense expansion of this field came from the Second World War, which suddenly swept vast, virtually unknown regions of Oceania, of Australasia and the Far East into the vortex of the world's life and death struggle.

Art and architecture have inspired many travelers—Ruskin studying the stones of Venice, Henry Adams from Mont-Saint-Michel and Chartres building the spiritual fabric of the Middle Ages. E. V. Lucas' "Wanderer" books, with their graceful, expert commentaries on art, architecture, historical and literary associations of famous cities, are on the border line between the book of travel and the guidebook. James Bone's *London Perambulator*, which Christopher Morley calls "one of the most beautiful books ever written about the world's greatest city," penetrates through the obvious into the core of London; and there are many books devoted to tracing and describing scenes celebrated in literature or places associated with the work of great writers—such as Jaccaci's *On the Trail of Don Quixote*, Rawnsley's *Literary Associations of the English*

Lakes, or travel studies of the England of Dickens or the Dorset of Hardy's novels. Such travel studies merge indistinguishably into essays—as represented by Hudson's *A Traveller in Little Things*.

The literature of travel is thus of widely varying kinds and types. It may be best surveyed when broadly grouped according to distinctive form, scope, and method.

History and bibliography of travel are not extensive. There are no analyses and appraisals of the art of travel writing, such as exist for the art of the biographer and of the historian. For the beginnings of travel literature C. B. Firestone's delightful volume, *The Coasts of Illusion*, offers summary and characterization, bringing together the tales, half legend, half myth, that made the travel truth of ancient times, and setting before us the earth and its inhabitants as man accepted them before the modern world had taken its full shape in maps and natural histories. This "study of travel tales" gives in its final chapters a survey of the travel tales of mankind and a selective bibliography of famous narratives and collections, from Marco Polo to Hakluyt, in which this lore has come down to us; it is an enlightening accompaniment to history and a lure to imagination and to literature.

There are various general works on travel in its aspect of geographic science and as world discovery and exploration. There are specialized historical studies, such as Dunbar's exhaustive *History of Travel in America*, a treasure store of valuable and interesting material on changing social and economic conditions; or Richardson Wright's panorama of the traffic of the road through three hundred years, *Hawkers and Walkers in Early America*, which covers in organized condensation an immense field of curious and picturesque information; both works with bibliographies that guide to the fuller literature of their subject. Mead's *The Grand Tour in the Eighteenth Century* is a more concentrated study, in which the conditions of European travel two hundred years ago are set forth in quaint and curious (and rather appalling) detail. And, of course, the travelers themselves furnish material for the history of travel—as Montaigne in his journals describes the inns, the roads, and the fare encountered during his pilgrimages in search of health—and this is often made available in compression and selection, in such works as Mesick's *The English Traveller in America, 1785-1835*, or Roget's *Travel in the Two Last Centuries of Three Generations*.

Not only specific travel conditions, but the historical past in its customs, patterns of thought, and everyday living are illuminated by the descriptive, critical, and comparative observations of travelers. Rich in descriptive detail of people and places (chiefly New York, Norfolk, and Philadelphia) and in unbridled scandalmongering concerning manners and customs, is the journal kept by a French Revolutionary refugee during his five-year exile in America, which, 150 years later, edited and translated by Kenneth Roberts, was made available to American readers as *Moreau de St. Méry's American Journey (1793-1798)*. Much early contemporary travel material is found in the ever increasing anthologies and collections which represent so dominating a trend in current literature. Vilhjalmur Stefánsson's substantial volume, *Great Adventures and Explorations from the Earliest Times to the Present, as Told by the Explorers Themselves*; E. P. Hanson's *Highroad to Adventure*, bringing together selections from twenty-three works by noted explorers and scientific adventurers; and Blair Niles' distinctive *Journeys in Time, from the Halls of Montezuma to Patagonia's Plain*, in which selections by twenty-six writers dealing with the humanity and literature of Latin America from 1519 to 1942 are woven into a deep-dyed tapestry of nature and man, are significant examples. Good selective bibliographies are a feature of many of these anthologies; also among them there is much variety of method as well as of scope. George Bradshaw's *Collection of Travel in America*, for example, belies its title by drawing from many sources (Mark Twain, Thoreau, and Ring Lardner among them) which are not books of travel. Philip Rahv reverses the customary approach in *Discovery of Europe*, a selection of writings by Americans, from Franklin and Jefferson to Thomas Wolfe, on their impressions of the European scene.

Bibliographies and reference aids are less satisfactory for travel than for many other classes of literature. In general and current selection for smaller libraries, chief dependence must be placed on the *A.L.A. Catalog* volumes, the *Standard Catalog*, the *Booklist*, and *Book Review Digest*. The *Bookman's Manual* chapter devoted to "Travel" is a fine achievement in selective comprehensiveness, including literary and historical maps and atlases, guidebooks, and travel series, as well as a discriminating gleaning from older and recent travel literature.

Of importance in comprehensive scholarly selection and historical research is the *Reference Guide to the Literature of Travel, including Voyages, Geographical Descriptions, Adventures, Shipwrecks and Expeditions* (Seattle, University of Washington Press, 1935-38), a momumental work by Dr. Edward Godfrey Cox, of the University of Washington. The first volume, devoted to Old World travel, appeared in 1933; the second, covering New World voyages, expeditions, and travels, followed in 1938; a third and concluding volume, devoted to Great Britain and Ireland, is in course of publication. This is a bibliography with selective limitations and somewhat uneven, but distinctive for scholarly devotion and literary quality. Chronological in arrangement, material is listed from the earliest ascertainable date through the year 1800, in broad class and country divisions, with frequent annotations giving biographical and bibliographical detail. In the second volume concluding chapters on "General Reference" and "Bibliographies" list many series and works about travel published to 1936, and are excellent for reference use; an author index is included. An old but useful suggestive aid for any extended survey or selection is found in Part 2 of Sonnenschein's *Best Books*. Here Class E, devoted to Geography, brings together an extremely interesting collection of works that represent all aspects of the subject—ethnography, topography, local history, atlases and maps, collections and voyages, travel and adventure, and biographies of voyagers and discoverers. Further literature of travel is scattered through the classes devoted to History and Antiquities. Careful examination and checking of Sonnenschein, indeed, seems to me indispensable to expert selection in this broad subject, as it is for other divisions of literature.

There is fascination for the general reader as well as reference value for any library in *The Story of Maps* (Little, 1949), a history of cartography by Lloyd A. Brown, who, beginning with Strabo and his great *Geography*, written in the first century B.C., carries the story of mapmaking from the ancient world to the present. This is a work of knowledge and enthusiasm, rich in scholarship and also in narrative allure, conveying with unflagging interest the ever enlarging sweep of man's knowledge and mastery of "this goodly frame, the earth."

Atlases, maps, guidebooks, and handbooks for travelers make a group in which the chief requirements are exactitude of information, convenience of arrangement, and timeliness. While older standard publications are of continuing value in much reference work and study, for current usefulness maps and guidebooks must be up to date. The war changed boundaries all over the globe, extinguished former national states, brought others into being, obliterated historic monuments and created new ones; and transformed the medium, scope, and mechanics of travel, as the great airways were added to the world's land and waterways. Most of the standard guidebooks were thus made obselete, and revised editions were impracticable until conditions became more stable. Not until the late 1940's, as the tide of international travel rose again, was there a mounting inflow of familiar guides, manuals, and handbooks in fresh revision and of new, attractive, and authentic travel companions—such as Roger Roumagnac's collaborative *France: Paris and the Provinces*, with its charming color illustrations, its alluring section of gastronomic guidance.

In this general group travel as literature is represented by the "literary maps" that have become increasingly popular, and by what may be called "glorified guidebooks," such as those of Lucas, Hare, Esther Singleton, Helen Henderson, and Clara Laughlin. Literary maps are really decorative accessories for libraries, schoolrooms, or homes, and do not demand attention in book selection; but their charm and ingenuity and the fillip they give to reading interest, especially for young people, make a few good examples desirable in any library. It is difficult to draw distinctions between the "glorified guidebook" and the less utilitarian, more original work of the widely informed and discriminating traveler. The official type of guidebook (such as Baedeker, the "Blue Guides," the "Murray Handbooks") organizes its encyclopedic detail into timetable compactness and abbreviation. Clara Laughlin's "So You're Going" volumes—which represent the popular "glorified" type—take the form of informal, exuberant exposition, conveying essential travel information and working out itineraries with a direct personal appeal and interweaving of historical, literary, art, and descriptive material. Helen Henderson's "Loiterer" volumes are of this general pattern, but with more leisurely and specialized detail. So are H. V. Morton's books, imbued with personal sympathy and descriptive charm (especially evident in his linked volumes on *London*). Lucas' "Wanderer" books, still less formalized, like Hare's chronicles of his "Walks," represent rather the responses of a richly stored mind to contacts and associations with the world's heritage of beauty and the pageant of human history.

The United States and Latin America are the countries upon which the mounting tide of present-travel guides and works of regional and general exposition rose earliest and spread most widely. Foremost here are the serried volumes of the "American Guide Series," elsewhere noted,[1] indispensable in all library collections; and the great body of closely related but independent series and individual works for the American traveler, covering regions, states, cities, main-traveled roads and picturesque byways—from the "Look at America" guide volumes, begun in 1946, to the Duncan Hines guides to food and lodging for motorists (*Adventures in Good Eating, Lodging for a Night, Vacation Guide*) kept up to date in revised editions. The bulletin, *Travel USA*, attractive and useful monthly, edited by R. B. Lattimore, designed to stimulate travel to and within the United States, began publication in October, 1948, for free distribution by the Travel Division of the National Park Service, United States Department of the Interior. Be-

[1] See above, pp. 240–41.

sides descriptive and informational articles, it offers a travel calendar for each month, and descriptive listing of new travel books about the United States: good grist for the travel collection in any school or small public library.

For Latin America, the *South American Handbook*, which issued its 24th annual edition in 1947, is the standard English yearbook and guide, emphasizing tourist interests and business developments and covering in separate chapters the twenty-three countries south of the Rio Grande. Sydney A. Clark's *All the Best in South America*, in two companion volumes (*East Coast* and *West Coast*) first published in 1940 and 1941, appeared in revision in 1947; and for individual volumes the flow of travel manuals becomes constantly more varied and more extensive. Erna Fergusson's vigorous, sympathetic volumes on Cuba and Guatemala; Anita Brenner's *Your Mexican Holiday;* Frances Toor's *New Guide to Mexico*, in late revision; *The Land of Short Shadows*, Erle Stanley Gardner's full-length exploration tour of the little known peninsula of Baja California, exemplify diversity of method and of scope.

Descriptions of countries, not recording any special journey or personal experience, usually take the form of comprehensive expositions, giving social, political, historical, and topographical information as well as description. There are infinite variations in subject, scope, and method. Nearly all countries are included in this type of travel writing, which is especially prevalent in well-known older travel series. Here America is strongly represented by critical analyses and interpretations of national life and ideals studied against their physical backgrounds, centering on social and economic injustice, race cleavages, and minority problems, and continuing the revulsion from traditional standards which found previous expression after the First World War. Many of these books belong as much in social science as in travel. Nearly all are part of the movement toward discovery of America by Americans, inspired by the depression and the war. There is much work of high excellence, thought-provoking and stimulating—the strongest trends being toward illumination of national backgrounds, toward deepened social consciousness, toward sharper awareness of problems and conflicts born of world-change. The most common weakness is overbalance, either of undue disparagement or (more rarely) of indiscriminate praise. Carey McWilliams' *Southern California Country*, for example, in the "American Folkways" series, is factually accurate, fascinating in vivid transmission of scene, but so satirically critical that fair values are obscured. John Gunther's *Inside U.S.A.* stands on a pinnacle of its own: an impressive achievement in creative travel narrative. Informal, absorbing, warmly human, though not always factually correct, it mingles sweeping perspectives with sharp detail, shrewd analysis with perceptive interpretation, forthright criticism with deserved praise. Here, in the full compass of the forty-eight states, in a pervasive spirit of friendliness for people and confidence in the enlargement of the democratic process, is evoked the substance and nature, the far-reaching diversity and the underlying basic unity of "the greatest, craziest, most dangerous, least stable, most spectacular, least grown-up, and most powerful and magnificent nation ever known."

Narrative or descriptive rendering of personal observation and experience is the most familiar and the most flexible form. It prevails in the best current and standard travel literature and in most of the "classics of travel." Its variations are endless, ranging from the plain logbook record of the adventurous seaman to the brilliant word pictures of the literary artist and the meditations of the traveling philosopher. The work of travel that is a fine work of literature always possesses individual personality and reflects or transmits human experience; it usually possesses also definite structural form, ordered development of interest, and unity in the composition as a whole. These qualities may be discerned and analyzed in most of the books included in the selective list that accompanies this chapter. Their recognition is necessary in any intelligent selection from the diversity and multiplicity of current travel literature.

Every purpose, every interest, every preoccupation known to humanity, serves as incentive to the traveler. Some years ago a sightless tourist wrote of a blind traveler's impressions of Europe; and I recall a volume called *Round the World by an Oculist* and another entitled *A Pilgrimage with a Milliner's Needle*, by an enterprising pilgrim who made hats in every stopping-place to cover her expenses. Artists travel for background, novelists for material, scientists for research. Every purpose and mode of travel has offered excuse for a book. There are the youths who tramp, or bicycle, or hitchhike across continents; there is he who rounded the globe on a wooden leg; he who swam the Panama Canal; there are human birds of the air, winging their way over the poles and the seven seas; flocks of motor tourists, and an army of round-the-world voyagers. In travel literature, as in travel itself, there is always a difference between travelers and tourists. Stella Benson says:

Travelers are people who want to see far places; tourists want to say they have seen far places. Travelers come home and gape dreamily when you ask where they have been; tourists bring back souvenirs in order to prove to indifferent friends that they have actually trodden on a pyramid hard enough to knock this very chip off, or dried their faces on this very towel in the hotel at Peking. These tourists may be men or women. They are, however, more often women than men, because so many women, unfortunately, have more time to waste than men.

So great are the range and variety of the books that fall within this group that only a few significant types can be indicated.

Day-to-day record or adaptation of diary notes give the basis for many famous narratives—such as Dana's *Two Years before the Mast* and Kinglake's *Eöthen*, both, after a hundred years, perennial in charm and vitality. Journals and letters in their original form may convey immediate individual experience, or may be used as foundation material for a more unified narrative. In Keyserling's *Travel Diary of a Philosopher*, almost entirely a record of subjective experience, the journal form is consistently maintained and transmits an intimate and vivid sense of place to the reader. Doughty's magnificent *Travels in Arabia Deserta*, on the other hand, was built up through ten years of work from the notes collected and hidden in his bosom during his two years of Arabian wanderings. In its colossal structure are imbedded immense minutiae of detail; its prose is archaic and scriptural in dignity, but it also conveys the same sense of living, day-to-day experience that a diary imparts.

Travel as accessory to specialized knowledge branches out into every field. Here are expeditions made for exploration and scientific research, places visited for historical or literary associations, journeys taken for economic or sociological investigation. Alexander von Humboldt's *Personal Narrative of Travels* has been source material for historians of Hispanic America for nearly a century; Stephens' *Incidents of Travel in Central America* set the first milestone in modern study of the Mayan civilization. Many famous books are of this type, and its importance and value will be obvious from what has been said of the interrelation of travel with other classes of literature.

Scene painting in words is a type that fuses literary artistry with keen sense impressions and poetic insight. It is most often manifest in short pictorial sketches, brilliant, powerful or delicate, dramatically sharp-cut or traced with sensitive impressionism. Gertrude Bell's glowing *Persian Pictures* is an example of this mingling of descriptive, poetic, and literary art; so are the beautiful travel studies of Lafcadio Hearn and Pierre Loti; so is Antoine de Saint Exupéry's flight into the magic world of the air, in his *Wind, Sand, and Stars*—luminous sequence of exotic scenes, of moments of peril or vision, of friendships born from ordeals suffered in common, all infused with rare spiritual insight.

Romantic and adventurous travel possesses some of the qualities of the pictorial type, but more often employs the novelist's art to intensify and sustain its narrative of exciting, unusual experiences. It merges into fiction, as in Herman Melville's *Omoo* and *Typee*, or Stoddard's *South Sea Idyls*, where romantic episodes and actual experiences are interwoven; and into biography, as in Burnham's *Scouting on Two Continents*, which tells the life story of the modest soldier-adventurer, frontiersman, and pioneer, whose experience ranged from the Klondike to South Africa. Often this type of travel-adventure claims an authority it does not possess, and its texture of actual experience is overloaded with embroidery of exaggeration or imagination. Ossendowski's spectacular narratives are examples of this. A little-known example of fictional chronicle frequently accepted as authentic is *Journey of the Flame*, by Antonio de Fierro Blanco, mythical Mexican chronicler, which, in fact, was written by the late Walter Nordhoff, father of Charles B. Nordhoff, coauthor with James Norman Hall of *Mutiny on the Bounty* and other books on Polynesia.

Foreigners' impressions of other countries belong naturally in groups or types already mentioned, but these books are so numerous and so distinctive that they almost form a class by themselves. An American's impressions of Germany, a Frenchman's study of England, an Englishman's observation of Russia, are likely to bring out aspects disregarded or unrealized by native writers, but significant in world relationships. Foreigners' impressions of America hold, of course, special interest for American readers; and few countries have been privileged to study themselves as others see them so constantly and from as many different angles as has the United States. For more than a hundred years, from Mrs. Trollope and Charles Dickens to the latest visiting lecturer, the impressions of curious and sharp-eyed observers have been set forth in many volumes representing every point of view—caustically critical, effusively flattering, cogent, commonplace, witty, or dull. One of the most comprehensive gleanings of such observations and appraisals is Allan Nevins' substantial volume first published in 1923 as *American Social History as Recorded by British Travelers*, and revised in 1948, under the title *America through British Eyes*, with admirable introductions and an extensive annotated bibliography. A significant recent trend, born of war and postwar international relationships, is toward specialized analysis and evaluation of why Americans are as they are. This is exemplified in *The American Character*, Denis W. Brogan's brisk, thought-provoking historical-psychological study; and in Geoffrey Gorer's pungent "psycho-cultural" exposition, *The American People: a Study in National Character*, which bases on anthropology and psychoanalysis, and is akin to Margaret Mead's wartime classic, *And Keep Your Powder Dry*. Effective book selection should glean from these varied materials for self-study that which is illuminating and stimulating and holds constructive values.

In all contemporary travel literature, changing trends of intention and method are evident. The strong influences of anthropology and psychoanalysis have been noted. There is a growing tendency toward race study and race interpretation through sympathy and shared experience. The superficial, flippant, critical traveler who sees everything unfamiliar as ridiculous is less in evidence nowadays; the amused aloofness of Kinglake contrasts curiously with Aldous Huxley's realization, in *Jesting Pilate*, that "doubt of one's own omniscience is the one certain fruit of knowledge and experience." Effects of the war are seen in the diminution of trivial chronicles by ingenuous tourists; in more general and searching observation of social problems, economic contrasts, political conditions, and race relations; and in a steadily deepening recognition that, however deeply opposed in convictions and beliefs, the peoples of the postwar world share a common need, a common hope—for peace, for security, for a better life.

Thus, travel literature can become a medium for understanding man's unity in diversity—a means to evaluate and turn into a common fund of knowledge all racial qualities and racial history. Keyserling's *Travel Diary of a Philosopher* is a manifestation of this. So, in more thorough scientific exactitude and broader intellectual perspective, is Julian Huxley's *Africa View*, one of the great works of far-reaching importance in a dozen different fields of knowledge. A significant though minor supplement to this is Eslanda Robeson's *African Journey*, diary of a trip through South and Central Africa in 1936: vivid, forthright, and penetrating presentment of the native peoples, seen—not as servants or slaves or as "primitive minds," but as people, with their own abilities, their own capacities for development—through the eyes of an American Negro who is also a woman of intellectual attainments, a trained anthropologist, proud of her race and aware that the "Negro problem" is not limited to the problem of the 173,000,000 black people in Africa, America, and the West Indies, but includes "the problem of the 300,000,000 Indians of India, the problem of the 450,000,000 Chinese in China, as well as the problem of all minorities everywhere." Special consideration in selection should be given to the work of writers who visualize and interpret the regions and peoples—Africa, the Far East, China, Korea, Australia, the world of the Pacific—brought by the war into the orbit of America and in their future holding the destiny of civilization. *Without Bitterness: Western Nations in Postwar Africa*, the remarkable work in which Orizu, cultured and tolerant Nigerian prince, writes of the continent and peoples of Africa and their relation to the rest of the world; *Richer by Asia*, Edmond Taylor's "mental log" of two years in India and provocative commentary on western conceptions of the East and vice versa; Richard Lauterbach's *Danger from the East*, vigorous report of observations in Japan, Korea, and China—these are examples of books that help build stronger foundations of global understanding in the postwar world.

A few practical points to consider in judging the merits of travel literature may be briefly noted:

Form or type.—To be judged according to the suggestions previously made.

Qualifications of author.—Consider whether the book is written from adequate observation or from hasty and unverified impressions; whether it is the work of a novice, a veteran adventurer, a traveler of general culture and experience, or an observer of special training and authority. The latter is particularly important in books that deal with original explorations or travel pursued for scientific research, where the traveler's authority and veracity are as essential as are the same qualities in the historian.

Point of view.—The trustworthy traveler is fair-minded, tolerant, and interested. A biased point of view or strong personal prejudices are among the most common defects of travel literature. Only when a book has great vividness or unusual value from other aspects are these defects offset. There should always be sympathy, or at least fair play, toward the life the traveler depicts. An aggressive

Protestant is unlikely to interpret a Roman Catholic country with entire fairness. A militant W.C.T.U. tourist should not describe a French vintage festival. A highly antiseptic sanitarian will probably be blind to the picturesque aspects of life among the gypsies. Katharine Mayo's *Mother India* is a devastating example of reformist ardor condemning an entire ancient civilization for a recognized and age-old evil. Strong antagonisms—personal, ideological, or political—dominating descriptive and interpretative books on Soviet Russia (John Fischer, V. A. Kravchenko are examples) should be balanced by more sympathetic, equally authentic work, such as that of Albert Rhys Williams, Edgar Snow, Hewlett Johnson, and Walter Duranty. Many books by missionary travelers are warped or narrowed by the writers' extreme distrust or dislike of any religion other than their own. There are, too, the provincial-minded travelers, innocent of contact with history or literature, complacent, prosperous, conscious only of the absence of accustomed accessories of living. Like Mr. and Mrs. Haddock, they "get to go abroad" in bodily peregrination, but in psychological truth they never leave their native habitat, nor can guidebooks nor steamship and railway tickets lavishly employed extend their boundaries.

Importance or interest of subject.—As in biography, the subject of a travel book must be interesting in itself, or made interesting. A brilliant or charming writer can invest a familiar subject with freshness and allure; a writer of less ability commands interest when he deals with a subject that is comparatively unknown. A book on travel in England or France, for example, demands higher literary art or more original or specialized point of view than does a book recording a sojourn in Mongolia or a journey to Tierra del Fuego. Travel, especially today when so few regions of the globe are still unexplored, must reveal new aspects or enlarge horizons of knowledge. Avoid the travel writers who treat a hackneyed subject in a hackneyed way: the dreary narratives of egotistical persons who are inspired by crossing the ocean to tell the rest of the world many things it already knows; the sprightly, superficial recitals of *What I*

Saw in Italy; the shallow pronunciamentos that dispose of world-shaking social forces on the authority of two weeks of travel in Russia or India. Timeliness, however, is always a factor in selection: a book that deals with an unfamiliar region suddenly brought to public attention is invested with immediate importance. Sven Hedin's *Jehol*, published just as that unknown "city of emperors" became a focus of Japanese-Chinese conflict, is an example of the value and interest timeliness gives to a book that except for world events would appeal to comparatively few readers.

Literary quality.—Travel literature should not be travel only; it should be literature also. There must be some sap of originality; some flavor, or color, or savor, to enrich it, to give it piquancy and a reason for existence. In travel books, "manner makyth man." There should be clear or graceful or forceful style, graphic power, ability to interest. There must be effective organization of material, discrimination in what is presented: a barren record of meals, hotel accommodations, weather, and train connections is not a book of travel. All travel literature of permanence possesses literary quality.

Textual features.—Excellence of textual and physical characteristics will often turn the scale in decision between two books dealing with a kindred subject. Illustrations are always an attraction; good photographs often help to assure the authenticity of a narrative. Maps are always useful and often indispensable. Bibliographies or citation of authorities are useful as references for selection of other books on the subject or as suggestions for personal reading. Notes and appendixes often give valuable aid to more extended study of the subject.

Veracity.—Truthfulness in travel literature demands a further word. Although the tests that have been noted should help in distinguishing the spurious from the genuine travel chronicle, this is, in fact, often extremely difficult to determine. Veracity, of course, is of less importance in narratives of personal experience in more or less familiar regions; but it is of very great consequence in works that purport to be authoritative record of travel in little known countries, or explorations undertaken with scientific purpose. Dr. Cook's report of his discovery of the North Pole in 1908 is one of the most famous examples of conflicting claims to priority made by rival explorers. In the bitter controversy that followed Robert E. Peary's report of his discovery of the Pole on April 6, 1909, the bulk of evidence supported Peary, whose discovery received official recognition from Congress and has had permanent acceptance; Dr. Cook, however, had considerable support from some of the well-known Arctic explorers, and in numerous reference books his claim is cited as not conclusively disproved. There have been many notable fabricators, whose work, although exposed as unveracious by geographical and scientific authorities, long received popular acceptance. A. H. Savage Landor's narrative, *In the Forbidden Land*, is an interweaving of exciting and highly improbable incidents with threads of veracious experience. A comparison of this book with *Trans-Himalaya*, Sven Hedin's record of exploration in the same region, will make clear the contrast between the sensation-mongering travel adventurer and the conscientious explorer. To many reviewers and a large proportion of the reading public the veracity of a thrilling travel tale is of minor importance; indeed, there is always a certain enjoyment in believing impossible things; but in any serious appraisal of values the truth of a travel narrative is as important as the art with which that truth is conveyed. The romanticized and misleading "yarns" and "tall tales" that masquerade as genuine travel experience (*Trader Horn* and Welzl's *Thirty Years in the Golden North* are examples of many) should be accepted only for what they are and find no place among accredited travel records that are valuable and trustworthy materials of knowledge.

There are many travel series that demand attention in selection. Some of these are reprint series of older travel literature; others are devoted to the encyclopedic work of a single expositor—such as the many-volumed sets of "Carpenter's World Travels" or the "Stoddard Lectures"; others, again, offer a sequence of books by different authors, each covering a single field—as the "Invitation to Travel Series," and the "English Countryside Series." In all selection, however, discriminating choice of individual volumes according to their intrinsic interest and literary quality is preferable to inclusive acceptance of an entire series.

Good travel literature is of perennial interest and appeal. It combines both romance and knowledge. It is informational and recreational, and often inspirational too. It enlarges the reader's mental horizon and sharpens his intelligence. It has particular interest for men and boys, and offers the most effective bridge from stereotyped "westerns" to more worthwhile reading. Books of travel can impart to any individual reader the sense of changing and stimulating experience, given by travel itself, that is expressed by W. S. Maugham:

I travel because I like to move from place to place, I enjoy the sense of freedom it gives me, it pleases me to be rid of responsibilities, duties; I like the unknown; I meet odd people who amuse me for a moment . . . I am often tired of myself and I have a notion that by travel I can add to my personality and so change myself a little. I do not bring back from a journey quite the same self that I took.

All who are concerned with bringing together books and people —whether in book selection, in relationship with readers, or in the many other fields of book use, should become familiar with the range of travel literature, should know of their own knowledge its classics, and keep in touch with the ever enlarging values of present-day illumination and perspectives directed upon "this world so wide," so complex, so increasingly interdependent. To give a reader a poor book when a better one is available is one of the worst sins of commission in the code of library service.

TEN CLASSICS OF TRAVEL

Burton, Sir Richard Francis. Personal Narrative of a Pilgrimage to al-Madinah and Meccah. 1855–56.
Curzon, Robert. Visits to Monasteries of the Levant. 1849.
Dana, Richard Henry. Two Years Before the Mast. 1840.
Darwin, Charles Robert. Charles Darwin's Diary of the Voyage of H.M.S. "Beagle." 1839.
Doughty, Charles Montagu. Travels in Arabia Deserta. 1888.
Irving, Washington. Astoria, or Anecdotes of an Enterprise Beyond the Rocky Mountains. 1836.

King, Clarence. Mountaineering in the Sierra Nevada. 1872.
Kinglake, Alexander William. Eöthen, or Traces of Travel Brought Home from the East. 1844.
Polo, Marco. Travels. 1579.
Scott, Robert Falcon. Scott's Last Expedition. 1913.

FIFTY BOOKS, OLD AND NEW, THAT REPRESENT ASPECTS OF TRAVEL

Adams, Henry. Mont-Saint-Michel and Chartres. 1904.
Ayscough, Florence. A Chinese Mirror. 1925.
Benson, Stella. The Little World. 1925.
Bone, James. The London Perambulator. 1925.
Buck, Peter. Vikings of the Sunrise. 1938.
Cable, Mildred, and Francesca French. The Gobi Desert. 1944.
Cherry-Garrard, Apsley. The Worst Journey in the World: Antarctic, 1910–13. 1922.
Covarrubias, Miguel. Mexico South: the Isthmus of Tehuantepec. 1946.
Dobie, J. F. A Texan in England. 1945.
Duff-Gordon, Lady Lucie. Letters from Egypt. 1863.
Emerson, Ralph Waldo. English Traits. 1856.
Farrer, R. J. On the Eaves of the World. 1926.
Greene, Graham. Journey without Maps. 1936.
Gruber, Ruth. I Went to the Soviet Arctic. 1939.
Gunther, John. Inside U.S.A. 1947.
Hakluyt, Richard. Principal Navigations, Voyages, Traffiques, and Discoveries of the English Nation. 1589.
Hare, A. J. C. Walks in Rome. 1883.
Hawthorne, Nathaniel. Our Old Home, and English Notebooks. 1863.
Hearn, Lafcadio. Glimpses of Unfamiliar Japan. 1894.
Hedin, Sven. Trans-Himalaya. 1910–13.
Hudson, W. H. Idle Days in Patagonia. 1893.
Humboldt, Alexander von. Personal Narrative of Travels to Equinoctial America. 1881.
Hutton, Graham. Midwest at Noon. 1946.
Huxley, Aldous. Jesting Pilate. 1926.
Huxley, Julian. Africa View. 1931.
Johnson, Hewlett. Soviet Russia since the War. 1947.
Keyserling, Count Hermann. Travel Diary of a Philosopher. 1925.
Lomax, John A. Adventures of a Ballad Hunter. 1947.
Lucas, E. V. A Wanderer in Florence. 1912.

TRAVEL

McPhee, Colin. A House in Bali. 1946.
Mead, Margaret. From the South Seas. 1939.
Mears, Helen. Year of the Wild Boar: an American woman in Japan. 1942.
Moreau de St. Méry, M. L. E. Moreau de St. Méry's American Journey, 1793–1798; trans. and ed. by Kenneth Roberts. 1947.
Nansen, Fridtjof. Farthest North. 1897.
Parkman, Francis. The Oregon Trail. 1849.
Powys, Llewellyn. Black Laughter. 1924.
Poncins, Gontran Montaigne. Kabloona; in collaboration with Lewis Galantière. 1941.
Rama Rau, Santha. Home to India. 1945.
Robeson, Eslanda. African Journey. 1945.
Schweitzer, Albert. On the Edge of the Primeval Forest; and More from the Primeval Forest. 1931, 1948.
Snow, Edgar. Red Star over China. 1938.
Stark, Freya. The Arab Island: the Middle East, 1939–45. 1945.
Stein, Sir Aurel. On Ancient Central-Asian Tracks. 1933.
Steinbeck, John. A Russian Journal. 1948.
Stevenson, R. L. Travels with a Donkey in the Cevennes. 1879.
Tomlinson, H. M. The Sea and the Jungle. 1912.
Trollope, Mrs. F. M. Domestic Manners of the Americans. 1832.
West, Rebecca. Black Lamb and Grey Falcon: a journey through Yugoslavia. 1941.
Wood, Thomas. Cobbers. 1940.
Young, Arthur. Travels in France during the Years 1787, 1788, 1789. 1792.

15. Nature and Science

> The bomb that fell on Hiroshima fell on America too.
> It fell on people.
> Not a few hundred thousand only, but one hundred and thirty-five million.
> It did not set them afloat over New York, Kansas City or Los Angeles.
> But it set them afloat on currents of chance which no man may navigate or know the direction of.
>
> Hermann Hagedorn: "The Bomb that Fell on America"
>
> The dominant fact of our time is the towering place of the machine, of applied science, in the lives of mankind. And the great issue of our time, with which the peoples of the whole world will be at grips day in and day out for the rest of our lives, is simply this: Are machines and science to be used to degrade man and to destroy him, or to augment the dignity and nobility of humankind? How can men use and direct science and the machine so as to further the well-being of all men and the flowering of the human spirit?
>
> David Lilienthal: "Science and the Human Spirit," in *A.L.A. Bulletin*, September 1, 1946

THE TRANSFORMATIONS effected in life and thought during the last hundred years are greater than all that came to pass between the dawn of history, so-called, and the middle of the nineteenth century. Modern science has built the modern age—scientific, mechanical, industrial, and social—and has enforced reorientation of the whole intellectual outlook upon the nature and meaning of life. The continuing revisions of the fourteenth (1926) edition of the *Encyclopaedia Britannica*, witness to the mounting velocity and impetus of this transformation. The preceding complete revision of the Encyclopaedia was made in 1910. Various supplements appeared at succeeding intervals, but by 1926 no addenda could cover the increment of the previous sixteen years; complete revision, entire renovation, was necessary. In the 1910 edition, for example, the article on the atom represented a conception now completely discarded; the electron received only a few lines; biology was covered in two pages; the article on aviation was negligible, and so was that on radio (known only as "wireless"); motion pictures were in their first experimental stages, and talking pictures were unknown. Politically and geographically also the world was in another era; but the revolutions and displacements that are historic aftereffects of war are less immediately potent in reshaping human life than are the forces controlled and released by science.

Henry Adams, in his essay, "The Rule of Phase Applied to History," suggests phases or changes through which human thought has passed. He sees first the Phase of Instinct, or control by the automatic drive of animal nature, lasting unbroken for millions of years. Then, with "the leap of nature from the phase of instinct to the phase of thought," he sees the Religious Phase dominating the world, until, in 1500, with the introduction of printing, the discovery of America, the invention of the telescope, the writings of Galileo, Bacon, and Descartes, and the opening of new intellectual vistas, there came a distinct change in direction and form of thought, and a new phase, the Mechanical Phase, appeared, to prevail for three hundred years. With the invention of the dynamo in 1870, there followed the Electrical Phase, with an enormously accelerated intensity of thought-energy in applied science—physics, electricity, astronomy. He says:

The world did not double or treble its movement between 1800 and 1900, but measured by any standard known to science—by horse-power, calories, volts, mass in any shape—the tension and vibration and volume and so-called progression of society were fully a thousand times greater in 1900 than in 1800—the force had doubled ten times over, and the speed, when measured by electrical standards as in telegraphy, approached infinity and had annihilated both space and time.

Last in his vision was to open (in 1917) the Ethereal Phase, "which for half a century science has been promising." Further than that he did not go: "Nothing whatever is beyond the range of possibility." And he adds: "If man should continue to set free the infinite forces of nature, and attain the control of cosmic forces on a cosmic scale, the consequences may be as surprising as the change of water to vapor, of the worm to the butterfly, of radium to electrons." Henry

Adams died in 1918. His Ethereal Phase has not yet risen. But on August 6, 1945, the atomic bomb dropped on Hiroshima by the United States Army Air Force signalized that man for his own destruction had attained control of cosmic forces; and that, in Adams' terms, the world had entered the Atomic Phase of history.

However fanciful may be this application of a scientific formula to the course of human history, there can be no question of the dominance of science in the world today. Its literature grows constantly in volume and variety, keeping pace with the manifold developments of science in theory and in application, and with the rising tide of popular interest. As the whole field of science widens, its specialization intensifies. Original research concentrates more and more minutely upon a single detail. It is from the multitude of infinitesimal threads, discerned, traced, and tested by individual patience, assembled, retraced, retested, combined and recombined, that the fabric of knowledge is woven.

The record of these minutiae of research constitutes the fundamental literature of science. Monographs, treatises, periodicals, society transactions, reports, bulletins, and cognate publications bring to workers in every field the methods and results of specialized, intensive study, in a ceaseless process of utilization, verification, and expansion. This is both source material and working specifications of the scientist: a highly technical organization and formulation of knowledge that in method and terminology conveys its meaning only to the trained student and specialist. It forms the chief content of every specialized scientific library, and must have as full representation as practicable in any large general collection that provides adequately for specialized use. Its bulk is so vast that even in the greatest scientific libraries no "complete" collection is possible. Some idea of its extent may be gained when it is noted that the *Catalogue of Scientific Papers*, compiled by the Royal Society of London, recording material published during the years 1800 to 1900, fills nineteen volumes; that more than five thousand serial publications are regularly examined for entries in the current issues of *Bio-*

logical Abstracts and approximately seven thousand for *Chemical Abstracts*.

Specialized inclusive selection in the grand divisions of science does not come within present consideration. Research workers and advanced students in all the major branches of science (biology, chemistry, physics, astronomy, zoology, and the rest) depend for working material in their subjects chiefly upon the highly developed scientific departments of university and college libraries and upon the collections of institutions and organizations devoted to scientific research. All the leading observatories, for example, maintain their own libraries, devoted to subjects fundamental to astronomical research. Only special medical libraries, or the medical departments of a few large special libraries, such as the John Crerar Library of Chicago (the largest public library devoted to scientific and technical literature), attempt to provide the body of technical literature necessary to professional study, research, and practice in medicine. The ordinary library collection, as a rule, provides only medical works designed for the information of laymen, for nurses, for household use or general reference. Industrial and mechanical technology receives extended representation in general library service, because in every community books in the useful arts are becoming more and more the tools of practical workers in varied fields and crafts, the means of acquiring and developing individual proficiency in many different skills, and to these users the public library is the freest, most accessible source of information, the readiest and most flexible agency of vocational study. However, any extended selection in either science or technology requires expert, specialized proficiency and large and varied bibliographical equipment.

Science was the dominating force of the Second World War. It brought enormous expansion of specialized research, development of new substances, new methods, in chemistry, in biology, in medicine; it captured the speed of sound, the infinite radiations of light; and it thrust upon the world tremendous new problems of international relationship on the solution of which human survival depends.

In mathematical physics, fission of the atom was no longer the working out of abstruse theories in laboratory experiment, but an inexorable means to military victory and a controllable force for the destruction or the service of mankind. Control and use of atomic energy, not for world war but for world peace, thus became the one great world issue, resolvable only by international cooperation to ensure security against humanity's destruction. Albert Einstein, producer of the famous equation which is at the root of atomic fission, said: "This basic power of the universe cannot be fitted into the outmoded concept of narrow nationalism. For there is no secret and no defense; there is no possibility of control except through the aroused understanding and insistence of the peoples of the world."

The great mushroom of yellowish smoke that rose over Hiroshima still casts upon the world a deepening shadow of rival national sovereignties and international power politics and a continuing threat of atomic war. Information and warning have been poured out upon the public by leading men of science and by many writers of knowledge and authority. Distinguished physicists who shared in the project which produced the bomb unified their strength and knowledge in an Emergency Committee of Atomic Scientists, to carry on a campaign of public enlightenment through scientific and educational organizations, libraries, and all available publicity channels. Their monthly *Bulletin of the Atomic Scientists* is an indispensable current source of authoritative information on problems of control and research, on scientific fact and method, on govermental relations, national and international; and on the pivotal importance of the United Nations in the world responsibilities involved. It brings directly to the public the purpose and the spirit of their campaign: "The responsibility to see that atomic energy is used for the benefit and not the destruction of mankind is ours—and *yours*." There can be no cessation of this campaign until international control of atomic energy is achieved and the elimination of war becomes possible. Every library, in book selection and book service, must recognize the part that science plays in human life today; must realize that under the compulsions of the atomic age man's survival depends on reason, not on violence; and must seek to strengthen and illuminate public intelligence to act not for death but for life.

There is a steadily widening general reading public for books in science. Colleges and universities are turning out thousands familiar with the more advanced aspects of physics, chemistry, and biology. Among nearly all young people a clearer understanding of science spreads. In spite of the addiction to "scientific fiction" and wonder tales of planetary travel and atomic automobiles, they have a matter-of-fact acceptance of the new conceptions and changed values that science is bringing into life. In 1946 Harlow Shapley reported that 10,500 science clubs in American schools were linked up with the national organization of science clubs—a group from which will come the scientists of the next generation, "representing a social movement in a scientific age." Adult response to books in science comes from an enlarging public of more or less intelligent laymen. Many are students and teachers, not specialists in science, but familiar with its development and aware of its significance; many are men and women seeking to reconcile traditional convictions and loyalties with the findings of science; and many are everyday citizens absorbed in the business of daily living and unaccustomed to mental exercise, but dimly conscious that modern science is the most important factor shaping the course of modern life. Impact of the atomic bomb sharpened that consciousness; and its vibrations run through the world's social and political struggle for unity, through religious and philosophic concepts, and through every field of creative literature. There is a mounting inflow of books in which science is made intelligible to the layman, and a growing popular acceptance for even the abstruse aspects of scientific research. The present chapter is concerned with the literature of natural science in which this public may find interest and satisfaction, rather than with the pure content of scientific research in technical rendering or with the literature of technology.

As the term natural science is here used it conveys unavoidable generalization. For the so-called exact, physical, natural, and applied sciences all blend and merge in a way that makes close delimitation impossible in any broad survey. The older sciences change, expand, and proliferate. New sciences emerge, as certain branches of knowledge become more generalized, systematized, and verified. Chemistry, for example, has been recognized as a science during less than two centuries. Physics has developed from the so-called "natural philosophy" of a century ago into an exact science which is the fundamental basis and component of modern astronomy and of many of the applied sciences. Psychology in certain aspects (such as psychiatry and psychoanalysis) is transforming and enlarging into one of the great branches of biological science. Definitions and classifications of science have been made by philosophers and scientists from Aristotle to Karl Pearson, in the effort to organize all knowledge into a coherent whole; but no rigid demarkation, no single systematic arrangement, has won general acceptance. The Dewey classification, though it serves in most American libraries as the general frame into which science is to be fitted, is in many respects inflexible and illogical, and if used for closely specialized collections requires both modification and elaboration.

A glance at some of the divisions of science will make their interdependence and interrelation more evident. "Exact" science, "pure" science, "abstract" science, are terms applied to those sciences that on their theoretical side are fundamentally dependent upon mathematics—which is itself abstract or pure science and the foundation both of the most abstruse creations of philosophic thought and of the material structure of modern civilization. Physics belongs here. By the mathematical-physicist are formulated the laws which direct the exploration of the universe through astronomical research and have established the applied sciences of electronics and supersonics, which brought the "electric eye" into electric engineering, the service of radar into radio, the guided missile into aeronautics. Chemistry and astronomy are assigned both to "exact" science and to "physical" science—which is the term commonly applied to those branches of knowledge that deal with nonliving things (mechanics, for example), in contrast to the "natural" sciences, which are concerned with living things. Biology in all its ramifications (botany, zoology, anthropology) is natural science, as are geology and paleontology in their record of past life on earth. Astronomy, dealing with the developing universe, also merges into this division; and so does chemistry, which in biochemistry and in other branches is tracing, analyzing, and testing the origin and substance of living matter. Medical science is a vast domain of its own, but it belongs to biology in the most exact meaning of the term—the science of life. Biology, indeed, is a pivotal factor in modern thought. Concerned with man's relation to his environment, reaching into the nature of human personality, it is transforming the conception and interpretation of history, of religion, of political and social science. Thus science as a whole is an integrated structure. Julian Drachman, in his *Studies in the Literature of Natural Science,* groups the sciences under four headings, as the mental, the physical, the natural, and the human sciences, and says: "One cannot place any one science at the foundation, because each can be seen to derive from the one just before it and to sustain the next one following in an endless cycle."

Virtually all pure or abstract science, in varying degree, leads to, or links with, applied science. Minute particles of knowledge coalesce with other particles, and little by little is formed a medium through which nature is controlled or daily life reordered or reshaped. Haldane says, "It is only the applicable portions of science which are reasonably sure to survive."

But the applicability of science to practical life is not the first concern of scientific research, nor does it affect the scientific point of view. Truth is the lodestar and the touchstone, the one concern, of the worker in science. His business is to see things as they are, free from the glamor of hope or desire; to discern, sift, classify and reclassify, test and retest with endless patience facts assembled in laborious and minute detail. The emotional and the ethical have no place in the scientific attitude. Science does not seek to determine what is right or wrong; it simply demonstrates processes and consequences. Its spirit is the spirit of logical, impersonal thought, of power to suspend judgment. Its highest value is its liberative value in dissipating ignorance, in freeing man from superstitions and prejudices. And it should be added that only science can judge science. Qualities of style, of clarity, of interest, may be fairly estimated by any competent critic or intelligent reader, but the value and validity of scientific content can be made known only by the verdict of scientists themselves.

Literature of natural science, in general presentation and in special fields, takes different forms suited to different kinds of use. There are manuals or textbooks for elementary or advanced use; monographs and treatises for the scientific investigator or scholar; simple, popularized introductions and "outlines" for the inexperienced general reader; essays and studies of literary charm; "classics" that have won permanence both as science and as literature (from Lucretius' poem, "On the Nature of Things," to Augustus De Morgan's *Budget of Paradoxes*); and works of sound scientific authority that with ability and literary skill are "humanizing" knowledge. Each form has its own special requirements and characteristics, but for all there is one prime qualification. Truth and art together establish permanence as literature; but in the field of science truth is the first necessity. And truth in science (exactitude of fact, precision of detail) depends in large measure upon the time factor. The classics of science are milestones in scientific progress; they established the foundations of knowledge upon truth discerned and captured by minds far in advance of their day; but in contemporary scientific literature the more recent a publication is, the more valuable it is likely to be. So rapid are the modern developments in research, experimentation, discovery, and invention that new material constantly changes and enlarges the body of knowledge. This, of course, is particularly true in applied science; but in all fields of science the latest harvests are the richest.

So-called "nature books" form a broad, ill-defined group in the literature of natural science. In them the observation of nature and the study of animal life are invested with emotional, aesthetic, and imaginative implications that are inherent in creative literature. Thus they lie in a borderland between science as the record of ascertained fact, and literature as writing whose value lies in beauty of form or emotional effect. They merge almost indistinguishably into fiction, according to the pattern set by Ernest Thompson Seton in 1898. They belong also to the genre of essay literature that draws ethical and philosophical reflections from communion with nature, as Thoreau practiced it, with Burroughs and Muir among his successors; or that links a casual commentary, poignant, thoughtful, or whimsical, with the vivid, accurate observations of a naturalist, as in the nature essays of W. H. Hudson and Richard Jefferies. They blend into travel in the journals and narratives of naturalists and scientific explorers, as in Sanderson's *Animal Treasure* or Levick's *Antarctic Penguins*. They are of the substance of science in so far as they present exact and definite knowledge of the facts of nature, based on genuine observation and set forth with simple directness. The natural history essays of Hudson and Muir are valid as science and delightful as literature. Comparison of Fabre's study, *The Mason-Bees*, with Maurice Maeterlinck's *Life of the Bee* makes clear the distinction between books of natural science that have the qualities of fine literature and works of literature that find in natural science material for metaphysical thought and poetic emotion. Maeterlinck's *Life of the Ant*, set beside Julian Huxley's *Ants*, offers a similar and even more illuminating contrast between the exercise of the literary imagination upon a scientific theme and the fine literary expression of scientific truth.

The natural history essay and the fictionized or emotionalized study of animal life represent the most familiar and popular kind of nature literature. Nature essays are delightful to a great many readers of cultivated taste and fine sensibilities who have little conscious interest in science. Their effect is chiefly to give esthetic pleasure and induce a certain meditative serenity, yet in developing esthetic responsiveness to nature they are also an influence toward appreciation of more scientific nature study. In this genre Donald Peattie's *Almanac for Moderns* stands as a modern classic: a "daybook" of observations and reflections on nature and science and the men who have revealed their truth and beauty, by a scientist who is also nature-lover, historian, poet, novelist, and rational-minded philosophic thinker.[1]

Nature books and animal stories for children contain much allowable fancy and romance, valuable in establishing sympathy and a sense of human kinship with all living things. But the sentimental "make-believe" nature writing that invests all wild life with human emotions, sensations, and faculties is fiction, not natural history. Animal psychology has become one of the most significant modern fields of natural science. Its effect was evident, in a measure, in the animal fiction of Thompson Seton and C. G. D. Roberts, and it gained deepening emphasis and value in later work, such as Henry Williamson's *Tarka the Otter*. Sally Carrighar's studies of the life vicissitudes of wild creatures in the High Sierras; Gustav Eckstein's varied, brilliant sketches of the nature and behavior of the lesser creatures of the world, from canaries to cockroaches; Edwin Way Teale's vivid word and camera portrayals of insect and plant life; and Haig-Brown's *Return to the River*, saga of the Columbia River salmon, are examples of fine present-day work in this field. There still linger, however, in many popularized or fictional "nature books" vestiges of the fables and traditions that have come down from the medieval "bestiaries" which preserved ancient myths and symbols. Most of our familiar animal similes (bold as the lion, tender as the dove, wily as the serpent, sharp-eyed as the lynx) are simply survivals of this ancient lore. The valid, brilliant, fascinating work of modern scientific observers—Fabre's accurate and beautiful rendering of insect life-drama, W. H. Hudson's illuminating synthesis of the natural instincts in his study, *A Hind in Richmond Park*, Dr. Levick's detailed record of the penguin world that so strangely parallels the human one, and many other books of kindred authority—have deeper interest and value for any intelligent reader, young or old, than the sugared or mysticized anthropomorphizing compositions of literary sentimentalists.

[1] Peattie's *The Road of a Naturalist* (pp. 275–81) contains illuminating retrospect and characterization of the enduring qualities of popular "nature writing."

Astronomy and biology are the divisions of natural science that today command the widest popular interest and have enlisted the largest corps of skilled and authoritative interpreters. The great modern developments in physics, the theory of relativity, and the theories and experimentations concerning the atom, as Eddington says, "are not merely discoveries as to the content of the world; they involve changes in our mode of thought about the world." Modern astronomical research, based as it is on physics, is projecting into the common mind an ever deepening knowledge of the universe that is penetrating and influencing philosophy, religion, ethics, education, and creative literature, just as nineteenth-century research in natural science, establishing the principle of evolution of life, penetrated and transformed thought concerning man's history in the world of living matter. Today we have a conception of the universe that embraces myriad universes in which ours is a minor and unimportant system; "solid" matter no longer exists, but is replaced by rushing currents of atoms and incessant whirls of electrons, ever dissolving and merging; fixed time, vacant space, are abolished, and time and space assimilated in a unified, ever moving cycle; gravitation is not what we thought it. The entire universe is transformed from the old static conception into a universe finite but unbounded, requiring a different time sense, demanding different mental similes, new symbols of measurement and meaning, and in lengthening vistas carrying man from a more remote past to a more distant future than the imagination ever before conceived.

These new conceptions of space, matter, and time—so different from the "classical" astronomy of even a generation ago—are the product of recondite exact science, but are made intelligible to laymen through many books of high authority and clear graphic exposition. Hale, Jeans, Shapley, Eddington are among the leaders in modern astronomy who present its substance of knowledge in a manner that can be understood by any reader even slightly acquainted with the vocabulary and technique of the science. There are other excellent presentations, more condensed and simplified, freed so far as possible from technical and abstruse phrasing and sound in scientific fact. Gamow's *The Birth and Death of the Sun* is such a popularization from the standpoint of atomic physics, of first rank in authority, pleasantly informal and not too difficult for the amateur. Professor Turner's *A Voyage in Space*, though one of the older works, is a delightful simplification that conveys the charm and personality of a great man of science. Unusual in appeal to young or uninformed readers is Lillian and Hugh Lieber's *Einstein Theory of Relativity*, combining lucid text, carefully worded for swift and easy reading, and skillful diagrams and cartoon drawings that effectively interpret the subject. Lincoln Barnett's *The Universe and Dr. Einstein* also is unusual in kindred qualities of lucidity, conciseness, and arresting, illuminative expression which make this compact exposition relating the work of Einstein to man's whole concept of the universe intelligible and impressive to readers from high school age to maturity. In the leading comprehensive histories and untechnical handbooks of science, such as Thomson's *Outline of Science* and Wells' *Science of Life*, this fascinating chapter of modern research receives, as a rule, authentic and effective treatment.

In biology probably the strongest popular interest attaches to books in which the findings of science that relate to man in his physical and mental nature are made available to the nonscientific reader. The origin and nature of life, the structure and processes of the human organism, the growth of the brain, the sources and mechanism of human behavior, the manifestations of individual psychology—these are subjects in which modern science is constantly increasing the sum of knowledge. This knowledge is establishing means to the control of human life and the solution of many problems of human relationship; it is a force working for intelligence, for rationalism, and for social reorganization. Only as it is understood and accepted by the public at large can it be fully utilized. While the application of science to the material and mechanical accessories of living is eagerly accepted by the multitude, the scientific attitude of mind, the scientific pursuit of truth concerning human beings and the objectives of human life, meet with widespread, strong, and threatening opposition. The principle of evolution, though now established for nearly a century, in its demonstration of man's animal background and relationship to the rest of the physical world is still evaded or ignored in much public education and has hardly penetrated at all into certain domains of traditional religion and moralism. In spite of the dominance of science in the present-day world, the general diffusion of scientific knowledge is only beginning. Books that are humanizing and popularizing scientific research increase constantly in number and meet a steadily growing demand. Many of them rise quickly to best sellers; but an enormous reading public remains to be reached.

Every general library collection should be, so far as possible, a means of disseminating scientific knowledge and promoting the scientific attitude of mind. Wells' encyclopedic work, *The Science of Life*, for example, should be in even a small collection, for it sets before any untrained reader the whole structure of life, begins with and culminates in man, and brings together the discoveries and accumulated facts of science that ought to energize and revolutionize general human intelligence. So should *Science for the Citizen*, Lancelot Hogben's monumental compendium, which centers on the theme that science is inextricably related to social growth, that this relationship is the new "social contract," and that the makers of the new social contract will be the makers of a new social culture. Planned as a "self-educator," not only in scope and substance but in organization, this is a book not "written down" to the untrained mind, but so brilliant and lucid that it will rouse all the latent abilities of such a mind. Brilliancy, lucidity, and brevity are combined in J. B. S. Haldane's *Science Advances*, a small volume of ninety short essays, in which the famous English biologist discusses scientific and technical developments that relate to men, animals, plants, physiology, evolution, medicine, hygiene, and inventions—a remarkable achievement in simplification for untrained readers, in impeccable scientific fact, and in the dominating conviction that "Marxism is the application of scientific method to the widest field so far achieved by man."

Such books as H. W. Haggard's *Devils, Drugs, and Doctors* and R. H. Shryock's *The Development of Modern Medicine*, vividly tracing that long pursuit of truth which suddenly within less than a life span brought in sight the goal of conquest over disease and human suffering; Logan Clendening's wise, pungent exposition of the structure and mechanism of *The Human Body;* and H. M. Parshley's comprehensive, detailed study, *The Science of Human Reproduction*, are of cardinal importance and interest, and ought to be known to that great public which lives in either a fog of transcendental or superstitious beliefs about the human organism or in an obscurity of ignorance due to traditional pruderies and interdictions.

That public, however, is diminishing, as the light of science in steadily increasing volume is directed on the subject of sex and on the application of psychosomatic medicine to common ills of mind and body. The so-called "Kinsey Report," *Sexual Behavior in the Human Male*, published in January, 1948, is foundation stone of a massive structure of sex knowledge, objective, factual, explicit, in which collective data from some hundred thousand contributors are in process of record, analysis, and integration. Originated and carried on by Dr. Alfred C. Kinsey and associates at Indiana University, sponsored by the National Research Council, and financially underwritten by the Rockefeller Foundation, the impact of this work upon the public was immediate, its influence far-reaching. It became at once a continuing best seller, opened frank general discussion of a subject long taboo, precipitated an avalanche of reviews, articles, and commentary, and evoked a varied succession of interpretative, expository, and critical studies. Among these, *Sex Habits of American Men*, a symposium by specialists, edited by Albert Deutsch, and *About the Kinsey Report*, a similar compilation, edited by Donald Porter Geddes and Enid Curie, issued in the 25-cent "New American Library," gave prompt, competent summary and appraisal. Of the value and importance of the Kinsey Report in the study of complex social problems there can be no question. Its findings are still partial; final judgment of defects and qualities must await fuller scientific assessment. But it is a sincere, determined, objective advance toward a worthy goal, which the preface clearly indicates: "As long as sex is dealt with in the current confusion of ignorance and sophistication, denial and indulgence, suppression and stimulation, punishment and exploitation, secrecy and display, it will be associated with duplicity and indecency that lead neither to intellectual honesty nor human dignity."

Psychosomatic medicine, in which the principles and methods of psychoanalysis are merged with those of medical pathology, has risen rapidly, though less explosively, to public attention, as the newest, most important, and most fascinating field of medical science. Now thoroughly established, a book club is maintained to disseminate "Basic Books" related to its subject; it has had sound, informative popularization in such books as Dr. L. E. Hinsie's *The Person in the Body*, and Dr. Helen Flanders Dunbar's *Mind and Body*, which link to the work done by Zilboorg and Menninger in humanizing for the intelligent layman the problems and principles of scientific psychology.

More technical, but of far-reaching significance and value, is H. S. Jennings' volume, *The Biological Basis of Human Nature*, one of the ablest presentations of the problem of heredity and environment that has yet appeared. It represents deep knowledge, patient experiment guided by acute reasoning, constant caution in drawing inferences—the genuine scientific attitude. As with Frederick Tilney's study of the origin, development, structure, and powers of the human brain, *The Master of Destiny*, the course of evolution may here be followed as a continuing process of development in which the emergence of new factors, the operation of new forces, affect the organism, the mind, the behavior, and bring about progressive transformation. Such books and others of like value are not "written down" to adult infants, but are addressed to thoughtful and intelligent though nonscientific readers. They demand concentration and purpose, but they offer the finest fruits of modern scientific research.

It is often difficult to maintain the best standards of selection in the provision of books in science for the general public. Popular demand, as a rule, has little relation to scientific value. For the rapid development of modern science has established what John Langdon-Davies called a "new age of faith," in which a great mass of lay worshipers make no discrimination between pseudoscientific theories and vagaries and the less readily understood, more modestly advanced, achievements of specialized research in science. How far obscurantism should be fostered and public intelligence retarded by supplying the demand for so-called "scientific" literature that disseminates fallacies and encourages "wishful thinking" is a problem of library book selection that has received very little thoughtful consideration and even less frank discussion. Matthew Arnold defined the aim of education as "the getting to know on all matters which concern us the best that has been thought and said in the world, and through this knowledge turning a stream of fresh and free thought upon our stock notions and habits." It is true that a stream of fresh thought turned suddenly upon an unexpectant mind may only have the effect of rousing violent indignation. But if the library is the chief public agency for self-education through life, it must give the genuine materials of knowledge priority over those which are inferior or spurious.

Varied manifestations of pseudoscience, of vagary and delusion, are indicated in a book that should be familiar to all concerned with selection in the field of science. Augustus De Morgan's *Budget of Paradoxes* is a classic in literature as well as in science. In record and commentary it gleans from the mass of books, pamphlets, and correspondence that came to Professor De Morgan's attention during his years as scientific editor of the London *Athenaeum*. Here squarers of the circle, discoverers of perpetual motion, exponents of esoteric cults, eccentric prophets, astrologers, geomancers, inventors of strange devices, submitted their arguments and conclusions, and here De Morgan's encyclopedic learning and inexhaustible wit play over the medley, exposing dross, disclosing a jewel now and then, appraising and summarizing all with expert knowledge, logic, and irresistible common sense. Somewhat similar in general purport, evoked by the prevalence of myth and folklore among presumably intelligent people, is Bergen Evans' pungent, witty *Natural History of Nonsense*, a provocative, hard-hitting demolition of popular fallacies concerning the animal kingdom (including man). His satire plays vivaciously over the maternal instinct in birds, the physical superiority of savages, the statistical analysis of "extra-sensory perceptions," and many other subjects; it takes on impressiveness and eloquence in dealing with traditional beliefs about Negroes, with anti-Semitism, with the theory of a pure race, the inferiority of "the poor," and the immorality of primitive peoples.

Joseph Jastrow's *Wish and Wisdom: Episodes in the Vagaries of Belief*, however, must rank as De Morgan's successor and complement. Concerned not so much with the pretensions of pseudoscience as with the conflict between the delusions and obsessions of wishful thinking and the logical discipline of reason and tested knowledge, this thought-provoking volume is a tonic to reason, an antidote to adult infantilism. Here in seven divisions is a high-lighted survey of the psychological factors "that bend wisdom to wish and lead the thinker astray." First, is Credulity, the will to believe, which makes the human race eternally gullible. Then, Magic and Marvel, expression of wonder in man's mind, seeking thrill of awe and mystery to inject a stimulant into belief. Transcendence follows: acceptance of the claim of supernatural powers. Then, in order: Prepossession, in which the mind finds what it looks for; Congeniality of conclusions; Cult and vagary; and last, Rationalization, which is "assigning good reasons for weak thinking." Such are the "seven inclinations" that deflect the mind from the path of wisdom by yielding to wish. They are manifested in a varied sequence of historic episodes, of miracle-mongers, of cultists, of strange cosmologies born of fanaticism and self-hallucination, which reach their pinnacle in the imperishable story of the "scientific" origin and purpose of the Jaeger Sanitary Woolens.

Science as ordered knowledge, slowly pursued and patiently studied, is, of course, in natural opposition to an intuitive perception, an emotional acceptance, of an intangible truth. For this reason, the scientific mind is sometimes prone to sweep away as confusion or vagary thought and speculation that are legitimate enough as imaginative symbolism or as philosophical or ethical theory, and that do not assume to deal with the factual or material. And although science directs its energies upon evidence, not opinion, upon fact, not speculation, it must also be remembered that scientists themselves are not immune to prejudices and fixed ideas. A specialist absorbed in some single line of research often links observed facts with theory; gradually theory becomes dogma, and what should have been open-minded research becomes the propagation and dissemination of some particular doctrine, some individual obsession. In any continued familiarity with the literature of science the propagandist is soon recognized. Appraisal of his work must denote its unreliability as a complete or fairly proportioned body of knowledge and allow for its peculiar bias, whether it be the unalterable recurrence of "cycles" in the life of the universe, or the attribution of every human trait and condition to ductless glands, or the consideration of man's organism and history solely as the effect of climate, or the advocacy of human sterilization as the solution of every social and political problem. Much doctrinaire and propaganda science attains to wide popularity; but in discriminating selection, works of sounder balance should be given preference.

A few specific points for consideration in the selection of books in science may now be summarized:

Form (such as textbook or manual, elementary or advanced; reference work; anthology; professional monograph or treatise; presentation for the general reader); *subject* (general or particular); and *scope* (complete, partial, highly specialized) indicate the fundamental character and organization of the work. Remember that there is a growing body of nonspecialized users for texts and manuals popularized to meet the demand for self-education aids—which is the basic purpose of the "How to" books in their endless variations and disguisements.

Author's qualifications are of prime importance, in denoting both scientific authority and degree and kind of research represented. Work of firsthand authority in science is as a rule closely specialized; a biologist does not write on geology, an astronomer does not expound eugenics. But there are many works that represent summary or synthesis or interpretation rather than original research, and knowledge of the author's scientific background is a guide in appraisal of their authority. Sir J. A. Thomson's *Outline of Science* by its editor's eminence in natural history conveys implication of excellence. Wells' *Science of Life* would convey much less assurance of authority if it were not produced in collaboration with Julian Huxley, one of the most distinguished present-day biologists. The work of authors whose qualifications are chiefly educational or literary or journalistic is often of much value in popularizing science for untrained readers; but specific scientific collaboration or supervision enhances its authority, and the importance of such collaboration is more and more realized by publishers. The successful popularizations of science by E. E. Slosson were the product of a carefully developed system of scientific authority that expanded into Science Service, the institution sponsored by the National Academy of Sciences, the National Research Council, and the American Association for the Advancement of Science, which supplies syndicated scientific news articles to many American newspapers. Hackwork popularizations of science, superficial and inferior, though less common than formerly, still exist, and form one of the difficulties encountered in building up a dependable science collection for the general reader. Authors who produce a new book every year, each volume in a different field of knowledge, are usually of questionable authority and their work should have close critical examination.

Basis of work, though often implied in an author's qualifications, should be clearly understood. As in the case of history, it may represent source material of firsthand research, exact experimentation, and trained observation; or material of firsthand value drawn from untrained observation; or secondary material presented with skill and authority, or weakened by superficial or ill-balanced handling. It should be remembered that the source material of science is rarely comprehensible to the nonscientific reader. To effectively "humanize" knowledge, it must be made readable and interesting.

Purpose, if not sufficiently indicated in *form*, should be ascertained—whether it is to record observations and results, to disclose a special body of knowledge, to summarize and generalize in broad survey, to expound a theory, to analyze or criticize the work of others, or to express a particular point of view, appeal to a particular group of readers.

For *manner of treatment* and for *qualities* of structure and expression, the tests suggested for history are suitable. All effective presentation of science demands logical organization, ordered progression, precision of statement, and a direct, explicit style. "Literary" qualities (charm or vigor of style, imagination, fervor, humor, ease) give wider value and more assured permanence to any scientific work, but are important only as they are freighted with the true ore of science. Predominant use of technical and specialized terminology is an impediment and disadvantage in communicating scientific information to the layman—Darwin, Huxley, and other great men of science were able to write in a thoroughly scientific manner yet with sparing use of such terms—just as, at the other end of the scale, journalistic exaggeration, triviality, and sentimentality are the chief sins of overpopularization.

Date and *publisher* are important. New trends and achievements in all fields of modern science should have prompt recognition; and for applied science satisfactory library service depends upon up-to-date material; recent editions of standard works are to be preferred to older ones. Publisher's imprint often conveys implication of value: scientific and technological books issued by publishers of first rank must as a rule conform to high standards of accuracy and competence.

Such *textual and physical characteristics* as illustrations, charts, diagrams, tables, bibliographies, full and exact indexes, clear typographical presentation, are essential features in the exposition of scientific fact. They must be considered in relation to the form and purpose of the work and their significance to readers.

These are points that, noted in brief examination, help toward generalized comparison and selection among books of varying merit;

but they cannot determine full or final values. Nor can such values be determined from the general literary reviews or the enthusiasm of nonscientific readers. Selection in this field must constantly utilize the judgment of specialists, as it is made available through standard aids, through reviews in the scientific periodicals, and through use of the extensive, varied, and elaborate bibliographical equipment of science.

While extensive specialized selection is beyond the scope of this chapter, its range and character should perhaps be indicated. The fundamental materials of knowledge of current scientific research consist in the original contributions in the myriad periodicals, serials, and other publications issued by scientific institutions and organizations. Thus, indexes and contents abstracts of these publications, prepared and sponsored by scientific authority, constitute the most important bibliographical record of science. Such a record of all materials of research in atomic energy is now in process of development by the Atomic Energy Commission, the federal agency responsible for the United States atomic energy program, in cooperation with the Research Information Service of the John Crerar Library of Chicago. By a contract made in 1948, that library does the abstracting of scientific books and periodicals necessary to the atomic energy research being carried on under the sponsorship of the Commission. A special staff studies the 3,500 scientific periodicals received by the library for relevant material, translates it where necessary, abstracts it, and makes it immediately available to the Commission for distribution to its affiliated research laboratories.[2]

In the field of general science two important works are: the *Catalogue of Scientific Papers*, compiled by the Royal Society of London, already mentioned, and the *International Catalogue of Scientific Literature*, published from 1902 to 1921 for the International Council by the Royal Society of London. Of the latter, it was planned to issue seventeen volumes a year, each volume indexing contributions in a specific field of science. From 1914, however, war and postwar conditions obstructed or prevented the work of the

---

[2] *Library Journal*, 73:1163 (Sept. 1, 1948), p. 1163.

various regional bureaus, and in 1921 publication was suspended on account of these difficulties and of steadily increasing bulk and cost. This catalogue is a definitive reference and selection aid in all the branches of science it deals with. *Science Abstracts,* published monthly in London in two sections, "Physics Abstracts" and "Electrical Engineering Abstracts," are devoted to abstracts of articles in current scientific periodicals and proceedings. *Biological Abstracts, Chemical Abstracts,* and other publications of similar type, are the current working tools of scientists in different fields. Van Hoesen and Walter's manual, *Bibliography,* in the chapter devoted to "Religion, Philosophy, Sciences," and the bibliographical appendix, gives an excellent, compact résumé and record of the important bibliographies, indexes, abstracts, and lists in the various divisions of science. The great Poggendorff bio-bibliography, covering the life and works of scientists in every field, of all countries and all times, which for nearly a hundred years has been the most important aid for bibliographical research in science, is today given extended availability through the lithoprinted facsimile edition published by the Edwards Brothers of Ann Arbor.

And in any advanced reference and research there should be some acquaintance with that wonderful monument of scientific knowledge and scholarship, Dr. George Sarton's *Introduction to the History of Science.* Lifetime achievement of one of the great world historians of science, and published for the Carnegie Institution of Washington, the first massive volume, *From Homer to Omar Khayyám,* appeared in 1927. A second volume, in two equally massive parts, followed in 1931, in which the weaving of man's deep-piled ever-enlarging fabric of knowledge is carried *From Rabbi Ben Ezra to Robert Bacon.* And in 1947, volume III, also in two parts (each covering more than 1,000 pages) presented *Science and Learning in the Fourteenth Century*—the whole a still continuing progression through time that, in Lord Acton's words, reveals "the logic of discovery, the demonstration of the advance of knowledge and the development of ideas, which, as the earthly wants and passions of men remain almost unchanged, are the charter of progress and the vital spark in history."

For more limited general selection, the standard aids, with *Booklist* and *Book Review Digest* for current publications, are often the main dependence; but further guidance is desirable. Shaw's *List of Books for College Libraries* gives basic material in specific fields of science, particularly for study and reference use. Of indispensable value in the whole field of science and technology is the annotated list of *Scientific, Medical and Technical Books Published in the United States of America, 1930–1944*. Issued in April, 1946, and distributed by the Bowker Company, this is a cooperative undertaking in which publishers, scientists, teachers, and the government contributed services and support. It was sponsored by the State Department, editorially organized by the National Research Council, and prepared under the editorship of R. R. Hawkins, chief of the New York Public Library science and technology division. Limited to American and Canadian authors, its 1,114 pages include more than 6,000 selected titles, arranged in fifty-odd major divisions and many subdivisions. For each book, table of contents are listed and for many a brief note denotes importance, purpose, and use. Successive supplements at three-year intervals are planned to keep the list up to date. There should also be acquaintance with the *Science News Letter*, weekly current summary of science, published by Science Service, which offers frequent reviews of important current books in science; with the reviews and annotated lists of new books which appear in the *Scientific Monthly;* with the *Bulletin of the Atomic Scientists;* and with the extensive informational and bibliographical service maintained by the National Research Council at Washington.

Series are important from several aspects of selection. There are many old-established standard series carried by leading general and technological publishers that are constantly drawn upon in any extended selection in pure and applied science. Of general interest and importance in the wide range and accepted authority that make them a semiencyclopedic current record of the sciences are the biennial volumes (the fifth appeared in 1948) of "Science in Progress" (Yale University Press), devoted to the national lectureships sponsored by Sigma XI, honorary scientific fraternity, in which leading scientists present surveys of recent progress in their respective fields. The "Harvard Monographs in Applied Science" is an impressive, highly specialized series, initiated in 1948 in cooperation of Harvard University Press with the John Wiley Publishing firm, under the supervision of an editorial committee of five Harvard faculty members; it consists of abstruse technical and theoretical studies, running to from 100 to 200 pages, dealing with applications of engineering to seismology, the modern network theory, and kindred acroamatic topics. "Harvard Books in Astronomy" (Blakiston) have through more than a decade covered important phases in their field of science and proved their standard usefulness. One of the most significant projects in American scientific publication was launched on December 2, 1948, when the first completed volume of the "National Nuclear Energy Series" was published by McGraw-Hill, under a contract with Columbia University as representative of the Atomic Energy Commission; a first copy of this volume was presented to David Lilienthal, chairman of the commission, on that day, signalizing the sixth anniversary of the operation in Chicago of the first atomic pile. The series is expected to run to about sixty volumes, prepared chiefly at Oak Ridge from documentary material and printed wholly by offset process by Edwards Brothers, Ann Arbor, Michigan. Additional volumes will probably be prepared and printed by the government and held under close restrictive control. In popularized selection for non-specialist readers it must be remembered that, among the various older series of small readable volumes designed as sound and illuminating introductions to science and useful arts, many volumes are now outdated and their serviceability is to that degree impaired.

Anthologies in science, as in other fields of literature, have increased immensely in number, range, popularity, and usefulness. They offer timely and authoritative discussion of recent progress, current problems, and controversial aspects; they glean from the classics of science and from older or little known literature not readily available elsewhere; often they present the progression of science in its historical development and its relation to society. They are among the most effective aids to popularization of scientific information. In general library selection they should have the fullest practicable representation, always with emphasis on comparative authority, scope and organization of material, timeliness, and stimulative quality.

Important anthologies often appear in series as "source books" or "readings"—as with "Source Books in the History of the Sciences from the Renaissance to the End of the Nineteenth Century" (McGraw-Hill), in whose successive volumes devoted to astronomy, mathematics, physical and biological sciences, under distinguished editorship, the progress of science unfolds in the words of its makers. A similar historical progression is compressed into the anthology, *Autobiography of Science*, edited by F. R. Moulton and J. J. Schifferes (Doubleday, 1945). Anthologies and symposiums have been a chief medium for the most immediate and important information on the atomic bomb and its related problems. Foremost here is *One World or None*, published early in 1946, a symposium participated in by some fifteen eminent physicists (eleven of whom had shared in the project which produced the bomb), admirably edited by Dexter Masters and Katharine Way, and still one of the best compact, illuminating presentations for the lay reader. Also of value are: *The Scientists Speak* (Boni & Gaer, 1948), in which Warren Weaver has organized by subject, in 14 chapters, 81 talks by distinguished scientists given over the radio during intermissions of the New York Sunday afternoon Philharmonic-Symphony concerts—the whole forming a compendium of enlightening little essays on present-day science; *Physical Science and Human Values*, symposium of papers and discussions offered at one of the conferences organized to celebrate the Princeton University bicentenary in 1947; and *Readings in the Physical Sciences*, edited by Harlow Shapley, Helen Wright, and Samuel Rapport, which is the revised

(1948) edition of the same editors' notable *Treasury of Science*.

Familiarity with book reviews in scientific periodicals is a chief factor in discriminating current selection. In selection for large or highly specialized collections, reviews in an immense number and variety of scientific and technical periodicals are constantly drawn upon. Even in limited general selection, from the reviews that appear in *Nature* and *Science*, the two leading general scientific periodicals, may be gained valuable acquaintance with the appraisals made by science of its own literature. *Nature*, weekly scientific journal published in London since 1869, is the most important medium of such appraisal. It covers the whole field of natural science (applied science is also represented), chiefly through reviews and critical commentary on current literature. Its wide range, its interest, the distinction and authority of its contributors, and its spirit of fair-minded critical judgment will give to anyone who reads it regularly a sound background of general scientific information and a clear understanding of the standards and viewpoint of science itself. *Science*, the American weekly journal, also deals particularly with natural science; it publishes more articles and reports than reviews, but gives brief selective record of current publications.

Some background acquaintance with the literature of science is necessary if it is to be wisely chosen and effectively used. Through Julian Drachman's *Studies in the Literature of Natural Science* (Macmillan, 1930), this background may be established or developed, not only for any worker in books, but for any intelligent reader. Here the rise and spread of scientific literature during the nineteenth century is recorded, the qualities and characteristics of the books themselves are made clear, and their effect upon public opinion is shown. Rich in information, sound in literary judgment, this volume combines the personal history of great men of science, past and present, and the denotation, sympathetic appraisal, and bibliographical record of their published work, both as science and as literature. It reveals the fine literary quality that is inherent in classics of science, often not intended for popular reading at all, and it brings out both in implication and analysis many of the values and distinctions that are fundamental in discriminating book selection.

To open the great domain of science more fully to public exploration and acceptance is an inspiring enterprise. The advance of science continues through the modern world; but only as its aims are understood and its results known can the knowledge it releases be infused into common living. Through the provision and dissemination of the books that diffuse this knowledge the library, more vitally perhaps than any other agency, participates in bringing the purpose of science to unpredictable fulfillment. As Dr. Jennings has said:

> What is to come in the future is not predictable from what has occurred in the past. The laws of nature are not immutable, in the sense that new laws shall not be exemplified as new conditions arise. Because things have occurred in a certain way in the past, it does not follow that they must thus occur in the future. This has not been the history of evolution in the past; there is no ground to expect it in the future. . . . There is nothing in legitimate science or scientific method that makes it unreasonable to hope for the appearance in the future of what has not been seen in the past. Nothing in science is incompatible with striving to realize ideals that have never yet been realized.[3]

TWENTY-FIVE BOOKS ON NATURE AND ANIMAL LIFE

Beebe, William. Nonsuch, Land of Water. 1932.
Borland, Hal. An American Year: country life and landscapes through the seasons. 1946.
Bouvier, E. L. Psychic Life of Insects. 1922.
Burroughs, John. Ways of Nature. 1905.
Carrigher, Sally. One Day on Beetle Rock. 1944.
Eckstein, Gustav. Lives. 1932.
Evrard, Eugène. Mystery of the Hive. 1923.
Fabre, J. H. The Insect World of J. Henri Fabre; interpretive comments by Edwin Way Teale. 1949.
Fairchild, D. G. The World Grows Round My Door. 1947.
Haig-Brown, R. L. Return to the River. 1941.
Hornaday, W. T. Minds and Manners of Wild Animals. 1922.
Hudson, W. H. Book of a Naturalist. 1919.

[3] H. S. Jennings, *The Biological Basis of Human Nature* (Norton, 1930), p. 376.

Huxley, Julian. Ants. 1930.
Jefferies, Richard. Wild Life in a Southern County. 1879.
Kieran, John. Footnotes on Nature. 1947.
Levick, G. Murray. Antarctic Penguins: a study of their social habits. 1914.
Muir, John. Mountains of California. 1894.
Peattie, D. C. The Road of a Naturalist. 1941.
Roulé, Louis. Fishes: their journeys and migrations. 1933.
Sanderson, Ivan T. Animal Treasure. 1937.
Saunders, C. F. Western Wild Flowers and their Stories. 1933.
Stewart, G. R. Storm. 1941.
Thoreau, H. D. Walden, or Life in the Woods. 1854.
Walton, Izaak. The Compleat Angler. 1653.
White, Gilbert. Natural History of Selborne. 1789.

FIFTY BOOKS IN MODERN SCIENCE

Andrews, R. C. On the Trail of Ancient Man. 1926.
Arrhenius, S. A. Destinies of the Stars. 1918.
Bell, E. T. The Magic of Numbers. 1946.
Blackett, P. M. S. Fear, War, and the Bomb. 1949.
Bragg, Sir William. The Universe of Light. 1933.
Candolle, A. L. P. de. Origin of Cultivated Plants. 1883.
Cohen, I. B. Science, Servant of Man: a layman's primer for the age of science. 1948.
Daly, R. A. Our Mobile Earth. 1926.
Dampier, Sir William C. A History of Science. Rev. enl. ed. 1949.
Dantzig, Tobias. Number, the Language of Science. 1930, 1939.
Darwin, Charles. On the Origin of Species by Means of Natural Selection. 1859.
De Kruif, Paul. Microbe Hunters. 1926.
Dunbar, Helen Flanders. Mind and Body: psychosomatic medicine. 1948.
Eddington, A. S. The Nature of the Physical World. 1929.
Einstein, Albert, and Leopold Infeld. The Evolution of Physics. 1938.
Faraday, Michael. Six Lectures on the Chemical History of a Candle. 1861.
Galton, Sir Francis. Natural Inheritance. 1889.
Gamow, George. Birth and Death of the Sun. 1940.
Gregory, W. K. Our Face from Fish to Man. 1929.
Haldane, J. B. S. Science Advances. 1947.

Herrick, C. J. Brains of Rats and Men. 1926.
Hogben, Lancelot. Science for the Citizen. 1938.
Hooper, Alfred. Makers of Mathematics. 1948.
Hoskins, R. G. The Tides of Life: the endocrine glands in bodily adjustment. 1933.
Huxley, Julian. Evolution. 1942.
Huxley, T. H. Man's Place in Nature. 1863.
Jastrow, Joseph. The Story of Human Error. 1936.
Jeans, Sir James. The Universe around Us. 1931.
Jennings, H. S. The Biological Basis of Human Nature. 1930.
Kinsey, A. C., and others. Sexual Behavior in the Human Male. 1948.
Laurence, W. L. Dawn over Zero: the story of the atomic bomb. 1946, 1947.
Menninger, W. C. Psychiatry in a Troubled World: yesterday's war and today's challenge. 1948.
Millikan, R. A. The Electron. 1917, 1925.
Montagu, M. F. Ashley. Man's Most Dangerous Myth: the fallacy of race. 1942.
Morgan, T. H. The Theory of the Gene. 1926.
One World or None: a report to the public on the full meaning of the atomic bomb. Ed. by Dexter Masters and Katharine Way; foreword by Niels Bohr; introd. by A. H. Compton. 1946.
Osborn, Henry F. Men of the Old Stone Age. 1915.
Parshley, H. M. The Science of Human Reproduction. 1933.
Pearson, Karl. The Grammar of Science. 1891.
Shapley, Harlow. Flights from Chaos. 1930.
Shryock, R. H. The Development of Modern Medicine. 1936.
Singer, Charles J. The Story of Living Things. 1931.
Smyth, Henry DeWolf. Atomic Energy for Military Purposes. 1945.
Tilney, Frederick. The Master of Destiny; a biography of the brain. 1930.
Turner, H. H. A Voyage in Space. 1926.
Tyndall, John. On Sound. 1867.
Wells, H. G., and others. The Science of Life. 1931.
Whitehead, A. N. Science and the Modern World. 1925.
Zilboorg, Gregory. Mind, Medicine and Man. 1943.
Zinsser, Hans. Rats, Lice, and History: life history of typhus fever. 1935.

16. Sociology; The Social Sciences

> There is nothing mysterious about the foundation of a healthy and strong democracy. The basic things expected by our people of their political and economic systems are simple: They are: equality of opportunity for youth and for others; jobs for those who can work; security for those who need it; the ending of special privilege for the few; the preservation of civil liberties for all; the enjoyment of the fruits of scientific progress in a wider and constantly rising standard of living.
>
> These are the simple and basic things that must never be lost sight of in the turmoil and unbelievable complexity of our modern world. The inner and abiding strength of our economic and political systems is dependent upon the degree to which they fulfill these expectations.
>
> Franklin Delano Roosevelt: "Four Freedoms" speech, January 26, 1941

> Socialists who want to have everything socialized, Liberals who want to have everything Cobdenized, Conservatives who want to have nothing changed, and people who are unaware that all civilization is based on a foundation of Communism and a surrender of individual liberty in respect of totalitarian agreements to do or not to do certain fundamental things, should be disfranchised. Some of them should be sent to mental hospitals. Every competent citizen should be Communist in some things, Conservative, Liberal, and even Capitalist in others all at once, before he or she can rank as a competent citizen.
>
> George Bernard Shaw: "Art Workers and the State," in *Atlantic Monthly*, November, 1947

SOCIOLOGY is the term established in library usage for the literature that deals with organized human society in all its conditions and relations. First used by Auguste Comte and brought into popular acceptance by Herbert Spencer, it is a name that has never been wholly acceptable, either to scholars in the fields with which it deals or to purists in language, who protest it as bad Latin. There is a growing tendency to replace it by the term, "the social sciences," which conveys the collective nature of political, economic, and social studies that range through infinite variations of content and aspect, and indicates the increasing dominance of scientific method in social research. As Sociology it holds permanent place as the third category of the Dewey classification, embracing political science, economics (formerly political economy), law, administration, associations and institutions, education, commerce, customs, and folklore. Its domain cannot, however, be confined even within these boundaries. Fundamentally interrelated with ethics and psychology, Sociology merges also into natural science as social studies draw more and more fully on anthropological research, it extends into religion as origins of human culture are traced in primitive belief and ritual, and is inherent in the philosophical systems and speculations in which through the ages man has sought a cure for life's ills. It is a basic component of history, not only in its political phases but as the integration of all aspects of life; and it impinges upon biography in studies of political leadership and life experiences of political or social import.

Much argument has been expended to prove that sociology is not science in any exact meaning of the term, because the student of human society cannot analyze, test, retest, prove, and compare his material under the invariable control of laboratory experiment as the physicist or the biologist can. As knowledge scientifically constituted, however, penetrates any aspect of life, organizes elements and principles, tests and verifies assumptions, science comes into being. Thus, political science and economics (Carlyle's "dismal science") have established themselves within little more than a century. Thus, education is taking shape as a science; and thus in increasing number different phases of life are brought under control of the scientific spirit, under the application of the scientific method, and become legitimate "social sciences."

With the impact of the atomic bomb came realization that today science is a conditioning force, setting up revaluations and establishing new concepts in all fields of knowledge. As this realization deepens and wider understanding of its implications prevails, problems of human behavior, conflicts in group relations, opposed national or world issues—the mass material of sociology—are more and more approached and explored under the discipline of science, which resolves its problems independently of our desires and wills, by investigation of facts, rigorously examined in laboratory technique, from observation, experience, repetition, and comparison.

Stuart Chase, in *The Proper Study of Mankind*, makes a comprehensive, clarifying "inquiry into the science of human relations," which he sees emerging from the collective, cooperative work done in cultural anthropology, social psychology, sociology, economics, and political science. Such scientists, he says, should concentrate not on winning wars, but on study of "the dynamics of peacetime." "Social engineers should be ready to leave their desks to study a big strike, a hearing of the Un-American Activities Committee in Congress, a mine disaster, a series of sex crimes in a city suburb, a heated session of the United Nations Assembly at Lake Success." When the Science of Human Relations is operative, "no government department, large corporation, big national union, or benevolent enterprise, no powerful community leader, will think of making important decisions without consulting social scientists or their findings." Mr. Chase's informal, trenchant survey and analysis is valuable and stimulating background material for any intelligent reader. Correlating it is Robert Lynd's provocative critical study, *Knowledge for What?* in which the inconsistencies, contradictions, and facile assumptions that impede and frustrate application of the social knowledge already acquired are set forth as incentives to clearer thinking and more logical action.

No field of literature, not even science, has shown such great recent development in volume and in popular interest as is evident in the social sciences. After the First World War, problems of international relationship, of political purpose and method, of economic rehabilitation, of social adjustment, became the most important problems confronting the world. They were no longer seen as problems of somewhat remote governmental or academic or other specialized concern, but recognized as crucial, complex issues, vital to the organization and continuance of individual living. The culmination in 1929 of the economic breakdown of the nation, and the succeeding "depression years" that brought reversal of living conditions, insecurity, and privation to millions, wakened the public mind as never before to realization of the necessity of an improved technique of human relationships and contacts. The processes of national reorganization made public policies the supreme concern of the individual. Revivification of the national spirit was inspired by President Roosevelt's leadership. The processes of rehabilitation and reconstruction established under that leadership by the forces of imagination, sympathy, ingenuity, devotion, and humanitarianism brought fundamental transformations in the social structure, for the common welfare of the common people. The New Deal set new designs for living in almost every field: social security, provision for old age, provision for youth and childhood, strengthening of organized labor, safeguarding of bank deposits, fair employment practices and freedom from race discrimination, slum clearance and model housing, adjustment of agricultural production, national development and control of electric power, these were projects built into the framework of government and society which enormously expanded and diversified the literature of the social sciences.

Up to the full tide of the Second World War this expansion and diversification continued, waning as military and technical phases of a war-centered economy rose to their peak in 1942. Wartime trends were toward intensification of applied science as an instrument of victory and a means for repair of broken bodies and damaged minds, toward national and international unity in resistance to world conquest, and toward optimistic charting of proposed pathways to peace. The United Nations, established at the San Francisco conference of fifty nations in June, 1945, as the war ended in Europe, was symbol and promise of permanent global peace, to be attained through world cooperation and the substitution of political agreement for armed force. The hope it offered was soon belied, as the postwar years brought mounting turmoil of nationalistic prides and jealousies, racial fears and prejudices, conflicting dogmatisms of conviction and purpose. Between the Soviet Union and the United States, suspicion and hostility deepened, evoking on one side increasing dogmatic rigidities, on the other fostering world armament and energizing war tensions. Power politics dominate world affairs. War has left its wake of turbulence in every land, and fear of a third world war is still the pervading shadow of the atomic age.

"In the representative individual and in the human community," says L. L. Whyte, "traditional ideas have failed to maintain even a minimum of unity; the other aspects of human nature are now in the open; in place of a stabilizing conviction there is distortion, conflict, confusion, and indifference; the constructive tendencies of human nature are at work as always, but they are relatively ineffective, because disorganized. The old ideals are felt to be valid, but they are known to be no longer adequate. When conflict becomes too intense partial ideals lose their power and the desire for unity rises into dominance. Ideals which imply conflict must fade when the supreme need is for a balanced order." [1] New trends of social, economic, and political adjustment are emerging over the disintegrating patterns of the past; and as these are known and sanctioned by public opinion they must in time bring collective acceptance of universal standards of social justice. To strengthen and advance these trends through clearer public understanding and wider knowledge is the great present responsibility of librarianship.

Of course, trends of public interest are always reflected and stimulated in current literature and library service. During the depression years book production statistics showed a decline in proportion of fiction published, and library reports attested the enormously increased use of books that dealt with economic, political, social, and industrial problems.[2] The postwar tensions that still prevail are keyed to controversy and confusion, obscuring and distorting issues and policies that must shape the future. Only through more education, clearer understanding, and wider knowledge can the people know and accept the conditions that must be satisfied, the compromises that must be made, to evoke a tolerable world order, not another world war. Our public libraries must provide the Ameri-

---

[1] L. L. Whyte, *Everyman Looks Forward* (Holt, 1948), p. 38.
[2] The figures of publications recorded in sociology and economics in the *Publishers' Weekly* annual summaries make evident the sharp rise that followed after 1929: 1929, 484; 1930, 523; 1931, 632; 1932, 650; 1934, 674; 1935, 691; 1937, 753; 1939, 854; 1940, 876. In 1942 the number had dropped to 620, and the military and technological group took precedence with 791 titles. The war restrictions on book production are indicated by the totals for sociology and economics for the succeeding years: 1944, 321; 1945, 301; 1946, 311, with the postwar rise (to 387) beginning in 1947. The year 1948 brought 461; 1949, 548.

can people with material that offers historical perspective, ample information, neither biased nor fragmentary, contrasting interpretations, and valid conclusions. They must put emphasis on books that center on advancing social trends, on changing standards of political and economic orthodoxy. More books are being written and read on such subjects as race discrimination and race relationship, Negro participation in American life, anti-Semitism, the world rise of communism, the background and development of the Soviet state, socialism and capitalism, democracy and totalitarianism, censorship and civil liberties, freedom of the press, world cooperation and world disunity, support for the United Nations, the objective of world government. These are rising trends in current literature that move toward national and international cooperation and security.

This use of books has direct relationship to conditions of life for the individual, the community, the nation, and this close-knit interdependent world. It is the most obvious and immediate means by which men may hope to understand the causes and probable course of the situation in which they find themselves and may prepare to meet its exigencies. Much of it, of course, is superficial or random or influenced by personal limitations and vagaries; but it represents also a leavening of mass intelligence and a more widespread diffusion of knowledge concerning public policies and changing currents of social thought. All effective library service must accept the responsibility thus imposed, and must seek to provide to an ever-enlarging public the fullest, most varied, and best materials of information available.

As with science, the development of the literature of the social sciences to its present variety and extent has come about within little more than a generation. The two categories of the Dewey classification that have most constantly demanded extension and revision are the 300's and the 600's; because in these two classes the diversity and multiplicity of new knowledge, of new fields and methods of research, have overloaded and broken down the original framework. Its greatest growth has been since the opening of the twentieth century, but the literature of sociology in its general bulk is little more than a hundred years old.

The foundation "classics," the so-called "landmark" books in the development of social thought, take us back to ancient Greece —to Plato and Aristotle—and bring before us a few names of those who in later centuries sought to trace or establish principles of government and national life. Such are Machiavelli, with his treatise on the art of maintaining political power, *The Prince;* Jean Bodin, whose *Six Books of the Republic*, in refutation of Machiavelli, represented the first elaborate attempt in modern times to construct a system of political science; Sir Thomas More, whose speculative political essay, *Utopia*, linked with Plato's *Republic* in the past and was forerunner of Butler's *Erewhon*, Bellamy's *Looking Backward*, and many other imaginary commonwealths invented by philosophers and reformers; the philosopher Hobbes, who in his treatise, *The Leviathan* (its title symbolizing sovereign power), first developed the theory of the "social contract" by which the multitude establishes its ruler; and Montesquieu, whose *Spirit of the Laws* (in which were the deepest portents of the French Revolution) is regarded as the first example of the comparative historical method in social science.

By the close of the eighteenth century, social philosophers and rationalists had laid the foundations of modern political science and were developing and systematizing economic theories and principles. The writings of Rousseau and Thomas Paine gave inspiration and theoretical basis for the French Revolution. In Scotland Adam Smith revolutionized economic theories with his *Enquiry into the Nature and Causes of the Wealth of Nations*, published at the actual date of the American Declaration of Independence; while in England Jeremy Bentham enunciated the political and ethical theory of utilitarianism, which, combined with the later doctrine of *laissez faire*, was to influence economic and government policies for more than a hundred years.

Much of this early literature centered upon ethics and morals. It was philosophic and religious in tone rather than objectively concerned with social conditions and relationships. Not until the second quarter of the nineteenth century, when the reaction inspired by the excesses of the French Revolution had subsided and the problems created by the new industrial age had begun to develop, did an awakening interest in human welfare, the relationship and responsibility of man to man, mark the beginnings of modern social science. Among those whose work raised milestones in the broadening path was Rev. Thomas Malthus, who in his *Essay on the Principle of Population*, published in 1798, was first to advance the thesis that population increases more rapidly than food supply and that some positive checks upon its growth are necessary for social welfare. A hundred and fifty years later the Malthusian doctrine furnished the core of *Road to Survival* (Sloane, 1948), William Vogt's arresting, deeply foreboding study of the multiplying peoples of the world, of man's ruthless waste and abuse of earth's natural riches, and of ultimate, inevitable extinction of civilized life unless population pressures are reduced and natural resources maintained. Succeeding milestones were set by David Ricardo, who established the "law of differential rent," in which lay the germ of the later land value theories of Henry George; and John Stuart Mill, who crystallized the "classical" economic thought of the nineteenth century in his famous *Principles of Political Economy*, and whose political and social views, set forth in his essays "On Liberty" and "The Subjection of Women," are still more advanced in principle and application than are those of most modern radicals.[3]

Through the nineteenth century the scope of sociological interest and inquiry steadily widened. The rise of the modern social revolutionary movement may be traced from the Revolution of 1848, and the economic theories expounded twenty years later by Karl Marx. Generalization and formulation of existing ideas of social philosophy were made by Auguste Comte, who gave the name "Sociology" to the body of knowledge he sought to organize and established it as a science in his *Positive Philosophy*, which classified the sciences as mathematics, astronomy, physics, chemistry, biology

---

[3] Brilliant epitome of the teachings of these "philosophic radicals" and of other nineteenth-century exponents of economic doctrine will be found in Bertrand Russell's *Freedom versus Organization, 1814–1914* (Norton, 1934).

(including psychology), and sociology. Herbert Spencer incorporated it as a science in his *Synthetic Philosophy*, and in his later work brought encyclopedic material to bulwark his conception and interpretation of sociology as the synthesis of the evolutionary processes of human society. The third name associated with the building up of modern sociology is that of Lester Ward, whose philosophic conception emphasized evolutionary progress through education, and whose *Applied Sociology* is the capstone of his work.

In all this earlier development, sociological doctrine was primarily philosophical. Its emphasis was upon theory; upon principles, elements, systems; and it built up an elaborate esoteric vocabulary of its own. As specialization and research developed, the scientific attitude gained upon the philosophical and ethical point of view. The work that marks the application to the study of society of a technique derived from exact science is the vast treatise on general sociology, by the Italian sociologist, Vilfredo Pareto, published in Italy in 1916, and issued in a French translation in 1919, and in English translation (with title *The Mind and Society*) in 1935. Pareto, formerly an engineer and mathematician, dismisses the existing body of sociological principles and theories as based on the rationalizing of traditional beliefs and the acceptance of unproved assumptions, and seeks to establish in mathematical terms a precise, objective analysis of human behavior (drawn in large measure from cultural and anthropological research as developed by Frazer and Westermarck) as the basis for study of the development of human society.

Important in later theoretical sociology is the work of Pitirim Sorokin in its influence toward a merging of eastern and western countercurrents of social thought. Of Russian Revolutionary background, but anti-Bolshevist, Professor Sorokin was a member of the Kerensky government; later, released by Lenin from political imprisonment, he accepted self-exile, taught in Europe and in American universities, and in 1930 was appointed to the faculty of Harvard's Department of Sociology. His sociological doctrine, most fully presented in his four-volume work, *Social and Cultural Dynamics* (American Book Company, 1937–41), centers on the assumption of three different processes of social growth: "ideational," based on a supernatural concept of reality; "idealistic," offering an ideal synthesis of supernatural and natural; and "sensate," denoting scientific or materialistic domination of all social activities, each of these "supersystems" rising and waning in successive phases toward an ultimate evolutionary fulfillment.[4] There is kinship to Toynbee and Spengler in the far-ranging detail and abstruse terminology of Sorokin's ambitious sociocultural study, which ramifies into half a dozen related volumes offering forceful objective and suggestive thinking on the crises, transformations, and fateful vicissitudes of the present world era.

The present dominance of scientific method, of elaborate factual and statistical research into every aspect of contemporary society, came into being within a generation. Just as scientific discoveries and mechanical inventions since the opening years of the twentieth century transformed material conditions of living, and the advances of scientific research increased power to check disease and improve physical well-being, so a parallel transformation was effected in the attitude toward social organization, contacts, and relationships. The application of scientific method to social problems, the patient accumulation of facts, the testing and verification of data, the systematization and generalization of unbiased findings, apparently offered means through which society might be guided to know itself and to use and control the increased power which science and technology placed at its disposal. Thus the social sciences expanded in range and intensified in activities, bringing rapid development in formulation and standardization of laboratory method and of field practice, and in the collection and analysis of vast stores of information concerning social, industrial, and political problems.

Probably the greatest factor in this development has been the unprecedented flow of private wealth, within the present century, into noncommercial agencies for the advancement of knowledge, and

---

[4] The scope of Sorokin's foundational work may be indicated by the titles of its successive volumes: Vol. I, *Fluctuation of Forms of Art;* Vol. II, *Fluctuation of Systems of Truth, Ethic, and Law;* Vol. III, *Fluctuation of Social Relationship, War, and Revolution;* Vol. IV, *Basic Problems, Principles, and Methods.*

the consequent growth of organization and specialization in every branch of social study. The Carnegie Institution of Washington, with its magnificent range of publications in varied fields of knowledge, was established in 1902. The Carnegie Endowment for International Peace, which has brought into existence an entire literature of international relations, dates from 1910. The Russell Sage Foundation, responsible for the "survey" as an instrument of social research, began its work in 1907. The American Sociological Society, first formal organization of the sociologists of America, was founded in 1905; and in 1924 the establishment of the Social Science Research Council, linking with social research institutes in many parts of the country, gave national impetus to organized social surveys and fact-finding studies.

The Twentieth Century Fund, founded in 1919 by Edward A. Filene, specializes in economics, and includes Stuart Chase's series of popular "dollar books" on postwar problems among its many publications. Brookings Institution (established in 1927), also concerned with economics, especially in regard to business, labor relations, and social insurance, makes extensive statistical studies of more conservative trend in these and other subjects. Unusual in its time limitation was the Julius Rosenwald Fund, founded in 1917 with the provision by the founder that it must be expended, both principal and interest, within twenty-five years after his own death (which occurred in 1932), because, as he said, "We may be certain that the acute social need of tomorrow will be different from that of today and will doubtless call for a new kind of agency to meet it." This endowment, which ended in 1948, was important in opening higher education to Negroes and advancing the improvement of rural schools in the southern states. The Commonwealth Fund, one of the ten largest American foundations in size, publishes chiefly in medicine, public health, and mental hygiene; while the two organizations responsible for the greatest volume and variety of social research publishing maintained by financial grants are the Rockefeller Foundation, and the Carnegie Corporation of New York. These are the two largest foundations in existence, ranking also as foremost American publishers in the number and importance of publications that are by-products of the subsidized investigations they have sponsored in every field from studies of regional culture (Graham Hutton's *Midwest at Noon* was produced under a Rockefeller grant to the Newberry Library) to the four-year nationwide Public Library Inquiry undertaken in 1947 by the Social Science Research Council in cooperation with the American Library Association.[5]

There has been steadily increasing government participation in research in all these fields. The National Bureau of Economic Research, the various committees of the National Research Council, and the President's Committee on Civil Rights, whose report in 1947—epochal in American social history—reached the reading public through low-priced publication by Simon and Schuster under the title *To Secure These Rights*—these are among the many official groups helping to build up the enormous present-day accumulation of knowledge concerning economic, social, political, and industrial problems.

In its international aspects, such knowledge received worldwide stimulus from the immense range of publications sponsored by the League of Nations. Many of these still hold continuing validity and significance; and all are eventually to be taken over by the United Nations, with Columbia University Press official agent of distribution. Today the publications of the United Nations have become the most important source material through which are transmitted the urgency and impact of international problems, the intensifying world issues shaping human destiny. As source material, usually documentary, formalized and officialized in form and expression, they have limited appeal to the public that most needs them, although commanding specialized recognition. In library selection, therefore, especially in smaller public libraries and school libraries, effort should be made to emphasize those that possess immediate values of timeliness, to direct attention to specific projects, to make

---

[5] *American Foundations for Social Welfare*, by F. Emerson Andrews and Shelby M. Harrison (New York, Sage Foundation, 1946), gives full and interesting presentation of this subject.

evident the range and nature of the whole vast United Nations enterprise and the undercurrents of achievement that run below the surface. Activities of the various sections should be presented, such as Unesco (United Nations Educational, Scientific, and Cultural Organization) with its great project of Fundamental Education; World Health Organization, formed in 1946 to "help eliminate the ancient human plagues, such as malaria, cholera, tuberculosis and syphilis," and also concerned with formulation of a bill of rights for children; the Food and Agriculture Organization, surveyors for "the road to survival," working toward increase of food crops and improved food distribution all over the world; and the Economic and Social Council, with its Commission on Human Rights, which formulated the Universal Declaration of Human Rights, adopted on December 10, 1948, by the United Nations General Assembly. The *Yearbook of the United Nations* and the semimonthly *United Nations Bulletin* should be first choice in any limited selection; these, like all United Nations books, periodicals, and documents, are handled by the International Documents Service of Columbia University Press.

To clarify understanding of present world relations, to deepen realization that international cooperation is the only key to world peace, is a responsibility that rests today on the school and the public library. Simple, effective, comprehensive suggestions and help in meeting that responsibility are embodied in the volume, *Education for International Understanding in American Schools,* published in 1948 by the National Education Association. Although designed primarily for teachers, it has strong stimulative value for book selection and book service in school libraries and small general collections; the point of view is broad and constructive, presentation is interesting and vigorous, and the excellent classed bibliography of "aids and sources" offers a good model selective list.

In the literature of the social sciences there is an immense amount of pamphlet material. The findings of original research, the raw materials of information, must be sought in official and institutional reports, surveys, publications of societies and other organizations, monographs, propagandist or doctrinaire pronouncements of all kinds. Often new fields of social or economic inquiry are opened, new political or social credos promulgated, almost entirely through pamphleteering. Extremely useful series of pamphlets and leaflets, representing authoritative, compact discussion of subjects of current interest, are by-products of radio broadcasting, planned and sponsored by organizations affiliated in adult education. From literally thousands of associations and groups, from publicity mediums of every kind, from individual monitors, dogmatists, radicals and libertarians, there pours a continuing flood of free or low-priced literature, intended to inform the people on fundamental issues, to advance a cause, to shape public opinion. The Foreign Policy Association, the East and West Association, the Institute of Pacific Relations, the Congress of Industrial Organizations, the American Civil Liberties Union, the Anti-Defamation League, the Public Affairs Committee, the National Association for the Advancement of Colored People, the National Conference of Christians and Jews, are familiar examples of authoritative and representative exposition, while the more personal type of pamphleteering in the historic Tom Paine tradition may be exemplified in Louis Adamic's series of "Time and Tide" pamphlets.

Even in the most limited selection the importance of pamphlet material must be recognized. In any effective general library service it must be constantly gleaned and made available; and in specialized collections and college and university libraries it must be built up to large proportions, thoroughly organized, and continually drawn upon to reinforce and supplement information in newspapers, magazine articles, and books.

Whether pamphlet or book, every publication has its own particular form of presentation. In the social sciences, dominant forms parallel rather closely those most common in the field of science. The "classics" that mark the development of knowledge and that still hold vital substance of principle or theory are indispensable in serious study, and many of them (Plato's *Republic*, for example, and Mill's essays) have a continuing appeal to almost any intelligent reader. Textbooks range from simple introductions for elementary study to massive structures of close-packed detail; they may offer a general survey of a major subject, or an intensive exploration of a single subdivision. Treatises, monographs, or surveys on individual problems (such as crime, unemployment, social conditions) usually represent research based on statistical investigation or organized first-hand study for which the Lynds' *Middletown* set a continuing pattern. Expositions of principles and theories may be presented in authoritative, impersonal, comparative, and descriptive discussion; or more often infused with personal conviction, conservative or radical, propagandist or doctrinaire, championing or attacking a system, theory, or "cause." So far, there is less effective "humanization" of knowledge in the field of sociology than in that of science. Simplified, impersonal presentation of economic conditions, social problems, or public policies, made interesting and intelligible to the general reader, is rare. Nevertheless there is much work of brilliancy and vigor that possesses wide popular appeal (the books of Louis Adamic, Stuart Chase, Harold Laski, and Carey McWilliams offer examples of differing types); and an increasing number of thoughtful, soundly based works of social analysis (such as MacIver's *The More Perfect Union*) that make crucial problems and conflicting issues of the day cogent and vital to any responsive mind.

Specialized library service in sociology is given through many agencies. These may be departments in large public libraries—developed as municipal libraries, and in some cities maintained at the headquarters of the city government as departmental branches with the primary purpose of giving information to city officials on public questions and supplying material to aid in drafting new legislation or improving existing laws, or as civics or sociology departments carrying on broader and more varied activities; or they may be legislative reference libraries, established independently or as departments of state libraries; or they may be collections built up by institutions or organizations concerned with economic, political, or social research or with phases of public welfare (the Haynes Foundation of Los Angeles is an example). Some such specialization is important in all public library service. Even in the smallest communities the public library should be a central source of information, a repository of material, concerning local government and public affairs. Workers in these specialized fields must through experience and the use of all available bibliographical equipment develop expert proficiency in the collection, organization, and use of material that embraces every kind of current ephemeral literature, as well as government documents, court decisions, and many other works of specialized nature. Law, of course, like medicine, has its own body of literature, supplied for professional use through the collections of bar associations, law schools, legislative and administrative institutions and organizations, and not included within the range of general public library service. The varied, extensive literature of education, although an integral part of the entire body of knowledge and of importance in all general library service, also has its own specialized development, through departmental organization in larger public libraries, or through school and university libraries and other special collections.

Consideration of selection in the whole domain of sociology cannot be attempted in the present survey. A few aspects of its literature have been broadly outlined. As in the case of the literature of science, this chapter is concerned chiefly with the "humanizing of knowledge" through selection in a few representative fields where the impact of the "revolution of our time" is opening a new era of human history.

Political science focuses upon the reshaping of the structure of government into novel patterns; on capitalism, socialism, communism, fascism, collectivism, democracy, and totalitarianism as elements of the postwar world conflict; on international relations; on the influences of nationalism; and the power struggle between the United States and Russia. These are immediate political problems, studied and interpreted in a vast body of current literature that reveals the crises, mutations, compromises, intransigencies, opposed forces and principles, succeeding one another in the slow convalescence of a war-poisoned world.

Selection for the general public should emphasize books that present with authority and vitality variant aspects of these phases of a changing age. Such, for example, are Edward Hallett Carr's short study, *The Soviet Impact on the Western World*, illuminating the five specific impacts—political, economic, social, international, and ideological—which, launched by the Bolshevik revolution, have left their impact on Europe and America; or Julian Towster's detailed, scholarly survey and analysis of *Political Power in the USSR, 1917-1947*—both valuable counterbalances to the invective and distortion that turn into war tinder so much controversial United States-Soviet literature. Bertrand Russell's thought-provoking volume, *Power*, analyzes the exercise of power by man over man in its diverse forms, and forces that foster it or bring its decline, and the means that may curb excesses of power and bring tolerance and cooperation into government. In his *Shall Not Perish from the Earth* Ralph Barton Perry gives inspiring expression of the philosophy that underlies faith in democracy; Harold Laski's massive work, *The American Democracy*, in its all-inclusive survey of the political and intellectual life of the United States, offers a reincarnation of De Tocqueville, as conceived by English socialism and born of Marxian philosophy, rich in substance, erudite, readable, and challenging; and *Socialist Britain*, by Francis Williams, former member of the British Labour Ministry, gives a vigorous, optimistic survey of the historical background, the aims, methods, and leaders of the socialist government which came to power in the elections of 1945. These are few of the many books from which the individual caught in the fast-spinning coil of events may gain at least some realization of world forces in action, some intimation of ways in which it may be possible to control or adapt inevitable processes of change.

Economics, in orthodox definition "the practical science of production and distribution of wealth," has today brought within its compass nearly all political, industrial, and social problems. Stemming from the rising world movement toward socialism in its many different kinds and degrees are the most immediate issues, the most insistent trends, of a crucial transition period. Here violence of opposed convictions, clash of controversy, prevail. "Planning" under governmental control has given us the Tennessee Valley Authority, in whose achievements David Lilienthal records "democracy on the march." But in the gospel of individualism and "free enterprise" expounded by Hayek, "planning" opens "the road to serfdom." Sir William Beveridge's *Full Employment in a Free Society* is a blueprint for the social security foundation being built into Britain's national structure. But to John Jewkes, also a distinguished English economist, such a blueprint means "ordeal by planning," and must inevitably lead to economic collapse or totalitarianism.

The irreconcilable antagonisms that rage today through once arid regions of Sociology are akin to those that for centuries inspired the wars of religion. To understand an issue, whatever it may be, "the other side" must be known and weighed by reason and an adequate sense of values, not by passion. Thus, in the locked battle between capitalism and communism that now divides the two great world powers, materials of both defense and attack must be freely available for public information and study. This responsibility should be maintained in library selection. Even in limited collections, besides literature that upholds American principles of democracy and freedom, there should also be authentic exposition of Marxian doctrine from the Marxist viewpoint, the tractates by Lenin and Stalin which are standard expressions of Soviet theory and practice, and Sidney and Beatrice Webb's *Soviet Communism: a New Civilization?*, which since 1936, in its various editions, has been basic to study of the subject by American readers. Andrei Vyshinsky's massive, militant exposition of *The Law of the Soviet State*, though too expensive for smaller general collections, is of foundational value to any reader who wishes to understand the structure of the Soviet state and the uncompromising dogmatism of Soviet political and economic doctrine. This is probably the most notable volume in the "Russian Translations Project," organized in 1944 by the American Council of Learned Societies (with the aid of a Rockefeller Foundation subsidy and publication by Macmillan) and devoted to "the translation into English of significant Russian works in the fields of the humanities and the social sciences which provide an insight into Russian life and thought." In *The Philosophy of Peace* (Gaer, 1949), thoughtful study of United States–Soviet relations, John Somerville says:

There will never be even the possibility of a normal attitude on the part of our people until they receive as much responsible information and instruction about Soviet Russia—its history, philosophy, literature, language, institutions and culture, as they do about France and Germany. It may even be that in the world of today a background on Russia is more necessary than on France or Germany.

Most acute and insidious of American social problems in its international and domestic implications is the problem of race relations. The "second-class citizenship" that is the lot of Negro Americans, the lower class status of Filipino, Indian, Mexican, Oriental, and other minority groups, and the discriminatory practices that set up political, industrial, educational, and social barriers against equal participation of all citizens in the nation's life, deny our national heritage and ideals and invite the ironic skepticism of other peoples toward our international role as champions of democracy. The simple facts of American race discrimination, says Dr. MacIver, "constitute a momentous danger to everything for which the United States stands before its own citizens and in the eyes of the world." Before the irresistible mass trend of countries which contain more than half of the population of the globe, the code of "white supremacy" has been superseded: in India, in Asia, in Malaysia—all over the world except in South Africa and the United States.

And in the United States, in spite of the deep regional cleavages that are seedbeds of continuing conflict, the trend toward equality and social justice steadily gains momentum. There has been an immense increase in the literature of race relations. Sociologists, social psychologists, anthropologists, economists, historians, scientists, scholars, dramatists, poets, and novelists attack terror and intimidation, seek to aid governmental and legislative effort to protect the political and civil rights of Negroes and other minorities, and to eliminate segregation. Our public libraries in general hold firmly to the American tradition of free opinion and democratic equality; through books they aim to resist intolerance, to deepen knowledge and clarify understanding. Many, as previously mentioned, maintain organized effort for improvement of race relations and for cooperation with other groups and agencies working for solution of minority problems. Book selection in this field should be both broad and intensive, drawing from the rich stores of contemporary material with understanding of its varied range, its distinctive values, and its human appeal.

Gunnar Myrdal's monumental treatise, *An American Dilemma*, is fundamental in any collection; and the excellent one-volume condensation by Arnold Rose makes it widely available. The criticism and confutations evoked by Myrdal's work should also be fairly represented, as in the socio-ethnic analytical study, *Caste, Class and Race*—winner of the second (1947) George Washington Carver Award—in which Oliver Cromwell Cox sets forth with scholarship and uncompromising logic the Marxist thesis that race prejudice is essentially racial exploitation. A later bulwork of knowledge on this whole subject is E. Frazier Franklin's comprehensive sociological study, *The Negro in the United States*. Walter White's appalling *Rope and Faggot*, with its ironic subtitle, *Biography of Judge Lynch*, holds permanent value as an objective documentary record of what President Roosevelt called "that vile form of collective murder, lynch law." His autobiography, *A Man Called White*, focuses on the building of the National Association for the Advancement of Colored People into an organized international movement toward the goal of complete equality. The story of that organization's forty-year battle against the "walls of intolerance, prejudice, injustice, and arrogance" is told with dramatic simplicity in *The Walls Came Tumbling Down*, by Mary White Ovington, guiding spirit in its history from its founding in 1909. There should be emphasis on present-day conditions and forms of segregation

(*The Negro Ghetto*, by Robert C. Weaver; *Black Metropolis*, by St. Clair Drake and Horace Cayton);[6] on contrasts and comparisons, as in Donald Pierson's revealing study, *Negroes in Brazil;* and on presentation of traditional influences, as in Katharine Lumpkin's graphic, sympathetic autobiographical study, *The Making of a Southerner*, which reveals in penetrating and sensitive perspective the background in which the theory of white supremacy and black inferiority is a natural growth. Lillian Smith's *Killers of the Dream* presents the same background with arresting intensity and uncompromising attack upon the root evil of segregation. There should be constant response and recognition to the many writers through whose work, as Roi Ottley expresses it, "the legend of the Negro's 'place' is swiftly tumbling into the limbo of legends, shattering the traditional outlook of white and black alike."

Preservation of civil rights and maintenance of civil liberties are vital issues of the day. They are closely linked to the problem of censorship, which has had previous consideration, and in their relationship to library service the Library Bill of Rights has established basic principles, which the A.L.A. Committee on Intellectual Freedom and its allied state committees have reinforced by cooperation and publicity.

If librarians use every opportunity to work with teachers, authors, publishers and others interested in preserving free thought and expression in America, if library schools encourage their students to study the principles involved in this problem, and if librarians are alert and quick to report attempts at censorships, perhaps the necessity for action by intellectual freedom committees will decrease. This should be the hope of all librarians.[7]

These are but a few obvious present trends of mass interest. There are many others. Freedom of the press, labor and labor unions, housing, unemployment, juvenile delinquency, the economic status of

---

[6] Of cardinal importance is the "Report of the National Committee on Segregation in the Nation's Capital" (4901 Ellis Ave., Chicago, January, 1949), which lays bare "the anatomy of discrimination in the Federal Government," and records that in Washington "one-quarter of the population is segregated according to color."

[7] David K. Berninghausen, "Publicity Wins Intellectual Freedom," *A.L.A. Bulletin*, February, 1949, pp. 73-75.

women, are among the insistent problems of common experience that are also problems of the social scientist. Books that treat these problems with authentic factual knowledge, that maintain the scientific spirit but preserve also a sense of social justice, tempered by understanding of human nature, must slowly foster the clear, dispassionate public thinking in which lies the best hope of social advance.

There is probably a greater medley of values in the literature of the social sciences than in that of any other field of knowledge. This is natural enough. The rigorous qualifications and methods demanded of the research worker in natural and physical science cannot be applied to expositors of social phenomena; nor can the phenomena be subjected to laboratory analysis, to X-ray or spectroscope. Anyone can form an opinion on political, economic, and social questions, can amplify that opinion in reasoning or rhetoric, bulwark it by statistics or historical similitudes, proclaim it as a philosophy, a theory, or a system, draw adherents, and inspire other enthusiasts to kindred or divergent opinions. Thus, propaganda, dogma, and polemics stand side by side with impersonal research and reasoned judgment; partisanship and personal bias are inextricably involved in almost any sponsorship of theories and doctrines. Work that displays limitations of knowledge or of temperament, that challenges sanity and common sense, is carried to popular acceptance by fervor of championship or brilliancy of expression. The enthusiast imbued with imagination and the conviction that salvation lies in his chosen gospel promises the millennium to his followers if his system is set in operation. The thoughtful, balanced exposition of that same doctrine, based on scrupulous investigation of facts and thorough study, can promise no Utopian fulfillment, and so draws no such ardent following.

In judicious general selection, however, these conflicting values cannot be escaped. There should be no insistence upon preferred viewpoints, no actual or implied repression of legitimate opinion or of recognized tenets. Conservative, liberal, radical, and revolutionary schools of thought demand balanced representation in any present-day collection. In controversial questions, each side is entitled to a hearing. The movement toward the "left" in social, political, and economic thought now finds expression in every field of literature. Marx, Freud, and Darwin are the dominant influences of the modern world. Even a small library collection should make available books through which the ordinary intelligent reader may understand the fundamental principles of the Marxian doctrine and study the political, economic, and social forces that it has set in operation. As James Harvey Robinson has said:

The sensible question to ask about a book is obviously whether it makes some contribution to a clearer understanding of our situation by adding or reaffirming important considerations and the inferences to be made from them. Such books could be set off against those that were but expression of vague discontent or emulation, or denunciation of things because they are as they are or are not as they are not.[8]

Specific points for consideration in selection of works of sociology differ little from those previously noted in dealing with books of science. Determination of *form, subject*, and *scope;* of *author's qualifications and point of view;* of *informational basis, manner of treatment*, and *qualities of literary expression* will generally establish a sufficient foundation for judgment. In closer analysis of comparative values the following questions may be found useful:

Is the work of value as presentation of theory—or as application of principle or theory to practical experience?

Does the description of facts show keen insight and reliable analysis through direct observation—or is it generalized and confusing, or elaborately statistical and technical, or an exaggeration or sensationalization of a single aspect?

What is the author's standing among others in his particular field: does he belong among recognized authorities, doctrinaires, conservatives, extremists, or fair-minded synthesizers and interpreters? Some sympathies, some personal trend of opinion, must exist, except in dehydrated compounds of pure information; but dogmatization and intolerance are always defects.

[8] J. H. Robinson, *The Mind in the Making*, p. 217.

Does the work show candor, poise, sanity, sincerity? Many books that have intense sincerity have little poise or sanity. Sincerity, indeed, is a somewhat doubtful claim to consideration—aside from the sincerity of mental delusion and fixed ideas, there is unquestionable sincerity in many works that are erroneous in fact and defective in expression.

What are the strongest features of the work? What its most evident weaknesses? What its specific contribution, if any, to knowledge of its subjects? Does it apparently hold promise of becoming a standard work, or is it of transitory or fortuitous significance?

Style is always of importance, although excellence of literary expression is probably more lacking in the literature of sociology than in any other kind of writing. What Fowler calls "the periphrastic malady" is a common affliction of economists and sociologists; its chief symptom an uncontrollable addiction to "strings of abstract nouns depending upon one another and the use of compound prepositions." The heaviness and formlessness that often overweight work of cardinal importance are evident, for example, in the writings of Thorstein Veblen. Probably no modern economist exerted a more powerful influence in the overthrow of the older philosophic and ethical attitude and the development of the analytical biological approach to economic problems. It is, however, an influence transmitted chiefly through the writings of others able to penetrate Veblen's obscure, involved sentences and transmit their searing purport. Probably the best presentation of Veblen for general popular use is through *The Portable Veblen* (Viking, 1948), edited by Max Lerner, whose selections provide an orderly presentation of Veblen's writing, and whose long introduction gives clear, sympathetic exposition of the political and economic theories originated by "the most creative mind American social thought has yet produced."

Forcefulness, clarity, and candor are chief requirements in books that present or interpret to the general reader the findings of social research; and in appraisal of works that are otherwise fairly equal in authority and value the predominance of these qualities should turn the scale. But it must be remembered that all specialized knowledge has its own technical terminology, its own professional method of demonstration, and that in its original materials matter, not manner, is the essential thing. Veblen contributed high explosive to the substance of economic thought; the fact that his formula is more or less illegible does not affect its intrinsic potency. The expert must possess capacity, training, specific qualifications; he should make no pretenses, indulge in no vague generalizations, be cautious of opinion. If, in addition, he possesses sensitive perceptions and vigor or magnetism in expression, his work is likely to take its place not only among the materials, but in the literature of knowledge.

Date demands attention according to the purpose of selection. Any representative selection, of course, must be comprehensive, though selective, of both older and newer literature, so that historical backgrounds may be studied and the development of ideas traced. But enlightenment concerning the present is what most readers seek, and this can be conveyed only through books that reflect and record the present. It can fairly be said that no work on economics published before 1935 can adequately present the general economic and industrial situation as it exists today. Certainly, the breakdown of old stabilities, the swift momentum of emerging mass movements, the succeeding crises of world relationships and national affairs, make it more and more necessary to provide the timeliest and most up-to-date information possible concerning the causes, effects, and portents of the problems that confront the world we are living in.

What has been said concerning the value of series in current selection of science applies equally to selection in sociology. Older standard series are numerous and varied. They range from publications of universities, research organizations, and associations (such as "Harvard Economic Studies" or the publications of the National Conference of Social Work), to texts and treatises and specialized studies (such as Macmillan's "Social Science Textbooks" or Crowell's "Social Science Series"). As regards more popularized presentation, however, the trend is toward independent individual volumes, rather than toward the specialized sequence of readable, concise, expository little books in a given subject field, which set an earlier pattern.

In judicious selection there must be use of specialized aids and of reviews and abstracts appearing in journals, bulletins, and other publications devoted to the several groups of social studies. The *American Economic Review*, for example, is useful for authoritative appraisal or summary of current publications in its field; so are the leading journals of education for reviews of current educational books; and the *Survey* offers timely comments on books of varied sociological range. *Crisis*, monthly organ of the National Association for the Advancement of Colored People, includes useful reviews of books on race relations, and *Common Ground* (quarterly), devoted to the democratic ideal as applied to social questions, also gives special emphasis to racial equality as basis for democratic principles and processes. *Facts on File*, weekly news digest with cumulative index, provides a continuing information service of indispensable reference value concerning world events. The quarterly, *Foreign Affairs*, published in New York by the Council of Foreign Relations, contains useful selected and annotated lists of books on international relations, which are consolidated in succeeding volumes of *Foreign Affairs Bibliography:* that covering publications from 1919 to 1932, edited by W. L. Langer and H. F. Armstrong; that for 1932 to 1942, edited by Robert G. Woolbert (Harper, 1945); both essential aids in any broad selection.

Important reference works must be drawn upon. The great *Encyclopaedia of the Social Sciences* (Macmillan), with a bibliographical apparatus that ranges from exhaustive bibliographies for major subjects (such as "land tenure") to brief bibliographic notes appended to shorter articles, is a source of suggestion in building up foundation material on every phase of social science—which as here interpreted seems to include virtually everything outside the domain of "exact" science. Useful background knowledge of the social science field may be drawn from *Society in Transition*, Harry Elmer Barnes' comprehensive volume devoted to "problems of a changing world" (Prentice-Hall, 1939; 8th ed., 1946), antitraditional in point of view, readable in treatment. Harry W. Laidler's *Social-Economic Movements* (Crowell, 1944) combines a revision of his *History of Socialist Thought* with comparative scrutiny of other systems of social reconstruction; while the collective volume, *European Ideologies: a Survey of 20th Century Political Ideas*, edited by Feliks Gross (Philosophical Library, 1948) contains valuable material by able American and European contributors on Panslavism, Agrarianism, Falangism, and other exceptional movements. Anthology, reference tool, and series volume are combined in *Masterworks of Government*, edited by L. D. Abbott (1947), in Doubleday's "Masterworks Series," which offers digests of thirteen classics of political thought, from Plato to Lenin.

No adequate indication can here be given of the full bibliographical equipment to be utilized in extended selection. For comprehensive, condensed record of its range and diversity the student is referred to Van Hoesen and Walter's manual, *Bibliography* (Chapter IV, "Historical and Social Sciences").

Two works of exceptional importance should, however, be noted. A monumental achievement that must rank almost as the universal bibliography of its subject is *The London Bibliography of the Social Sciences*, undertaken by the London School of Economics and Political Science, carried to completion under the direction of its librarian, B M. Headicar, and published in 1932 in four massive volumes. It records in a single subject catalogue (in alphabetical arrangement) the contents of seven important special collections, including the 250,000-volume library of the School of Economics, the economic library of the University of London, and the collection of the Royal Statistical Library, reaching a total of more than 600,000 separate items. Well printed, readily usable, its fourth volume devoted to author indexes and lists of periodicals, this is a foundation work of bibliographical reference and guidance, although the great collections on which it was built were almost wholly destroyed in the bombing of London in the Second World War.

For both extended and limited selection, one of the effective and widely used aids is the "Public Affairs Information Service," which with the publication of its *Annual Cumulated Bulletin for 1948* completed its thirty-fourth year in print. Organized in 1913 as a cooperative group of librarians (there were forty original members), in 1914 it was established in the office of the H. W. Wilson Company, with its own editor; and its *Bulletin*, previously mimeographed, became a printed publication, cumulated five times a year, under the familiar Wilson form and bibliographical arrangement. Four years later the editorial work was transferred from the Wilson office to the Economic Division of the New York Public Library, and since 1923 all managerial, editorial, and financial functions have been maintained by the publication committee (whose chairman is chief of the library's Economic Division) from its own office in the New York Public Library building, with printing and distribution carried on in continuing cooperation by the Wilson Company.[9] There were, in 1945, four hundred subscribers to the "Public Affairs Information Service," and the number steadily increases. The *Bulletin*, published weekly, is a current bibliography of selected material in English relating to economic, social, and political affairs: articles in periodicals, papers in proceedings of trade, labor, and professional associations; books or chapters and essays in books; government documents, pamphlets, and typewritten or mimeographed compilations by libraries or organizations. Session laws of legislative bodies are indexed. There is constant reference usefulness in the directory of publishers and organizations covered, as this gives quick guidance to names and addresses of many trade, economic, technical, and statistical bodies, while the list of publications analyzed is in itself a valuable specialized bibliography. In range and value this is probably the most important current aid in its field. Correlation of the *Bulletin* with the "Vertical File Service" maintained by the Wilson Company, makes available almost the

---

[9] See "Success Story: the Public Affairs Information Service," by R. A. Sawyer, chief of Economics Division, New York Public Library, *Library Journal*, 71:98-100 (Jan. 15, 1946).

whole body of current ephemeral printed matter that is fundamental material of information in so many fields of social study.

The standard aids are the main reliance in selection for smaller general collections. *A.L.A. Catalog, 1926*, and its supplements for 1926–31, 1932–36, and 1937–41; the *Standard Catalog for Public Libraries*; and Sonnenschein, Part II, will give a basis for representative older and contemporary selection. The *Booklist* and *Book Review Digest* are dependable for current guidance; the *Booklist*, indeed, since 1932, has given enlarged representation to sociology and printed many useful special lists on topics of timely interest. In any library that can afford it the "Vertical File Service" aids the systematic accumulation of inexpensive but vitally useful material. Helpful suggestions may be garnered from the *A.L.A. Bulletin;* from the *Library Journal* "New Book Appraisals" department and special lists; from *Wilson Library Bulletin, Special Libraries*, and the inflowing stream of library lists and bulletins. And in the use of current reviewing periodicals there should be attentive gleaning of appraisals that bear a stamp of expert authority, and of titles that may have escaped attention elsewhere.

However limited selection may be, there should be elasticity in range, response to changing currents of interest, and a controlling purpose to enlarge and stimulate public use of the books that best amplify and revise knowledge of the social, political, economic, and industrial conditions of the day. The vital principle has been stated by James Harvey Robinson:

We must look forward to ever new predicaments and adventures. Nothing is going to be settled in the sense in which things were once supposed to be settled, for the simple reason that knowledge will probably continue to increase and will inevitably alter the world with which we have to make terms. The only thing that might conceivably remain somewhat stabilized is an attitude of mind and unflagging expectancy appropriate to the terms and the rules according to which life's game must hereafter be played. We must promote a new cohesion and cooperation on the basis of this truth.[10]

[10] J. H. Robinson, *The Mind in the Making*, p. 212.

FIFTY BOOKS ON QUESTIONS OF THE TIMES INDICATING TRENDS AND TENDENCIES

Adamic, Louis. A Nation of Nations. 1945.
Allen, R. S., ed. Our Fair City. 1947.
Arnold, Thurman. The Folklore of Capitalism. 1937.
Barzun, Jacques. Teacher in America. 1945.
Beard, Charles A. The Republic. 1943.
Beck, H. P. Men Who Control Our Universities. 1947.
Beveridge, Sir W. M. Full Employment in a Free Society. 1945.
Brogan, D. W. Government of the People: a study in the American political system. 1944.
Brooks, R. R. R. When Labor Organizes. 1938.
Chafee, Zechariah. Free Speech in the United States. 1941.
Chase, Stuart. The Proper Study of Mankind. 1948.
Commission on Freedom of the Press. A Free and Responsible Press. 1947.
Conant, J. B. Education in a Divided World. 1948.
Dolivet, Louis. The United Nations: handbook of the new world organization. 1946.
Epstein, Abraham. Insecurity: a challenge to America. 1933.
Fowler, B. R. The Co-operative Challenge. 1947.
Griffith, Beatrice. American Me. 1948.
Harris, Herbert. American Labor. 1938.
Harvard University. General Education in a Free Society. 1945.
Hayek, F. A. The Road to Serfdom. 1944.
Joughin, G. L., and E. M. Morgan. The Legacy of Sacco and Vanzetti. 1948.
Laski, Harold J. The American Democracy: a commentary and an interpretation. 1948.
Leighton, Alexander E. The Governing of Men. 1945.
Liebling, A. J. The Wayward Pressman. 1948.
Lilienthal, David. T.V.A.: Democracy on the March. 1944.
MacIver, R. M. The More Perfect Union. 1948.
McWilliams, Carey. Brothers under the Skin. 1943.
——— A Mask for Privilege: anti-Semitism in America. 1946.
Mills, C. W. The New Men of Power. 1948.
Mumford, Lewis. Technics and Civilization. 1936.
Myrdal, Gunnar. An American Dilemma: the Negro problem and modern democracy. 2 vols. 1944.

Myrdal, Gunnar. The Negro in America: a condensation of An American Dilemma, by Arnold Rose. 1948.
Osborn, Fairfield. Our Plundered Planet. 1948.
Parkes, James. The Jewish Problem in the Modern World. 1946.
Peterson, Florence. American Labor Unions. 1945.
President's Committee on Civil Rights. To Secure These Rights: report of Committee. 1947.
Ross, Malcolm. All Manner of Men. 1948.
Schuman, F. L. Soviet Politics at Home and Abroad. 1946.
Sigrist, Henry. Medicine and Human Welfare. 1941.
Simmons, E. J., ed. U.S.S.R.: concise handbook. 1947.
Somerville, John. The Philosophy of Peace. 1949.
Straus, Nathan. The Seven Myths of Housing. 1944.
Strong, Anna Louise. Tomorrow's China. 1948.
Vogt, William. Road to Survival. 1948.
Wallace, Henry A. Sixty Million Jobs. 1945.
Weaver, R. C. The Negro Ghetto. 1948.
Wecter, Dixon. The Age of the Great Depression. 1948.
Whyte, L. L. Everyman Looks Forward. 1948.
Williams, Francis. Socialist Britain: its background, its present, and an estimate of its future. 1949.
Wooton, Barbara. Freedom under Planning. 1946.

17. Religion; Philosophy

> Man imperishably stands
> through his thousand destinies.
> There are planets in his eyes
> there are aeons in his hands,
>
> Time in him is ever now;
> yesterday is in his veins
> And tomorrow in his loins.
> And forever on his brow.
>
> Dilys Bennett Laing: "The Eternal";
> in her *Another England* (1941)

The genius of man lies in his growing faculty for enchantment without illusion. As man develops, the less need inspiration feed on illusion. Every fresh inspiration is born of a new discovery of unity, and every major step in development from the discarding of illusion. According to the state of man this process may appear in two contrasted forms: as the rejection of old limitations or as the acceptance of new ones. Traditional restrictions may prove illusory and the spirit of man may break through them in a proud outburst. Or an old freedom may be discovered to be an illusion and a new limitation be accepted as the condition of a more extensive achievement.

Lancelot Law Whyte: *The Next Development in Man*

RELIGION is one of the dominating classes of literature, perhaps larger in extent and variety than any other. The earliest records of every race are religious records (prayers, exorcisms, invocations, ascriptions) as found in the roughly notched sticks of primitive tribes, in the hieroglyphs or sculptures of the Central American races, in the clay tablets of Chaldea and Babylonia, in the papyrus rolls of Egypt. It is easy to understand how this must necessarily have been so: how the earliest speculations of man would be concerned with the preservation of the self, with the differences between life and death, with how and why the spirit departs from the body, and with nature's mysterious powers for good and ill. From the roots of wonder and fear sprang worship and ritual, to flourish in primitive cults and to expand in overshadowing world religions, each passing through a similar process of development, each in the broad outline of its history resembling the other. Born out of the terrors, experiences, and beliefs of primitive man, religion is a continuing force in human life. It has been an unfathomed, unfathomable source of power, surging in barbarities and destruction, flowing in tenderness, pity, and healing; transforming individual lives, submerging peoples, shaping the course of nations.

Religion is not primarily intellectual. It is based chiefly upon tradition and feeling. As men's minds passed from the control of custom and authority to question, to doubt, to challenge and examine—in a word, to the exercise of thought upon the nature and meaning of life—philosophy came into being. Its domain embraced alike the world of ideas and the physical world. Moral philosophy sought to define and establish conceptions of human qualities, to solve the problems of good and evil; natural philosophy sought to penetrate the phenomena of nature, the substance of the universe, the tangible manifestations of life. In both aspects the relationship to religion was long a dominating one. Indeed, religion itself is the "divine philosophy" that Milton praises:

> How charming is divine philosophy!
> Not harsh and crabbèd, as dull fools suppose.

As the processes of intellectual development came more and more under the sanctions of experimental knowledge, ethics and psychology superseded the religious element in so-called moral philosophy, and the old natural philosophy found itself transformed into natural science. Philosophy, thus, is the child of religion, and science is the child of philosophy, in the continuing evolution of thought.

So closely allied are philosophy and religion that distinction between the two must often be arbitrary. Within the carefully differentiated framework of the Dewey classification many books may be placed with virtually equal correctness either in the 100's (in Metaphysics, Philosophical Systems, or Ethics) or in the 200's (in Philosophy of Religion, Natural Theology, or Religious History). Walter Lippmann's *Preface to Morals*, commonly assigned to Ethics, is an analysis of modern disillusion concerning former orthodoxies and a formulation of principles that modern intelligence can accept in framing a valid code of morality. There is little distinguishable difference between its essential purport and that of R. W. Sellars' volume, *Religion Coming of Age*, tracing the naturalistic and humanistic development of religious thought, which is classed as Religion. The composite volume, *Living Philosophies*, and its successor, *I Believe*, in which leaders in various fields make their personal "confessions of faith," are classed as Philosophy; yet these statements of individual conviction on life and death, faith, skepticism, and ideals are essentially religious, though most are nonacceptant of theologies. The dialogues of Plato are specifically Greek philosophy; but many of them (the Crito, the Phaedo, the Apologia) are in their essence religious meditation.

In the general class of religion is included the varied literature of mythology, that of the evolution of religion from nature analogies and tribal customs, and thus the wide domain of primitive religion, as set before us in such works as Frazer's *Golden Bough*. Natural theology impinges upon psychology, through the literature of conscience, immortality, mysticism, and the many ramifications into esoteric cults; while psychology unfolds into psychoanalysis and psychiatry, exploring the labyrinthine corridors of the unconscious, sifting and recording elemental data of personality, and seeking to discover what are the undercurrents which determine the religious evolution of mankind. History also forms part of religion—as in such enormous subjects as Jewish history, or history of Christianity, treated by theologians and historians in every possible aspect, or as in the immense outpouring of literature upon a single religious movement, such as the Reformation.

In biography religion finds manifold expression—in life experiences of religious leadership or endeavor, and in the spiritual autobiographies, confessions, letters, and diaries that have contributed to literature some of its most beautiful and enduring human documents and have also supplied problem material to modern psychologists. Religion in its relation to science established that nineteenth-century battleground from whose conflicts the modern age rose to power;

still, against a changing background, this relationship yields continuing argument, controversy, and discussion. Religion's concern with society finds strong present-day manifestation in the social sciences. It has its own relationship to art, music, travel, examples of which will occur to everyone familiar with books: handbooks and studies of sacred and legendary art, works devoted to medieval cathedrals, books that deal with religious music of all faiths, travel studies of regions identified with religious history. Religion in literature lives in the creative works of every age—in the sagas of the Norseland, the mystical, contemplative narratives of the Orient, the *Divine Comedy* of Dante, the *Vision of Piers Plowman,* the writings of Bunyan; in poetry, in drama, and in fiction.

Although it overpasses so many boundaries, the literature of religion falls into its own distinctive areas, according to the kinds of religion or the particular religious systems with which it deals. There is the literature of primitive religion, of the ethnic or race religions, of the great world religions (Judaism, Christianity, Buddhism, Mohammedanism) all branching into myriad diversities of structure, cult, and sect, and each with its varied, far-reaching relationships to history and to culture.

Christianity is the religion of our western world, and about it has been built the structure of our religious literature. Until within the last two hundred years this literature held supremacy. Works of Christian faith and doctrine outnumbered all others in medieval times. The libraries of the eighteenth century were filled with theological tomes. Even today annual American and English book production statistics show that the number of religious books published each year exceeds publications in other classes of literature except fiction and sociology. Probably the greater part of this production finds specialized dissemination through religious organizations and their members; at any rate, no predominant religious interest is evident in general reading, nor is it reflected in library selection. Reading interests range too widely in other fields. Religion and philosophy together constitute but 6 percent of the titles included in the *A.L.A. Catalog* volumes of 1904 and 1926 and in the supplement for 1926–31, 7.2 percent in 1932–36, and only 5.6 percent in the wartime supplement of 1937–41. Only half as many titles in philosophy as in religion were listed in 1904, but by 1931 the two classes were represented equally.

A decline of public interest in religious literature from the turn of the century to 1921 was indicated in the report of the President's Committee on Social Trends,[1] by an analysis of the religious book titles indexed in the *United States Catalog* in ratio to all other nonfiction titles and a similar analysis of the religious articles indexed in the *Readers' Guide*. This showed that religious interest as reflected in book publication reached its highest point in 1903–5, and its lowest in 1918–21. "The Bible," it was pointed out, "receives less than half the attention it had twenty-five years ago"; and the general conclusion reached was that "religious sanctions have been largely displaced by scientific sanctions."

From 1920 to 1939, according to Charles Gosnell's twenty-year chart of United States book production in *Publishers' Weekly* for January 18, 1941, publications in philosophy and ethics decreased slowly from 242 in 1920 to 102 in 1939. Religion also lost during these years, though more unevenly, with lowest ebb of 501 in 1921, a vigorous increase in the predepression period (1924 to 1930), retrogression through the four depression years, and a succeeding rise to the high mark of 843 in 1940. During the war years there was decrease in both categories, and the postwar rise in publication was more marked in philosophy and ethics than in religion.[2]

From 1946, existence of the atomic bomb and the sweeping rise of communism were dominating influences in the literature of religion and philosophy. Conceived by man's enlarging mastery of nature, born of world war and world revolution, these forces expressed and symbolized the shattering of accepted foundations of belief, the failure to achieve peace, the chaos and conflict and fear

[1] Hornell Hart, "Changing Social Attitudes and Interests," Chapter VIII: President's Research Committee on Social Trends, *Recent Social Trends in the U.S.* (McGraw-Hill, 1933).
[2] *Publishers' Weekly* annual summary of trade statistics records show: Philosophy and ethics, 1946, 192; 1947, 290; 1948, 308; 1949, 325. Religion, 1946, 530; 1947, 630; 1948, 677; 1949, 720.

that shadowed the world. They evoked counterforces, flowing from every level of religious conviction, purpose, and feeling, charged with humanity's passionate desire for peace, yet fused with a fear of world destruction which was incentive to power politics and continuing war tensions rather than to international understanding and a unified world. Religion became in the public mind an immediate and momentous issue. The disillusioned, cynical attitude, strong in the literature of the prewar and Depression years, was succeeded by changed spiritual allegiances or championship of the Christian faith on the part of many writers whose fame had been won as ironic realists.

All aspects of Christian belief and multiple phases of philosophic, ethical, and esoteric thought were reflected in the books poured forth as munitions of the conflict between the two great systems of social organization that now divide the world. Intensities of polemic, clash of opposed dogmas, militant warfare upon heretic and unbeliever, emerged from the limbo to which reason and common sense had long consigned them. The classics of Greek and early Christian philosophy were brought to thousands of readers enlisted in the Great Books discussions carried on in public libraries and schools all over the country. In "Neo-Orthodoxy" old theological dogmas, such as original sin, the operations of grace, predestination and free will, were revived by modern scholarship for application to present problems. The resurgence of Catholic mystical philosophy found brilliant expression in the work of Jacques Maritain; the fundamental tenets of orthodox Christianity were expounded in the kaleidoscopic color and sharp outlines of C. S. Lewis' attacks along all fronts of skepticism; in the earnest, provocative polemics of Dorothy Sayers; and in many other books of high intellectual and literary quality. Deepening interest was evident in distillations of Oriental philosophy; and there was increasing acceptance of the fusion of psychiatry into religion and ethics as a fundamental element in the development of personality. Strongest trends to be noted are: the movement of the Protestant churches to strengthen unity among themselves, to work together for the relief of human suffering, for international understanding and world peace and the development of the World Council of Churches; advance of the Catholic Action movement, bringing a flow of fervent converts to the faith and marshaling the power of the church to preserve and extend its religious authority in relation to the policies and institutions of the state; and the rising world struggle between the ideologies of Christianity and communism.

In general, religious reading trends are toward books that deal with moral and spiritual problems in Christian living, that convey an inspirational impulse toward personal self-adjustment, that place their emphasis on social, ethical, or scientific considerations. Significant is the growing response to the socializing and secularizing of religious activities, the endeavor to strengthen youth in moral faith, in the principles of justice and equality unrestricted by color, race, or creed, rather than to instill the rigidities and self-complacencies of inflexible sectarianism. Wide acceptance has been established for the evolutionary concept of religion as a changing sequence of spiritual insights attained in succeeding stages of human history; and many books of rich and varied content offer variations of this theme. Here the color, vitality, and warm human qualities of *This Believing World*, Lewis Browne's sympathetic study of comparative religion, hold continuing popularity through more than a quarter-century. Emma Hawkridge, in *The Wisdom Tree*, neither overpopularized nor doctrinaire, combines clear, readable history of religions of the western and eastern worlds with thoughtful analysis of fundamental similarities in origins and practice. *The Eleven Religions*, edited by Selwyn Gurney Champion, is presentation in unusual anthology form of the teachings and proverbial lore of Buddhism, Christianity, Confucianism, Hebraism, Hinduism, Islam, Jainism, Shinto, Sikhism, Taoism, and Zoroastrianism. A section for each religion is devoted to proverbs and sacred quotations (4,890 in all, indexed by key words and subjects) and preceded by an essay on the origins and teachings of that faith, each essay by a different writer of authority in his field. Eustace Haydon's *Biography of the Gods* is the vigorous, compelling work of a humanist who sees religion as simply a phase of natural human life experience, rooted in and shaped by the social needs and aspirations of men. The gods spring from man, not man from God; their biographies, traced in the great world religions, follow a continuing death process. "More needful than faith in God is faith that man can give all his beloved moral values embodiment in human relations. Denial of this faith is the only real atheism."

Frankness in the expression of individual viewpoint becomes constantly more familiar in the realm of religious beliefs and opinions. Every observer today must admit the waning of orthodoxy, the pushing aside of mufflings of acceptance and conformity which are the traditional garb of religious convictions. Thus, popular interest responds to books that deal with religious subjects in a fresh and unconventional way. Skillful, vigorous iconoclasm commands public attention and often stimulates fruitful discussion. H. L. Mencken's *Treatise on the Gods,* after eighteen years of profane evangelism, in 1948 won survival as a modern classic in its field, with a second edition, "corrected and rewritten," ingrained even more deeply with ribald analogies and caustic derision. *Generation of Vipers*, Philip Wylie's Freudian jeremiad, is its postwar successor, a furious castigation of sins and outrages he sees as prevailing today, rather than a Menckenish debunking of "religiousness" in history and practices; while in *Man against Myth* Barrows Dunham liquidates in clear, caustic solution of logic, common sense, and constructive thought some of the social, ethical, and political myths that limit man's knowledge of his own nature and his power to control his destiny.

What may be called the professional literature of religion (exegetical and doctrinal material, sermon material, manuals for theological study, texts for Sunday-school teaching) is of less importance in general library selection than is the literature that is of interest to lay readers. As in the case of medicine and law, the public library does not attempt to build up a professional collection in theology. It confines itself in this field to works that are of general reference value or wide scholarly usefulness. However, there are specialized trends of religious interest that as elements in community demand must have representation. The varied organizations of church workers and the many study groups in history of religion, missions, and kindred subjects, should find in the library books that will enlarge knowledge and vitalize understanding of the subjects on which their interest is directed. To individual religious leaders and ministers the best current literature of religious thought should be made available. Such subjects as the relationship of religion and science, study and interpretation of the character of Jesus, new renderings of the Bible, relationship of the church to present social problems, changing factors in mission work, the application of psychology to religious education, and religion as revealed in biography demand continuing attention. The perennial conflict between fundamentalism and liberalism, between the absolutist and the evolutionary point of view, has been responsible for a mass of contemporary literature that ranges from sectarian dogmatics to philosophical subtleties and requires careful selective gleaning. The element of specialized demand that exists in the membership of the various religious bodies, Catholic, Protestant, and Jewish, and in that of many groups and cults whose trend is toward the metaphysical and the transcendental, will vary according to the character, size, and special interests of the community. The volume of this demand must, in large measure, determine the representation it receives.

In the literature of religion more, perhaps, than in any other class, library selection must be broad, tolerant, without partisanship or propaganda, yet consistently directed toward the choice of the best books as regards authority, timeliness, and good literary quality. The library is a supporter of no race, faith, or cult. It is an agency of public education, not a religious institution; and as an agency of education, while it recognizes the obligation to provide books in accordance with public demand, its chief aim must be to enlarge knowledge and enrich culture. Religion, as the source of inspiration and beauty in personal living, is an agency of spiritual education; in its integral relationship to human life, it is part of the history and development of culture; on these aspects library selection places emphasis. Toward the bitter antagonisms of opposed beliefs, the deep animosities engendered by works of destructive criticism, however authoritative and dispassionate they may be, the library must remain impersonal.

A consistent and reasoned attitude must be maintained toward the efforts so constantly made to control library selection of controversial material. Such efforts have already been mentioned. Libraries must meet the danger of censorship and control by constructive and preventive cooperative action, based on the Library Bill of Rights. And book selection and book service in a field that is the battleground of man's most passionate presumptions must maintain objectivity and fair proportional balance. The library, it should be remembered, gives impartial recognition to conflicting points of view; but extreme sectarianism, violent propaganda, the pronouncements of obvious charlatanry and delusion, have no place in judicious selection. Controversial and doctrinal and other material that would not justify purchase is often offered to the library as a gift, and when practicable, should be politely accepted. By such acceptance, and by general public understanding that such gifts may be made, propagandists are pacified and the library establishes a legitimate way of escape from the onus of unfair discrimination or exclusion.

While demand is a controlling factor in current selection, it must be remembered that demand is always influenced by supply. If a reader finds no means available for adventure in unexplored fields, the impulse toward such adventure dies. General selection in religious literature should be as broadly inclusive as possible. Religion should be regarded in its universal aspect, rather than as a particular dispensation of faith. Even a moderate-sized library should provide the Bible in at least the most important English versions. These are: the Douay (including the remarkable new translation from the Vulgate by Father Ronald Knox); the King James Authorized; the American Revised; its recent successor, the Revised Standard Version of the New Testament; and the (Old Testament) Jewish version, *The Holy Scriptures*, published in 1917, and practically the first Jewish Bible in English. There should also be some distinctive modernized version (as Smith and Goodspeed's "American translation," and E. S. Bates' rearrangement "designed to be read as living literature)." Devotional books of other religions should be included: the Bhagavad-Gita, in separate form and in its matrix, the Mahabharata, and the Upanishads, brought together from the Vedas as the first book of the so-called Hindu "Old Testament," in translation by Swami Nikhilananda; the Koran; the "sayings" of Confucius; the teachings of Lao-Tzu. In the smallest collection there should be at least a compact summary of world religions, with extracts from their sacred writings, such as Ballou's *Portable World Bible*.

Histories and studies of comparative religion, of primitive religion (Frazer's *Golden Bough*, in the one-volume abridged edition, is fundamental in any collection), and of the religions of the ancient world, should have such representation as to convey realization of the power, the sweep, and the changing manifestation through time, of an earlier era in man's thought. The classics of Christian faith and devotion, treasures of spiritual experience as well as of literature, are necessary not only for historical importance but for their continuing power of inspiration.

In general selection, emphasis should be maintained on the American tradition of religious freedom, on democracy, and brotherhood. There should be balanced representation of the three great religious groups, Protestant, Catholic, and Jewish, and effort to include books that transmit a sense of the substance and appeal of different faiths. Mary Ellen Chase does this in *The Bible and the Common Reader*, vivid, illuminating presentation of the charm and power of the literature of the English Bible. It is conveyed by many autobiographic and biographic studies, such as Thomas Merton's *The Seven Storey Mountain* and William Manners' family chronicle, *Father and the Angels*. In spite of the blinding fires of prejudice that shut off perspective in today's battle of opposed beliefs, constructive, reasoned thought, tolerance, cooperative effort toward unity, and deepening response to ethical ideals are strong currents in present-day religious literature—expression of the advancing trend toward what Albert Schweitzer calls "the elementary and universal conception" of Reverence for Life: "namely, that good consists in maintaining, assisting, and enhancing life, and that to destroy, to harm or to hinder life is evil." Books that strengthen and enlarge this trend are aids to the survival of civilization.

Much of the contemporary literature of religion may be grouped roughly into four broad divisions: historical; interpretative and doctrinal; practical and informational; devotional and inspirational. There are many books that can properly find place in several of these groups; and often it is the manner in which a subject is treated, rather than the subject itself, that determines the group to which it appears to belong—studies of the life of Jesus, for example, may be preponderatingly historical, or doctrinal, or devotional.

In the historical group there must be judicious representation of varying *forms*, from the compendium or textbook and the definitive work of scholarship and authority to popularizations which, though necessarily superficial, have a fair measure of accuracy, are vivid, readable, and temperate in tone. Many extensive works of enduring importance, though indispensable in specialized study, can seldom be included in limited general selection. Tests for selection in this group, which would include history of religions, Bible history, church and sectarian history, and history of religious movements, are in a measure similar to those previously outlined for history. That is, it is necessary to consider scope, whether complete or partial, exhaustive, brief, or in balanced proportion; authority and kind of material on which the work is based, and the scholarship that it represents; point of view, as regards bias, partisanship, specific faith or purpose; treatment, as impersonal, controversial, popularized, informal, erudite; and qualities of logical organization, literary skill, and interesting, pleasing or forceful style. Scholarship and inspirational appeal are qualities of first importance in the literature of religion, whatever its particular subject or manner of treatment.

In the interpretative and doctrinal group is found the mass of exegetical literature; biblical commentaries, studies and paraphrases; expositions and interpretations of creeds and systems of faith. Here the controversial aspect is strongly in evidence, and selection should give emphasis to work of definite authority or inspirational value. In small general collections the many-volumed biblical commentary is now usually superseded by a good religious encyclopedia and other specialized reference works. Hastings' *Encyclopedia of Religion and Ethics*, the *Catholic Encyclopedia*, and the *Jewish Encyclopedia*, for example, are indispensable in any effective collection; and there is great value in a careful gleaning of pertinent anthologies, such as Henry Bettenson's selection of *Documents of the Christian Church* in the "World's Classics, Galaxy Edition." Attention should be directed to works of broad general appeal (such as Dinsmore's *The English Bible as Literature* and Fosdick's *Modern Use of the Bible*), and to representative interpretations of Jewish, Catholic, Protestant, and other doctrines (Milton Steinberg's *Basic Judaism*, Cardinal Gibbons' *Faith of Our Fathers*, G. P. Hedley's *The Christian Heritage in America*, are examples), and of current religious movements that enlist public interest. Here authority and scholarship demand consideration; so do point of view (whether conservative, liberal, or radical), treatment (scientific, emotional, or rational), and prevailing tone (whether dispassionate, argumentative, controversial, or violently provocative).

The practical and informational group contains much of the modern literature that deals with administration of religious organizations and with religion in its application to present-day social conditions, and that often merges into sociology. Important here is the omnibus volume devoted to the first assembly of the World Council of Churches, held at Amsterdam in August, 1948. Entitled *Man's Disorder and God's Design*, it contains the forty-two papers delivered by delegates to the conference, with discussions and reports. This work represents the first significant postwar step to bring the whole Protestant church into closer relationship with the social forces that are today reshaping the world. Both capitalism and communism are condemned; Christians are asked "to recognize with contrition that many churches are involved in forms of economic injustice and racial discrimination which have created conditions favorable to the growth of communism, and that the atheism and anti-religious teaching of communism are in part a reaction to the checkered record of a professedly Christian society." The churches are urged to explore "the middle ground" and seek for "creative solutions which do not allow either justice or freedom to destroy the other"; and the solution most clearly indicated is that of a democratic socialism. In the practical and informational group, there is a continuing demand for works on religious education and on activities relating religion to movements for community welfare. This group demands consideration of authority and experience in the fields dealt with, relationship to economics or sociology, tolerance of spirit and understanding of human nature; point of view and specific purpose are also to be regarded.

Writing that is predominantly devotional or inspirational must be tested chiefly by its spiritual and literary quality; by whether there is evidence of sincerity and high purpose; whether originality or exaltation or dignity of thought, beauty or power of expression, are discernible. In any adequate collection, place must be made for the treasures of the spirit enshrined in the devotional and contemplative writings that have lived through the ages—the simplicities of Saint Francis, the counsel of Thomas à Kempis, the wisdom of Sir Thomas Browne, the utterances of others who belong in their company. From the contemporary literature of personal religion there should be chosen books that hold spiritual reinforcement for many present-day readers, such, for example, as *Peace of Mind*, in which Rabbi Joshua Liebman draws from religion, psychiatry, and understanding of human nature thoughtful, stimulating counsel on problems of personal adjustment to life. Norman V. Peale's *A Guide to Confident Living* strikes a similar note of psychiatry as complement of religious faith, and H. A. Overstreet's *The Mature Mind* offers challenging psychological insights on mind, emotions, and social outlook; while a heartfelt, profound, and ardent approach to religion as the meaning of life is made by Edith Hamilton in *Witness to the Truth*, directed at the rediscovery of Christ as he is given in the Gospels.

Years ago, in an essay on religious books in his volume, *Books and Reading*, Dr. Noah Porter summarized shrewdly the qualities of religious literature. He divided it into *good* religious books, which have merits of thought, feeling, and diction, and invariably bear marks of having originated in a gifted mind; *goodish* books, which possess secondhand goodness, are an imitation and dull variation of good books, and are frequently couched in extravagant religious phraseology or redolent of cant; and *good-for-nothing* books, which are stupid in thought, feeble in mind, false in imagery, vulgar in illustration, or elementary in education. It must be remembered that the chief test by which good books may be distinguished from those that are inferior is the test of individuality, of fresh and original thought. Every original, distinctive writer has hosts of imitators following in his footsteps. The works of the great spiritual thinkers and philosophers are wells whose waters have been dipped out by thousands of later minds and diluted through hundreds of thousands of dull and commonplace pages.

Philosophy, as a specific class of literature, traditionally includes logic, aesthetics, ethics, politics, metaphysics, and psychology. According to the Dewey classification, aesthetics and politics are assigned elsewhere, but a place is found for an indeterminate area between metaphysics and psychology, designated as "Mind and Body." In its essential nature, of course, philosophy is an attitude and exercise of the mind—a method of thinking directed upon the nature and meaning of life, that produces a reasoned conception of the whole cosmos and a reasoned insight into the values and purposes of human life. Its scope embraces any aspect of knowledge and culture upon which reflective thought is directed in the endeavor to make a unified, consistent interpretation of its elements and values. Thus, there is a philosophy of religion, a philosophy of science, a philosophy of law, of politics, of art, and of conduct. A "philosophy" of anything may be said to be the theory of its first and most fundamental principles, arrived at by critical and constructive thinking. A "science" of anything may be defined as a formulation of knowledge arrived at through exact analysis and description of perceived facts.

The literature of philosophy offers fewer difficulties in selection than does that of religion. It opens no such general battleground of age-old conflict; nor does it make the same appeal to the mass mind. It is primarily intellectual, not emotional; it demands an intellectual response, or at least a reflective, reasoned attention. In its best and most permanent expression it offers the quintessence of human wisdom—compounded of the reason that organizes and universalizes the data of sense experience, and the creative imagination that illuminates and interprets the mind's quest for ultimate reality. Wisdom is a precious deposit that apparently neither changes nor increases greatly through the ages. Despite two thousand years of advancing knowledge of man and the universe, the race has never surpassed the ancient Greeks in powers of abstract thought. The problems upon which Plato and Aristotle meditated are still fundamental problems of philosophy, and most of the important philosophies of the present day are based upon the foundations laid, the patterns traced, by Greek genius. In its modern development the range of philosophy has, of course, been greatly narrowed. The key to our knowledge of the material world is held by the physical sciences. Psychology, as it discloses the processes of the mind, is penetrating problems once veiled in philosophic theorizing; and in ethics a new body of authority, practical and confident, offers through psychological adjustment and scientific understanding of individual physical and mental capacities a guidance to the conduct of life formerly assumed by philosophy and religion.

Any adequate selection of philosophy, even for a small collection, must include the historic classics and the works that are part of the framework of modern philosophic thought. Only in large or specialized collections can there be extended representation of the bulk of philosophic literature. Every system and school of philosophy erects an immense structure of exposition, commentary, explanation, paraphrase, condensation, and extension. In limited selection, the fundamental formulation of a specific philosophic doctrine, with a clear interpretative commentary, is more satisfactory for general use than is a more elaborate text, which, though essential to scholars and important to students, is frequently prohibitive in cost and difficult to acquire. The complete writings of Spinoza, for example, in themselves fill several volumes and they have produced an immense body of contributory literature; but his teachings have their culmination in his master work, the *Ethics*—the completion of a structure of thought that after two hundred and seventy-odd years holds expression of the most advanced scientific-ethical philosophy of the present day. From Spinoza in direct succession proceed Einstein and the other modern mathematical-philosophic explorers of the universe, no less than the ethical philosophers (Emerson, Royce, James, Russell) who seek to establish the principles of the "good life" on reason and advancing knowledge. Spinoza's *Ethics* is to be had in various standard English editions, as are several of his other treatises. These, supplemented and interpreted by such a commentary as Sir Frederick Pollock's *Life and Philosophy of Spinoza*, or H. H. Joachim's *Study of the Ethics of Spinoza*, and by Lewis Browne's simple, vivid biography, will provide material sufficient for the needs of any ordinary student or general reader. The modern philosophy of Benedetto Croce, important in its theory of art and history, will be better understood by the average reader through the compact interpretative study by H. W. Carr than through the several English translations that present Croce's work. Thus, in selection of philosophy particular attention must be given to the auxiliary material that best summarizes and interprets specific doctrines.

The *Dialogues* of Plato, preferably in the Jowett translation, Aristotle and Plotinus, in at least partial form, should be found in even a closely restricted representation of philosophy. In enduring wisdom Marcus Aurelius and Epictetus are part of the living inspirational literature of the world's sages. Saint Thomas Aquinas, greatest of the medieval philosophers, who sought to reconcile faith and reason and effected adaptation of the Aristotelian system to Christian dogma, is the foundation stone of Catholic philosophy, and a supreme influence in the present-day revival of Catholic scholasticism. Through Bacon and Descartes to Spinoza, the experimental and scientific foundations of modern philosophy are assembled and coordinated. In the doctrines of later philosophers, from Locke, Berkeley, Mill, Hegel, Kant, Spencer, and Nietzsche to Havelock Ellis, Bertrand Russell, John Dewey, and Whitehead, the modern development of science, psychology, education, ethics, government, and sociology may be traced in conception and in principles. In an adequate collection there must be expression of this relationship of philosophy to the present stream of thought— for example, the close relationship to religion that is apparent in the writings of Plato, of Marcus Aurelius, of William James, of Santayana, and of Royce; the relationship to science in the writings of Comte, Spinoza, Fiske, and Whitehead; the relationship to sociology and ethics in the writings of Mill, Marx, and Bertrand Russell; the relationship to education in the writings of John Dewey.

Marxian philosophy as a rising force in the world's life today demands specific consideration. Germ plasm of socialism and communism in their myriad radiations through more than a century, it is based on the work of Karl Marx and Friedrich Engels, evangelists of the materialist-evolutionary concept of human history. Both gave life service to their evangel, but Marx was its creator and it rightly bears his name. His purpose was to make socialism scientific, not utopian; revolutionary, not romantic; to transform it into an instrument for gauging the changing patterns that history stamps on fundamental human relationships and to apply that instrument to reconstruction of social life. Bertrand Russell calls Marx "the last of the great system builders," successor to Hegel and like him "believer in a rational formula summing up the evolution of mankind." That formula (which has developed into what is currently known as communism) Marx called Dialectical Materialism, a name on which the curse of unintelligibility still rests. For both words are drawn from the terminology of ancient philosophic contention.

"Materialism" does not mean realism or objectivity in the modern sense, but denotes the ancient controversy between philosophers who believed that matter (substance) came before idea (thought), and those who held that a Divine Creator "thought" the universe before it came into being. "Dialectic" is even more obscure; it has no relation to language, but is defined in its original meaning as the art of discussion, consisting of statement (thesis), contradictory statement (antithesis), and a third statement (synthesis) that presents revision or compromise; it implies continuing argument or movement of thought. In the view of Marx, as of Heraclitus, all things are in flux, in constant process of movement, development, transformation—a process attested by science and registered by history. Thus, an approximately valid definition of dialectical materialism might be: philosophy of the ceaseless evolutionary progression of life.

From the foundations laid by Marx has risen the vast, complex, social and political structure of communism, which in its many different phases today dominates half the globe and challenges the traditional structure of western civilization. Indeed, a double challenge confronts the world, as hostility deepens between the two dominant powers of the postwar era: the United States, exponent of a capitalistic economy, supporter of religious faith, dedicated to the preservation of personal, individual freedom through democratic processes; the Soviet Union, exponent of a collective economy, resistant toward the elements of religion which it regards as a survival of supernaturalism, dedicated to the equality of rights of all peoples "irrespective of their nationality or race." Only as unity of understanding and a controlling will to peace replace unity of hate and persistent fostering of ignorance and fear can the world turn from pursuit of its own destruction to reconstruction and human well-being. No attempt can be made here to survey this fateful problem of present and future. But libraries must make such survey—as fair, as free from sensational distortion as possible —available for the great body of American readers, to most of whom communism stands for a fantastic devil realm of cruelty and oppression. Of indispensable value here is John Somerville's *Soviet*

Philosophy (Philosophical Library, 1945), an exposition of the basic structure of Marxism, in Soviet theory and practice, sympathetic in approach, authoritative in background, and opening valuable, extensive material for comprehensive study. This may well be supplemented by *Human Nature: the Marxian View*, by Vernon Venables (Knopf, 1945), which is a clear, interesting, and unprejudiced presentation of the original theory of Marx and Engels, that history establishes a behavior pattern of human nature which can be studied and controlled by "scientific socialism." Unqualified attack, reprobation, and denunciation are usually strongly represented in general library selection in this subject, but it must be remembered that any philosophy of life, to be understood, must be approached with a certain amount of sympathetic imagination. John Somerville makes this point, when he says:

If any philosophic work emanating from another culture is read primarily with the desire to discover *prima facie* absurdities, exaggerations and inconsistencies, it can easily be made to appear ridiculous because of different language patterns, the general deficiencies of earlier stages in the development of knowledge, and the widespread readiness to take it as a self-evident truth that our own peculiarities are pleasantly humorous, whereas those of others are deplorable perversions.

The constant outcropping of new or revisionary philosophies, outcome of war and postwar conflict and the effort to readjust man's thinking to a changed world, must have judicious consideration. Existentialism as a philosophic theory is interwoven in the modern development of philosophic thought from the metaphysical and symbolic to the factual and existent. As a specific philosophic doctrine, however, formulated by Jean-Paul Sartre, in the grim war years when France lay prostrate in the shackles of the German Occupation it brought strength and incentive to the "underground" of the French Resistance, in its stoic rejection of escapism, inertia, and trust in God, its stern insistence that man is free, that he alone controls his destiny, that "to live is to will to live." In *Humanism as a Philosophy*, Corliss Lamont sets forth his own warmly human philosophy as "a man-centered theory of life, the viewpoint that men have but one life to lead and should make the most of it in creative work and happiness." Based on Marxian realism, on the inseparability of body and mind and the power of human beings to be masters of their destiny by reason and scientific method, he ignores classes and the class struggle but accepts the necessity of a cooperative economic order and a democratic social structure. Somewhat akin, but more centered on scientific and historical perspectives is *The Next Development in Man*, in which Lancelot Law Whyte, British physicist, advances his theory of Unitary Man—the development of a growing unity of thought from the underlying unity of form established by "the unchallengeable movement of science as common knowledge."

The unitary world will be formed because it is implicit in the continuity of the historical process. Nor is this particular prediction the expression of an individual's desire. The unitary world trend will be realized because the time has spoken to a thousand million men. Soon there will be a consensus of opinion in Asia, and in parts of the West, such as has never been seen before. This is no apocalyptic misuse of language, but a sober deduction from present social, economic, and technical facts. Russia has already proved its possibility, China is awake, and India is stirring. It is within the setting of these major facts that the next generation of the English-speaking peoples will have to shape their lives and thoughts.

The rising currents of thought, the fresh winds of confidence and purpose, that are today ruffling the great expanses of religion and philosophy should open enlarging vistas to all who seek to know the dangers and the hopes that are setting the course of our civilization.

General selection in philosophy offers fewer problems than does selection in religion. But there is one pitfall that can rarely be avoided. It lies in the two subsidiary divisions of the Dewey classification to which are assigned "Metaphysical Topics" (the 120's) and "Mind and Body" (the 130's). Here the literature of psychic vagary, cultism, necromancy, fraud, and delusion is garnered for an eager and credulous public. In almost every community a demand exists for manuals of numerology, for astrological lore, for spiritualist and psychic and occult revelation. Like the literature of pseudoscience, of which it is a part, this material represents a problem in library book selection that should have fuller and franker discussion than it has yet received. The library's obligation to respond to demand and to maintain tolerance and catholicity toward every point of view needs reconsideration if it is supposed to justify the purchase and dissemination of books that strengthen ignorance and foster charlatanism. Selection in these fields should be cautious and critical, and standards of proportion and of quality should be maintained that will necessarily limit supply. In the literature of spiritualism, for example, F. W. H. Myers' monumental study, *Human Personality and Its Survival of Bodily Death*, represents fine literary powers, scholarship, and research, and is a foundation for later investigators. Elaborate psychological experiments carried on by Dr. J. B. Rhine, of Duke University, to establish validity of "extra sensory perception" (or "E.S.P.") as a human capacity to communicate thoughts and perceive physical objects without sensory aids are presented in his volumes, *Frontiers of the Mind* (1937) and *The Reach of the Mind* (1947); they have commanded the attention of psychologists and hold continuing controversial interest, but have failed to win general scientific acceptance. There is work of kindred character that justifies the interest it may command; but the mass of this material in its most familiar manifestations—the pretentious, crude literature of "spirit origin," the communications of mediums, the compendiums of astrologers, numerologists, and professional soothsayers in general—has no place in discriminating selection.

Consideration of form is important in selection of philosophy. Outlines and interpretative summaries, as already mentioned, are of value for nonexpert general readers who would like to have clearer understanding of systems and schools of thought that influence present conceptions of man's nature and destiny. Durant's *Story of Philosophy*, for example, though partial and superficial, has continuing popular usefulness as an effective and readable "humanization" of famous philosophic teachings. It has interested thousands of people in philosophy who were formerly indifferent to the subject, as Wells' *Outline* has done for history, and has thus opened paths to individual exploration and discovery. Broadly akin, but on a much higher scholarly plane, is Bertrand Russell's *History of Western Philosophy*, in which the ablest philosopher of our day makes manifest his power of synthesis, his logic and crystalline clarity, and his pervading play of ironic wit. This volume seems to me his masterwork. Its scope runs from the earliest times to the present; its basic theme is to show that philosophy is an integral part of political and social life and has been both cause and effect of the character of the various communities in which different philosophical systems flourished. Encyclopedic knowledge, elaborate organization and detail, are here fused into luminous summary and analysis, at once effortless and sparkling. There is no pedantry, no "writing down" to the mental illiterate; but direct, almost conversational narrative, deceptively simple, vigorous and provocative, conveys in vivid characterization famous figures and historic epochs, challenges tradition, extracts ore from the great philosophic quarries of past and present, and stimulates critical thought, for Russell is a skeptic and iconoclast whose lambent irony is seldom tempered and whose rapier thrusts strike deep. *Preface to Philosophy* by W. E. Hocking, in collaboration with three other professors of philosophy (Blanshard, Hendel, and Randall), presents a clear, simple, and comprehensive world panorama of philosophic thought. To almost any reader these three books will give a foundational interest in philosophy. In extended and specialized selection, of course, the structure of contemporary thought must be built in the fullest range and closest detail practicable.

Many of the specific tests indicated for appraisal of books in religion and the social sciences are equally applicable to philosophy. Perhaps the chief requisites here, especially in current literature, are originality, clarity, and excellence in expression. The classics and masterworks in philosophy are fruits of human reason at its highest organizing power, its most exalted point of creative energy. All the great philosophic doctrines that have helped in shaping man's enlarging vision of his universe have had originality, in concept or in the organization and development of correlated principles. Vital philosophic thought today must also flow from springs of intellectual power and creative insight. Speculation is not thought; solemn reiteration of truisms is not philosophy. Indeterminate sapience, obscure sonority, are characteristics of would-be philosophers and pseudo-sages. The problems of philosophy demand the philosophic attitude of mind, and this involves penetrating, critical, and logical thinking, the ability to see all aspects of a subject, and a realization of fundamental values. "Sustained thinking on the major issues of nature and life," says Irwin Edman, "if it is to be more than vague soothsaying, must subject its vision to discipline, observe the meaning of what it thinks and the consequences logically involved in what it proposes as an avenue to truth." In work that is not original, but that synthesizes and interprets, there should be logical organization and clear development of the subject, as little technical terminology as possible, and skill and vigor in expression.

Anthologies flow today in a never-ending stream through all the domains of literature. Their extent and variety give them multiple usefulness in both general and special selection, and require discriminating appraisal and ample representation. Only briefest indication can here be given of their comprehensive range and the effective presentation they offer of different types of religious and philosophical writing. Many historic classics and important contemporary standard works are made available in authoritative selective form (as in the "Basic" volumes devoted to Aristotle, Saint Augustine, Saint Thomas Aquinas, and Sigmund Freud), in the various volumes of "Readings," supplementing notable works by individual scholars (as T. V. Smith's *Philosophers Speak for Themselves*, and Muelder and Sears' *The Development of American Philosophy*) and in the "digests" of ancient and modern masterworks. From stores of forgotten learning, anthologies excavate precious deposits and make them common currency of knowledge and inspiration: such are *The Talmudic Anthology*, by Louis Newman; Lin Yutang's unsurpassed gleanings of *The Wisdom of China and India; A Treasury of Russian Spirituality*, edited by G. P. Fedotov. Many anthologies illuminate specific tenets of belief, as does *And the Third Day*, Sir Herbert Grierson's rich gathering of varied expressions of man's faith and hope centering on the Christian doctrine of resurrection. Aldous Huxley's *The Perennial Philosophy* seeks to record the ultimate reality envisioned by saints, philosophers, thinkers and seekers of every age and every clime. There is a strong trend toward anthologies that distill the personality of religious teachers and spiritual pilgrims, past and present, and bring them new friends and followers. Distinctive and very different examples are: *A Kierkegaard Anthology*, edited by Robert Bretall, gleaning from sixteen of the most important works of the mid-nineteenth-century Danish theologian in whose interpretation of life through self-examination and meditation lay the seed of existentialism; *Albert Schweitzer, an Anthology*, in which C. R. Joy conveys the many-sided genius expressed in religion, in philosophy, in music, in medicine, and in daily living by the remarkable man whose creed of "reverence for life" inspired his years as missionary-physician in his hospital for natives of equatorial Africa; and the little anthology, *George MacDonald*, in which C. S. Lewis distills from the writings of the Scottish poet and novelist the pure passion of religious faith that became his own life influence.

Series demand consideration in selection of both religion and philosophy. The more important series devoted to religion are, as a rule, scholarly or doctrinal or historical. Many of these present lectures or addresses delivered on endowed foundations for universities or religious organizations. The famous Gifford Lectures (Macmillan), for example, maintained by the four great Scottish universities and devoted to consideration of natural theology without reference to creeds, have engaged the powers of the foremost theologians, philosophers, and scientists of the day. The Bampton Lectures (Oxford), originally devoted to closely specified theological subjects and given annually at Oxford since 1780 (with the proviso that the same person shall never preach them twice), have enlisted the most famous Anglican divines. Their scope has broadened during a century and a half, and the first series (four lectures) to be delivered at Columbia University was given in April, 1948, by Arnold Toynbee, on "The Prospects of Western Civilization," based on material to appear in the concluding volumes of his *Study of History*. The Hibbert Lectures (Scribner) devoted to the philosophy of religion; the William Belden Noble Lectures at Harvard, which embrace almost every aspect of religion in life; the Ingersoll Lectures (Houghton), concerned with belief in immortality, and the Hoover Lectures on Christian Unity (Harper) are of wide range and interest. A monumental series of enduring specialized importance is "The Fathers of the Church" (Fathers of the Church, Inc.), in which 80 Catholic scholars have embarked on a modern translation of some 300 patristic works embodying more than five centuries of Christian thought, to appear in 72 volumes (the first two in 1947) and to be completed within five years. Jewish classical literature and significant works by contemporary Jewish authors have notable presentation in the small attractive volumes of "The Schocken Library Series," which continue for American readers work of the Schocken publishing firm, long identified with the best bookmaking of pre-Hitler Germany. Here, in religious utterances, folklore, history, biography, and unusual fiction (as in the unfinished historical novel by Heinrich Heine) the tragedy, the unquenchable faith, and inextinguishable vitality of fundamental Jewish experience receive picturesque, poignant, and penetrating expression.

In limited and popularized selection, familiar low-priced and reprint series are of constant usefulness. "The World's Classics" in its new "Galaxy Edition" (Oxford) brings to a larger public Henry Bettenson's admirable collection, *Documents of the Christian Church*. S. E. Frost's *Basic Teachings of the Great Philosophers*, in the "New Home Library" is highly valuable as a compact, interesting, and sound popular summary. There are many manuals and texts in church history, Bible and mission study, that may be drawn upon for specialized demand, and many low-priced series offer good practical editions of the classics of religious meditation and philosophic thought. In all general selection it is preferable to choose from a series individual volumes that meet a particular need or have distinctive general usefulness, rather than to be unnecessarily inclusive.

The most useful series in philosophy are those that present the works of leading philosophers in satisfactory form for the general reader, that offer the history of philosophy in compact readable presentation, or that give clear summary and interpretation of important philosophic doctrines. The "Philosophy Series" of the "Modern Students' Library" (Scribner) is excellent in compactness and readability. Unusual in plan and of continuing timeliness is the "Library of Living Philosophers," published by Northwestern University, begun in 1939. Each volume presents a single philosopher in a compact biography, followed by an extensive selection of descriptive essays; then follows the philosopher's "answer" to the criticisms or comments made, and a bibliography. John Dewey, Santayana, Whitehead, and Bertrand Russell were among the first philosophers thus presented. The well-known "Library of Philosophy" (Macmillan), with its scholarly and exhaustive presentation, is important in building up a representative collection, but unsuited to developing popular interest in philosophy. Of arresting general appeal, in the varied, extensive series, "Columbia Studies in American Culture," is H. W. Schneider's *History of American Philosophy*, thought-provoking comprehensive survey and interpretation of the ideas and influences which have taken root in this country from colonial times to the present. Here also, selection should, as a rule, glean individual volumes, with regard to form, treatment, readability, and the purpose they are to serve in relation to the collection as a whole.

Aids in selection in religion and philosophy range from bibliographies of all degrees and types of specialization and review journals both popular and scholarly, to the familiar general standard and current guides. In limited selection, the *A.L.A. Catalog* volumes, the *Standard Catalog*, and Sonnenschein (Part I) are the chief reliance for older and standard works. The *Bookman's Manual* is indispensable, with a chapter on Bibles, which includes the chief texts of the non-Christian religions, an extended presentment of Bible versions, translations, editions, publishers, books about the Bible, and a wealth of varied related information and detail. Equally notable is the succeeding chapter on Philosophy and Psychology, guiding to important reference books, to general and specialized histories and the leading works and authors in ancient and modern philosophy, and to suggestive, selective representation of the contemporary literature of psychology and psychoanalysis. Current selection depends chiefly on the *Booklist* and *Book Review Digest;* but the bulletin issued by the Religious Book Club, the various lists of books recommended for Catholic readers,[3] and the many excellent reviews that appear in *Information Service*, published weekly by the Federal Council of the Churches of Christ in America, are constantly useful, as are the review columns of the *Christian Century* and the *Commonweal.* The *Review of Religion*, published quarterly by Columbia University, is almost entirely devoted to reviews of wide range and scholarly authority; the *Journal of Religion* (quarterly, University of Chicago), claims consideration; and the scholarly quarterly *Hibbert Journal* is of special value not only in its regular review coverage but in its occasional extended surveys of philosophical and theological literature.

In more extended selection, the bibliographies found in the great religious encyclopedias are of much value. The fundamental guide to the older literature of philosophy is still the "Bibliography of Philosophy, Psychology, and Cognate Subjects," compiled by Benjamin Rand and published in 1905 in two substantial volumes as Parts 1 and 2 of the third volume of Baldwin's *Dictionary of Philosophy and Psychology*. Long out of print, these bibliographical volumes are not included in the two-volume offset reprint of Baldwin's *Dictionary* published by Peter Smith in 1940; in the text volumes of the *Dictionary*, however, many bibliographical references are interwoven in the subject matter. The Philosophical Li-

---

[3] "White lists" of recommended books appear in the *Book Survey*, published quarterly by the Cardinal Hayes Literature Committee, at 23 East 51st St., New York.

brary publishing company of New York is identified with many contemporary reference books in this general field. Among them, *The Dictionary of Philosophy*, edited by Dagobert Runes (1942), putative successor to Baldwin, contains much useful and interesting material but lacks authoritative comprehensiveness and integration. *Twentieth Century Philosophy: Living Schools of Thought*, also edited by Dr. Runes, possesses the same qualities, of assembling much varied, useful information, the same defects of inadequate organization and uneven authority. And this is true of Virgilius Ferm's *Religion in the Twentieth Century*, which, however, has much reference value in the great number and variety of religions and cults it includes. The philosophy section of Shaw's *List of Books for College Libraries* is particularly useful in proportional balance and excellent representation of critical commentary and interpretation. A practical, frequently used aid is the *Bibliographical Guide to the History of Christianity*, by S. J. Case (University of Chicago, 1931), in which 2,500 representative titles, without annotations, are recorded in a clear classed arrangement. *Psychological Abstracts*, published monthly, is the indispensable guide to current publications, reviews, and articles in its particular field. More specific guidance to most of these and to other specialized bibliographies is given in Van Hoesen and Walter's manual, *Bibliography* (Chapter VI).

A national movement to increase public interest in religious literature was initiated in 1921, when an annual "religious book week" was organized, in further manifestation of the "book week" idea expressed in "poetry week," "drama week," and "children's book week." Sponsored by religious and educational bodies, the book trade, and many libraries, its activities were conducted by a co-denominational Religious Book Week Committee, which included Presbyterian, Methodist, Baptist, Congregational, Catholic, Jewish, and several general publishers. Cooperation of churches was extended through sermons and lectures; libraries cooperated by display of special exhibits and preparation and distribution of lists. For several years the movement was maintained with fair success, but gradually lapsed. Revived in May, 1943, in memory of the Nazi book-burnings in Berlin ten years before, and sponsored by the National Conference of Christians and Jews, Religious Book Week was marked by the issue of a yearly *Religious Book List*, prepared by committees representing the Jewish, Catholic, and Protestant faiths, and listing some two hundred titles. After 1948 Religious Book Week was discontinued, but in 1950 some of its activities were included in those of Brotherhood Week, originated in 1934 and also sponsored by the Conference. The pamphlet *Books for Brotherhood*, issued in 1950, lists fifty-one books chosen as were those in *Religious Book List*, some on intercultural understanding and some of religious interest. It is hoped that the Conference—founded in 1928 to show that those who differ deeply in religious beliefs can work together for understanding among themselves and for peace, social justice, and religious liberty—may again expand its activities in the religious book field.[4] Useful and suggestive in any library are the annual list of "Fifty Books of the Year" recommended for library use by the Religious Round Table of the A.L.A. and the religious book number of *Publishers' Weekly*, which has appeared every spring since Religious Book Week began.

FIFTY BOOKS, OLD AND NEW, IN RELIGION, PHILOSOPHY, ETHICS

Famous Older Works

Aristotle. Basic Works; ed. by R. P. McKeon. 2 vols. 1941.
Augustine, Saint. Basic Writings; ed. by W. J. Oates. 2 vols. 1948.
Bacon, Francis. The Advancement of Learning.
Browne, Sir Thomas. Religio Medici.
Confucius. The Analects; trans. by Arthur Waley. 1939.
Descartes, René. Philosophical Works. 2 vols. 1911.
Emerson, Ralph Waldo. The Conduct of Life.
Epictetus. Moral Discourses.
Francis of Assisi, Saint. Little Flowers of Saint Francis.

---

[4] The National Conference of Christians and Jews maintains headquarters at 381 Fourth Ave., New York.

Hegel, G. F. W. Selected Writings.
Kant, Immanuel. Critique of Pure Reason.
Lao-Tzu. The Way of Life According to Laotzu; trans. by Witter Bynner. 1944.
Law, William. Selected Mystical Writings . . . and 24 studies in the Mystical Theology of William Law and Jacob Boehme; foreword by Aldous Huxley. 1948.
Locke, John. Essay Concerning the Human Understanding.
Lucretius. On the Nature of Things.
Marcus Aurelius Antoninus. Meditations.
Nietzsche, Friedrich. Thus Spake Zarathustra.
Pascal, Blaise. Pensees, and Provincial Letters.
Plato. Dialogues and Discourses.
Plotinus. Ethical Treatises and Enneads; trans. by Stephen McKenna. 1917.
Schopenhauer, Arthur. Philosophy; ed. by Irwin Edman.
Spinoza, Benedictus de. Ethics.
Thomas à Kempis. Of the Imitation of Christ.
Thomas Aquinas, Saint. Selected Writings: ed. by A. C. Pegis. 2 vols.
Upanishads; trans. by Swami Nikhilananda. 1949.

Modern Works

Bergson, Henri. Creative Evolution. 1907.
Breasted, J. H. The Dawn of Conscience. 1934.
Browne. Lewis. This Believing World. 1926.
Dewey, John. Reconstruction in Philosophy. Rev. ed. 1949.
Dimnet, Ernest. The Art of Thinking. 1929.
Dixon, W. Macneile. The Human Situation. Reissue, with introd. by H. C. Luccock. 1949.
Durant, W. J. The Story of Philosophy. 1926.
Ellis, Havelock. The Dance of Life. 1923.
Fosdick, H. E. On Being a Real Person. 1943.
Frazer, Sir. J. G. The Golden Bough: a study in magic and religion. 1-vol. abridged ed. 1923.
Freud, Sigmund. Basic Writings; trans. and ed. by A. A. Brill. 1938.
Hamilton, Edith. Witness to the Truth. 1948.
Haydon, A. E. Biography of the Gods. 1941.
Hocking, W. E., and others. Preface to Philosophy. 1946.
James, William. Varieties of Religious Experience. 1902.

Jones, Rufus. The Radiant Life. 1944.
Lewis, C. S. The Screwtape Letters. 1943.
Liebman, Joshua. Peace of Mind. 1946.
Niebuhr, Reinhold. The Nature and Destiny of Man: a Christian interpretation. 1941–43.
Russell, Bertrand. A History of Western Philosophy. 1945.
Santayana, George. The Idea of Christ in the Gospels, or God in Man. 1946.
Schneider, H. W. A History of American Philosophy. 1946.
Sellars, R. W. Religion Coming of Age. 1928.
Steinberg, Milton. Basic Judaism. 1947.
Whitehead, A. N. Essays in Science and Philosophy. 1947.

TWENTY-FIVE BOOKS INDICATIVE OF EMERGENT TRENDS IN RELIGION, PHILOSOPHY, ETHICS

Bennett, John C. Christianity and Communism. 1948.
Blanshard, Paul. American Freedom and Catholic Power. 1949.
Braden, C. S. These Also Believe: study of modern American cults and minority religious movements. 1949.
Comfort, William Wistar. Quakers in the Modern World. 1949.
Dawson, Christopher. Religion and Culture: Gifford Lectures, delivered in University of Edinburgh. 1948.
Dunham, Barrows. Man against Myth. 1947.
Howells, William. The Heathens: primitive man and his religions. 1948.
Isherwood, Christopher. Vedanta for the Western World. 1946.
Kierkegaard, Soren. Point of View. 1947.
Koestler, Arthur. Insight and Outlook: an inquiry into the common foundations of science, art, and social ethics. 1949.
Kunkel, Fritz. In Search of Maturity. 1946.
Lamont, Corliss. Humanism as a Philosophy. 1949.
Laski, Harold J. Faith, Reason, and Civilization: an essay in historical analysis. 1944.
Lecomte de Noüy, Pierre. Human Destiny. 1947.
Liebman, Joshua, ed. Psychiatry and Religion. 1948.
Miller, Alexander. The Christian Significance of Karl Marx. 1947.
Northcott, Cecil. Religious Liberty. 1949.
Northrop, F. S. C. The Meeting of East and West. 1946.
Reik, Theodor. Ritual: psychoanalytical studies; introd. by Sigmund Freud. 1947.
Roth, Cecil. The Jewish Contribution to Civilization. 1940.

Sartre, Jean-Paul. Existentialism. 1947.
Schweitzer, Albert. The Decay and the Restoration of Civilization. 1932.
Somerville, John. Soviet Philosophy: a study of theory and practice. 1947.
Whyte, L. L. The Next Development in Man. 1948.
World Council of Churches. Man's Disorder and God's Design: papers delivered by delegates to the Amsterdam Conference of the World Council of Churches. 1949.

18. Literature; Essays

> We have our responsibilities as readers and even our importance. The standards we raise and the judgments we pass steal into the air and become part of the atmosphere which writers breathe as they work. An influence is created which tells upon them even if it never finds its way into print. And that influence, if it were well instructed, vigorous and individual and sincere, might be of great value now when criticism is necessarily in abeyance; when books pass in review like the procession of animals in a shooting gallery . . . If behind the erratic gunfire of the press the author felt that there was another kind of criticism, the opinion of people reading for the love of reading, slowly and unprofessionally, and judging with great sympathy and yet with great severity, might this not improve the quality of his work? And if by our means books were to become stronger, richer, and more varied, that would be an end worth reaching.
>
> Virginia Woolf: *The Common Reader*, Second Series

LITERATURE, in familiar library classification and definition, embraces the whole domain of imaginative and creative writing as well as the history, philosophy, and art of literary expression and various distinctive forms in which literary art finds manifestation. Essays, poetry, drama, fiction in all its patterns, are components of Literature in the classification of knowledge. In the Dewey classification fiction is fundamentally thus organized, but in library practice it has been broken off into a separate class. Literature, thus, is placed with the arts (such as music, the theater, and the other so-called fine arts) in differentiation from the sciences which seek to establish knowledge through fact, and from the exercise of thought which centers on philosophic and religious verities. The term *belles lettres* was formerly often applied to literature, in the sense of works of imagination and literary art; but its vagueness and flavor of affectation seem to have doomed it to extinction, and it is now seldom used except in allusion or by "literary" reviewers. Fowler admits that it may serve usefully to denote "the lighter branches of literature or the aesthetics of literary study," but adds: "We could in fact do

LITERATURE AND ESSAYS 419

very well without it and still better without its offshoots 'belletrist' and 'belletristic.' "

In extent the field of literature, ranging as it does through every country and every language, is so great as to be beyond full representation in any library collection. World literature, even in broadest definition, is only a selection from the thought of the race recorded through time, a selection determined by majority verdict; and majority verdict always goes to that which has the closest personal familiarity and the strongest penetration to common experience. Thus, the stream of world literature as it is known to American and English readers flows down through the dominant European languages—Greek, Latin, English, French, German, Spanish, Italian—and conveys the traditional and historic influences that have been dominant in the development of western Europe. Every race, every country, has a literature of its own, whether or not this has become part of what we call world literature. Many literatures are shut away behind language barriers. Wales, for example, has an ancient, rich, and varied literature, little known outside its own boundaries. Every history of an individual national literature contains hundreds of names of writers unknown to readers in other countries. Jewish literature, Arabic literature, the literatures of the oriental races, these are immense regions in which most American and English readers know only a few isolated landmarks.

All the great libraries have their special, extended collections of certain literatures, and for research and comparative study the specialist must go to such collections—to the Library of Congress for Russian literature, to New York for Yiddish, to Yale for Arabic, to Cornell for Icelandic, and so on.[1] Aside from such special collec-

---

[1] A list of *Special Collections in Libraries in the United States*, by W. D. Johnston and Isadore Mudge, was published in 1912, as a bulletin of the U.S. Bureau of Education. It is, of course, much out of date, but still useful as a guide to many older collections. The third volume ("Bibliographies") of the *Literary History of the United States* guides to this general field in its summary of national bibliographical centers of information, of important library holdings, and union lists. There are also numerous records of special collections in the publications of library, bibliographical, and historical organizations; among these, recent notable contributions are: Robert Downs, *Resources of Southern Libraries* (American Library Association, 1938); *Special Library Resources*, ed. by Rose Vormelker (3 vols. and index,

tions, even the larger public libraries usually attempt only to supply works of world literature as comprehensively as possible, to build up good selective representation of works in certain foreign languages, to range widely through the chief literatures available in English translation, and to offer the fullest possible representation of English and American literature. The smaller the library collection, the more limited selection necessarily becomes; but in all library book selection, endeavor should be made to go beyond narrowly national restrictions and to cover, at least in reference material, in anthologies, and other selective form, as broad a range of foreign literature as possible. Present consideration must be limited to works in a few familiar groups, and to essays as one of the most widely interesting subdivisions of Literature. Poetry, drama, and fiction follow in separate survey and characterization.

One point, however, to be noted here, as applicable to selection in all these divisions of literature, and in other classes as well, is that works which have received the distinction of national or special literary prize awards should, whenever practicable, be given representation. The Pulitzer Prize Awards in Letters, granted since 1917 to books chosen each year as representing the best American work in poetry, drama, fiction, history, and biography; the Nobel Prize for Literature, awarded yearly since 1910 to "the most distinguished work of an idealistic tendency"; the Hawthornden Prize, that since 1919 has gone annually "to an English writer under forty-one years of age for the best work of imaginative literature" published during the year; the James Tait Black Memorial Award, founded in England in 1919 for recognition of important work in biography and fiction; the French awards—such as Le Prix Goncourt, granted each year to "the best work of imagination in prose . . . that best exemplified youth, boldness, and talent," and Le Prix Femina–Vie Heureuse, bestowed annually on the work of imagination, prose or poetry, most suitable and worthy of translation into English—these are but

---

Special Libraries Association, 1941–46); John Van Male, *Resources of Pacific Northwest Libraries* (Pacific Northwest Library Association, 1943). In all these, however, emphasis is on general and historical material, not on specific literatures of countries or regions.

a few of the many awards through which in nearly all modern countries literary work of creative quality or scholarly distinction receives encouragement and recognition.

In the United States, literary awards of every kind, degree, and character increase and multiply. As incentive to writers, they represent each year an impressive growing total of money rewards through publishers' prize contests and "literary fellowships" aimed at the discovery or encouragement of promising new writers. Universities, organized groups, and individual sponsors also seek by prizes, citations, and similar acknowledgment to encourage authorship and stimulate public interest in books. There is much significance in the establishment of the National Book Award, first given in 1950, which was originated cooperatively by the Book Manufacturers Institute, the American Book Publishers Council, and the American Booksellers Association. It was founded as an annual award to the most distinguished book in each of the three fields of fiction, nonfiction, and poetry published in the previous year. Designed to direct public interest to serious books, it is the first official award to be made to American authors by the entire book industry.[2]

Foreign, continental, and international literary awards indirectly bring to American readers greater familiarity with universal qualities of literary art and better understanding of present world backgrounds and portents. A prize award in itself is evidence that a book is believed to possess merit or significance, and a book which receives a national award in any country is likely to be chosen for English translation and thus made available for general library use. Latin American literature in English is still too scantily represented in most American public libraries, and current Russian literature in translation hardly exists. But national literary awards are made in virtually all Latin American countries; and in Russia the Stalin prizes, instituted in 1939 and first awarded in 1941, have gone to

[2] The National Book Award grew out of, and absorbed, the Book Manufacturers Institute's Gutenberg Award for "the book which had most strongly affected progressive thinking in America," which had its first and only presentation in 1949 and was given to Robert Sherwood for his *Roosevelt and Hopkins*. Winners of the N.B.A. in 1950 were: fiction, Nelson Algren; nonfiction, Ralph L. Rusk; poetry, William Carlos Williams.

many books in varied fields, including drama, the dance, fiction, art and letters. Fuller American knowledge of the current literature of these and other countries, developed through book trade and public library cooperation, could be a mounting influence toward better international understanding, could strengthen support of the United Nations, and materially enrich the content of our libraries. The yearly list of "Literary Awards," which appears in the "Annual Summary" number of the *Publishers' Weekly*, published in January, is the simplest practical source of current information. It should be bulwarked by the standard aid, *Literary Prizes and their Winners*, first published by Bowker in 1936, revised and enlarged under the editorship of Anne Richter in 1946, which records and characterizes the prizes offered in the United States, in England and the British Commonwealth, Continental prizes (including Russia), and Latin American prizes. Careful regular gleaning of *Books Abroad* yields current clues and commentary for discriminating selection.

There is an aspect of book use from which the works that fall within the specific class of literature are of special importance in a public library collection. To all who work with books, books are the indispensable working materials. A carpenter can do his work acceptably and profitably even if he never reads a book on his trade (though such reading will undoubtedly increase his skill); but a writer cannot do his work without the use of other books, for verification, for incentive, for correlative material, for a thousand points of reference or illumination. The writer's craft is still too commonly regarded, not as a craft, but as a natural gift. It is, of course, as every craft should be, the expression of a natural gift or predisposition; but its practice is chiefly a matter of continued, pertinacious labor. Poets must study poetry and know the work of other poets; essayists must live in books; dramatists draw structure and pattern from the literature of drama; novelists are constantly building on the work of other novelists. "The literary mind," as John Macy says, "is strengthened and nurtured, is influenced and mastered, by the accumulated riches of literature." The library is the supply station and the workshop of all who write, and should aid them in every way possible, for it is their work that leavens thought and enlarges understanding. New spiritual and social currents find their first presage in creative literature. Poetry, drama, and fiction catch and transmit "the little noiseless noise among the leaves" that sooner or later in rising force is to shake the forest.

Books on authorship, the art of writing, history and meanings of words, qualities and usages of literary expression, range from simple manuals for beginners to philosophic-linguistic profundities of semantics. Selection, even for a small public library, should give judicious representation to these different aspects, for there are few American communities today in which literacy is divorced from a desire "to write." In such selection, emphasis should be on practical values and interest of presentation. Stuart Chase's *Tyranny of Words* brings to the novice a more immediate realization of the motivation of human behavior through long-accepted interpretation of words which stand for ideas than can be gained from a first impact of Korzybski's philosophy of semantics, *Science and Sanity*, which is its fountainhead. Ivor Brown's delightful Siamese twin of word lore (*A Word in Your Ear and Just Another Word*) has a stimulus to imaginative understanding of the raw material of literature that is rarely found in the guides or manuals designed to enlarge vocabulary and clarify allusions. Books by writers, recording their own experiences as warning or encouragement to others, have wide appeal and usefulness; there are many of sound authority and literary distinction. Vera Brittain's manual for writers, *On Being an Author*, seems to me one of the most interesting and useful works in this special field, in its combination of practical exposition, high ideals, and broad personal experience in different kinds of writing. She presents with earnestness, sincerity, and candor the problems, encouragements, and opportunities of the writing profession that she has encountered through the years; she covers an immense range of informational detail, including comprehensive record of literary awards in the British Commonwealth and the United States and an admirable selective bibliography listing separately British and American publications of continuing reference value. To her, the obligation that rests upon writers today is "to give our readers more awareness than they would otherwise possess of the realities they confront, the human beings amongst whom they move, and the direction in which they are being carried by this apocalyptic age which embraces us all."

For the library's own equipment and service, works that give full and varied information concerning literature are indispensable. Even in a collection of moderate size there should be as ample provision as possible of dictionaries, encyclopedias, and histories of literature, different representative editions of classics and standard works, and a wide range in the literature of contemporary criticism. Works that demand special consideration in selection fall roughly into four groups. These are; bibliographies and lists, dictionaries and encyclopedias, history and study of literature, study and practice of literary criticism. These groups should be represented with all practicable fullness in every library collection, from the small deposit or branch collection and the school library to the large library that can select with little limitation of choice.

Bibliographies and lists have already been surveyed in part, for these include aids and guides that are necessary to book selection in every field. There are many "best book" lists that are good selective bibliographies of standard literature, designed chiefly for guidance of the individual reader, but often useful in library selection. Here Asa Don Dickinson's "Best Books" volumes have unusual basic selective value, for they are built on an impersonal collective choice arrived at by collation of many authoritative lists and computation of specific points of excellence. The variety, extent, and judicious characterization of the lists cited (many of them unhackneyed), the apt annotations to individual titles, the indexes that guide to different angles of use, and the informality of warm personal interest, bear witness to the background of book knowledge and book love, fused in a lifetime of librarianship, of which these volumes are the product. First of the series, *One Thousand Best Books*, with subtitle, "the household guide to a lifetime's reading," was published by Doubleday in 1924 and reprinted, with some changes, by Wilson in 1931; in 1931 Wilson published *The Best Books of Our Time, 1901–1925*, covering the first quarter of the present century; followed in 1937 by *The Best Books of the Decade, 1926–1935;* and in 1948 by a similar volume for the decade 1936–1945 thus setting the series firmly in the Wilson bibliographical structure. One of the most compact, comprehensive, and stimulating of present publications in this field first appeared in pamphlet form in 1932, as *Good Reading: a Guide to the World's Best Books,* prepared by the Committee on College Reading of the National Council of Teachers of English. In succeeding years it went through thirteen printings, was issued in 1947 in a "Pelican-Mentor" edition and in regular trade format, and has become a standard reference aid in many schools and colleges and a continuing incentive to self-education. Somewhat akin, but centering on the treasure store of English literature from Beowulf to James Joyce, is the modest book list issued in 1943 by the National Book Council of England as *An English Library: an Annotated Guide to 1300 Classics.* Edited by F. Seymour Smith, with foreword by Edmund Blunden, it offers expert inventory and illuminating appraisal of the English literary heritage, in which are included American classics and present-day authors no longer living.

Such lists as these, of course, really belong in general bibliography. And in that vast region we can here note only one great landmark recently set up along the path to expert book selection. The four solid volumes of *The Cambridge Bibliography of English Literature* (Volume IV is devoted to the Index) record by authors, titles, and editions "all writings," says the preface, "in book form (whether Latin or English) that still have literary interest, written by natives of what is now the British Empire up to 1900." Edited by F. W. Bateson and a small army of specialist scholars, in preparation for nearly twenty years, published in 1941 by Cambridge University Press (in the United States by Macmillan), this great work is the first attempt since Watt's *Bibliotheca Britannica* in 1824 to bring the whole of English literature within the bounds of a single work of reference. It is in a measure a descendant of the famous *Cambridge History of English Literature* (1907–16), in which each chapter is supplemented by a bibliography; for these bibliographies furnished part of the material here integrated and perfected to completeness. Arrangement is chronological, in five period groups: Anglo-Saxon, Middle English, Renaissance to Restoration, Restoration to Romantic Revival, Nineteenth Century; and these groups are subdivided according to kinds of literature and subject fields. This is a monumental achievement; every worker with books should at least know of its existence and realize its inexhaustible values. For American literature there is no comparable general bibliography; but the bibliographies and reference lists appended to standard histories of literature and to many specialized studies in contemporary criticism are of constant usefulness in rounding out, checking or comparing selection, and in suggesting specialized reading.

In any extended selection the *Annual Bibliography of English Language and Literature,* edited for the Modern Humanities Research Association by American and English scholars and published for the association in England, was of sustained interest from its beginning in 1921 until discontinuance in 1939. Here was winnowed the entire production of creative literature in English during each calendar year, including all studies and material on English language. Essays, poetry, drama, and fiction were brought within its field; besides works in book form it included articles and book reviews in nearly two hundred publications. While the usefulness of this bibliography was greatest to students and writers and for reference information, its successive issues provided a comprehensive bibliographical guide to the materials of contemporary English literature. Its cessation seems to have been a war casualty, in the fact that the 1939 volume was the last to appear and was not available to American libraries until 1948. Like so many of the prewar works of permanent value, it may be hoped that this too will survive, in rebirth or renewal.

Dictionaries and encyclopedias of literature should include the chief standard works and current ones distinctive in content or excellence. Discriminating choice is necessary, for there is always an inflow of more or less superfluous compendiums and reference works, revamping familiar material, sapless and reiterative. Among the "old reliables," Moulton's *Library of Literary Criticism* holds perennial primacy; nothing else combines record of the works of English and American authors up to and through the nineteenth century with examples of the contemporary criticism evoked by those works. *The Warner Library of the World's Best Literature*, though dimmed in pristine indispensability, still proves its usefulness. And that famous centenarian, *Chambers' Cyclopedia of English Literature*, now under the Lippincott imprint, presents its rich inheritance in a 1938 revision.

The Readers' Encyclopedia, edited by William Rose Benét, is successor (in 1948) to *Crowell's Handbook for Readers and Writers*, double in bulk, expanded in content, well organized and well presented, and keeping kinship to the pattern set by the immortal Dr. Brewer, in its fascinating miscellany of "world literature and the arts": plots and characters of novels and plays, summaries of poems, biographical facts, literary and journalistic terms, and mythological, classical, and biblical allusions. Joseph T. Shipley's *Dictionary of World Literature: Criticisms, Forms, Technique*, published by the Philosophical Library in 1943, is a substantial compendium of variegated information, somewhat heterogeneous by lack of organization of its combined dictionary-encyclopedia technique. There is a corps of 264 contributors, and sound information is given on phrases, definitions, allusions, authors, titles, countries, institutions, forms of literary composition, foreign quotations, and what have you. If the medley recalls the contents of Merlyn's bedroom, as recorded in T. H. White's tale, *The Sword in the Stone*, the whole mass yields much information not readily found elsewhere. The two-volume *Encyclopedia of Literature*, also edited by Joseph T. Shipley for the Philosophical Library (1946), surveys all literature from ancient Egypt to the present time, draws contributions from more than a hundred writers, and is arranged alphabetically under names of countries. An ambitious undertaking, it is, perhaps necessarily, superficial and uneven, but its enormous range makes it practically useful for quick reference. Also encyclopedic in scope though within narrower form limitations is *Thesaurus of Book Digests*, edited by Hiram Haydn and Edmund Fuller, with a staff of fifteen notable specialists (Crown, 1949). This contains two thousand digests of books that have taken a place in world literature, from the Babylonian and Egyptian civilizations to the present. Devoted entirely to books, it gives no separate treatment to authors, but there are outlines under author of important related work; while an eighteen-column index to authors and a thirty-four-column index to characters give added keys to the content. Readable and well integrated, this is of general usefulness and reference value.

But the *Columbia Dictionary of Modern European Literature*, published in 1947, must take first place in this group. Edited by Horatio Smith, head of Columbia's Romance Languages Department, who did not live to see it published, this 900-page volume is moderate in weight, legible in type, masterly in proportionate organization, and vitalized throughout by that warm current of sympathetic appreciation that flows through channels of immediate personal understanding. "Thirty-one literatures are represented," says Dr. Smith, "because that is how many there are, and 239 specialists have done the work because that was how many were qualified and available." There are 1,167 articles, the shortest (350 words) on the Faeroe Islands, the two longest (10,000 words each) on France and Russia. They include contemporary movements and changing forms in literary expression, and summaries of national literatures; with record and characterization of "the chief books of the important literary artists of all continental Europe in the twentieth century and the preceding two decades." Psychoanalysis has seven pages; Russian literature, like that of France, receives clear, fair-minded consideration in fourteen pages. "Soviet literature," it is pointed out, "has scarcely begun to realize its vast potentialities, but its present vitality, positive affirmation, and soaring faith, give promise of a great future." There are included 200 French authors, 150 Germans, 100 Russians, 100 Italians, 50 Poles, 40 Czechs, and many of other nationalities—Scandinavian, Spanish, Yugoslav, Turkish, Greek, among them. Literatures virtually unknown to most Americans are here, their qualities discerned and distilled by scholars who know and respond to them, and who are able to convey their radiations of strength and enlightenment. This is a volume indispensable in every library, not only for a public that sorely needs widened world horizons, but because the flow of creative power that runs through its pages brings new perceptions of the universal qualities of literary art, and deeper realization of this universality as an influence toward international understanding.

There are older and recent works of continuing usefulness that should have a passing word. Among them, the *Oxford Companion to English Literature* (Oxford University Press, 1932; 2d ed., 1937) is of constant service to all users of English books, whether in libraries, in class rooms or editorial offices, as writers or readers: a desk book as requisite as the dictionary. Although its range is limited as regards living authors, and adequate treatment of American literature was reserved for later handling, it is so rich in varied knowledge, in wealth of information on curious or obscure details, that it holds continual allurement for all who know and love literature; and for the novice or for the reader who seeks a quick answer to a specific question, it offers both satisfaction and invitation. Its younger brother, the *Oxford Companion to American Literature,* born in 1941, has the same qualities of comprehensive knowledge and mastery of detail, with an added analytical originality evidenced by the double-column chronological index, which breaks into a parallel sequence the literary history and social history imbedded in the volume itself. In 1584, for example, the birth of John Cotton is literary history, the founding of Roanoke is social history; in 1941, United States lend-lease aid to Britain is social history, books by Marquand, MacLeish, Upton Sinclair, and six others are literary history. Each event and personality registered in this index, it is believed, "in some way constitutes a milestone in the progress of the American nation and its culture." This volume also maintains its indispensability in a second edition, revised and enlarged, published in 1948.

Works on the history of literature often merge into the foregoing group, or they may maintain an individual focus, or follow varied ramifications. The *Literary History of the United States,* published by Macmillan in 1948, is the finest achievement yet realized in over-all presentation of the development of American literature as it has shaped and recorded the nation's history. Both a landmark and a milestone, it builds a cooperative structure of history, inclusive in scope, in which the progression of political and social change takes on arresting perspective and vivid immediacy. Also with critical insight it illuminates understanding of the writers who have enlarged the boundaries of our literature from traditional limits to the ultimate measure of human experience. Distinguished historians, scholars, and critics have here worked together in an organizational plan based on research, perspective, and balanced judgment. Robert E. Spiller, Willard Thorp, Thomas H. Johnson, Henry Seidel Canby are editors; Howard Mumford Jones, Dixon Wecter, Stanley T. Williams are associates, and there are forty-eight contributors. Five years were devoted to the writing, two more to editing and publishing. Of the three massive volumes, two are divided into ten sections that in their sequence epitomize the whole evolutionary course: the Colonies, the Republic, the Democracy, Literary Fulfillment (Emerson, Thoreau, Hawthorne, Melville, Whitman), and Crisis—as the fateful lightning is loosed from the terrible swift sword. Then come Expansion, the Sections, the Continental Nation, the United States, and World Literature. The narrative throughout is smooth, expert, often brilliant, and so unified that collaborative individuality can be determined only from a separate table of contributors. There can be few American readers to whom these volumes would not open a thrilling adventure into unrealized actualities that have shaped the age in which they are living. The third volume, "Bibliographies," is a gift of God to librarians, libraries, bibliographers, students, and research workers. Thomas H. Johnson's impressive bibliography, covering in a comprehensive classed record the subjects presented in the text, belongs among indispensable reference works (and is sold separately as well as with the set). Two hundred individual authors, past and present, are included. Our national bibliographical centers of information and their literary resources are summarized, as are important library holdings, union lists, and special collections.

An important new undertaking is the twelve-volume *Oxford History of English Literature,* begun in 1946, under editorship of F. P.

Wilson and Bonamy Dobree, which is planned to embrace all the arts and the body of philosophic, political, scientific, and social thought that finds expression in literature. More centralized and compressed is another newcomer, *A Literary History of England*, which enlists five American scholars in collaboration, with Albert C. Baugh as both editor and contributor, and appears in a single 1,600-page volume (Appleton-Century-Crofts). Broad in scope but well proportioned, it is sound in authority, leavened by perceptive insights and spontaneous appreciation of literary values, and excellent in brief bibliographical references.

Among standard works, the great *Cambridge History of English Literature*, available in reprint without the bibliographies, still maintains pre-eminence, and the *Cambridge History of American Literature* has now special significance as precursor of the *Literary History of the United States*. Garnett and Gosse's familiar history, *English Literature*, still holds perennial charm and value in the wealth and interest of the illustrations. And John Macy's *Story of World Literature*, which is to me the most vital and inspiring popularization of literature yet brought to the general public, still flourishes in the Black and Gold Library reprint edition after a quarter-century of pleasing usefulness.

Many older works still valid and needed were victims of the wartime restrictions on book production which enforced destruction of plates and elimination of editions to meet military needs for metal and paper. Among them were Mrs. Botta's *Handbook of Universal Literature*, after half a century of library usefulness; Magnus' *Dictionary of European Literature*, covering the period from the twelfth to the twentieth centuries and an important pioneer in this field; Barrett Wendell's *Traditions of European Literature from Homer to Dante*, masterly survey of world influences on our literature; and Brandes' monumental study, *Main Currents in Nineteenth Century Literature*. Of more immediate significance is Parrington's deep-rooted analytical survey of *Main Currents in American Literature*, which gave impetus to the twentieth century's rising leftward currents of radicalism and democracy. Its three massive volumes, the third left unfinished by the author's untimely death, were brought together in one, in 1930, and for twenty years Parrington's great work has held its place as a foundation stone of modern American literary criticism. Ludwig Lewisohn's brilliant, controversial *Expression in America*, centering on psychoanalysis and sex repression as conditioning factors in our literature, and Calverton's doctrinaire thesis, *The Liberation of American Literature*, the first Marxian exposition of our literary history, are among the striking early examples of critical writing—dynamic, interpretative, strongly biased—that gave sign and portent of the violent postwar conflict between opposed ideological and aesthetic doctrines which is fertilizing and transforming American literary art.

Literary criticism has had brief consideration in its relation to building up background of book knowledge and as an element of book reviewing. But attention must also be given to the so-called Modern Criticism, or New Criticism, or Scientific Criticism (the terms are interchangeable), which within a generation has brought entirely different principles and techniques into the study and appraisal of literature. The principles are rooted in semantics, or the philosophical and psychological analysis of words in their many-layered meanings; they are drawn from insights given by anthropology into origins and evolution of human behavior, by the social sciences and the Marxian dialectic into the influences of environment, the concept of class status, the effects of social change and social conflict; and they have taken over the findings of psychoanalysis in its various schools, from Freudian dream analysis to psychosomatic medicine. The techniques are based predominantly on the laboratory method; objective, detached from emotional response and acceptance for "traditional literature," centering on textual analysis, indifferent to the creative process and the relation of the work to the reader.

I. A. Richards' *Principles of Literary Criticism*, in 1924, set the original framework within which Modern Criticism shapes its materials. T. S. Eliot, with his first collection of critical essays, *The Sacred Wood*, in 1920, and his long poem "The Waste Land," in 1922, initiated the New Criticism (so christened by John Crowe Ransom) and has remained its sponsor and high priest. There is often great erudition and fine scholarship in this criticism, brilliant legerdemain with words, and arresting disclosure and interpretation of symbolic expression. Its molding influence on present-day poetry is touched on in the following chapter, and its impress is evident in drama and fiction. But its interest is chiefly for students, teachers, experimentalists in writing, and fellow critics—whether friends or foes. To the lay reader it is apt to give the impression of a specialized aesthetic-literary cult, split into many divergencies—humanist, naturalist, realist, symbolist—engaged in self-centered controversial argument and exposition in a verbiage of its own, with no recognition of literature as the inexhaustible source of one of the greatest, most enduring pleasures of life. Representation in library selection will vary according to the nature of demand and use, but in even a small collection there must be indication of these new intellectual currents that are opening fresh channels in the stream-bed of literature.

Of great usefulness in establishing a background of familiarity is S. E. Hyman's comprehensive study, *The Armed Vision* (Knopf, 1948). This is a survey, commentary, and appraisal of Modern critical method covering its rise, intentions, and accomplishments, remarkable for inclusiveness, for detail, and for sharply accented characterizations; enriched by an admirable bibliography. The core of the book is a thoroughgoing analysis of twelve leading American and English critics, each linked to a different aspect of Modern Criticism. They are Edmund Wilson, Yvor Winters, T. S. Eliot, Van Wyck Brooks, Constance Rourke, Maud Bodkin, Christopher Caudwell, Caroline Spurgeon, R. P. Blackmur, William Empson, I. A. Richards, and Kenneth Burke. There is a dynamic drive in Mr. Hyman's presentation that reflects his own intensity of interest. He sweeps into his commentary almost every literary critic of the day. His judgments are incisive, illuminating, often personal and peremptory, and his own "armed vision" is directed at an integration or synthesis of multiple methods and variant viewpoints that will establish a valid collective body of criticism: "From the interplay of many minds, even many errors, truth arises." Reinforce Hyman by R. W. Stallman's anthology-textbook-bibliography, *Critiques and Essays in Criticism, 1920–1948* (Ronald, 1949), which draws its substance from British and American critics and covers criticism of criticism, poetry, fiction, and aesthetics, and the groundwork will be laid for discriminating selection.

Contemporary criticism that is not specifically Modern, or New, or Scientific, is in broad characterization of three general types: that which is primarily concerned with the aesthetics of literary art; more personal critical analysis and comparison of books and writers; and informal literary commentary, personal and responsive rather than critical. Within each type there is infinite variation in subject and point of view, from the intellectual classicism of Pater and Arnold to the iconoclasm of Mencken, the aesthetic sensitivity of Virginia Woolf, the psychological preoccupation of Rebecca West, the perceptive magnetism of Lord David Cecil, the mellow historicism of Van Wyck Brooks, and the Marxian undertones of Malcolm Cowley. All these types meet and merge with one another; they overlap on one side into literary biography and interpretative history of literature, on the other into essays. Indeed, the essay is one of the most important forms of criticism; the finest and most significant analyses and appraisals of literature are found in the work of the great essayists of an older day—Arnold, Carlyle, Hazlitt, John Morley—and of their modern successors, among whom are Gosse, Sherman, Canby, Krutch, and Virginia Woolf.

In all consideration of the literature of criticism the difference between textual scholarship and creative criticism must be recognized. Textual research, detailed comparative study of great works of literature, give the basis of full understanding of their import, their relationship, their place in the structure of thought. Creative criticism implies insight and wisdom in revealing principles of literary art, truths to which it gives form and expression, and aspects these truths assume in the minds that receive them. The finest critical writing possesses both scholarship and creative power. It conveys judgment based on knowledge, it discerns hidden beauties, discovers fresh aspects, frees unrealized potencies, and in doing this it exercises a skilled literary art.

Essays are not amenable to rigorous classification. Irrepressibly elastic, they cannot be confined within specific boundaries; for in one aspect the essay merges into the short story; in another it puts on the laughing mask of burlesque or comedy sketch; in another it offers ironic or polemic commentary; in another it is turned to meditation and self-communing; in another it disseminates information; and in another it engages in moral or philosophic discussion. Its common characteristic is that it is small in size; but even this is relative to dimensions in other classes of literature. For in size the essay ranges from the ample work of the great nineteenth-century essayists (Huxley's solidly packed pages of *Lay Sermons*, or Matthew Arnold's 150 pages *On Translating Homer*) to the sparkling cobweb "paragraph-essays" of *Trivia*, that Pearsall Smith invented in the dawning 1920's. It has, however, an organic constitution of its own. It might, perhaps, be defined as a unicellular prose organism in the body of literature. It encloses a central thought or idea, general or typical, which however applied or metamorphosed does not enlarge its entity: undue development of subject, expansion of treatment beyond inherent limits—and the essay is no longer an essay, but a biography, a novel, or a philosophic, or religious, or social, or scientific treatise.

The essay is a self-conscious exercise of literary art, a highly civilized form of literature. It is an expression of experience and of culture. Montaigne must be accepted as its inventor; the first edition of his essays appeared in 1580, seventeen years before the first publication of Bacon's essays. In its formal aspect of philosophic and moral disquisition (as Bacon practiced it) the essay existed in classic literature at its period of highest development—as in the writings of Plutarch, Plato, Cicero, and Seneca. But it was Montaigne who gave to the essay its organic constitution and infused it with the magic of individual personality which is the secret of its development and appeal. Whatever its theme, whatever its point of view, personality is its indispensable attribute. This spirit of personality, expressed with informality and intimacy, has become the hallmark of the modern essay. The older, more formal, objective type still flourishes, but it does not convey what the present-day reader expects an essay to give. The "familiar essay," as it has come to perfection in French and English literature, was born when in his book-lined tower room, nearly four hundred years ago, a quiet French gentleman determined to know himself and to make known his discoveries. He sought to "essay," to probe or test, his "imperfections and natural form." As he tells us, "myself am the groundwork of my book."

To the English literary genius the essay is especially congenial. To trace its development is to trace the succession of the best and most cultivated English writers. Whether they give us the more formal and objective essay, as do Bacon and Dr. Johnson, Macaulay, and Huxley, or the familiar essay of informality, humor, sentiment, vivacity, and wisdom, as do Addison, Steele, Lamb, Holmes, Stevenson, and Christopher Morley; or the manifold types between, as do Emerson, Thoreau, Jefferies, Lowell, Russell, and Mencken—the rich flavor of personality is always present.

Concentration, personality, and finished literary art are, thus, dominant characteristics of the essay. However rambling and discursive it may be, it must focus on its central thought, on the special phase or aspect of life, the particular character or trait of character, with which it deals. There must be a foreshortened perspective; events and materials must be chosen and disposed, not to effect completeness but to transmit an aspect, to render an impression. It should be neither expository nor violent; but it can, and does, command formidable weapons of attack and defense in the arena of opposed opinion. The continuing "revolution of our time" brings new patterns into all literary expression. On the art of the essay, as of the short story, the *New Yorker* magazine has left its own impress: a light, probing, candid ruthlessness, weighted with fact, sharpened with sophistication, infused with ironic humor; *New Yorker* "profiles" have given new dimensions to the biographic essay, and in descriptive and character sketches have accented psychoanalytical perceptiveness. To the reader the appeal of the essay is that of thought-provoking or entertaining conversation: personal, direct, apparently casual, but striking hidden chords of shared experience or glancing lightly from many angles of thought. The texture of words that conveys, in the small compass of an essay, charm of personality, mellowness of wisdom, impact of thought, grace of humor, and shades of sensitive perception, is woven only by the accomplished literary artist.

So varied in range is the essay that it takes its place in every class of literature. The "psychographs" of Gamaliel Bradford, the character studies of Lytton Strachey, are essays that introduced new methods in biography. T. R. Glover's mellow essays, *The Challenge of the Greek*, Tomlinson's strong, thoughtful judgment of *The Turn of the Tide* in the surging torrents of the Second World War, are interpretations of history. The essays of Richard Jefferies, of John Muir, of William Beebe, are significant in the literature of natural history. Trends in modern science and social ethics may be traced in essays by Haldane and Bertrand Russell. Philosophy and religion have always stirred essayists to thought, from Bacon, Emerson, and Carlyle to Aldous Huxley and George Santayana. There are essayists whose work belongs to the interpretation and criticism of art, music, and drama (such as Ernest Newman and Virgil Thomson); essayists, many already mentioned, who have established the existing body of literary criticism; essayists of travel, of book collecting, of gardening, of walking, talking, dining, cooking, and mountain-climbing—of all social and intellectual and professional activities. Its variety makes the essay adaptable to different moods. Its size fits it to broken or limited time for reading. It is the best of bed-books; the most friendly, modest, and comfortable of traveling companions. All libraries should endeavor to provide good older and recent collections of essays and to keep a generous representation of individual essayists of originality and distinction.

Determination of type of essay, in differentation from subject, often gives guidance in selection. Essayists may be roughly grouped as those who instruct or inform, those who stimulate thought and provoke opinion, those whose work is introspective, meditative, and reflective, and those who write primarily to entertain. The finest essays possess the qualities of several or all of these types. W. H. Hudson's essays, for example, combine the precision and knowledge of the scientific naturalist with the intuition of the poet and the meditative wisdom of the philosopher. J. B. S. Haldane's essays convey authority of scientific knowledge, stimulate thought, and provoke opinion. Much brilliant specialized literary criticism may be found in the second group; while essays that entertain offer examples in the absurdities of Robert Benchley, the deadly satire and hilarious common sense of James Thurber, and the intimate warm friendliness of Christopher Morley, who in his earlier years brought the modern "familiar essay" to near-perfection in American literature.

In all selection of essays first consideration must be given to the author's standing as a writer and the quality of his literary art. Qualifications such as may be expected of biographers, historians, and other writers who deal with the literature of information are not applicable to writers whose work is creative rather than factual. The work of a novelist, a poet, a dramatist, is not judged by the writer's academic or scientific attainments. It stands or falls according to its creative power, human validity, and literary art. This is in large measure true of the essayist, except, of course, that writers whose work has specialized significance must necessarily have gained mastery of their subject through experience and knowledge. Distinction won in any field of literature carries an assurance of authority and skill. Essayists of significance or charm have, as a rule, published much of their work in periodicals or newspapers before it appears in book form. It is hardly possible for an unpracticed writer to command or deserve attention as an essayist, though this is less true of a novelist or a poet.

Other points to consider are:

Kind of essay.—Whether general or specialized, serious or familiar, stimulating or trivial, pungent or trite, commonplace or original. Above all, whether it is of a kind already amply represented in fuller-bodied and more finished work.

Interest or value of the subject.—An essay on a familiar subject must have a fresh point of view or display originality or unusual charm in treatment. Shun stereotyped subjects treated in imitative fashion—feeble Lamblike gambols, mild Morleyish murmurings, over such topics as open fires, old books, middle age, or vacation days.

Style.—There are essays that are simply designs in word building—mosaics of elaborate composition presenting nothing of importance to the mind. There are essays that are commonplace sermonizings. There are essays that utter only trivialities or sentimental platitudes. There are essays that are like pleasing, witty, stimulating conversation. It must be remembered that although in essays style is the stamp of excellence, even a master of style must have something to say that is worth saying.

The tidal wave of anthologies that today inundates the book world is probably more overwhelming in Literature than in any other general class. Here problems of selection center on kind, substance, organization, qualities, and practical usefulness. There are many pitfalls and blind alleys. Excessive duplication of material stamps a monotonous sameness on many anthologies, increases cost, and irritates users. Superficial or defective editorship mutilates text, omits selections in part, without indicating the cuts, repeats over and over timeworn subjects upon which commonplace anthologies are built. But there is always stimulation and pleasure in anthologies that venture into fresh fields or enlist the devotion and enthusiasm of an editor who knows and loves his subject. There should be a watchful eye for anthologies of little known literatures—such as *Hundred Towers*, F. C. Weiskopf's Czechoslovak anthology of creative writing, prose and poetry, during the last fifty years (Fischer, 1945), or Joshua Kunitz's panoramic-historical anthology, *Russian Literature since the Revolution* (Boni and Gaer, 1948), which is conceived and organized as a "people's autobiography."

Essays, like poetry, plays, and the short story, are happy hunting ground for the anthologists. Collections of older, standard, contemporary essays, essays of particular type, essays representative of different periods and literatures, are published in ever increasing numbers. Judiciously gleaned, such collections have practical suitability for library use, for they make available in compact and inexpensive form representative work of many essayists and so reduce the cost and number of individual volumes. Especially in small libraries, where it would be impossible to purchase many of the books of individual essayists, a few well chosen anthologies will make the reader free to range through the most important older and present-day essay literature. In choosing collections of essays, the purpose of the collection and the fitness of its editor are of first importance. While formalized classroom texts have no place among books intended to attract and satisfy the general reader, there are many collections for student use that are both valuable to the student writer and pleasing to the reader without a purpose. Thus, *The Modern Omnibus*, comprehensive anthology-text, edited by F. P. Rolfe, W. H. Davenport, and Paul Bowerman (Harcourt, 1946), presents analysis and examples of the techniques of exposition in literary art as an interesting, carefully chosen sequence of selections covering the essay in its "models and ideas," biography, the short story, drama, and poetry. The whole field of literary criticism has been judiciously gleaned by J. H. Smith and E. W. Parks in their anthology, *The Great Critics* (Norton), first published in 1932, revised and enlarged in 1939. Morton D. Zabel's solid, carefully organized volume, *Literary Opinion in America* (Harper, 1937), brings together fifty critical essays that illustrate methods, problems, and rising trends of criticism in the United States, from the First World War era to 1937.

It is to be remembered that the editor sets the keynote of a collection. Anthologies sponsored by editors of rich experience and recognized personality are always to be preferred to those that offer no such promise. But it must also be remembered that unknown names often convey fine achievement and that well-known names sometimes convey little more than a publicity gesture; when this seems indicated careful comparison and verification of values are called for. Variety in the content of collections is always important. Of course, certain essays are likely to be chosen more frequently than others, but it is not desirable to have the same material served up in a dozen different containers. So selection should imply a sharp eye for duplications and an endeavor to choose volumes that supplement one another in representation of periods or phases of essay writing and that display freshness and wide range in choice of individual essays.

The most important bibliographical aid in the selection of essays is the *Essay and General Literature Index,* published by the Wilson Company. This began with the great single cumulated volume for the period 1900–1933 (which, in its turn, was successor to the *A.L.A. Index to General Literature, 1900–1910,* brought out in 1914 and long out of print). A seven-year cumulated volume followed for 1934–1940; and the sequence continues with semiannual supplements, annual and three-year cumulations, and a seven-year cumulated volume. The 1900–1933 "foundation volume" indexes 40,000 essays and articles in 2,144 volumes. The seven-year cumulated volume for 1941–1947 covers 32,226 essays and articles in 2,023 volumes of collections. Essays in all fields are included, as are an immense variety of sketches, studies, and articles that otherwise would be difficult to trace. The prefatory lists of works indexed are in themselves a fairly comprehensive guide to selection; in many libraries these are checked, so that volumes not in the collection may be considered for purchase. Next to this, as mainstay and guide in selection, I would place the revised (1948) edition of the *Bookman's Manual,* which overflows with rich and rewarding information and suggestion in the whole field of Literature. Its scope and values have already been mentioned, but the chapters on "Essays," on "Anthologies of Poetry and Prose," on "British and American Humor," on "French Literature," and on "Russian Literature" offer fresh and stimulating accompaniment to the consideration of general literary history and criticism, of essays and anthologies, which forms the substance of the present chapter.

Letters (in the sense of works on letter-writing and collections that exemplify the art; personal letters are primarily part of the literature of Biography), literary miscellany, oratory (in which are found also texts on rhetoric and public speaking), satire, and humor, are subdivisions commonly included in the class of Literature. Satire and humor, of course, also filter through all the divisions of literature and find expression in the work of many essayists. However manifested, they should have recognition and generous representation in selection. All readers welcome books that smile at human foibles and touch life with gayety. The field of humor has narrowed as the world has gained keener sensitiveness to suffering and a more instinctive shrinking from brutality. The full-bodied humor of an earlier age—the practical jokes that delighted Tom Jones and his friends, the hearty guffaws of Mr. Midshipman Easy—has lost much of its savor. Yet humor is the salt of life. There is no such solvent to remove shams, to show up pretenses, to reveal unpleasant truths. It still serves as the king's jester, whose quips and gibes concealed the philosopher's commentary on the foolishness and conceits of mankind. In present-day literature its seasoning is conveyed in light satire, in whimsical and absurd and fantastic sidelights on people and things, in a sophisticated and quizzical wit, in hilarious burlesque, or in caustic, mordant irony. Though fashions in humor change and its past glories fade —even Mr. Dooley failed to achieve immortality—it has its own continuing succession; and in even a small library collection there should be place for its hierarchy: for Leacock, Benchley, Don Marquis, Oliver Herford, Ogden Nash, James Thurber, E. B. White; for vital older figures and promising newcomers.

TWENTY-FIVE BOOKS REPRESENTATIVE OF SIGNIFICANT MODERN CRITICISM

Blackmur, R. P. The Experience of Greatness. 1940.
Brooks, Van Wyck. The Flowering of New England, 1815–1865. 1936, 1937.

Burke, Kenneth. The Philosophy of Literary Form: studies in symbolic action. 1941.
Campbell, Joseph, and H. M. Robinson. A Skeleton Key to Finnegans Wake. 1944.
Daiches, David. A Study of Literature for Readers and Critics. 1949.
Eliot, T. S. Selected Essays, 1917–32. 1932.
Empson, William. Seven Types of Ambiguity. 1930.
Hicks, Granville. The Great Tradition. 1935.
Hyman, Stanley E. The Armed Vision: a study in the methods of modern literary criticism. 1947.
Jones, Howard Mumford. Ideas in America. 1944.
Kazin, Alfred. On Native Grounds: an interpretation of modern American prose literature. 1942.
Krutch, Joseph Wood. The Modern Temper. 1929.
Lewisohn, Ludwig. Expression in America. 1932.
Lowes, John Livingston. The Road to Xanadu. 1927.
Macy, John. The Spirit of American Literature. 1908.
Matthiessen, F. O. American Renaissance. 1941.
Maugham, W. S. The Summing Up. 1938.
Orwell, George. Dickens, Dali and Others. 1947.
Parrington, Vernon. Main Currents in American Thought. 1924.
Read, Herbert. Collected Essays in Literary Criticism. 1938.
Richards, I. A. Principles of Literary Criticism. 1924.
Tate, Allen. Reason in Madness: critical essays. 1941.
Tindall, William York. Forces in Modern British Literature. 1947.
Wilson, Edmund. The Wound and the Bow: seven studies in literature. 1941.
Winters, Yvor. In Defense of Reason. 1947.

FIFTY VOLUMES OF ESSAYS, CHIEFLY CONTEMPORARY, ILLUSTRATING TYPES AND CHARACTERISTICS

Atherton, Gertrude. Can Women Be Gentlemen? 1938.
Baker, Ray Stannard. The David Grayson Omnibus. 1946.
Baring, Maurice. Have You Anything to Declare? 1937.
Barzun, Jacques. Teacher in America. 1945.
Beerbohm, Sir Max. Mainly on the Air. 1947.
Belloc, Hilaire. Selected Essays. 1936.
Butler, Samuel. Note-Books; selections ed. by H. F. Jones; introd. by Francis Hackett. 1917.

Cather, Willa. Not under Forty. 1936.
Chesterton, G. K. What's Wrong with the World. Reissue, 1942.
Cohn, Alfred Einstein. No Retreat from Reason, and other essays. 1948.
Connolly, Cyril. The Condemned Playground. 1944.
Conrad, Joseph. Notes on Life and Letters. 1921.
Day, Clarence. After All. 1936.
Edman, Irwin. Philosopher's Holiday. 1938.
Emerson, Ralph Waldo. Essays. 1841.
Glover, T. R. The Challenge of the Greek, and other essays. 1942.
Green, Paul. The Hawthorn Tree: some papers and letters on life and the theatre. 1943.
Hall, James Norman. Under a Thatched Roof. 1942.
Hudson, W. F. A Traveller in Little Things. 1921.
Huxley, Aldous. Do What You Will. 1929, 1931.
Huxley, Julian. On Living in a Revolution. 1944.
Lamb, Charles. Essays of Elia. 1823.
Lawrence, D. H. Phoenix: posthumous papers. 1936.
Leacock, Stephen. Last Leaves. 1945.
Liebling, A. J. Mink and Red Herring. 1949.
Lin Yutang. The Importance of Living. 1937.
Mann, Thomas. Essays of Three Decades. 1947.
Mencken, H. L. A Mencken Chrestomathy; ed. and annotated by the author. 1949.
Morgan, Charles. Reflections in a Mirror. 1st and 2d series. 1945, 1947.
Morley, Christopher. Essays, 1918–1927. 1928.
Nock, Albert J. Free Speech and Plain Language. 1937.
Parsons, Alice Beal. The Mountain. 1944.
Peattie, Donald C. An Almanac for Moderns. 1935.
Powys, Llewellyn. Earth Memories; with introd. by Van Wyck Brooks. 1938.
Quiller-Couch, Sir Arthur Thomas. Studies in Literature. 1st and 2d series. 1918–22.
Repplier, Agnes. To Think of Tea! 1932.
Roberts, Kenneth. For Authors Only, and other gloomy essays. 1935.
Rowse, A. L. The English Spirit: essays on history and literature. 1944.
Russell, Bertrand. In Praise of Idleness, and other essays. 1935.
Saintsbury, George. A Saintsbury Miscellany: selections from his essays and scrapbooks. 1947.
Santayana, George. Little Essays, drawn from his writings, by Logan Pearsall Smith. 1920.

Smith, Alexander. Dreamthorp. 1863.
Smith, Logan Pearsall. All Trivia. 1934.
Stevenson, Robert Louis. Virginibus puerisque. 1881.
Thoreau, H. D. Walden, and selected essays; introd. by G. F. Whicher. 1947.
Thurber, James. Let Your Mind Alone! and other more or less inspirational pieces. 1937.
Tinker, C. B. Essays in Retrospect. 1948.
Tomlinson, H. M. The Turn of the Tide: reflective essays. 1947.
White, E. B. One Man's Meat. (New enlarged ed.) 1944.
Woolf, Virginia. The Moment. 1948.

19. Poetry

> That everything which comes into being must pass away; that all is fleeting, all is moving; that to exist is to be like the fountain and have a shape because one is never still—is the theme of all art because it is the texture of reality. Man is drawn to life because it moves from him; he has desires as ancient and punctual as the stars; love has a poignant sweetness and the young life pushes aside the old; these are qualities of being as enduring as man. Man too must pass away.
>
> Therefore the stuff of art endures as long as man. The fountain dwindles away only when men are rent and wasted by sterile conflict, and the pulsing movement of society is halted. All this movement is creative because it is not a simple oscillation but a development unfolded by its very restlessness. . . . Thus art is one of the conditions of man's realization of himself, and in its turn is one of the realities of man.
>
> <div style="text-align:right">Christopher Caudwell: <i>Illusion and Reality</i></div>

> The bedlam of persuasions, personal creeds,
> Opposing forms, methods of dialectics,
> And their subjoined esthetics might be classed
> Together under the heading *Criticism*.
> By criticism I do not mean the art
> Of judging art, but the complex of mind
> Which has beset the modern writer, that
> Which is expressed through self-dependent pride
> In thought, act and invention . . .
> . . . Love of evidence and fact
> Has narrowed vision and imagination
> In poetry to the vanishing point.
>
> <div style="text-align:right">Karl Shapiro: in his <i>Essay on Rime</i></div>

IN POETRY creative literature attains its pinnacle. It is not only the highest but the oldest form of expression. Rhythm, meter, word imagery, naturally and instinctively convey among primitive peoples the emotions of worship, of battle, of grief, and of joy. Poetry is subjective, emotional; it is imagination playing upon the material world, tapping the secret currents of the self, seizing and applying to its own uses the sanctions of the mind. The ancient Egyptian ritual, the Greek myths, the Hebrew Scriptures, the Christian doctrines, are poetry. It is an art older than recorded history, because rhythm is the elemental channel through which man dramatizes his conception and experience of nature and of human life. Prose comes later, as the medium (unemotional, unrhythmic) for the expression of reason and for plain factual record. No prose lives as literature unless it possesses some infusion of poetry. The art of the dramatist and that of the novelist have, of course, closest kinship with the art of the poet; but the philosopher, the historian, the biographer, the essayist, the naturalist, the astronomer, must have some share of the poet's gift of creative imagination if they are to shape the materials of knowledge into structural beauty and invest them with intensity of meaning.

To make clear the complete, precise nature of poetry is difficult, though many great poets and great critics have given wise and illuminating definitions. The *Concise Oxford Dictionary*, in terms of the obvious, says that it is "the elevated expression of elevated thought or feeling in metrical form." To William Blake, prophet and mystic, poetry was "one of the chief ways of conversing with Paradise"; and John Masefield, in affinity with Blake, says:

I believe that the best poetry has always been a radiant perception of the life of the universe, of its persons, its powers, and its laws, as they exist eternally, and that the mood of poetry in which they are perceived is an undying mood, existing eternally, as the heart of life; and that true poetry, which is a living in that mood and a setting down of its truth, is necessarily eternal, too.

This is the definition of the mystic and idealist, that accepts "inspiration" as the explanation of poetry. But "inspiration" itself remains unexplained—the unsolved mystery of creative force, the essence of being pulsing within the ego and flowing forth in what we call genius: in the cadences of poetry, the harmonies of music, the sublimities of religion, in the immanence and realization of beauty. "A. E.," the Irish poet, in his little volume, *Song and Its Fountains*, studies these hidden springs of poetic inspiration, tracing and recording them in his own inner life. Like Blake and Masefield, he shares the age-old belief in the dualism of the universe; that is, in human life, the cleavage between the spiritual and the material, the mind and the body. He traces the awakening and development of his own poetic art to a childhood joy in color, a continuing process of introspection, and a constant study of and surrender to dreams and visions that projected into his normal consciousness pictures and themes fashioned into words by an art "with which the working brain had little to do." He says: "I think as we go inward images and ideas begin to glow as transparencies"; and although his study is throughout individual and personal it is nevertheless an illuminating analysis of the creative imagination that is the source of poetry.

Perhaps the most widely accepted definition of poetry is that offered by Theodore Watts-Dunton, in the essay (originally prepared for the *Encyclopaedia Britannica*) that established his reputation as a critic: "Absolute poetry is the concrete and artistic expression of the human mind in emotional and rhythmic language." This conveys the dual nature of poetry (content and form) and its infinite range and variation. Matthew Arnold's famous definition centers on a narrower aspect, but remains for much poetry a touchstone of critical judgment. To him, "poetry is, at bottom, a criticism of life: the greatness of a poet lies in his powerful and beautiful application of ideas to life—to the question: "How to live." Wordsworth in somewhat similar fashion defined it as the overflow of powerful feelings about man and nature. Coleridge gave a broader, less concentrated definition, when he said: "Good sense is the body of poetic genius, Fancy its drapery, Motion its life, and Imagination the soul that is everywhere, and in each; and forms all into one graceful and intelligent whole." These definitions are basic and valid. But they are incomplete today, as the twentieth-century revolution against nineteenth-century literary tradition sweeps through the mainstream of poetry. It is the same revolution that we encounter in philosophic, religious, and social thought, in science, in all the literature of human relations. And it is part of the present remaking of the fabric of civilization that seeks to replace myth and legend by fact and experience, to turn man outward toward social consciousness, and constrain him to look the world steadily in the face.

Differentiation is often made between poetry that is, in Arnold's phrase, "criticism of life"—that expresses an ethical, religious, or intellectual theme and conveys a personal experience—and "absolute" or "pure" poetry, which simply transmits emotional realization of experience or sense-perception of beauty. Lord Dunsany says: "Of pure poetry there are two kinds, that which mirrors the beauty of the world in which our bodies are, and that which builds the more mysterious kingdoms where geography ends and fairyland begins." George Moore and John Freeman, in discussion of what constitutes "pure" poetry, decided that it must not be subjective nor expository nor hortatory nor moralistic. It must be objective, or rather it must have the form of "dream flowers." It must be magical and beautiful and a *thing*, like a cloud or a flower. It must be poetry that a poet creates out of his own personality; and for examples they turn to Shakespeare and the Elizabethan lyrics, to Shelley, Coleridge, Blake, Poe, Swinburne, and Emily Dickinson. This is an arbitrary and narrow judgment, for it confines "pure" poetry almost entirely to lyric expression. Indeed, there seems little reason for any specific differentiation between "pure" poetry and "ethical" poetry, for in much of the most beautiful and enduring poetry the qualities of each are fused. The region of fine poetry is broad and diversified. Its vistas may be starred with the delicate "dream flowers" and glittering crystals of the lyric; they may echo to the chime of the ballad, or rise to the grandeur of the epic, or open upon the ordered loveliness of the sonnet, or sweep from the heroic heights of the saga to the grim cadences of war, destruction, and despair that chant civilization's doom. But constantly they expand into new perspectives and disclose the ever changing never ceasing flow of life.

Poetry is both content and form; or we may say, in traditional analogy, that it has a spiritual nature and a material one. Spiritually, it is the operation of the creative imagination *impelled* by intuitions, emotions, and instincts rooted in the subjective consciousness, *working upon* the materials of knowledge and experience, *directed* by concentrated and purposed exercise of the mind. Materially, it is a compound of words and rhythms, harmonized into an art of sounds closely akin to music but addressed directly to the understanding rather than to the ear. It is neither casual nor spontaneous (though lines and images may flow without conscious volition into a poet's mind), but an art perfected by the most expert ingenuity, the most rigorous control. Words are its medium —words that must convey immediate, precise, emotional values, that must be used with the utmost compression, in exquisite adjustment to one another, and in a harmonious and prearranged pattern. There can be no fine exercise of poetic art, no sound critical appreciation of poetic values, without study and understanding of the meanings, implications, and potencies of words.

Rhythm, meter, and rhyme are the most obvious characteristics of poetry. Rhythm, which is the measured rise and fall of sound that summons and expresses emotion, exists in all poetry. Meter, which is the formalized framework of rhythm, and rhyme, which repeats and accents tonal harmonies, are less essential. They give structural finish to poetic art; but they also furnish a pseudopoetic disguise for verse, as differentiated from poetry. The most popular poetry, so-called, is not poetry but verse; usually verse which with strongly marked sing-song of rhyme and simple, familiar words stamps stereotyped patterns (domestic, patriotic, sentimental, or religious) of mass emotion. Such verse has little appeal to experienced readers or to those of sensitive perceptions, and it seldom approaches the border line where distinctions between poetry and verse become more or less dogmatic assertion of personal tastes and opinions. For the higher levels of verse and the lower levels of poetry merge and are often indistinguishable. There is delicate, witty, fanciful, or dramatic verse that has qualities of poetry; there is pretentious, portentous poetry that is really pedestrian verse. Distinctions between extremes are obvious enough; but border lines are always variable and debatable.

It is, thus, virtually impossible to establish rigid lines of demarkation between fine poetry and that which is uneven and mediocre, between poetry and good verse, between passable verse and elementary rhyming. Perhaps the most useful aid is to remember that poetry is essentially poetic, verse essentially prosaic. A great deal of verse is fluent enough, but commonplace; it conveys no originality of thought, no freshness of imagination, no arresting visualization of scene, but transmits familiar images and traditional sentiments to literal or undeveloped minds. Through verse, however, many readers enter the heritage of poetry. Youthful minds, especially, respond to the swing of even crude or noisy rhythm and are stirred to imaginative perception by imagery that may be timeworn or commonplace, but that comes to them with the freshness of discovery.

In poetry, as in all art, there must be perpetual cross currents, constant variation and experimentation. Convention, accepted forms, can never continue unchanged. There is always the impulse to revolt, the uprush of originality, the ardent pursuit of the new-beckoning light. Beneath cross currents and variations are the foundations on which art rests; and the art that endures is built on them.

When on September 23, 1912, Harriet Monroe published in Chicago the first (October) issue of *Poetry: a Magazine of Verse* a new era began in American poetry. Within the next five years Vachel Lindsay, Edgar Lee Masters, Carl Sandburg, E. A. Robinson, Robert Frost, Edna Millay, Amy Lowell, W. R. Benét, and other adventurers and experimenters had established a body of "new poetry" extraordinary in vigor, vitality, and inventiveness. They sought to infuse new life into poetry, to cast off the older molds, to break away from a technique that had become stale, and to seek and use media, rhythms, and words that are part of modern life and expression. Thus, augmented and developed through succeeding years, was born the strong and fecund body of contemporary poetry that was, in fact, not a "renaissance," as it was often called, but an integral manifestation of the creative impulse engendered by a changing world. Harriet Monroe's little publication was both a challenge and a portent. It brought instant repercussions, enthusiasm, recrimination, praise, and attack. But it flourished, enlisted faithful supporters, drew to its pages poets from all over the world, and was an arena and proving-ground for all the innovations, experiments, and "movements" that flowed through continuing years of transition and revolution. Among poets of present-day significance there is probably no one whose name has not appeared in the columns of *Poetry;* to many their first recognition, their continuing encouragement, came in this way. The strength and vitality of the magazine lay in the instinctive, unerring critical perceptions and the pervading catholicity that characterized Harriet Monroe's editorship and welcomed all radiations of form and meaning—the bizarre, the baroque, unique experimenting, and strange adventuring in words. When she died in 1936, she believed that *Poetry* would not survive her; but support was maintained, and the magazine, through many editorial changes, remains an undaunted exponent of contemporary poetry, both in hieratical elucidation and in the uninhibited expression of the poets themselves. Her candid, simple autobiography, *A Poet's Life: Seventy Years in a Changing World* (Macmillan, 1938) is personal history of an undefeatable spirit, and a fascinating source book in the history of contemporary poetry. Her personal collection of manuscripts and correspondence, first editions, inscribed copies, critical prose, biographies and anthologies was bequeathed to the University of Chicago, and is there maintained as a permanent "modern" collection.

All poetry has one quality in common: it is interpretation of life. Sometimes life is interpreted through beauty of nature, sometimes through the emotion of love; sometimes through everyday aspects of human experience; sometimes through tragedy, irony, or a sardonic smile; sometimes through philosophic meditation or religious idealism; sometimes through fantasy or legend or romance; sometimes through a kaleidoscope of brilliant, grotesque, or harsh and glaring patterns. Although in one sense the appeal of poetry is universal, for minds of every caliber respond in varying degree to rhythm and the time-beat of words that in themselves are charged with emotional values, it must be remembered that poetry, and particularly the finest and most interesting poetry, is not easy to understand, and only to a mind and spirit capable of meeting its requirements can it fully communicate what it has to give. Consider briefly the demands that poetry makes upon the reader.

It requires a background of fundamental general information. For example, a knowledge of Greek mythology and the themes of the Greek tragedies is assumed in much of the finest poetry of the past and present, from Chaucer to Robinson Jeffers. John Masefield's vivid, story-poems assume knowledge of the tale of Troy, the Arthurian epic, and the romantic backgrounds of historic legendry. Kipling's ode to France assumes knowledge of the relations of France and England through past history. Amy Lowell's poems in *Can Grande's Castle* assume knowledge of American and European history. Benét's *John Brown's Body* assumes general knowledge of the Civil War period and familiarity with its campaigns and leaders, while Archibald MacLeish's *Conquistador*, itself a rendering of Bernal Díaz' narrative, demands some background knowledge of Cortez' conquest of Mexico. Even Edwin Arlington Robinson's pastoral and philosophic poem, "Isaac and Archibald," assumes knowledge of Homer and the tale of Troy.

It requires familiarity with miscellaneous allusions from literature, art, history, and science. References to the Bible are woven into all English poetry; words and phrases are drawn from the whole racial store of the past and from every present phase of life and thought, and if we don't know what they mean the effect produced is of benumbment or confusion. Robert Bridges' *Testament of Beauty* weaves the complex strands of a lifetime's experience and knowledge into a close-textured fabric that is rich in beauty and wisdom to the perceiving mind, but a dull and impenetrable mass to one that is undeveloped or unresponsive. The poetry of Yeats and James Stephens is steeped in Irish legend and history, and deeply tinged with oriental philosophy and religious mysticism. The work of Elinor Wylie, T. S. Eliot, Edith Sitwell, Conrad Aiken, W. H. Auden, and Archibald MacLeish overflows with erudition and is almost a shorthand of allusion.

It always requires receptive attention and often demands extreme concentration. For poetry is the most highly concentrated form of expression; it crystallizes meaning; distills the essence of emotion. In all great poetry the meaning is deep, underlying, woven through the whole structure of the poem, which is not just a soothing or stimulating sequence of harmonious sounds, vivid images, inspiring ideas, and varying emotions, but a profound, unified interpretation of life. This is especially true of the poetry of Edwin Arlington Robinson, among poets of today, but it applies also to Masefield, to Frost, to De la Mare, to A. E. Housman, to Edna Millay, to James Stephens, to Yeats, and to many others.

It requires either experience of life, personal knowledge of the fundamental realities of living—love, hate, frustration, joy, pain, fear, grief, labor—or it requires the sympathetic imagination by which this experience can be understood. Without such insight, however it be attained, the greatest poetry will never reveal its full significance. Life must be fulfilled, in understanding and ideal, through experience.

> Each life's unfulfilled, you see;
> It hangs still, patchy and scrappy:
> We have not sighed deep, laughed free,
> Starved, feasted, despaired—been happy.

But this fulfillment may also be vicariously attained through the great literature of emotion.

So the ore of poetry yields its full value only to the skilled assayer. No superficial or indifferent reading can give understanding of all its implications, its full beauties, its depths, or its concentrated rendering of thought and emotion. Poetry enriches and invigorates any individual life that can absorb it. It trains and stimulates the imagination and thus gives the power of entering into experiences not our own, of comprehending moods and ways of thought that we do not share, of living many lives besides the one that constrains us, perhaps, within narrow bounds. It deepens consciousness of earth's beauty and of nature's timeless ministry that offers solace or strength in the dark storms of the spirit. It liberates mind and heart from petty trammels of custom and opinion, for it reveals all the forces, ideals, and emotions that have stirred the spirit of man, and so establishes relationship with the whole of human consciousness.

While the values of poetry are never fully recognized, it is always a creative power in the world. Foreshadowings of world change now taking shape are in the poetry of the last thirty-five years, foreshadowings of change to come are in the poetry of today. Since 1914, war and revolution have swept poetry through intensive phases of negation, acceptance, affirmation, hope, frustration, and disillusion, have fragmentized or reshaped form and content, and in recent years have drawn it toward a self-centered obscurantism and an esoteric verbiage that seal it from common understanding. The contrast in the reactions of an earlier and later generation of poets to this era of world violence and insecurity is illuminated in two English anthologies dedicated to the First and Second World Wars. *The Spirit of Man* expressed in its title the essence of faith and inspiration that Robert Bridges in 1915 distilled from the literature of the past. In 1940, *Fear No More: a Book of Poems for the Present Time* brought together eighty-three poems by English poets then living—utterances molded in a different matrix, turning not to religious symbol and ritual but to the power of the mind to maintain spiritual strength; the self-sacrificial ardor of Rupert Brooke was absent, fortitude and joy in beauty were the dominant tones, and the keynote was touched in the lines,

> . . . Our proper place
> Is now our proper selves. The only hope
> For man is still man.

By unanimous agreement the poems were printed without names of the authors, to form a unified expression of man facing himself and drawing confidence from his own time, his own people.

Consciousness of the new forces shaping human destiny is evident in different phases that mark the course of poetry during these years of change, crisis, and conflict. The shock of the First World War was reflected by most of the younger poets in a mood of disillusionment, bitterness, and dismay. Desire for peace, for beauty, for happiness, confronted by the stark realities of war, brought to many conviction that civilization was doomed, that life was sterile, futile, and ignoble, and that human beings were a graceless, contemptible breed. From this reaction, with its deepening scorn for the industrialization of society, and under the influence of Ezra Pound and T. S. Eliot, what may be termed the Waste Land phase was evoked in 1922, by Eliot's poem of that name, and a new pattern of theme and structure from which rise unending variations was set in the framework of poetry. The Revolutionary Phase, as significant as that which a century before had kindled the ardor of Shelley and Wordsworth, had its inception as the Russian Revolution transformed the empire of the tsars into the fatherland of socialism; and by the early 1930's much contemporary poetry had donned a red mantle and acclaimed Marx as prophet and forerunner of "this Time's change." This phase was in part due to revulsion from the ugliness and debasement of modern society emphasized by Eliot and Pound; it challenged the existing order and voiced ideals of equality and brotherhood. Stephen Spender struck the keynote in the lines,

> No spirit seek here rest. But this: No man
> Shall hunger; Man shall spend equally.
> Our goal which we compel: Man shall be man.

Here early leadership lay with the brilliant, vigorous Oxford group of young English Marxists—W. H. Auden, Stephen Spender, Day Lewis, foremost among them. But the long, desperate tragedy of the Spanish civil war enlisted other English and many American poets in the struggle against fascism. These included Christopher Caudwell, (pen name of Christopher St. John Sprigg), English Marxist, who at twenty-eight joined the International Brigade and was killed in action in 1937, leaving in press for posthumous publication the most important work of Marxist literary criticism: *Illusion and Reality*, an exploration of poetry as a product of society in continuous active relationship to the life of man.

As the decade closed, the ardors and aspirations of the Revolutionary phase were crushed by the avalanche of war, spreading desolation and enthroning death in "a common world of great slaughter and much sorrow." The phase of Pessimism followed—of longing for past certainties and serenities, of craving for some new uplift of faith, of bitter, sardonic disillusion and haunting fear of the future. This has dominated what Auden calls "the age of anxiety," when, after victory, the high hopes of peace and a united world were lost to power politics, rival imperialisms, and rekindled nationalisms of the two great world powers, and the atomic bomb had become a tribal obsession of military policy-makers. These phases and many others move and mingle in the never ceasing inflow of poetry, which is broken into cross- and counter-currents and under the incessant and shifting pressures of our own time is continually opening new channels regardless of the past. Ours is still the age of anxiety. Tensions, perturbations, controversy are conveyed in every medium of communication, and in none is transmission as intensified as in poetry. Today the poetry of protest and revolt has gained in maturity and expanded in range, focusing more strongly on social and economic struggle than on militant revolution. For bitter revulsion to war and ineradicable longing for peace underlie postwar poetry in spite of superpatriotic chauvinism; as May Sarton says,

> The poet, scientist, and teacher know
> How fast the seeds of hate and fear can grow,
> What passions can take over peaceful nations,
> What anguish lurk in the safe reservations.

Most of the younger poets belong to the left wing, but among those who count themselves as on the right or in the center there are few whose vision does not pierce below familiar surfaces to a core of human experience. Even in the poetry of ardent religious affirmation inspired by the conflict of opposing faiths and divided loyalties there is, I think, a note of rising confidence in man, as seeker and finder of interdependence in the flux of things.

Modern poetry is highly complex. It requires standards of technical excellence, understanding of and some relationship to the ideologies of this period of transition and revolution. Indifferent to tradition, it has cast off romanticism, concentrates on the object, deepens consciousness of inescapable realities, and directs its power toward understanding the compulsions of motive and revealment of hidden deficiencies and values. It reflects the changes and conflicts of the modern mind, the preoccupation with psychoanalysis, the absence of religious certitudes, the injection of metaphysics into science, and the ruthless exploration of sex. It is sometimes brutal, sometimes pathological. It is a product of the machine age and the material environment of its own day. It regards the poet as released from the necessity of being poetical in any conventional fashion, as free to explore the whole physical and mental world and record his findings in any way that seems needful. In expression it transmits every grade of contemporary speech, adopts complicated syntax or is starkly laconic, juggles with inscrutable collocations of words, applies words to meanings they have never before conveyed, and too often abandons intelligible communication of thought to deal in words as sounds or symbols whose meaning is evident only to the mind that conceived them. Here are two lines from Kenneth Patchen:

> Arms. Milk. Legs. Water. Seven.
> Wall. Sea. Blue. Push. Coax.

—ten words listed perhaps in a code message; but one that no reader is likely to crack. Kenneth Rexroth sets a different verbal exercise:

> And now surprised by lunar mountain avatars
> The avid eyes of gravid mice entice
> Each icy nostrum of the zodiac.

—and this to most readers adds up to nonsense.

These are among the Unintelligibles. They represent the more extreme group advancing along the pathways of the New Poetry under supervision of the New Criticism, of which T. S. Eliot is still guide and teacher. And to some degree their characteristics mark the work of the most highly praised, brilliant, and distinctive poets of the day. Wallace Stevens, E. E. Cummings, Marianne Moore, Hart Crane, have been formative influences in this poetry of verbal sleight of hand, mysterious linking of word-sounds and word-meanings, with infinite variations in individuality, in mood, in form, which reached the apogee of sadistic obsession in *Lord Weary's Castle*, Robert Lowell's comminatory poems directed at his native New England—winner of the Pultizer Prize in 1947.

The last few years have seen an immense expansion in the study of poetry. University and college courses, poetry workshops, poetry clinics, writers' conferences, flourish and multiply; high schools all over the country publish yearly anthologies of student verse; and in almost every community earnest poetry groups meet to discuss and compare their product. At the same time there is a marked lessening of public interest in poetry as one of the great cultural and ethical influences in life. The attitude of the majority of the population is always one of indifference; but more and more intelligent and cultivated readers have turned in boredom or aversion from current poetry that has wakened critics' enthusiasm. By the cult of unintelligibility and the technique of analytical pedantry, the poets themselves and their devoted expositors have raised a barrier that shuts out the reading public from the poetry of its own day. It is the situation, previously summarized, that exists in the application of Modern literary criticism to the appraisal of literature. But poetry offers more opportunity for impressive incommunicability; and behind its self-erected barrier we see the New Poetry as a victim of high word pressure and cryptological infections, and the New Criticism as ministrant psychoanalyst, charting ambivalences and interpreting complexes. The chief reason why the general reader has been alienated from poetry was made evident, I think, in the "Glossary of the New Poetry," published by *Poetry,* in the issues for November, 1948, to January, 1949. Here are a few examples: "Argument: the paraphrasable idea of the poem; autotelic: pertinent to the poem, having teleology or end-purpose in itself; concrete-universal: paradoxical union of the concrete, specific, and unusual, together with the universal and general; affective fallacy: a confusion between the poem and its results." Few who seek the beauty or strength or solace of poetry are likely to linger long in such airless alleyways as these.

The episode of the Bollingen Award should have a word here. For it expressed the protest of poets as well as of readers against the dictatorship of the New Poetry, and remains significant indication that the power of poetry lies in its ethical and intellectual responsibility, its transmission of beauty and of understanding sympathy for common humanity. The first (original) award of the Bollingen Award (of $1,000) was made in January, 1949, by the Fellows of the Library of Congress in American Letters: a group of fourteen distinguished writers appointed in 1944 by the Librarian of Congress (then Archibald MacLeish) as honorary advisers in developing the strength and usefulness of the library collections. Their selection was Ezra Pound's volume, *The Pisan Cantos*, chosen as "the highest achievement of American poetry in 1948," and completed while Pound was in an American Army prison camp in Italy on a charge of treason to the United States in broadcasting Nazi, Fascist, and anti-Semitic propaganda. Later returned to the United States under indictment, he was adjudged insane and confined in a mental hospital in Washington. Uncompromising attack on the award was opened in the *Saturday Review of Literature* for June 11, by Robert Hillyer, winner of the Pulitzer Prize for poetry in 1934; successive articles, editorials, and a flood of letters kindled widespread indignation; and in August official action was taken by the Library Committee of the Senate and House (ultimate authority in Library of Congress administration) providing that in the future no cultural awards may be given in the name of the Library of Congress. As to the award itself, it must, I think, remain an example of the distorted aestheticism and false values which can prevail among poets of fine abilities, who have given their accolade to a work disordered and incoherent, lightened now and then by a flash of beauty or of tragic insight, but reeking with hatred, imbued with brutal anti-Semitism, and finding cynical satisfaction in ugliness.[1]

The established leaders of the New Poetry are still often characterized as "the younger poets," but the term has little factual validity as

---

[1] For fuller record of this controversy, see *Saturday Review of Literature*, issues for June 11, June 18, July 2, July 30, Sept. 3, 1949; and *The Case against the Saturday Review of Literature* (Chicago, Modern Poetry Association, 1949). Administration of the Bollingen Award was taken over in 1950 by Yale University.

the mid-twentieth century relentlessly tells its tale of years. From poetry's rising generation will come the younger poets by whom the schism between Old and New must be resolved, and communication between poet and reader restored. Many who accept the laws of conventional rhyme and meter and seek simplicity and humanness of appeal are doing work that is original, vital, and infused with understanding of the present. Karl Shapiro (self-styled "anti-critic"), Peter Viereck, Rolfe Humphries, Dilys Laing, John Betjeman, Helen Bevington, Byron Vazakos, are among later comers who should help to restore to poetry its former audience of sympathetic friends and intelligent companions.

It must always be remembered that however cryptic, however disconcerting, it may be, poetry is constantly constructing. Much that repels or bewilders the reader of today will be welded into the poetic metal of tomorrow. For poetry, like history, like life, is a continuous cycle of successive experience, ever changing yet ever the same. We speak of the New Poetry, as a "modern" newcomer, trampling down older forms; but if we look back over the generations of English poetry alone, from Chaucer to Tennyson, we see a succession of changing fashions, each new pattern regarded at first as daring and dangerous. Poetry lives by defiance more than by acquiescence. In the eternal rhythm of life the new becomes accepted, the accepted stiffens into convention, convention breeds defiance, which in its turn produces the new, and the cycle endlessly repeats itself. So in dealing with the vagaries of poetry in our own day, with the strange utterances of poets seeking a different mode of expression, there should be catholicity of judgment and responsiveness of mind. Poets today are striving for adjustment to the complex mental and emotional experiences of a new age in which the irresistible flow of scientific knowledge has transformed all the older conceptions of man's nature and place in the universe—conceptions that are still rooted in the subconscious mind and still live in the words that transmit intellectual and emotional experience. Whatever transformations it may undergo, poetry will remain. The great poetry of the past lives on, transmitting and illuminating the eternal elements of human experience; and in the poetry of the present and the poetry of the future, through new concepts and advancing knowledge, those eternal elements will still find recognition and interpretation.

In considering the literature of poetry that is of special importance in library selection, a few practical points should be noted.

It is desirable, especially for smaller libraries, to build up a good collection of anthologies. One of the prime reasons for this is the purely utilitarian one that such a collection provides a quantity and variety of older and contemporary poetry in inexpensive selective form. The work of present-day poets when published in book form usually appears in frequent small volumes, seldom containing more than a hundred pages each and rarely costing less than two dollars. A good anthology offers representative poems of from fifty to more than a hundred such poets at a cost of from three to five dollars, and even less in reprint editions. The economic argument for anthologies is therefore a sound one.

Also, anthologies bring together poetry of distinctive kinds and in almost every specialized field. They collect jewels from the past that would otherwise be known only to scholars, and they sift the whole increment of the present for precious or semi-precious fragments. There are anthologies of the sea, of travel, of the outdoors; of poetry of different countries and races, of different religious faiths, and of different poetic forms (sonnets, lyrics, carols, humorous verse); of peace and war; of birds, horses, cats, and animals in general. They please and stimulate varied tastes, and they make available in compact form an immense amount of poetry much of which would not otherwise be accessible in a small library. It is true that an anthology gives only a limited representation to any single poet's work, but for the majority of minor poets such gleanings are sufficient to convey understanding of qualities and values, and for poets of established standing individual or "collected" volumes should be adequately represented.

There is charm and lure for almost any reader in anthologies. From them all who know and love books choose some treasured companion. It may be the *Oxford Book of English Verse,* or *Come*

Hither, or Oscar Williams' overflowing *Little Treasury of Modern Poetry, English and American*, or Aldous Huxley's sensitive and provocative *Texts and Pretexts*, with its subtle, penetrating commentary; or any other similar precipitation of beauty and invigoration for the mind. They are the most permanent and indispensable influences in any home, in childhood and in youth.

The steadily mounting inflow of anthologies demands careful discrimination in selection. There must be close consideration of scope and value, and disregard of collections that simply repeat what other anthologies already give in more effective presentation. The most important factor in selection is the editor or compiler. For example, Walter De la Mare's anthologies, *Come Hither* and *Love: a Garland of Prose and Poetry*, arrest immediate attention because they represent the selective judgment of a poet of exquisite discernment. Richard Aldington's fine anthology, *The Viking Book of Poetry of the English-speaking World*, carries out a long-cherished purpose with authority and discriminating taste; its selection of poems by more than three hundred poets, its admirable historical introduction and valuable index give it both permanence and personal appeal. *The Poetry of the Negro, 1746–1949*, anthology edited by Langston Hughes and Arna Bontemps, has unusual historical and biographical values in addition to the varied and moving human qualities made manifest by editors of fine poetic gifts and deep-rooted understanding. Anthologies edited by Conrad Aiken, Louis Untermeyer, Joseph Auslander, W. R. Benét, Edith Sitwell, Selden Rodman, John Drinkwater, or by other poets of standing and critical writers of imaginative and literary gifts, are by that fact of presumptive value. But even here, in the present anthological floodwaters, there should be a general comparative "screening" of respective qualities.

Besides consideration of editor or compiler, of subject and scope, attention should be directed to the arrangement of the anthology: its effective organization, simplicity, and clearness; the number of poets represented and the number of poems chosen for each; and whether or to what extent the collection as a whole duplicates material already available in similar form. Some duplication is, of course, desirable, as it helps to meet readers' demands; but there should be an element of differentiation that possesses a value of its own. If bibliographical or critical material is included, its fullness, accuracy, and the manner in which it is presented should be observed. Compactly and unobtrusively handled, this is always a useful accessory; but an elaborate classroom paraphernalia of appendixes and references and a peppering of pages with intrusive explanatory footnotes are fatal to the reader's free participation in what is offered by the poetry itself. Interpretative commentaries or introductions are always important; often they illuminate beauty and meaning and convey fine critical analysis. Walter De la Mare's charming fanciful prologue to *Come Hither* and the delightful notes that enrich and amplify the body of that collection are of integral value and significance. The introduction to George Moore's *Anthology of Pure Poetry* is a clarifying critical discussion that has stimulation and enlightenment for any reader sensitive to poetry. Indeed, some of the most thoughtful and perceptive writing on poetry is to be found in the introductions to anthologies prepared by poets and scholars. The *Bookman's Manual* (6th edition) gives rich coverage to Poetry in six chapters, one of them devoted to anthologies, all alluring and indispensable aids to selection in their selective lists, their range of information, and their comprehensive indication of the extent and variety of the field.

Good editions of older and standard poetry are important. The larger the library, the fuller and more well-balanced should be the poetry collection, and the more effort should be made to include different and variant editions of the better-known poets. The beautiful definitive edition of Milton, for example, published by subscription by Columbia University Press, which embraces in its eighteen volumes all the poetry and prose regarded as genuine, is an unattainable luxury in limited selection, but of fundamental importance in any large library that desires to provide the materials for scholarly study of English literature. Even a small library should have as rounded a collection as possible of the older names in poetry—Chaucer, Spenser, Milton, Blake, Scott, Byron—in readable and undefaced editions. It is pitiful to see in many small libraries the abject, bloated derelicts of the 1860's and 1880's, with small blurred type packed into dingy double-column pages (gifts or salvage) that are the only texts in which Herrick or Pope or Byron or Hood or Burns, or other poets of an earlier day, are offered to readers. Judicious replacement and selection need not be an expensive process, for there are many good low-priced editions of standard poetry. For English poetry, particularly, the Oxford standard editions are excellent and inexpensive, partly because Oxford University Press regards it as a national duty to provide good editions of great English literature at moderate cost.

Every library should have an adequate collection of present-day poetry. "Standards" alone are not sufficient. Recent poetry, work that represents immediate trends and tendencies of the day, is very important. It is a constant present influence for imagination, intelligence, and invigorating discussion. Even in a small town, women's clubs, study groups, high school and college students will use much modern poetry, and they should find it in the public library. In larger libraries one of the most valuable and appreciated services to readers of poetry is the provision in duplicate reference copies of all the distinctive current books that are available for circulation. This means that a desired volume may be examined or consulted at any time, whether or not it has already been issued for home reading. Poetry and printed plays are especially subject to such emergency demands, and the certainty that they can be promptly satisfied strengthens the bond between the library and its public. Almost any library that meets demands and realizes the possibilities of group study programs is likely in time to build up an excellent collection of modern poetry. While much of this is made available through anthologies, poets of recognized standing should have individual representation; their "collected" work is of particular importance and should be bought whenever possible. When a poet appears in the definitive form of a one- or two-volume "collected edition," it means that he has "arrived," that his work has justified bringing together its previous scattered manifestations into unified, dignified, and permanent form. The "collected poems" of Gerard Manley Hopkins, T. S. Eliot, E. E.

Cummings, Hart Crane, James Stephens, "H. D.," D. H. Lawrence, Elinor Wylie, W. H. Auden, William Carlos Williams, and others achieving this recognition, should be in even a small library.

Work of minor present-day poets may usually be sufficiently supplied through anthologies; and for the more ephemeral verse of this type the various "annuals" of college verse, of "best" poems chosen from current sources, are useful. Much of this verse, however, appears in the numerous "vanity" anthologies, which require subscriptions from those whose contributions are printed. Such publications seldom justify library purchase; if they happen to possess local interest, they can almost always be readily obtained by gift. The publisher's imprint, indeed, is of special importance in selection of current poetry; for in poetry more than in any other class of literature there is a constant inflow of books printed privately or issued by obscure publishing firms at the author's expense. Now and then work of fine quality thus appears, to be later sought for as a "collector's item," but in general such publications may be ignored in library selection, unless for some definite local reason.

Minimum requirements in selection of current poetry may be broadly stated as: an author whose name has become familiar at least through appearance in the magazines and to whose work reviewers have conceded qualities of beauty, or power, or originality; and a publisher of recognized standing. Exceptions, of course, must be made. They apply chiefly to the rare instances where beauty and promise are discovered shining in obscurity; and to the considerable body of verse that is not poetry in any true sense but that appeals to a wide public of undiscriminating readers. The verse of "Eddie" Guest, known and loved by more inhabitants of the United States than have made the acquaintance of John Masefield or Edna Millay, is the most familiar example. Don Blanding, his runner-up and possible successor in mass popularity, is on a more colorful level, with an ingratiating note of vagabondage against Hawaiian backgrounds, and a more sophisticated idiom. On a lower level of primitive rhyme-beat and pietistic-domestic sentimentalism are the daily hundred-word typeblocks of James J. Metcalfe, syndicated in many newspapers and also brought together in book form. In general, such work is elementary in content and form, but it deals with common experience and homely topics in common terms, imparts a certain emotional satisfaction, and gives pleasure and content to multitudes. Of it little more can be required than fluent rhyme, simplicity of theme, and absence of blatant vulgarity. It should form a very small part of a representative poetry collection.

Books about poetry are indispensable. They clarify and strengthen the critical and intellectual perceptions of experienced readers, and they reveal the beauties of poetry to many who would not discern them without interpretation. Their range is varied, their values diverse. Perhaps the most obvious differentiation is between writing concerned with the more abstract nature and elements of poetry; that which is primarily critical analysis; that which conveys appreciation and interpretation rather than criticism; and that which deals specifically with the technique of poetry—its structure, form, and word usage. Work of enduring importance exists in each of these groups. Studies of poetry by poets themselves nearly always transmit to the reader a sense of sudden electric contact with "the current of radiant energy" that runs through fine poetry. The older scholarly criticism defines and denotes poetry's established structure and fundamental values. Modern criticism challenges conventions and directs upon the older structure, the traditional values, a contemporary sensibility which finds its expression in the symbols and obscurities of modern poetry. Even in the arid field of technique there is stimulus and support for those who are adventuring and experimenting in poetic composition.

The use of all this literature is constantly increasing. "Poetry Week," first launched in May, 1927, receives each year widespread school, civic, and library observance. Numerous sporadic organizations of poetry adherents have taken shape through the years. Among them, the League to Support Poetry, with headquarters in New York, celebrated its tenth anniversary in 1947, and launched a magazine of its own, *The New Quarterly of Poetry*, but survived only through that year and left no direct successor. Those interested in such poetry movements are not readers primarily, but an ever growing number, particularly of young people, who are themselves making verse a medium of expression. It is for the library to help strengthen and develop these innate capacities for poetic experience, and enable every responsive mind to enter into its full heritage of poetry.

A significant departure toward this end, which links with many audio-visual activities in library service, is the presentation of "Twentieth Century Poetry in English," in the series of "Contemporary Recordings of the Poets Reading Their Own Poems," initiated in 1949, sponsored by the Bollingen Foundation, and sold only by the Library of Congress. Five albums compose the first series, one devoted entirely to recordings by T. S. Eliot, the others each covering a group of five poets—giving a total representation of sixteen leading exponents of today's poetry. The records are intended primarily for listening and will be an impressive addition to school, club, or other poetry group-programs; but they have special values as accessory library material. Gerald McDonald says:

> This is the ideal way to publish poetry: to record the poet's own reading of his verse and to accompany it with a printed text to assist the lazy ears of an audience accustomed to silent reading. Except for the most skilled reader, the practice of silence limits the experience which the poet would share with his audience.... This series of records, remarkable for technical excellence, should be in all libraries where the printed words of these poets are to be found.[2]

It is hardly possible to indicate specific tests that will aid in determining values in poetry. What has been said concerning the qualities and characteristics of poetry, the demands it makes upon its readers, and the enrichment it imparts, should give understanding of the foundations upon which discriminating judgment must be based. It may be added that comparison is one of the most effective means of making critical distinctions obvious. Compare, for example, Chesterton's glorious ballad, "Lepanto," with the turgid sentimentalism of Service's "Ballad of the Northern Lights." Set the smooth, dignified obviousness of Henry Van Dyke beside the complexity and deep-

[2] *Library Journal*, September 15, 1949, p. 1327.

veined philosophic wisdom of Edwin Arlington Robinson. Turn from the simple rustic verse of Riley to Robert Frost's equally simple but beautiful and profound poetry of New Hampshire pastures. Compare older and now conventional poetry with more modern work—the gentle artificiality of Aldrich with Sara Teasdale's radiance of emotion and artistry; or the grandiose pomposity of Joaquin Miller with the surging syncopated chant of Vachel Lindsay. In any consideration of poetry, determine through what medium its interpretation of life is conveyed and what aspect this interpretation assumes; or, in other words, recognize its form, its character, and spirit, and in so doing establish a sense of the personality that exists, vital and distinctive, in every poet's work.

True understanding, sound critical judgment, of poetry can be developed in any individual only as poetry makes its appeal to the individual consciousness, and as, through reading, intellectual responses are strengthened and emotional responses are clarified and deepened. Wide comparative reading is indispensable. This reading must include interpretation and criticism of poetry as well as poetry itself. It seems suitable, therefore, to close this chapter by indicating a limited amount of reading that will give perhaps the best basis for understanding and appreciation of poetry. Matthew Arnold's famous essay, "The Study of Poetry," I would put first; this is included in his *Essays in Criticism, Second Series*, available in "Everyman" and Oxford editions, and is also reprinted in part in Mallory's *Backgrounds of Book Reviewing*. While it deals entirely with the older English poets, it presents with precision and authority the aesthetic principles that apply to all poetry. Second in order, I suggest John Livingston Lowes' *Convention and Revolt in Poetry*, one of the best analyses of the cycle of change in poetic expression. For modern poetry, as a base read Amy Lowell's *Tendencies in Modern American Poetry*, which is definitive and illuminating, although unduly dogmatic; and follow it with Untermeyer's *American Poetry Since 1900*, as enlightening interpretative commentary. Then, for the quintessence of the whole matter, read Elizabeth Drew's two modest, delightful volumes: *Discovering Poetry*, which with simplicity and sensitive perception conveys the qualities and significance of poetry in the continuity of human experience; and *Directions in Modern Poetry*, with its clear, magnetic analysis and interpretation of the variety and significance of the poetry that since 1922 has revealed the transformation effected in society and individual thought and brought radical revision of the existing conception of poetry.

From this reading there should be stimulus to further exploration. If so, I recommend *Modern Poetry and the Tradition*, Cleanth Brooks' development of T. S. Eliot's canon of allegiance to "the literature of the great ages, the sixteenth and seventeenth centuries." Brooks' study is notable for its "close reading" of individual poets, its technical exploration of poetic structure, its eclecticism, and the stimulating insights offered into fundamental relationships of the traditional and the contemporary. Karl Shapiro's phenomenal *Essay on Rime* should come then, as a brilliant, provocative critical summary of contemporary English and American poetry in form, content, and language. Poured forth in skillful, flexible verse, lucid, cogent, easy to follow, this is a *tour de force* in basic comparative analysis of prosody: "a tract on the treble confusion in modern rime," covering thumbnail characterizations of poets of yesterday and today, generally valid in judgment, good-tempered, lightened with humor, vigorous and forthright.

These background-building suggestions may close with mention of Christopher Caudwell's seminal volume, *Illusion and Reality*, which sets up milestones new to most American readers as it traces the course of poetry from the primitive past through an obscured present to an idealized future. A work of creative genius and encyclopedic range, this is the first comprehensive attempt to work out a Marxist theory of art. As the subtitle makes clear, it is not a study of poetry but a study of "the sources of poetry"; and it finds those sources in the social life of man, as this is shaped by environment, by instinctive forces of consciousness, and by pervading, restricting influences of class domination, for the unyielding absolutism of Marxist doctrine receives emphasis throughout. Ardor of enthusiasm and universality of learning give fascination to this remarkable exposition, which centers on the ideological conflict of the present day and closes in glowing prophetic assurance of a future in which the poet will enter as never before into "realization of all the values contained in the relations of human beings in real life." The book went almost unnoticed when it was first published in London in 1937, just after the author's death, but within a decade had been recognized as a Marxist classic. If, as Hyman indicates, Caudwell is to stand as "the most genuinely important Marxist cultural thinker of our time," it is desirable that his work should be known to librarians and made available in libraries.

There is no single comprehensive bibliographical aid in the selection of poetry; but the great variety of existing lists and the representation given to the subject in the standard aids afford adequate guidance and suggestion. The *Bookman's Manual* in the already mentioned chapters covers the better-known older, standard, and contemporary English and American poets, and provides a fine basis for personal study or for limited selection.

A FEW BOOKS AND ESSAYS ABOUT POETRY [3]

Arnold, Matthew. "The Study of Poetry." In his *Essays in Criticism: second series.* New York, The Macmillan Company, 1924.

Auslander, Joseph, and F. E. Hill. The Winged Horse: the story of the poets and their poetry. New York, Doubleday, 1927; Odyssey, 1929.

Brooks, Cleanth. The Well Wrought Urn: studies in the structure of poetry. New York, Reynal & Hitchcock, 1947.

Caudwell, Christopher. Illusion and Reality: a study of the sources of poetry. New York, International Publishers, 1947.

Coffin, Robert P. Tristram. The Substance That Is Poetry. New York, The Macmillan Company, 1940.

Coleridge, S. T. Biographia literaria. (Particularly, chapters 14, 16, and 18). New York, E. P. Dutton & Co.: "Everyman's Library."

Day-Lewis, Cecil. A Hope for Poetry: a reprint with a postscript. Forest Hills, N.Y., Transatlantic Arts, 1936; 5th ed., 1942.

De la Mare, Walter. Poetry in Prose: the Warton lecture on English poetry, 1935. New York, Oxford University Press, 1936.

[3] In the "List of Twenty-five Books of Significant Modern Criticism," given in the preceding chapter, the books by Blackmur, Eliot, Empson, Lowes, Read, Tate, and Winters are equally relevant to Poetry.

Drew, Elizabeth. Discovering Poetry. New York, W. W. Norton & Co, 1933.
—— and J. L. Sweeney. Directions in Modern Poetry. New York, W. W. Norton & Co., 1940.
Eastman, Max. The Enjoyment of Poetry. New ed. New York, Charles Scribner's Sons, 1939.
Gregory, Horace, and Marya Zaturenska. A History of American Poetry, 1900–1940. New York, Harcourt, Brace & Co., 1946.
Housman, A. E. The Name and Nature of Poetry. New York, The Macmillan Company, 1933.
Lowell, Amy. Tendencies in Modern American Poetry. Boston, Houghton Mifflin Company, 1917.
Lowes, John Livingston. Convention and Revolt in Poetry. Boston, Houghton Mifflin Company, 1921.
MacNeice, Louis. Modern Poetry: a personal essay. New York, Oxford University Press, 1938.
Masefield, John. Poetry. New York, The Macmillan Company, 1932.
Poets at Work: essays based on the modern poetry collection at the Lockwood Memorial Library, University of Buffalo, by Rudolf Arnheim, W. H. Auden, Karl Shapiro, Donald A. Stauffer. New York, Harcourt, Brace & Co., 1948.
Rylands, G. H. W. Words and Poetry. New York, Payson & Clark, 1928.
Russell, George ("A. E."). Song and Its Fountains. New York, The Macmillan Company, 1932.
Stauffer, Donald A. The Nature of Poetry. New York, W. W. Norton & Co., 1946.
Watts-Dunton, Theodore. Poetry and the Renascence of Wonder. New York, E. P. Dutton & Co., 1916.
Wells, Henry Willis. New Poets from Old: a study in literary genetics. New York, Columbia University Press, 1940.

FIFTY NAMES CHOSEN TO INDICATE PATTERNS AND VARIATIONS IN MODERN POETRY

Aiken, Conrad. The Kid. 1947.
Auden, W. S. The Age of Anxiety: a baroque eclogue. 1947.
Benét, Stephen Vincent. Western Star. 1943.
Bevington, Helen. Dr. Johnson's Waterfall, and other poems. 1946.
Bridges, Robert. The Testament of Beauty. 1930.

POETRY

Crane, Hart. Collected Poems: in "Black and Gold Library." 1948.
Cullen, Countee. On These I Stand. 1947.
Cummings, E. E. Collected Poems. 1938.
Davies, W. H. Collected Poems; introd. by Osbert Sitwell. 1946.
Day-Lewis, Cecil. Short is the Time: poems 1936–1943. 1945.
De la Mare, Walter. The Burning-Glass: new poems, including "The Traveller." 1945.
Dickinson, Emily. Bolts of Melody: new poems; ed. by Mabel Loomis Todd and Millicent Todd Bingham. 1945.
Eliot, T. S. Four Quartets. 1943.
Fearing, Kenneth. Afternoon of a Pawnbroker, and other poems. 1943.
Frost, Robert. Complete Poems. New collected ed. 1949.
Godden, Rumer. In Noah's Ark. 1949.
Graves, Robert. Poems, 1938–1945. 1946.
"H. D." (Hilda Doolittle). Collected Poems. New ed. 1940.
Hopkins, Gerard Manley. Poems; ed. by Robert Bridges. 2d ed. 1937.
Housman, A. E. Collected Poems. 1940.
Hughes, Langston. Fields of Wonder. 1947.
Humphries, Rolfe. The Wind of Time. 1949.
Jeffers, Robinson. Selected Poetry. 1938.
Lowell, Robert. Lord Weary's Castle. 1946.
MacLeish, Archibald. Conquistador. 1932.
MacNeice, Louis. Springboard: poems, 1941–1944. 1945.
Miles, Josephine. Lines at Intersection. 1939.
Millay, Edna St. Vincent. Collected Lyrics. 1948.
Miller, Alice Duer. The White Cliffs. 1940.
Moore, Marianne. Nevertheless. 1944.
Nash, Ogden. Many Long Years Ago: poems from five early volumes. 1945.
Pound, Ezra. The Cantos, I through LXXXIV. 1947.
Ransom, John Crowe. Selected Poems. 1945.
Robinson, Edwin Arlington. Collected Poems. New ed. 1937, 1946.
Rukeyser, Muriel. The Green Wave. 1948.
Sandburg, Carl. The People, Yes. 1936.
Schwartz, Delmore. In Dreams Begin Responsibilities. 1938.
Shapiro, Karl. Essay on Rime. 1945.
Sitwell, Edith. Street Songs. 1942.
Spender, Stephen. Poems of Dedication. 1947.
Stevens, Wallace. Ideas of Order. New ed. 1936.
Taggard, Genevieve. Calling Western Union. 1936.
Tate, Allen. Poems, 1922–1947. Definitive ed. 1948.

Thomas, Dylan. Selected Writings; introd. by J. L. Sweeney. 1946.
Viereck, Peter. Terror and Decorum: poems, 1940–1948. 1948.
Walker, Margaret. For My People: foreword by Stephen Vincent Benét. 1942.
White, E. B. The Fox of Peapack, and other poems. 1938.
Williams, William Carlos. Selected Poems; introd. by Randall Jarrell. 1949.
Wylie, Elinor. Last Poems. 1933.
Yeats, W. B. Collected Poems. 1933.

20. Drama

> Modern tragedy does not deal with wrong and just vengeance, which are both, if conceived absolutely, pure fictions of our deep-rooted desire for superiority and violence. It is inspired by compassion. And it seeks to derive the tragic element in human life from the mistakes and self-imposed compulsions, not from the sins, of men. . . . In the serener realm of art the modern idea of tragedy is very sure to make its gradual appeal to the hearts of men. Guilt and punishment will be definitely banished to melodrama, where they belong. Tragedy will seek increasingly to understand our failures and our sorrows.
> Ludwig Lewisohn: "A Note on Tragedy,"
> in *A Book of Modern Criticism*

THERE ARE SEVERAL aspects from which library selection in the literature of drama demands consideration. Drama as a whole is a subject of steadily growing extent and importance. Within a quarter century its public has enormously increased and it has become established as one of the most vital influences in community life and in education. Its significances and relationships are manifold—as literature, as art, as a profession, as a craft, and as a social force. Fundamentally, drama is one with poetry and the dance, as the oldest form of emotional expression, conveyed through the combination of words, music (rhythm), and bodily motion. Under accepted library classifications these components are separated: music is one of the great divisions of the Fine Arts; the technique of the theatre, in costume, stagecraft, mechanics of production, and the actor's art, is also placed among the Fine Arts, as is the technology of the moving picture (the rising star of television finds its orbit mainly in Useful Arts); drama, in the sense of the play itself as a work of creative literary art and in the sense of dramatic history, commentary, and criticism, is one of the subdivisions of Literature. There is, of course, constant interrelation between books that deal with the art of the theatre and the literature of drama in which that art finds expression, and many works may with equal propriety be assigned to either class; but the distinction between the two is obvious. Both must be included in any survey of the extensive and varied literature from which even a small library should seek to satisfy existing demands and develop the potential interest of a public which is more and more awakening to the aesthetic, social, and intellectual influences of drama.

The place that drama holds in American life today has been established through the continued and mounting activity of the noncommercial theatre movement, with its evolutionary advance from "little" theatres, "art" theatres, and producing groups of every size and kind to the "community" theatres that justify their name in cities and towns all over the country; through the development of play writing, acting, and play production in schools, colleges, and universities; and through the immense increase in the supply of printed plays and in the public that reads and discusses them.

Much of this early development was due to the activities and influence of the Drama League. This organization, founded in 1910, had for its objectives the encouragement of drama as a high form of art, the support of such plays as were considered worthy of approval, the dissemination of information concerning drama and its literature, and the fostering of all means that would aid in the development of drama in the life of the people as a medium of individual expression and community cooperation. During the first few years of the League's work its chief endeavor was to increase playgoing and thus build up public support of good drama. This was followed by effort to foster the study of drama through cooperation with study clubs and libraries throughout the country, and by systematic encouragement of the Little Theatre movement, initiated at the Drama League convention of 1913. When that convention was held only three or four "little theatres" were in existence in the United States. In 1929, Kenneth Macgowan, in his *Footlights across America*, estimated that approximately 13,000 noncommercial organizations or groups were engaged in "little theatre" or kindred dramatic activities, that some 335,000 workers were enlisted in these various theatrical avocations, and that the audiences to which they appealed numbered some twelve million persons.

This was at the glittering peak of the first postwar prosperity era. Then came sudden downfall from the pinnacle of self-deluding pride and success into the abyss of penury, unemployment, privation, bewilderment, and despair. The Great Depression strewed wreckage through the professional world of the theatre, but it seeded and fertilized the growth of drama in vast areas of everyday living and released creative forces of truth, of imagination, and of social consciousness that opened new paths to recovery and broadened the horizon of the arts. Of special significance was the Federal Theatre Project initiated in August, 1935, under the Works Progress Administration, with Hallie Flanagan, head of Vassar's experimental theatre, as director. *Arena*, published in 1940, is her vivid, moving report of the accomplishments and vicissitudes of this memorable enterprise, which, by implication at least, remains a step toward a national theatre. This, with its allied undertakings—the Writers Project, the Art Project, the Music Project—was part of President Roosevelt's great reconstruction campaign of practical inventiveness, bold experiment, unflagging devotion, and deep humanitarianism, which reached into millions of damaged lives and brought them hope and incentive. It came into being, says Hallie Flanagan, because the government "took the position that the talents of these professional theatre workers, together with the skills of painters, musicians, and writers, made up a part of the national wealth which America could not afford to lose." The Federal Theatre was brought to an end by act of Congress in midsummer of 1939, mainly as a political scapegoat for red-baiting legislators. Its four years of dynamic existence tried out new forms and original methods of production, turned immediate problems of the day into thought-provoking visualization, brought work and opportunity to approximately 12,500 actors, gave unstinted recognition to the talents of Negro players; carried its performances to all parts of the country, from northern lumber settlements and far-western prairies to deep South bottom land, and reached an audience of from twenty to twenty-five million persons, most of whom had never before seen an "acted play."

The Federal Theatre was planned to be a "free uncensored adult theatre," and in large measure fulfilled this purpose. Its effect on the stage, on playwriting, on social consciousness and political thought can only be estimated in the perspective of history-in-the-making, but certainly it was the most far-reaching influence for social reform measures ever released with such concentration and such impact. Plays new and old were drawn upon; classic and experimental drama alike found representation. Colorful patterns of regional folk-life, grim social problems of oppression and persecution, were brought to vivid actuality in the original work of young playwrights. And technical innovations turned current events into exciting drama. Most notable was the "living newspaper," a dramatic form mingling techniques of theatre, radio play, and documentary newsreel, in which living actors, music, light, movement conveyed, in *Power*, the transfer of natural resources into power, and the struggle for control of that power, with the ideals and development of the Tennessee Valley Authority as underlying theme; in *One-Third of a Nation*, the degradation and evils of slum living and beginning of government effort for slum clearance.

These were years of protest and revolt. So-called "radicalism" intensified as the harsh realities of the Depression merged into the deepening conflict of fascism and democracy and the cataclysm of the Second World War brought the opposed forces of communism and capitalism together in alliance and victory. Left-wing drama evoked all phases of the conflict, from Clifford Odets' flashlight shots of union terrorism in *Waiting for Lefty*, and the unmitigated tragedy and horror of his *Till the Day I Die*, set in Hitlerized Berlin, to Irwin Shaw's poignant fantasy, *Bury the Dead*, in which six dead soldiers refuse to be buried until the living are wakened to realization of the horror and waste of war. Marxism is a strong element in present-day drama, as it is in every aspect of literature, and the work of many leading playwrights of the war and postwar period is communist in sympathies. Effective propaganda drama has intense theatrical vitality; has drive and electric thrill of emotional conviction. It stirs feeling; it often instills a realization of man's cruelties and stupidities that incites to remedial action. But also propaganda sets forth only a single aspect of its theme; it magnifies and distorts, eludes balanced judgment and offers only material—however valuable—chosen to prove its thesis. There should, however, be no contemptuous dismissal of propaganda drama. There should be recognition that its values depend upon its objectives, its ethical standards; and upon how honestly and usefully it presents realities and clarifies confused judgment.

Many and ingenious are the means by which community interest in drama has been stimulated and extended. The Drama League was founded as a national organization, with local centers in all communities that desired to establish them. From its educational department it launched study courses and lectures to cooperating groups and gave impetus to the demand for printed plays. It published an official monthly bulletin, established prizes for play writing, and fostered competitive play production contests. Through its local centers it published also local bulletins and developed a special "Little Theatre Service," with monthly play lists and news-letters. In 1922 it initiated "national drama week," still observed each year by schools, colleges, churches, and little-theatre groups. The twenty years from 1910 to 1930 cover its useful functioning. Since then a pervasive process of decentralization and interdependence has brought the enlarging body of little theatres, community theatres, and other amateur dramatic organizations into fruitful coordination and cooperation.

From the first National Little Theatre Tournament, organized in New York in 1923, has developed a network of competitive play production events, interscholastic, intercollegiate, and intercommunity, conducted through cooperating organizations and groups throughout the country. The National Theatre Conference, since 1936 the leading group representative of college and university theatres (with headquarters at Western Reserve University), directs its energies toward the development and extension of the nonprofit community theatre and the stimulation of public familiarity with the best in dramatic literature. Latest comer in the field, dedicated to the achievement of a vital national theatre for the United States, is the American National Theatre and Academy, known as ANTA. Established by act of Congress in 1935, when its charter was signed by President Roosevelt on July 5, this was defined in the preamble as "a people's project, organized and conducted in their interest, free from commercialism, but with the firm intent of being as far as possible self-supporting." The professional theatre was not represented among its incorporators. No appropriations were asked from Congress, and for the eleven years during which first the Federal Theatre and then World War II held the national stage ANTA remained dormant. Reorganized and revitalized in 1946, with Vinton Freedley, Robert Sherwood, Gilbert Miller, Rosamond Gilder, and C. Lawton Campbell officers of its directorate, and with quarters at 139 West 44th Street, New York, it carries on multifarious activities: revival of the New York Experimental Theatre, sponsorship of regional projects, surveys and reports on productions, plans for state theatres, for a national yearly drama festival, for regional and national awards for playwrights. It maintains close cooperation with other theatre organizations, such as the National Theatre Conference, the American Educational Theatre Association, and the National Association of Teachers of Speech. Far-reaching among the plans taking shape was the designation of March, 1950, as International Theatre Month, to be devoted, under sponsorship of Unesco in cooperation with ANTA, to a nationwide program enlisting theatre organizations of every form and kind and centered on the theme of peace through international understanding and the universal rights of man. This idea was launched at the International Theatre Congress in Zurich in the summer of 1949, and its worldwide application is envisioned by Unesco as a means of strengthening the mutual understanding and good-will that alone can achieve and maintain world peace.

The sustained impulse to the study and practice of dramatic art given by the colleges and universities has been a vital factor in all

DRAMA 481

this development. Creative work in drama, long encouraged at Harvard and Yale, has taken root and flowered throughout the world of education. Fresh, vigorous young talent is poured into playwriting, into theatrical designing and direction, while acting by the student body as a whole not only stimulates appreciation of drama as literature and art but is fostered as one of the most effective means of imparting grace and ease in diction and manner. From Professor Baker's famous "47 Workshop," at Harvard—the first American university to make study and technique of the drama a part of its regular curriculum—may be drawn a long list of the playwrights who have made the modern American theatre; and today there are few universities that do not count the dramatic laboratory and the theatrical workshop as within their orbit. The playwriting and production of the University of Wisconsin groups, the folk-play achievements of the University of North Carolina, the range of dramatic work done at the University of Washington are notable among the many far-spreading seedbeds from which drama has been implanted into American life.

Effective library service sustains and reflects this community interest in drama. Indeed, the community theatre movement in its present nationwide sweep has an integral relationship to the public library as an institution for and of the people, democratic, nonprofit, educational, social, and recreational, representing a cross section of the entire community drawn together by a common interest. It is part of a development that through many different channels—music, art, architecture, city planning, public recreation—is bringing beauty and imagination into American life; holding promise also of that illumination and enrichment of individual capacities in which the public library may fulfill its purpose and ideal. Many of the larger libraries maintain an extensive "drama service," designed to meet the needs of professionals and amateurs alike and to attract and interest the general reader. Besides full and varied representation of the literature of the stage and of drama in its diverse aspects, theatrical periodicals, bibliographies, indexes, and reference aids, such material as clippings, pictures, programs, bulletins, play analyses, and lists, is organized and made accessible. The extent and specialization of such a collection depends, of course, upon the "drama consciousness" of the public it serves. But in a community where interest in drama finds any manifestation whatever, even the smallest public library should stimulate and strengthen that interest by building up a well-chosen and serviceable, even though closely limited, drama collection.

So extensive is the literature that deals with dramatic art and the stage that only a few of its varied phases can here be indicated. Its volume constantly increases. The motion picture, of course, has brought an inflow of books on the various mechanical aspects of the cinema, as well as on its history and influence, on scenario writing and production, and on present developments and future possibilities in television, sound projection, and other invention and experimentation. Radio has its own distinctive literature in "radio plays," either original or condensed or abstracted from other material, but most of this requires minor representation. With the revival of puppetry has come an appreciable increase in the literature devoted to that ancient art, in its earlier and modern manifestations. And there is always the fundamental "background" literature, older, standard, and contemporary—aesthetic, historical, biographical, and critical —not to mention the vast stores of printed material that have been built up about such subjects as Greek drama, medieval miracle and mystery plays, or the work of Shakespeare.

The scope of a representative drama collection in a large library may be roughly summarized as including history of drama, essays and studies on the theatre, dramatic criticism, theatrical biography, single plays, collections of plays, manuals of playwriting and dramatic technique, works on amateur theatricals, community drama and pageantry, puppetry and pantomime, Shakespeare, opera, scenario writing, motion pictures, lists of plays, reference books, and bound periodicals. Such a collection would include works about the Greek, English, French, German, Italian, Spanish, Yiddish, Russian, Chinese, Japanese, and Javanese theatres; and examples of drama from classic, oriental, and nearly all European languages, as well as

Hebrew and Yiddish. Its books would almost surely range in date through at least the last three centuries; with some curious or valuable or interesting publications of the eighteenth century and a considerable bulk of standard nineteenth-century works, besides the dominant body—as widely varied and judiciously balanced as possible—of contemporary and current literature.

In smaller libraries the supply of background literature will be necessarily much more limited. Here selection must center upon obvious and immediate interests of the library users. It should be directed also to establishing foundations for the understanding and appreciation of drama, not only as a means of individual self-expression, or as emotional recognition of familiar experience, but for illumination of the new directions and dimensions of human history taking shape today, and as stimulus to deeper realization of the universals of human nature, to clearer thinking, and to a more ordered living.

In its most exact and deepest significance the true literature of drama is the play itself: the art and achievement of the playwright. From the ancient Greeks to Eugene O'Neill, great plays have been great literature; like great poetry, like great fiction, they are the expression in words of the creative imagination. They live as literature long after time has abolished the stage on which they made their first appeal. Indeed, the reading and discussion of contemporary plays is virtually the reading and discussion of contemporary literature. Dramatists are novelists and poets quite as often and as notably as they are dramatists; such names as Shaw, Galsworthy, Barrie, Ervine, Maugham, Dunsany, Capek, Bynner, Tarkington, Wilder, Saroyan, Steinbeck, are evidence of this interrelationship. Today important plays are issued in book form as soon as they are produced, sometimes, as in the case of O'Neill's *Lazarus Laughed*, before their stage presentation; and they are as promptly reviewed and as widely discussed as are new novels.

The rise of the printed play to popularity with an ever widening reading public has been one of the striking incidents of modern book history. Until 1910 very few plays appeared in book form and there were few good collections of the drama of the day. It was in that year that Clayton Hamilton, in his critical study, *The Theory of the Theatre*, remarked: "Very few plays are printed nowadays, and those few are rarely read: seldom do they receive as careful critical consideration as even third-class novels." Comparison of the *A.L.A. Catalog, 1904*, with the *A.L.A. Catalog, 1926*, affords significant contrast. In the 1904 volume, American drama was represented only by two of W. D. Howells' farces. The 1926 volume records forty-two titles, with many more indicated in the annotations. In the 1904 volume, English drama including Shakespeare received thirty-two entries; in 1926, there were one hundred and fifty entries.

Consider how rich, how diversified, this literature of drama is. It ranges from the symbolic dramatic poem, the airy wisp of fantasy, to the clear-cut acting play that is visual and emotional, but not literary. It draws from the racial store of the whole world, sets before us with humor, irony, passion, and understanding the ebb and flow of human experience, and reflects and interprets human problems that, however individual their manifestation, are yet universal. Contemporary drama is like contemporary poetry and contemporary fiction. It has cast off formalism and convention to expand in diversity and anarchy and has become a mold into which almost anything may be poured—opinion, sermon, tract, theory, fancy, fact. Its one compulsion is the compulsion to interest; to illuminate, to interpret, some aspect of life, some fundamental quality of human nature. There is much more fine drama today than ever before, except in the flowering time of the Greeks and the Elizabethans. Compare modern drama with that which prevailed through most of the nineteenth century: the contrast between them is like that of a living, surging, eddying stream beside an artificial lake, shallow, stagnant, and carefully diked.

All literature today reflects the immense breaking up of past stabilities. It was said of *The Education of Henry Adams* that Boston for a million three hundred thousand years lay in the ice age; then came the Adamses. With the coming of the twentieth century our ice age has broken fast; few surfaces remain uncracked. And the great ice breakers, who questioned, challenged, and thrust aside old compulsions and traditions, were Henrik Ibsen, George Bernard Shaw, and H. G. Wells. They were inspirers and thought molders of a generation that has seen its own life shadows lengthen and strange new portents rise on changed horizons. And of the three, the two dramatists, Ibsen and Shaw, were the first to crack and upheave the ancestral ice.

Ibsen's centenary was celebrated in 1928. Recognition of his plays in England came in the early nineties, and before the turn of the century his somber ruthless reason, his logic and realism, had begun to affect English and American thought. His plays went to the roots of living: relentlessly he showed hypocrisies and falsities and deliberate blindness warping marriage, sapping the family, corrupting civic affairs. His plays no longer carry their stunning impact: established in the accepted dramatic literature of the world, they have now a timeworn familiarity; but the seed he sowed still germinates. Shaw must be counted as the next great influence to Ibsen. He was Ibsen's first expositor in England (in his *Quintessence of Ibsenism*, in 1899), his disciple, and a builder on Ibsen's foundations. Through his plays, with their mercurial wit, audacity, irresponsibility, scorn, satire, and paradoxical absurdities, he overturned conventional and traditional attitudes toward marriage, sex, relations of parents and children, medicine, religion, law, and social problems in general. Never consistent, he was yet always the reformer, biting, sardonic, bound by no scruples. For all the sparkle of his humor, there is little joy in Shaw, no tenderness, no sympathy with minor human foibles and indulgences, but a keen, piercing penetration of social weaknesses and shams, and a dauntless unquenchable spirit, often turned to freakishness because unable to grasp the meaning of modern science in relation to the modern world. The influence of Wells, running alongside that of Shaw, has been exercised in large measure through his novels, but particularly through his *Outline of History*. It is an influence that carried further into the immediate present than has Shaw's, because it recognized science as the instrument through which truth must be studied and tested. To the work of these three iconoclasts may be traced many of the strongest undercurrents that have shaped the course of present-day dramatists and novelists.

Effect of the Depression on American drama has been indicated as intensifying protest against social injustice, strengthening proletarian revolt and stimulating communism. The war years that followed brought drama that differed strongly from the plays of the First World War. Then the most representative opposed responses were made by Robert C. Sherriff's *Journey's End*—poignant but gentle realism infused with self-sacrifice—and *What Price Glory?* where Maxwell Anderson and Lawrence Stallings with disillusioned realism, lush profanity, and barracks ribaldry evoked the private enmities and underlying comradeship of two hardboiled fellow soldiers, though a different note was struck in Robert Sherwood's *Idiot's Delight*, portent of the grim war shadow then (1936) fast rising over Europe.

In the plays of World War II there was a broader range into political backgrounds. With disillusion, bitterness, and pity there was a deep sense of the heroic in common human nature, and a fundamental realization of the tragic irony and futility of war as a solution for the world's problems. Lillian Hellman's *The Searching Wind* was both retrospect and indictment; her *Watch on the Rhine*, humanly vital anti-Nazi drama, set in Washington, maintained absorbing tension without sensationalism. Maxwell Anderson's *The Eve of St. Mark*, the first notable play to deal with the United States at war, gave thoughtful expression to the common experiences and responses of an everyday New York State family—clear, coherent, truthful, with remarkable insight into the hidden, almost unrealized, loyalties and ideals that send men to death and make those who love them accept loss and sacrifice.

Plays of the early postwar years seem to have found their dominating note in the disintegration of basic values of human life under the influences of a capitalistic society, through class violence and race discrimination, through poverty, ignorance, and degradation of living, and through psychosexual abnormalities, perversions, and violences; while in virtually all present-day drama the sex element receives an uninhibited expression and an audience acceptance which reveal the transformation in social standards and general mores that has come into being since the turn of the century. Arthur Miller's *Death of a Salesman*, Lillian Hellman's *Little Foxes* and *Another Part of the Forest*, O'Neill's *The Iceman Cometh*, Tennessee Williams' *The Glass Menagerie* and *A Streetcar Named Desire* are representative of the drama that applies ruthless shock treatment to a society seen as festering in greed, or despair, or self-created tragedy. Indeed, these undercurrents of social consciousness run through nearly all postwar drama, from serious play to musical comedy—as witness the ripples of whimsical satire that in *Finian's Rainbow* sparkle on America's racial dilemma, and that in the tropical charm and gayety of *South Pacific* glint with ironic understanding on inborn or acquired prejudice against race or color.

So varied and far-ranging in content and form is drama today that older conventional definitions seem no longer adequate. Such characterizations as tragedy, melodrama, comedy, farce, are too limited for the literature in which Shaw clashes the cymbals of mountebank and scatters the ashes of denunciation and prophecy; or Sean O'Casey, with poetic mysticism, biting humor, and turbulent realism brings the red roses of communism in tribute to youth divided by revolution and united by death; or O'Neill lifts the mask beneath which man's inner selves writhe in conflict; or Pirandello offers subtle bewildering answers to the enigma of personality. Thus there has been constant multiplication and differentiation in forms and types. The major forms—such as realistic drama, poetic drama, symbolic drama, historical drama—have flourished, branched out, and borne new fruit of many colors and exotic flavors. The problem play, the thesis play, the satirical fantasy, the social comedy, all the familiar types, are still with us, but transformed, diversified, invested with different meanings, penetrating with the X-rays of modern psychology always more deeply into life and human nature.

In discriminating selection there must be understanding of the particular type of drama to which a play belongs, or the aspect of life with which it is concerned. Historical drama is a form that in its implications carries us back to Shakespeare, to Schiller, to Bulwer; but it includes many variant and opposed types, from Drinkwater's *Abraham Lincoln*, in which are mingled pageant, epic, and symbolic drama, and Sherwood's *Road to Rome*, with its satirical rendering of a historic theme in terms of present-day speech and ironic gayety, to Maxwell Anderson's many-faceted tragedy of Anne Boleyn, *Anne of the Thousand Days*, absorbing, valid study of two historic personalities brought to impetuous life. Finer differences and distinctions may be drawn by comparison of plays dealing with the same theme—say, Shaw's *Saint Joan*, with its double thread of historic fact and modern social and intellectual significance, and Edward Garnett's *Trial of Jeanne d'Arc*, which by its very historical exactitude fails to convey the emotional intensity necessary for stage success. History merges into biography in the literature of drama just as it does in the literature of fact. The impulse given by Lytton Strachey that brought Queen Victoria and Queen Elizabeth to life on the stage is delightfully evident in the two substantial volumes of short plays, *Victoria Regina* and *The Golden Sovereign*, in which Laurence Housman has enshrined the Victorian age. Here are both retrospect of history and distillation of character study, firm in historical authenticity, keen in psychological insight, illuminating with humorous perception shadowy familiar figures that were landmarks in a past not so remote in years but now quaintly prehistoric.

"Drama of ideas" is a broad term, covering much work of modern playwrights that stems from the older days of so-called "problem" or "thesis" plays. All of Galsworthy's plays are plays of ideas; ideas that in their essence are subversive of most of the complacencies and acceptances that we call civilized. So are the plays of Maxwell Anderson, whether in the noble verse he has made his chosen medium or in the idiom of common speech. *Winterset*, his memorial echo of the Sacco-Vanzetti tragedy, takes from materials of contemporary life the failure of justice and the futility of both crime and revenge, and molds them into drama which replaces stark realism and harsh prose by the tragic poetry that was the medium of the great dramatists of the past. *Both Your Houses* with gusto, realism, and ruthless humor offers irrefutable and devastating commentary on processes of democratic government, as it follows through a Congressional committee the course of an appropriations bill manipulated into a pork barrel measure. Here also Eugene O'Neill, Ervine, Maugham, Sidney Howard, Priestley, Lillian Hellman, are among the accomplished playwrights who render with varying shades of power, skill, and irony problems of experience and complexities of character, and challenge evils of economic injustice, of class and race conflict.

Primarily subjective in theme and treatment is the "cerebral drama," essentially intellectual rather than emotional, applying metaphysical and psychological subtleties to crucial human problems, often tinged with symbolism or fantasy, unusual in expression. Pirandello is a master here of the theme of man's creation of illusion in unconscious endeavor to escape self-identity. But Eugene O'Neill stands supreme as begetter of the drama built on the framework of the Freudian psychology which has infused its interpretation of human character and conduct into every branch of literature, art, and science. O'Neill's plays, so strong in tragic realism, seek also to transcend literal realism by some ultimate gleam of joy and beauty. A letter quoted by George Jean Nathan in his *Intimate Notebooks* gives O'Neill's own indication of his purpose:

The playwright today must dig at the roots of the sickness of today as he feels it—the death of the old God and the failure of science and materialism to give any satisfying new one for the surviving primitive religious instinct to find a meaning for life in, and to comfort the fears of death with. It seems to me that anyone trying to do big work nowadays must have this big subject behind all the little subjects of his plays or novels, or he is simply scribbling around the surface of things.

In closest relationship to this subjective drama are the expressionistic plays, perhaps the most striking modern development of the playwright's art. The mechanical ingenuities of modern stagecraft, which have so mastered the production of illusion by the use of light, have been chief factors in their stage success; but stagecraft alone cannot make expressionistic drama. It represents the effort of the playwright to set before us a state of mind, to visualize thoughts, to invest ideas and imaginings and abstract principles with the intensity of actuality. O'Neill did this in *The Emperor Jones*, where memories and terrors, the product of experience and race heredity, are made as vivid to the perceptions of the audience as they are to the tortured mind of the fugitive. The expressionism of Elmer Rice in *The Adding Machine* visualized both individual thoughts and impulses and abstract principles. Through these and other early examples (with German and Russian playwrights as pioneer influences) expressionism established the modernistic drama that in its extreme manifestations, such as the plays of E. E. Cummings and John Dos Passos, is a sort of visual, symbolic shorthand, as obscure and elliptic as the work of the extreme experimentalists in poetry and in fiction. Here Jean-Paul Sartre, leader of the French existentialists, plumbs ultimate depths of horror in *No Exit*—where after death three people live on in the hell they had made for others, trapped forever in a room with no exit.

Much poetic drama of fantasy and imagination however, remains little affected by expressionism. Barrie has his domain here, with the delicate haunting emanations of *Dear Brutus* and *Mary Rose;* Lord Dunsany, his wonder world of enchanted destiny; Yeats, his legendry of fairyland. Sean O'Casey, in *Within the Gates*, set a more complex pattern, combining poetic fantasy, pageant, epic, and melodrama into what might be called a futurist morality play. Allegory, satire, and warning were brilliantly conveyed in Capek's *R.U.R.*, which with electric impact projected the word "robot" into the world's social and political vocabulary. And simple allegory of freshness, charm, and delightful absurdity wove a thread of philosophic truth into Thornton Wilder's delicate, fantastic fable, *The Skin of Our Teeth*, in which man's course on earth is traced from ice age and Deluge through world war, horror, and reign of death, to emergence with the unconquerable will, the inextinguishable purpose, of building a new world. None of these characterizations quite fit the plays of William Saroyan, compounded of laughter, pity, adolescence, wisdom, and unintelligibility, and defined by George Jean Nathan as "a vaudeville of humanity that goes deep under mankind's grease-paint."

One of the richest fields of contemporary drama is that in which racial traits, deep-rooted folkways, and race psychology are revealed by playwrights native to the life they portray. Here are many famous older plays: of Björnson, of Hauptmann, of Echegaray, of Tolstoy, of Chekhov, whose *Cherry Orchard* remains the amber matrix in which lies imbedded the moth-winged soul of a vanished Russia. Here the flooding genius and inexhaustible vitality of Soviet drama (Martin Flavin called it "the only real living theatre in the world today") poured out by Mayakovsky, Korneichuk, Leonov, Ivanov, Simonov, Afinogenov and many more, is becoming more available in English translation, particularly in anthologies. Contemporary Spain is glimpsed in the plays of Benavente, ironic and satirical or fierce torrential tragedy, and in Martínez Sierra's delicate, wistful idylls of Catholic faith. Irish life is seen in many aspects through the work of Lady Gregory, Synge, O'Casey, Lennox Robinson. Yiddish folk drama offers harsh, simple, sordid scenes, picturesque customs, and strange traditions of race experience, imbued with emotional intensity.

Chinese drama, sweeping back into a legendary past, steeped in tradition, belongs to a national symbolic art rather than to a national literature. It has increasing significance today as an influence in general theatrical technique and as China's importance in world culture is more widely recognized. For Chinese plays, rarely available in English translation, distill Chinese character and Chinese history. Lin Yutang says:

Through its immense popularity, the theatre has achieved a place in the national Chinese life very nearly corresponding to its logical place in an ideal republic. Apart from teaching the people an intense love of music, it has taught the Chinese people, over ninety percent of whom are illiterate, a knowledge of history truly amazing, crystallizing, as it were, the folklore and entire historical and literary tradition in plays of characters that have captured the heart and imagination of the common men and women.

An excellent introduction and guide is the volume, *Famous Chinese Plays*, translated and edited by L. C. Arlington and Harold Acton, which includes in translation and synopsis thirty-three plays of perennial popularity. Published in Peiping in 1937 (Henri Vetch), this is not commonly found in American libraries, and should justify a reprint edition.

Just as foreign fiction in English translation helps to remove the barriers of provincialism that shut out understanding and sympathy for other ways of living and different patterns of thought, so the many translations of foreign drama help to widen knowledge of other backgrounds than our own, and may contribute in time to building a stage of civilization above the plane of national hatreds.

American folk drama gains constantly in volume and significance. It should have careful attention in selection. Just as in "local color" American fiction the immense and vivid panorama of our national life unrolls its pictures from the bayous of Louisiana to the plains of Wyoming and the glaciers of Alaska, so our native drama is drawing rich substance from the medley of race strains, the deep race roots of local custom, the sharply contrasted influences of different environments. It is building up a body of native folk drama, homely and earthborn, that reveals and interprets the strangely assorted elements, the fundamental diversities, of a nonhomogeneous people whose unity is a slow welding process enforced by time, by purpose, and by ideal. Much of this is literature more than it is drama; that is, it is suited for reading or for the little-theatre rather than for the professional stage. *Carolina Folk Plays*, edited by F. H. Koch; Percy MacKaye's *Kentucky Mountain Fantasies; Lonesome Road*, Paul Green's volume of plays for a Negro theatre; the first Oklahoma plays of Lynn Riggs (whose roadside idyl, *Green Grow the Lilacs*, of 1931, had its transfiguration in 1943 as the brilliant, poetic musical folk play, *Oklahoma!*), all are earlier examples that, while often crude in structural development or weak in sustained dramatic quality, nevertheless indicate the picturesque variety of scene and setting, the character vitality, and the pristine vigor that give power and beauty to the more perfected work of dramatists whose plays are indigenous to the environment they depict.

In the rich profusion of plays that transmit the American scene in its multifarious shapes and moods, its people, "assorted, human, warious," its speech, idiosyncrasies, taboos, aspirations, credos, I can note only two among the many that have become theatre classics: Thornton Wilder's *Our Town* (1938), sensitive, wistful, serene unfoldment of birth, life, love, marriage, and death in the little New Hampshire community of Grover's Corners, its stagecraft modeled on the Chinese fashion of *The Yellow Jacket*, its atmosphere a sublimation of the universals of living; and *Life With Father* (1939), the dramatization by Howard Lindsay and Russel Crouse of Clarence Day's imperishable family chronicle, which proved the most successful play in the history of the American theatre—"its enormous appeal," as Ward Morehouse says, "to be attributed to its universality and to the fact that everyone in the audience at every performance sees in the play something of himself or herself."

It is not strange that the printed play has come to wide popularity among readers. That popularity reached its peak in 1930, when the Cleveland Public Library reported that plays were being read in greater numbers than ever before, that readers, especially young people, were growing to like them as a form of literature, perhaps because they were all in dialogue, and that "play reading may now be dignified as a 'trend' of popular taste." Today, supplanted by radio and television, play reading represents a well established public interest, rather than an advancing trend. It has strong individual and personal appeal, and still keeps the place formerly held by the short story for reading aloud, at home or in groups, while the short story remains more limited to individual personal reading and to study for story-writing technique.

Probably a chief reason for the popularity of play reading is that the most original and important plays of the day must make their widest appeal in this way rather than through the theatre. Such plays seldom command commercial success except in the metropolitan areas. Indeed, it is only through their translation to the screen, in which process their full significance is too often lost or diminished, that they are likely to receive any commercial production whatever, outside the larger cities. Thus, plays that represent the most distinctive work of contemporary dramatists reach their largest audiences through either little-theatre or community productions, or through reading. Everyone who has access to a library may maintain his own private and personal theatre, in which the most comfortable chair is without price, the performances start on schedule time, the actors are always perfect, and the repertory offers the cream of the plays produced and admired at home and abroad, the play of the moment, and the revival of great drama of earlier days.

There is a double appeal in play reading. Those who know plays as literature usually desire whenever possible to see the plays they have enjoyed reading; and those who have seen plays that provoked thought or brought some unusual interpretation of life, are more fully satisfied if they are able to read them also and get a clearer and more penetrating apprehension of their lines, for the ear is less immediately impressible and transmits its message less instantly and coherently to the mind than does the eye. When a play is seen, its power, stimulus, enjoyment, come chiefly through the vision as it conveys color, emotion, and movement to the mind. When a play is read, meanings, beauties, and implications are almost always discovered in the lines themselves that were not fully apprehended in hearing them. Shakespeare, of course, is the fundamental example of this; but the plays of Bernard Shaw and of Eugene O'Neill certainly require to be read, quite as much as to be seen and heard.

A few groups or subjects in the literature of drama that demand special consideration in ordinary library selection may be briefly noted.

Collections of plays as varied and as extensive as possible are of first importance. There must be discriminating representation of different types, such as standard full-length plays, short plays, one-act plays, plays of different countries, different races, different historical periods, and different dramatic form, plays for church and classroom use, plays for women, and other selections made to meet specific needs. These collections have a twofold appeal to the public. They appeal to readers who find them more interesting and attractive than short stories, and they offer to all concerned with drama working material for amateur production, for group reading, for teaching, and for study. Both these aspects of use should be recognized and provided for. Just as with anthologies of essays, poems, and short stories, the great number of drama anthologies published enforces careful comparison and appraisal. While some duplication of contents is desirable, as a means of appeasing the continuous demand for certain individual plays and certain types of plays, it is more desirable that so far as possible collections should supplement one another and enlarge the whole field covered. In comparison of individual anthologies, the purpose, competence, and authority of the editor; the number of plays included, their variety, individual excellence, and the readability and effectiveness of their arrangement; and the interest and value of any accompanying critical, biographical, or bibliographical material, are the chief points to be considered.

There are, of course, standard anthologies such as those edited by Brander Matthews, W. A. Neilson, Montrose Moses, and T. H. Dickinson, that are foundation stones in any collection. There are specialized anthologies that have acquired permanent significance, such as Professor Baker's *Harvard Plays*, the *Provincetown Plays*, *Wisconsin Plays*, F. H. Koch's *Carolina Folk Plays*, his *American Folk Plays*, with settings in seventeen states, Canada, and Mexico; and the plays of the Moscow Art Theatre. Varied types of importance would include the anthologies of one-act plays by Frank Shay, Helen Cohen, Margaret Mayorga's annual volumes, *The Best One-Act Plays*, which began as biennials in 1941; William Kozlenko's collections, which embrace stage and radio plays; Betty

Smith's two volumes of nonroyalty one-acters; Gassner and Nichols' *Twenty Best Film Plays;* Norman Corwin's several volumes of radio plays; and Archibald MacLeish's experimental "verse plays for radio," with his later experiment at historical narrative via radio dramatic exposition, *The American Story: Ten Broadcasts* (1945). In any library the most indispensable anthology, which is index and reference aid as well as anthology, is Burns Mantle's series, "The Best Plays," in annual volumes published since 1920 and two ten-year volumes (1899–1909, and 1909–19). This gives for each year the compiler's selection of "the ten best plays" produced in New York, each play presented in summary and partial text, with a compact, comprehensive record and commentary for the other productions of the period. Burns Mantle, who founded and carried on this historic enterprise, died on February 9, 1948, and the succeeding volumes are edited by his former fellow-worker, John Chapman. The whole series is used so constantly and so variously that whenever practicable it should be made available in libraries both for circulation and for reference.

Individual plays require judicious representation. Particularly important are "collected plays" of established contemporary dramatists and distinctive work of newer playwrights that is not sufficiently accessible in anthologies. The individual plays of Dunsany, Synge, Anderson, Sherwood, Sidney Howard, and other first-rank dramatists, which have not appeared in group or collected form, should be in even a small library. Playwrights whose work has won the distinction of literary awards should have representation. Attention should also be paid to fine or unusual foreign drama appearing in English translation (Ansky's *The Dybbuk*, Werfel's *Goat Song*, and Molnar's *Liliom* are notable examples), and to current plays that in their stage success awaken interest in books. Besier's *The Barretts of Wimpole Street* drew many readers to the lives and work of the Brownings, just as *The Green Pastures* was an influence toward wider appreciation of the richness and significance of Negro folk literature. In selection for small libraries, however, the practical economy made possible by use of the anthology must be remembered, and plays that receive anthology representation need not ordinarily be purchased in individual form.

The classics; Shakespeare: Much of the great drama of the past has today become literature (or poetry) rather than drama. The Greek dramatists and the Elizabethans are more widely read by lovers or students of literature than by the public interested in present-day dramatic art. Only in large collections can this literature be fully represented; more limited selection should seek to provide satisfactory, readable editions of work that possesses established and continuing importance—the Greek dramatists in several of the best renderings, famous older continental and English drama, and a careful gleaning from the immense literature of Shakespeare. There must be generous and varied provision of Shakespeare's works. Even in a very small collection a good play-to-a-volume edition, a complete one-volume edition (duplicated for reference), and one of the standard editions in three or more volumes (preferably based on the Globe or Cambridge text) are minimum essentials, to be developed whenever possible to more representative proportions.

In dealing with the constant inflow of books about Shakespeare, freshness of viewpoint, sound scholarship, and spontaneity and interest in presentation are of first importance. Formalized, trite expositions, freakish theorizings, the delusions and cryptograms of Baconian and other "fixed-idea" enthusiasts, should be avoided in any limited selection. But as generous representation as possible should be given to the many and varied books that enrich and stimulate general and personal appreciation of Shakespeare. Pearsall Smith's informal commentary, sensitive, piquant, and sagacious, *On Reading Shakespeare;* and J. Dover Wilson's stimulating, soundly-based brief study, *The Essential Shakespeare* are examples of matter and manner that offer interest and pleasure to any intelligent reader. In the same category are *The Approach to Shakespeare,* J. W. Mackail's delightful lecture-directives to the pleasures and rewards of reading Shakespeare; and *Shakespeare without Tears,* Margaret Webster's animated discussion of the plays and the Elizabethan theatre, fruit of her rich background of theatrical experience and her conviction that Shakespeare should be enjoyed rather than revered.

Very different, a work of original scholarship, indispensable to students and of absorbing fascination to anyone who cares for literature, is Caroline Spurgeon's volume, *Shakespeare's Imagery and What It Tells Us*, which I should like to see in the Shakespeare collection of every library, large or small. Here—product of ten years' labor—is organized the result of an elaborate scientific analysis of the imagery found in all of Shakespeare's work, set in comparison with a similar analysis of the writings of Marlowe, of Bacon, and a group of leading Elizabethan writers, and revealing the personality, the mind and nature, of Shakespeare as it is expressed in his work. A remarkable set of colored charts enables the reader to trace and compare for himself contrasts and similarities in the work of Shakespeare and his chief contemporaries and to follow a new, significant approach to Shakespeare. But the cardinal value of Miss Spurgeon's work is that with lucent finality it sounds the death knell of the Baconian and kindred cryptogrammatic or acrostical hypotheses of Shakespeare's identity.

History of drama, books about the theatre, dramatic criticism and commentary need a varied representation that will both accord with demand and stimulate and develop interest. The list of "Fifty Books on Drama and the Theatre," that closes the present chapter, gives partial indication of the range, variety, and radiating values of the contemporary literature in these fields, which in its endless progression must have consideration in library book selection. In all limited selection, range and differentiation rather than repetition of subject are important. Thus, three books each dealing acceptably with a different phase in the history of drama (say, the American stage, continental drama, the Irish theatre) are preferable to three books devoted to the same specific subject (say, history of drama in America) and offering material that is fundamentally similar, though with variations in detail. It must be remembered, however, that as a collection expands or as specialized demand develops (and this is true in every field of literature) there must be continuous increment of material that judiciously supplements, amends, and enlarges its own substance of knowledge. Theatrical biography conveys both history and technique of dramatic art as well as personal experience. Here, as with dramatic criticism and commentary, experience and personality of the author, authority, originality, and charm of literary expression are chief considerations.

Manuals of playwriting (now usually inclusive of screen writing) are constantly in demand. Here sound authority, effective organization of material, and clear exposition are of prime importance, while mature critical judgment or provocative appraisal give confidence or incentive to playwrights and to students. Older basic works, such as Archer and Baker, hold their values, and attention should be paid to new editions that have been brought to date by important fresh material. John Howard Lawson's exhaustive, illuminating, and explorative study, *Theory and Technique of Playwriting and Screenwriting*, is an example here. Originally published in 1936 without the last two words of the present title, the revised edition (1949) adds a comprehensive section covering in brilliant, incisive analysis the development and problems of the motion picture from its American beginnings in 1908; and the whole text, by introduction and summations, has been given a fresh impact of immediacy in its penetrating exposition of the opposed ideological, social, and economic influences that find expression in present-day dramatic art.

Technical and professional aspects of drama that enlist a widening popular interest must have adequate representation, with particular attention to stagecraft for amateur and little-theatre groups, and to the intimate, individual art of puppetry, which seems to have gained in favor as the predilection for pageants and pageantry has waned.

Excellent aids are available in the selection of drama. Indexes to plays, particularly, are abundant and varied, indispensable not only in library selection but in the choice of plays for individual current needs. Foremost here is Ina Ten Eyck Firkins' comprehensive *Index to Plays, 1800–1926* (Wilson, 1927), which records 7,872 plays by

2,203 authors; its *Supplement, 1927–1934* (Wilson, 1935), indexing 3,284 plays by 1,335 authors. Miss Firkins' index is of first importance in the tracing of individual plays, which are given both in separate form and as found in anthologies and collections; it thus serves as an index to the standard dramatic anthologies. The *Dramatic Index* (Faxon), in substantial annual volumes, records since 1909 material concerning plays and players (dramatic criticism, reviews, articles, and portraits) appearing in two hundred American and English periodicals, and texts of plays whether published in book or magazine form. A useful companion and supplement to these—of special interest in its careful indication of subject-range in individual play content—is Ruth Gibbons Thomson's *Index to Full-Length Plays, 1926 to 1941* (Faxon, 1946). *A Guide to Play Selection*, by Milton M. Smith, published by the National Council of English (Appleton-Century, 1934) is a descriptive index of full-length and one-act plays, intended primarily for directors of educational dramatics, but useful to libraries and to amateur or professional groups for standard older material. One-act plays are effectively covered in the *Index to One-Act Plays*, by Hannah Logasa and Winifred Ver Nooy, published by Faxon through more than a quarter-century. The first volume covered the period 1900–24, and indexed 5,000 plays; the *Supplement: 1924–1931* (1932) included 7,000; the *Second Supplement: 1932–1940* appeared in 1941, with no specific indication of the number of plays indexed, but prefatory mention that "it includes over 500 collections, a great many separate pamphlet plays and a large number that have appeared in periodicals." Throughout, plays are indexed under title, author, subject, and number of characters in each play listed. In close relationship to these indexes is John H. Ottermiller's *Index to Plays in Collections*, covering in author and title record plays appearing in collections published between 1900 and 1942 (Wilson, 1943).

For literature of drama in its general and special aspects the comprehensive aid is Blanch M. Baker's *Dramatic Bibliography* (Wilson, 1933), supplement and complement to the Firkins index. This is an annotated list of about four thousand titles chosen from the books of the last fifty years and limited (except for a few volumes on costume) to works available in English. It covers in four broad divisions Drama and Theatre (history and criticism, but not plays); Production and Stagecraft; Pageantry, Religious drama and Entertainment; Anthologies (including "collected" or grouped plays of individual playwrights), Bibliographies, and Directories. Under each division, in closer subsidiary grouping, books are listed by title —a practice for which there seems little justification and which retards quick tracing of works by known authors. There are confusions and inadequacies in arrangement and in detail; but as a whole this aid meets ordinary requirements in the selection of standard and contemporary literature in its field, except for unusually large or specialized collections. Its full record of bibliographies is especially valuable. Librarians hope for a revised edition, brought to date and improved in detail.

The *Bookman's Manual*, in the revised (sixth) edition, is the indispensable aid in selective representation of the chief literature of drama, including work of leading older and contemporary playwrights. Seven chapters given to the subject present: general reference material on drama (bibliographical, historical, technical, critical, and anthologies); Classical drama; William Shakespeare (remarkable in range and compression of essential informative detail); Early English drama; Modern English drama; American drama; Modern continental drama. In each, salient aspects are set forth in logical sequence with clear, compact characterization and bibliographical effectiveness. These chapters are life lines for any inexperienced worker with books and welcome navigation charts to the more proficient.

An aid that is still effective in building a small collection valuable to students in the history, theory, and practice of the theatre is the concise bibliography by Rosamond Gilder, *A Theatre Library* (Theatre Arts, Incorporated, 1932), which records one hundred carefully chosen titles; and with this links the "international handbook," by Rosamond Gilder and George Freedley, *Theatre Collections in Libraries and Museums*, published under auspices of the

New York Public Library and the National Theatre Conference, with the cooperation of the A.L.A. (Theatre Arts, 1936). As a general reference aid often useful in selection, Bernard Sobel's all-inclusive *Theatre Handbook and Digest of Plays,* in the sixth revised edition (1948), has special helpfulness in a small library; and in similar limited selection George Jean Nathan's pungent, individualistic commentary in his annual *Theatre Book of the Year,* by strident distaste or enthusiastic approbation often modifies or strengthens selective judgment. Remember that many important books devoted to drama and most of the texts concerned with playwriting contain bibliographies of general or specialized interest that offer useful suggestions in selection—an outstanding example is the fascinating collective volume, *A History of Modern Drama,* edited by Barrett H. Clark and George Freedley and published by Appleton-Century in 1947. These should be noted and drawn upon; as should the play lists of dramatic publishers (*Samuel French's Catalog of Plays,* with its frequent supplements, is an indispensable aid) and the varied, extensive lists and bibliographies to be found in library bulletins and kindred publications.

FIFTY BOOKS ON DRAMA AND THE THEATRE

Andrews, John, and Ossia Trilling, eds. International Theatre. London, Sampson Low, Marston & Co., 1949.

Baker, George Pierce. Dramatic Technique. Boston, Houghton Mifflin Co., 1919.

Bentley, Eric R. Playwright as Thinker: a study of drama in modern times. New York, Reynal & Hitchcock, 1946.

Block, Anita. The Changing World in Plays and Theatre. Boston, Little, Brown & Co., 1939.

Boleslavski, Richard. Acting: the first six lessons. New York, Theatre Arts, 1933.

Brown, John Mason. Seeing Things. New York, McGraw-Hill Book Co., 1946.

Chambers, Sir Edmund K. The Elizabethan Stage. 4 vols. New York, Oxford University Press, 1923.

——— The Mediaeval Stage. 2 vols. New York, Oxford University Press, 1903.

DRAMA

Cheney, Sheldon. The Theatre: three thousand years of drama, acting and stage-craft. New York, Longmans, Green & Co., 1929.

Clark, Barrett H. A Study of the Modern Drama. New York. D. Appleton & Co., 1925; 2d rev. ed., New York, D. Appleton–Century Co., 1938.

—— and George Freedley, eds. A History of Modern Drama. New York, Appleton-Century-Crofts, 1947.

Clurman, Harold. Fervent Years: the story of the Group Theatre and the thirties. New York, Alfred A. Knopf, 1945.

Dean, Alexander. Fundamentals of Play Directing. New York, Farrar & Rinehart, 1941.

Dolman, John. The Art of Acting. New York, Harper & Brothers, 1949.

Drew, Elizabeth. Discovering Drama. New York, W. W. Norton & Co., 1937.

Fergusson, Francis. The Idea of a Theater. Princeton, N. J., Princeton University Press, 1949.

Freedley, George, and John A. Reeves. A History of the Theatre: from pre-Greek days to modern America. New York, Crown Publishers, 1940.

Flanagan, Hallie (Mrs. P. H. Davis). Arena. New York, Duell, Sloan & Pearce, 1940.

Gagey, Edmond McAdoo. Revolution in American Drama. New York, Columbia University Press, 1947.

Gassner, John. Producing the Play; with The New Scene Technician's Handbook by Philip Barber. New York, The Dryden Press, 1941.

—— Masters of the Drama. New York, Random House, 1940; 2d rev. ed., New York, Dover Publications, 1945.

Gorelik, Mordecai. New Theatres for Old. New York, Samuel French, 1940.

Granville-Barker, Harley. Use of the Drama. Princeton, N.J., Princeton University Press, 1945.

Harbage, Alfred. Shakespeare's Audience. New York, Columbia University Press, 1941.

Henderson, Archibald, ed. Pioneering a People's Theatre. Chapel Hill, University of North Carolina Press, 1945.

Houghton, Norris. Moscow Rehearsals: an account of methods of production in the Soviet theatre; introd. by Lee Simonson. New York, Harcourt, Brace & Co., 1936.

Isaacs, Edith J. R. The Negro in the American Theatre. New York, Theatre Arts Books, 1947.

Jones, Robert Edmond. The Dramatic Imagination. New York, Duell, Sloan & Pearce, 1941.

Krutch, Joseph Wood. The American Drama since 1918. New York, Random House, 1939.

Lawson, John Howard. Theory and Technique of Playwriting and Screenwriting. New York, G. P. Putnam's Sons, 1936; new ed., 1949.

Macgowan, Kenneth. Footlights across America: towards a national theatre. New York, Harcourt, Brace & Co., 1929.

Mantzius, Karl. A History of Theatrical Art in Ancient and Modern Times; trans. by Louise von Cossel and Charles Archer. 6 vols. Philadelphia, J. B. Lippincott Co., 1903–21; reprint ed., New York, Peter Smith, 1936.

Mayorga, Margaret. A Short History of the American Drama: commentaries on plays prior to 1920. New York, Dodd, Mead & Co., 1932.

McPharlin, Paul. The Puppet Theatre in America. New York, Harper & Brothers, 1949.

Morehouse, Ward. Matinee Tomorrow: fifty years of our theatre. New York, McGraw-Hill Book Co., 1949.

Moses, Montrose J., and John Mason Brown, eds. The American Theatre, as Seen by Its Critics, 1752–1934. New York, W. W. Norton & Co., 1934.

Nathan, George Jean. Encyclopedia of the Theatre. New York, Alfred Alfred A. Knopf.

—— Theatre Book of the Year. Annual, 1942 to 1948–49. New York, Alfred A. Knopf.

Nicoll, Alardyce. The Development of the Theatre. New York, Harcourt, Brace & Co., 1927; new rev. ed., 1948.

Odell, G. D. C. Annals of the New York Stage. 15 vols. New York, Columbia University Press, 1927–49.

Oenslager, Donald. Scenery, Then and Now. New York, W. W. Norton & Co., 1936.

Priestley, J. B. Theatre Outlook. London, Nicholson & Watson, 1947.

Pudovkin, V. I. Film Technique and Film Acting; trans. by Ivor Montagu; introd. by Lewis Jacobs. New York, Lear Publishers, 1949.

Quinn, Arthur Hobson. A History of the American Drama from the Civil War to the Present Day. Rev. ed., New York, F. S. Crofts & Co., 1936.

Raphaelson, Samson. The Human Nature of Playwriting. New York, The Macmillan Company, 1949.

Rourke, Constance. The Roots of American Culture; ed. and with preface by Van Wyck Brooks. New York, Harcourt, Brace & Co., 1942.

Simonson, Lee. The Stage Is Set. New York, Harcourt, Brace & Co., 1932; reprinted, 1947, by Dover Publications.

Stanislavski, Constantin. An Actor Prepares; trans. by Elizabeth R. Hapgood. New York, Theatre Arts Books, 1936.

—— Building a Character; trans. by Elizabeth R. Hapgood; introd. by Joshua Logan. New York, Theatre Arts Books, 1949.

Thompson, Alan Reynolds. Anatomy of Drama. Berkeley, University of California Press, 1942; 2d ed., 1946.

21. Fiction Today

> If the novelist's power of presenting character is multiplied (as it is in fact) by his power of presenting time and space, and to it is added his power of comment, there becomes visible his tremendous, his almost unrivalled—I myself believe it quite unrivalled—power, his amazingly extensive scope, in the presentation of life. Because his medium is a fictitious narrative, a blend of summary and scene, the novelist is able to tell us what people did, where they did it, when they did it, how they did it, why they did it, and what the writer thinks about it as well. There is nothing in life—no landscape however vast, no feeling however minute and subtle, no piece of action however lengthy or complex—which a novelist cannot put into his novel, provided only that his talent is equal to the task.
>
> Phyllis Bentley: Some Observations on the Art of Narrative

WITH FICTION we close our enterprise of exploration and discovery in the great domains of literature. It has been kept until the last for two reasons. One is because the survey and characterization of books in other classes, and the indication of methods of analysis applicable to them, should establish an understanding of basic principles of selection that will clarify the difficult task of appraising current fiction. The other is because present-day fiction in its range, variety, and relationship to public demand offers more opportunities and greater problems in library selection than do other classes of literature. Two chapters are therefore devoted to fiction, one centering on the development and salient characteristics of the modern novel and upon principles that will aid in its appraisal; the other giving consideration to certain aspects of fiction that have special significance in library use.

Any attempt within such limitations to survey and characterize fiction must be inadequate. It must concentrate, synthesize, and generalize too arbitrarily; must disregard much that should command attention; and can convey but little realization of the full dimensions, the far-reaching influences, of the form of creative art that most comprehensively expresses human experience. Havelock Ellis said: "Fiction is our modern popular art. After all, it is the human soul in its myriad and ever changing aspects which is the one permanently interesting thing. And that is why novels have a significance that is not exhausted in the brief hour of amusement that they give us—a significance which, if we see it rightly, goes deep down to the roots of our life."

There is increasing need of sensible, comparative, and sympathetic studies of fiction from the point of view of library selection and reader values. *What's in a Novel*, published in 1942, was directed toward meeting this need, and also intended to serve as companion and aide to *Living with Books*. So perhaps brief characterization of its scope and purpose is fitting here. Both are implied in the title. *What's in a Novel* is not a question but a statement, intended to answer a questioner's scornful emphasis ("What's in a *novel?*"), or skeptical accent ("What's *in* a novel?"), or simple desire for information ("*What's* in a novel?"). Well, in the novel today will be found: the changing course of history surging through the world; the conflict of tyranny and justice, of freedom and subjection, as it prevails in the nature of man and in life experience; the evolutionary conflict of our era in religion, politics, and industry; world revolution and world reconstruction; challenge of social injustice and expansion of social awareness; advance of women; dominance of science; interests and activities in every profession, calling, and walk of life; backgrounds of the past, aspects of the present, portents of the future. And in the work of our contemporary novelists will be found deeper psychological insight, more thorough factual exactitude, a larger measure of basic authenticity, often of personal knowledge and experience, and a more varied and exhaustive literary art than has ever existed before.

If there is need in library literature for fuller exposition of the many values that novels hold for the reading public there is even greater need among librarians for a broader background of personal familiarity with fiction, a deepened responsiveness to the qualities and influences of the novelist's art. The apologetic attitude so commonly maintained toward the existence and reading of novels in public libraries is one of the vestigial remains of traditional moralism. In the present day, of variety and mastery in technique of literary expression and broadening appreciation of literature, the only fiction collection that demands apology is one in which trivial, inane, inferior, and vulgar books predominate. Through the half-century now closing world revolution increases in momentum, and the portents, tragedies, confusions, and fears that shadow the world are reflected in the creative art of fiction as it penetrates with insight and power into man's external and internal violence and disintegration. This fiction is properly part of the library's apparatus of public enlightenment, and libraries should approve its values, as they should be proud of the manifold influences for intelligence and imagination and sympathy and simple pleasure—surely a great gift—that they are radiating through fiction.

In the world of literature today the novel dominates. Fiction records, mirrors, interprets, every aspect of modern life, its activities, surroundings, interests, convictions, ideals, and problems. From religion to hotel management every conceivable subject furnishes a theme to the novelist. The novel has subdued to itself all other forms of literary expression; it supplies current coin of conversation; to the great majority of readers it is synonymous with literature. In its immediate manifestation it is the product of its day; but it constantly renews, reshapes, and modifies older patterns, and its methods and materials, in all their bewildering diversity, have come into being through a process of creative evolution. Anyone who has made even a superficial study of the development of modern fiction must be impressed by the transformation effected within a century in the range, depth, and skill of the novelist's art. Some understanding of this development, of the increasing extension and variation of scope, the multiplication of types, is necessary to establish a basis for reasoned judgment of the qualities and defects of current fiction and to appreciate its hold upon the reading public. The universal appeal of the novel rests on its relation to life; and it is as its depiction of life has become more truthful, more varied, more vivid, that the power of the novel has so wonderfully grown.

Characteristics of ordinary English fiction as it existed over a hundred years ago may be indicated from a glance at the Hammond collection of old novels in the possession of the New York Society Library. This collection contains about 1,850 novels, published approximately between 1790 and 1833, which originally formed part of a circulating library maintained in Newport, Rhode Island, in 1835. It is well known to students of literary history, and has been used for source material by many who have written on early American fiction. Titles gleaned from this collection indicate the moralistic-grandiose fashion of that day and the prevalence of the double-header title, which held its popularity until late in the nineteenth century. Here you will find: *Abelino, the Bravo of Venice; Albinia, or, The Young Mother; The Bandit's Bride, or, The Maid of Saxony; Edward, or, Various Views of Human Nature; Eliza, or, The Pattern of Virtue; The Hapless Orphan, or, The Innocent Victim of Revenge.*

These are the forebears of Faith Baldwin, of Lloyd Douglas, of Frances Parkinson Keyes, of Taylor Caldwell, and Clarence Budington Kelland. They represent the mass of ordinary popular novels, creatures of their own little day, soon gone and soon forgotten, paralleling the mass fiction of fifty years ago, of ten years ago, of today. Chief among their characteristics is lack of verisimilitude in background, and absence of descriptive detail that conveys locality. Mainly by English writers, they make London their favorite scene of action, but in many the setting is not indicated at all. Often, when it is indicated, it is done in the fashion of the Elizabethan stage, where a tree in a box symbolized a countryside background, or a central throne an imperial presence-chamber. Many of the romances offer a fantastic farrago of history and geography that shows how little heed was given to what have become first requisites in fiction with historical background. When we recall the mass of reference material that went to building up Charles Reade's novels, not *The Cloister and the Hearth* alone, but his novels of humanitarian and social purpose also; the accuracy and detail of Weir Mitchell's fictional studies of revolutionary Philadelphia; the re-creation of medieval life and environment achieved by Sigrid Undset; Robert Graves' close factual detail even in his fabulized pre-historical chronicles; and the authority and scholarship represented in Naomi Mitchison's transference to fiction of pre-Christian and early Christian history, we realize how great has been the transformation effected in the factual authenticity of the novelist's work.

In construction, these old novels are awkward, formal, slow-moving, couched in long-drawn-out narrative, infused with conventional religious sentiment; high-flown, sentimental, and pietistic in phrasing. Most of them deal in a romanticized, objective fashion with love; they are without subjectivity, devoid of the analyzings, questionings, candor, and far-reaching variations that characterize the modern conception and handling of the subject. Sex, in present-day acceptance, does not exist in them; yet it is hardly paradox to say that they are more absorbed in consciousness of sex than are the novels of today, for their puppets move only toward ultimate matrimony or ultimate death from a broken heart. Man is inexorably presented as the intellectual superior, woman as either a "charming trifler" or an angelic being existing on noble sentiments. The whole realm of everyday contacts, of working or professional association, of free companionship between men and women, is unknown; eighteen is the deadline for female hopes of life fulfillment. The atmosphere is muggy with moral instruction, and the idealism, probably genuine enough, is saccharine and pietistic.

Yet these old novels were stepping-stones to a more skilled art. In any random collections of the novels of the next quarter-century a much larger proportion would undoubtedly give evidence of increased vitality, significance, and interest; and this proportion steadily enlarges as the years advance. There is a constant heightening, deepening, and perfecting of craftsmanship in literary art, although apparently the great single masterpieces of creative genius are more infrequent. As Stephen Leacock said: "The age of individual eminence has given place to the world of universal competence."

With the opening of the nineteenth century the first names that convey profound influences in the development of English fiction are those of Jane Austen and Walter Scott. Although Jane Austen was Scott's contemporary her earlier work preceded his by a few years. Her novels, published from 1811 to 1818, though composed ten years earlier, mirror the life and environment she knew in images that have remained undimmed and vital through successive generations. She brought to fiction the spirit of social comedy, that, light and impersonal, points individual personality, uncovers character, illuminates human nature. The true spirit of comedy is to survey with ironical amusement the words, actions, illusions, and self-contradictions of persons who know only what they are doing, saying, or experiencing, but do not see the situation or event as a whole. The comic spirit hovers over the whole scene and realizes the curious, ironical, absurd, or pathetic interlocking or interrelationship which is unrealized by the persons concerned. This comic spirit is the familiar genius of Jane Austen. Her influence took on masculine power, tragic irony, and deeper insight in George Meredith's *Egoist,* a spring from which modern fiction has drawn potencies of psychological analysis. It broadened into the chronicles of Barsetshire, in which Trollope imbedded his solid segments of English life; and brought into being the twentieth-century Barsetshire of Angela Thirkell pervaded by a more acrid postwar disillusion than the kindlier Victorians knew. Ellen Glasgow drew from the same source the satiric elixir of *The Romantic Comedians* and *They Stooped to Folly.* So, against their own English backgrounds, did "Elizabeth" (Countess Russell), in true Austen succession, and Humphrey Pakington, whose later work has a postwar touch. Jane Austen is still the idol and model of most of the novelists who deal with social comedy.

Walter Scott's first novel was published in 1814, his last in 1831. His genius is the greatest force that has appeared in English fiction.

In his work the romance of adventure and the drama of history are combined with the homeliest realism and with a portrayal of character surpassed only by Shakespeare. Historical characters as he presented them stamped their enduring likeness on the mind. His power of tragic emotion, though restrained by the formalism of his era, is unextinguished by time. The permanence of Scott's novels lay in the power and truth of their relation to life; from his day on the stream of Victorian fiction rises, expands, and deepens, and its greatest names, consciously or unconsciously, carry some indebtedness to him. Those names, in their turn, convey leavening and transforming influences in the development of modern fiction. Such are Dickens, transmitting vital forces of humor, of sympathy, of actuality; Thackeray, bittersweet commentator on the contrasts between the surface and the inner experience of living; Hawthorne, who sowed the seed of analysis of man's inner nature, as it has germinated and flourished in modern fiction, and whose insight still penetrates and reveals; the Brontës, first to render woman's emotional intensity into honest and open expression; George Eliot, isolating and analyzing the individual self; Meredith, iconoclast of tradition, practitioner of modern psychology; Hardy, whose creative genius struck the note of today in the fiction of the late Victorian era.

A steady gain in depth, freedom, and flexibility marks the development of fiction from the middle to the close of the nineteenth century. There was increasing preoccupation with individual personality (so evident in the novels of Hawthorne and George Eliot), a continuing endeavor to analyze mind and emotions, to present not simply actions but the impulses and motives that produced them, which later under the influence of modern psychology was to launch the novel on the dark stream of the unconscious. A rising spirit of democracy was manifest in the portrayal of men and women in every kind of environment according to their own character and experience, and in the gradual diminution of that glamour of the "upper classes" which so long pervaded English fiction. The advance of science, with its requirement of exactitude in observation and record of perceived facts and its impersonal pursuit of truth concerning life and human nature, brought into fiction a corresponding demand for accuracy in factual details and for truth in the reflection and interpretation of human experience. The advance of woman into constantly enlarging activities and relationships released an influence that in three-quarters of a century revolutionized fiction, opened immense new regions of observation and experience, and is only beginning to assume its full significance.

From these influences arose others, in ceaseless germination, growth, and transition. Through the first quarter of the twentieth century development of the novel was particularly significant in three directions. In a sustained movement toward intensified subjectivity novelists sought to study and capture the protean self that lurks in the conscious and unconscious mind. Based on principles and methods of psychoanalysis, with dominant emphasis on sex as motor and motive, this endeavor involved also an attempt to register the continuous flow of instinctive, emotional, and volitional sensation which is the "stream of consciousness." Here the work of James Joyce, D. H. Lawrence, Virginia Woolf, Dorothy Richardson, and others, in direct succession to the earlier subjective fiction of Henry James and Joseph Conrad, indicates the multiplication and variation of types emerging from earlier forms as fiction moved on to new issues.

Revolt against the established social order set the direction of the second movement. Partly, this was aftermath of bitterness and disillusion from World War I, but even more it was ground swell of the oncoming social and intellectual revolution that was to overthrow the old order of established sanctions and accepted boundaries. Under leadership of H. G. Wells, Theodore Dreiser, and Sinclair Lewis attack on materialism and commercialism, assault on capitalism, arraignment of traditional religion and conventional morality, marked the course of this battle for a better world and enlisted a vigorous and able body of younger writers. Proletarian fiction, stimulated by Upton Sinclair and Jack London, came of age in strength and militancy, centering on the labor strike and the struggle to bring union solidarity to unorganized and exploited workers; poverty and unemployment were beginning to assume economic as well as human aspects. Reaction from World War I fostered cynical indifference to political leadership, while at the same time the anti-Bolshevik "red scare" traced a coercive pattern of repression prophetic of the deeper menace to intellectual freedom that was to confront the nation in another quarter century. These were the years of "flaming youth," with Scott Fitzgerald as their prophet, when the lure of after-the-war prosperity shone ever more brightly, when national prohibition taught boys and girls to drink, brought gangsterism into fashion, revolutionized social behavior, and corrupted personal integrity on all levels of living.

Experimentalism in expression was the third trend of fiction in these pregnant years. As in the "new" poetry, the purpose was to enlarge and vitalize the medium through which the writer conveys thought, emotion, and action; and by bizarre, variable, often complex word usage and structural form to indicate the occurrence of many different events at the same moment of time, and to transmit consciousness as it is experienced. Thus, novels of Virginia Woolf and John Dos Passos reflected in different fashions the conception advanced by modern physics: they sought to realize and present the timelessness of being and the atomic composition of matter, instead of rendering substantial figures against static backgrounds.

Through the second quarter of the century these trends were dominant, in that constant transition, variation, and self-renewal which makes fiction the reflection of life. With them, innumerable other currents rose and overflowed and succeeded one another in the stream of current literature, while the tidal wave of world catastrophe advanced in irretrievable course. Novels of social protest expanded and intensified as the mirage of everlasting prosperity faded before the gathering storm of economic disaster. With unsparing insistence these novels visualized for remote and indifferent Americans evils crippling the lives of millions of other Americans, workers in mines, in lumber and textile mills, in automobile factories, in commerce, and in agriculture. They illuminated the infinite injustices of race discrimination, the vicious undertow of hopeless poverty, the subhuman living that existed along Tobacco Road. Their impress struck deep and still lingers. In many, communism was the gospel that offered hope and confidence and pointed the way out of the jungle of industrial conflict, the quicksand of ruthless exploitation, to a firm and fertile ground of cooperation and mutual well-being. Their influence, together with the harsh impact of the Depression, strengthened radical political doctrines, and made Marxism groundwork for novels of moving social import. As a whole this body of fiction, which finds human beings, however poor and humble, however illiterate, distorted by poverty or degradation, worthy or inspiring subjects for the novelist's art, has meant the extension of democracy to literature on a scale never known before.

As the Depression waned world problems ranging far beyond local and regional boundaries rose in the foreground. Novelists of the First World War—Hemingway, Remarque, Dos Passos, many more—in disillusion and distrust had registered the universal tragedy of war in terms of human suffering, futilities, and stupidities, and helped to create a pervasive pacifism that was blind to the later advancing German drive to world conquest, "neutral" under the collapse of France and Britain's single-handed battle for survival, and faced reality only when Pearl Harbor plunged the nation into global war. Not until after the war had been won and in the winning the world had been promised total annihilation at any time that military supremacy might determine, did fiction become fully recorder, clarifier, and interpreter of an era in dissolution. The earlier war novels, unshadowed by the atomic bomb, reflected simpler poignant realities: the common heroism of common people, exemplified by the unshaken fortitude and confidence of Britain under German bombing, is pictured in Nevil Shute's sensitive, warmly human renderings of actuality; Louis Golding's *Mr. Emmanuel* and Phyllis Bottome's *The Mortal Coil* glimpse a Germany settling in the Nazi mold; Czechoslovakia, despoiled and degraded in the grip of Nazi despotism, is visualized in the tragic, inspiring novel of Maurice Hindus, *To Sing with the Angels*.

Victory in Europe held presage of that "one world" of international cooperation and understanding which was vision and incentive for the United Nations, so hopefully and earnestly planned and begun. But the guiding hand, the keen, far-seeing vision, that could reconcile, control, and unite warring human elements, was gone. With President Roosevelt's death the world scene again darkened. Victory in Japan had been achieved, but the atomic bomb remained; the glow of hope chilled, fear and suspicion congealed, and the "cold war" benumbed the human brain in the irrational, fear-ridden limbo of a two-power world. Fiction is, I think, the only medium that can reveal with vivid, immediate, and continuing actuality the incredible changes brought into the world's life and into human experience during the second quarter of the twentieth century. Postwar novels in constantly increasing numbers enlist fresh, vigorous talent which draws from backgrounds of personal knowledge and stamps unforgettable impress of the compulsions, violences, and infections of disintegrating social relationships. These novels strike below the surface into the effect upon the human mind of the dehumanization of man, the mass mechanization of death, the worship of war and violence, the acceptance of sadism as a natural human characteristic. They possess high powers of narrative, recognize obscenity and sexuality as basic realities of life, and record in clinical objectivity physical sufferings and psychological abnormalities. With all its hard-boiled realism, its sexuality and frequent emotional overbalance, this fiction has, I think, more genuine seriousness, a deeper compassion and more human sympathy than prevailed in the novels of World War I. There is also a deeper vein of decadence than in the 1920's: a hopeless submergence in defeatism of spirit and in aberrations of eroticism. But in counter-influence there is a rising sense of confidence in man's own powers of self-mastery and self-renewal.

In postwar fiction the war novels demanded and received first attention. *The Naked and the Dead*, Norman Mailer's grim, overpowering evocation of inhumanity, corruption, and military fascism in the American capture of a small Japanese island in the Pacific, stands foremost in this fiction of civilized savagery. Irwin Shaw's *The Young Lions*, James Cozzens' *Guard of Honor*, center on bitter ironies of racial injustice in army service; John Horne Burns, in *The Gallery*, gives graphic, sympathetic characterization of Naples under American occupation; and Stefan Heym's *The Crusaders* integrates the American army in its European campaign in a rounded, absorbing, dramatic, and richly human novel of men in war. This is just a single trend—varied, complex, full of significance for the understanding of present and emergent influences and realities.

No attempt can be made here to summarize the range and diversities of current fiction. But I would refer the reader to the illustrative list appended to the present chapter, in which fifty postwar novels have been chosen to indicate background, trends, and dominant themes in a cross section of representative fiction. Look over that list and observe the themes, ranging into all the interests and issues of our day.

It is clear that fiction has so widened its scope that today it presents almost every kind of literature that formerly required separate and distinctive literary forms. Perhaps a few immediate trends that convey insistence in reader demand, however, should be noted. Religion, in continuing exposition since 1888, when *Robert Ellesmere* gave up the church to accept mid-nineteenth-century science, has, under the impact of the atom and communism, become one of the strongest trends in general reader interest. Its fiction ranges from the intellectual universality of Mann's *Joseph*, the biblical scholarship and epical power of Sholem Asch, the hortatory moralism of Lloyd Douglas, to the brilliancy and doctrinal evangelism of *The Screwtape Letters*, the bizarre, symbolic fantasies of Charles Williams, and the crystalline distillation of man's ideals of compassion and human brotherhood in *Cry, the Beloved Country*—with infinite variations and proliferations.

Psychology and psychoanalysis are infused in almost all contemporary fiction, and psychopathology is an increasing element. Novels of insanity represent a trend that has deep human appeal and significant social values, as influences for institutional improvement and for individual sympathy and understanding. *The Snake Pit*, by Mary Jane Ward, and Fritz Peters' *The World Next Door*, are distinctive and different examples. Child psychology and adolescence, subjects of ever growing public interest, are steadily enlarging the scope of fiction's mirror, clarifying problems and obscurities of personality and revealing springs of character and behavior. Carson McCullers' *The Member of the Wedding*, William Maxwell's *The Folded Leaf*, represent the sensitivity, candor, and vitality of the many novels in this field that give charm and refreshment as well as enlightenment to the reader. A very different trend, born of disillusion and fear and embittered resentment of world change is manifest in novels of savage anger and sardonic satire. George Orwell's *Nineteen Eighty-Four*, anti-Utopian fantasy of a world transformed by "socialism" into a power-crazed totalitarian state of brutish enslavement and fiendish cruelties, stems in a measure from Aldous Huxley's earlier work, but is paranoia, not literature. There is sounder balance and deeper meaning in Albert Camus' summing up of his appalling war allegory, *The Plague*: "What we learn in a time of pestilence is that there are more things to admire in men than to despise." Social comedy has been touched by a somewhat similar infection, as in the novels of Ivy Compton-Burnett, a Jane Austen turned to sadism and melodrama, whose dozen novels (only four as yet published in the United States) flow calmly through traditional English family living, in unalterable dialogue and a withering, irresistible humor that discerns only the egotistical, the vindictive, and the contemptible in human nature.

Race relations and race discrimination, crucial problems of America's national and international life, have become as important in fiction as they are in the literature of history and sociology. From the early 1930's Negro novelists with deepening literary art have visualized tragic, simple, and complex aspects of common

Negro experience and revealed with power and understanding the nature and qualities of their people. An increasing number of white writers also in arresting, thought-provoking novels are carrying on the battle to eradicate the evils of segregation, race prejudice, and anti-Semitism, and fulfill the tradition of a democratic America with freedom and equal opportunity for all. Such fiction should have support and encouragement in all public library book selection and reader service. Lillian Smith's *Strange Fruit*, thoughtful, poignant, deeply honest rendering of everyday actualities of the South's many-sided dilemma; and *The Other Room*, Worth Hedden's clear-minded, warm-hearted novel of broadening racial understanding, are both by white women of Southern heritage, whose convictions and sympathies link their books to the more challenging firsthand experiences of humiliation and injustice that are the dramatic substance of William Gardner Smith's *Last of the Conquerors*, novel of a young Negro soldier in the American army in Germany, and Ann Petry's unforgettable evocation of *The Street*—the squalor, poverty, and degradations of Harlem's 125th Street.

A trend that poses the question of the library's legitimate response to popular demand is the mass addiction to so-called "science fiction"—inevitable product of the atomic age. Jules Verne and H. G. Wells set the pattern for these fictional flights into fantasy which uses facts or theories of experimental or accepted science as vehicles for planetary adventure, for travels-in-time to Utopias or Gehennas that hold portent of man's ultimate destiny, for spectacular visualization of atomic energy used to reconstruct or destroy the material world, to shift or populate the planets, and particularly for fear-inspiring narratives of earth's invasion by aggressors from other worlds (often of Russified aspect), equipped with death-dealing scientific paraphernalia, from bacteria to cosmic rays. Much of this fiction bears the stamp of the cruder comics and pulp magazines; in elementary workmanship and infantilism of violence and repetitiousness it fails, I think, to justify provision as library material. But the skillful and arresting work that steadily increases in volume and variety is comparable as " 'escape' literature" to the crime-detection fiction which has become an accepted literary form; and this has values both as recreational reading and as giving to readers valid scientific backgrounds for rocket ships, supersonic flight, mechanical brains, and other concepts of superscience today.[1]

Nearly all forms and trends in fiction may, in broad generalization, be resolved into a series of types of novels that, although constantly dissolving, merging, and re-forming, yet maintain distinctive characteristics. Discrimination in selection is greatly helped by familiarity with important types, by appreciation of the essential differences between them, and by realization that qualities which give value to one type are not necessarily to be required of another. The everyday product of the competent craftsman cannot be expected to match the finest work of the literary artist. In judicious current selection there must be representation of types that will satisfy divergent tastes of readers of all ages and different degrees of intelligence, but there must also be sustained endeavor to choose the best from different types, according to sound standards of critical judgment.

Fuller analysis and characterization of types of fiction are presented in *What's in a Novel* than can be attempted here, and to that presentation the reader must be referred. But a few of the more familiar types should be briefly noted. Among them, the mid-Victorian domestic novel, centering on character depiction, on everyday scenes, sentiments, and perplexities, ramifying into social comedy and social disintegration, finding postwar expression in work of Angela Thirkell, Ivy Compton-Burnett, Henry Green, Elizabeth Cadell, and Margery Sharp, merges, as it always has done, into another important and familiar type, the biographic novel.

The biographic (often autobiographic) novel has enlisted the ablest novelists of the day, and is also a dominant type in regional and historical fiction. It merges with increasing insistence into manifold psychological and psychoanalytical studies of personality

---

[1] For compact, useful comment on this subject, see Lyn Hart, "Science Fiction," in *Booklist*, Nov. 1, 1949, p. 73. *What's in a Novel*, pp. 214-15, summarizes the remarkable novels of Olaf Stapledon.

that explore problems of childhood, of adolescence, of marriage, and of sexual abnormalities. The stream-of-consciousness type with its corollary of experimentalism in technique has already been indicated. Its fountainhead is James Joyce's *Ulysses*, which has transfused its influence through myriad manifestations and remains a monumental landmark in the development of modern fiction. Joyce's work, published in Paris in 1922, was forbidden publication or circulation in England and the United States. It remained under government censorship as obscene literature in the United States until 1933, when the American censorship was lifted by a judicial ruling, which characterized the book as "a sincere and serious attempt to devise a new literary method for the observation and description of mankind." [2] In 1936 a special edition was printed by John Lane in London; the subsequent trade edition (1937) was never acted on by the authorities, and so the ban was tacitly removed. *Ulysses*, together with several other Joyce titles, is still, however, forbidden publication or circulation in Ireland.

Novels of fantasy and symbolism, poetic or satiric, are still a salient type in modern fiction. James Branch Cabell's intricately patterned ironic renderings of sex instinct which first developed in the American reading public the continental attitude toward erotic literary art no longer titillate or shock a public inured to sex consciousness in every field of literary expression. Fantasy, allegory, and symbolism are now chiefly directed toward the ideological conflict of the time, religious, philosophic, political, and social; the repercussions of war, and man's quest for peace. There are many examples. Diverse in patterns and in qualities, they range from the imaginative penetration and philosophic wisdom of Robert Nathan's *Jonah* and *Road of Ages*, the brilliant religious allegory of C. S. Lewis' *Out of the Silent Planet*, to the ironic pessimism of Aldous Huxley, and the savagery of George Orwell. Other types strongly represented in current fiction include novels of art and music; professional and vocational novels, centering on business, the theatre,

---

[2] Text of Judge Woolsey's decision is given in full in the authorized American edition of *Ulysses*, published by Random House, New York, 1934, pp. ix–xiv.

sports, and almost every specific human interest and activity; novels of the sea; adventure novels, with their subdivision of "westerns" and their close integration with historical fiction; novels of crime and detection, in immense present-day expansion; and what may be called "cocktail novels" of sophistication and sensual excitation. Types, indeed, may be multiplied at will; there is constant emergence of new patterns, constant application of new methods to old materials. And all these types take on many different forms (romantic, realistic, naturalistic, impressionistic, idealistic) as older or newer modes of expression prevail in the individual writer's work.

Consider now a few principles and methods that should aid in determining values of individual novels. Some of these have already been indicated in previous chapters [3] and a little repetition is perhaps unavoidable. It is not my purpose to enter into subtleties of literary criticism; but rather to note certain standards and indicate a few specific points of analysis useful in the development of sound critical judgment, good literary taste, tolerance, and common sense.

Five familiar tests that aid in establishing a sound basis of judgment if applied in the critical consideration of fiction are: the test of time, the test of compensation, the test of significance, the test of effect on reader, and the test of comparison.

The *test of time* expresses in other words the principle that the greatest art is that which gives the most lasting pleasure to the greatest number of people. Compare, for example, the number of readers who have received, and continue to receive, pleasure from *Robinson Crusoe* (1719), or from *Pickwick Papers* (1836), or from *The Scarlet Letter* (1850) with the number who have found pleasure in any contemporary "best seller" (even *Gone with the Wind* or *Anthony Adverse*) whose term of life seldom outlasts a decade. This test of permanence of appeal is the decisive and enduring test of creative art. Unfortunately, we cannot apply it to the products of our own day; its immediate value is in deepening perspectives and discounting facile certainties.

The *test of compensation* poses the question: Does this book

[3] See above, pp. 54–55, 127, 131–32.

contain enough truth, beauty, pleasure, or active good to make it worth my while? In other words, it asks us to consider whether sufficient profit of any kind ensues from reading the book to compensate for the time spent on it instead of on a different book. It is the test implied in Ruskin's warning, "Remember, if you read this, you cannot read that." There is need of elasticity in its application, for there are different kinds of "compensation," each with values of its own. The compensation of mental escape and refreshment found by so many readers in mystery and detective fiction, for example, has its value, though it differs from the compensation of the beauty that permeates *The River*, Rumer Godden's studies of childhood in India, and from the "active good" of deepened understanding of human problems that may be found in the abnormality of Radclyffe Hall's *The Well of Loneliness*.

What is the value of the book as an interpretation of life? This is the *test of significance*—of prime importance in consideration of current fiction. Many books that we may personally find unpleasant or to the spirit of which we object are of value according to this test, and so are others in which at first sight we may see only fantastic absurdity or imaginative make-believe. Thus, whether or not *The Lost Weekend* offends the individual reader, its significance as a vivid reflection of a phase of social history cannot be denied. Budd Schulberg's *What Makes Sammy Run?*, in a medium steeped in blatant vulgarity, conveys corruptive elements in character and living with power, understanding, and dynamic social significance. Zora Hurston's uninhibited novels of Negro life have significance as interpretations of race experience that justify the earthiness and naturalism that are abiding folk elements.

Does the book leave any kind of fine or wholesome feeling in the mind of one who reads it? This is the *test of effect on reader*. It needs broad interpretation, for many books of power, beauty, and significance (from *Jude the Obscure* to *The Grapes of Wrath*) leave the immature or mentally inelastic reader bewildered, depressed, or repelled. It must be applied with understanding of the point of view of the reader to whom the book does appeal and at the same time with appreciation of the book's intrinsic quality as literary art.

The *test of comparison* asks: How does the book I am judging measure up, quality by quality, alongside works of the same kind that have passed the test of time? It is one of the most useful aids to discriminating judgment, but demands a broad background of book knowledge. For example, the ability to set in immediate mental comparison such a historical novel as *The Cloister and the Hearth* with a new historical novel, such as *The Black Rose*, or to instinctively compare Conrad's *Chance* with McFee's *Harbourmaster*, gives a more authoritative approach in the analysis of the more recent book. Always in such comparison there must be recognition of changes in spirit and in convention brought about by time, and realization that current fiction is the mirror of its own day.

The two great requirements of a novel are truth and art. Truth implies vitality in the rendering of human beings, valid psychology, consistency in the relationship of cause and effect and of motive and action, verisimilitude of backgrounds. Art implies skill in workmanship: sound structure and good style. To aid in appraisal of fiction for library use specific test questions have been formulated, partly drawn from the methods and practice of literary criticism, partly from immediate problems of library selection. A few such questions that serve to bring out qualities of a novel have been indicated in a previous chapter,[4] but should be noted here. They are:

Is it true to life? Sensational? Exaggerated? Distorted?

Has it vitality and consistency in character depiction? Valid psychology? Insight into human nature?

Is the plot original? Hackneyed? Probable? Simple? Involved?

Is dramatic interest sustained?

Does it stimulate? Provoke thought? Satisfy? Inspire? Amuse?

Questions that center on the requirement of art and that are equally applicable to any work of creative literature are:

[4] Above, p. 54.

Does the work show any degree of creative power?
Is the form appropriate to the thought?
Has it originality of conception? Of expression?
Has it a clear and graphic style? Charm? Profundity? Imaginative power?

Questions of this kind are readily framed, and undoubtedly help to test the validity of a novelist's materials and the excellence of his manner of presenting them. To elaborate their detail, however, and apply them indiscriminately to current fiction of different types and characteristics is obviously absurd. Only a masterpiece would possess all the desired qualifications; and indeed, many of the qualifications suggested are mutually incompatible, or debatable in themselves. To disapprove "morbidity," to question rigorously as to distinctions between "right and wrong," is to confuse, not clarify, critical perceptions. "Morbid" is a convenient term often complacently applied to anything of which we desire to remain ignorant. Dostoyevsky's greatest novels are submerged in morbid psychology; Aldous Huxley's *Point Counter Point* and most of D. H. Lawrence are deeply tinged with morbidity; modern fiction primarily concerned with instinctive, introspective, and subjective aspects of human experience is intolerably "morbid" to those whose reading of life is determinedly objective and "wholesome." So far as test questions aid in denotation of a novel's substance, structure, and spirit, they have practical usefulness; so far as they furnish specifications for moralistic judgment, they are, I think, to be distrusted.

Two points upon which attention may most usefully be directed are consistency in character creation and excellence of expression; in other words, a novel's truth to human nature and its workmanship as a piece of literary art.

It is in its rendering of human beings that fiction holds the mirror up to life. Character depiction in a novel, therefore, should stand the test of consistency with the individual portrayed and with probability according to the broad principles and processes of human nature. The reader following the acts of the characters should be able to link motive logically to action, to discern valid reasons and influences as responsible for developments set forth. Readers whose critical taste is undeveloped will not distinguish between consistency and inconsistency; and this is why many novels without genuine merit, but with sentimental or sensational appeal, achieve ready popularity, quickly die, and leave no trace. They are full of unnatural yet time-worn situations, or preposterous, inadequate, and inconsistent motives; but immature or unobservant readers are untroubled by their falsities and find a transient satisfaction in their synthetic compound. Here we find the heroes and heroines who spurn fortunes; the heroes who destroy evidence of their own innocence; the heroines who accept an undeserved stigma (usually accompanied by a baby) for the sake of an erring sister and conceal their innocence from the one person to whom they would indubitably have revealed it; the heroes who agree to marry a girl they do not love who has been seduced by another, when they do love someone else; the books of such novelists as Kathleen Norris, Harold Bell Wright, A. S. M. Hutchinson, and multitudes of lesser degree, abound in these conventionalized inconsistencies. However, it must be remembered that in real life almost nothing is incredible. It is not consistency of action that makes a novel true to human nature and human experience, but consistency of motives and of character. Human beings are constantly inconsistent in thought, word, and deed; but these inconsistencies arise from temperamental qualities, from circumstantial or psychological causes, and are logically related to motives and to events.

Excellence of expression means simply that a novel possesses good literary style. Every author has his style; read a page of Hawthorne and a page of Meredith, and the difference of texture is instantly apparent; a paragraph from Henry James and a paragraph from Ernest Hemingway could never be thought to be from the same pen. Or compare the artificial elaboration, the ironic sophisticated filigree, of James Branch Cabell with the slow, confused verbosity of Theodore Dreiser—the clumsy utterance of a great writer who never learned to write, but whose work holds slow-burning fires of truth and power. The style of the practiced literary craftsman is always evident. It may be felt instantly when, after reading many crude, poorly written novels, one takes up a book by a master workman, such as Edith Wharton or John Galsworthy or Willa Cather. Compare a page of one of them with a page of Ethel Dell, or Lloyd Douglas, or Faith Baldwin, and observe the difference.

Style is really more than an author's mode of expression; its springs are in the author's personality. Stevenson and Hardy are examples of this, the swift vividness and gaiety of one in contrast with the somber power, the earthborn beauty, the inner heartbreak, of the other. Style can be imitated by any clever writer; Meredith was long a copybook for many ambitious beginners; Conrad furnished a model to others of a later day; from patterns set by Hemingway, by Virginia Woolf, by Thornton Wilder, have been made stencils in widespread use today. But imitation has no roots of its own; either the copyist finally evolves his own individual, distinctive manner or his work perishes from lack of vitality. Style must have more than mere skill in words; there must be thought, sensitivity, sympathy, beneath its surface. Nowadays almost all writers have acquired technical facility; even third-rate novelists possess definite narrative skill. With this steady rise in the style level of current fiction, cheapness, crudity, and wanton vulgarity should be ruled out from consideration in library selection. So also should the dead commonplace, the vague footlessness, the "sweet" inanity, that produces what Professor Rogers called "the cold boiled macaroni of literature."

By undeviating application of the test of consistency and the test of style probably most novels of inferior quality could be eliminated from consideration; but the element of popular demand complicates the problem of selection. A large and faithful body of public library readers finds satisfaction in commonplace, idea-less fiction, conventional in pattern, mildly romantic or tepidly sensational, "pleasant" to undeveloped taste—fiction associated with such names as Ethel Dell (who wrote a book a year from 1911 until her death in 1939, and sold over three million in the United States), Temple Bailey, Margaret Pedler, Lida Larrimore, and Grace Livingston Hill. Such novels are never condemned as immoral, never excite Boston's watchful warders. In general, they are permeated by piety, by complacent inconsistencies, by inane saccharine sentimentality. Of different kinds and on varying levels, they are usually of low standards in craftsmanship and lower values in useful reading relationships. But they command continuing demand and approval from readers (chiefly feminine), and are accepted by many librarians as "harmless"—satisfying to consumers and saving the time and trouble of discriminating selection. I find it difficult to justify their inclusion in a fiction collection of desirable standards and useful reading relationships. There is also constant, insistent demand for novels innocent of any values of substance or structure that apparently hold inspiration for their own elect; as, for example, *Carmen Ariza*, incredible compound of infantile melodrama, fatuous sentimentality, and thoroughgoing fanaticism, which still keeps its place on "reserve" lists. At the opposite pole is the inflow of popular fiction in which vulgarity and sexuality infiltrate content and method and present a problem of selection to be touched on in the next chapter.

The indiscriminate popularity of romantic-adventurous fiction, of "westerns," of mystery and detective novels, is an expression of the desire to find in mental diversion or absorption surcease or escape from everyday living. There is always also a formidable shifting volume of demand created by the commercial machinery of book publicity, that centers upon the novels (whatever their individual qualities may be) that are receiving the most intensive "promotion" at the moment. It must always be remembered that primarily fiction is read for pleasure; it is recreation, solace, entertainment, free and accessible to all; and in the service the public library renders to its community, recreation is an indispensable component.

The importance of this component is evidenced by Bernard Berelson's statement, in his study *The Library's Public*, Report of the Public Library Inquiry, page 56, that "fiction makes up 60 to 65 percent of the circulation of the American public library." This proportion, it should be remembered, is set by the public and is often questioned or opposed by library authorities. But if accepted as a norm, maintained and strengthened by perceptive and responsive selectivity, it could, I think, enable the public library through the creative art of fiction to "enlarge the entire range of human experience" and greatly extend public education and enlightenment.

How then is discriminating selection to be reconciled with public demand? This is a problem that cannot be solved by rigid formulation of standards or uncompromising enunciation of principles. It requires flexibility and tolerance. There should be a gradual but steady leavening of the lump of mass demand—an intelligent effort to replace inferior fiction by more excellent work of the same general type. A novel by Lloyd Douglas should satisfy, on a superior level, even a devotee of Harold Bell Wright. The work of Betty Smith, Agnes Turnbull, Dan Wickenden, Margaret Banning, Albert Idell, and many others, certainly holds more pleasure for uncritical readers than do the inferior productions they complacently absorb. Skillful, well-constructed, unbrutalized novels of crime detection are manifold; there are "westerns" in which sensationalism is tempered by genuine flavor of time and place. Careful and intelligent selection can provide fiction that will satisfy mass demand for entertainment and excitement, and yet avoid the banal, the rowdy, and the brutal.

Thus, a broad grouping of novels according to their type and the application to different types of the standards most appropriate to them, gives probably the best practical basis for general library selection. The biographic novel, for example, or the novel of intensive character portrayal, demands an insight into human nature and a vitality of individual character creation that are of less importance (though they impart added value) in the novel that centers upon sustained dramatic or sensational plot interest, for which ingenuity or originality are chief requirements. The novel of local color demands truth and vividness of setting and a distinctive characterization expressive of the environment it deals with. In the novel of social purpose, championing a cause or a theory, the reality of the problem, the interest of the theory propounded, and the effectiveness or verisimilitude with which it is presented, are of particular importance. In novels that center upon exploration of individual personality, there will necessarily be emphasis upon sex and upon psychopathology. The novel of imaginative fantasy or poetic symbolism is unfettered by the requirement of truth to reality in setting or in character creation, but must have something of the poet's magic, or the philosopher's insight, or the two-edged vigor of the satirist-moralist. The novel of specific factual basis, centering on art, or music, or the theatre, or medicine, or business, or any specialized activity, and the historical novel also, must evince knowledge and authority in the treatment of its particular subject, even though adapting it to a story-teller's purpose.

The continuous surging inflow of new novels (1,102 were published in 1948, 1,019 in 1949) and the close economy necessary in library expenditures impose rigorous limitation in selection. But this limitation should not be directed toward reduction of the fiction collection as a whole below the proportionate ratio its public use justifies. It should be exercised to eliminate mediocre, crude, and inferior fiction from current selection and replacement, to improve quality, maintain variety, and give judicious recognition to public demand. It must be remembered that to select fiction with discrimination and to develop its intelligent and fruitful use by readers requires not only knowledge of critical principles and much practice in analysis of individual books, but also an innate love of books, wide reading of novels, still wider reading of the better literary reviews, and a realization of the influences and values inherent in the form of literature that more than any other holds in solution the substance of human experience.

DEVELOPMENT OF MODERN ENGLISH FICTION INDICATED IN A CHRONOLOGICAL SEQUENCE OF FIFTY NOVELS

1813   Pride and Prejudice. Jane Austen.
1814   Waverley; or, 'Tis Sixty Years Since. Walter Scott.
1826   The Last of the Mohicans. J. Fenimore Cooper.
1847   Jane Eyre. Charlotte Brontë.
——   Wuthering Heights. Emily Brontë.
1848   Vanity Fair. W. M. Thackeray.
1850   David Copperfield. Charles Dickens.
——   The Scarlet Letter. Nathaniel Hawthorne.
1851   Moby Dick. Herman Melville.
1857   Barchester Towers. Anthony Trollope.
1859   Adam Bede. George Eliot.
——   The Ordeal of Richard Feverel. George Meredith.
1860   The Woman in White. Wilkie Collins.
1876   The Adventures of Tom Sawyer. Mark Twain.
1878   The Return of the Native. Thomas Hardy.
1881   The Portrait of a Lady. Henry James.
1882   Treasure Island. R. L. Stevenson.
1884   The Rise of Silas Lapham. W. D. Howells.
1894   Trilby. George DuMaurier.
——   Esther Waters. George Moore.
1895   The Red Badge of Courage. Stephen Crane.
1897   The Nigger of the Narcissus. Joseph Conrad.
1900   Sister Carrie. Theodore Dreiser.
1901   Kim. Rudyard Kipling.
1903   The Way of All Flesh. Samuel Butler.
1905   The House of Mirth. Edith Wharton.
1906   The Man of Property. John Galsworthy.
1908   The Old Wives' Tale. Arnold Bennett.
1909   Tono-Bungay. H. G. Wells.
1913   Sons and Lovers. D. H. Lawrence.
1915   Of Human Bondage. W. S. Maugham.
1919   Jurgen. James Branch Cabell.
——   The Tunnel. Dorothy Richardson.
1920   Main Street. Sinclair Lewis.
1922   Ulysses. James Joyce.
1923   A Lost Lady. Willa Cather.

1924 A Passage to India. E. M. Forster.
1926 Manhattan Transfer. John Dos Passos.
1928 Point Counter Point. Aldous Huxley.
1929 Look Homeward, Angel! Thomas Wolfe.
—— A Farewell to Arms. Ernest Hemingway.
1930 As I Lay Dying. William Faulkner.
1931 The Waves. Virginia Woolf.
—— The Good Earth. Pearl Buck.
1937 The Late George Apley. J. P. Marquand.
1939 The Grapes of Wrath. John Steinbeck.
1940 Native Son. Richard Wright.
1944 A Bell for Adano. John Hersey.
1948 The Naked and the Dead. Norman Mailer.
—— Cry, the Beloved Country. Alan Paton.

TWENTY-FIVE BOOKS ABOUT FICTION: CHOSEN TO CLARIFY JUDGMENT AND STIMULATE APPRECIATION OF THE MODERN NOVEL [5]

Beach, Joseph Warren. American Fiction, 1920–1940. New York, The Macmillan Company, 1941.
Critical and analytical study of eight novelists whose work has stamped patterns and opened paths in contemporary fiction, in which changes in social thought and changes and developments in literary art have found distinctive expression.

Bentley, Phyllis. Some Observations on the Art of Narrative. New York, The Macmillan Company, 1947.

Bowen, Elizabeth. English Novelists; with 8 plates in color and 19 illustrations in black and white (Britain in Pictures Series; ed. by W. J. Turner). London, William Collins, 1942.
Graceful, perceptive commentary, by an accomplished English novelist, writing "as a pleasure-seeker and not as a judge."

Brewster, Dorothy, and Angus Burrell. Modern Fiction. New York, Columbia University Press, 1934.
Fifteen chapter-essays on distinctive modern novelists, American,

---

[5] The list of "Twenty-five Books Representative of Significant Modern Criticism" appended to Chapter 18 (pp. 442–43) contains a number of enlightening studies of modern fiction; among them, *On Native Grounds: an Interpretation of Modern American Prose Literature,* by Alfred Kazin, has particular relevance to the present list.

English, and European. Underlying purpose is the recognition and understanding of "perspectives"—perspectives in the reader's own background and nature, and in the background and nature of the novelist as expressed in his work; this is set forth in first chapter. In final chapter the perspective of the reader and his response to the novelist and his work is considered as the essential factor to be recognized in understanding "fiction as experience"—i.e., the character and value of the experience that fiction gives to its readers. These two chapters will repay attention by librarians confronted by the perennial controversy over the effect of fiction upon human behavior.

Cross, Wilbur L. The Modern English Novel: address before the American Academy of Arts and Letters. New Haven, Yale University Press, 1928.

English fiction, "from around 1890" to 1928, is surveyed in a delightful, fleeting, retrospective glance.

Daiches, David. The Novel and the Modern World. Chicago, University of Chicago Press, 1939.

Forster, E. M. Aspects of the Novel. New York, Harcourt, Brace & Co., 1927; reissue, 1947.

Fox, Ralph. The Novel and the People. New York, International Publishers, 1937, 1944.

Published after the death of the young English author, who was killed fighting with the Loyalists in the first months of the Spanish Civil War, this is one of the first modern studies of fiction based on Marxist principles. Earnest, stimulating, and unpretentious, it urges the need of an epic fiction that shall draw its strength and truth from the energies and ideals emerging from the revolution of our own time, and discards the body of contemporary fiction that centers on character and emotion instead of social environment.

Garaudy, Roger. Literature of the Graveyard: Jean Paul Sartre, Francois Mauriac, André Malraux, Arthur Koestler. New York, International Publishers, 1948.

Brief, ardent affirmation of communist ideals linked with scathing critical attack on the four writers chosen as symbols of the decadence, skepticism, despair, and disintegration of a "dying world."

Geismar, Maxwell D. Writers in Crisis: the American novel between two wars. Boston, Houghton Mifflin Co., 1942.

Akin to Beach's *American Fiction, 1920–1940*, but centers on six instead of eight novelists, all but one (Ring Lardner) also covered by Beach. While too closely framed on an arbitrary pattern, gives effective indication of the strong rising current of social consciousness from 1929, leading to an almost absolute change of attitude and to the beginning of more ample, more humane work.

Glasgow, Ellen. A Certain Measure: interpretation of prose fiction. New York, Harcourt, Brace & Co., 1943.

Gustafson, Alrik. Six Scandinavian Novelists: Lie, Jacobsen, Heidenstam, Selma Lagerlöf, Hamsun, Sigrid Undset. Princeton, Princeton University Press; American-Scandinavian Foundation, 1940.

Haines, Helen E. What's in a Novel. New York, Columbia University Press, 1942.

Considers range and values of contemporary fiction, chiefly from the point of view of library book selection, with characterization of novels in many different type-groups. Designed as a companion to *Living with Books*.

Lavrin, Janko. Introduction to the Russian Novel. New York, Whittlesey House, 1947.

Leavis, F. R. The Great Tradition: George Eliot, Henry James, Joseph Conrad. New York, George W. Stewart, 1949.

Michaud, Regis. The American Novel Today. Boston, Little, Brown, 1928.

Still cogent, valid, and interesting.

Monroe, N. Elizabeth. The Novel and Society: a critical study of the modern novel. Chapel Hill, University of North Carolina Press, 1941.

Interesting and suggestive studies of five women novelists: Undset, Lagerlöf, Wharton, Glasgow, Cather. Catholic point of view prevails.

Muller, Herbert J. Modern Fiction: a study in values. New York, Funk & Wagnalls Company, 1937.

Applies term "modern" to the fiction of the last 60 years; covers a great number of the writers of this period but concentrates on those who have been a focus of controversy, who have "consciously or unconsciously adjusted their art to a changing order, faced in new directions, suggested new patterns of experience, or been, in any important sense, prophets or pioneers." Most comprehensive and useful of any recent study of modern fiction, in its sweeping birdseye view that brings out the range and tendency-currents of present-day fiction, with insight and seasoned judgment, although with a somewhat stereotyped attitude of mind.

O'Connor, William Van, ed. Forms of Modern Fiction: essays collected in honor of Joseph Warren Beach. Minneapolis, University of Minnesota Press, 1941.

Twenty-three essays by different writers, varied in range but chiefly concerned with forms and techniques employed by modern novelists.

Ortega y Gasset, José. The Dehumanization of Art; and Notes on the Novel. Princeton, Princeton University Press, 1948.

Two essays originally published in Madrid in 1923 and still thought-provoking. Emphasis is on structure and psychology as the two most important elements of the novel. Very interesting and suggestive analytical comment on Dostoyevsky and Proust.

Pritchett, Victor S. The Living Novel. New York, Reynal & Hitchcock, 1947.

A fresh approach to novels of the past and present, by a critic with a contagious enthusiasm for living books.

Reavey, George. Soviet Literature Today. New Haven, Yale University Press, 1947.

Of the eight chapters, three are wholly devoted to Soviet fiction.

Saurat, Denis. Modern French Literature, 1870–1940. New York, Doubleday & Company, 1947.

The French literary scene surveyed with a critical eye.

Stebbins, Lucy Poate. A Victorian Album: some lady novelists of the period. New York, Columbia University Press, 1946.

Taylor, Walter Fuller. The Economic Novel in America. Chapel Hill, University of North Carolina Press, 1942.

Study of the novels evoked by the industrialization of American society, from the 1870's to the turn of the century. Special emphasis is on Mark Twain, Hamlin Garland, Edward Bellamy, Howells, Frank Norris. Establishes interesting, significant background for the later fiction of social consciousness.

Van Doren, Carl. The American Novel, 1789–1939. Revised and enlarged ed. New York, The Macmillan Company, 1940.

Comprehensive survey and appraisal of history of American fiction through 150 years; excellent in compression and characterization. Very useful and illuminating in showing general conditions of life and opinion in America in their relation to development of the novel: rise of different types of fiction, changing interests and methods. One of the practical foundation stones for American librarians in building up knowledge of values and use of fiction.

FIFTY POSTWAR NOVELS, CHOSEN TO INDICATE BACKGROUNDS AND TRENDS OF A WORLD IN TRANSITION

Algren, Nelson. The Man with the Golden Arm. 1949.
Balchen, Nigel. The Small Back Room. 1945.
Bottome, Phyllis. Survival. 1943.
Bright, Robert. The Life and Death of Little Joe. 1944.
Burns, John Horne. The Gallery. 1947.
Chevalier, Haakon. For Us the Living. 1948.
Compton-Burnett, Ivy. Bullivant and the Lambs. 1948.
Cozzens, James G. Guard of Honor. 1948.
Fast, Howard. Clarkton. 1947.
Graham, Gwethalyn. Earth and High Heaven. 1944.
Hedden, Worth Tuttle. The Other Room. 1947.
Hersey, John. A Bell for Adano. 1944.
Heym, Stefan. The Crusaders. 1948.
Hobson, Laura Z. Gentleman's Agreement. 1947.
Jackson, Charles. The Lost Weekend. 1944.
Koestler, Arthur. Thieves in the Night. 1946.
La Farge, Christopher. The Sudden Guest. 1946.
Lewis, C. S. The Screwtape Letters. 1943.
McCullers, Carson. The Member of the Wedding. 1946.
Mailer, Norman. The Naked and the Dead. 1948.
Marquand, J. P. Point of No Return. 1949.
Miller, Arthur. Focus. 1945.
Miller, Merle. The Sure Thing. 1949.
Moon, Bucklin. Without Magnolias. 1949.
Motley, Willard. Knock on Any Door. 1947.
Paton, Alan. Cry, the Beloved Country. 1948.
Peters, Fritz. The World Next Door. 1949.
Petry, Ann. The Street. 1946.
Sayre, Joel. The House without a Roof. 1948.
Schneider, Isidor. The Judas Time. 1947.
Schulberg, Budd. What Makes Sammy Run? 1941.
Shaw, Irwin. The Young Lions. 1948.
Shute, Nevil. No Highway. 1948.
—— The Chequer Board. 1947.
Sinclair, Jo (Ruth Seid). Wasteland. 1946.
Sinclair, Upton. O Shepherd, Speak! 1949.

Singer, Jeanne. This Festive Season. 1943.
Smith, Lillian. Strange Fruit. 1944.
Smith, William Gardner. Last of the Conquerors. 1948.
Stewart, George R. Earth Abides. 1949.
Sylvester, Harry. Moon Gaffney. 1947.
Trilling, Lionel. The Middle of the Journey. 1947.
Turnbull, Agnes S. The Bishop's Mantle. 1947.
Ullman, James. The White Tower. 1945.
Wakeman, Frederic. The Hucksters. 1946.
Ward, Mary Jane. The Snake Pit. 1946.
Weaver, John D. Another Such Victory. 1948.
Weller, George. The Crack in the Column. 1949.
Williams, Charles. Many Dimensions. 1949.
Young, I. S. Jadie Greenway. 1947.

22. Aspects of Fiction

> At this time of day a civilized person, male or female, should be unshockable . . . Being shocked means that reason has been dethroned. Prudery, like fear, comes between a man and his impartial judgment, pulls this way and that, and perplexes the issue . . . Had anatomists been so disgusted by the sight of a dead human body that, averting their eyes, they had refused to proceed with their dissections, we should to this day be in a state of complete biological ignorance. And how should those who refuse to consider and, if possible, understand disagreeable, that is unfamiliar, tastes, habits and tendencies, physical and emotional extravagances—how should they, starting away, screaming, "I am shocked, I am shocked," ever come to know anything of psychology or ethics? The causes and consequences of what distresses them they will not examine. They never see, steadily and whole, the thing itself, because some physical qualm or hard-dying taboo—which they are pleased to call "moral indignation" or a "sense of decency"—surges up and blinds them. They cannot touch a snake; it gives them creeps. So it may; so much the worse for them; but do not let them make a virtue of a physical disability, or condemn snakes and snake-students on that account. This prudery, unlike fear, which is often a means to self-preservation and may well be founded on reason, springs wholly from superstition when it is not a mere physical qualm.
>
> <div align="right">Clive Bell: <i>Civilization: an Essay</i></div>

HISTORICAL FICTION was not included among types previously considered. Indeed, it is a broad class rather than a specific type, for within it are many different types: the biographic, the study of character and environment, the romantic, the realistic, the adventurous or melodramatic, and the symbolic or imaginative reweaving of historical legendry. Far-reaching influences, continuing appeal, emanate from this cross-fertilization of fiction with history, which links to literature in many fields of knowledge and establishes intimate relationship to History, Biography, Travel, Poetry, and Drama. In the enlarging orbit of historical fiction more and more attention turns to aspects of history that have immediate significance today and that are presented with realistic precision rather than romantic glamour. In public library service, in school librarianship, and in the teaching profession there is need of broader knowledge and more constructive realization of the values and use of the historical novel.

Perhaps the simplest, most explicit definition of the historical novel is that it is a novel which depicts actual periods, persons, or events of history in such a manner that they can be readily identified. Such depiction may be complete or partial, specific or generalized. Many novels are rendered historical by their evocation of the background and "atmosphere" of a period, rather than by presentation of specific historical characters or events, as in Gogol's magnificent epic of sixteenth-century Cossack life, *Taras Bulba*, Hewlett's vignettes of Renaissance Italy, *Little Novels of Italy*, Hawthorne's background of colonial New England in *The Scarlet Letter*. Others again, in the depiction of their own day (such as *Tom Jones* and *Evelina*), become historical with the passing of time—just as *Ann Vickers*, if it should survive until 2030, will then be a novel of distinctive historical American twentieth-century background. For the great body of historical fiction the more rigid definition is valid. The historical novel offers a re-creation of the past at once imaginative and realistic, it imbues famous figures of history with immediate vitality and emotional significance, and it enables present-day readers to realize conditions of living as they were known to men and women of a vanished day.

"Historical novel" is a term often used by critics and reviewers in a slurring fashion, as if this were a hybrid or inferior form of fiction. On the contrary, it is a form that has exercised the talents of the greatest masters of fiction, whose art has helped to mold and develop it; it will be found generously represented in any list of the great novels of the world. Among English novelists alone, Scott, Thackeray, Dickens, George Eliot, Bulwer, the Kingsleys, Charles Reade, Walter Besant, Walter Pater, Stevenson, Conrad, Doyle, Hewlett, Walpole, Robert Graves, and Naomi Mitchison have brought power and skill to the weaving of history into the tapestry of fiction. Among present-day American novelists Joseph Hergesheimer, James Boyd, Esther Forbes, Willa Cather, Elizabeth Roberts, and Susan Ertz have found in American history material for novels of distinction and beauty; Kenneth Roberts, Hervey Allen, Margaret Mitchell, and many others have brought epical drama and pictorial reality to the re-creation of periods and events; and Evelyn Scott drew from the Civil War, theme and substance for her endeavor in *The Wave* to render into fiction simultaneous human experiences caught, carried to intensity, and swept under by the wave of war.

The critical warfare waged over historical fiction had its origins in the opposed ideals and methods of romanticism and realism in literary art. This perennial controversy was strongest in Victorian days, when powerful currents of realism were sweeping into a body of fiction dominated by the romantic and the sentimental. Sir Leslie Stephen was probably the bitterest opponent of the historical romance; Howells, also, was an uncompromising and consistent adversary. The distinction between the romantic and the realistic spirit in fiction still exists, and each still enlists its adherents; but there is now more general realization of the ceaseless alternating currents that make the rhythm of literature, as of life. Also an aggressive realism, fostered by the material and spiritual destructiveness of the Depression years and two world wars, and by a postwar world under deepening shadow of doom, has succeeded the cheerful, confident optimism of the pre-atomic age. In briefest summary, the chief charges brought against the historical novel are that it has no legitimate right to exist at all; that the romantic convention, to which primarily the historical novel belongs, means inaccuracy and distortion of fact; that even the best historical novels abound in anachronisms and misstatements, that they mislead the ignorant and irritate the well informed, and that the very attempt to re-create a past period is absolutely and necessarily impossible. The only real historical novel, according to these critics, is the novel that pictures in detailed verity the life of its own day and thus in the course of time becomes a valid historical record.

There are ample rejoinders to these contentions. Although the ideal of history is truth, this ideal, like many others, can never be fully realized; in the work of the greatest historians there is always some alloy of prejudice, partisanship, or emotional emphasis. The great appeal of history does not lie in the enumeration of facts, but in the unrolling of a panorama of human action, in the delineation of conditions of living and of the development and destinies of human beings, as individuals and in mass. The able historical novelist unrolls this panorama and offers this delineation, without assuming the authority of the historian yet with a sincere effort to convey the color and pattern of life in the past and to give immediate reality, charm, and meaning to its human figures. It is true that Shakespeare was a boy of eleven in the year that Scott (in *Kenilworth*) depicts him as a player at Elizabeth's court; true that the Young Pretender never came to England in such a conspiracy as Thackeray weaves in *Henry Esmond*. Nevertheless, Scott's recreation of Elizabethan pageantry and intrigue, Thackeray's panorama of the days of Addison and Steele and of the hopes and plots of Stuart adherents that centered about Queen Anne, give the life and color of those two periods as few would realize them from history alone. Nor can history alone illuminate and humanize remote and unfamiliar segments of the past as can the historical novel. Eleanor Dark did this in *The Timeless Land*, her creative historical novel of Australia's beginnings, which weaves the full web of human experience from the thread of recorded fact. The first five years of English settlement, in authentic substance of history, gives the material base for an epic of human struggle, submergence, and emergence that conveys the evolutionary process of civilization as it involves the native race, the white man, and the land itself, timeless and immobile, constraining man to its own nature. A good historical novel demands the painstaking research of the historical student, the keen analysis and dramatic instinct of the novelist, and the gift of creative imagination that can infuse life into the dust of yesterday. Such a novel reaches the mass of readers as history cannot; it kindles an interest and offers a lure that lead many to pursue for themselves exploration and discovery in history and biography.

In good historical fiction the most important elements are truth, graphic power, consistent character portrayal, and sustained dramatic or human interest. It is work of imagination, not of fact;

authoritative history is not expected; but it should satisfy broad requirements of historical truth and probability. Other things being equal, the more sound and thorough the historical basis the deeper and more enduring is the value. Naomi Mitchison's magnificent novel, *The Corn King and the Spring Queen*, which unfolds the pageant of the ancient world in the second century before Christ, displays not only the skill and insight of the novelist, but scholarship and authority in history, archaeology, and anthropology. Sigrid Undset's *Kristin Lavransdatter* re-creates the life of medieval Norway, not only with the intensity of immediate emotional experience, but with a rich historical knowledge founded on long and specialized research. The historical novel of romantic adventure, stemming from Dumas and Stevenson, at its best keeps its thread of historical truth as clear and strong as possible.

With the many virtues of the historical novel there are also many faults. This is one of the most tempting forms to the immature writer, and one of the most common vehicles chosen to serve some ulterior purpose—to prove an author's thesis, to vindicate or condemn a person or a cause, to expound a fixed idea or cherished theory. Crude, sensational, trivial, and deeply prejudiced historical novels abound; and the lack of intelligent, critical but fair-minded reviewing that exists concerning them makes discriminating selection difficult. Chief among defects are flagrant distortion of history; the focusing upon a single exaggerated theme; superabundance of costume and dearth of flesh-and-blood people; elaborate descriptive detail, with all life buried under antiquarian furniture; affectations in language, with speech turned into timeworn, archaic jargon; and the injection of an entirely modern spirit and present-day colloquial phrasing in the portrayal of people and times with which they are entirely inconsistent. The two latter weaknesses are now much diminished, for historical fiction today is developing a smooth and lively technique that conveys thought and action suitably to the modern reader, but is neither oppressively antiquarian nor preposterously modern.

Factual accuracy based on sound historical data has become an accepted responsibility. Many histories and biographies that receive wide acceptance are less well documented, less carefully grounded on authoritative material, than are the historical novels of Kenneth Roberts, Neil Swanson, Esther Forbes, Elizabeth Page, and many others. Few readers realize how much care is taken to verify incidental details and guard against anachronisms. *Gone with the Wind* received, during eight months before publication, so rigorous a checking of facts that verification from four reference sources was required for every statement of fact before it was incorporated in the text. But this research and factual accuracy have little relation to a novelist's theme and point of view; his work in its nature is fiction, not history, and he is free to choose any subject that interests him and write about it from any point of view. Kenneth Roberts' *Oliver Wiswell*, for example, is an intensely partisan presentation of the Loyalist side in the American Revolutionary War. The Revolution is regarded as conceived in iniquity and born of evil, directed by conscienceless political tricksters, rabble-rousing demagogues, and crazy theorists, "turning all our colonies into madhouses," supported by brutal mob violence, and carried out by a shambling, pock-marked, cowardly rabble that ran like rabbits whenever firmly encountered. This indicates the "revisionist" trend to unsparing realism which has found strong expression in literature and thought. But whatever the values of this trend in illuminating many unregarded realities of the past, the violent one-sidedness of *Oliver Wiswell* remains a novelist's distortion of history.

The expansion and revivification of historical fiction that has given the historical novel its immense popularity with American readers for the past quarter century came, I think, not as a surface wave of escapism from the stresses of the Depression, but as a deep unconscious movement toward national homogeneity. It was part of the revival of interest in American things that became manifest as the fight against the Depression got under way and recognition of evils and weaknesses in our social structure brought clearer vision of the American heritage and stronger purpose for its fulfillment. All people must meet adversity from resources within themselves, and it was inevitable that Americans should turn instinctively to the American past, rooted in conviction of the dignity of man; to the American scene, in its continental richness and variety; to America's power of welding human diversity into unity. The flood of American historical fiction that began its rise in 1930 drew from the richly diversified backgrounds of that past a succession of changing, contrasting figures, in colorful, arresting evocation and interpretation. Two phenomena were born of those floodwaters. *Anthony Adverse*—creation of picaresque world adventure rather than of specialized historical fiction—appeared in July, 1933, and had sold 275,000 copies by the year's end; and in 1936 the advent of *Gone with the Wind* set a world record that remains unique. Margaret Mitchell's only novel stands by itself in Civil War fiction; one of those rare novels that in sheer storytelling quality commands absorbed interest and spontaneous emotional response. There are defects in characterization and strong partisanship, and a high-colored romanticism dominates, but the book has flesh-and-blood reality, magnetic power, and genuine historic substance.[1] While the flood tide of our historical novels has waned, they are still the most popular form of American fiction and their influence has been more than transitory. American historical novels have gained a maturity of art and method they never possessed before; they are producing, in their own measure, the background-making values that English historical novels have so long held, creating the strong sense of a common past that integrates a people, and making the heritage of American memories a test for the present and an inspiration for the future.

It must be remembered that in its full range the historical novel makes every country and every age its tributary. Masters of English and European fiction have laid its foundations and molded its development. The work of even minor present-day writers, con-

---

[1] *Golden Multitudes*, by Frank Luther Mott (Macmillan, 1947) gives admirable comment on these two novels. Indeed, Dr. Mott's volume, in its well-marshalled, swift-paced cavalcade of the books that through three hundred years (from 1662 to 1945) have been best sellers in the United States, offers pleasure and enlightenment to all who know or enjoy books.

stantly improving in historical authority and in flexibility of technique, has freshness and energy in bringing to light obscure materials and emphasizing aspects of the past that take on special significance for our own times. What this fiction can do in strengthening and vitalizing individual background knowledge of history is not sufficiently realized. In almost every country native novelists have used their art to weave from the fibers of their country's past a tapestry of national experience that imbues with life, color, and immediacy historic traditions, events, crises, famous figures, the conditions of men and women through earlier generations. Nearly every age and epoch finds representation and interpretation in this form of fiction. The ancient world—Crete, Egypt, Palestine, Asia, Greece, Rome in power and decay—has been evoked in brilliant, pictorial realism by an enlarging body of modern novelists. The medieval world, the world of the Renaissance, the far-expanding horizons of the Western Hemisphere, the new vistas of our own age opening in the Eastern Hemisphere and in ancient Oriental civilizations, receive similar, more widely radiating illumination. The great panorama of history in fiction sweeps down through more than three thousand years of man's recorded progress through time.

So much fine historical fiction comes from European writers that the subject leads naturally to another important aspect of contemporary fiction. This concerns the values that exist for American readers in foreign fiction in English translation, regarded from the point of view of illumination and interpretation—historical, social, pictorial—of the world's life, past and present. The whole flood of English fiction, of course, has been fed from the springs of world literature. In its development are to be traced influences derived from the medieval French romances, the early Spanish narratives of roguery and adventure, the German introspective romanticism of Jean Paul (Richter) and *Wilhelm Meister*, the universality of Balzac (Gulliver among the pygmies, as Henry James calls him), the technique of Flaubert and Anatole France, the naturalism of Zola, the sensuous power of D'Annunzio, the psychological revelation of Dostoyevsky, the prophetic vision of Tolstoy. Knowledge of these and other influences that have helped to mold the thought and expression of English and American writers is necessary to any understanding of modern English fiction. Every cultivated person must have some background familiarity with the world masters of creative literary art; and librarians dealing with the dominant creative literary art of our own day should have the widest possible acquaintance with the contemporary foreign fiction made available to American readers in good English translation.

Not only does foreign fiction include many of the greatest works of world literature, but in range and variety it brings the English reading public to virtual first-hand acquaintance with human life and character all over the world. Through contemporary novels by foreign writers familiarity with history, with national, social, and political backgrounds, is deepened, narrow personal horizons are enlarged, provincialism is reduced, and clearer understanding is instilled of the rise of conflicting mass forces that, unrealized and uncontrolled, can foredoom humanity. Only through knowledge and association, whether direct or vicarious, do we realize the kinship of the human family and see our own emotions and experiences repeated or interpreted in the emotions and experiences of another branch of the race. Complacent isolation is likely to develop a mentality incapable of imaginative or intellectual apprehension of ways of thinking and living outside personal experience. To a dogmatic provincialism all it is accustomed to is good; all that is unfamiliar is undesirable and probably evil. The sweep of world catastrophe since 1940 brought Americans into immensely increased contact with the human tragedies, the uprooted, displaced, and replanted lives of Europe; nevertheless, this provincialism, in some degree, exists among the rank and file of American readers, whose attitude toward foreign fiction, if not one of entire ignorance and indifference, is still likely to be one of distrust or predetermined distaste. The public that accepts and appreciates foreign fiction has enormously enlarged, but it is still chiefly a public of higher intellectual abilities than the mass, or of more cosmopolitan background, or of foreign heredity or extraction.

First among the difficulties encountered by many Americans when they begin to read the work of foreign novelists is distaste for books that are not set in familiar scenes and written in familiar form. This distaste often exists even for English fiction: the backgrounds are unfamiliar; the social structure portrayed is irritating; the people and their environment are unreal and uninteresting. Such readers are generally of limited education or undeveloped literary taste. In foreign fiction the most formidable obstacle that confronts the inexperienced American reader is the unfortunate fact that the authors, the characters, the places, all have foreign names, unnecessarily unintelligible and much less satisfying than such comfortable and familiar names as Kathleen Norris, Zane Grey, or Walla Walla, Washington. There are obstacles of subject and style. Foreign novels usually have a theme, philosophic or ethical or psychological; or they may be genre novels, portraying life in simple pictures, plotless, with little or no action. The most widely popular American and English fiction tells a story and gives its readers plot, action, and dialogue. In style foreign novels may seem odd and unpleasing: disconnected and bewildering, or overemotional and confusing, or tiresome and monotonous in long analyses or descriptions. In reality much foreign fiction represents perfected technique in literary art. It has its own beauty and power: delicate pencillings, passionate intensities, austere clarity; it takes for granted or implies what English fiction expounds or explains. Foreign writers seldom care for "happy endings"; they are interested in crises, emotional complexities, tangled skeins of purpose and motive; subjects that the provincial-minded reader is likely to regard as "unpleasant," if not "immoral"; in what Unamuno calls "the tragic sense of life." Unconcerned by any adolescent problem, they regard fiction as intended for mature readers, and mature readers are supposed to accept any exposition of a subject or to avoid it if it is distasteful to them, but not to supervise it for other mature readers. This Continental point of view has come more and more to prevail in the United States as America's participation deepens in the conflict, disintegrations, struggles, and confusions of a world in transition.

Ever since the First World War, which first made Europe real to modern America, the work of the leading foreign novelists has flowed in a swelling current into our literature; there is wide diversity and expansion in supply and steadily growing volume of use. That such novels as Hamsun's *Growth of the Soil*, Reymont's *The Peasants*, Undset's *Kristin Lavransdatter*, should have taken their place among American best-sellers, is evidence of the steady improvement in reading tastes that (in spite of standardization and mediocrity) is in process in the United States today. From French and Italian, Spanish, Balkan, Belgian, Dutch, and German writers the European scene has been built before us; from Scandinavia and the north has come work of beauty and power, stimulus to thought and feeling—novels from Copenhagen, from Oslo, from Finland and Iceland. The Russian genius, emerged from the eclipse of revolution, again flashes its portents against the clouds. From the Orient and South America we receive more frequent and varied manifestations of a rich and diversified literary art.

But the whole world scene has changed and darkened from the clear and confident vistas of the dawning twentieth century. In the mirror of fiction is reflected a civilization engulfed for a decade in war, ruin, misery; struggling through incredible horrors of violence and suffering toward visioned goals of peace and self-fulfillment, but carried by the undertow of military power rivalry toward a world cleavage that invites man's complete self-destruction. Only by mutual responsibility, accommodation, and concession can continuing world catastrophe be escaped and swelling currents of fear, suspicion, and hatred be abated by reason, tolerance, and acceptance of unity in diversity. The fifty contemporary foreign novels in English translation with which the present chapter closes were chosen as indication of the presage and impact of world war and revolution in Europe. Perhaps from these novels American readers may draw fuller realization of their own inescapable participation in one of those revolutionary periods of human history when forces long accumulating have intensified to explosion point.

Thus foreign fiction illuminates world vistas. By reading a limited but intelligently chosen group of books by novelists of a given country any American can gain understanding of that country's history and design for living more vivid and more responsive than is likely to be produced by the conscientious perusal of any textbook summary or even by more ambitious works of formal history. Educators and scholars constantly urge universal literacy, broader education, and respect for all races as holding the only solution for the problems we are facing today. Libraries have important responsibilities toward such solution. The iron curtain of mutual ignorance and distorted judgment that shuts off contact between American and Soviet mass minds might be made less impenetrable by fuller representation in our general library selection of novels by Soviet writers that reveal Soviet concepts, Soviet experience, in their own past and present way of life. Such a selection need comprise only half a dozen novels: opening, say, with Alexei Tolstoy's trilogy, *The Road to Calvary*, definitive novel of the revolution, from its foreshadowings in Saint Petersburg in 1914 through the painful building of a new society; then Sholokhov's two-volume sequence, *The Silent Don*, panorama of the fratricidal civil war of 1917–21, portrayed with understanding and insight for Reds and Whites alike; the same writer's *Seeds of Tomorrow*, picturing the communist effort of 1930 for collectivization of the land of Cossack farmers; *Road to the Ocean*, Leonid Leonov's many-colored evocation in realism and fantasy of the early years of Soviet development; *The Storm*, Ilya Ehrenburg's powerful panoramic exposition of the Second World War, from Paris in 1939 to victory in 1945; and Konstantin Simonov's *Days and Nights*, story of the defense of Stalingrad, austere, unforgettable record of unending fighting in the rubble of city streets, when days and nights were indistinguishable and men lived or died without sleep. As a postscript I would add *The Train*, Vera Panova's short, warmly human novel of the Russian hospital train rushing back and forth between the front and its base. Such vistas can be extended and diversified, carried more fully through a country's history or opened for almost any country, in novels that bring realization of the movement, color, and depth of the world's life, rising, changing, and passing in ceaseless cycle of forms.

Points of chief importance in the selection of foreign fiction are the writer's claim to consideration, the merit of the translation, the degree and trend of community interest, and I would add the power of the book to aid international understanding. As a rule, novelists who have won wide recognition in their own country have qualities that will command the attention of readers elsewhere. The Nobel Prize, of course, confers international distinction, and the various novelists who have received it belong in any adequate collection of fiction. The many literary awards of national significance also give guidance in selection, for they represent work that by virtue of style or originality or some particular appeal stands out above the ordinary level. The importance of good translation can hardly be overestimated. This has previously been emphasized; it demands particular attention in the selection of fiction. A novel that in the original may have admirable qualities, but that is available only in a crude and garbled English rendering, does not belong in a well chosen collection. The amount of representation given to foreign fiction must vary according to possibilities of demand. In larger cities and cosmopolitan communities there will be much wider and stronger interest than in small towns and rural regions; but even the smallest public library should provide fiction that will appeal to minority race groups in the community, and that for cultivated readers, for study clubs, for all interested in world affairs, will extend mental horizons beyond provincialism.

We come now to the most difficult and controversial aspect of fiction from the point of view of library selection. This is the aspect of its ethical influence upon readers and the attitude toward censorship that is involved. Traditional moralism has waned today, but there still lingers widespread belief in the prevalence and evil influence of "immoral fiction." This is in part the result of our moral heritage. The harmful influence of novels was a tenet of most moral and religious teaching from the days of the beginnings of the English novel, a tenet partly rooted, of course, in that ancient puritan conviction that whatever is pleasant is pernicious. Nowadays, fiction that is part of the background of literature stirs little controversy; but from lecture platforms and pulpits there still come denunciations of the modern novel, of its repulsive themes, its iconoclasm, its flaunting and brazen impudicity, its morbidity of subject and treatment. Many library trustees and leaders in public and educational affairs (by most of whom all imaginative literature is regarded as distinctly inferior to "serious" reading) share these opinions; and in every American community there is a large reformist element, eager to serve as self-constituted protectors of public morals. Thus a more definite attitude of censorship exists toward fiction than toward any other class of literature; its selection for library use is hedged with difficulties and perplexities; and librarians themselves are often too timorous or too rigorous to make their fiction collections representative of the spirit of the age and of the most stimulating and significant tendencies and developments of literary art.

Concern over the ethical influence of fiction concentrates upon its treatment of sex. As a matter of fact, there are many other elements that may make a novel undesirable; but this is the one that arouses the strongest, most widespread reprobation. Nevertheless, today sex must be accepted as a legitimate and integral element of fiction; it is one of the primary life forces, a crucial factor in all human experience; and the novel as literary art is welded from the raw material of life experience. In the intellectual revolution that has taken place since the opening of the century the older attitude toward sex as solely related to moral questions has been discarded; it is now a field of scientific study through biology and psychology, a subject of popular exposition and discussion from many points of view, and an immediate, practical problem of everyday experience. Through newspapers, magazines, and moving pictures its sensational and offensive features have become so familiar that fiction which presents the same aspects, while meretricious and deteriorating in its effect on public taste, can hardly be regarded as in itself a destructive ethical influence. Fiction of this type has no place in intelligent selection; but dominance of a sex theme, preoccupation with sexual psychopathology, blunt characterization of the "facts of life," intensive analysis of sex emotion, are common attributes of the best fiction of the day.

In discriminating selection there can be no wholesale winnowing of what used to be called "sex novels." But there must be differentiation between fiction that in dealing with sex possesses sincerity, social significance, and values as literature, and that which represents simply sensationalism and lubricity. The change in attitude that has taken place today toward the whole body of sex literature should aid in this differentiation. During the last quarter-century a flood of erotic fiction opened new channels in the American book world. It began with the so-called "erotica," at first distributed in semi-surreptitious fashion in high-priced subscription and "de luxe" editions, later launched into immense general popularity through "remainders" and cheap flashy editions, filling drugstore windows and department store counters; while at the same time the more distinguished works in this field, long restricted from general circulation, were published in standard low-priced series. By various legal decisions the ban of official censorship was lifted or relaxed, both as regards informational works concerning sex and novels once adjudged obscene. In fact, virtually the whole orchard of forbidden fruit in literature was suddenly made accessible to the public. The result has been that the lure of the illicit simply as illicit has weakened; the classics that have lived as mirrors of an earlier age or as outpourings of animal spirits or ribald ironies by writers of genius are more generally seen in their true proportions; and for the mass of erotic fiction everyday readers can discover for themselves the deadly dullness, the nauseous reiteration, to which its provocative hints and mysterious beckonings invite.

It must be recognized that much current fiction receiving general acceptance today from critics and readers would have been pilloried and prohibited a few years ago. *Strange Fruit* was adjudged obscene (the judgment later reversed) from the use of one four-letter word; four-letter words are now the vitamins of novelists who cherish the delusion that only strong words can express strong emotions. The war novels first released the tide of profanity that flows through fiction today, and dredged from the oozy bed of the unconscious strange monsters of frustration, lust, and sadism, which roam now uninhibited through novels of love, of marriage, and of adolescence. Sex obsession has not yet, apparently, passed its peak. Most of its manifestations—pathological, neurotic, bawdy, phallic, and the rest—are now so familiar that their shock power has diminished and there can be fairer discernment of individual values; and these values do exist. Recognized and accepted as an indispensable element in any valid study or interpretation of human nature, it seems fair to expect that sex will eventually command less exaggerated emphasis, to be treated in more ordered proportion by novelists proficient in their art.

Fiction may be rendered defective and undesirable by other characteristics than its treatment of sex. Equally open to condemnation in any broad consideration of ethical influences is the fiction that seeks to intensify race and national hatreds; that invests dramatic plots of crime, of underworld or picaresque adventure with callous brutality and deliberate sadism; and that is steeped in a sardonic, jeering contempt for human beings as doomed animals or determinist machines. Such fiction is much less an object of public criticism and protest, but it demands as definite an application of standards of selection as does that which offends in its treatment of sex.

Discriminating and broad-minded selection will not fully solve the public library's fiction problem. There always remains the argument that much modern fiction of high literary art and distinctive value is harmful to immature minds, and that the public library with its open shelves must protect young readers from this influence. This is the bulwark behind which the volunteer censors of a community chiefly entrench themselves. The argument is open to question. Most young people today through school courses in biology and physiology and the extramural instruction of the movies are more familiar with sex than were the adults of an earlier generation;

it receives from them a more matter-of-fact acceptance. Dr. Kinsey has reached a large adolescent audience. Also much of the fiction that it is believed might be harmful to them either will not be fully understood; or will be regarded as unutterably dull and left undisturbed; or will be already familiar from other sources. Any young person who wants to read and will read *Strange Fruit* is not likely to derive moral injury from so doing. The garish vulgarity of *Forever Amber* was less, I think, the reason for its whirlwind popularity than was the vivid story-telling drive that gave to immature readers a cheap, high-colored chromo of Defoe's two famous originals.

Public libraries in general, however, accept this argument. It has resulted in the practice of restricting to limited adult use much current fiction that may by some protestant be regarded as questionable or objectionable. There is no consistency discernible in the practice of restriction, nor is any very high degree of common sense evident in its application. In many communities it is probably a necessary expedient. But it should be definitely recognized as intended only to protect young readers, and any adult should have free range in choice of the fiction that the library finds worthy of selection. Too often "restricted" books are invested with an illicit flavor; the mature reader who wishes to read *The Well of Loneliness*, or *Ulysses*, or even *Madame Bovary*, is made to feel under suspicion as a degenerate or a libertine. Fiction is an adult art, and most novels are intended for men and women. There is no reason why books that may fairly be withheld from adolescents should not be available without question for mature readers; and one of the most common difficulties of library service in relation to modern fiction would be much nearer solution if such a course as this could be consistently followed.

One of the most useful contributions to this subject is the short *Library Journal* article (February 15, 1949), "It Takes Courage to Stock 'Taboos'," in which Roger P. Bristol summarizes with wit and common sense "what librarians do when faced with books that are hot to handle." The books dealt with were "the K-bomb of 1948," in other words, the Kinsey Report, *Sexual Behavior in the Human Male*, and Norman Mailer's *The Naked and the Dead*, both leading and continuous best-sellers; and the decisions concerning them were made in eleven public libraries near Boston that serve populations from 11,000 to 100,000. The divergencies in practice, the various factors in decision, and the methods of dealing with "taboo" books are clearly and tersely noted. "The basic conflict," says Mr. Bristol, "seems to be between two conceptions of the librarian's job: (1) maintaining taboos of society, and (2) providing wide variety of community fare, even including material personally repugnant to the librarian." "There are two cross-pulls in libraries now," it is added: "greatly increased frankness in books and magazines, and the native conservatism of libraries." Mr. Bristol's own conclusion holds promise for the future: "In no library have the taboos increased; at most, some libraries have stood pat." It is to be hoped that other librarians more interested in books than in mechanization techniques concerning them, may supply from time to time kindred studies of other novels that pose a similar problem of existent or non-existent public values. John O'Hara's *A Rage to Live*, Budd Schulberg's *What Makes Sammy Run?*, Nelson Algren's *The Man with the Golden Arm* might be potential subjects.

Selection, not censorship, is the library's responsibility. For the best advantage of its community it must select from the mass of current fiction that which is adjudged the best according to standards of literary value and by practical standards of usefulness, or timeliness, or popular demand. In selection it must, perforce, draw from the books that are. You cannot get a contemporary literature made to order. What is new, untried, startling, in fiction today is simply manifestation of the eternal youth of literature, constantly reborn of the spirit of its day and stamped with the pattern of its time.

One of the important divisions of fiction is that of the short story. A distinct fictional form, with its own qualities, characteristics, and wide popular appeal, its relationship to the essay has already been noted, and it should command more attention than this brief summary can give. The short story may be, perhaps, best defined as the equivalent in fiction to the lyric in poetry and the one-act play in drama: the intensified, concentrated expression of an idea or a theme that is presented in more detail and more leisurely exposition in the novel. There is clear differentiation between the short story and the novelette, though dimensionally both may be placed in the same category. The novelette is a novel reduced in its dimensions; the short story is an entity in itself, compact, brilliant or pellucid, powerful or moving, on a single key of feeling. The novel paints life on a canvas of any preferred amplitude; it may include many characters, may linger on scenery, on incidents not vital to its theme, may moralize, analyze, or describe at leisure. It is, as a rule, chiefly, or in large measure, concerned with love. In all these points the short story differs; its chief characteristic is implied in its name; it is essentially incident (of fact, of imagination, of romance, of realism, of terror, of adventure); many of the finest short stories do not touch upon love at all.

Requirements of the short story may be epitomized as structure, style, imaginative power. Built on a single incident, or theme, or plot-climax, it must achieve unity of effect. It demands greater, but less sustained, mastery of style than does the novel; its pattern may be pricked in a swift staccato fusillade or traced in delicate word shadowings. It permits use of vague suggestions and fancies too delicate in texture for a novel; and it is also the legitimate medium for the portrayal of the horrible, the morbid, the evocation of terror; the thrill of horror imparted would become an intolerable nightmare if drawn out through the length of a novel. It may pose problems without answering them; need not trace cause and effect in logical development or work out a conclusion; may make beauty out of the horrible and turn the commonplace into poetic symbolism. These opportunities exist in the novel, but are more difficult of accomplishment; the brevity of the short story, while it limits, also makes for freedom. At the same time the short story lacks much that the novel possesses; it does not require the even balance, sustained power, the sanity and breadth of view. Most first-rank novelists have written short stories of merit, but the masters of the short story are less often first-rank novelists.

Popular interest in the short story has lessened within recent years, in part undoubtedly owing to the rise of the printed play in public favor; but short stories are in perennial use by at least two large groups—those who for themselves or for invalids desire reading that will give refreshment and relaxation for a few hours at a time, that can be picked up at odd minutes and quickly finished; and those who are either students of literature or of the technique of short-story writing. To meet this demand an adequate fiction collection should provide the best work of individual authors and a good range of anthologies, and in current selection should glean from new publications in both kinds. The gleaning should be highly selective. In individual collections, the standing of the author is of first importance; writers whose work is virtually unknown or highly experimental are as a rule sufficiently represented in the anthologies.

For short-story anthologies the principles that apply in selection of collections of plays will prove suitable. Works included in the standard short-story indexes have, of course, special usefulness. Anthologies that group stories by type (ghost stories, sea stories, mystery stories, dog stories, and so on) are likely to repeat familiar material, so that a varied range of types is preferable to many examples of a single type.

The various annual anthologies, with their emphasis on experimentalism and originality, appeal to the literary student and would-be writer rather than to the general reader. Oldest and most widely known of them are: The *Best American Short Stories* (Boston, Houghton), edited by Martha Foley since the death of Edward J. O'Brien, who founded this annual in 1914; and *Prize Stories*, chosen by the O. Henry Memorial Award Committee, edited by Herschel Brickell, and published for the Society of Art and Letters by Doubleday & Company. Particular interest attaches to *Story: the Fiction of the Forties* (New York, Dutton, 1949) in which Whit and Hallie Burnett, editors of the magazine *Story*, have assembled fifty-one stories printed in that magazine from 1941 to

1948, when, as Whit Burnett says, "all angels departed" and the magazine was suspended; and to the companion volumes, *Short Stories from the New Yorker*, 1925–40, and *55 Short Stories from the New Yorker* (New York, Simon & Schuster, 1940, 1949). As has been previously mentioned, the impress of the *New Yorker* has imparted a quality of transitional allurement to much contemporary writing—an ironic evasion of emotional challenge or commitment, a cynical or hilarious sophistication, and a sympathetic insight that disintegrates social pretenses and penetrates undercurrents of personality. In the general field of fiction anthologies are legion, in multitude probably rivalling the anthologies of plays and poetry. Every form and every type of writing is drawn upon; the whole world and the seven ages of man are reflected with intensifying realism and a deepening sense of opposing social forces. Amid the routine of fiction selection there should be constant watchfulness for fresh, well edited collections that have value as examples of distinctive writing or that illuminate unfamiliar, remote but crucial realities of the world's life—as do the two volumes, *Contemporary Chinese Stories*, translated by Chi-Chen Wang (New York, Columbia University Press, 1944), and *Stories of China at War*, edited by the same Chinese scholar and from the same press in 1947.

There are many excellent aids available in selection of fiction. Those in which annotations are a feature are of special usefulness, for they give clue to content and often indicate quality of books that are unfamiliar. In limited selection, of course, the standard general aids (*Booklist, Standard Catalog, Book Review Digest*) are chief reliance. Annotations in the *Booklist*, representing evaluation from the library point of view, are generally accepted as decisive appraisal; those in the *Book Review Digest*, indicating consensus of literary reviewers' opinion, are useful as basis for consideration but often register approval of books that do not justify library selection.

The Wilson *Fiction Catalog: 1941 Edition*, published in 1942, is probably the most practical and effective American bibliographical tool yet provided for the constructive use of fiction, in broad contemporary range, in general library service. Technically a volume in the "Standard Catalog Series," succeeding the *Standard Catalog: Fiction Section* of 1931, it is a new and different work that represents a compromise between the original "Standard Catalog" plan and the comprehensive subject index to fiction long desired by librarians. Such an index was considered by Wilson soon after the publication of the *Standard Catalog: Fiction Section* and questionnaires were sent to librarians to determine the degree of comprehensiveness that was needed. Apparently, the extent and complexity of the field proved too formidable, and it was decided to expand the former *Fiction Section* to serve both as a buying list and selective aid and for reference use as a subject index to fiction. This is the fullest bibliographic guide to fiction that has as yet appeared in the United States; 5,520 titles are included, of which 5,050 receive full entry and 470 are referred to in the notes. The dictionary form makes for prompt, practical efficiency. Virtually all titles receive annotations; these, drawn from many sources, are predominantly descriptive and factual, uneven in quality, with little differentiation between novels of high quality and those of minor merit. Technical detail is adequate and precise, and out-of-print titles are wisely given liberal representation. A *Supplement, 1942–46*, appeared in 1947, and a second period-volume, *Fiction Catalog: 1950*, is in preparation. The *Fiction Catalog* will repay study for the diversity of subject radiations registered for individual novels; *Anthony Adverse* appears under sixteen valid headings. It holds continuing usefulness to librarians, teachers, readers' advisers, and workers with books in every field, and is evidence of the increasing realization of the value of fiction as a medium of public education.

This realization finds masterly expression in Elbert Lenrow's *Reader's Guide to Prose Fiction* (New York, Appleton-Century, 1940), in which 1,500 novels, chosen with catholicity and high literary discrimination, are listed and characterized in far-ranging topical classification. Prepared for the Commission on Secondary School Curriculum of the Progressive Education Association, it is modern in outlook, mature in selective range, and perceptive throughout of the varieties and realities of experience, the intricacies of personal problems, on which the novel today casts illumination. Within a more restricted field but extremely valuable in fresh and dynamic selectivity is the classed and annotated check list, *America in Fiction*, by Otis W. Coan and Richard G. Lillard (Stanford University Press). First published by planograph in 1941, and proving its permanence in the third edition, revised and brought skillfully to date in 1949, this is designed "to aid students of American civilization—adults using the facilities of public libraries, college undergraduates, and young people in the eleventh and twelfth grades." There is a breadth and maturity in selection that offers striking contrast to older school and library standards of reading list suitability. As a presentation of a cross section of American novels that interpret the American social scene, this list effectively fulfills the compilers' aim "to help readers understand their country better through imaginative writings which present specific human beings in realizable situations."

Two older aids, invaluable in selection and reference use, are Baker's *Guide to the Best Fiction, English and American*, and its companion volume, *Guide to Historical Fiction*. These are the work of Ernest A. Baker, veteran English librarian and bibliographer—work carried on for thirty years with the cooperation of W. S. Sonnenschein. The *Guide to the Best Fiction*, first published by Macmillan in 1903, was brought out (with James Packman as co-author) in its third revised and enlarged edition in 1932, transformed into a virtually new work. Comprehensive rather than "autocratically critical," its six hundred pages through 1930 record 7,696 books by English and American writers and by foreign authors in translation. The annotations, descriptive and in a measure critical, give fair, compact appraisal of the character and quality of a book, and often have a graphic compression and high quality of literary appreciation that set a standard rarely reached in American aids. Arrangement is in a single alphabetical author list, to which an elaborate index (112 four-column pages) is key, guiding to titles, subjects, historical names and allusions, places, characters, national fiction, and many other valuable points of information. The companion

Guide to Historical Fiction was published by Macmillan in 1914, as a development from an earlier work, called *History in Fiction*, published in two small volumes in 1908. Although so long out of date (also out of print), this is the best annotated list of historical fiction yet published; and librarians cherish hope that the perennial announcement of a new edition in preparation may eventually have fulfillment. Another familiar aid important in this field is Jonathan Nield's comprehensive *Guide to the Best Historical Novels* (5th edition, New York, Macmillan, 1929), which in its arrangement by countries and periods, with author-and-title and subject indexes and brief descriptive annotations, is particularly helpful in suggesting fiction to correlate with historical reading.

Two later volumes give further aid in selection of historical fiction. *English History in English Fiction*, by Sir John Marriott (New York, Dutton, 1941) is the delightful survey and summary by a distinguished historical scholar of each successive period in English history as it is elucidated and vitalized by historical fiction. Written *con amore*, with charm and gusto, Sir John's avowed aim that "readers of all ages may be encouraged to use historical novels as complementary to their study of history," should be successfully achieved. Ernest E. Leisy's thorough, carefully organized volume, *The American Historical Novel* (University of Oklahoma Press, 1950), is, so far as I know, the only full-length, descriptive, critical, and chronological study of the subject. An introductory chapter ("History Vivified") defines and clarifies the development of the historical novel with understanding of its defects and warm appreciation of its qualities. The body of the book consists of five main period sections: Colonial America, the American Revolution and its aftermath, the Westward Movement, the Civil War and Reconstruction, National Expansion; within each period related novels in topical sequence are discussed and evaluated in smooth, readable narrative; publication date is given for all novels mentioned, but there is no other bibliographical detail. A forty-two-page appendix is devoted to "additional historical novels," listed in chronological accompaniment to the chapters of the main section; and the full index is a connecting link. The volume, interesting and suggestive as selection background, should have special reference usefulness as the fullest available chronological record of American history reflected by and interpreted in fiction. Characterization of individual novels is consistently fair-minded, generally adequate, and often illuminating in conveying contrast between the run-of-the-mill product and the beauty and insight of the novel of fine literary art. In this same field there should be mention of Hannah Logasa's excellent reading outline, *Historical Fiction*, designed for high schools, which in its fourth revised, enlarged edition (Philadelphia, McKinley, 1949) contains titles of mature significance provocative of forum or other controversial discussion.

In selection of foreign fiction in English, whether for a large or small collection, Agnes Camilla Hansen's volume, *Twentieth Century Forces in European Fiction* (A.L.A., 1934), still offers suggestion, stimulus, and valuable information. Here in carefully organized presentation are more than five hundred novels by European authors, written since 1900 up to or through 1932, available in English translation, and chosen as representative of "concepts, forces, and phenomena characteristic of twentieth-century civilization." The text, in discerning analytical commentary, summarizes the trends and phases expressed in fictional rendering. Few readers who now turn these pages can escape realization that this fiction foreshadowed universal ideas to come, "ideas which are taking possession of all mankind" as the twentieth century moves on its resistless course. In today's perspective this thoughtful little book makes clearer the values for American readers that lie in the rich stores of world fiction.

There are many lists that may be used to advantage. The *Gold Star List of American Stories,* published annually for many years by the Syracuse Public Library, covers selected American fiction since 1821, classified by subject, with notes; the 1949 edition includes 749 titles, old and new, currently in demand by readers. The Newark Public Library list, *A Thousand of the Best Novels* (revised edition, 1939) has long been popular for distribution to readers and as suggestive basis for small collections. Indeed, in selection of fiction there should be constant collection and use of bulletins and lists issued by libraries and educational institutions. The "white lists" of the Catholic *Book Survey*, the lists for students' reading prepared by the National Council of Teachers of English, the excellent classed list, "Introduction to the World of Books," published as a *Scripps College Bulletin* in July, 1934, and many kindred lists issued by colleges and universities all offer suggestion and help to clarify appraisal. Of unusual interest are the short reading lists of novels compiled by William H. F. Lamont, of Rutgers University, some of which have appeared in various literary publications. His list of "One Hundred Great Novels" has special significance, as it was submitted to more than fifty American, British, and foreign scholars and revised in the light of their recommendations. In the third version (1947), printed in *Books Abroad*, the authors chosen represented nineteen different nationalities (British, 19; French, 15; Russian, 13; German, 12; American, 11; with thirty titles from fourteen other countries). The *Bookman's Manual* is a bulwark here, as elsewhere, with five admirable chapters devoted to British and American fiction, one each to French literature and Russian literature (predominantly fiction), and one to "Other Foreign Fiction" (including bibliographies and novels in English translation from twenty nationalities). The *Reader's Digest of Books*, the *Oxford Companion to English Literature*, and the *Thesaurus of Book Digests* (New York, Crown, 1949) often give guidance in careful and accurate plot summaries of novels past and present; and many of the texts used in English courses offer both bibliographic aid and stimulation of critical judgment.

Selection of current fiction demands constant wide reading of literary reviews, with an eye for new novels of timeliness and merit; but it must be remembered that, in the field of fiction particularly, review opinion is often favorable toward books that are trivial, meretricious, or otherwise undesirable for library use. Fiction by untried writers, and, indeed, new fiction in general that seems to demand consideration should, so far as possible, be examined before purchase and appraised according to library standards, fortified by all available information and review opinion.

For short stories, the comprehensive, indispensable aid is Ina T. Firkins' *Index to Short Stories* (2d edition, Wilson, 1923), with its two supplements (1929, 1936). The second supplement only is now available, and the parent volume will be succeeded by the *Short Story Index*, in preparation. These volumes include all older short stories commonly in demand in libraries, and while their first and greatest usefulness lies in giving clues to stories readers desire, their record of works indexed guides to basic material for any representative collection.

BRIEF PANORAMA OF HISTORY AS PRESENTED IN CHRONOLOGICAL ORDER IN FIFTY HISTORICAL NOVELS

B.C.

1400	Egypt	Joseph and His Brothers	Thomas Mann
	Egypt, Crete, Syria	The Egyptian	Mika Waltari
1225	Greece	Hercules, My Shipmate	Robert Graves
480	Greece, Persia	Arrogance: the conquests of Xerxes	Louis Couperus
240	Carthage	Salammbô	Gustave Flaubert
218	Spain, Rome	Sonnica	Vicente Blasco Ibáñez
200	Scythia, Greece, Egypt	The Corn King and the Spring Queen	Naomi Mitchison
166	Judea: the Maccabees	My Glorious Brothers	Howard Fast
52	Britain, Gaul, Rome	The Conquered	Naomi Mitchison

A.D.

1st cent.	Egypt	The Tour	Louis Couperus
	Rome	I, Claudius	Robert Graves
		Blood of the Martyrs	Naomi Mitchison
		Josephus (Sequence)	Lion Feuchtwanger
2nd cent.	Italy	Andivius Hedulio	Edward Lucas White
4th cent.	Roman Empire	The Death of the Gods	D. S. Merejkowski
5th cent.	Alexandria	Hypatia	Charles Kingsley
6th cent.	Italy: the Lombards	The Unspeakables	Laverne Gay
11th cent.	England	Hereward the Wake	Charles Kingsley
		The Golden Warrior	Hope Muntz
12th cent.	Crusades	The Talisman	Sir Walter Scott
		Life and Death of Richard Yea and Nay	Maurice Hewlett

	France	The World Is Not Enough	Zoé Oldenburgh
		Peter Abelard	Helen Waddell
14th cent.	Norway	Kristin Lavransdatter	Sigrid Undset
	England	Long Will	Florence Converse
15th cent.	France	Quentin Durward	Sir Walter Scott
		Notre Dame de Paris	Victor Hugo
	Florence	Romola	George Eliot
		Romance of Leonardo da Vinci	D. S. Merejkowski
	Europe	The Cloister and the Hearth	Charles Reade
16th cent.	Scotland	The Abbot	Sir Walter Scott
		The Queen's Quair	Maurice Hewlett
	England	Kenilworth	Sir Walter Scott
		The Lily and the Leopards	Alice Harwood
17th cent.	France	Colas Breugnon	Romain Rolland
	England	The Power and the Glory	Phyllis Bentley
	France, England	The Three Musketeers	Alexandre Dumas
	Italy	The Star-Gazer	Zsolt de Harsanyi
		The Betrothed	Alessandro Manzoni
	Canada	Shadows on the Rock	Willa Cather
18th cent.	England	Henry Esmond	W. M. Thackeray
	Scotland	Kidnapped	Robert Louis Stevenson
	England, France	Tale of Two Cities	Charles Dickens
	France	Ninety-three	Victor Hugo
		The Gods Are Athirst	Anatole France
		Proud Destiny	Lion Feuchtwanger
19th cent.	Napoleon, Russia	War and Peace	L. N. Tolstoy
	Napoleon, Europe, America	Anthony Adverse	Hervey Allen
	U.S. Civil War	Gone with the Wind	Margaret Mitchell

FIFTY CONTEMPORARY FOREIGN NOVELS IN ENGLISH TRANSLATION

Chosen to indicate presage and impact of world war and revolution in present-day Europe. A more comprehensive survey and characterization of foreign fiction in English may be found in *What's in a Novel*, Chapter VII: "Vistas in European Fiction."

Aragon, Louis. The Bells of Basel; trans. by H. M. Chevalier. 1936.
Asch, Sholem. Three Cities; trans. by Willa and Edwin Muir. 1939.
Baroja y Nessi, Pío. The Struggle for Life; trans. by Isaac Goldberg.
  (Sequence.)[2] 1923–24. 1: The Quest; 2: Weeds; 3: Red Dawn.
Berto, Giuseppe. The Sky Is Red; trans. by Angus Davidson. 1948.

[2] Several novels, separately titled, that together form a single work under the collective title here given.

Blasco Ibáñez, Vicente. The Cabin; trans. by F. H. Snow and B. M. Mekota. 1919.
Borgese, Giuseppe Antonio. Rubè; trans. by Isaac Goldberg. 1923.
Broch, Hermann. The Sleepwalkers; trans. by Willa and Edwin Muir. 1932.
Camus, Albert. The Plague; trans. by Stuart Gilbert. 1947.
Duhamel, Georges. The Pasquier Chronicles; trans. by Béatrice de Holthoir. (Sequence.) 5 vols. in 1. 1938.
—— Cécile Pasquier; trans. by Béatrice de Holthoir. (Sequence.) 3 vols. in 1. 1940.
Ehrenburg, Ilya. The Storm; trans. by J. Fineberg. 1949.
Feuchtwanger, Lion. Success; trans. by Willa and Edwin Muir. 1940.
Gide, André. The Counterfeiters; trans. by Dorothy Bussy. 1927, 1947.
Gorky, Maxim. The Life of Clim Samghin; trans. by Alexander Bakshy. (Sequence.) 1930–38. 1: Bystander; 2: The Magnet; 3: Other Fires; 4: The Specter (left uncompleted).
—— Mother; introd. by Howard Fast; rev. trans. by Isidor Schneider. 1921, 1947.
Hasek, Jaroslav. Good Soldier, Schweik; trans. by Paul Selver. 1930.
Hesse, Hermann. Steppenwolf; trans. by Basil Creighton. 1929, 1947.
Kafka, Franz. The Trial; trans. by Willa and Edwin Muir. 1937.
Kesten, Hermann. The Children of Guernica; trans. by Geoffrey Dunlop. 1939.
Koestler, Arthur. Darkness at Noon; trans. by Daphne Hardy. 1941, 1946.
Leonov, Leonid. Road to the Ocean; trans. by Norbert Guterman. 1944.
Malraux, André. Man's Fate; trans. by H. M. Chevalier. 1938.
Mann, Thomas. The Magic Mountain; trans. by H. T. Lowe-Porter. 1927, rev. 1938.
—— Doctor Faustus; trans. by H. T. Lowe-Porter. 1948.
Martin du Gard, Roger. The World of the Thibaults; trans. by Stuart Gilbert. (Sequence.) 1941. 1: The Thibaults; 2: Summer, 1914.
Mauriac, François. Therèse; trans. by Gerard Hopkins. 1928, 1947.
Meersch, Maxence van der. Invasion; trans. by Gerard Hopkins. 1937.
Moberg, Vilhelm. The Earth Is Ours; trans. by Edwin Bjorkman. 1941.
Nexö, Martin Andersen. Pelle the Conqueror; trans. by Jessie Muir and Bernard Miall. 1913–16. 4 vols. in 1, 1930.
Panova, Vera. The Train; trans. by Marie Budberg. 1949.
Plivier, Theodore. Stalingrad; trans. by Richard and Clara Winston. 1948.

Proust, Marcel. Remembrance of Things Past; trans. by C. K. Scott Moncrieff and Frederick A. Blossom. (Sequence.) 2 vols. 1934, 1941.
Ramuz, Charles Ferdinand. When the Mountain Fell; trans. by S. F. Scott. 1947.
Remarque, Erich Maria. All Quiet on the Western Front; trans. by A. H. Wheen. 1929.
Romains, Jules. Men of Good Will; trans. by W. B. Wells and Gerard Hopkins. (Sequence.) 14 vols. 1933–46.
Sartre, Jean-Paul. Roads to Freedom; trans. by Eric Sutton. (Sequence.) 1947. 1: The Age of Reason; 2: The Reprieve.
Seghers, Anna. The Seventh Cross; trans. by J. A. Galston. 1942.
Sender, Ramón. Seven Red Sundays; trans. by Sir C. P. Mitchell. 1936.
Sholokhov, Mikhail. The Silent Don; trans. by Stephen Garry. (Sequence.) 1941. 1: And Quiet Flows the Don; 2: The Don Flows Home to the Sea.
—— Seeds of Tomorrow; trans. by Stephen Garry. 1935.
Sillanpaa, F. E. Meek Heritage; trans. by Alexander Matson. 1938.
Silone, Ignazio. Bread and Wine; trans. by Gwenda David and Eric Mosbacher. 1937, 1946.
Simonov, Konstantin. Days and Nights; trans. by Joseph Barnes. 1945.
Smirnov, V. A. Sons; trans. by Naomi Y. Yohel. 1947.
Svevo, Italo (Ettore Schmitz). The Confessions of Zeno; trans. by Beryl De Zoete. 1930, 2d ed., 1948.
Tolstoi, Aleksei N. Road to Calvary; trans. by Edith Bone. 1946.
Vittorini, Elio. In Sicily; introd. by Ernest Hemingway; trans. by Wilfrid David. 1949.
Werfel, Franz. The Forty Days of Musa Dagh; trans. by Geoffrey Dunlop. 1934.
Zweig, Arnold. The Case of Sergeant Grischa; trans. by Eric Sutton. 1928.
—— The Axe of Wandsbek; trans. by Eric Sutton. 1947.

Epilogue

> Reading, in short, is a form of experience without which writing is an empty exercise; for the poet has never lived who, without books, be they only primitive laws and hymns and Bibles, has attained a universal point of view. By means of reading alone, half the writers of history have fitted themselves for the parts they have played in history, for through books they have arrived at standards of comparison which they have brought to bear upon themselves and the unenlightened worlds in which they moved; through books they have learned how to pull their wits out of the ruts of peasants, of impotent and blundering social misfits, getting out of themselves and into the great currents of life and a sense of the range of human possibility.
>
> Van Wyck Brooks: "On Reading,"
> in *Sketches in Criticism*

WE HAVE BEEN ENGAGED in foundation building for library service. In the foregoing chapters the purpose has been to establish a groundwork of principle, method, and understanding on which the student or inexperienced worker may build an individual and ever-growing structure of expert book knowledge. Much that must find place in that structure has necessarily been omitted or too lightly touched upon. Attention has been focused upon books as the object of selection, rather than upon bibliographical minutiae of selective processes. This consideration of books in broad survey and characterization has passed over various important classes of literature. The great body of general reference works, books in the fields of art and music, of technology and useful arts, have received no attention. To these classes most of the general principles and methods of selection are applicable; but they are essentially specialized fields, and it has been made clear that in every specialized field of book selection specialized proficiency must be established. Such proficiency must be developed from specialized training and experience, although based on the fundamentals of general book selection.

In closing summary, a few points that have been implied rather than specifically considered should, perhaps, be noted. First of all, there is no magic formula by which prompt and certain distinction may be made between a good book and a poor one. All the principles and tests and suggestions that can be formulated may be applied with an insensitivity that renders them useless or a wavering uncertainty that nullifies them. Only by living with books in the spirit as well as in material contact and use, by sharing intellectually and emotionally their many-sided relationship to people and life, does reasoned judgment become instinctive and assured; but such judgment never assumes infallibility. Authority (which is knowledge) and flexibility (which is sympathy) are the two great requirements for bringing to readers the books which are the best for them. They are also the requirements most needed in the adjustment of problems of selection precipitated into library service by violence of opposed public opinion or eddying currents of propaganda. Many of these problems have been indicated; in number and variety they are endless. Some of them are solved as time brings its changes; as old interdictions are lifted and new avenues of knowledge are opened to common use. In dealing with such problems of selection there must be a mind responsive to the transformations in process in human history, a sustained impartiality toward variant purpose and opinion, and an acceptance of those free processes of self-education for which the public library stands.

Another salient point is the importance of the new as compared with the old, in the present day of transition, when former stabilities and assurances no longer prevail. As the reading public grows in number and with increasing eagerness turns to books for guidance in thought and action, it becomes more necessary than ever before that library selection should maintain the highest standard of book values in terms of present-day thought. Between the older standard work that has lost its significance and appeal to the readers of today, and the new book (perhaps of less original importance) that offers vital present interest, that interprets immediate experience, and reflects the spirit of the time in its own mode of expression, choice must turn to the new rather than to the old. Present-day emphasis on the mechanics of library administration which tend to reduction or undue limitation of library book funds can make this a serious problem in selection. In any event, it involves close comparative study of essential book values; less replacement of older literature whose pristine qualities have faded; and in current selection more thorough elimination of the commonplace, the trivial, and the spurious.

But whatever checks or limitations are to be overcome in library book selection, the importance of library service in American life must necessarily increase. With more and more readers seeking through books to find strength and new vision with which to meet the challenges and exigencies of the future; and with added leisure brought to millions, which should be used to enrich, not to degrade, living, the library has already entered into its highest opportunities. Without books there can be no transmission of the values and energies that bring life to new issues. In the fateful adventure in living that is opening today the service that releases books to their fullest influence in common life cannot be dispensed with. Professional librarianship is bringing books into the mind and work and common interests and individual development of people young and old; kindling interest in books and fostering interest that is latent; stimulating intelligent use and enjoyment of books and strengthening through books the power of the common man to overcome or solve the problems that all of us must encounter today. From books modern life has built its structure, and books are the materials of its future development.

In book selection for library service the ideal to be maintained is the ideal that Clive Bell makes the definition of civilization: "A sense of values and reason enthroned."

Index

"A.E." *See* Russell, George William
A.L.A. *See* American Library Association
A.N.T.A. *See* American National Theatre and Academy
Abbott, Leonard Dalton, 380
Abbreviations, 146
About Books (bulletin), 89
About the Kinsey Report (Geddes and Curie), 338
Abraham Lincoln (Drinkwater), 488
Abramowitz, Isidore, 230
Abridgment and abridged editions, 220n, 228-30, 235
Abstracts: biology, 327-28, 346; chemistry, 327, 346; science, 345-46; sociology, 379
Accent (periodical), 116, 117n
Accessions, 92
Acton, Harold, 492
Acton, John Emerich Edward Dalberg-Acton, Lord, *quoted*, 346
Adamic, Louis, 239, 367, 368
Adams, Charles Kendall, 286-87
Adams, Donald, 113
Adams, Henry Brooks: autobiography, 256; Cram, Ralph Adams, 148; *History of the United States*, 280; human thought phases, 325-26; *Mont-Saint-Michel and Chartres*, 298, 305
Adams, James Truslow, 283, 288
Adams, John and Abigail, 254
Adams, Leta E., 48-49
Addams, Jane, 254
Adding Machine, The (Rice), 490
Adler, Mortimer Jerome, 34, 43, 57n, 60
Admiral of the Ocean Sea (Morison), 51
Adolescence, 518, 553-54
Adult education, 34
Advertising, 90, 107, 121, 208
Aesthetics of literary art, 434
Africa View (J. Huxley), 316
African Journey (Robeson), 316-17
Age of Jackson, The (Schlesinger), 283
Age of the Great Depression, The (Wecter), 283

Aiken, Conrad Potter, 454, 463
Album of American History (J. T. Adams), 288
Aldington, Richard, 163, 244, 463
Aldis, Harry Gidney, 209
Aldrich, Thomas Bailey, 469
Aldus Manutius, 186
Aley, Maxwell, 18
Algren, Nelson, 421, 555
All the Best in South America (Clark), 311
Allegory, 521
Allen, Frederick Lewis, 130, 278
Allen, (William) Hervey, 270, 540; *Anthony Adverse*, 168, 522, 544, 559
Almanac for Moderns (Peattie), 333-34
Amberley Papers, The (Russell), 167, 260
America in Fiction (Coan and Lillard), 560
America through British Eyes (Nevins), 315
American (Linderman), 252
American Association for Adult Education, 34
American Book Publishers Council, 421
American Booksellers Association, 112, 421
American Catalogue (1876), 82, 83, 87
American Catalogue (1890-1895), ix
American Character, The (Brogan), 315
American Civil Liberties Union, 367
American Council of Learned Societies, 371
American Democracy, The (Laski), 370
American Dilemma, An (Myrdal), 373
American Economic Review, 379
American Fiction, 1920-1940 (Beach), 532, 533
American Folk Plays (Koch), 495
American Foundations for Social Welfare (Andrews and Harrison), 365n
"American Guide Series," 240, 310
American Historical Association, 286, 288
American Historical Novel, The (Leisy), 561

American Humor (Rourke), 141
American Institute of Graphic Arts, 172, 182, 183
American Library Association: adult education, 34; book binding, 180n; *Booklist*, 69; *Bulletin*, 382; censorship, 188n; conventions, ix; fiftieth anniversary, 67; Fifty Religious Books of the Year, 414; foreign book lists, 202; *General Literature Index*, 441; Haines, Helen, viii, ix; Intellectual Freedom Committee, 374; motto, 23; organization, ix; postwar planning program, 20, 30; reading interests survey, 17; *Subscription Books Bulletin*, 206; typography, 171
—— Catalog, 76, 78, 79; annotations, 69, 73, 139; editions, 219; history, 286; literature classes, 46, 62; religion and philosophy, 388-89, 411; sociology, 382; travel, 308
—— Catalog (1893), 66
—— Catalog (1904), 62, 66-68; annotations, 147-48; drama, 484; literature classes, 251
—— Catalog (1926), 67-68; annotations, 73, 148; arrangement, 72; biography, 253; drama, 484; history, 253; literature classes, 62, 251
—— Catalog (1926-1931), 62, 68
—— Catalog (1932-1936), 62, 69
—— Catalog (1937-1941), 62, 69
American life, in English literature, 85
American National Theatre and Academy, 480
American News Company, 116
American Novel, The, 1789-1939 (Van Doren), 535
American Novel Today, The (Michaud), 534
American People, The: a Study in National Character (Gorer), 315
American Poetry Since 1900 (Untermeyer), 469
American Sociological Society, 364
American Story, The: Ten Broadcasts (historical dramatic expositions for the radio by Archibald MacLeish), 496
American Tragedy, An (Dreiser), 133
Americanisms, 153
Americans, as readers, 17, 19-20
Americans from Holland (Mulder), 239
America's Stake in Britain's Future (Soule), 143

Amiel, Henri Frédéric, 259
Ancient Maya, The (Morley), 303
Ancient Times (Breasted), 290
And Keep Your Powder Dry (Mead), 315
And the Third Day (Grierson), 409
Anderson, Maxwell, 486, 488, 489, 496
Anderson, Sherwood, 37
Andrews, F. Emerson, 365n
Andrews, Roy Chapman, 304
Animal life, books on, 332-34, 351-52
Animal Treasure (Sanderson), 333
Ann Vickers (Lewis), 539
Anna and the King of Siam (Landon), 253
Annals of American Bookselling, 1638-1850 (Boynton), 212
Anne of the Thousand Days (Anderson), 488
Annotations and annotation writing, 137-55; *A.L.A. Catalog*, 69, 73; *A.L.A. Catalog (1904)*, 66; *A.L.A. Catalog (1926)*, 67; Adams' Manual, 287; *Best Books*, 87, 424; *Book Review Digest*, 71, 73; *Booklist*, 70, 73, 139-40; cataloguing, 155; construction, 137; definition, 65, 124-25, 137; dogmatism, 147; fiction, 140, 149-50, 558-61; fiction, foreign, 150-51; librarians' notes, 138-40; *Library Journal*, 139, 140; literary taste, 123; *Literature of American History* (Larned), 286-87; nonfiction, 147, 149, 154; personal opinions, 146; phrasing, 137; *Publishers' Weekly*, 83; purpose, 65-66; readers' notes, 138-40; *Standard Catalog for Public Libraries*, 80; *United States Quarterly Book List*, 139; word choice, 147
Annual Bibliography of English Language and Literature, 426
Annual Library Index (1905), x
Another Part of the Forest (Hellman), 487
Anshen, Ruth, 283
Antarctic Penguins (Levick), 333
Anthologies, 168; *Accent*, 117n; book reviews, 104; drama, 491, 494-97, 501; essays, 440-41; foreign literature, 420, 439; literature, 439; *Partisan Reader*, 117n; philosophy, 408-9; poetry, 455, 462-63, 465, 466; science, 348-50; short-story, 557-58; travel, 307
Anthology of Pure Poetry (Moore), 464
Anthony, Katharine, 269

INDEX 573

Anthony Adverse (Allen), 168, 522, 544, 559
Anthropology, 277, 305, 316
Anti-Defamation League, 367
Anti-Semitism, 341, 359, 519; Pound, Ezra, 460
Ants (Huxley), 333
Appeal, permanence of, 522
Appendixes, 165
Appleton-Century-Crofts, 192, 198, 206, 207
Applied Sociology (Ward), 362
Appraisal of books. *See* Evaluation
Approach to Shakespeare, The (Mackail), 497
Aquinas, Saint Thomas, 401-2
Arabic literature, 419
Archaeology, 277, 302-3
Archer, John, 180*n*
Archer, William, 244
Arena (Flanagan), 477
Aristotle, 400, 401; tragic plot, *quoted* on, 142
Arlington, Lewis Charles, 492
"Armed Services Editions," 197-98
Armed Vision, The (Hyman), 433
Armstrong, Hamilton Fish, 379
Army, 197-98, 517
Arnold, Matthew: culture, *quoted* on, 15; education, the aim of, 340; essays, 49; literary criticism, 58, 61, 100, 434; poetry, 469, *quoted* on, 448-49; translator's art, 233, 435
Art: *A.L.A. Catalog*, 251; illustrations, 179; purpose, 29; religion, 388; reviews, 101; selection principles, 568; travel, 304, 305
Art of Plain Talk, The (Flesch), 153
Art of Thinking, The (Dimnet), 8, 45, 130
Artzybasheff, Boris, 182
Asch, Sholem, 517
Ashton, Helen, 265
Askling, John, 167
Aspects of Biography (Maurois), 272
Aspects of the Novel (Forster), 533
Association of American University Presses, 199
Astrology, 405, 406
Astronomy, 330, 331, 335, 348, 447
Athenaeum, Boston, Mass., 90
Athenaeum (periodical), 118-19, 340
Atlantic Monthly, 115
Atlas of American History, 288

Atlases, 304, 309
Atomic age, 324, 326, 328-29, 516, 519
Atomic Energy Commission, 345, 348
Auden, W. H. (Wystan Hugh), 454, 456-57, 466
Augustine, Saint, 260
Auslander, Joseph, 463
Austen, Jane, 511
"Author meets critics," 106-7
Authority: biography, 267; book reviews, 107-8; books of information, 51; definition, 569; fiction, 149; history, 295-96; nonfiction, 53-54, 55; review slips, 129; science, 342-43; sociology, 376; subject series, 241; travel, 317
Authorized editions, 230-31
Authors: copyrights, 189, 190; essays, 438; ghost-writing, 208; property rights, 189; publishers, 205, 207-8; publishing of his own books, 57; qualifications, 55, 56. *See also* Authority; Literature classes; and the names of individual authors
Authors and the Book Trade (Swinnerton), 216
Autobiography, 253, 255-62, 271; Adams, Henry, 256; Cellini, 254, 256, 257; definition, 255; dullness, 257; fiction, 520; Franklin, Benjamin, 255-56; Goldman, Emma, 269-70; selection, 267, 268; verbosity, 268; Woolf, Virginia, *quoted* on, 249. *See also* Biography
Autobiography of America (Van Doren), 289
Autobiography of Science, 349
Axel's Castle (Wilson), 131

Background and background-building, 5, 57-58, 61
Bacon, Francis: essays, 435-36; knowledge, division of, 50; Shakespeare's identity, 498
Baedekers (guide books), 310
Bailey, (Irene) Temple, 527
Bain, Robert Nisbet, 253
Baker, Blanch Merritt, 500-501
Baker, Ernest Albert, ix, 560
Baker, George Pierce, 481, 495
Baldwin, Faith, 509, 527
Baldwin, James Mark, 412
"Ballad of the Northern Lights" (Service), 468
Ballou, Robert Oleson, 395
Balzac, Honoré de, 131, 235, 545

INDEX

Bampton Lectures, 409-10
Banning, Margaret Culkins, 529
"Bantam Books," 223, 244
Barck, Oscar Theodore, 278
Baring, Maurice, 265
Barke, James, 266
Barnes, Harry Elmer, 285, 288, 379-80
Barnett, Lincoln, 336
Barretts of Wimpole Street, The (Besier), 496
Barrie, Sir James Matthew, 261, 490
Barrington, E. (pseud.), 265
Barzun, Jacques, 32, 153
Bascom, Elva L., 48n, 76
Basic History of the United States (Beard), 296
Basic Teachings of the Great Philosophers (Frost), 410
Bates, Ernest Stuart: autobiography, 271; translations, 237, *quoted* on, 218
Bateson, Frederick Wilse, 425
Baugh, Albert Croll, 431
Beach, Joseph Warren, 532
Beagle expedition, of Darwin, 304, 321
Beard, Charles Austin, 280, 295, 296
Beard, Mary Ritter, 280, 295, 296
Becker, May Lamberton, 112
Bed: books, 437; reading in, 60
Beebe, Charles William, 304, 437
Bell, Clive, *in full* Arthur Clive Howard, *quoted* on civilization, 538, 570
Bell, Gertrude Margaret Lowthian, 260, 314
Bellamy, Edward, 360
"Belle Dame sans Merci, La" (Keats), 231
Belles lettres, 418-19
Belloc, Hilaire, 144, 269, 272
Benavente y Martinez, Jacinto, 491
Benchley, Robert Charles, 438
Benedict, Ruth Fulton, 305
Benét, Stephen Vincent, 453
Benét, William Rose, 111, 427, 451, 463
Bennett, (Enoch) Arnold: book reviewers, *quoted* on, 108; reading, *quoted* on, 8
Benson, Arthur, 268
Benson, Stella, *quoted* on travelers and tourists, 313
Bentham, Jeremy, 360
Bentley, Eric, 120
Bentley, Phyllis Eleanor, 532; fiction writing, *quoted* on, 506
Berelson, Bernard, 18n, 43, 528

Berlin, Germany, book-burnings in, 186-87, 414
Berlin Diary (Shirer), 259
Berninghausen, David Knipe, 374n
Besant, Sir Walter, 539
Besier, Rudolf, 496
Best American Short Stories, The, 557
"Best books," futility of selecting, 7
Best Books (Dickinson), 424
Best Books, The: a Readers' Guide (Sonnenschein), 86-88, 94; annotations, 146, 149; history, 286; philosophy and religion, 411; sociology, 382; travel, 308
Best Books of Our Time, The, 1901-1925, 424
Best Books of the Decade, The, 1926-1935, 425
Best One-Act Plays (Mayorga), 495
Best Plays, The (Mantle), 496
Best sellers, 107, 195n, 544n, 548
Bestiaries, 334
Betjeman, John, 461
Bettenson, Henry, 397, 410
Beveridge, Albert Jeremiah, 268, 298
Beveridge, Sir William, 371
Bevington, Helen, 461
Bhagavad-Gita, 395
Bible, The, 389, 394-95; *Bookman's Manual*, 411-12; Pater, *quoted*, 51
Bible and the Common Reader, The (Chase), 395
Bibliographical Guide to the History of Christianity (Case), 413
Bibliography and bibliographic aids, 63-77, 78-95; essays, 441; history, 286-88; library usage, 47, 424-26; plays, 499-500; travel, 306-9; value and importance, 165-66
Bibliography of Philosophy, Psychology, and Cognate Subjects, 412
Bibliography, Practical, Enumerative, Historical (Van Hoesen and Walter), 212; history, 288; philosophy, 413; science, 346; social sciences, 380
Bibliotheca Britannica (Watt), 425
Bieber, Ralph, 290
Big Yankee, The (Blankfort), 253
Billings, John Shaw, 60
Bindings, 55, 160, 179-81, 183
Bio-bibliography, 346
Biochemistry, 331
Biography (*speculum vitae*), 249-74; *A.L.A. Catalog*, 62, 251; annotations, 144; authority, 267; Black Memorial

Award, 420; boys, 252-53; censorship, 269-70; classification, 50, 52, 53, 302; collective, 261, 262-63, 270n; debunking, 264; definition, 255; Dickinson, Emily, *quoted* on, 249; essay, 263, 437; evaluation, 57; examples, 273-74; fiction, 520, 529; fictionized, 265-66; headlines, 178; historical, 283; history, 277, 297-98; illustrations, 179; imagination, 447; indexes, 57; individual, 261-62; influence, 6; life, 250; Maurois, André, *quoted* on, 249; *New Yorker* "profiles," 436-37; publications (1926-1949), 252; Pulitzer Prize, 420; religion, 387; reprints, 220; reviews, 103; series, 239; Woolf, Virginia, *quoted* on, 249

Biography and the Human Heart (Bradford), 271
Biography of the Gods (Haydon), 391
Biological Abstracts, 327-28, 346
Biological Basis of Human Nature, The (Jennings), 339, 351
Biology, 327-28, 330-31, 335-37, 346, 349
Birth and Death of the Sun, The (Gamow), 336
Birth control, 187, 254
Björkman, Edwin August, 244
Black (James Tait) Memorial Award, 420
"Black and Gold Library," 222, 242, 431
Blackwood, William, 200
Blake, Nelson Manfred, 278
Blake, William, *quoted* on poetry, 447
Blanding, Don, 466
Blankfort, Michael, 253
"Blue Guides," 310
"Blue Ribbon Books," 222, 242
Blunden, Edmund Charles, 425
Blunt, Wilfred Scawen, 259
"Blurbs," on book jackets, 182
Bodin, Jean, 360
Bodkin, Maud, 433
"Bohn Libraries," 163, 202, 218, 221
Bollingen Foundation, 459-60, 468
Bone, Edith, 244
Bone, James, 305
"Bonibooks," 222
Bontemps, Arna, 463
Book, The (McMurtrie), 210-11
Book and author luncheons, 112
Book clubs, 18, 19, 102, 106
Book in America, The (Lehmann-Haupt), 214

Book industries and trade, 106, 185-217
Book Industry, The (Miller), 215
Book jackets, 121, 180-82
Book Manufacturers' Institute, 18, 421
Book of Modern Criticism, A (Lewisohn), *quoted*, 475
Book of the Small Souls (Couperus), 168
Book Review Digest, 70-72, 78, 79; annotations, 73; fiction, 558; pamphlet material, 91; philosophy and religion, 412; plus signs over minus signs, 102; scientific writing, 347; selectivity, 83-84; sociology, 382; travel, 308
Book reviewing. *See* Reviewing
Book Reviewing (Drewry), 104
Book selection. *See* Evaluation; Selection
Book Selection (Drury), xv, 48
Book Selection: Its Principles and Practice (Wellard), 32-33, 44
Book Survey, 412n, 563
Book talks, 126
Book trade. *See* Book industries
Book week idea, 413
Booklist, 78, 79; *A.L.A. Catalog*, 69; annotations, 70, 73, 139-40; editions, 219; fiction, 558; pamphlet material, 91; philosophy and religion, 412; scientific writing, 347; selectivity, 83-84; sociology, 382; travel, 308
Booklist Books, 69-70
Booklists, 79
Bookmaking, 159-84
Bookman's Glossary, 82, 94
Bookman's Manual, 73-76, 78-79, 82; best sellers, 195; biography, 270; drama, 501; editions, 219-20; essays, 441; fiction, 563; history, 287; philosophy and religion, 411-12; poetry, 464, 471; reference books, 75; travel, 308
Book-of-the-month clubs, 36
Book-order meetings, 122-23, 125
Books: bulked-up, 169; burning of, 186-87, 414; clumsiness, 168; distinction, 242; examination technique, 57n; good, 569; living with, xvi, 569; microfilm editions, 174; overbulked, 168; page margins, 176; physical aspects, 159-84; poor, 569; production, 196-97; repairing and care, 180n; small, 170, 220; textual aspects, 159-84
Books Abroad, 117, 202, 422, 563
Books and Reading (Porter), 399

"Books by Offset Lithography" (exhibit), 172
Books in Print, an Index to the Publishers' Trade List Annual for 1948, 81-82, 93
Bookseller, 85
Booksellers and bookselling, 10, 73-74, 107, 185-217
Borrowers, 18. *See also* Demand
Boston Evening Transcript, 114
Boston Public Library, 89
Boswell, James, *quoted* on catalogues and the backs of books in libraries, 78
Both Your Houses (Anderson), 489
Botta, Anne Charlotte Lynch, 431
Bottome, Phyllis, 515
Bourke-White, Margaret, 179
Bowdler, Thomas, 228
"Bowdlerization," 228
Bowen, Elizabeth Dorothea Cole, 532
Bowerman, Paul, 440
Bowker, Richard Rogers, 83
Bowker (R. R.) Company, 82-83. *See also* names of their individual publications
Boyd, Ernest Augustus, 235, 245
Boyd, James, 298, 539
Boynton, Henry Walcott, 212
Bradford, Gamaliel, 272; biography, 265, 271, *quoted* on, 250; biography, collective, 263-64; essay, 437; journal, 263*n*
Bradshaw, George, 307
Brandes, George Morris, 431
Breasted, James Henry, 290
Brenner, Anita, 245, 311
Bretall, Robert, 409
Brewster, Dorothy, 532
Brickell, Herschel, 557
Bridges, Robert Seymour, 453, 455
Bristol, Roger P., 554
British Museum: catalogue eyestrain, 172; copyright law, 190
British National Bibliography, 85
Brittain, Vera, 423-24
Broadus, Edmund Kemper, 175
Brogan, Denis William, 315
Bromfield, Louis, 195; book reviewing, *quoted* on, 102
Brontë sisters, 270, 512
Brooke, Rupert, 455
Brookings Institution, 130, 364
Brooklyn Library, 90
Brooks, Cleanth, 470
Brooks, Cyrus, 236*n*

Brooks, Van Wyck, 433; criticisms, 58, 61, 434
Brown, Edwin R., 115
Brown, Ivor, 423
Brown, John Carter, 215
Brown, Karl, 47*n*
Brown, Lloyd Arnold, 309
Browne, Lewis, 391, 401
Browning, Robert, 231
Bryan, Alice Isabel, 31, 43
Bryce, James, 280
Buck in the Snow, The (Millay), 168
Budget of Paradoxes (De Morgan), 340
Bulletin of the Atomic Scientists, 328, 347
Bulosan, Carlos, 38
Burlingame, (William) Roger, 164, 213
Burnett, Whit and Hallie, 557-58
Burnham, Frederick Russell, 314
Burns, John Horne, 517
Burns, Robert, 266
Burrell, Angus, 532
Burroughs, John, 333, 351
Burton, Sir Richard Francis, 321
Bury, John Bagnell, 165, 232
Bury the Dead (Shaw), 478
Business books, 101, 199
Bussy, Dorothy, 245
Butler, Samuel, 360
Buying and ordering, 48
Buying of books, American public, 19
Byron, George Gordon, 230, 267

"c." (abbreviation), use of, 131
Cabell, James Branch, 521, 526
Cadell, Elizabeth, 520
Caldwell, Erskine, 179
Caldwell, (Janet) Taylor, 509
California Library Association, x
Calverton, Victor Francis, 148, 432
Cambridge Bibliography of English Literature, The, 425
Cambridge History of American Literature, 431
Cambridge History of English Literature, 425-26, 431
Cambridge University Press, 200, 202; classics, 242; histories, 288, 290-91; "poets series," 227, 231, 242
Campbell, C. Lawton, 480
Camus, Albert, 518, 566
Canada, 79, 190, 347
Canby, Henry Seidel: criticism standards, 106; essays, 434; *Literary History*

of the United States, 430; reviewers, quoted on, 99; *Saturday Review of Literature*, 110-11
Cancel title, definition, 162
Cannan, Gilbert, 245
Canterbury Tales (Chaucer), 232
Capek, Karel, 490
Capitalism: communism and, 293, 371, 403, 478; current literature, 359; postwar world conflict, 369; World Council of Churches, 397-98; World War I (post), 513
Care and Binding of Books and Magazines, 180n
Care and Repair of Books, The (Lydenberg and Archer), 180n
Carey, Mathew, 199
Carey-Thomas Award, 199
Carlson, Pearl Gertrude, 219
Carlyle, Thomas: essays, 263, 434; *French Revolution*, 282; reading, quoted on, 3
Carmen Ariza (Stocking), 528
Carnegie Corporation, 19, 31, 75, 364
Carnegie Endowment for International Peace, 91, 364
Carnegie Institution of Washington, 346, 364
Carnegie Library of Pittsburgh, 90
Carolina Folk Plays (Koch), 492, 495
"Carpenter's World Travels," 320
Carr, Edward Hallett, 370
Carrighar, Sally, 334
Carroll, Marie J., 289
Carswell, Catharine, 266
Carter, John, 209
Cartography, 309
Caruso, Dorothy Benjamin (Mrs. Enrico), 253
Case, Shirley Jackson, 413
Casing of books, 180
Cassell, John, 221
Caste, Class and Race (Cox), 373
Catalog of Reprints in Series, 219
Catalogue of Scientific Papers, 326, 345
Catalogues, library, 90; annotations, 155. *See also* American Library Association
Catalogues, publishers', 64-65, 79, 81, 82; British, 84-85
Cather, Willa Sibert, 150, 527, 539
Catholic Church: book selection, 395; books recommended, 412; Catholic Action movement, 391; *Catholic Encyclopedia*, 397; *Commonweal*, 115; "Fathers of the Church" series, 410; fiction, 563; *imprimatur*, 189; Maritain, Jacques, 390; philosophy, 390, 395, 402; religious book week, 413-14
Caudwell, Christopher [Sprigg], 433, 456, 470-71; poetry, quoted on, 446
Caxton, William, 186
Cecil, Lord Edward Christian David, 434
Celebrities, 262
Cellini, Benvenuto, 254, 256, 257
Cellulose, 173
Censor Marches On, The (Ernst and Lindey), 214
Censorship, 214; American Library Association, 374; biography, 269-70; China, 186; controversial material, 394; current literature, 359; definition, 187; England, 214; expurgation, 228, 229; fascism, 186-87; fiction, 550-52; historical collections, 292; librarians, 555; obscenity, 214, 552-53; political opinion, 187-88; religion, 187; sex, 187, 551-52; *Ulysses*, 521; World War I (post), 514
Century of Publishing, A (Waugh), 217
Certain Measure, A (Glasgow), 533
Challenge of the Greek, The (Glover), 437
Chambers, Robert, Scottish publisher, 200, 202, 221, 427
Chambers' Cyclopedia of English Literature, 427
Champion, Selwyn Gurney, 391
Chapman, John, 496
Chapman and Hall (publishers), 200, 202, 217, 230
Chapter headings or titles, 57, 178
Charles XII and the Collapse of the Swedish Empire (Bain), 253
Chase, Mary Ellen, 395
Chase, Stuart, 368; *Mexico*, 130, 166; *Proper Study of Mankind*, 356; *Tyranny of Words*, 423
Chater, Arthur, 245
Chaucer, Geoffrey, 232
Chekhov, Anton Pavlovich, 491
Chemical Abstracts, 327, 346
Chemistry, 327, 330, 346
Cheney, Orion Howard, 213
Cherry Orchard (Chekhov, 1904), 491
Chesterton, Gilbert Keith, 468
Chevalier, Haakon M., 245

578 INDEX

Chicago Sun Book Week, 114
Chicago Sunday Tribune Magazine of Books, 114
Children: familiarity with good literature, 58; reading disabilities, 60n
Children's books: *A.L.A. Catalog*, 62, 68; animal stories, 334; bindings, 180; biography, 252-53; library budgets, 47-48; nature books, 334; offset printing, 172; poetry, 463; purchase file, 92; religious books, 414; review slips, 126; westerns, 321
China: censorship, 186; drama, 491-92; International Copyright Union, 191, 194; stories, 558
Choice of Editions, The (Carlson), 219
Christian Century, 412
Christian Science Monitor, 114
Christianity, 389-91, 398
Chronicles and chroniclers, 279, 280, 289
"Chronicles of America" (series), 240, 283, 291
Chrysanthemum and the Sword, The (Benedict), 305
Churchill, Winston Leonard Spencer, 259
Circa, use of, 131
Citizen 13660 (Okubo), 164
Civil liberties, 359, 374. *See also* Censorship
Civil War, in literature, 253-54, 298, 540, 544, 561
Clark, Barrett H., 502
Clark, Sydney Aylmer, 311
Classics: annotations, 144; editions, 218; Greek, 303, 390, 453, 497; Latin, 233-34; translations, 218, 233-34
Classics in Translation (Smith), 234
Clemens, Samuel Langhorne (Mark Twain), 60, 208, 268, 307
Clendening, Logan, 338
Cleveland Public Library, 493
Cloister and the Hearth, The (Reade), 298, 509
Coan, Otis W., 560
Coasts of Illusion, The (Firestone), 306
"Cocktail" novels, 522
Coleridge, Samuel Taylor, *quoted* on poetry, 448
Collection of Travel in America (Bradshaw), 307
Collectivism, 369
Colleges and universities: fiction, 560; libraries, 327; scientific training, 329

Collingswood, Robin George, 285
Colophon (inscription), 206
Color: bindings, 180; book jackets, 182; reproduction, 172
Columbia Dictionary of Modern European Literature, 428-29
Columbia-Lippincott Gazetteer of the World, 202
Columbia Studies in American Culture, 411
Columbia University Press, vii, xiii, 199, 202, 366
Columbia University Studies in Library Service, vii
Come Hither (De la Mare), 463, 464
Comedy: Austen, Jane, 511; drama, 487; fiction, 518
Comics, 519
Commercialism, and literary criticism, 120-21
Common Ground (quarterly), 379
Common Reader, The (Woolf), *quoted*, 418
Commonweal (periodical), 115, 412
Commonwealth Fund, 364
Communism: capitalism and, 293, 371, 403, 478; Christianity and, 397-98; current literature, 359, 369; dialectical or historical materialism, 277, 402-3; drama, 478, 487; exposition, authentic, need for, 371-72, 403-4; 477; fiction, 515, 533; information, impartial, need for, 293-94, 371-72, 403; *New Masses*, 114-15; *Partisan Review, The*, 116-17; phases, 403; public opinion, 294; religion and philosophy, 389. *See also* Marxian philosophy
Community and its libraries, 15-27, 93
Community theatres, 476, 479, 481-82
Compton, Charles H., 22n
Compton-Burnett, Ivy, 518, 520
Comte, Auguste, 361
Confederacy, 253-54
Confessions, definition, 260
Confucius, 395
Congress of Industrial Organizations, 367
Connolly, Cyril, 119-20
Conquered, The (Mitchison), 298
Conquistador (MacLeish), 453
Conrad, Joseph: historical novel, 539; publisher, 208; style, 527; subjectivity, 513; *Victory*, 152
Contemporary Biography (Longaker), 272

INDEX 579

Contemporary Chinese Stories, 558
Contents table, 165
Convention and Revolt in Poetry (Lowes), 469
Cook, Dorothy Elizabeth, 77, 94
Cook, Sir Edward, 271; indexes, *quoted* on, 166
Cook, Frederick Albert, 319-20
Cooper, Isabella M., 76
Copernicus, Nicolaus, 4
Copyright Law, The (DeWolf), 194
Copyrights and the copyright law: American, 190, 191, 193; British, 190; code, 193; date examination, 56, 164; international, 190, 191-95; libraries, 203; protection, 189-95; reprint editions, 224, 230
Corn King and the Spring Queen, The (Mitchison), 542
Correspondence and letters, 260-62, 313, 387
Corwin, Norman, 496
Coulter, E. M., 291
Council of Foreign Relations, 379
Council on Books in Wartime, 197-98
Couperus, Louis-Marie-Anne, 168
Cournos, John, 245
Cousins, Norman, 111
Cowley, Malcolm, 245, 434
Cox, Edward Godfrey, 308
Cox, Oliver Cromwell, 373
Cozzens, James, 517
Cram, Ralph Adams, 148
Crane, (Harold) Hart, 458, 466
Crerar (John) Library, Chicago, 327, 345
Crime and detective fiction, 519-20, 523, 528, 529
Crime of Sylvestre Bonnard, The (France), 235
Crisis (periodical), 379
Criterion (periodical), 120
Critical writing, 58-59. *See also* Literary criticism
Critiques and Essays in Criticism, 1920-1948 (Stallman), 434
Croce, Benedetto, 285
Cross, Wilbur Lucius, 533
Crothers, Samuel McChord, *quoted* on books, 63
Crouse, Russel, 493
Crowell's Handbook for Readers and Writers, 427
Crusaders, The (Heym), 517

Crusaders, The: Iron Men and Saints (Lamb), 147
Crutchley, E. A., 209
Cry, the Beloved Country (Paton), 517
Culture, 6, 15, 21
Cummings, E. E. (Edward Estlin), 458, 465-66, 490
Cumulation (process), 70-71
Cumulative Book Index, 79, 84, 94, 219
Cumulative Book Lists (Whitaker's), 85
Cuppy, Will (William Jacob), 112
Curie, Enid, 338
Current Biography, 262
Curtin, Jeremiah, 245
Czechoslovak literature, 439

Daiches, David, 106, 533
Dana, Richard Henry, 313
Danger from the East (Lauterbach), 317
Dark, Eleanor, 541
Darwin, Charles Robert, 51, 304, 321, 344, 376
Date slips, 40
Dates. *See* Copyrights; Editions
Davis, William Stearns, 298
Day, Clarence Shepard, Jr., 261, 493
Days and Nights (Simonov), 549
Days of a Man, The (Jordan), 268
De Kruif, Paul, 263
De la Mare, Walter, 454, 463, 464
"De luxe" bindings, 160, 181
"De luxe" editions, 225, 242, 552
De Morgan, Augustus, 340
De Onis, Harriet, 245
De Quincey, Thomas, 263
De Voto, Bernard Augustus, 109, 111
DeWolf, Richard, 194
Dear Brutus (Barrie), 490
Death Comes for the Archbishop (Cather), 129
Death of a Salesman (Miller), 487
Debs, Eugene Victor, 266
Debunking biographies, 264
Decadence, 516
Decency, sense of, 538
Decline and Fall of the Roman Empire (Gibbon): annotations, 147-48; Bury edition, 165, 232; editions, 56; evaluation, 279-80; Milman edition, 232
Decline of the West (Spengler), 281
Dehumanization of Art, The (Ortega y Gasset), 535
Dell, Ethel M., 527

Demand, 21-24; budget, 47; controversial material, 394; definition, 39; fiction, 528-29; plays, 465; poetry, 465; value, 39-40
Democracy: American principles of, 371, 403; current literature, 359; drama, 489; fiction, 512, 515, 519; postwar conflict, 369
Dent, Joseph Mallaby, 202, 213-14, 238; classical literature, *quoted* on, 218
Depression years: biography, 251; drama, 477-78, 486; fiction, 358, 515; historical fiction, 543; library budgets 48; library service, 358; publishing, 196, 198-99; reading, 33; realism, 540
Designed for Reading (anthology), 104*n*
Detective fiction. *See* Crime and detective fiction
Detroit Public Library, 90
Deutsch, Albert, 338
Development of English Biography, The (Nicolson), 272-73
Development of Modern Medicine, The (Shryock), 338
Devices, publishers', 206-7, 223
Devils, Drugs, and Doctors (Haggard), 338
Devotional books, 395-96, 398
Dewey, John, 402, 411
Dewey, Melvil: *A.L.A. Catalog*, 66, 76; public libraries, problem and purpose, *quoted* on, 23
Dewey classification: *A.L.A. Catalog* (1926), 72; biography, 302; *Bookman's Manual*, 74, 75; fiction, 418; literature, 418; philosophy, 386, 399, 405-6; religion, 68, 386, 405-6; science, 330; sociology, 354, 359-60; travel, 302
Dialectical materialism, 277, 402-3
Dialogue, 265
Dialogues (Plato), 122, 387, 401
Diaries: definition, 259-60; history, 253; religion, 387; travel, 313
Dickens, Charles (John Huffam): fiction, 512; Forster's life of, 267; Gadshill edition, 162, 207; historical novel, 539; *Pickwick Papers*, 522; travel books, 315
Dickinson, Asa Don, 424
Dickinson, Emily (Elizabeth): biography, *quoted* on, 249; letters, 260
Dictionaries, 170, 424, 426

Dictionary of American Biography, 206, 262
Dictionary of American History, 288
Dictionary of European Literature (Magnus), 431
Dictionary of Modern English Usage, A (Fowler), 153
Dictionary of National Biography, 262
Dictionary of Philosophy, 413
Dictionary of Philosophy and Psychology (Baldwin), 412-13
Dictionary of World Literature: Criticisms, Forms, Technique (Shipley), 427
Didacticism, 153
Dimnet, Abbé Ernest: *Art of Thinking, The*, 8, 45, 130; Brontë sisters, 270; note-making, 8; reading the best books, *quoted* on, 45
Dinsmore, Charles Allen, 397
Directions in Modern Poetry (Drew), 470
Discovering Poetry (Drew), 469
Discovery of Europe (Rahv), 307
District of Columbia Public Library, 35*n*
Divine Comedy, The (Dante), Pater, *quoted* on, 51
Dobree, Bonamy, 431
"Doctrinal adhesions," 37
Documentation, 295-96
Documents of the Christian Church (Bettenson), 397, 410
Dodd, William Edward, 259
Dodd, Mead and Company, 192, 198, 208
"Dollar books," 220
Doolittle, Hilda, pen name "H.D.," 466
Dos Passos, John (Roderigo), 148, 490, 514, 515
Dostoyevsky, Fyodor, 152, 525, 535, 545
Douay Bible, 394
Doubleday and Company, 198, 201-2, 206, 208
"Doubleday Illustrated Library," 242
Doughty, Charles Montagu, 313-14
Douglas, Lloyd, 195, 509, 517, 527, 529
Downs, Robert, 419*n*
Doyle, Sir Arthur Conan, 539
Drachman, Julian, 331, 350
Drama, 475-505; background-building, 5; books on, 426, 502-5; classification, 50, 52; criticism, 433, 498; "datedness," 56; definitions, 487; English, 426; influ-

INDEX 581

ence, 423; Pulitzer Prize, 420; religion, 388; titles, 131
Drama League, 476, 479
Dramatic Bibliography (Baker), 500-501
Dramatic Index (Faxon), 500
Dreiser, Theodore: *American Tragedy, An*, 133; autobiography, 257; public libraries, *quoted* on, 38; style, 526; World War I (post) revolt, 513
Drew, Elizabeth, 469-70
Drewry, John, 104
Drinkwater, John, 463, 488
Drums (Boyd), 298
Drury, Francis Keese Wynkoop, xv, 48
Duffus, Robert Luther, 19-20, 21
Dumas, Alexander, 542
Dunbar, Dr. (Helen) Flanders, 339, 352
Dunbar, Seymour, 306
Dunham, Barrows, 392
Dunsany, Lord, on poetry, *quoted*, 449
Durant, Will (William James), 59, 406
Duranty, Walter, 318
Dust wrappers, 181-82
Dutton (E. P.) and Company, 202, 204
Dyslexia (reading difficulty), 60*n*

Early Western Travels (Thwaites), 290
East and West Association, 367
Eastman, Max, 144
Eckstein, Gustav, 334
Economic and Social Council, 366
Economic Survey of the Book Industry, 1930-1931 (Cheney), 213
Economics, 361, 370-71; history, 277; "periphrastic malady," 377-78; publications statistics, 358*n*; Twentieth Century Fund, 364
Eddington, Sir Arthur Stanley, 335
Edge, Sigrid, 33, 43
Edinburgh Review, 100
Editions, 218-46; abridgment, 220*n*, 228-30, 235; American, 203-4, 231; authorized, 230-31; Bible, 412; bindings, 181; books of accepted value, 56; classic, 218, 497; de luxe, 225; definition, 161-63, 223; English, 190, 203-4, 231; facsimile, 225; first, 56, 162; hard-bound, examples, 242-44; *Herald Tribune*, 112; incomplete, 230; limited, 224, 225; microfilm, 174; new, 224; *New York Times*, 113; paper-bound, 220-21, 244; poetry, 464-65; publication dates, 56; publishers, 207, 208; rag paper, 174; reprint, 236, 238; school, 224, 228; science, 334; selection, 184, 227-32; Shakespeare, 218; special, 224; trade, 224; translations, 235; type, 171; unabridged, 229
Editor's authority, 231
Edman, Irwin, *quoted*, 408
Education: adult, 34; books and, 3; definition, 15; fiction, 551; library, 26; literature on, 369; mass, 22; patois of, 153, 154; reading and, 9, 20, 21; reviews, 101; veterans, 18. *See also* Textbooks
Education for International Understanding in American Schools, 366
Education of Henry Adams, The (Adams), 484
Edwards Brothers, Ann Arbor, Michigan, 198, 225, 346, 348
Egoist (Meredith), 511
Ehrenburg, Ilya, 549
Eighteenmo, 170
Einstein, Albert, 328, 336
Einstein Theory of Relativity (Lieber), 336
Electrical Engineering Abstracts, 346
Elephant folio, 168
Eleven Religions, The (Champion), 391
Eliot, George, 512, 539
Eliot, T. S. (Thomas Stearns): allusion, 454; Brooks, Cleanth, study of, 470; collected poems, 465; *Criterion*, 120; critical essays, 432; erudition, 454; Hyman, S. E., study of, 433; literature of the great ages, 470; New Criticism, 432, 458-59; recordings, 468; *Waste Land* phase, 456
Elizabeth. *Pen name* of Countess Elizabeth Mary Russell, 511
Elizabeth and Essex (Strachey), 130
Elizabethans, 497-98
Ellis, (Henry) Havelock, 402; fiction, *quoted* on, 507
Elzevir family, 186
Emergency Committee of Atomic Scientists, 328
Emerson, Ralph Waldo: "Bohn's libraries," *quoted* on, 221; essays, 436; journals, 259-60
Emperor Jones, The (O'Neill), 490
Empson, William, 433
Encyclopaedia Britannica, 35; revisions, 324-25
Encyclopaedia of the Social Sciences, 379

582　INDEX

Encyclopedia of Literature (Shipley), 427

Encyclopedia of Religion and Ethics (Hastings), 397

Encyclopedias: literature, 424, 426; religious, 397, 412; subscription selling, 206

End papers, 180

Engels, Friedrich, 402, 404

English Bible as Literature, The (Dinsmore), 397

English books and literature: American editions, 203; bibliographies, 79, 425-27; book paper, 173, 175, 176; book-trade tools, 84-88; censorship, 214; copyright, 190; criticism, 120; *Cumulative Book Index*, 79; English editions, 231; essay, 435, 436; fiction, 509, 512, 545-47, 560, 563; historical novels, 544; libraries, 203; literary awards, 420, 422; printer's imprint, 164; Prayer book, 189; production, 196-97, 200; publishers, 200-201; publishing center, 173, 197; reprints, 192-93, 195, 238-39; review publications, 72, 100, 117-18; translations, 236

English Catalogue of Books, 85

"English Countryside Series," 320

English History in English Fiction (Marriott), 561

English Institute Annual: 1942, 271

English Library, An: An Annotated Guide to 1300 Classics, 425

English Literature (Garnett and Gosse), 431

"English Men of Letters" (series), 239

English Novelists (Bowen), 532

English Traveller in America, The, 1785-1835 (Mesick), 307

Enquiry into the Nature and Causes of the Wealth of Nations (Smith), 360

Enrico Caruso: His Life and Death (D. Caruso), 253

Eöthen (Kinglake, *1844*), 313, 322

Epic of America (Adams), 283

Epictetus, 401

Epigraphy, 276

Erewhon (Butler), 360

Ernst, Morris Leopold, 214

Erotica, 552

Erskine, John, 34

Ertz, Susan, 539

Ervine, St. John Greer, 489

Escape literature, 519-20

Esparto (grass), 173, 175

Essay and General Literature Index, 441

Essay on Rime (Shapiro), 470

Essay on the Principle of Population (Malthus), 361

Essays, 418, 434-41; America, 426; anthologists, 440-41; classification, 435; English, 426; examples, 443-45; imagination, 447; intrinsic qualities, 55; natural history, 333; nature, 333; poetry, 471-72; sociology, 361; travel, 306

Essential Shakespeare, The (Wilson), 497

Ethics (Spinoza), 401

Ethics, books on, 414-17

Eugénie Grandet (Balzac), 131

European fiction, 544-50

European Ideologies: a Survey of 20th Century Political Ideas, 380

Evaluation, 122-36; definition, 124; fiction, 154; reading of the book, 129. *See also* Annotation; Reviewing; Selection; Value

Evans, Bergen, 340-41

Eve of St. Mark, The (Anderson), 486

Evelyn, John, diary, 259

Everett, Louella D., 113

Everyman Looks Forward (Whyte), 358n

"Everyman's Library," 242; American distribution, 202, 242; Dent, J. M., 213; Hakluyt narratives, 229; Keats, 231; make-up uniformity, 163; size, 238; volumes, number of, 221-22

Evolution, 187, 337

Existentialism, 404

Experimentalism, 514

Exploration, 303, 304-5, 314

Expression in America (Lewisohn), 165, 432

Expressionism, 490-91

Expurgation, 228, 229

Eye fatigue, 171

Fables, 334

Fabre, Jean Henri, 334

Facsimile, definition, 225

Facts on File, 379

Fadiman, Clifton, 106

Fairfield, Cicely Isabel. *See* West, Rebecca

"Fake" authorship, 208

Famous Chinese Plays (Arlington and Acton), 492

Fantasy: drama, 489; fiction, 521
Far Away and Long Ago (Hudson), 256
Farrer, Reginald, 304
Fascism, 186-87, 369
Father and Son (Gosse), 256
Father and the Angels (Manners), 395
"Fathers of the Church, The," (series), 410
Faust (Goethe), 233
Fear No More: a Book of Poems for the Present Time, 455
Federal aid, 21
Federal Council of the Churches of Christ in America, 412
Federal prose, 154-55
Federal Theatre Project, 477-78
Federal Writers Project, 240-41, 477
Fergusson, Erna, 311
Ferm, Virgilius, 413
Fiction, 538-67; *A.L.A. Catalog*, 62, 68, 251; America, 426, 509, 563; annotation, 140, 141, 149-51; autobiography, 520; background-building, 5; Bentley, Phyllis, *quoted* on, 506; "best novel of the year," 102; best sellers, 195; biography, 253, 264-66, 520; Black Memorial Award, 420; *Book Review Digest*, 71; books about, 532-35; character delineation, 131; classification, 50, 52; criticism, 433; "datedness," 56; depression years, 358; Ellis, Havelock, *quoted* on, 507; English, 426, 509, 545-47; ethical influence, 550-51; evaluation, 131-32, 154; examples (*1813-1948*), 530-32; factual authenticity, 509-10; foreign, 150-51, 544-50, 562-63, 565; formalism and convention, 484; historical, 150, 253, 265, 298, 538; history, 277, 507; "immoral," 550-51; influence, 6, 423; library budgets, 47-48; life, 249; lists, 562-63; literary qualities, 131; local color, 492; London *Times*, 118; Marxist, 515, 533; National Book Award, 421; nature books, 333; notices, 105; oral reviewing, 134; plot, 134; possible purchase file, 92; psychoanalysis, 265; psychological insight, 507; Pulitzer Prize, 420; readers, 36, 251; rebinding, 180; religion, 388; reprints, 220; restricted, 554; review slips, 126, 129, 134; reviewing of, 102, 103, 132, 133; scientific, 329; selection, 506; series, 227; shelf space, 169; *Standard Catalog for Public Libraries*, 80; structure, 131; subjects, 132; tests for, 54-55, 522-24; titles, 131; "trash," 36; value, 40, 42; Victorian, 512
Fiction Catalog: 1941 Edition, 80, 558-59
Field, Eugene, 8
Fierro Blanco, Antonio de, 315
"Fifty Books of the Year," 183
55 Short Stories from the New Yorker, 558
"Fig-Leaf Edition," of Montaigne, 233
Filene, Edward Albert, 364
Fine arts, *A.L.A. Catalog* (1904-41) proportional representation, 62
Finian's Rainbow, 487
Firestone, Clark Barnaby, 306
Firkin, Ina Ten Eyck, 499-500, 564
First edition: definition, 162; translation, 236
First printing, definition, 162
Fischer, John, 318
Fitzgerald, Edward, 231
Fitzgerald, F(rancis) Scott (Key), 514
Flanagan, Hallie, 477
Flaubert, Gustave, 235, 554
Flavin, Martin, 491
Flax cellulose, 173
Flesch, Rudolf, 153
Fletcher, William I., x
Flexner, Jennie Maas, 33, 43
Flores, Angel, 245
Florio, John, 56, 233
Folded Leaf, The (Maxwell), 518
Foley, Martha, 557
Folio, 169
Folk drama, 492
Food and Agricultural Organization, 366
Footlights across America (Macgowan), 476
Footnotes, 165; poetry, 464; reader irritation, 165
Forbes, Esther, 539, 543
Ford, Henry, 269
Foreign Affairs (quarterly), 379
Foreign Affairs Bibliography, 379
Foreign literatures, 202; anthologies, 420; drama, 491-92, 496; fiction, 563, 565-67; translations, 492
Foreign Policy Association, 367
Foreign readers, 25
Forever Amber (Winsor), 195, 554
Format, 161, 163; definition, 161; margins, 176; wartime, 168-69

Forms of Modern Fiction (O'Connor), 534
Forster, Edward Morgan, 133, 533
Forster, John, 267
Forty-eightmo, 170
47 Workshop, at Harvard, 481
Fosdick, Harry Emerson, 397
"Foundation books," 47
Four-letter words, 552-53
Fowler, Henry Watson, 153; *belles lettres, quoted* on, 418; "periphrastic malady," 377
Fox, George, 259
Fox, Ralph, 533
France, Anatole, 235
France: Paris and the Provinces (Roumagnac), 309
Franklin, Benjamin, 221, 255-56, 307
Franklin, E. Frazier, 373
Franklin Delano Roosevelt: a Memorial, 223
Frazer, Sir James George, 229, 387
Freedley, George, 501, 502
Freedley, Vinton, 480
Freedom versus Organization, 1814-1914, (Russell), 361n
Freeman, Douglas Southall, 253-54
Freeman, John, on poetry, *quoted*, 449
Frémont, Jessie Benton, 265-66
French books and literature, 201-2, 220, 428, 563. *See also* names of individual authors
French Revolution (Carlyle), 282
French's (Samuel) Catalog of Plays, 502
Freud, Sigmund, 269, 376
Froissart, Jean, 281, 284
From Homer to Omar Khayyám (Sarton), 346
From Rabbi Ben Ezra to Robert Bacon (Sarton), 346
Frontier in American History, The (Turner), 295
Frontiers of the Mind (Rhine), 406
Frost, Robert Lee, 451, 454, 469
Frost, S. E., 410
Full Employment in a Free Society (Beveridge), 371
"Full sets" fetish, 41
Fuller, Edmund, 427
Fuller, Margaret, 269
Furnace, Horace Howard, 232

G. & D. Specials, 242
G. I. Bill of Rights, 18
Galantière, Lewis, 106, 245
Gallery, The (Burns), 517
Galsworthy, John, 165, 488, 527
Gamow, George, 336
Gangsterism, 514
Gannett, Lewis, 112
Garaudy, Roger, 533
Garceau, Oliver, 31, 43
Gardiner, Samuel Rawson, 281
Gardner, Erle Stanley, 311
Garnett, Constance, 245
Garnett, Edward, 488
Garnett, Richard, 431
Gassner, John, 496
Gateway to History, The (Nevins), 285-86
Geddes, Donald Porter, 338
Geismar, Maxwell D., 533
General Bookbinding (Groneman), 180n
Generation of Vipers (Wylie), 392
Genre novels, 547
Genteelisms, 153
Geography, 304
Geography of Reading, The (Wilson), 20-21
Geology, 331
George, Henry, 361
George MacDonald (Lewis), 409
George Washington (Woodward), 267
Ghost writing, 208, 268, 286
Gibbon, Edward, 49, 56, 279-80, 291; autobiography, 256. *See also* Decline and Fall of the Roman Empire
Gifford Lectures, 409
Gift-book bindings, 181
Gifts, 41, 394, 465, 466
Gilbert, Stuart, 245
Gilder, Rosamund, 480, 501
Gladstone, William Ewart, 49, 253, 268
Glasgow, Ellen (Anderson Gholson), 511, 533
Glass Menagerie, The (Williams), 487
Global war, impact of, 6-7
"Globe Editions," 243
Glossy paper, 172, 175
Glover, Terrot Reaveley, 437
Godden, Rumer, 523
God-forsaken volumes, that are admired and acquired by people otherwise of good taste and culture, 160
Goethe, Johann Wolfgang von, 233
Gogh, Vincent van, 265

INDEX

Gogol, Nikolai Vasilievich, 539
Gold Star List of American Stories, 562
Gold-Beetle, The (Poe), 231
Goldberg, Isaac, 245
Golden Book, The (McMurtrie), 159, 210-11
Golden Bough, The (Frazer), 387, 395; abridgment, 229
Golden Multitudes (Mott), 544n
Golden Sovereign, The (Housman), 488
"Golden Treasury Series," 243
Golding, Louis, 515
Goldman, Emma, 269-70
Goncourt, Edmond de, 260
Goncourt, Jules de, 260
Gone with the Wind (Mitchell), 522, 543, 544
Gooch, George Peabody, 285
Good Reading: A Guide to the World's Best Books, 425
Goodbye to All That (Graves), 257
Goodrich, R. M., 289
Gorer, Geoffrey, 315
Gosnell, Charles, 389
Gosse, Sir Edmund William, 256, 431, 434
Government and public affairs, 369
Graham, Bessie, 73-76
Grand Tour in the Eighteenth Century, The (Mead), 306
Granniss, Ruth Shepard, 214-15
Grass Roof, The (Kang), 142-43
Graves, Robert Ranke, 257, 510, 539
Gray, William Scott, 17, 29, 43
Great Books Discussion Groups, 226, 390
Great Books Extension program, University of Chicago, 34
Great Books Foundation, 34-35, 226
"Great Books of the Western World," 35, 225-26
Great Critics, The (Smith and Parks), 440
"Great Illustrated Classics," 243
Great Prisoners (Abramowitz), 230
Great Tradition, The: George Eliot, Henry James, Joseph Conrad (Leavis), 534
Greek literature, 166, 233-34, 303, 390; drama, 497; mythology, 453
Green, Henry, 520
Green, John Richard, 281, 291
Green, Paul, 492
Green Grow the Lilacs (Riggs), 492

Green Mansions (Hudson), 165
Green Pastures, The (Connelly-Bradford), 496
Grey, Zane, 547
Grierson, Sir Herbert, 409
Gross, Feliks, 380
Grote, George, 303
Group study programs, 34-35, 465
Growth, definition of, 4
Growth of the Soil (Hamsun), 548
Grummon, Stewart Edgar, 245
Guard of Honor (Cozzens), 517
Guedalla, Philip, 147, 272; biography, 265, quoted on, 266-67
Guerard, Albert, 106
Guerney, Bernard Guilbert, 245
Guest, Edgar Albert, 466
Guide books, 240-41, 304, 309-10
Guide to Confident Living (Peale), 398
Guide to Historical Fiction (Baker), 560-61
Guide to Historical Literature, 286-87, 297
Guide to Play Selection, A (Smith), 500
Guide to Reference Books (Mudge), 88, 286
Guide to the Best Fiction, English and American (Baker), ix, 560
Guide to the Best Historical Novels (Nield), 561
Guided Group Reading, 34-35
Guizot, François Pierre Guillaume, 281
Gunther, John, 312
Gustafson, Alrik, 534
Gutenberg, Johann, 186
Gutenberg Award, 421n

"H. D." (Hilda Doolittle), 466
Habits in reading, 29-42
Hacker, Louis Morton, 289
Hackett, Francis, 104
Hackneyed phrases, 153
Hagedorn, Hermann: *Brookings: A Biography*, 130; Hiroshima bomb, quoted on, 324
Haggard, Howard Wilcox, 338
Haig-Brown, Roderick Langmere, 334
Haines, Helen Elizabeth, vii-x, 238, 507, 534
Hakluyt, Richard, 229, 306
Haldane, John Bourdon Sanderson, 331, 337, 437, 438
Haldeman-Julius "Little Blue Books," 220

586 INDEX

Hale, George Ellery, 335
Half-tone illustrations, 175
Hall, James Norman, 315
Hall, Radclyffe, 523, 554
Halsey, F. W., 113
Hamilton, Clayton, 484
Hamilton, Edith, 399
Hamilton, James Alexander, 60*n*
Hammond fiction collection, 509
Hamsun, Knut, 548
Handbook of Universal Literature (Botta), 431
Handbooks for travelers, 309
Handling of books, 168
Hannum, Alberta, 172
Hansen, Agnes Camilla, 562
Hanson, Earl Parker, 307
Happy endings, 547
"Harbrace Modern Classics," 243
Hardy, Thomas, 512, 527
Hare, Augustus John Cuthbert, 309, 310, 322
Harper, Joseph Henry, 214
Harper and Bros., 192, 198, 201, 204, 207
"Harper Dollar Library," 243
Harrison, Shelby M., 365*n*
Harsanyi, Zsolt de, 299
Hart, Albert Bushnell, 290
Hart, Hornell, 389*n*
Hart, Lyn, 520*n*
"Harvard Books in Astronomy," 348
"Harvard Monographs in Applied Science," 348
Harvard Plays (Baker), 495
Harvard University, drama, 481
Hastings, James, 397
Hawkers and Walkers in Early America (Wright), 306
Hawkins, Reginald Robert, 347
Hawkridge, Emma, 391
Hawthornden Prize, 420
Hawthorne, Nathaniel, 203, 207, 230, 512, 522, 539
Haydn, Hiram, 427
Haydon, Benjamin, 257
Haydon, Eustace, 391
Hayes (Cardinal) Literature Committee, 412*n*
Haynes Foundation of Los Angeles, 368
Hazlitt, William, 100, 434
Headicar, B. M., 380
Headley, Leal Aubrey, 60
Headlines (running-heads), 177-78

Hearn, Lafcadio, 235, 245, 314
Hedden, Worth, 519
Hedin, Sven, 319-20
Hefling, Helen, 270*n*
Hegel, George William Friedrich, 402
Height of a book, 167, 170
Hellman, Lillian, 486, 487, 489
Hemingway, Ernest, 203, 515, 526, 527
Henderson, Helen, 309, 310
Henry Esmond (Thackeray), 541
Henry (O.) Memorial Award Committee, 557
Heredity, 250
Hergesheimer, Joseph, 539
"Heritage Editions," 243
Herodotus (5th cent. B.C.), 280
Heroes, 280
"Heroes of the Nations" (series), 207, 253
Hewlett, Maurice Henry, 539
Heym, Stefan, 517
Heyward, DuBose, 151
Hibbert Journal, 412
Hibbert Lectures, 410
Highroad to Adventure (Parker), 307
Hill, Grace Livingston, 527-28
Hillyer, Robert, 460
Hind in Richmond Park, A (Hudson), 334
Hindus, Maurice, 516
Hines, Duncan, 310
Hinsie, Dr. Leland Earl, 339
Hiroshima, 325, 326, 328
Historian and Historical Evidence, The (Johnson), 285
Historical drama, 487, 488
Historical fiction, 538, 561; annotation, 150; examples, 564-65
Historical Fiction (Logasa), 562
Historical materialism, 277
Historical Outlook, 288
Historiography, definition, 284-86
History, 275-301; *A.L.A. Catalog*, 62, 67, 251; annotations, 144; Bacon, Francis, 50; biography, 250, 253-54, 297-98; classification, 50, 52, 53; definition, 277, 278; distortion of, 542; drama, 498; examples, 299-301; fiction, 507, 545, 561; geography, 304; headlines, 178; illustrations, 179; imagination, 447; influence, 6; life, 249; Lowell, James Russell, *quoted* on, 275; Pulitzer Prize, 420; religion, 387, 395, 396; reviews,

101; series, 239; Sonnenschein, 88; travel, 298, 306. See also Historical fiction; Poetry
History (of books), 159, 160
History, Its Theory and Practice (Croce), 285
History and Historians in the Nineteenth Century (Gooch), 285
History as a Literary Art (Morison), 285
History of American Philosophy (Schneider), 411
History of Charles XII, King of Sweden (Voltaire), 253
History of England (Macaulay), 148
History of Greece (Grote), published (1846-1856), 303
History of Historical Writing (Thompson and Holm), 285
History of Modern Drama, A (Clark and Freedley), 502
"History of the American Nation," 290-91
History of the South, A, 291
History of the United States (Adams), 280
History of Travel in America (Dunbar), 306
History of Western Philosophy (Russell), 407
Hobbes, Thomas, 360
Hocking, William Ernest, 407
Hoffman, F. J., 117*n*
Hoffman, Hester R., 74, 76
"Hogarth Lectures on Literature," 272
Hogben, Lancelot, 337
Holden, John Allan, 94
Holm, Bernard, 285
Holmes, Oliver Wendell, 257
Holmes-Pollock Letters, 261
Holt (Henry) and Company, 198, 207, 208
Holy Roman Empire, The (Bryce), 280
Home reading, 10, 463
Homer, 233, 435
"Hoover Lectures on Christian Unity," 410
Hopf, Harry Arthur, 17-18
Hopkins, Byron Chandler, 33, 43
Hopkins, Gerard Manley, 245, 465
Horizon (periodical), 119-20
Horton, Marion, 76
Houghton Mifflin Company, 198, 201, 204, 207, 230, 231

House, Dr. Roy Temple, 117
House of Macmillan (1843-1943), The (Morgan), 215
Household hints, 91
Housman, Alfred Edward, 454
Housman, Laurence, 488
"How to" books, 342
How to Criticize Books (Jones), 153-54
How to Judge a Book (Shuman), 155
How to Read a Book (Adler), 34, 57*n*
How to Read Better and Faster (Lewis), 60*n*
Howard, Sidney, 489
Howells, William Dean, 109, 540
Huberman, Leo, 283
Hudson, William Henry: essays, 333, 438; *Far Away and Long Ago*, 256; *Green Mansions*, 165; *Hind in Richmond Park, A*, 334; nature, 333-34; *Traveller in Little Things, A*, 306
Hughes, Langston, 463
Hughes, Leora, 253
Hugo, Victor (Marie), 52, 235
Human Body, The (Clendening), 338
Human family, kinship of the, 546
Human Nature: the Marxian View (Venable), 404
Human Personality and Its Survival of Bodily Death (Myers), 406
Humanism as a Philosophy (Lamont), 404-5
Humboldt, Alexander von, 314, 322
Humor, fashions in, 442
Humphries, Rolfe, 461
Hundred Towers (Weiskopf), 439
Hurston, Zora, 523
Husbands, as biographers, 267
Hutchins, Robert Maynard, 34-35
Hutchinson, Arthur Stuart-Menteth, 526
Hutton, Graham, 365
Huxley, Aldous Leonard: *Jesting Pilate*, 316; Orwell, George, 518; *Perennial Philosophy*, 409; *Point Counter Point*, 525; reading, quoted on, 15; style, 130; *Texts and Pretexts*, 463
Huxley, Julian Sorell, 316, 333, 343, 344
Huxley, Thomas Henry, 435
Hyman, Stanley Edgar, 433, 471

I Believe, 387

Ibsen, Henrik, 485
Icelandic literature, 419
Iceman Cometh, The (O'Neill), 487
Idea of History, The (Collingwood), 285
Idell, Albert, 529
Idiot, The (Dostoyevsky), 152
Idiots' Delight (Sherwood), 486
Iles, George, 65, 72, 154
Iliad (Homer), 233
Illicit, lure of the, 552
Illiteracy, 17
Illusion and Reality (Caudwell), 470-71, quoted, 446, 456
Illustrations: book purpose, 55; halftone, 175; imagination, 183; offset lithography, 172; photography, 178-79; selection, 179
Immature minds, 553-54
"Imperial Editions," 243
Impression (or printing), definition, 162, 223
In My End Is My Beginning (Baring), 265
In Quest of the Perfect Book (Orcutt), 211
In the Forbidden Land (Landor), 320
Incidents of Travel in Central America (Stephens), 303, 314
Index to Contemporary Biography and Criticism (Hefling and Richards), 270n
Index to Full-Length Plays, 1926 to 1941 (Faxon), 500
Index to One-Act Plays (Logasa and Ver Nooy), 500
Index to Plays, 1800-1926 (Firkin), 499-500
Index to Plays in Collections (Ottermiller), 500
Index to Short Stories (Firkin), 564
Index translationum, 236
Indexes, 166-67; *A.L.A. Catalog* (1926), 72; *Best Books*, 87; *Book Review Digest*, 72; Cook, Sir Edward, *quoted* on, 166; definition, 166; humorous, 167; indispensability of, 55; omission of, 208; science, 345; testing of, 57; Wilson Company, 81-82
India paper, 175
Information (book of): definition, 50, 52; content table, 165; indexes, 166; knowledge popularization, 68; publication date, 56; tests, 55

Information Service (periodical), 412
Ingersoll Lectures, 410
Inside Out: an introduction to autobiography (Bates), 271
Inside U.S.A. (Gunther), 312
Inspiration (books of), 50-52, 54-56
Institute of Pacific Relations, 367
Intelligence, 4
Inter-American Congress for the Maintenance of Peace (1936), 89
International Catalogue of Scientific Literature, 345
International Copyright Union, 190-91
International Protection of Literary and Artistic Property, The (Ladas), 195
Inter-Traffic: Studies in Translation (Bates), 237n
Intimate Notebooks (Nathan), 489
Introduction to Bibliography for Literary Students, An (McKerrow), 210
Introduction to the History of Science (Sarton), 346
Introduction to the Russian Novel (Lavrin), 534
Introductions to books, 57, 164-65
Invalids, 557
"Invitation to Travel Series," 320
Irish drama, 491
Irving, Washington, 192, 207, 281
Issue, definition, 162, 223
"It takes Courage to stock 'Taboos'" (Bristol), 554
Ives, George Burnham, 233

Jackets (book), 121, 180-82
Jackson, Charles, *Lost Weekend*, 523
Jaeger Sanitary Woolens, "scientific" origin and purpose of, 341
James, Henry: Balzac, *quoted* on, 545; style, 526; subjectivity, 513
James, William, 402
Jamieson, John, 198
Japanese culture, 305
Jargon, vices of, 137
Jastrow, Joseph, 341
Jeans, Sir James Hopwood, 335, 353
Jefferies, Richard, 333, 437
Jeffers, (John) Robinson, *quoted*, 15
Jehol (Hedin), 319
Jennings, Herbert Spencer, 339
Jesting Pilate (A. Huxley), 316
Jesuit Relations (Thwaites), 229
Jesus, studies of the life of, 396

INDEX   589

Jewett, Charles Coffin, *quoted* on librarians, 15
Jewish Encyclopedia, 397
Jewkes, John, 371
Jews: authors, 294, 410; Bible, 394-95; *Jewish Encyclopedia*, 397; literature, 419; religious book week, 413-14; Yiddish folk drama, 491
Jim Bridger, Mountain Man (Vestal), 252
Joachim, Harold Henry, 401
Joeckel, Carlton Bruns, 43
John Brown's Body (Benét), 453
John o'London's Weekly, 118
Johnson, Allen, 285, 291
Johnson, Edgar, 272
Johnson, Hewlett, 318
Johnson, Thomas H., 430
Johnston, William Dawson, 419*n*
Jonah (Nathan), 203, 521
Jones, Howard Mumford, 106, 430
Jones, Llewellyn, 153
Jordan, David Starr, 268
Joseph (Mann), 204, 517
Journal: definition, 259-60; travel, 313
Journal of Religion, 412
Journey of the Flame (de Fierro Blanco), 315
Journey's End (Sherriff), 486
Journeys in Time, from the Halls of Montezuma to Patagonia's Plain (Niles), 307
Joy, Charles Rhind, 409
Joyce, James, 513, 521, 554
Juarez and His Mexico (Roeder), 298
Judging a book. *See* Evaluation
Judgment, 4, 58-59, 108, 132-33, 569
Juveniles. *See* Children's books

Kalish, A. H., 27*n*
Kang, Younghill, 142
Kant, Immanuel, 402
Kazin, Alfred, 532*n*
Keats, John, 231
Kelland, Clarence Budington, 509
Kelly, Grace, 31-32, 43
Kenilworth (Scott), 541
Kenton, Edna, 229
Kentucky Mountain Fantasies (MacKaye), 492
Kerr, Chester, 199
Keyes, Frances Parkinson, 509
Keyserling, Count Hermann Alexander, 313, 316

Kierkegaard Anthology, A, 409
Killers of the Dream (Smith), 374
Kingdom of Books, The (Orcutt), 211
Kinglake, Alexander William, 313, 316, 322
Kinsey, Dr. Alfred Charles, 338
"Kinsey Report," 338-39, 554-55
Kipling, Rudyard, 208, 453
Kirkus (Virginia) bookshop service, 115-16
Knight, Charles, 221
Knopf, Alfred A. (publisher), 198, 207
Knowledge, 50, 93
Knowledge for What? (Lynd), 356
Knox, Father Ronald, 394
Koch, Frederick Henry, 492, 495
Koran, 395
Korzybski, Alfred Habdank Skarbek, 423
Kozlenko, William, 495
Kravchenko, V. A., 318
Kristin Lavransdatter (Undset), 168, 510, 542, 548
Krutch, Joseph Wood, 106, 269, 270, 434
Kunitz, Joshua, 439

Labor unions, 26-27
Ladas, Stephen Pericles, 195
Laidler, Harry Wellington, 380
Laing, Dilys Bennett, 461, *quoted*, 385
Lamb, Harold, 147
Lamont, Corliss, 404
Lamont, William Hayes Fogg, 563
Land of Short Shadows, The (Gardner), 311
Landon, Margaret, 253
Landor, Arnold Henry Savage, 320
Lang, Andrew, 162
Langdon-Davies, John, 340
Langer, William Leonard, 379
Lao-Tzu, 395
Lardner, Ring, 307, 533
Larned, Josephus Nelson, 72, 286-87; on biography, *quoted*, 254-55
Larrimore, Lida, 527
Laski, Harold, 166, 368, 370
Last of the Conquerors (Smith), 519
Latin American literature, 237, 310, 421
Latin American republics, biographical information exchange, 89
Latin classics, 233-34
Lattimore, R. B., 310
Laughlin, Clara, 309, 310
Lauterbach, Richard, 317

Lavrin, Janko, 534
Law books, 205, 369
Law of the Soviet State, The (Vyshinsky), 371
Lawler, John, 81*n*
Lawrence, D. H. (David Herbert), 466, 513, 525
Lawson, John Howard, 499
Lay Sermons (T. H. Huxley), 435
Lazarus Laughed (O'Neill), 483
Leacock, Stephen Butler, *quoted*, 510-11
League of Nations, 235-36, 365
League to Support Poetry, 467
Leavis, Frank Raymond, 534
Lee, Jennie, 254
Lee, Muna, 245
Lee, Robert Edward, 253-54
Legacy of Greece, The, 166
Legibility, of type, 171
Lehmann-Haupt, Hellmut, 209, 214
Leigh, Robert Devore, 31, 43
Leisy, Ernest Erwin, 561
Lenrow, Elbert, 559-60
Leonard, William Ellery, 59
Leonov, Leonid, 549
"Lepanto" (Chesterton), 468
Lerner, Max, 377
Lettering, 183
Letters. *See* Correspondence and letters
Leviathan (Hobbes), 360
Levick, G. Murray, 333-34
Lewis, C. S. (Clive Staples), 390, 409, 517, 521
Lewis, Day, 456
Lewis, Norman, 60*n*
Lewis, Sinclair, 162, 195, 513, 539
Lewisohn, Ludwig: anti-Puritanism, 109; criticisms, 58, 61; *Expression in America*, 165, 432; tragedy, *quoted* on, 475; translations, 245
Leypoldt, Augusta Harriet, 154
Leypoldt, Frederick, 83, 87
Liberation of American Literature, The (Calverton), 148, 432
Librarians: book history, 160-61; book selection, 16-17; book talks, 126; book-trade familiarity, 208; community needs, 27; convention (1853), 15; copyright, 194; fiction, 507-8; formats of books, 163; interest, kindling and fostering, 570; leadership, 10; literary quality, insensitivity, 37; moral rigidity, 133; Negro, 26; newspaper reading, 27; printing, 210; public speaking, 135; purpose of, 15; responsibility evasion, 65; restricted books, 554-55; reviewers, 132; slim books, 169; successful, 28; taboos of society, 555; timorous and rigorous, 551; "trade familiarity," 82; training, 135; true measure of his service, 45

Libraries: administration, 569-70; annotated lists, 140; appropriation, 47; attendants, 57-58; bibliographical tools, 47, 78-95; book fund, 47-48; book reviews, 103; book-order meetings, 125; borrowing average, 19; budgets, 47-48; bulletins, 88-89, 138; censorship, 188; circulation, 19, 29-30, 39-40; collection comprehensiveness, 39-41; collections, 45-46; college, 75, 77, 327; community obligation, 393-94; conservatism, 555; controversial material, 394; definition, 393; demand, 21-24, 39-40, 47, 394, 465, 528-29; depression years, 358; drama service, 481; education, 26; English books, 203; everyday life, 9; federal aid, 21; fiction, 36, 528-29; foreign readers, 25; high school, 69, 75, 77; historical collections, 292; individual readers, 22; labor unions, 26; maps, 309; mass readers, 22-23; microfilming, 174; Negro population, 25-26; new books, 42, 78, 182; ordering, 92; personal relationship with readers, 23, 37; printed catalogues, 90; propaganda, 394; province, 16-17; public relations, 24; purpose, 16-17, 393; readers, knowledge of, 35-36; "readers' adviser" service, 33; rental, 19, 116; resources of other libraries in the community, 46-47; review slips, 92; reviewing, 92, 122-36; salaries, 47; school, 26, 80, 123; scientific, 326; self-education, xi; service, 16, 20-22, 37-38, 358; specialized libraries, 47; staff responsibility, 27-28; state, 89; state aid, 21; text books, vii; "trash," 21, 36; trustees, 551; writers, 422-23
Libraries (books in series), 218, 221, 226
Library Bill of Rights, 188*n*, 394
Library Curriculum Studies, 48
Library Demonstration Bill, 21*n*
Library Journal, 82, 83; American Library Association, ix; annotations, 139, 140; forthcoming books, 116;

INDEX 591

Haines, Helen, viii-ix, xv; sociology, 382
Library of Congress: *A.L.A. Catalog*, 66; Bollingen Award, 460; catalogue cards, 72-73, 90, 239; catalogues, eyestrain, 172; poetry recordings, 468; Russian literature, 419; *United States Quarterly Book List*, 89-90
Library of Literary Criticism (Moulton), 426
"Library of Living Philosophers," 411
"Library of Philosophy," 411
Library's Public, The (Berelson), 18*n*, 528-29
Lieber, Lillian and Hugh, 336
Liebman, Rabbi Joshua, 398
Life and Philosophy of Spinoza (Pollock), 401
Life of Gladstone (Morley), 49, 253, 268
Life of John Marshall (Beveridge), 268, 298
Life of the Ant (Maeterlinck), 333
Life of the Bee (Maeterlinck), 333
Life on a Mediaeval Barony (Davis), 298
Life with Father (Crouse and Lindsay), 493
Life with Father (Day), 261
Lilienthal, David, 348, 371; machines and science, *quoted* on, 324
Lillard, Richard G., 560
Limited editions, 224, 225
Lin Yutang, *quoted* on the theatre, 491-92
Lincoln, Abraham, 269-70, 298
Linderman, Frank Bird, 252
Lindey, Alexander, 214
Lindsay, Howard, 493
Lindsay, Vachel, 451, 469
Link, Henry Charles, 17-18
Linotype printing, 70
Lippincott (J. B.) Company, 202, 205, 206
Lippincott Gazetteer, 202
Lippmann, Walter, 386
List of Books for College Libraries (Shaw), 75, 77, 347, 413
List of Books for Girls and Women and Their Clubs (Leypoldt and Iles), 154
Literary awards. *See* Literary prize awards
Literary commentary, 99-121
Literary criticism: contemporary, 432-35, 440, 467; Eliot, T. S., 458-59; examples, 442-44; familiarity with, need for, 58-59; Marxist, 434, 456; nineteenth century, 100, 467; poetry, 433, 458-59, 467. *See also* Essays
Literary History of England, A (Baugh, ed.), 431
Literary History of the United States, The (Garnett and Gosse), 431
Literary History of the United States, The (Macmillan, *1948*), 429-30
Literary maps, 309
Literary Market Place, 82, 94
Literary merit, 128
Literary Opinion in America (Zabel), 440
Literary prize awards, 420-22, 550
Literary Prizes and their Winners, 422
Literary quality, 37, 59
Literary Recreations (Cook), 271
Literary Review, 110
Literature, 418-43; *A.L.A. Catalog*, 62, 251; annotation, 144; approach to, 133; classifications, 50; definition, 132; influence, contemporary, xii; purpose, 29; religion, 388; travel, 304. *See also* Drama; Essays; Fiction; Poetry, etc.
Literature of American History, The (Larned), 72, 286-87
Literature of the Graveyard (Garaudy), 533
Lithography, 172
"Little Blue Books" (Haldeman-Julius), 220
Little, Brown and Company, 192, 198, 205-8
Little Foxes (Hellman), 487
Little Magazine, The: a History and Bibliography (Hoffman), 117*n*, 164
Little Novels of Italy (Hewlett), 539
Little Theatre movement, 476, 492, 494, 499
Little Theatre Service, 479
"Living Library," 243
Living Novel, The (Pritchett), 535
Living Philosophies, 387
"Living Thoughts Library," 207, 239
Little Treasury of Modern Poetry, English and American (Williams), 463
Livingston, Arthur, 245
Locke, John, 402
Lockwood Memorial Library, University of Buffalo, 472
Locomotive God, The (Leonard), 59
Loeb, James, 234

"Loeb Classical Library," 234
Logasa, Hannah, 500, 562
Lolly Willowes, or the Loving Huntsman (Warner), 150-51
London, Jack, 513
London Bibliography of the Social Sciences, The, 380
London Mercury, 119
London Perambulator (Bone), 305
London *Times Literary Supplement*, 117-18, 119
Lonesome Road (Green), 492
Longaker, Mark, 272; biography, *quoted* on, 255
Longmans, Green and Company, 200, 207
"Look at America" guide volumes, 179, 310
Looking Backward (Bellamy), 360
Lord, Louis Eleazar, 282
Lord Weary's Castle (Lowell), 459
Los Angeles Public Library, x, xv, 38
Lost Men of American History (Holbrook), 263
Lost Weekend, The (Jackson), 523
Loti, Pierre, 314
Love: a Garland of Prose and Poetry (De la Mare), 463
Loveman, Amy, 111
Lowell, Amy, 451, 453, 469
Lowell, James Russell: criticism, *quoted* on, 108; history, *quoted* on, 275
Lowell, Robert, 459
Lowe-Porter, Helen Tracy, 245
Lowes, John Livingston, 469
Loyalty tests, 188
Lucas, Edward Verrall, 305, 309-10, 322
Lumpkin, Katharine, 374
Lust for Life (Stone), 265
Luther, Martin, 189
Lutz, Grace Livingston. *See* Hill, Grace Livingston
Lydenberg, Harry Miller, 180*n*
Lynd, Robert, 356, 368

Macaulay, Thomas Babington: descriptive detail, 281; enduring vitality, 279; essays, 263, 436; *History of England*, 148; literary criticism, 100
McCamy, James Lucian, 31
McColvin, Lionel Roy, 38-40, 43
McCullers, Carson, 518

McDonald, Gerald, *quoted* on poetry recording, 468
Macgowan, Kenneth, 476
Machiavelli, Niccolo, 360
MacIntyre, Carlyle Ferran, 233, 245
MacIver, Dr. Robert Morrison, 368, 372
Mackail, John William, 497
MacKaye, Percy, 492
McKerrow, Ronald Brunlees, 210
MacLeish, Archibald, 168, 453-54, 460, 496
Macmillan, Daniel P., 60*n*
Macmillan and Company, 198, 200, 202, 204, 207, 215
McMurtrie, Douglas Crawford, 159, 210
McWilliams, Carey, 312, 368
Macy, John Albert, 431; literary mind, *quoted* on, 422
Madame Bovary (Flaubert), 554
Madariaga, Salvador de, 145
Maeterlinck, Maurice, 333
Magazines: book reviews, 105-6, 114-16; essays, 438; history, 288; literary criticism, 100, 101; picture, 178; poetry, 450-51, 459, 466, 467; psychology, 413; publication statistics, 17; pulp, 174; reading habits, 30; reading of, 9, 17, 18, 21, 29-30; reading speed, 59; review periodicals, 72, 99-100, 108, 110; review periodicals, English, 85, 118-20; scientific, 350
Magic Mountain, The (Mann), 150
Magnus, Laurie, 431
Mahabharata, 395
Mailer, Norman, 517, 555
Main Currents in American Literature (Parrington), 431-32
Main Currents in Nineteenth Century Literature (Brandes), 431
Main Street (Lewis), 162
Mainstream (periodical), 114-15
Making of a Southerner, The (Lumpkin), 374
Making the Most of Books (Headley), 60*n*
Malthus, Thomas Robert, 277, 361
Man against Myth (Dunham), 392
Man Called White, A (White), 373
Man with the Golden Arm, The (Algren), 555
Mann, Thomas, 150, 204, 235, 517
Manners, William, 395
Man's Disorder and God's Design, 397

INDEX

Man's unity in diversity, 316
Mantle, Burns, 496
Manual of Copyright Practice for Writers, Publishers and Agents (Nicholson), 194
Manual of Descriptive Annotation for Library Catalogues (Savage), 155
Manual of Historical Literature (Adams), 286-87
Manufacturing clause, in American copyrights, 191, 193
Maps, 304, 309-10
Marcus, William Elder, 31, 43
Marcus Aurelius, 401, 402
Margaret Ogilvy (Barrie), 261
Margins, 173, 183, 238
Maritain, Jacques, 390
Markham, Reuben Henry, 296
Married people, reading habits of, 30
Marriott, Sir John, 561
Marshall, John, 268, 298
Martin, Lowell, 35n
Marx, Karl, 361, 402
Marxian philosophy, 402-4; American literature, 148, 432; Calverton, V. F., 148, 432; Caudwell, Christopher, 456, 470-71; Cox, Oliver Cromwell, 373; drama, 478; dialectic or historical materialism, 277, 402-3; fiction, 515, 533; Haldane, J. B. S., *quoted* on, 337; influence, 376, 402-4; Lamont, Corliss, 405-6; Laski, Harold, 370; library selection, 371-72, 376; literary criticism, 432; *Mainstream*, 114-15; poetry, 456, 470-71; *Science and Society*, 116; Somerville, John, 403-4; Venable, V., 404. See also Communism
Mary Rose (Barrie, *1920*), 490
Masefield, John: literary allusions, 453; poetry, *quoted* on, 447; reading demands, 454; *referred to*, 466
Mason-Bees, The (Fabre), 333
Mass thinking and emotion, 49, 280
Massee, May, 76
Masses & Mainstream (periodical), 115
Master Makers of the Book (Orcutt), 211
Master of Destiny, The (Tilney), 339
Masters, Dexter, 349
Masters, Edgar Lee, 269-70, 451
Masterson, James R., 154
Masterworks of Government (Abbott, ed.), 380
"Masterworks Series," 380

Mathematics, 349
Matson, Alexander, 245
Matthews, Miriam, 26n
Matthiessen, Francis Otto, 106
Mature Mind, The (Overstreet), 398
Maude, Aylmer, 245
Maude, Louise, 245
Maugham, William Somerset, 489
Maupassant, Guy de, 235
Maurois, André: biography, 265, 271-72, *quoted*, 249; biography of Byron, 267
Maxwell, William, 518
May, J. Lewis, 245
Mayo, Katherine, 130, 318
Mayorga, Margaret, 495
Mead, Margaret, 305, 315
Mead, William Edward, 306
Medicine: books published (*1930-1944*), 347; classification, 331; histories, 338; libraries, 327, 369; publishers, 204-5. See also Psychoanalysis; Psychosomatic medicine
Meeting of East and West, The (Northrop), 143
Melcher, Frederic Gershom, xvi, 83, 199
Melodrama, 487
Melville, Herman, 314
Member of the Wedding, The (McCullers), 518
Memoirs, 254, 258, 259
Memoirs of J. M. Dent, 1849-1926 (Dent), 213-14
Memoirs of the Second World War (Churchill), 259
Men: fiction, 512, 554; prudery, 538; reading habits, 30; westerns, 321
Mencken, Henry Louis, 392, 436
"Mentor Books," 222, 244
Meredith, George, 511-12, 526-27
Merton, Thomas, 395
Mesick, Jane Louise, 307
Metal binding, 181
Metcalfe, James J., 466
Meter (in poetry), 450, 461
Mexico (Chase), 130, 166
Miall, Bernard, 246
Michaud, Regis, 534
Microbe Hunters (De Kruif), 263
Microphotography, 172, 174
Middletown (Lynd), 368
Midwest at Noon (Hutton), 365
Miles, Hamish, 246

Mill, John Stuart, 361, 367, 402
Millay, Edna St. Vincent, 168, 451, 454, 466
Miller, Arthur, 487
Miller, Gilbert, 480
Miller, Joaquin, 469
Miller, William, 31, 215
Milman, Henry Hart, 232
Milton, John: definitive edition, 464; *Paradise Lost*, 51; philosophy, *quoted* on, 386
Mind and Body (Dunbar), 339
Mind and Society, The (Pareto), 362
Mind in the Making, The (Robinson), *quoted*, 376, 382
Mirror of Human Salvation, 249
Miserables, Les (Hugo), 51, 235
Misquotations, 153
Missionaries, 318
Mistletoe, John. See Morley, Christopher
Mitchell, Margaret, 540, 543, 544
Mitchell, Silas Weir, 510
Mitchison, Naomi Margaret, 298, 510, 539, 542
"Modern Age Series," 222
Modern and Contemporary European History (Schapiro), 290
Modern English Novel, The (Cross), 533
Modern Fiction (Brewster and Burrell), 532
Modern Fiction: a study in values (Muller), 534
Modern French Literature, 1870-1940 (Saurat), 535
Modern Humanities Research Association, 426
"Modern Library," 222, 229, 238, 243
Modern Omnibus, The (Rolfe, Davenport and Bowerman), 440
Modern Poetry and the Tradition (Brooks), 470
"Modern Students' Library," 411
Modern Translation (Bates), 237, *quoted*, 218
Modern Use of the Bible, The (Fosdick), 397
Monroe, Harriet, 451-52
Monroe, Isabel S., 94
Monroe, Nellie Elizabeth, 534
Montagu, Ashley, 305
Montaigne, Michel Eyquem de: essays, 435-36; Florio, John, translation, 56, 233; historians, *quoted* on, 283-84; travel, 306-7
Montclair (New Jersey) Public Library, 31
Montesquieu, 360
Mont-Saint-Michel and Chartres (Adams), 298
Moore, Anne Carroll, 112
Moore, George, 464; poetry, *quoted* on, 449
Moore, Marianne, 458
Moral indignation, 538
Moral philosophy, 386
Moral rigidity: librarians, 133; travel, 318
Morbidity, 525
More, Paul Elmer, 109
More, Sir Thomas, 360
More Perfect Union, The (MacIver), 368
Moreau de St. Méry's American Journey (1793-1798), 307
Morehouse, Ward, 493
Morgan, Charles, 215
Morison, Samuel Eliot, 285
Morley, Christopher Darlington: book catalogues, *quoted* on, 64; essays, 436, 438; greatness in books, *quoted* on, 7; *London Perambulator*, *quoted*, 305; Mistletoe, John, 111, reading, evolution in, 3; reviews, 103; *Saturday Review*, 111
Morley, John: *English Men of Letters*, 239-40; essays, 434; *Life of Gladstone*, 49, 253, 268; publishers, *quoted* on, 185; reading, *quoted* on, 4; *Recollections*, 166
Morley, Sylvanus, 303
Morris, William, 171, 176, 178
Mortal Coil, The (Bottome), 515
Morton, Henry Canova Vollam, 310
Mother India (Mayo), 130, 318
Motley, John Lothrop, 279, 282
Mott, Frank Luther, 544*n*
Moulton, Forest Ray, 349
Moving pictures: book interest stimulation, 24; books as a substitute for, 9; classification, 475; copyrights, 194; literature on, 482; playwriting, 499; reading, 36
Mr. Emmanuel (Golding), 515
Mudge, Isadore Gilbert, 88, 286, 419*n*
Muir, Edwin, 246
Muir, John, 333, 437

Muir, Willa, 246
Mulder, Arnold, 239
Muller, Herbert J., 534
Mumby, Frank Arthur, 215
Munroe, Ruth, 17, 29-30, 43
Murray, John, 200, 202, 230
"Murray Handbooks," 310
"Murray Hill Books," 243
Music publishing trades, 194
Mussey, Barrows, 246
My Fight for Birth Control (Sanger), 254
Myers, Frederic William Henry, 100, 406
Myrdal Gunnar, 373
Mythology, 387

Naked and the Dead, The (Mailer), 517, 555
Narrow-mindedness, 50
Nathan, George Jean: *Intimate Notebook*, 489; Saroyan's plays, *quoted* on, 491; *Theatre Book of the Year*, 502
Nathan, Robert, 203, 521
Nation, 103, 108, 114
Nation (English periodical), 118
National Association for the Advancement of Colored People, 367, 373, 379
National Book Award, 421
National Book Council of England, 425
National Bureau of Economic Research, 365
National Conference of Christians and Jews, 367, 414
National Council of Teachers of English, 425
National Education Association, 366
National Little Theatre Tournament, 479
"National Nuclear Energy Series," 348
National Opinion Research Center, 17
National Research Council, 347, 365
National Theatre Conference, 479-80, 502
Natural history, 437
Natural History of Nonsense (Evans), 340-41
Natural philosophy, 386
Natural science, 62
Nature (periodical), 350
Nature books, 332-34; examples, 351-52
Nature of the Physical World, The (Eddington), 60

Navy, 18
Neff, Emery, 285
Negro in the United States, The (Franklin), 373
Negroes: *A.L.A. Catalog*, 68; *African Journey*, 316-17; American life, 359; Federal theatre, 477; fiction, 518-19; plays, 492; libraries, 25-26; *Natural History of Nonsense*, 341; political and civil rights, 372-74; Rosenwald Fund, 364; "second-class citizenship," 372
Negroes in Brazil (Pierson), 374
Nelson (C. Oman), 167
"Nelson Classics," 243
Nemesis of Mediocrity, The (Cram), 148
Neo-orthodoxy, 390
Nevins, Allan, 285, 315
New American Library of World Literature, Incorporated, 222
"New Classics Series," 243
New edition, definition, 224
New England states, library circulation, 30
New English Weekly and the New Age, 119
New Found Land (MacLeish), 168
New History and the Social Studies, The (Barnes), 285, 288
"New Home Library," 410
New Larned History for Ready Reference, The, 288
New Masses, 114
New Quarterly of Poetry, The, 467
New Republic (magazine), 108, 114, 143
New Statesman and Nation, 118
New York Booksellers' League, 74
New York (City) Library Club, ix
New York *Evening Post*, 110
New York Experimental Theatre, 480
New York *Herald Tribune Weekly Book Review*, 110, 111-12
New York Libraries (July, 1911), *quoted*, 45
New York Library Association, ix
New York Public Library, 292; drama, 502; *Branch Library Book News*, 88-89, 138; photostat and microfilm, 175n; Public Affairs Information Service, 381; "readers' adviser" service, 33; Yiddish literature, 419
New York Society Library, 509
New York State Library, 66

New York *Times:* book reviews, 103, 110, 112-14; editorial bias, 108; index, 114; rag paper edition, 174
New Yorker (magazine): book reviews, 115; essay, 436; short stories, 558
Newark Public Library, 562
Newman, Ernest, 437
Newspapers: book reviews, 101-2, 104, 106, 111-14; essays, 438; history, 278; library and the public, 27; library book columns, 126; microfilm editions, 174; newsprint, 174-75; poetry, 466-67; publication statistics, 17; reading of, 9, 17, 18, 21, 30, 59; responsibility disclaiming, 146-47; sales, daily, 17
Next Development in Man, The (Whyte), 405
Nicholson, Margaret, 194
Nicolson, Harold, 272-73
Niebuhr, Barthold Georg, 279
Nield, Jonathan, 561
Nietzsche, Friedrich Wilhelm, 402
Nijinsky, Romola, 267-68
Nikhilinanda, Swami, 395
Niles, Blair, 307
Nineteen Eighty-four (Orwell), 518
Nineteenth Century and After, The (quarterly), 120
No Exit (Sartre), 490
No Time for Tears (Hughes), 253
"No; we don't have that" (blanket response), 65
Nobel Prize for literature, 420, 550
Noble (William Belden) Lectures at Harvard, 410
Nonfiction: annotations, 139-41, 147, 149, 154; best sellers, 195; bibliographical record, 72, 88; book reviews, 102; circulation statistics, 40; library budgets, 47-48; National Book Award, 421; note taking, 132; possible purchase file, 92; reading, 130-31; reading pace, 60; review slips, 126-28; reviewing, 103, 133; Sonnenschein, 88; *Standard Catalog for Public Libraries*, 80; tests for, 53-54
Nordau, Max Simon, 269
Nordhoff, Walter, 315
Norris, Kathleen, 526, 547
Northrop, Filmer Stuart Cuckow, 143
Norton, W. W., 197
Norway, Nevil Shute. *See* Shute
Note taking, 8-9, 130, 132, 134

Notes on the Novel (Ortega y Gasset), 535
Notice, definition, 100-101, 104-5
Notre Dame de Paris (Hugo), 52
Novel and Society, The (Monroe), 534
Novel and the Modern World, The (Daiches), 533
Novel and the People, The (Fox), 533
Novelette, 556
Novels. *See* Fiction
Numerology, manuals of, 405, 406

O'Brien, Edward Joseph Harrington, 557
O'Brien, Justin, 246
Obscenity, 552-53
Observatories, 327
O'Casey, Sean, 487, 490
O'Connor, William Van, 534
Octavo volume, 168-71
Odets, Clifford, 478
Odyssey (Homer), 233
Of Making Many Books (Burlingame), 164, 213
Offset printing, 172
O'Hara, John, 555
Oklahoma! (musical), 492
Okubo, Miné, 164
Oliphant, Laurence, 149
Oliver Wiswell (Roberts), 543
Oman, Carola, 167
Oman, Sir Charles William Chadwick, 285, 296n
Omnibus reviews, 104
"Omnibus volumes," 168, 175
Omoo (Melville, *1847*), 314
On Being an Author (Brittain), 423-24
On Judging Books (Hackett), 104
"On Liberty" (Mill), 361
On Reading Shakespeare (Smith), 497
On the Art of Writing (Quiller-Couch), 146, *quoted*, 137
On the Eaves of the World (Farrer), 304
"On Translating Homer" (Arnold), 233, 435
One Hundred Books about Bookmaking (Lehmann-Haupt), 209-10
One Mighty Torrent (Johnson), 272
One Nation (Stegner), 179
One Thousand Best Books, 424
One World (Willkie), 181
One World or None, 128, 181, 349, 353

INDEX

O'Neill, Eugene Gladstone: *Emperor Jones*, 490; expressionism, 490; Freudian influence, 489; *Iceman Cometh, The*, 487; *Lazarus Laughed*, 483; playwright today, 490, quoted on, 489; reading of, 494
Only Yesterday (Allen), 130, 278
"Open-Air Library" series, 227
Open-mindedness, 130
Oratory, 442
Orcutt, William Dana, 211; bookmaking, *quoted* on, 160, 183
Ordering and buying, 48, 92
Orizu, A. N. Nwafor, 317
Orlando (Woolf), 150
Ortega y Gasset, José, 535
Orthodoxy (Chesterton), 146
Orwell, George, 518, 521
Osgood, Herbert Levi, 282
Osler, Sir William, 8
Ossendowski, Ferdynand Antoni, 315
Other Room, The (Hedden), 519
Ottermiller, John H., 500
Ottley, Roi, 374
"Our Debt to Greece and Rome" series, 227, 240
Our Emergent Civilization, 283
Our Town (Wilder), 493
Out of the Silent Planet (C. S. Lewis), 521
Outline of History (Wells): contents table, 165; index, 167; information and inspiration, 52; knowledge popularization, 280, 295; perspective, 283
Outline of Science (Thomson), 336, 343
Oversize books, 170
Overstreet, Harry Allen, 398
Ovington, Mary White, 373
Ownership of books, 9-10
Oxford Book of English Verse, 462
Oxford Companion to American Literature, 429
Oxford Companion to English Literature, 429, 563
Oxford History of English Literature, 430
Oxford India paper, 175
"Oxford Standard Authors," 163, 243
Oxford University Press, 200, 202, 465

Pacific Coast, library circulation, 30
Pacifism, 515
Packman, James, 560

Page, Elizabeth, 543
Page, Walter Hines, 260
Page requirements, 176-78
Paine, Albert Bigelow, 268
Paine, Thomas, 360
Pakington, Humphrey Arthur, 511
Paleography, 276
Paleontology, 331
Palmer, Alice Freeman, 267
Pamphlet material, 91, 366-67
Panova, Vera, 549
Paper, 172-76; Bible paper, 175; bindings, 180-81, 220; bulk, 167; importance, 55; India paper, 175; kinds and qualities, 175-76; newsprint, 174-75; rag content, 173, 174; shortage, 171, 174; sizes, 170
Paradise Lost (Milton), Walter Pater, *quoted* on, 51
Paragraph-essays, 435
Paré, Ambroise, 4
Pareto, Vilfredo, 362
Parkman, Francis, 208, 282, 291
Parks, Edd Winfield, 440
Parrington, Vernon Louis, 431-32
Parshley, H. M., 338
Parsons, Geoffrey, 295
Partisan Reader, The (anthology), 117n
Partisan Review, The, 116-17
Passage to India, A (Forster), 133
Passos, John Dos. *See* Dos Passos
Patchen, Kenneth, *quoted*, 458
Pater, Walter Horatio; criticisms, 58, 434; greatness of literary art, *quoted* on, 51; historical novel, 539
Paterson, Isabel, 112
Paul, Eden and Cedar, 246
Peabody Institute of Baltimore, 90
Peace of Mind (Liebman), 398
Peale, Norman Vincent, 398
Pearl, Raymond, 167
Peary, Robert Edwin, 320
Peasants, The (Reymont), 151, 548
Peattie, Donald, 333, 334n
Pedler, Margaret, 527
"Pelican Books," 222
"Penguin Books," 222
People of the Serpent, The (Thompson), 141
"Peoples of America" series, 239
Pepys, Samuel, diary, 253, 259
Perennial Philosophy, The (A. Huxley), 409

"Permanent Library," 243
Perry, Ralph Barton, 370
Persian Pictures (Bell), 314
Person in the Body, The (Hinsie), 339
Personal integrity, 514
Peters, Fritz, 518
Petry, Ann, 519
Philadelphia Bookselling School, 73-74
Phillips, Wendell Brooks, 154
Philology, 62
Philosophy, 399-417; *A.L.A. Catalog*, 62, 68; Bacon, Francis, 50; biography, 250; definition, 399-400; essays, 437; examples, 414-17; imagination, 447; influence, 6; Sonnenschein, 88
Phonograph records, 194
Photography, 172, 178-79
Photomechanical printing, 172
Physical aspects of books, 159-84
Physical Science and Human Values, 349
Physics, 5, 330
Physics Abstracts, 346
Pickwick Papers (Dickens), 522
Pierson, Donald, 374
Pietistic-domestic sentimentalism, 466
"Pilot Omnibus" series, 243
Piracy, 189, 192, 193
Pirandello, Luigi, 487, 489
Pisan Cantos, The (Pound), 460
Plague, The (Camus), 518, 566
Planographic reproduction, 172
Plastic bindings, 181
Plato: annotations, his counsel applied to, 140-41; *Dialogues*, 122, 387, 401; *Phaedrus*, quoted, 122; philosophy, 400; religion, 402; *Republic*, 367
Plays and playwriting. *See* Drama
Playwriting manuals, 499
Plot, in fiction, 131, 134, 265
Plotinus, 401
Plutarch, 261, 262, 266
"Pocket Books," 181, 222-23, 244
Pocket-type books, 177
Poe, Edgar Allen, 269, 270
Poetry, 446-74; America, 426; Arnold, Matthew, *quoted* on, 448, 449; background-building, 5; Bacon, Francis, 50; books about, 467, 471-72; classification, 50, 52; Coleridge, *quoted* on, 448; criticism, 433, 458-59, 467; definition, 447-50; drama, 475; Dunsany, Lord, *quoted* on, 449; English, 426; essays about, 471-72; examples, 472-74; formalism and convention, 484; Freeman, John, *quoted* on, 449; history, 279; influence, 6, 423; intrinsic qualities, 55; life, 249; Moore, George, *quoted* on, 449; National Book Award, 421; *Prix Femina-Vie Heureuse, Le*, 420; Pulitzer Prize, 420; religion, 388; *Saturday Review*, 111; titles, 131; Watts-Dunton, Theodore, *quoted* on, 448; Wordsworth, *quoted* on, 448
Poetry: A Magazine of Verse, 450-51, 459
Poetry of History, The (Neff), 285
Poetry of the Negro, 1746-1949 (Hughes), 463
Poetry Week, 467
Poet's Life, A: Seventy Years in a Changing World (Monroe), 452
Poggendorff, Johann Christoff, 346
Point Counter Point (A. Huxley), 131, 525
Political censorship, 177-78
Political Power in the U.S.S.R., 1917-1947 (Towster), 370
Political science, 277, 369
Pollock, Sir Frederick, 401
"Popular Copyrights," 243
Porgy (Heyward), 151
Portable Veblen, The, 377
Portable World Bible (Ballou), 395
Porter, Dr. Noah, 399
Positive Philosophy (Comte), 361-62
Possession of books, 9-10
Possible order or purchase file, 92
Poster announcements, 182
Post-War Standards for Public Libraries (A.L.A.), 30, 47
Pound, Ezra, 456, 460
Powell, John, *quoted* on Guided Group Reading, 35
Power (Russell), 370
Powys, John Cowper, *quoted* on culture, 6
Practical Cogitator, The, 230
Praeterita (Ruskin), *quoted*, 256
Predmore, Richard Lionel, 303
Preface to Morals (Lippmann), 386
Preface to Philosophy (Blanshard, Hendel, Hocking and Randall), 407
Prefaces, 164
Prejudices, 49
Prescott, William Hickling, 279, 281
Present tense, biographical use of, 265

President Roosevelt and the Coming of the War, 1941 (Beard), 296
President's Committee on Civil Rights, 365
President's Committee on Social Trends, 389
Price-lists. *See* Catalogues, publishers'
Priestley, John Boynton, 489
Prince, The (Machiavelli), 360
Principles of Literary Criticism (Richards), 432
Principles of Political Economy (Mill), 361
Printed Book, The (Aldis), 209
Printer's imprint, 164
Printing: invention, 186; librarians, 210; offset, 172; Orcutt, W. D., *quoted on*, 160; paper sizes, 169; photomechanical, 172; type, 170-72
Printing (impression), 162, 223
Printing Types, Their History, Forms and Use (Updike), 211-12
Pritchett, Victor S., 535
Prix Femina-Vie Heureuse, Le, 420
Prix Goncourt, Le, 420
Prize Stories, 557
Professor's House, The (Cather), 150
Progressive Education Association, 559
Prohibition, 514
Proletarian fiction, 513-14
Promotion. *See* Publicity
Propaganda: drama, 479; libraries, 91, 394, 569; science, 342
Proper Study of Mankind, The (Chase), 356
Property rights in literature, 188-89
"Prospects of Western Civilization, The," lectures (Toynbee), 410
Protestant churches, 390-91, 395, 397; religious book week, 413-14
Proust, Marcel, 235, 535
Provincetown Plays, 495
Provincialism, 546, 547, 550
Prudery, 538
Pseudoscience, 340, 406
Psychiatry, 330, 387, 390
Psychoanalysis and psychoanalytic interpretation: biography, 265, 269; *Columbia Dictionary of Modern European Literature*, 428; confessions, 260; development, 330; fiction, 513, 518, 520-21; literary criticism, 432; philosophy, 387; poetry, 458; religion, 387; travel literature, 305, 316

Psychographs, 263
Psychological Abstracts, 413
Psychology: animal, 334; biography, 250, 261, 264, 266; development, 330; drama, 487, 489; fiction, 507, 511, 512, 516, 518, 520-21, 551; history, 277; influence, xii; philosophy, 387, 400; religion, 387; sociology, 355; travel literature, 305
Psychopathology, 518, 530, 552
Psychosomatic medicine, influence of, 338, 339, 432
Public Affairs Committee, 367
Public Affairs Information Service, 381
Public libraries. *See* Libraries
Public Library in the United States, The (Leigh), 31, 43
Public Library Inquiry (1947), 31, 43
Public morals, 550-51
Public relations, 24
Public speaking, 132-36, 442; Fowler's *Modern English Usage*, 153
Publication date, 56
Publicity: annotation writing, 138; book interest, 106-7; commercial, 90; literary criticism, 120-21
Publishers and publishing, 10, 185-217; bindings, 180; biography, 251-52; classes, 204-5; devices, 206-7; economics, 358; facts to know about, 206-9; fiction (1948, 1949), 530; imprints, 205, 207; Morley, John, *quoted on*, 185; plays, 483-84; poetry, 466; prize contests, 421; publicity, 90, 106-7, 120-21; religious books, 388-89; reputation, 56; reviewing, 107; science, 344; series, 226; sociology, 358; World War II, 19
Publishers' Circular, 85
Publishers' Trade List Annual, 81-82, 201, 239
Publishers' Weekly, 82-84; bookmaking, 183n; economics publications, 358n; Home School for Booksellers, 74; importance, 84; literary awards, 422; new publications, 83; pamphlet material, 91; philosophy and ethics, 389; reading of, 209; Religious Book Number, 414; sociological publications, 358n; titles, 72-73; use, 79
Publishing and Bookselling (Mumby), 215-16
Pulitzer Prize Awards, 420
Pulp magazines, 519
Pulpwood, 173-74

Purchase files, 92
Putnam, Samuel, 233, 246
Putnam (G. P.) Sons, 192, 198, 202, 207

Quarterly Review, 120
Quarto, 169, 170
Queens Borough (New York) Public Library, 32
Quigley, Margery Closey, 31, 43
Quiller-Couch, Sir Arthur Thomas, 146, 155, *quoted*, 137
Quintessence of Ibsenism (Shaw), 485

Rabelais, François, 228, 229, 233
Race relations, xii, 294, 359, 372-73; discrimination, 359, 398, 515, 518; hate, 553; prejudice, 25-26, 519; tolerance, 49
Radio: book appreciation, 24; copyrights, 194; Council on Books in Wartime, 197-98; library news, 24, 126; pamphlets, 367; plays, 482, 495-96; reading, 36; reviewing programs, 106, 126, 135; speaking, effective, 134
Rage to Live, A (O'Hara), 555
Rahv, Philip, 307
Rainbow Bridge (Farrer), 304
Rand, Benjamin, 412
Rapport, Samuel, 349
Rare books, 56, 113
Rascoe, Arthur Burton, 111
Reach of the Mind, The (Rhine), 406
Reade, Charles, 298, 509, 539
"Readers' adviser" service, 33-34
Readers' Choice of Best Books, 116
Readers' Digest of Books, 563
Readers' Encyclopedia, The, 427
Readers' Guide, 111, 389
Readers' Guide to Prose Fiction (Lenrow), 559-60
Reading: Brooks, Van Wyck, *quoted* on, 568; Carlyle, Thomas, *quoted* on, 3; evolution in, 3; expertness, 59-60; habits, 8, 29-42; in bed, 8, 60; indifference, 129-30; interest, 129-30; mechanics of, 60*n*; Morley, John, *quoted* on, 4; notes, 130; relaxation, 60; sympathy, 130; technique, 60; type, 171
Reading Interests and Habits of Adults, The (Gray and Munroe), 17, 29
Readings in the Physical Sciences, 349
Realism, 264, 405, 489, 540
Reavey, George, 535

Rebinding, 176-77, 180
Recipes, 91
Recollections (Morley), 166-67
Recordings, 468
Recreation (books of), 50-52, 54-56
Red Prussian, The: the Life and Legend of Karl Marx (Schwarzschild), 269
Reference books, 568; *Bookman's Manual*, 75; contents table, 165; history, 288-90; indexes, 166; possible purchase file, 92; size, 168, 170; subscription sale, 206
Reference Catalogue of Current Literature, 84-85, 94, 201
Reference Guide to the Literature of Travel, including Voyages, Geographical Descriptions, Adventures, Shipwrecks and Expeditions (Cox), 308
Reflections on the Revolution of Our Time (Laski), 166
Reissues. See Reprints
Religion, 385-417; *A.L.A. Catalog*, 62, 68; biography, 387; drama, 501; essays, 437; fiction, 507, 513, 517; history, 387; influence, 6; poetry, 457-58; reading list, 414-17; science, 387; series, 239; Sonnenschein, 88
Religion Coming of Age (Sellars), 387
Religion in the Twentieth Century (Ferm), 413
Religious Book Club, 412
Religious Book List, 414
Religious book week, 413-14
Remarque, Erich Maria, 515, 567
Reminiscences, 254, 258-59
Rental libraries, 19, 116
Reprints: classics, 218; copyright, 224; definition, 223-24; editions, 230, 236, 238; English books, 192-93, 195; excellence and abundance of, 220; *Herald Tribune*, 112; *New York Times*, 113; paper-bound, 221; "Pocket Books," 181; reissue, 121, 162; series, 222-23, 226, 410; translation, 236
Republic (Plato), 360, 367
"Reserves," made for individual books, 40
Resources of Pacific Northwest Libraries (Van Male), 420*n*
Resources of Southern Libraries (Downs), 419*n*
Restless India (Rosinger), 143
Restricted books, 554

Retail Bookseller's monthly "Almanac," 116
Return to the River (Haig-Brown), 334
Review of Religion, 412
Review slips, 125-29; examples, 127; fiction, 134; oral reviewing, 134
Reviewers: anti-Soviet "bloc," 109; Bennett, Arnold, *quoted* on, 108; Canby, H. S., *quoted* on, 99; editorial bias, 108; emotions, 105; English, 100; favorites, 109; identical sentences, 105; judgment, 108; kinds, 100-101; moral purpose, 132; professional, 105, 106; publicity agents, 106; publishers' advertising, 120-21
Reviewing, 99-121, 122-36; *Book Review Digest*, 70-72; commercial influence, 107; dullness, 108; fiction, 133, 563-64; fundamental qualities, 107-8; libraries, 92, 122-36; newspaper, 101-2, 104, 106, 111-14; oral, 133-34; periodicals, 72; personal prejudices, 132; plays, 483; poetry, 466; purchase of books, 63; radio, 135; review slips, 92; scientific periodicals, 350; selection of books, 63-64; sociology, 379. *See also* Annotations
Rexroth, Kenneth, 458
Reymont, Wladyslaw Stanislaw, 151-52, 548
Rhetoric, 442
Rhine, Dr. Joseph Banks, 406
Rhyme, 450, 461
Rhythm, 446, 450-52
Ricardo, David, 361
Rice, Elmer, 490
Richards, Eva, 270n
Richards, Ivor Armstrong, 36, 43, 432, 433
Richardson, Dorothy, 513
Richer by Asia (Taylor), 317
Richter, Anne, 422
Riggs, Lynn, 492
Riley, James Whitcomb, 469
Rise of American Civilization (Beard), 280, 295
"Rittenhouse Classics," 243
River, The (Godden), 523
"Rivers of America" series, 227
"Riverside Library," 243
Road of a Naturalist, The (Peattie), 334n
Road of Ages (Nathan), 521
Road to Calvary, The (Tolstoi), 549
Road to Rome (Sherwood), 488
Road to Survival (Vogt), 361
Road to the Ocean (Leonov), 549
Roberts, Sir Charles George Douglas, 334
Roberts, Elizabeth, 539
Roberts, Kenneth, 307, 540, 543
Robeson, Eslanda, 316
Robinson, Edwin Arlington, 451-54, 469
Robinson, James Harvey, 285, *quoted*, 376, 382
Robinson Crusoe (Defoe), 522
Rockefeller Foundation, 364-65
Rodman, Selden, 463
Roeder, Ralph, 298
Rogers, Robert Emmons, *quoted* on literature, 21
Rolfe, F. P., 440
"Rolls Series, The," 289
Roman Catholic Church. *See* Catholic Church
Romances, 509
Romanticism, 458, 540, 544
Roosevelt, Franklin Delano: A.N.T.A., 480; Beard, Charles, 296; books as weapons, 197; death, 516; "four freedoms," *quoted* on, 354; leadership, 357; lynch law, 373; a *Memorial*, 223; reconstruction campaign, 477
Roosevelt, Theodore, 295
Roosevelt and Hopkins (Sherwood), 421n
Rope and Faggot (White), 373
Rose, Arnold, 373
Rosenwald (Julius) Fund, 364
Roumagnac, Roger, 309
Rourke, Constance M., 141, 433
Rousseau, Jean-Jacques, 257, 260, 360
Rowse, Alfred Leslie, 286
Royal Society of London, 326, 345
Royce, Josiah, 402
Rubáiyát (Fitzgerald's version), 231
"Rule of Phase Applied to History, The," essay (Adams), 325
Runes, Dagobert, 413
Running headlines. *See* Headlines
R.U.R. (Capek), 490
Rural communities, 21, 24, 36
Ruskin, John: autobiography, 256; diction, *quoted* on, 122; *Praeterita*, *quoted*, 256; reading compensation, *quoted* on, 523; travel literature, 305
Russell, Bertrand Arthur William: *Amberley Papers, The*, 167, 260; essays,

Russell, Bertrand (*Continued*) 437; *Freedom versus Organization 1814-1914*, 361n; *History of Western Philosophy*, 407; influence, 402; "Library of Living Philosophers," 411; *Power*, 370
Russell, George William (A.E.), 448
Russian literature, 220, 419, 421, 563
Russian Literature since the Revolution (Kunitz), 439
Russian Translations Project, 371-72
Rust, Ralph L., 421

Sacco-Vanzetti case, 488
Sacred Wood, The (Eliot), 432
Sage (Russell) Foundation, 364
Saint-Exupéry, Antoine de, 245, 314
Saint Joan (Shaw), 488
St. John, Robert, 296
St. John's College, Annapolis, Md., 34
St. Louis Public Library, 23n
Samuel, Maurice, 246
Sandburg, Carl, 451
Sanger, Margaret, 254, 269-70
Santayana, George: criticism, 58, 61; history, *quoted* on, 278-79; influence, 402; "Library of Living Philosophers," 411; style, 130
Saroyan, William, 491
Sarton, Dr. George, 346-47
Sarton, May, *quoted*, 457
Sartre, Jean-Paul, 404, 490
Satire, 442
Saturday Review of Literature, 110-11; Bollingen Award, 460; *Designed for Reading*, 104; "Literature between Two Wars," 113
Saurat, Denis, 535
Savage, Ernest Albert, 155
Sayers, Dorothy, 203, 390
Scarlet Letter, The (Hawthorne), 522, 539
Schapiro, Jacob Salwyn, 290
Schifferes, Justice Julius, 349
Schlesinger, Arthur Meier, Jr., 283
Schliemann, Heinrich, 303
Schneider, Herbert Wallace, 411
"Schocken Library Series," 410
Schoeffer, Peter, 186
School editions, 224, 228
Schulberg, Budd, 523, 555
Schwarzschild, Leopold, 269
Schweitzer, Albert, 323, 409, *quoted*, 396

Science, 324-53; biography, 250; civilization, 7; fiction, 329, 507, 519-20; influence, 6; Lilienthal, David, *quoted* on, 324; reading list, 352-53; religion, 387; reprints, 220; reviews, 101; selection, 342; series, 239; Sonnenschein, 88; travel, 304
Science (periodical), 350
Science Abstracts, 346
Science Advances (Haldane), 337
Science and Learning in the Fourteenth Century (Sarton), 346
Science and Sanity (Korzybski), 423
Science and Society (quarterly), 116
Science clubs, 329
Science for the Citizen (Hogben), 337
"Science in Progress" (Yale), 348
Science News Letter, 347
Science of Human Reproduction, The (Parshley), 338
Science of Life (Wells), 336, 337, 343
Science Service, 343, 347
Scientific, Medical and Technical Books Published in the United States of America 1930-1944, 347
Scientific Monthly, 347
Scientific Religion: Higher Possibilities through Operation of Natural Forces (Oliphant), 149
Scientists Speak, The (Weaver), 349
Scott, Evelyn, 540
Scott, Sir Walter, 511-12, 539, 541
Scott Moncrieff, Charles Kenneth Michael, 246
Scouting on Two Continents (Burnham), 314
Screenwriting, 499
Screwtape Letters, The (Lewis), 517
Scribner's (Charles) Sons, 213
Scripps College Bulletin, 563
Scrutiny (quarterly), 120
Seagle, William, 214
Searching Wind, The (Hellman), 486
Second Empire (Guedalla), 147
Sectarianism, 391
Seeds of Tomorrow (Sholokhov), 549
Selection, 29-44; annotations, 137-38; balance, 46, 62; bibliographic aids, 63-77; bookmaking, 161; discrimination and broad-mindedness, 553; editions, 184, 227-32; illustrations, 179; knowledge, 45; librarians, 16-17; principles, xi, 29-44, 49, 50, 93, 163; purpose, 38, 49, 50; recording routine, 92-93; sub-

ject series, 241-42. *See also* Autobiography; Biography; Drama; Essays; Fiction; History; Philosophy; Poetry; Religion; Science; Travel
Selection of the Principal Voyages, Traffiques and Discoveries of the English Nation (Hakluyt), 229, 306
Self-education, 4
Sellars, Roy Wood, 387
Seltzer, Thomas, 246
Selver, Paul, 246
Semantics, 423, 432
Sensitivity, 4, 6
Series, 218-44; definition, 226-27; editions, 162-63; hard-bound, examples, 242-44; history, 291, 297; paperbound, examples, 244; philosophy, 409-11; plays, 496; publishers, 207-8; religion, 409-11; science, 347-48; sociology, 378; subject, 239-40, 297; travel, 320-21
Service, Robert William, 468
Seton, Ernest Thompson, 333-34
"Sets" of books, 218, 225-26
Seven Storey Mountain, The (Merton), 395
Sewanee Review (periodical), 116
Sewing (of books), 177
Sex, as a force in literature: censorship, 187, 551-52; emphasis on, 553; fiction, 510, 513, 516, 521, 528, 530, 551-53; "must be accepted," 551; nonfiction, 338-39, 432, 555; poetry, 458; reading interest, 36
Sex Habits of American Men (Deutsch), 338
Sexual Behavior in the Human Male (Kinsey), 338-39, 555
Seymour-Smith, F., 425
Shakespeare, William: *Bookman's Manual,* 501; editions, 218, 228, 232; expurgation, 228; first folio, 225; identity problem, 498; *Kenilworth,* 541; library needs, 497-98; reading of, 494; Scott, Sir Walter, 512, 541; study, quoted on, 7; Variorum edition, 232
Shakespeare without Tears (Webster), 497
Shakespeare's Imagery and What It Tells Us (Spurgeon), 498
Shall Not Perish from the Earth (Perry), 370
Shaping of the American Tradition, The (Hacker), 289

Shapiro, Karl, 461, 470, *quoted,* 446
Shapley, Harlow, 329, 335, 349, 353
Sharp, Margery, 520
Shaw, Charles B., 75, 77, 347, 413
Shaw, George Bernard, 485-88; communism, *quoted* on, 354; Ibsen, 485; reading of, 494; *Saint Joan,* 488; school editions, *quoted* on, 228; Terry, Ellen, 130, 261
Shaw, Irwin, 478, 517
Shelves and shelving problems: fat books and thin books, 169; inspection, 40; newspapers, 174-75; oversize formats, 170; paper quality, 173, 175; space between shelves, 170
Sheridan, Richard Brinsley, *quoted* on literary commentary, 99
Sherman, Stuart Pratt, 109, 111-12, 233, 434
Sherriff, Robert Cedric, 486
Sherwood, Robert, 421*n*, 480, 486, 488
Shipley, Joseph Twadell, 427
Shirer, William Lawrence, 259
Sholokhov, Mikhail Aleksandrovich, 549
Short History of the English People (Green), 281
Short stories, 555-58; definition, 556; essay, 435-36; index to, 564; *New Yorker,* 436, 538; reading of, 493
Short Stories from the New Yorker, 1925-1940, 558
Shryock, Richard Harrison, 338
Shuman, Edwin Llewellyn, 155
Shute, Nevil, 515
Signatures (bookmaking), 167, 170
"Signet Books," 222, 244
Silent Don, The (Sholokhov), 549
Silent People Speak, The (St. John), 296
Sillen, Samuel, 114
Simms, Myrna, 48*n*
Simonov, Konstantin, 549
Since 1900 (Barck and Blake), 278
Sinclair, Upton, 513
Singleton, Esther, 309
Sismondi, Jean Charles Léonard Sismonde de, 281
Sitwell, Edith, 454, 463; purpose of art and literature, *quoted* on, 29
Six Books of the Republic (Bodin), 360
Six Scandinavian Novelists (Gustafson), 534
Sixteenmo, 169, 170, 238

Sixty-fourmo, 170
Size of a book, 167-69, 238
Skin of Our Teeth, The (Wilder), 490
Slosson, Edwin Emery, 343
Smith, Adam, 360
Smith, Betty, 495-96, 529
Smith, F. Seymour. *See* Seymour-Smith
Smith, Horatio, 428
Smith, Lillian, 374, 519, 552, 554
Smith, Milton M., 500
Smith, Pearsall, 435, 497
Smith, Peter, 225
Smith, William Gardner, 519
Snake Pit, The (Ward), 518
Snow, Edgar, 318
Sobel, Bernard, 502
Social and Cultural Dynamics (Sorokin), 362-63
Social problems, 372
Social protest novels, 514-15
Social reminiscences, 258
Social Research, 116
Social Science Research Council, 31, 364
Social sciences, 354-84; *A.L.A. Catalog*, 251; history, 277
Social Studies, The, 288
Social-Economic Movements (Laidler), 380
Socialism, xii, 294, 369, 402
Socialist Britain (Williams), 204, 370
Society in Transition (Barnes), 379-80
Sociology, 354-84; *A.L.A. Catalog*, 62, 68; "periphrastic malady," 377-78; reading list, 383-84; religion, 397; series, 239; Sonnenschein, 88
Some Observations on the Art of Narrative (Bentley), 532, *quoted*, 506
Somervell, Professor D. C., 229, 281
Somerville, John, 372, 403
Song in the Green Thorn Tree, The (Barke), 266
Sonnenschein, William Swan, 86-88, 94, 560. *See also Best Books: A Reader's Guide*
Sorokin, Pitirim, 362-63
Soule, George, 143
"Source Books in the History of the Sciences from the Renaissance to the End of the Nineteenth Century," 349
Source material, 55
South: heritage, 519; libraries, 419*n*
South American Handbook, 311
South Pacific (musical), 487
South Sea Idyls (Stoddard, *1873*), 314

Southeast, 20-21
Southern California Country (McWilliams), 312
Southwest, 20-21
"Southwest Historical Series," 290
Soviet Communism: A New Civilization? (Webb), 371
Soviet Impact on the Western World, The (Carr), 370
Soviet Literature Today (Reavey), 535
Soviet Philosophy (Somerville), 403-4
Sparling, Halliday, on headlines, *quoted*, 178
Speaking, effective, 133-36
Special Collections in Libraries in the United States (Johnston and Mudge), 419*n*
Special edition, 224
Special Libraries (magazine), 382
Special Library Resources, 419*n*-420*n*
Spectator, 119
Speculum Vitae. See Biography
Speechmaking, impromptu, footless wanderings of, 134
Spencer, Herbert, 362, 402
Spender, Stephen, *quoted*, 456
Spengler, Oswald, 281, 363
Spiller, Robert Ernest, 430
Spin a Silver Dollar (Hannum), 172
Spinoza, 401, 402
Spiral bindings, 181
Spirit of Man, The (Bridges), 455
Spirit of the Laws (Montesquieu), 360
Spurgeon, Caroline, 433, 498
Stalin, Joseph, 269
Stalin prizes, 421-22
Stallings, Lawrence, 486
Stallman, Robert Wooster, 433-34
Stallybras. *See* Sonnenschein
Standard Catalog for High School Libraries, 75-77
Standard Catalog for Public Libraries, 69, 78-80, 94; editions, 219; fiction, 558-59; history, 286; philosophy and religion, 411; sociology, 382; travel, 308
"Star Books," 244
Star-Gazer, The (Harsanyi), 299
Star-News (Pasadena), x
Starkie, Walter, 246
State aid, 21
State guides, 240-41
Stebbins, Lucy Poate, 535
Stefánsson, Vilhjalmur, 307

INDEX 605

Stegner, Wallace, 179
Stephen, Sir Leslie, 100, 540
Stephens, James, 453, 454, 466
Stephens, John Lloyd, 303, 314
Stephenson, W. H., 291
Stern, G. B. (Gladys Bronwyn), 203
Stevens, George F., 111
Stevens, Wallace, 458
Stevenson, Robert Louis (Balfour): critical essays, 109; historical novel, 539, 542; style, 527
"Stock responses," 36-37
Stocking, Charles Francis. *See Carmen Ariza*
Stoddard, Charles Warren, 314
"Stoddard Lectures," 320
Stone, Irving, 195, 265
Stories of China at War, 558
Storm, The (Ehrenburg), 549
Story Magazine, 557
Story of America (Van Loon), 295
Story of English Literature, The (Broadus), 175
Story of Maps, The (Brown), 309
Story of Philosophy (Durant), 59, 406-7
Story of World Literature (Macy), 431
Story: The Fiction of the Forties (Burnett), 557-58
Strachey, Lytton: biography, 263-65; *Contemporary Biography* (Longaker), 272; *Elizabeth and Essex*, 130, 488; essay, 437; *Queen Victoria*, 488; style compared with Gibbon, 280
Strange Fruit (Smith), 519, 552, 554
Stream of History (Parsons), 295
Stream-of-consciousness writing, 521
Street, The (Petry), 519
Streetcar Named Desire, A (Williams), 487
Stuart, Henry Longan, 246
Studies in the Literature of Natural Science (Drachman), 331, 350
Study in the Ethics of Spinoza (Joachim), 401
Study of History, A (Toynbee), quoted, 275; abridgment, 229, 281
"Study of Poetry, The" (Arnold), 469
Style: definition, 53; evaluation through, 57; fiction, 526-27; hallmark, 130; importance, 53; sociology, 377
Subject balance, 46
Subject series, 226-27, 239-42, 297
Subject treatment, 55
"Subjection of Women" (Mill), 361

Subscription book publishers, 205-6, 226
Subscription Books Bulletin, 206
Subversive literature, 187
Sun Also Rises (Hemingway), 203
"Sun Dial Books," 244
Survey (periodical), 379
Sutton, Eric, 246
Swan of Usk, The (Ashton), 265
Swan Sonnenschein and Company, 86
Swanson, Neil, 543
Sward, Keith, 269
Swinnerton, Frank, book trade, 216, quoted on, 185
Symbolism: drama, 489; fiction, 521
Symonds, John Addington, 51
Sympathy, 317, 569
Synthetic Philosophy (Spencer), 362

Taboo books, 554-55
Tacitus, Cornelius, 280
Taras Bulba (Gogol), 539
Tarka the Otter (Williamson), 334
Taste in books and reading, 8, 58, 99, 549
Taylor, Edmond, 317
Taylor, Walter Fuller, 535
"Teach Yourself History" series, 239, 286
Teale, Edwin Way, 334
Teasdale, Sara, 469
Technical books, 347; annotations, 139; terminology, 378
Technology, 101, 199, 327, 568
Teggart, Frederick John, quoted on history, 278
Teixeira de Mattos, Alexander, 235, 246
Television, 475
"Temple Classics," 202, 213, 238
Tendencies in Modern American Poetry (Lowell), 469
Tennessee, books on evolution, 187
Tennyson, Lord Alfred, 267
Terry, Ellen, correspondence with G. B. Shaw, 130, 261
Testament of Beauty (Bridges), 453
Textbooks: history, 290; school editions, 224, 228; sociology, 368
Texts and Pretexts (A. Huxley), 463
Textual aspects of books, 159-84
Thackeray, William Makepeace, 512, 539, 541
Thane, Elswyth, 265
Theatre. *See* Drama
Theatre Book of the Year (Nathan), 502

Theatre Collections in Libraries and Museums (Gilder and Freedley), 501-2
Theatre Handbook and Digest of Plays (Sobel), 502
Theatre Library, A (Gilder), 501
Theology, 387, 392. *See also* Religion
Theory and Technique of Playwriting and Screenwriting (Lawson), 499
Theory of Book Selection for Public Libraries, The (McColvin), 39
Theory of the Theatre, The (Hamilton), 484
Thesaurus, use in annotation writing, 145
Thesaurus of Book Digests, 427, 563
Thickness (of books), 167-68
Thirkell, Angela Margaret, 511, 520
Thirty Years in the Golden North (Welzl), 320
This Believing World (Browne), 391
This Great Journey (Lee), 254
Thomas, Isaiah, 199
Thompson, Ernest Seton. *See* Seton
Thompson, James Westfall, 285
Thomson, Sir John Arthur, 336, 343
Thomson, Ruth Gibbons, 500
Thomson, Virgil, 437
Thoreau, Henry David, 307, 333
Thorp, Willard, 430
Thousand of the Best Novels, A, 562-63
Three Guineas (Woolf), quoted, 249
Thucydides, 282
Thurber, James, 195, 438
Thwaites, Reuben Gold, 229
Till the Day I Die (Odets), 478
Tilney, Frederick, 339
Time (magazine), 115
Time and Tide (periodical), 118
"Time and Tide" pamphlets (Adamic), 367
Timeless Land, The (Dark), 541
Title-page, 163-64; copyright, 189; editions, 230; examination, 56; Orcutt, W. D., quoted on, 183; translation, 235
Titles: annotation writing, 145; changing of, 203-4, 308; double-headers, 509; fiction, 131; headlines, 178; obscurity in, 145
Tito's Imperial Communism (Markham), 296
To Begin With (Pearl), 167
To Sing with the Angels (Hindus), 516
To the Pure: A Study of Obscenity and the Censor (Ernst and Seagle), 214
Tolstoi, Count Aleksei Nikolaevich, 549
Tolstoi, Count Lev, confessions, 260
Tomlinson, Henry Major, 130
Toor, Frances, 311
Totalitarianism, 359, 369
Toward Proficient Reading (Hamilton), 60n
Towster, Julian, 370
Toynbee, Arnold Joseph: Columbia University lectures, 410; history, quoted on, 275; Sorokin, P., kinship to, 363; *Study of History*, 229, 281
Trade editions, 224
Trade List Annual, 82
Trade series, 226
Trader Horn, 320
Traditions of European Literature from Homer to Dante (Wendell), 165-66, 431
Tragedy, 475, 487
Train, The (Panova), 549
Trans-Himalaya (Hedin), 320
Translations, 232-38; classics, 218; drama, 492, 496; fiction, 545, 548, 550, 562, 563, 565; *Herald Tribune*, 112; literary awards, 420, 421; Plato, 401; translators of distinction, 244-46
Translators' Guild, London, 236
"Trash," demand for, 21
Travel. *See* Travel literature
Travel Diary of a Philosopher (Keyserling), 313, 316
Travel in the Two Last Centuries of Three Generations (Roget), 307
Travel literature, 302-23; *A.L.A. Catalog*, 62, 251; annotations, 144; anthropology, 305; examples, 321-23; geography, 304; history, 277, 298; illustrations, 179; journal form, 260; letters, 260; religion, 388; reprints, 220; value testing, 53
Travel USA (bulletin), 310
Travelers, 313, 317-18
Traveller in Little Things, A (Hudson), 306
Travels in Arabia Deserta (Doughty), 313
Treasury of Biography, A (E. Johnson, ed.), 272
Treasury of Science, A, 230, 350
Treatise on the Gods (Mencken), 392
Trechmann, E. J., 233

INDEX

Trench, Herbert, 246
Trial of Jeanne d'Arc (Garnett), 488
Trivia (P. Smith), 435
Trollope, Mrs. Francis Milton, 215, 323
Trotsky, Leon, 269
Truth: pursuit of, 7; science, 332
Truth about Publishing, The (Unwin), 190, 216
"Tudor Books," 244
Tudor Wench, The (Thane), 265
Turn of the Tide, The (Tomlinson), 437
Turnbull, Agnes, 529
Turner, Frederick Jackson, 295
Turner, Herbert Hall, 336
Twain, Mark. See Clemens, Samuel Langhorne
Twelvemo, 168-70, 238
Twentieth Century Forces in European Fiction (Hansen), 562
Twentieth Century Fund, 364
Twentieth Century Philosophy: Living Schools of Thought, 413
"Twentieth Century Poetry in English," recordings, 468
Twenty Best Film Plays (Gassner and Nichols), 496
Twenty Years at Hull-House (Addams), 254
Twenty-fourmo, 170
Two Years Before the Mast (Dana, 1840), 313
Tyler, Ralph Winfred, 29, 30, 44
Type, 170-72, 183
Typee (Melville, 1846), 314
Typography, 185
Tyranny of Words (Chase), 423

Ulysses (Joyce), 521, 554
Unabridged editions, 229
Unamuno y Jugo, Miguel de, 547
Undset, Sigrid: *Kristin Lavransdatter*, 168, 510, 542, 548; translation, 235
Unesco. See United Nations Educational, Scientific and Cultural Organization
"Unintelligibles," 458, 459
Union of Soviet Socialist Republics: books about, 109, 318; communism, *see that heading;* drama, 491; Eastman, Max, 144; fiction, 535, 549; literature, 428, 439; political censorship, 187-88; religion and philosophy, 403-4; Stalin prizes, 421-22; United States, relations, 293, 371-72. See also Russian; Soviet
United Nations: atomic energy control, 328; current literature, 422; hope offered by, 357; library representation, 294; publications, 365-66; Roosevelt, F. D., 516; world government, 294, 359
United Nations Bulletin, 366
United Nations Educational, Scientific and Cultural Organization: A.N.T.A., 480; copyrights, 194, 217; education, 366; translations, 236
"United Nations Series," 240
United Nations Yearbook, 366
United Publishers' Association, Boston, 115
United States: books published, 79; copyright, 190, 191, 193, 194; democracy, *see that heading;* folk drama, 492-93; foreigners' impressions, 315; literary awards, 421-22; nonhomogeneous people, 492-93; political censorship, 187-88; pulpwood, 174; race discrimination, 372-73, 515; social justice, 372; social protest fiction, 514-15; Soviet Russia, relations with, 293, 371-72; travel books, 311-12; travel guides, 310
United States Catalog, 79; religion, 389; Shakespeare editions, 218-19
United States Quarterly Book List, 89, 139
Universe and Dr. Einstein, The (Barnett), 336
Universities. See Colleges and universities
University of California, x, xv
University of Chicago, 226
University of Chicago Press, 199
University of Southern California, x
University presses, 199-200
Unmarried, reading habits of the, 30
Untermeyer, Louis, 463
Unwin, Stanley, 190, 192, 216-17
Upanishads, 395
Updike, Daniel Berkeley, 211
Use of History, The (Rowse), 286
Useful arts: *A.L.A. Catalog*, 62; books in the, 327
"Useful Reference Series" (Faxon), 270*n*
Utopia (More), 360

Value in books, 38-39; biography, 270; book reviews, 102; comparative val-

Value in books (*Continued*)
ues, 65; critical judgment, 59; definition, 39; fiction, 40, 42, 507-8, 522; poetry, 455, 468; review slips, 128; testing, 45-61. *See also* Evaluation; Literary criticism; Reviewing; Selection
Van Doren, Carl, 535
Van Doren, Irita, 112
Van Doren, Mark, 289
Van Dyke, Henry, 468
Van Hoesen, Henry Bartlett, 212, 288, 413
Van Loon, Hendrik Willem, 203-4, 295
Van Male, John, 420*n*
Vanity anthologies, 466
Vanity publishers, 205
Variorum edition of Shakespeare, 232
Vaughan, Henry, 265
Vazakos, Byron, 461
Veblen, Thorstein Bunde, 377-78
Venable, Vernon, 404
Ver Nooy, Winifred, 500
Verne, Jules, 519
Verse, 450-51, 466, 469
Verso, definition, 164
"Vertical File Service," 81, 91, 381-82
Vestal, Stanley, 252
Veterans, 18
Victoria: Housman, 488; letters, 253; Strachey, L., 488
Victoria Regina (Housman), 488
Victorian Album, A (Stebbins), 535
Victorian fiction, 512, 520
Victory (Conrad), 152
Viereck, Peter, 461
Viking Book of Poetry of the English-speaking World, The (Aldington), 463
"Viking Portable Library," 230, 238, 244
Vocabulary building, 423
Vogt, William, 361
Voltaire, 253
Vormelker, Rose, 419*n*
Voyage in Space, A (Turner), 336
Vyshinsky, Andrei, 371

Waiting for Lefty (Odets), 478
Waldron, Gloria, 31, 43
Wales, literature of, 419
Waley, Arthur, 246
Wallace, Henry Agard, 114

Walls Came Tumbling Down, The (Ovington), 373
Walpole, Sir Hugh Seymour, 539
Walter, Frank Keller, 212, 288, 413
"Wanderer" books (Lucas), 305
Waples, Douglas, 29, 30, 36, 44
War and violence, worship of, 516
Ward, Lester, 362
Ward, Mary Augusta, *known as* Mrs. Humphry Ward, 166
Ward, Mary Jane, 518
Warner, Sylvia Townsend, 150
"Warner Library of the World's Best Literature," 427
Warren, Althea, vii-x, xiii
Wartime restrictions, 168-69, 171, 177, 358*n*
Washington, George, 267
"Waste Land, The" (Eliot), 432
Watch on the Rhine (Hellman), 486
Watt, Robert, 425
Watts-Dunton, Walter Theodore, *quoted* on poetry, 448
Waugh, Arthur, 217
Wave, The (Scott), 540
Way, Katharine, 349
We, the People (Huberman), 283
Weaver, Warren, 349
Webb, Sidney and Beatrice, 371
Webster, Margaret, 497
Wecter, Dixon, 283, 430
Weigall, Arthur Edward Pearse Brome, 269
Weight of books, 238
Weiskopf, Franz Carl, 439
Well of Loneliness, The (Hall), 523, 554
Wellard, James H., 32-33, 44
Wells, Herbert George: autobiography, 257; battle for a better world, 485, 513; *Outline of History*, 52, 165, 167, 280, 295; science fiction, 519; *Science of Life*, 336, 337, 343
Welzl, Jan, 320
Wendell, Barrett, 165, 431
West, Dorothy Herbert, 94
West, Rebecca (pseud. from Ibsen's *Rosmersholm*) of Cicely Isabel Fairfield, 434
Westerns, 522, 528, 529
Wharton, Edith Newbold, 527
What Makes Sammy Run (Schulberg), 523, 555

What People Want to Read About (Waples and Tyler), 29-30, 44
What Price Glory? (Anderson and Stallings), 486
What's in a Novel (Haines), vii, 507, 520, 534
Whitaker's Cumulative Book List, 85, 95
White, Carl Milton, xii
White, Newman D., 271
White, Walter, 373
"White supremacy," 372
Whitehead, Alfred North, 402, 411
Whitman, Walt, *Passage to India*, quoted, 302
Who Reads What (Compton), 22-23
Who's Who, 262
Whyte, Lancelot Law: genius of man, quoted on, 385; traditional ideas, quoted on, 358; unitary man theory, 405
Wickenden, Dan, 529
Wilder, Thornton Niven: *Our Town*, 493; *Skin of Our Teeth, The*, 490; style, 527
Wiley (John) and Sons, 192, 198, 204
Williams, Albert Rhys, 318
Williams, Charles, 517, 537
Williams, Francis, 204, 370
Williams, Oscar, 463
Williams, Stanley Thomas, 430
Williams, Tennessee, 487
Williams, William Carlos, 421, 466
Williamson, Charles Clarence, xvi
Williamson, Henry, 334
Willkie, Wendell, 181
Wilson, Arthur M., 271
Wilson, Edmund: *Armed Vision* (Hyman), 433; *Axel's Castle*, 131; criticisms, 106, 109
Wilson, Frank Percy, 431
Wilson, John Dover, 497
Wilson, Louis Round, 20-21, 49*n*
Wilson, Romer, 270
Wilson (H.W.) Company: "best books," 424-25; *Book Review Digest*, 70-72; current biography, 262; *Essay and General Literature Index*, 441; evaluation of their publications, 80-81; *Fiction Catalog*, 80, 558-59; fiftieth anniversary, 81; *Library Bulletin*, 80-81, 95, 116, 382; play indexes, 499-500; Public Affairs Information Service, 381; *Standard Catalog for High School Libraries*, 75-77; *Standard Catalog for Public Libraries*, 69, 80; *United States Catalog*, 79; "Vertical File Service," 81, 91, 381-82
Winchell, Constance, 88
Wind, Sand, and Stars (Saint Exupéry), 314
Wind that Shakes the Barley, The (Barke), 266
Winning of the West (Roosevelt), 295
Winsor, Kathleen, 195, 554
Winters, Yvor, 433
Winterset (Anderson), 488-89
Wisconsin Plays, 495
Wisdom Tree, The (Hawkridge), 391
Wish and Wisdom: Episodes in the Vagaries of Belief (Jastrow), 341
Within the Gates (O'Casey), 490
Without Bitterness: Western Nations in Postwar Africa (Orizu), 317
Witness to the Truth (Hamilton), 399
Wives, as biographers, 267
Wolfe, Thomas Clayton, 307
Women: fiction, 510, 512-13, 554; reading habits, 30; travel, 313
Wood pulp. *See* Pulpwood
Woodward, William E., 267
Woolbert, Robert Gale, 379
Woolf, (Adeline) Virginia: biography, quoted on, 249; *Common Reader*, quoted, 418; criticism, 434; experimentalism in expression, 514; *Orlando*, 150; readers responsibilities, quoted on, 418; "stream of consciousness" style, 513; style, 527; *Three Guineas*, quoted, 249; timelessness of being, 514
Woollcott Reader, 229
Woolman, John, 259
Word in Your Ear and Just Another Word, A (Brown), 423
Wordsworth, William, poetry, quoted on, 448
World Biography, 262-63
"World Books of Distinction," 244
World Council of Churches, 397
World Health Organization, 366
World in Books, The (magazine), 115
World literature, 419-20
World Next Door, The (Peters), 518
World War I: drama, 486; fiction, 513-14, 516; poetry, 455; political censorship, 187; reminiscences, 259
World War II: background books, 301;

World War II (*Continued*)
  fiction, 516-17, 536-37; history, 291-92; plays, 486; poetry, 455; publishing, 196-98; reminiscences, 259; restrictions, 168-69, 171, 177, 358*n*; science, 327-28
"World's Classics," 222, 244, 397, 410
Wormeley, Katharine, 235
Worster, W. W., 246
Wreath for San Gemignano, A (Aldington), 163
Wright, Harold Bell, 526, 529
Wright, Helen, 349
Wright, Richardson, 306
Writers in Crisis (Geismar), 533
Writer's Recollections, A (Ward), 166
Writing: Fowler's *Modern English Usage*, 153; imitators, 399; literary awards, 421-22; Quiller-Couch, Sir Arthur, 146, *quoted*, 137; working materials, 422-23. See also Biography; Fiction; Poetry, etc.
Writing of History, The (Oman), 285
Wroth, Lawrence C., 215
Wylie, Elinor Morton, 454, 466
Wylie, Philip, 130, 392

Yale Review, 117
Yale University Library, 419
Yeats, William Butler, 453-54
Yiddish literature, 419, 491
You Have Seen Their Faces (Caldwell and Bourke-White), 178-79
Young Lions, The (Shaw), 517
Youth, moral faith, 391

Zabel, Morton Dauwen, 440
Zeitlin, Jacob, 233

COLUMBIA UNIVERSITY STUDIES IN LIBRARY SERVICE

EDITORIAL COMMITTEE

CHARLES C. WILLIAMSON, Director Emeritus of Libraries, Columbia University, *Honorary Chairman*

CARL M. WHITE, Dean, School of Library Service and Director of Libraries, *Executive Chairman*

To serve until October 1, 1950

CARL W. E. HINTZ, Director, Natural History Museum Library, Chicago

DR. ANDREW D. OSBORN, Chief, Catalog Department, Harvard College Library

MISS MARY U. ROTHROCK, Specialist in Library Service, Tennessee Valley Authority, Knoxville

To serve until October 1, 1951

MR. WILLIS E. WRIGHT, Librarian, Army Medical Library, Washington 25, D.C.

MR. LOUIS M. NOURSE, Assistant Librarian, St. Louis Public Library

MR. JENS NYHOLM, University Librarian, Northwestern University, Evanston, Illinois

To serve until October 1, 1952

DR. CHARLES F. GOSNELL, Librarian, New York State Library, Albany

PROFESSOR LOWELL MARTIN, School of Library Service, Columbia University

DR. MAURICE F. TAUBER, Assistant Director, Technical Services, Columbia University Libraries